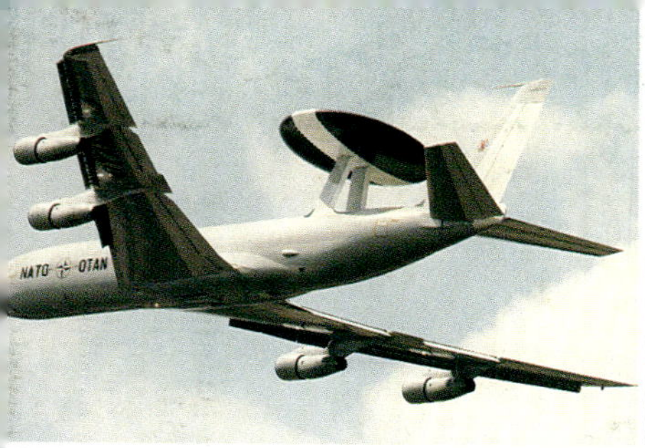
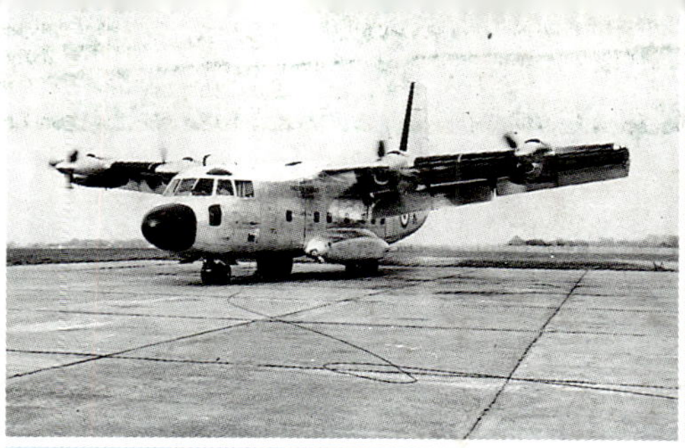
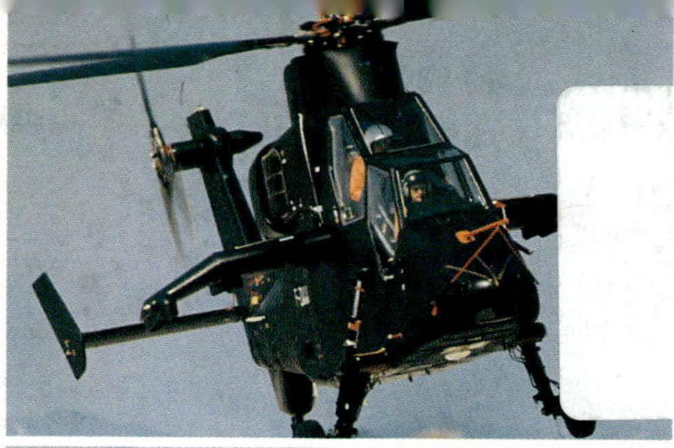

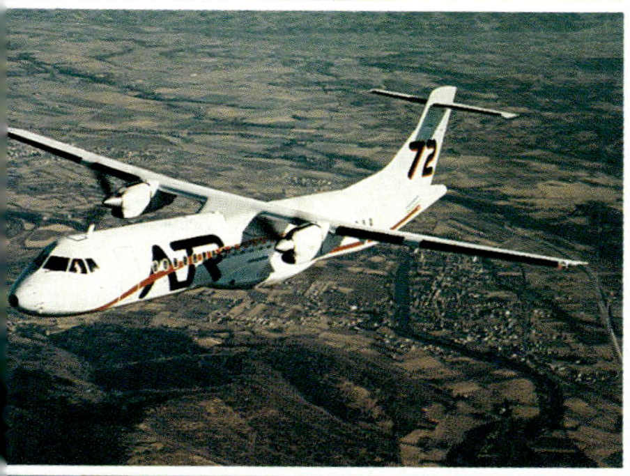
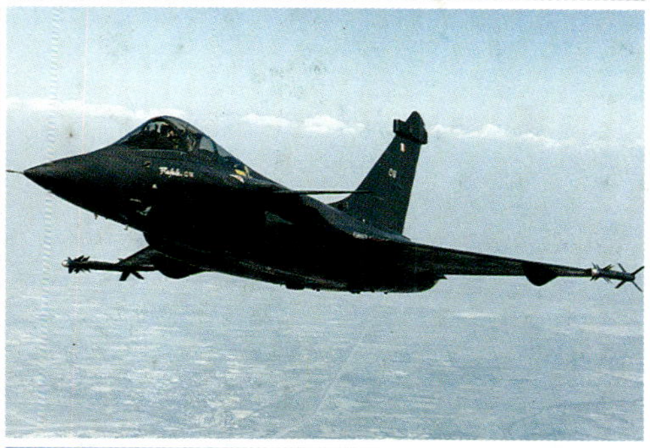
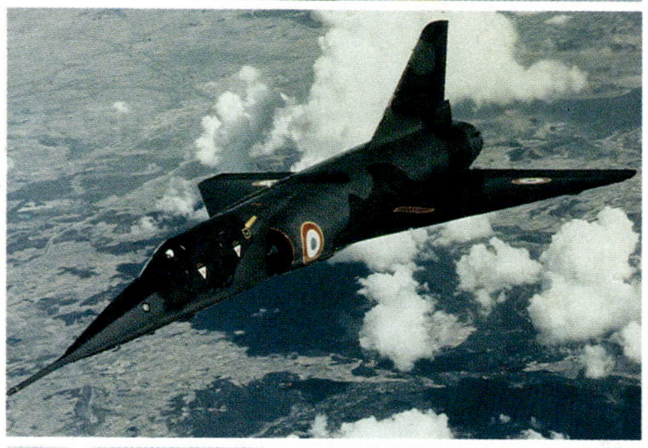
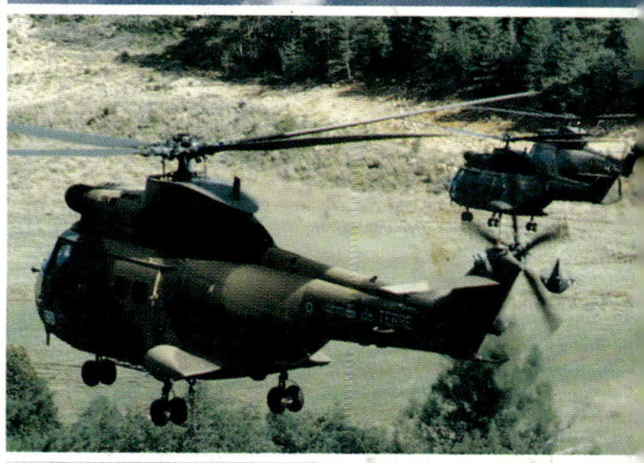
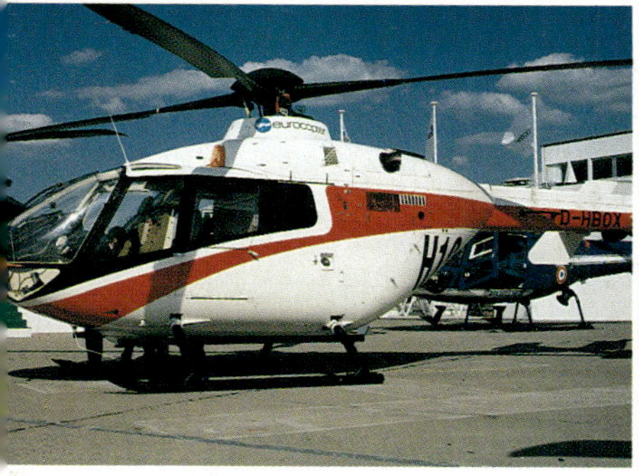
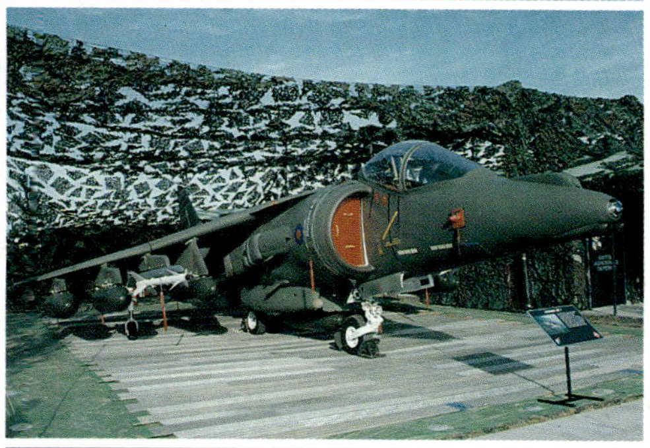
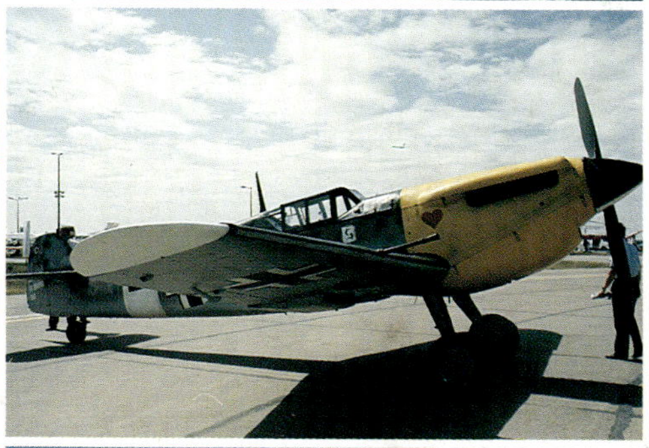
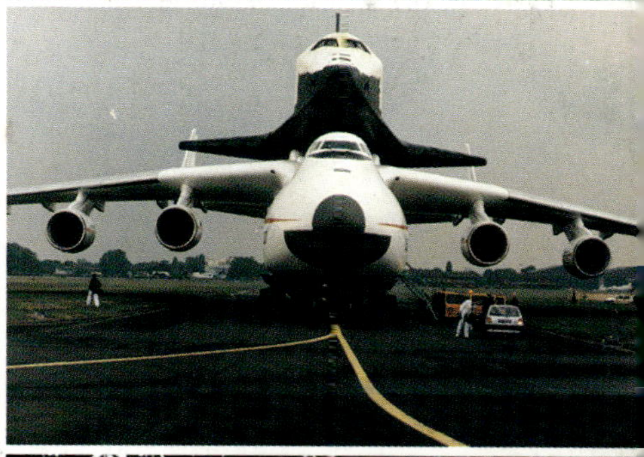
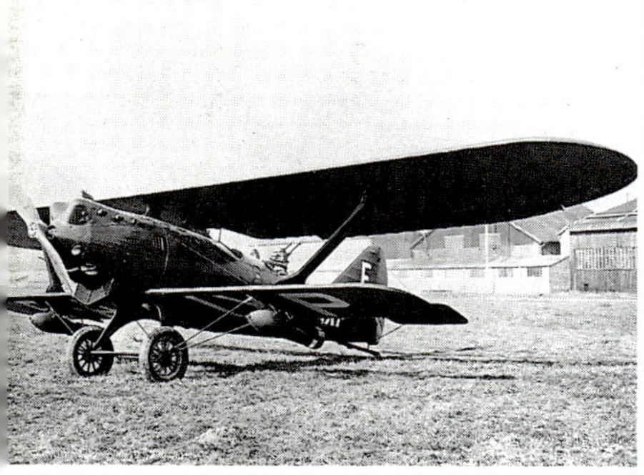
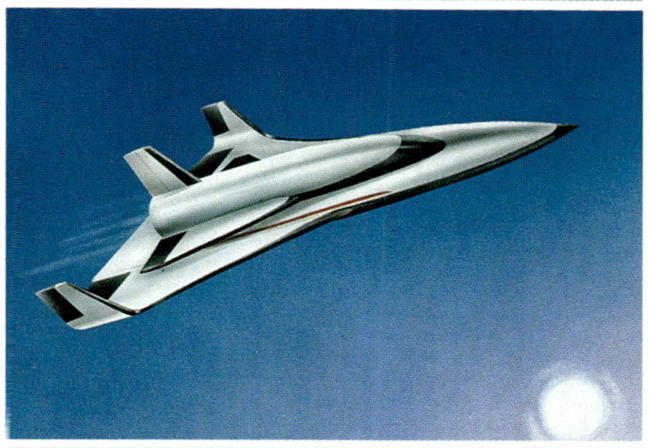
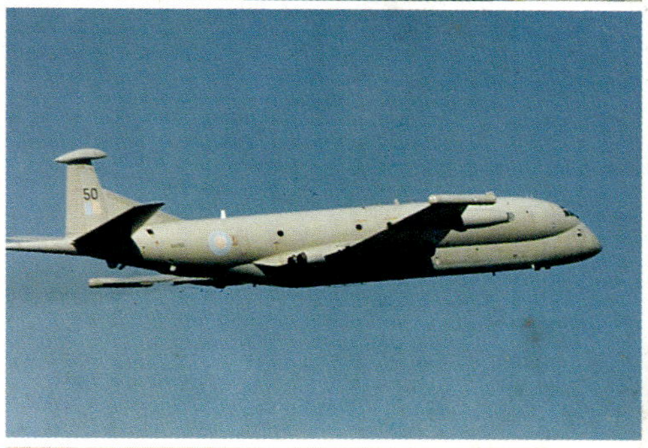
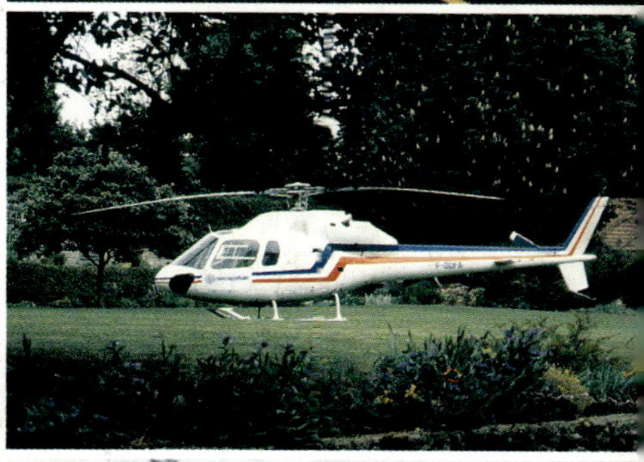
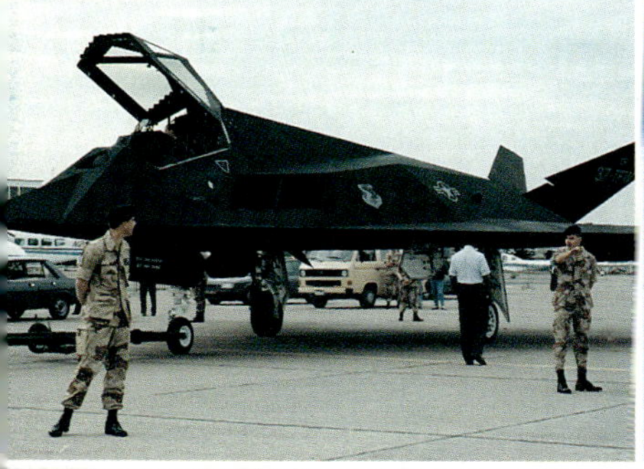
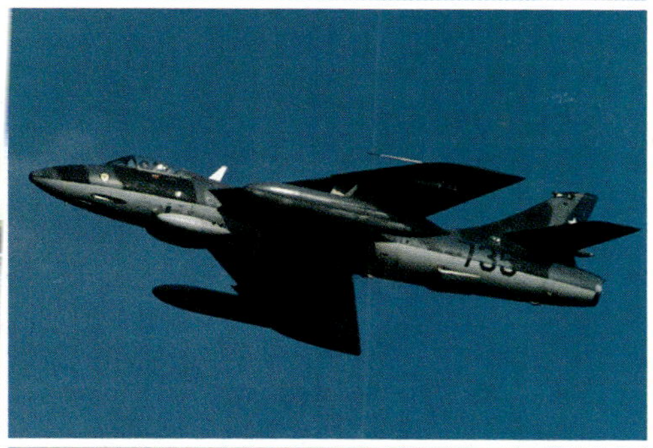
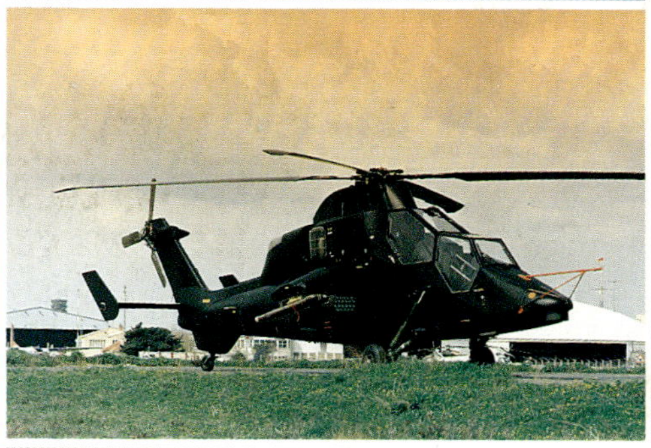
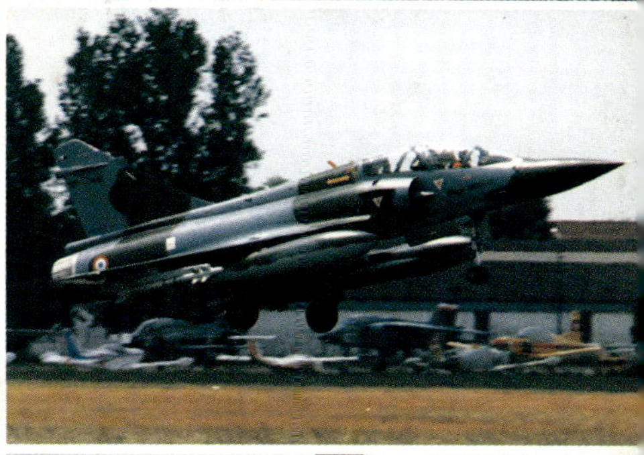
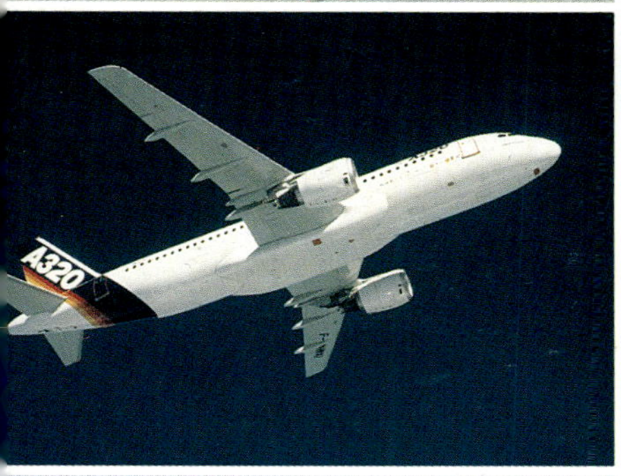
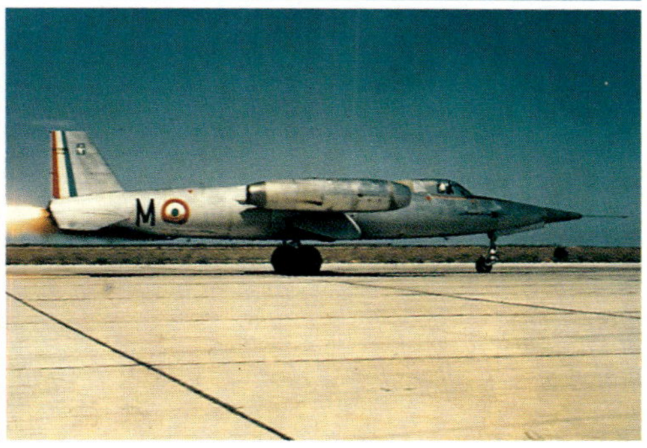
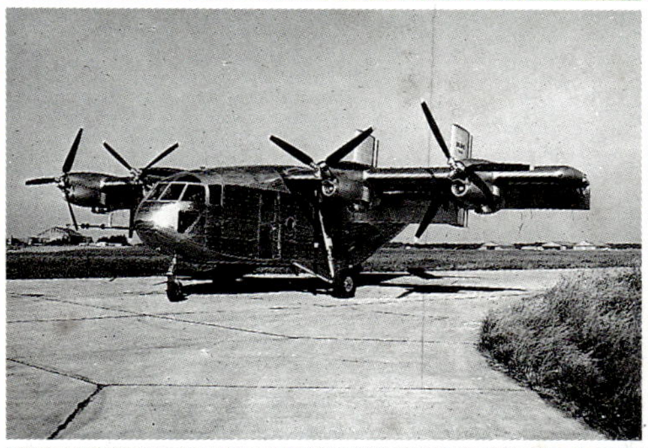
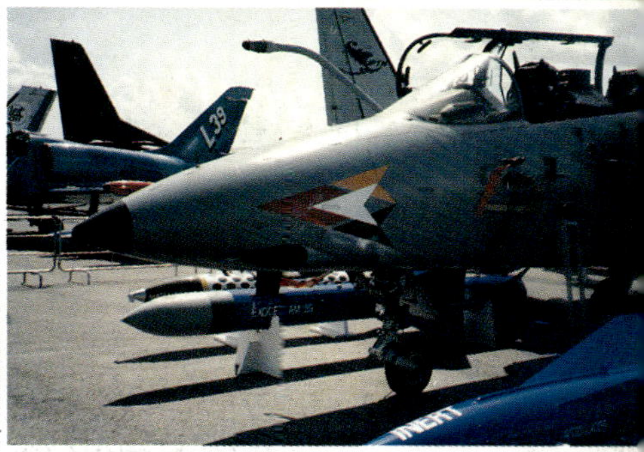
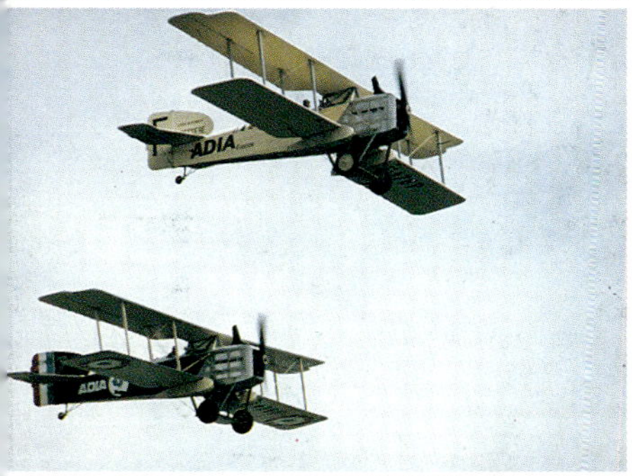
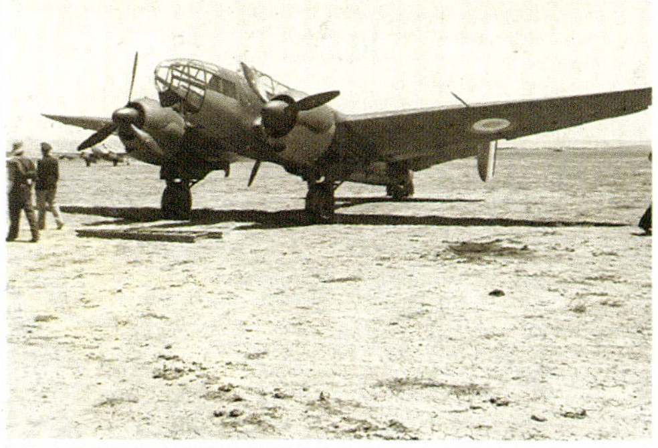
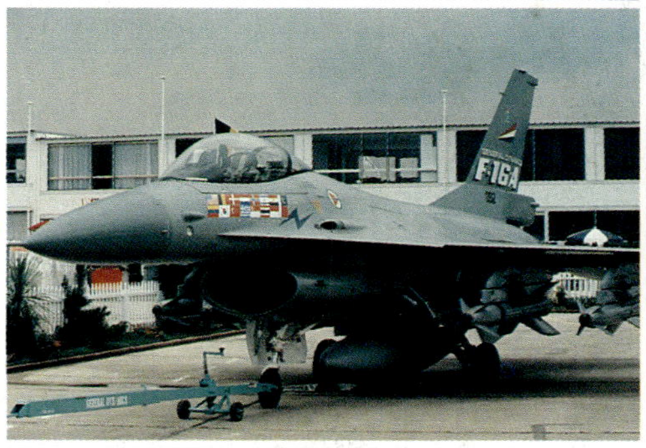
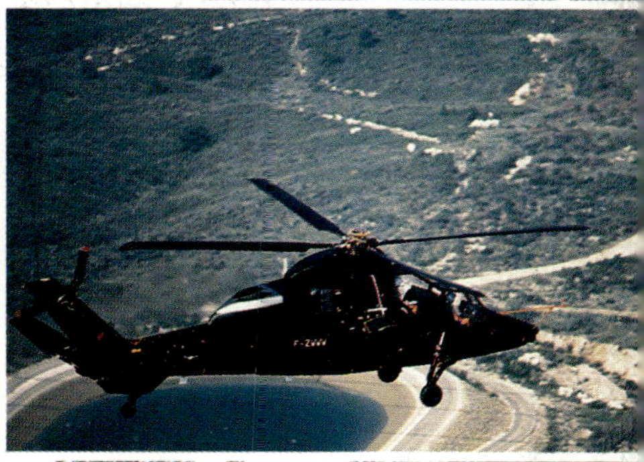
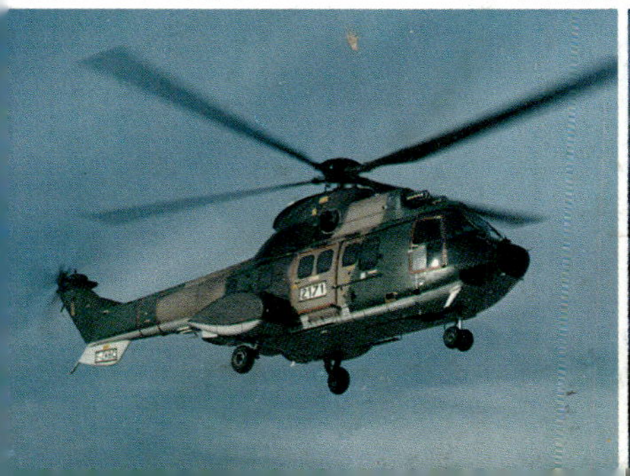
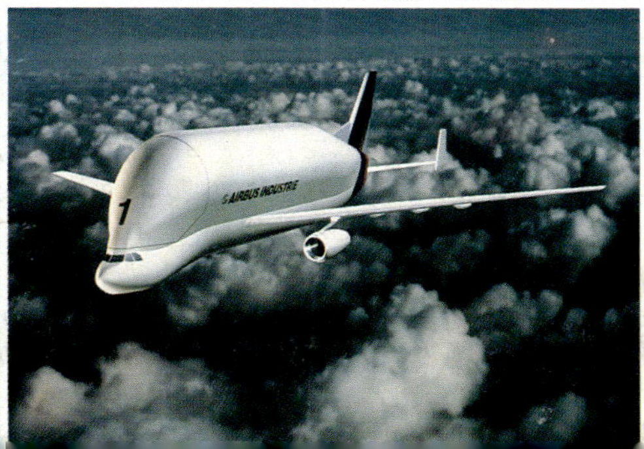
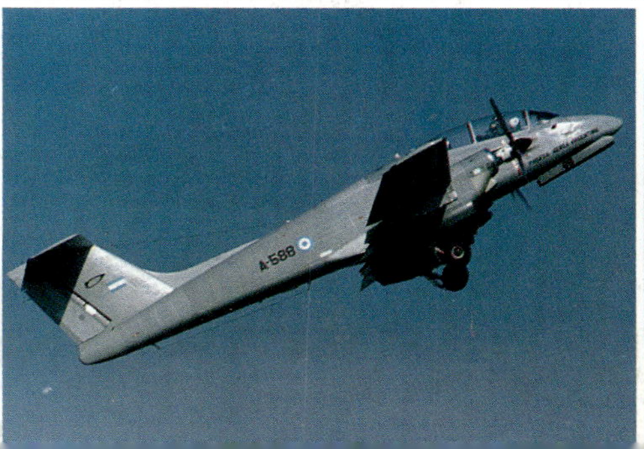
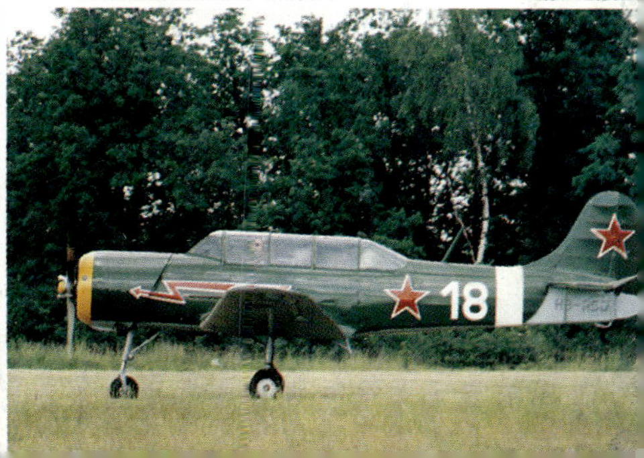

1001
IMAGES OF
AIRCRAFT

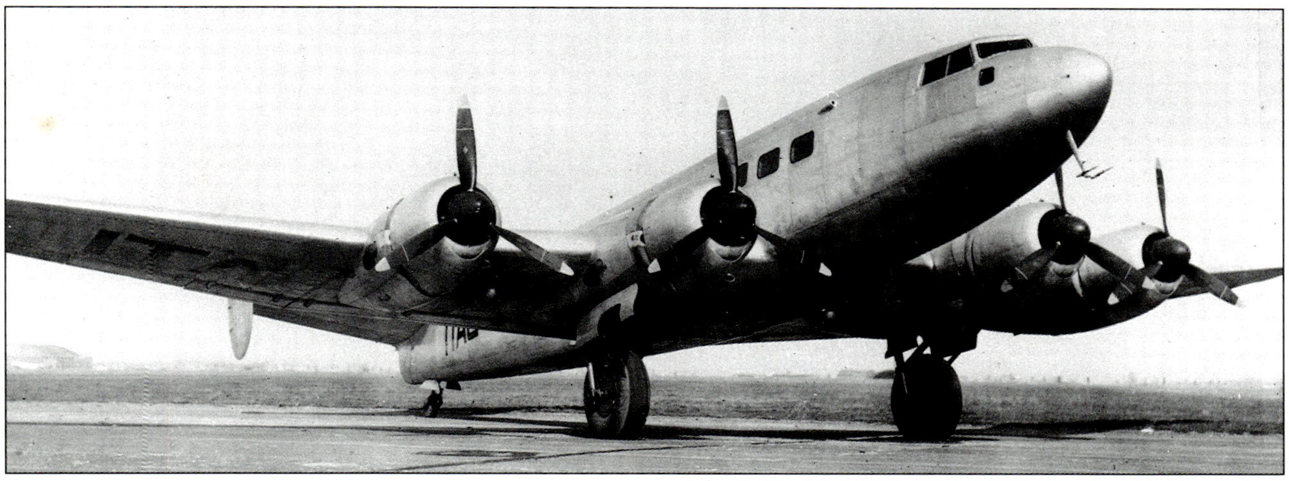

TEXT BY FRANÇOIS GROSS

Colour Library Books

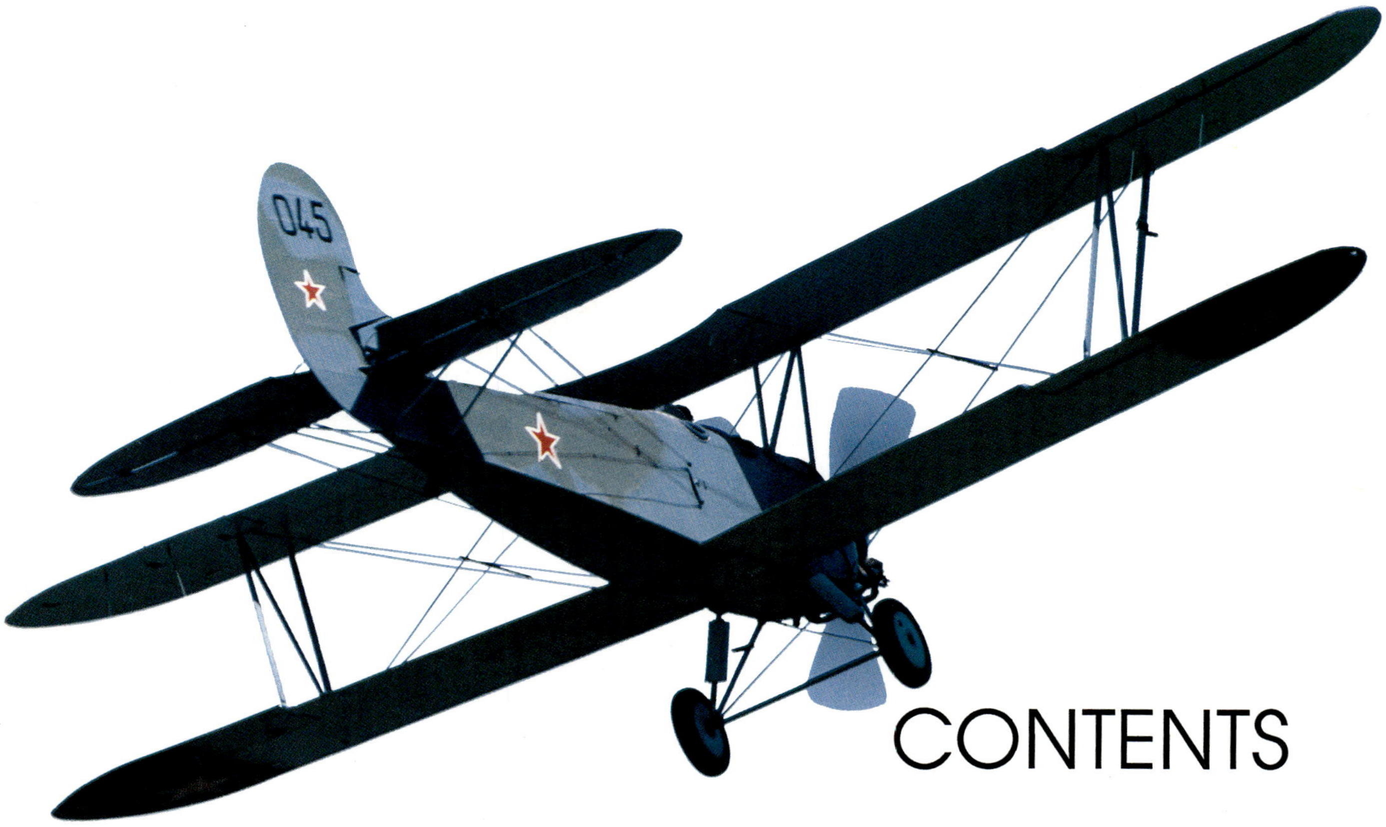

CONTENTS

FOREWORD

When Christopher Columbus made landfall in America five hundred years ago, Leonardo da Vinci was already considering the possibilities of human flight. To him we owe the first known studies for aircraft and the parachute. But it was nearly three hundred years before man at last became airborne – in a hot-air balloon – and another hundred before the first aeroplanes began to lift off the ground in Russia, France and England.

The race to conquer the skies – and then space – had begun. Before 1900 nobody could make more than a brief uncontrolled hop. The crucial step was taken by the Wright brothers on 17 December 1903, when their "Flyer" took to the air and flew for 12 seconds under pilot control. In 1909, the Channel was conquered by the Frenchman Louis Blériot and in 1913 the Mediterranean, by Roland Garros. But it was World War I that gave the major boost to aeronautics. Fighters reached ever higher altitudes (23,000 ft/7,000 m) and faster and faster speeds (145 mph/230 kph). Heavy bombers flew longer and longer distances (800 miles/1,300 km) to deliver heavier and heavier loads (3-4 tons).

After the war, bombers were converted to passenger use, giving rise to the first airlines. The routes they flew were pioneered by daring pilots setting distance records. In just a few years they had crossed the North and South Atlantic, conquered the Pacific and the African continent, and opened up the way to the Far East.

World War II accelerated the development of intercontinental aircraft and of the jet engine. Post-war commercial aircraft were designed to meet the demand for mass travel. So appeared the Boeing 747, the Airbus, and the supersonic Concorde. Combat aircraft were built to fly at two or three times the speed of sound, to deliver nuclear bombs to destinations thousands of miles distant, and to perform ever more complex and specialized tasks. Technological progress has led man to reach beyond the atmosphere and explore interplanetary and interstellar space. Constantly pushing towards new frontiers and accepting new challenges, he remains in thrall to an overriding passion: the urge to conquer his environment.

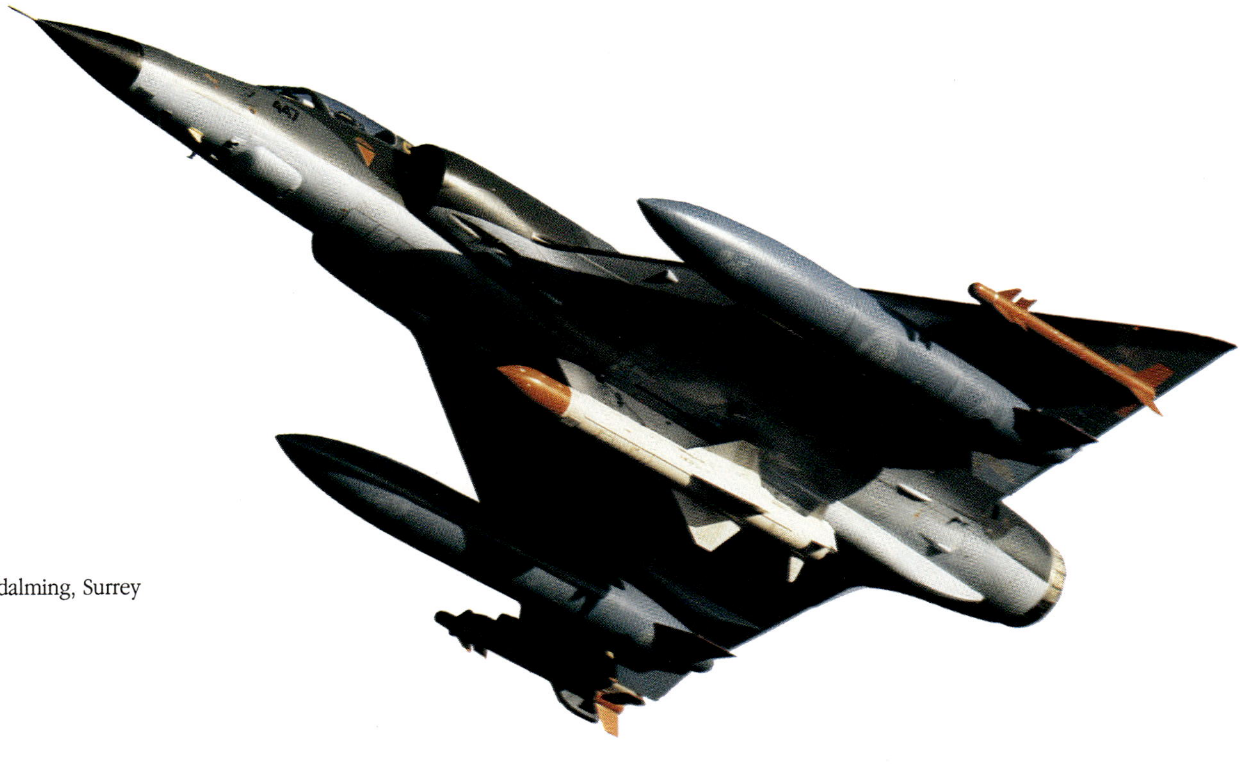

CLB 2896

Printed and bound in Malaysia

ISBN 1-85833-015-7

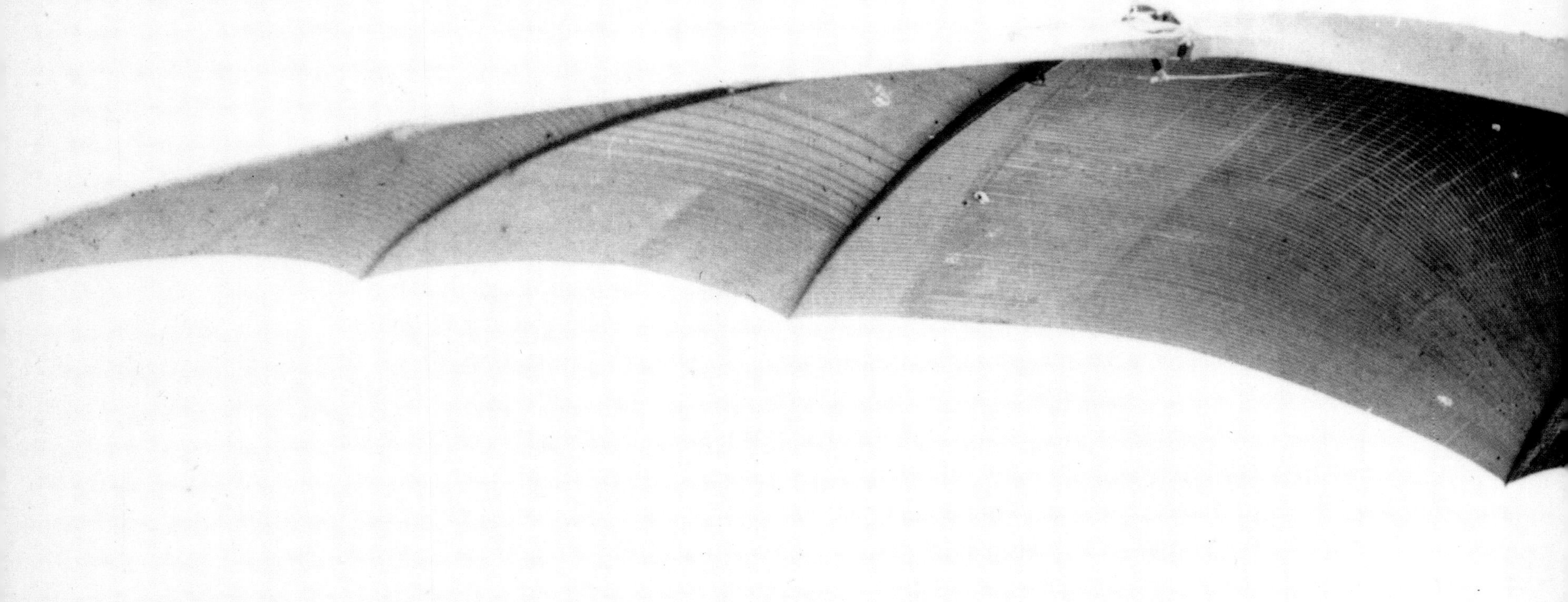

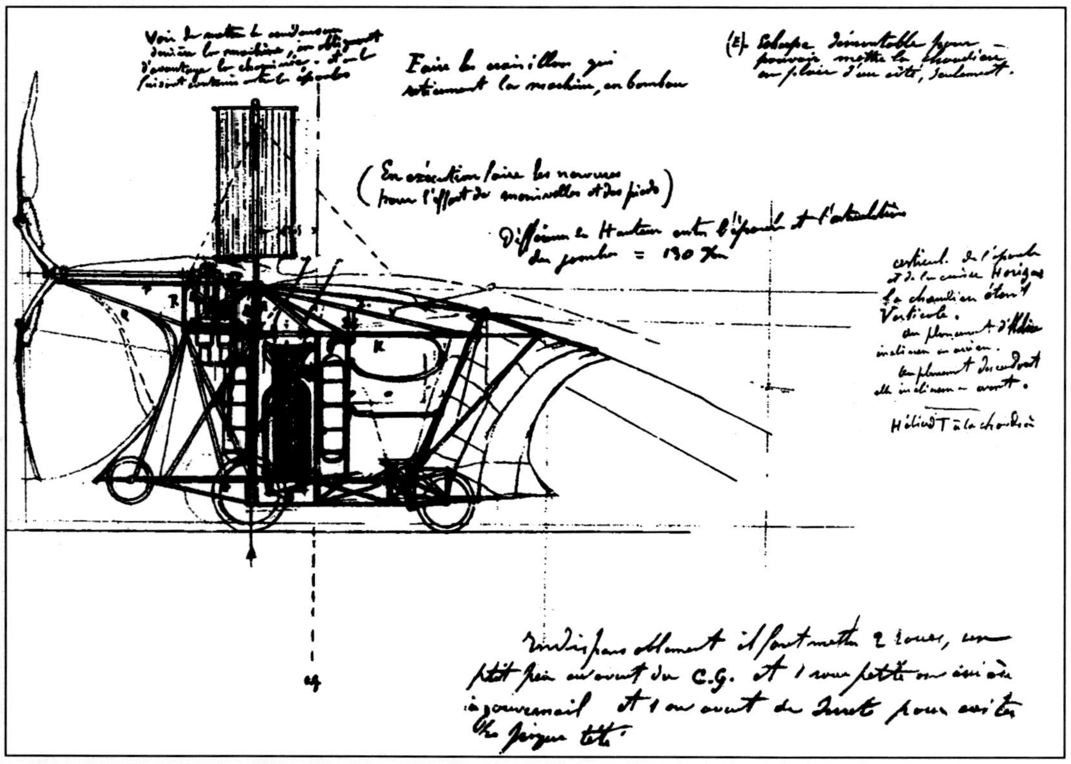
(En exécution faire les nervures pour l'effet de manivelles et des pieds)
Indispensablement il faut mettre 2 roues, un petit peu en avant du C.G.

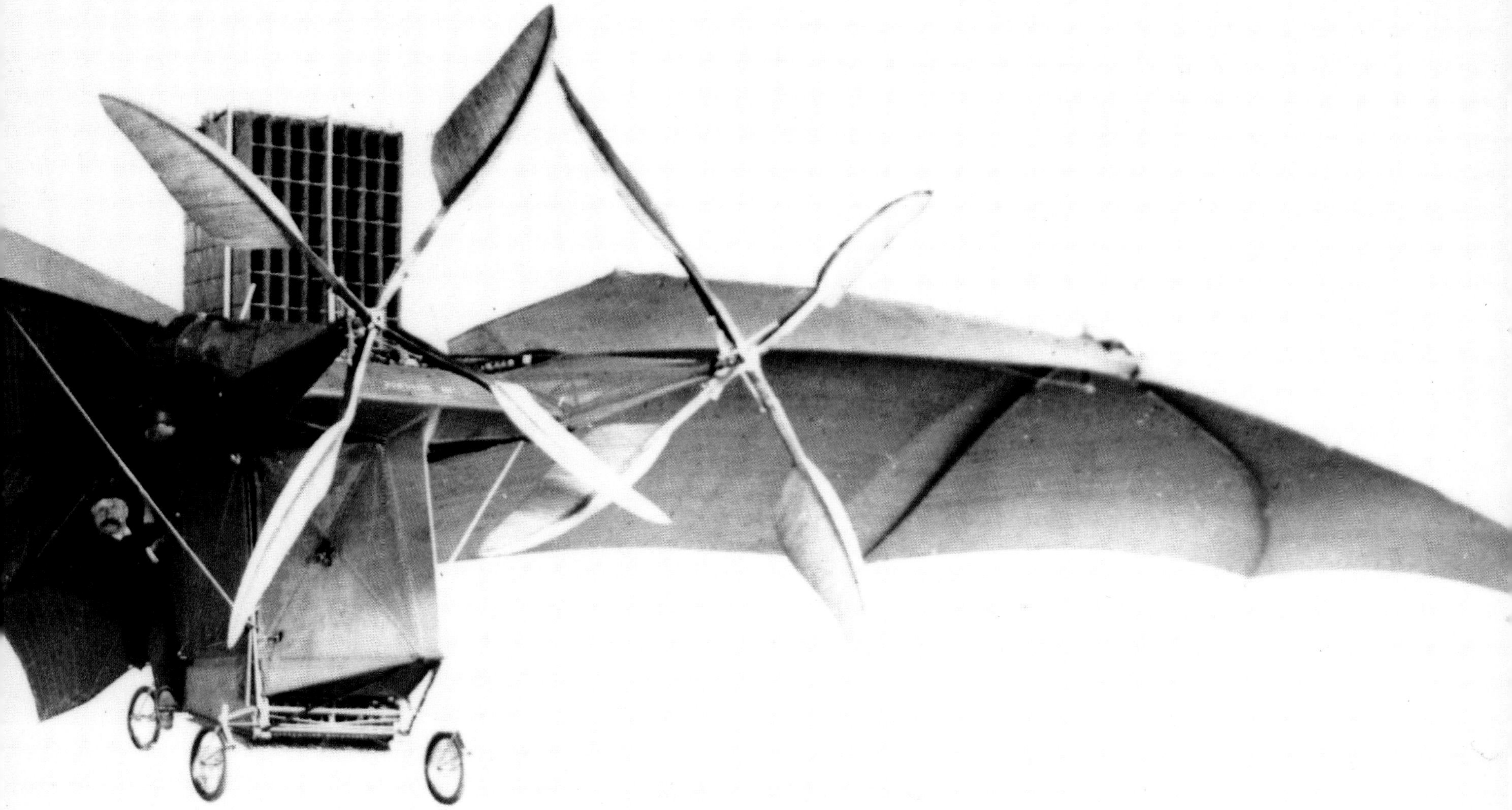

MAN'S FIRST ATTEMPTS AT FLIGHT

4

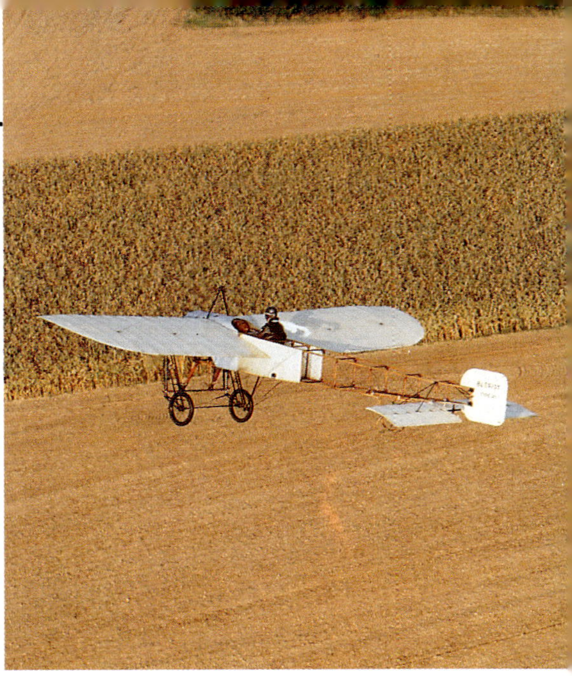

THE PIONEER AVIATORS

Since time immemorial, man has dreamed of flying like a bird, but as yet no bird-man has taken to the air, and attempts of this kind have often proved fatal. After many failures to follow in the wing-beats of Icarus and the angels, man's ambition has had to be satisfied by other means. Joseph and Etienne Montgolfier, papermakers of Annonay near Lyons, reasoned that, since smoke rises, its power might be harnessed to lift a lightweight structure clear of the ground. It is, of course, hot air that causes paper or fabric to rise and, on 4 June 1783, the principle they had discovered was used to lift their first unmanned ballon. Six months later, one of their fragile craft transported two passengers into the sky above Paris.

But the problem of getting a heavier-than-air machine to fly remained unresolved. It would seem that the first aeroplane to rise from level ground was made by another Frenchman, Clément Ader, whose steam-powered, bat-winged monoplane, the *Eole* (named after Aeolus, Greek god of the wind) briefly hopped a few metres in 1890, though he had no means of controlling it. In 1897 he built a second aircraft; nine years later he untruthfully claimed it had flown.

Meanwhile, a German engineer, Otto Lilienthal, was building gliders of all kinds and flying them himself. He realised that, to fly, one had to find a way to control the machine, and learn how to fly it. Lilienthal was the first pilot. In the years 1891 to 1896, he constructed over 2000 different machines and managed to fly a distance of nearly two miles. He eventually crashed to his death from a height of 50 feet. Wood, canvas and a four-cylinder engine driving two propellers were the main components of Wilbur and Orville Wright's *Flyer I,* which first took to the air at 10:30 A.M. on 17 December 1903 from the beach at Kill Devil Hill in North Carolina. Though the aircraft flew for less than a minute and covered little more than 200 yards, it was the first powered, sustained and controlled flight. Two years later came *Flyer III,* which was able to climb, dive and bank. In October 1905, this machine covered 25 miles (40 km) in approximately 40 minutes.

The conquest of the air had begun. In France, the Brazilian millionaire Santos-Dumont made notable progress in the years 1906 to 1909, while the brothers Charles and Gabriel Voisin, Henry Farman and Louis Breguet all appeared on the scene. Everywhere, aircraft designers were in a ferment. Throughout Europe and in the United States, steady improvements were being made by the likes of Avro, Rumpler and Curtiss. On 25 July 1909, Louis Blériot

1

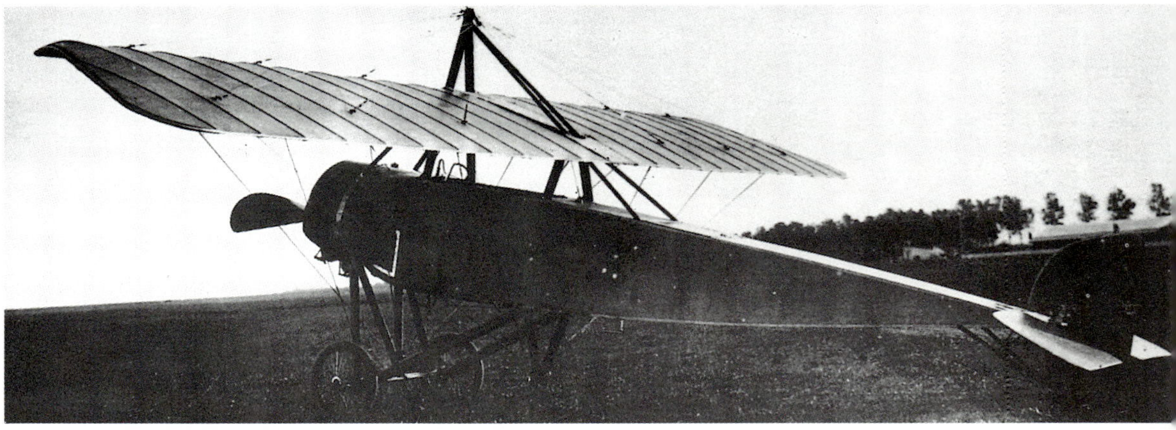

2

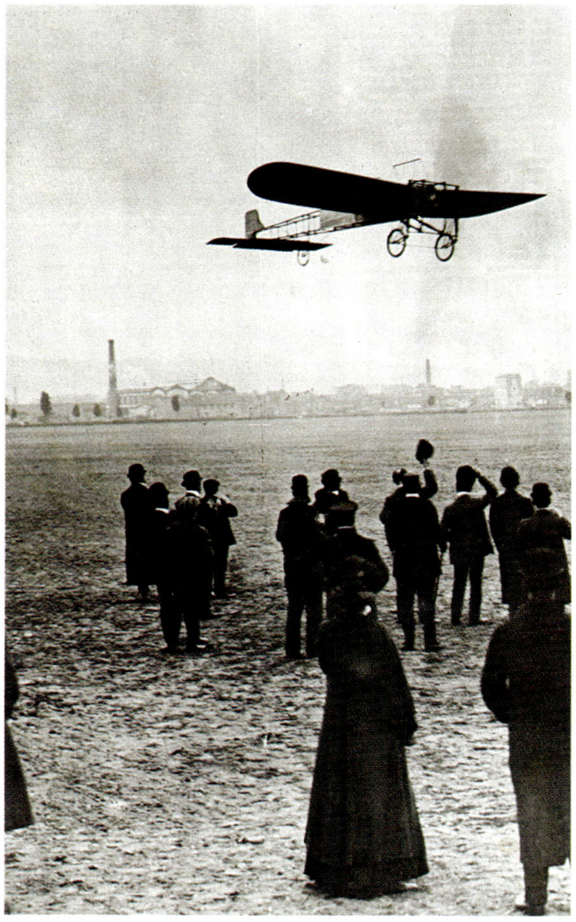

5

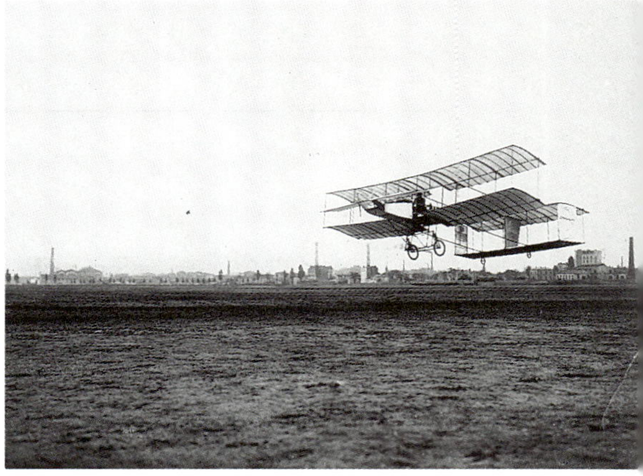

6

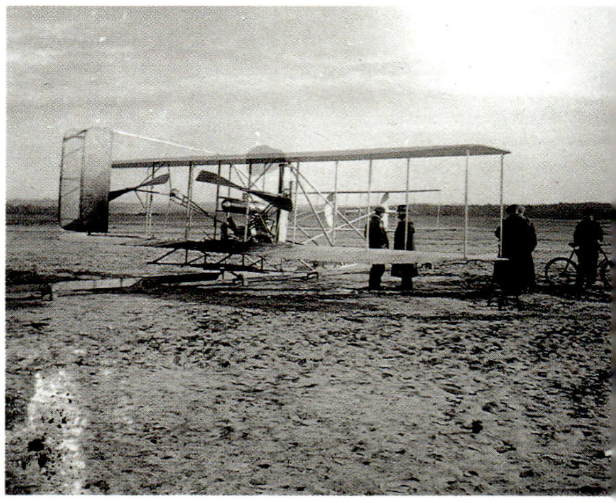

3

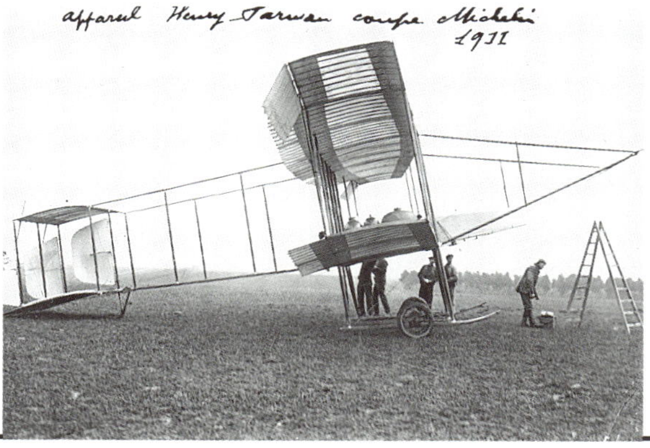

7

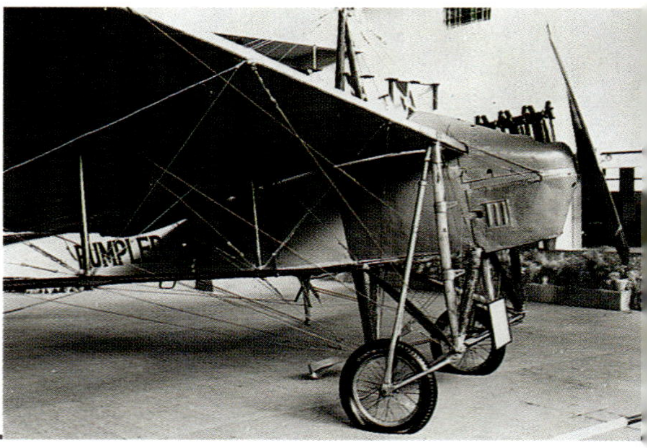

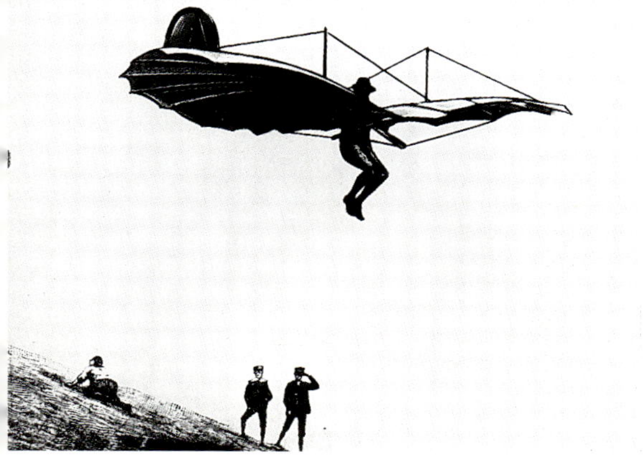
8

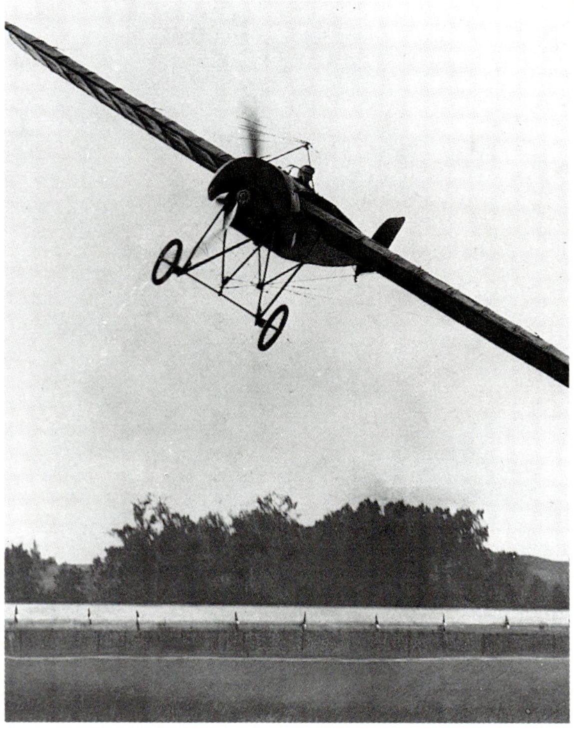
12

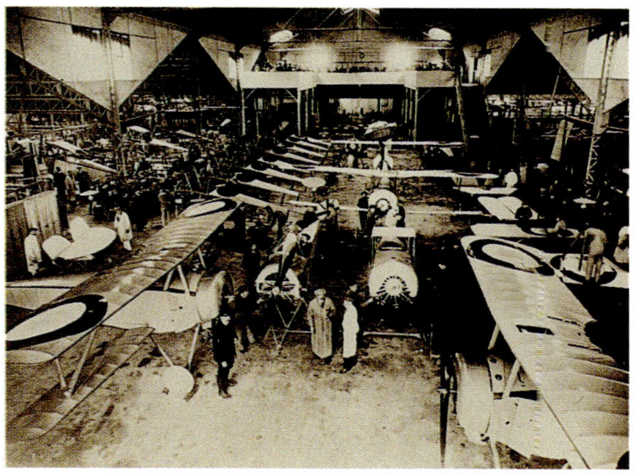
16

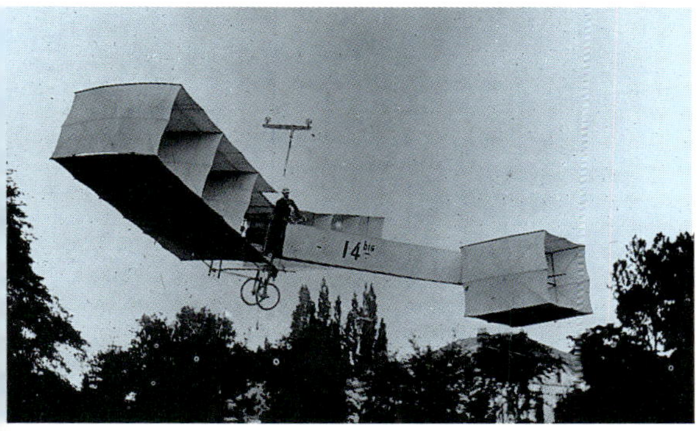
9

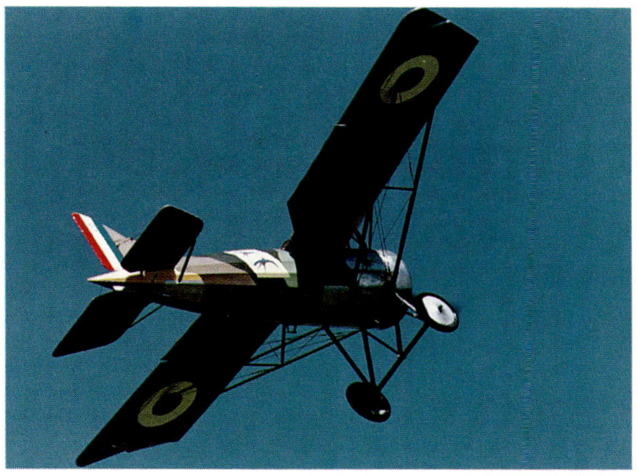
17

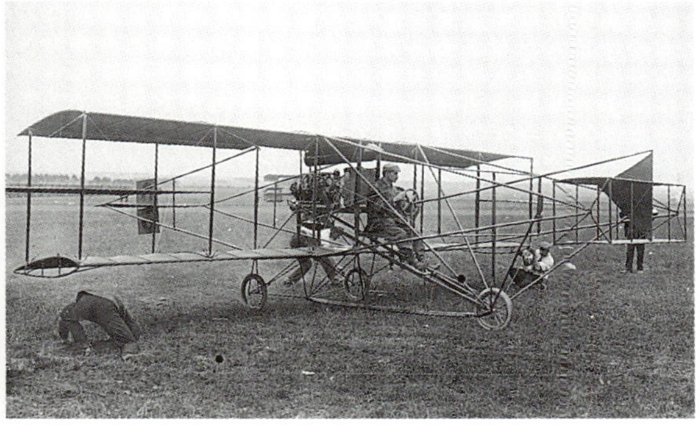
10

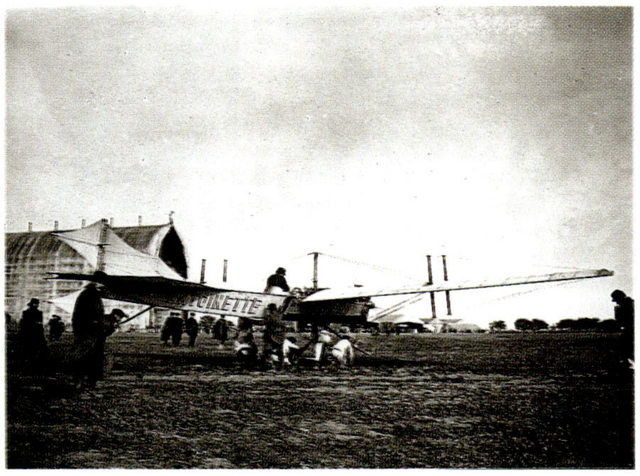
13

crossed the Channel from near Calais to Dover in his *Blériot XI* aircraft. Then, on 23 September 1913, Roland Garros conquered the Mediterranean flying a Morane-Saulnier Type H for 456 miles (730 km) from Saint-Raphaël to Bizerta in just under eight hours. On 29 September of the following year, at Rheims, the racing version of a Deperdussin reached the astonishing speed of 127 mph (204 kph).

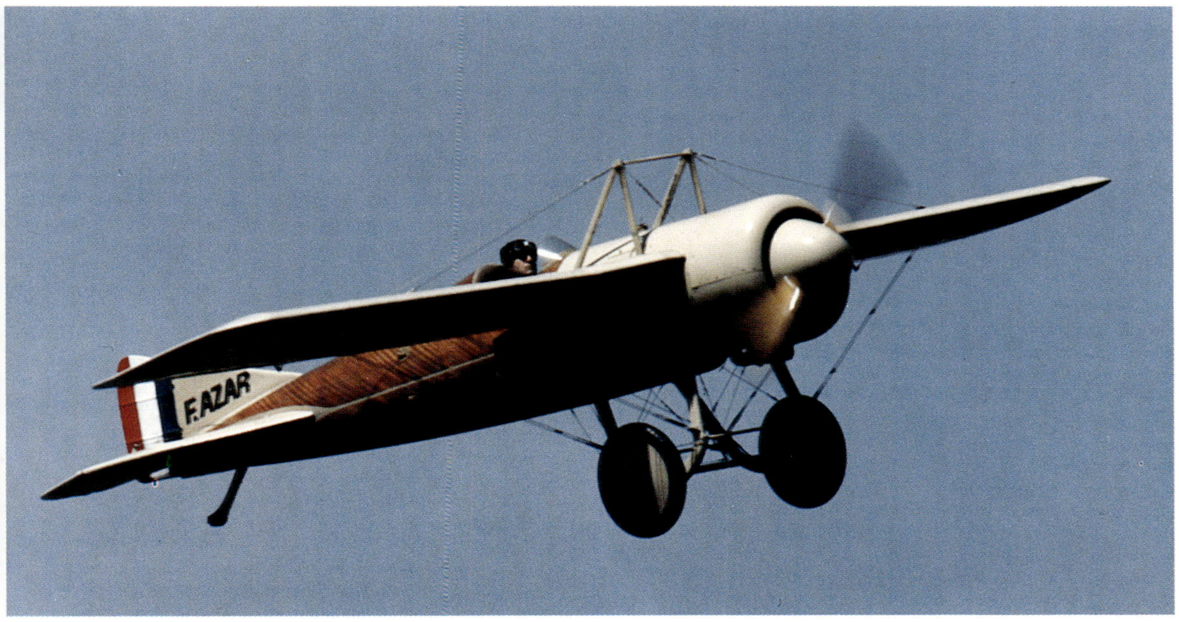

14

Photo No. 1: Morane Parasol (France)
Photo Nos. 2 and 4: Blériot XI (France)
Photo No. 3: Henry Farman III (Anglo-French)
Photo No. 5: Voisin biplane (France)
Photo No. 6: Wright Flyer (USA)
Photo No. 7: Rumpler Taube (Germany)
Photo No. 8: Otto Lilienthal glider (Germany)
Photo No. 9: Santos-Dumont's 14 bis (Brazilian-French)
Photo No. 10: Curtiss Golden Flyer (USA)
Photo No. 11: Santos-Dumont Demoiselle (France)
Photo No. 12: Morane-Saulnier flown by Roland Garros (France)
Photo No. 13: Antoinette IV (France)
Photo No. 14: Deperdussin, racing version (France)
Photo No. 15: Avro Triplane III (Great Britain)
Photo No. 16: Nieuport XI (France)
Photo No. 17: Morane-Saulnier AI (France)

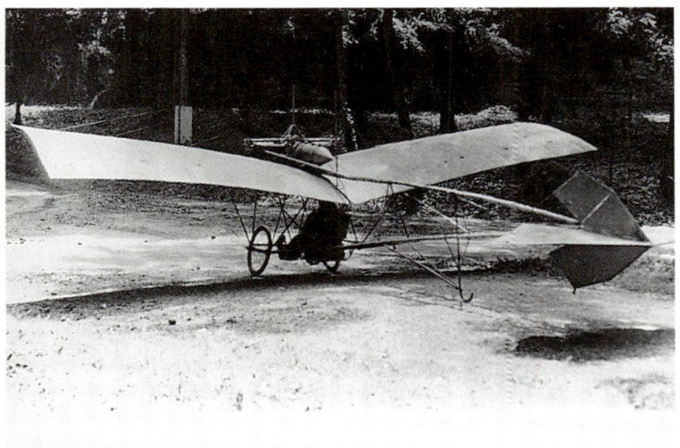
11

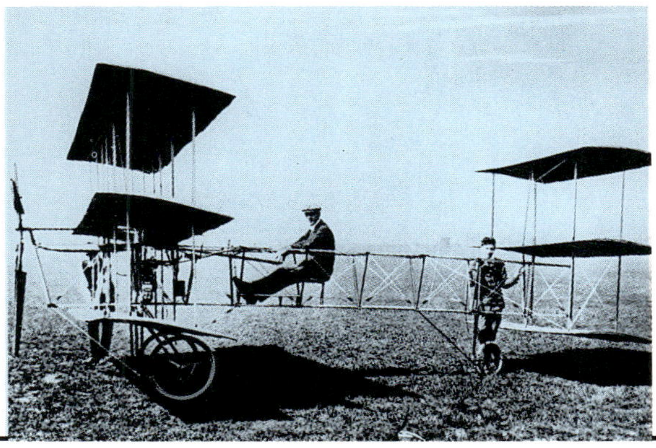
15

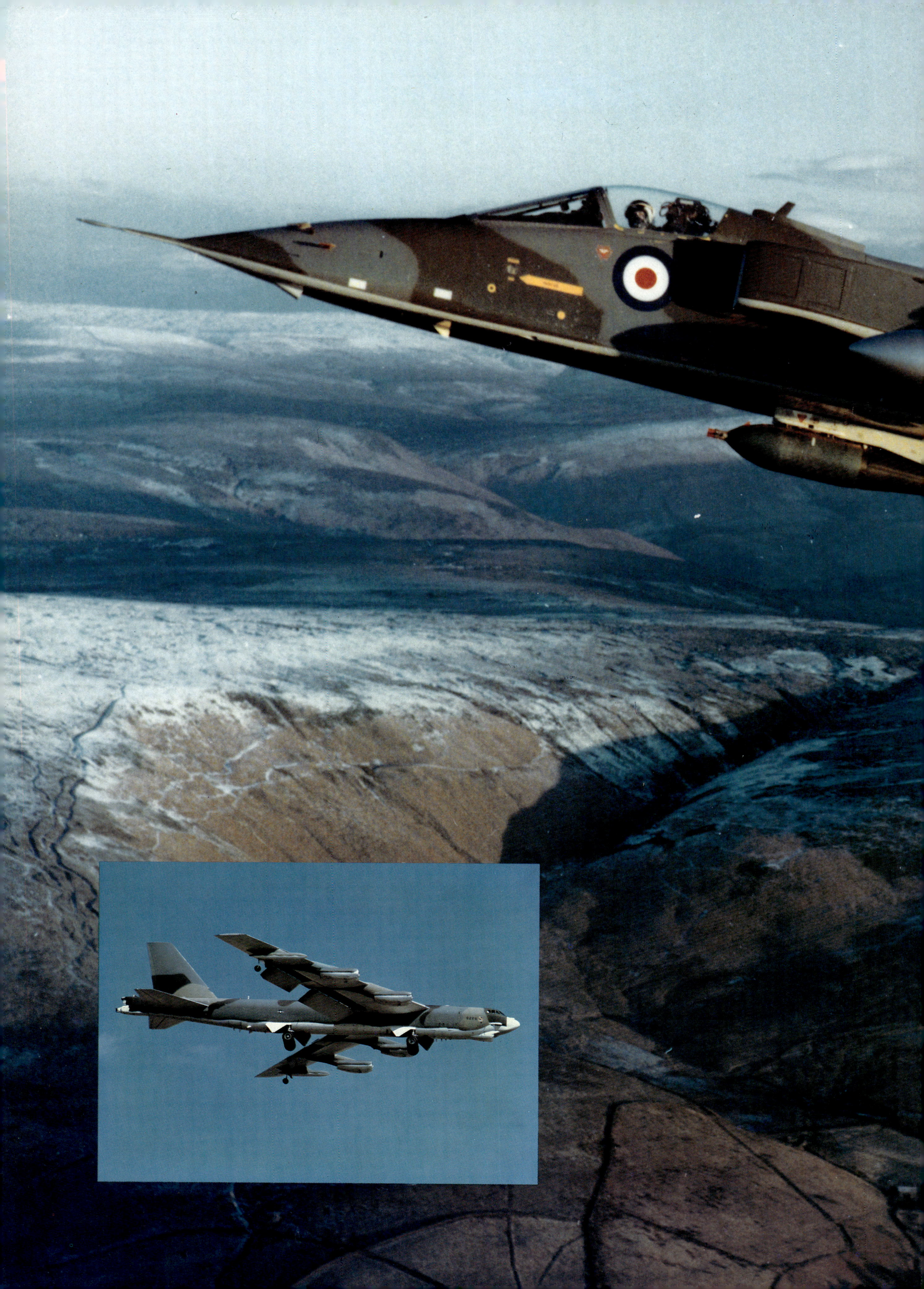

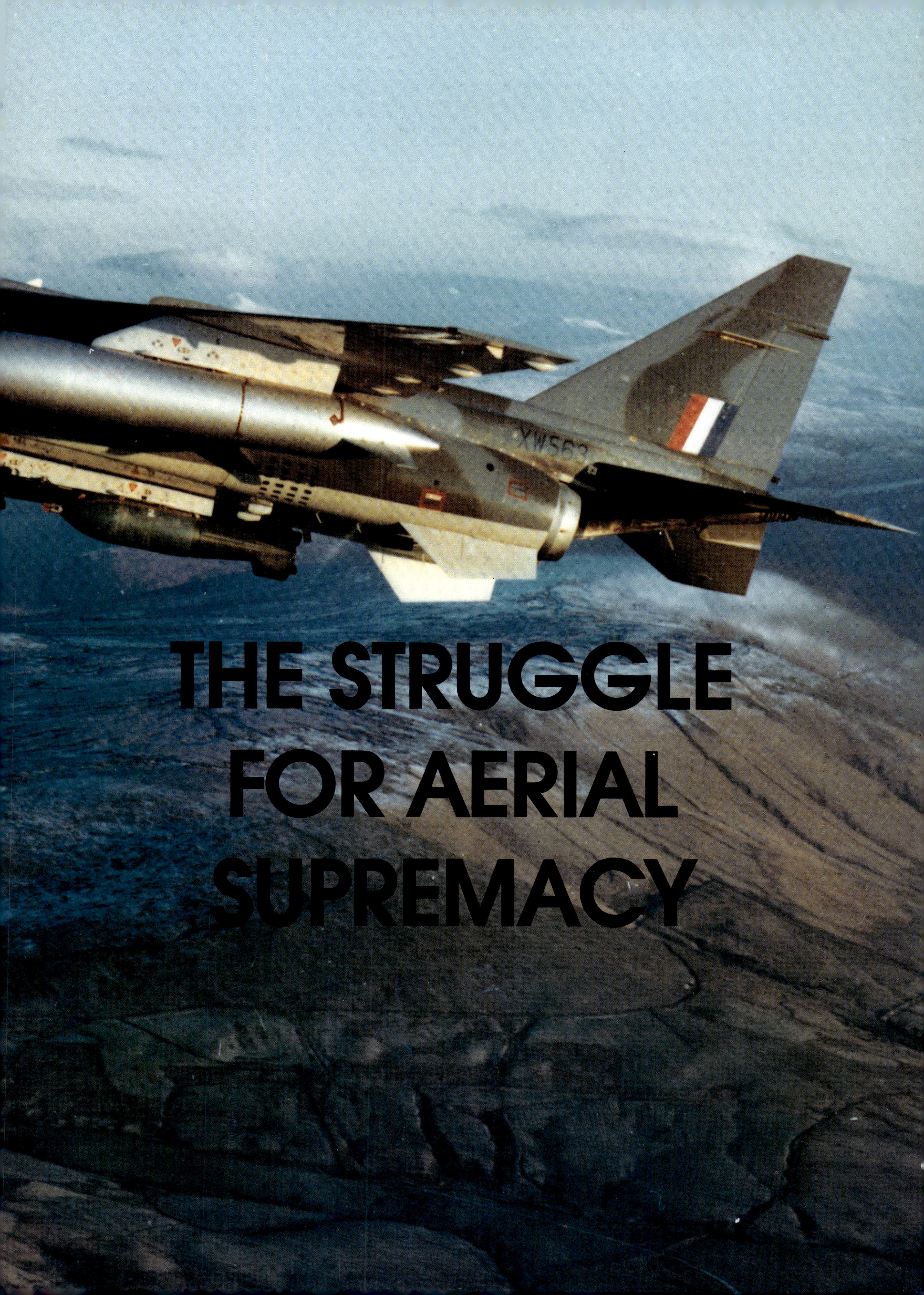

THE STRUGGLE FOR AERIAL SUPREMACY

FRENCH FIGHTER PLANES

4
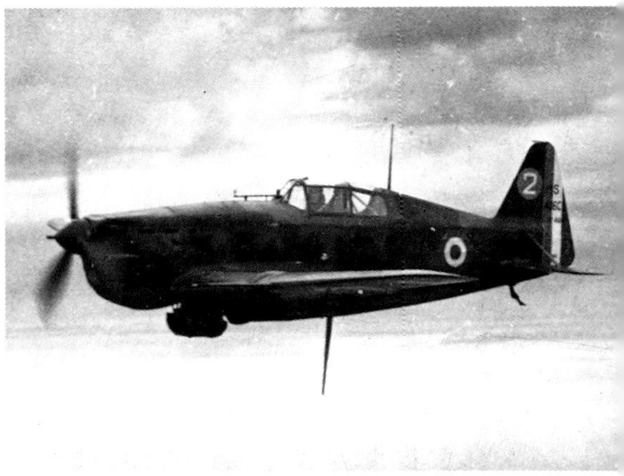

World War I was to transform the fragile box-kites of the early years into formidable fighting machines whose speed, flexibility and fire-power changed the face of warfare. First enlisted as an observer, the aviator quickly became an active combatant. The history of French fighter aircraft began on 5 October 1914, near Rheims, when sergeant-pilot Joseph Frantz and his observer Louis Quénault, flying a Voisin aircraft fitted with a machine gun, shot down a German Aviatik. Not until 1915 was their exploit repeated, when the crew of a Morane-Saulnier downed another Aviatik with rifle fire.

The first French fighter worthy of the name was the Morane-Saulnier Type N. It had a top speed of over 100 mph (160 kph), could climb to 9,840 ft (3,000 m) and – at the request of Roland Garros – was fitted with a machine gun which fired between the blades of the propeller. A few months later appeared the Nieuport Bébé, one of the most popular aircraft spawned by the war. But the most prestigious French machine, as flown by the fighter ace Georges Guynemer, was the SPAD VII, and its derivative, the XIII. This machine, capable of 137 mph (220 kph) and altitudes of over 21,300 ft (6,500 m), was armed with two machine guns.

Dewoitine, Breguet, Potez, Morane-Saulnier, Blériot-Spad and Bloch were some of the great names of French aeronautics until the nationalisations of 1936.

In 1939, the Armée de l'Air entered the war with some excellent fighters, though unfortunately too few in number. The Dewoitine D 520, derived from the D 500, was an outstanding aircraft, but less than 40 had been built at the time of the German offensive of May 1940. Another aircraft that took part in the battle was the less powerful Bloch MB 152, of which there were only 150. The mainstay of the French fighter force was therefore the Morane-Saulnier 406, over 1,000 of which were engaged in combat. Grossly inferior to the enemy Bf 109E, its 860-hp V12 engine gave it a top speed of 303 mph (485 kph), and it was armed with a 20-mm cannon and two machine guns.

After World War II the Armée de l'Air used British and American fighters while French jets were designed. Prototypes were built of the SO-6020 Espadon interceptor and, in 1953, the more daring SNCASO Trident: a jet fighter with a supplementary rocket engine propelling it at twice the speed of sound in level flight.

1
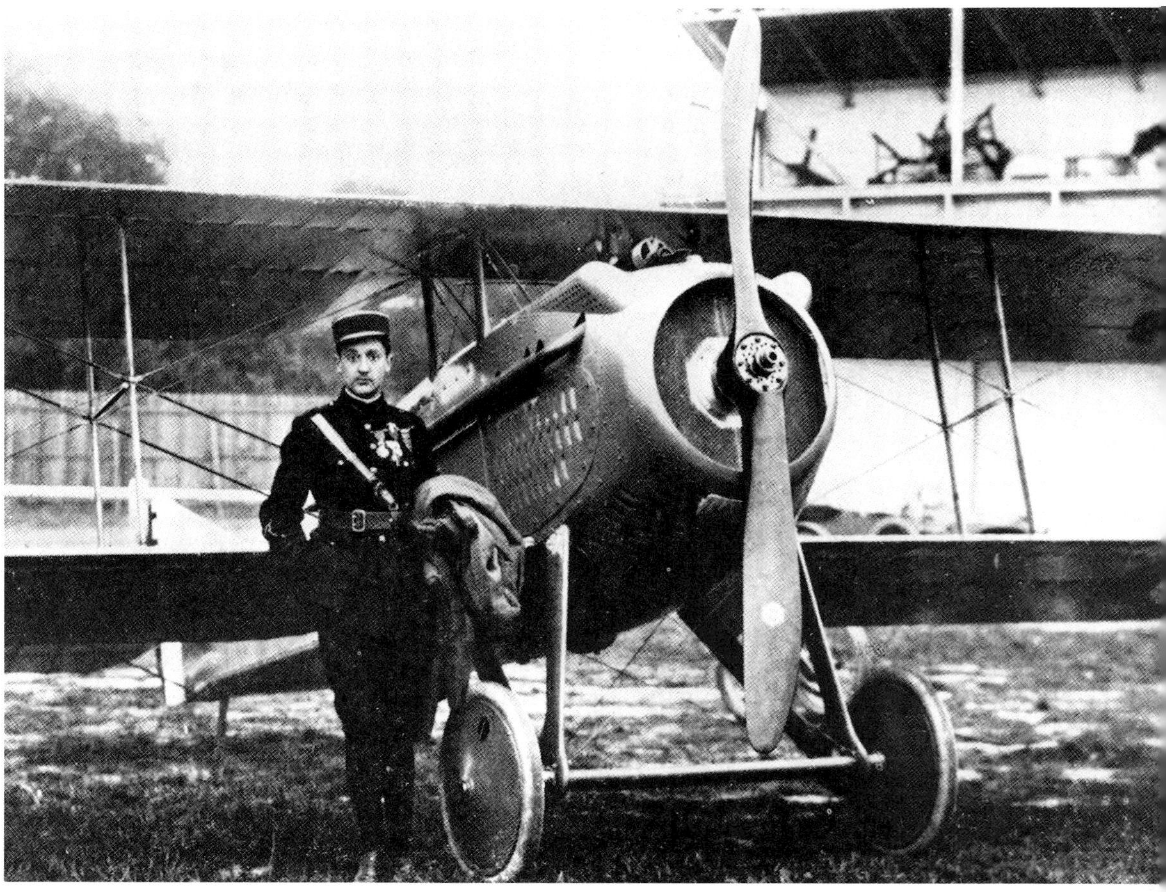

2
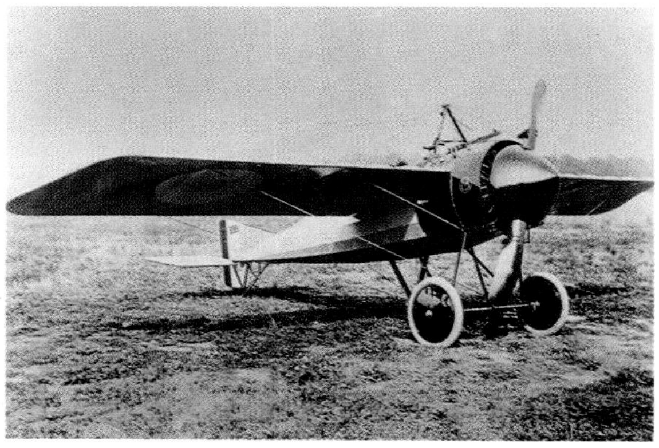

5
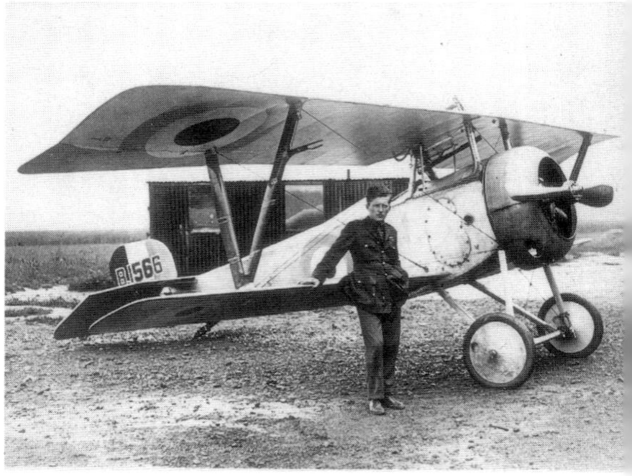

3
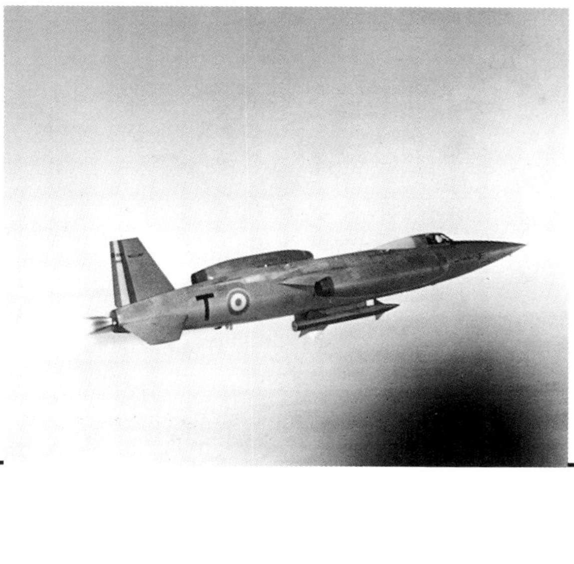

6
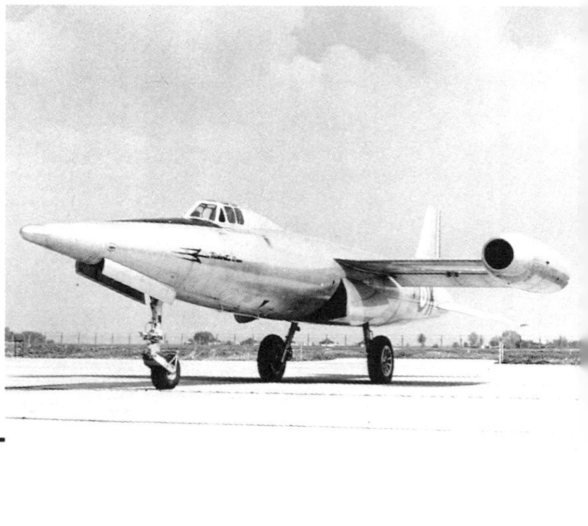

7

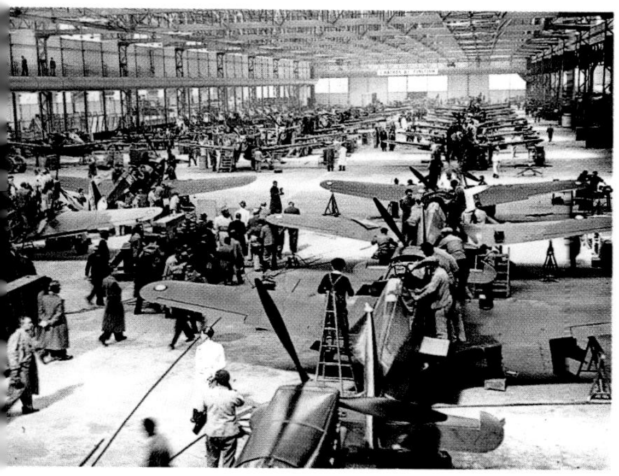

8

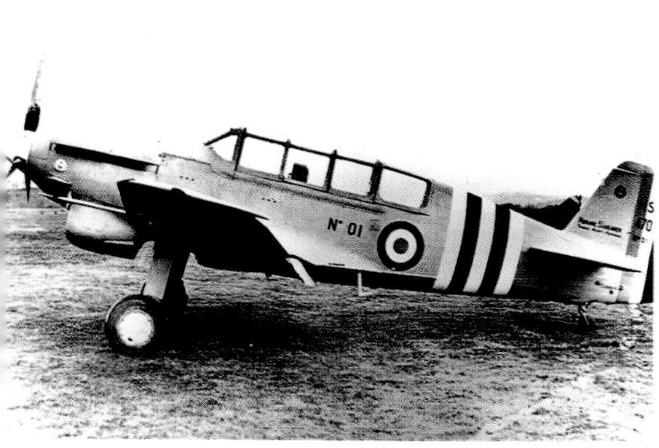

9

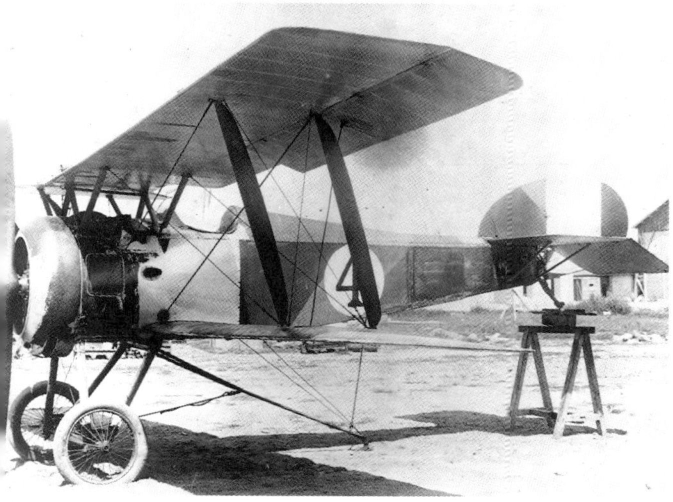

10

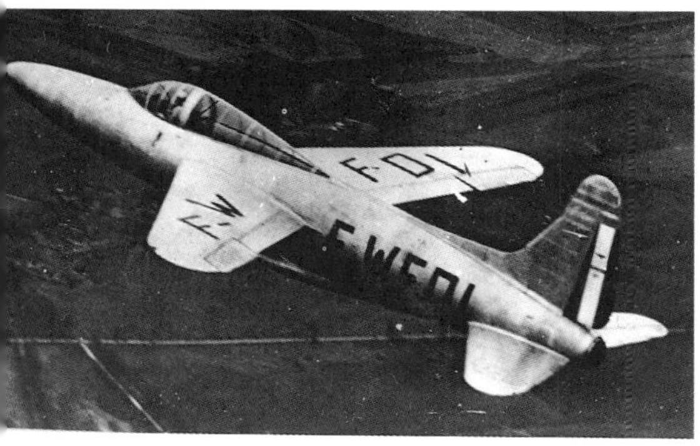

11

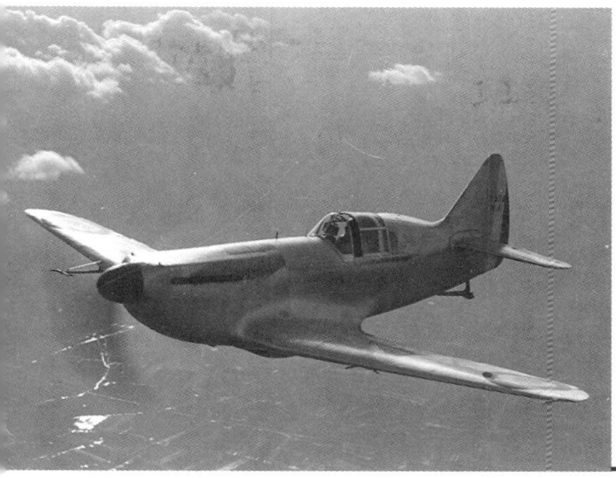

12

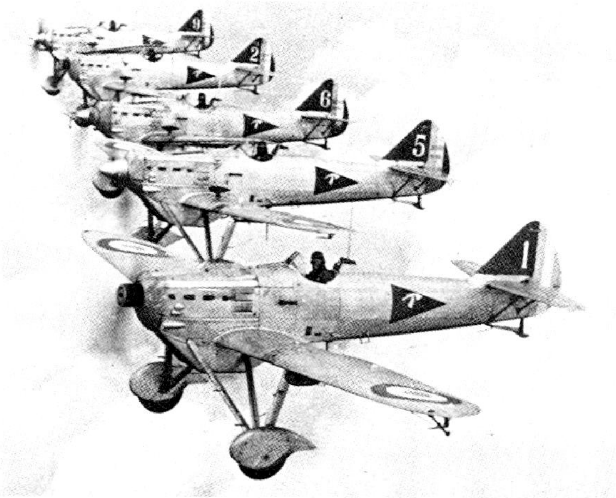

13

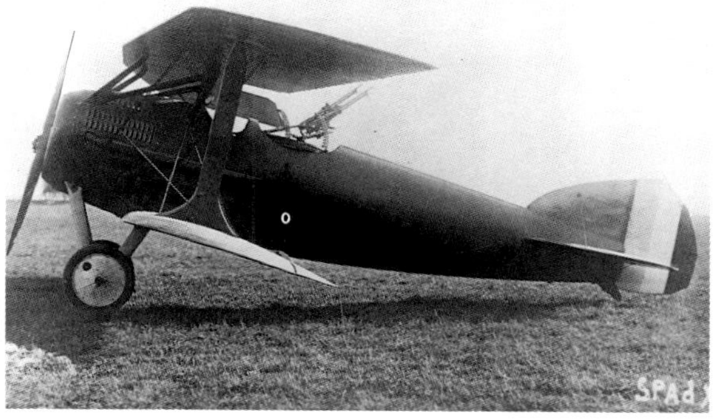

14

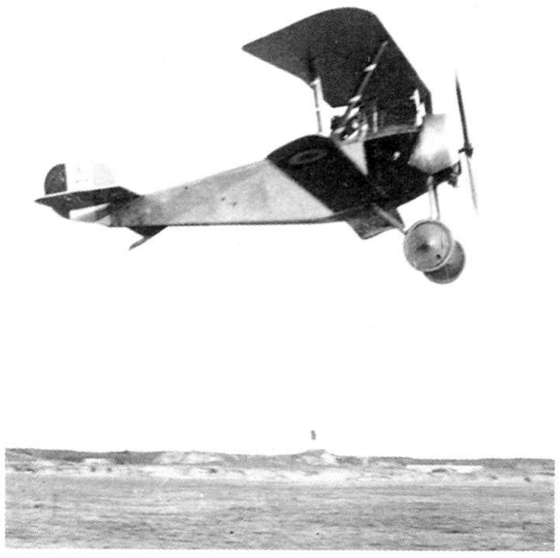

15

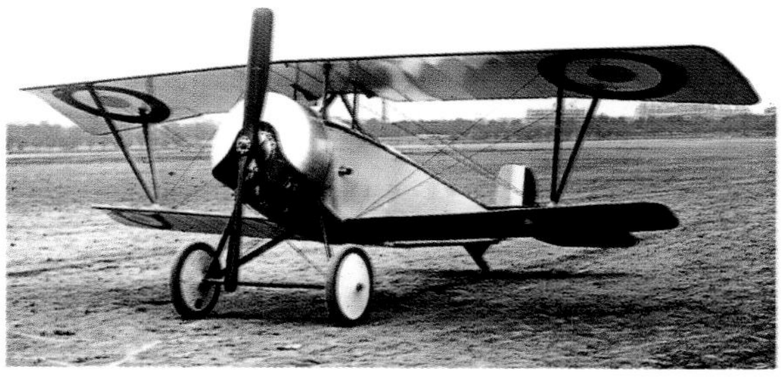

16

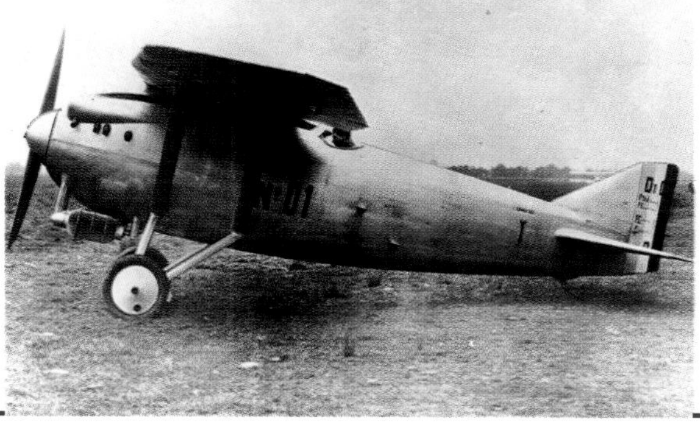

17

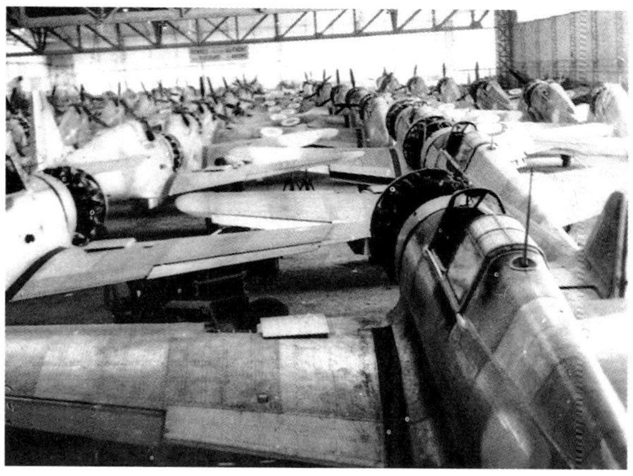

18

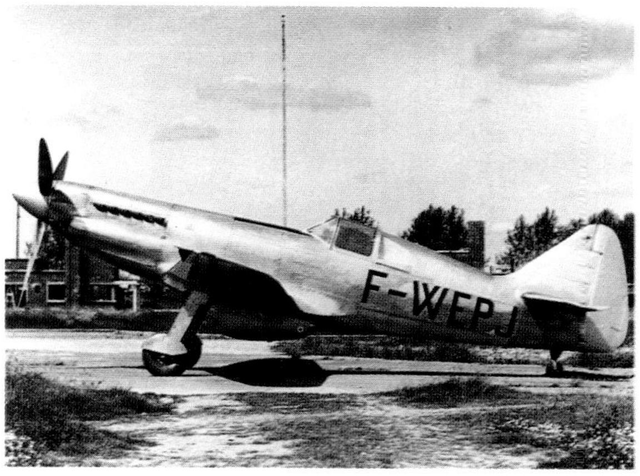

Photo No. 1: Georges Guynemer's Spad VII
Photo No. 2: Morane-Saulnier N
Photo Nos. 3 and 6: SNCASO Trident
Photo Nos. 4 and 7: Morane-Saulnier M.S. 406
Photo No. 5: Nieuport 17
Photo No. 8: Morane-Saulnier M.S. 470 trainer
Photo No. 9: Hanriot HD.1
Photo No. 10: SO 6020 Espadon
Photo Nos. 11: Dewoitine D 520
Photo No. 12: Dewoitine D 510
Photo No. 13: Spad XX bis
Photo Nos. 14 and 15: Nieuport Bébé
Photo No. 16: Dewoitine D1
Photo No. 17: Bloch MB 152
Photo No. 18: SE.520Z

FRENCH FIGHTER PLANES

The vitality of the French aeronautics industry was evidenced in the post-war period by a series of highly original aircraft. There was a proliferation of prototypes. In 1953, SNCASE brought out a fighter with no undercarriage: a rough-and-ready aircraft that took off from a trolley and landed on skates. It was intended for use on emergency airstrips just behind the front line.

The first French delta-wing prototype took to the air in January 1954. It was the SFECMAS Gerfaut, the first European aircraft to break the sound barrier in level flight. From it was derived an interceptor, the Gerfaut-II, which could climb exceptionally fast, reaching 29,000 ft (9,000 metres) in a little over 90 seconds. To rival the Gerfaut, SNCASE brought out the SE 212 Durandal, which made its maiden flight at Istres in 1956. But the most amazing aircraft of this period was undoubtedly the Nord Griffon, whose combined turbo-ramjet engine enabled it to fly at twice the speed of sound.

In 1949, the constructor Marcel Bloch – renamed Marcel Dassault – tested the first in a series of combat aircraft that were to make him world famous: the MD 450 Ouragan, 350 of which were eventually manufactured. It was followed by the swept-wing Mystère II, the Mystère IV and the Super-Mystère, all of which went into series production. Subsequently, Dassault launched the carrier-based Etendard fighter, then the long-lived Mirage family.

The first delta-wing Mirage III-Cs were delivered to the French air force in late 1960. This aircraft reached Mach 2.2, was armed with two 30-mm cannon, and in later versions could carry four tons of assorted weaponry beneath its wings. From the Mirage III were derived the simplified Mirage 5 and Mirage 50. The next member of the family was the Mirage F1, with swept-back wings replacing the delta shape to give greater range and manoeuvrability.

In the mid-1970s, Dassault began designing a new aircraft, of which two versions were actually built: a light, single-engined plane, the Mirage 2000, which was adopted by the French air force, and a heavier, twin-engined model, the Mirage 4000, which remained at the prototype stage. The 2000 is a multi-purpose supersonic combat aircraft capable of Mach 2.2. It is armed with two 30-mm cannon and six tons of missiles and other weaponry.

Dassault is currently engaged in developing the Rafale, which should enter service with the Armée de l'Air by the end of the century. A 21.5 ton twin-engined aircraft, it can fly at Mach 2, with an armament of cannon and missiles.

1

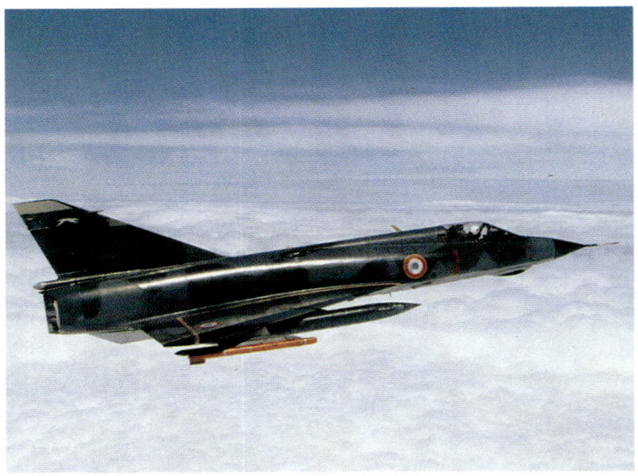

2

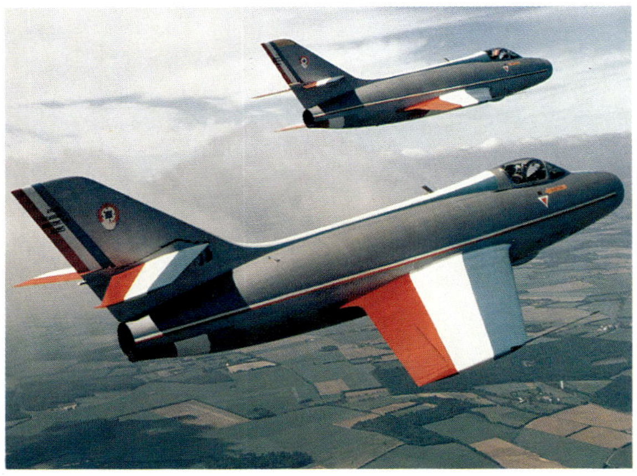

3

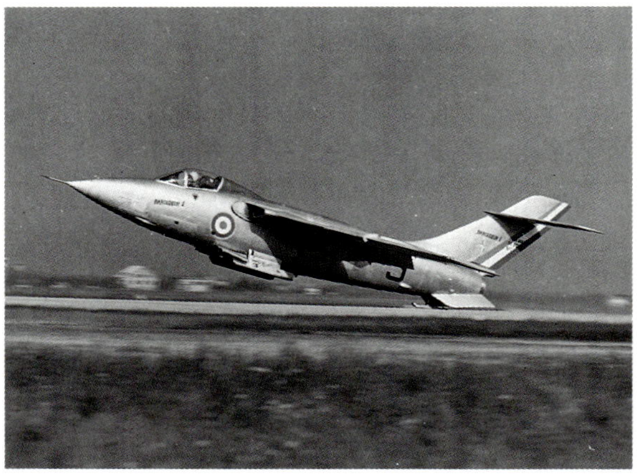

4

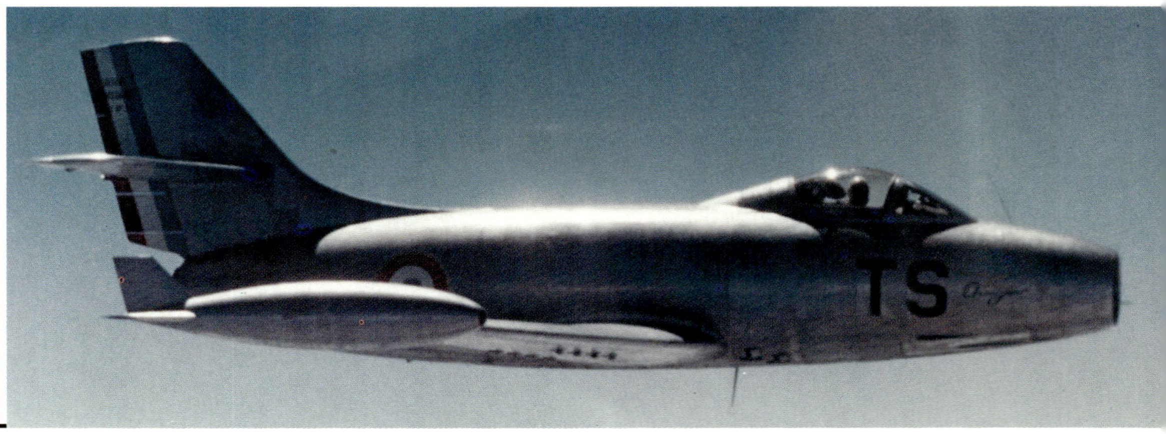

5

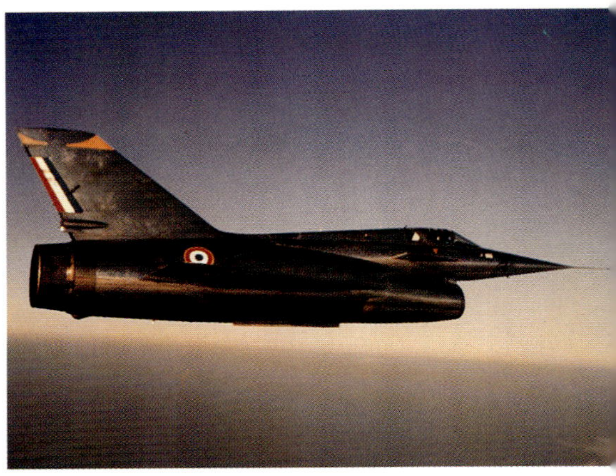

6

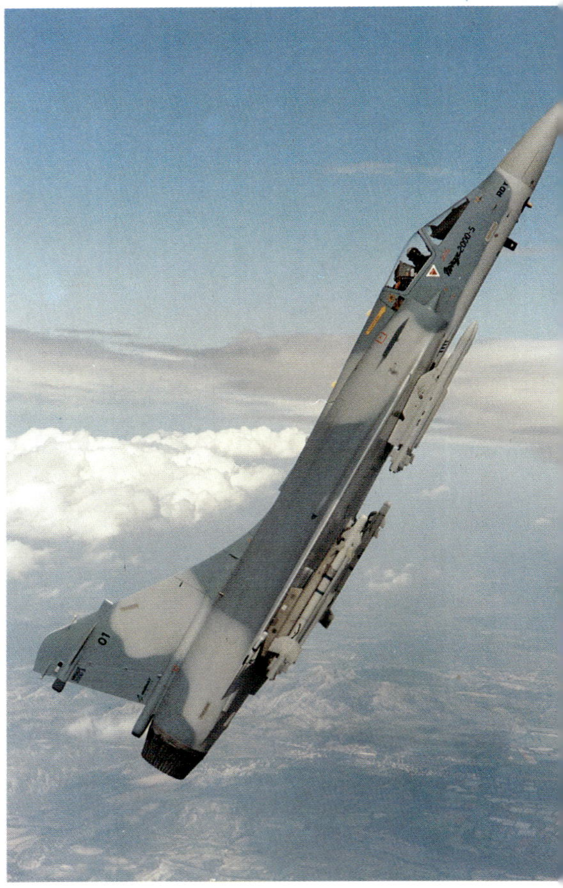

7

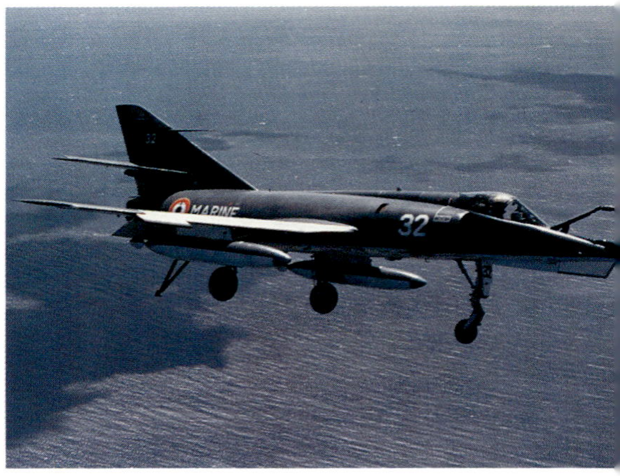

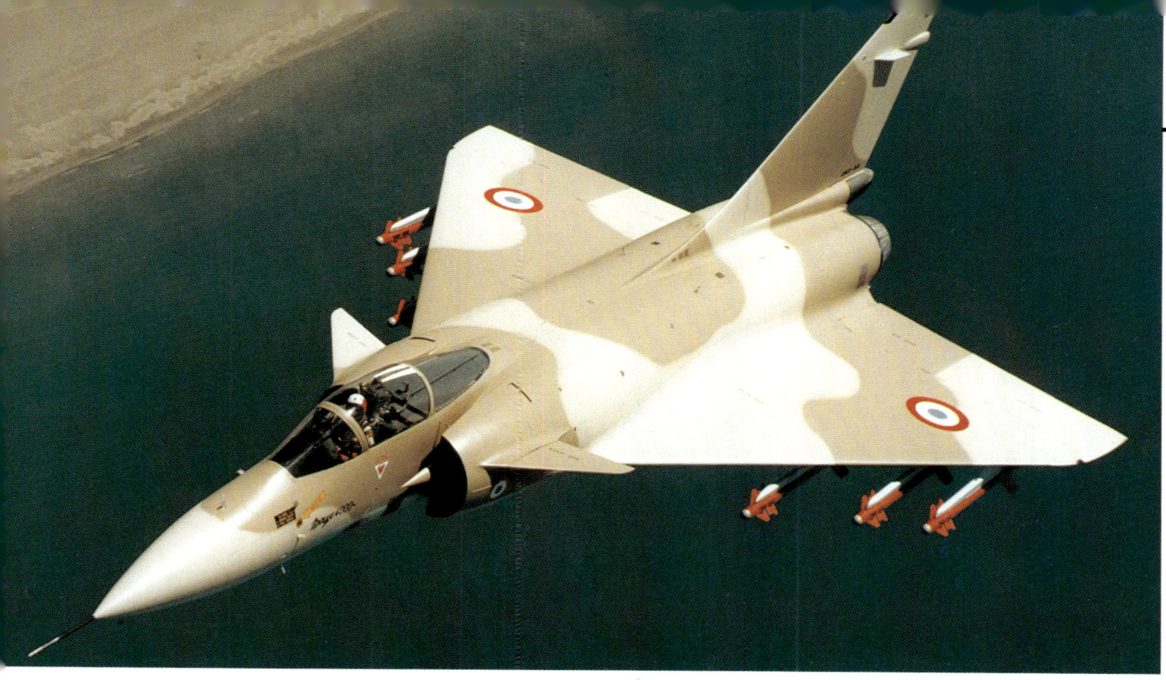

11

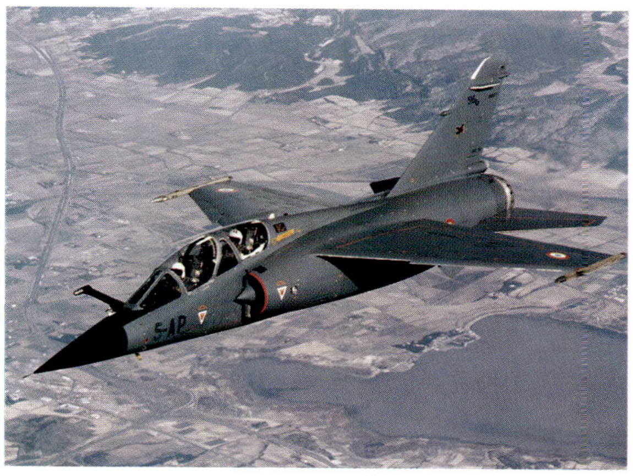

16

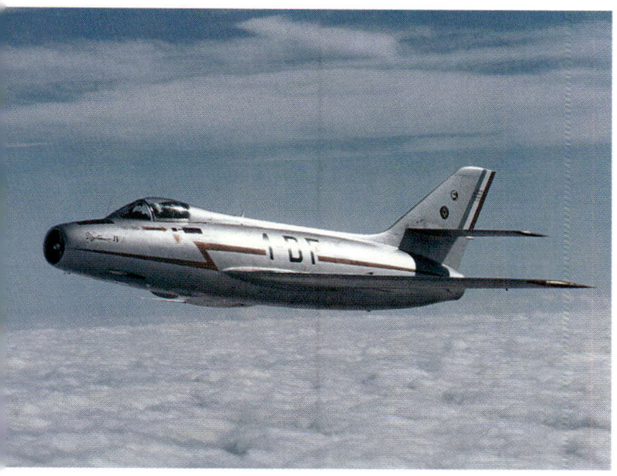

8

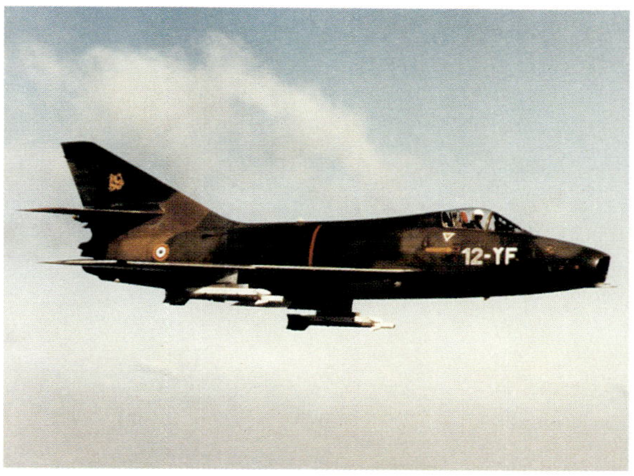

12

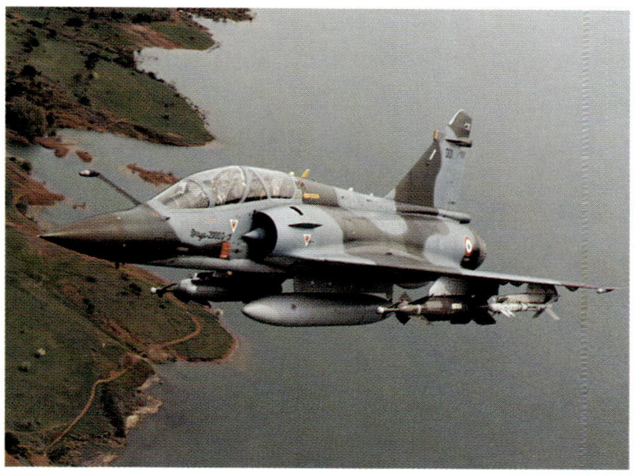

17

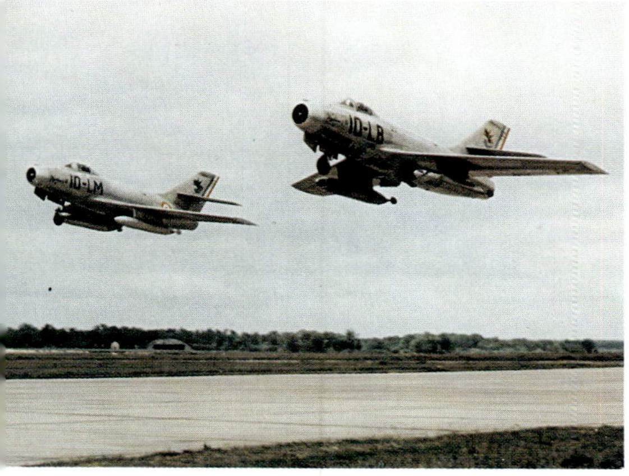

9

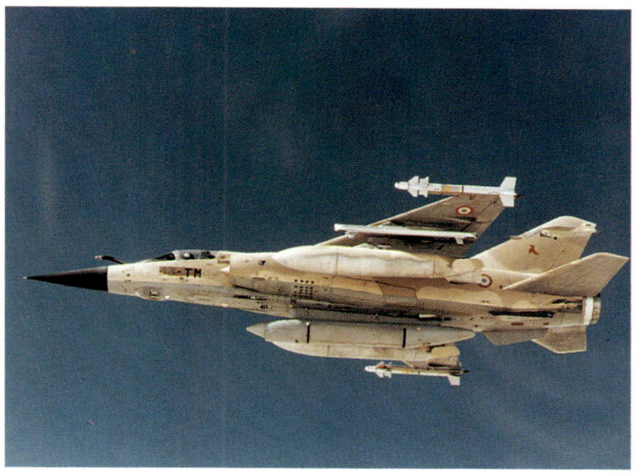

13

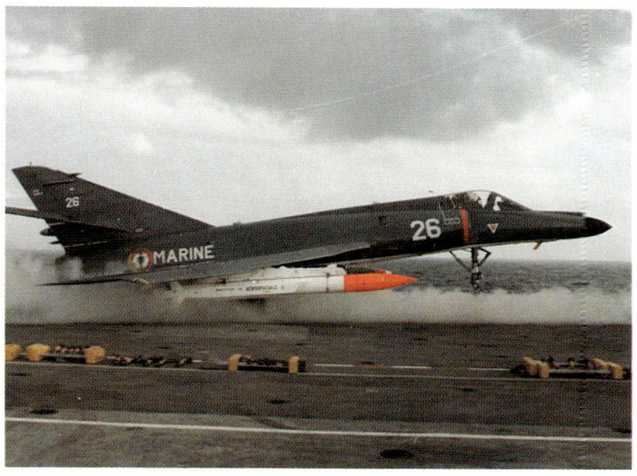

18

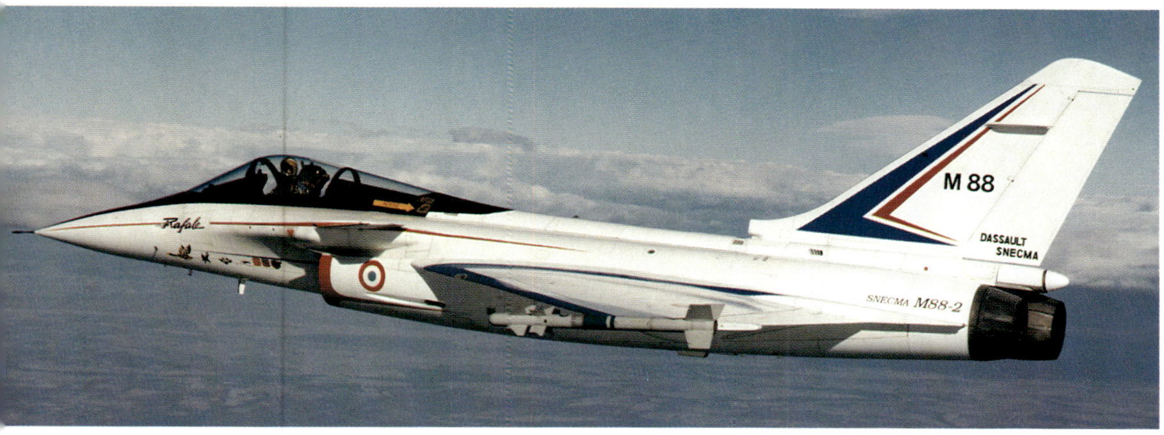

14

Photo Nos. 1 and 19: Dassault Mirage III
Photo Nos. 2 and 8: Dassault Mystère IVA
Photo No. 3: SNCASE Baroudeur
Photo No. 4: Dassault Ouragan
Photo Nos. 5: Nord Griffon
Photo Nos. 6 and 17: Dassault Mirage 2000
Photo Nos. 7: Dassault Etendard
Photo No. 9: Dassault Mystère II
Photo No. 10: SNCASE SE 212 Durandal
Photo No. 11: Dassault Mirage 4000
Photo No. 12: Super-Mystère B2
Photo Nos. 13 and 16: Dassault Mirage F1
Photo No. 14: Dassault Rafale
Photo No. 15: SFECMAS Gerfaut
Photo No. 18: Dassault Super Entendard

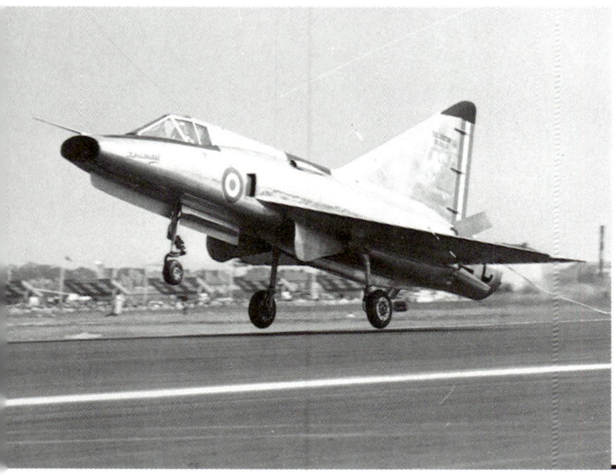

10

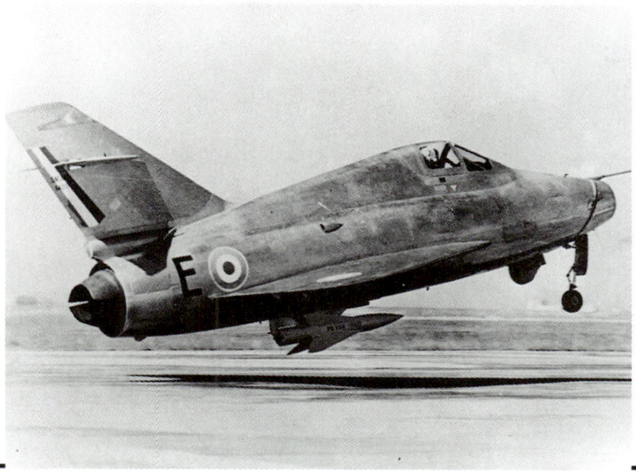

15

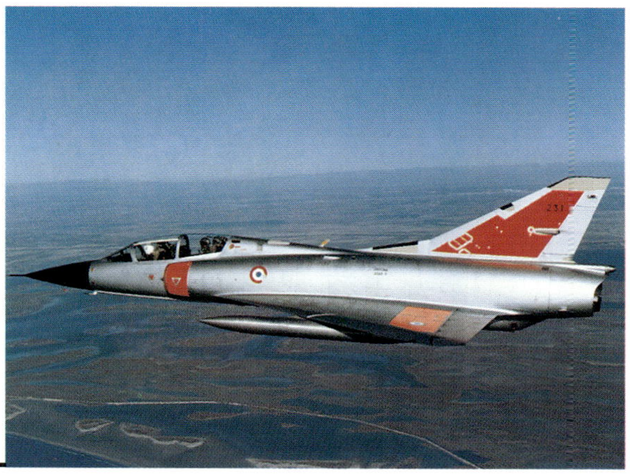

19

BRITISH FIGHTER AND ATTACK PLANES

4
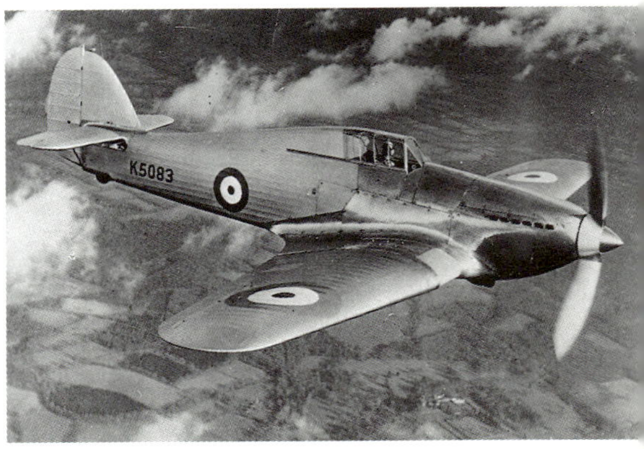

It was the British who created the first-ever fighter squadron, equipped with the first aircraft specifically designed to be armed with a machine gun: the Vickers FB 5 "Gunbus", which appeared in 1914. This plane had a top speed of 70 mph (113 kph) at an altitude of just over 4,920 ft (1,500 m). Like the larger F.E.2b, it had a pusher engine, with propeller located aft of the wings. These aircraft were quickly outclassed by three tractor biplanes, introduced in 1917, which proved to be among the best fighters of the war. The first was the Bristol F.2b, whose 275-hp V12 engine gave it a top speed of almost 125 mph (200 kph). A two-man machine, it was armed with three machine guns and could also carry over 220 lb (100 kg) of bombs. The second, the S.E.5a, of which 5,205 were built, was engaged on all fronts. It had a 200-hp V8 engine and flew at 137 mph (220 kph) at almost 19,700 ft (6,000 m). Its armament consisted of two machine guns. The third, the Sopwith Camel, was the successor to the Sopwith Pup and Triplane. It proved a fighter of superb quality, highly responsive and manoeuvrable, and in the hands of experienced pilots accounted for over 3,000 enemy aircraft in the 18 months from May 1917 to November 1918.

Between the wars and until the late 1930s, the fighters produced by the British aircraft industry retained the general configuration of World War I models: biplane wings, fixed undercarriage, two machine guns in line with the engine, and an open cockpit. As engines became more powerful and reliable, they were able to reach speeds of 190 mph (c.300 kph) and operate at altitudes of over 26,000 ft (8,000 m).

The final development of these biplanes was represented by the Gloster Gladiator. First delivered in 1937, it was already obsolete at the outbreak of World War II. Fortunately for the Royal Air Force, in 1934 the Hawker company had begun work on a monoplane fighter armed with eight machine guns: the Hurricane. Powered by a 1,000-hp engine, it could reach speeds of 312 mph (500 kph) and ascend to altitudes of over 32,800 ft (10,000 m). The more powerful Mk IIc version, which reached the RAF in 1941, approached 345 mph (550 kph) and was armed with four 20-mm cannon. Meanwhile, Hawker were perfecting the Typhoon, whose 2,200-hp 24-cylinder engine gave it a maximum speed of 406 mph (650 kph). It was widely used in 1944, supporting the Normandy landings with bombs and rockets. A later development of this aircraft, the Tempest, was even more manoeuvrable and could fly at 437 mph (700 kph), making it one of the most remarkable fighters of the latter part of the war.

1
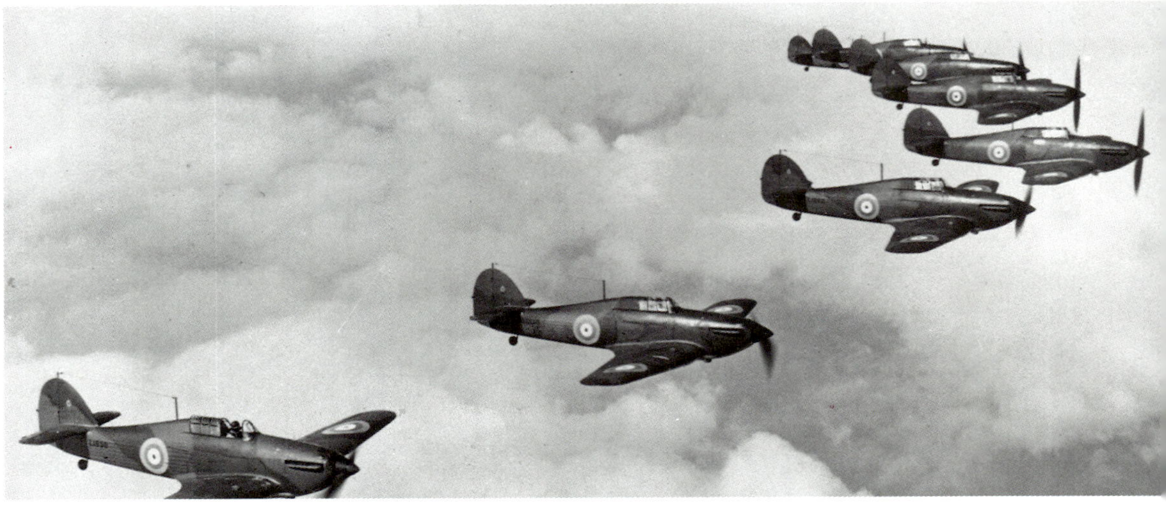

2
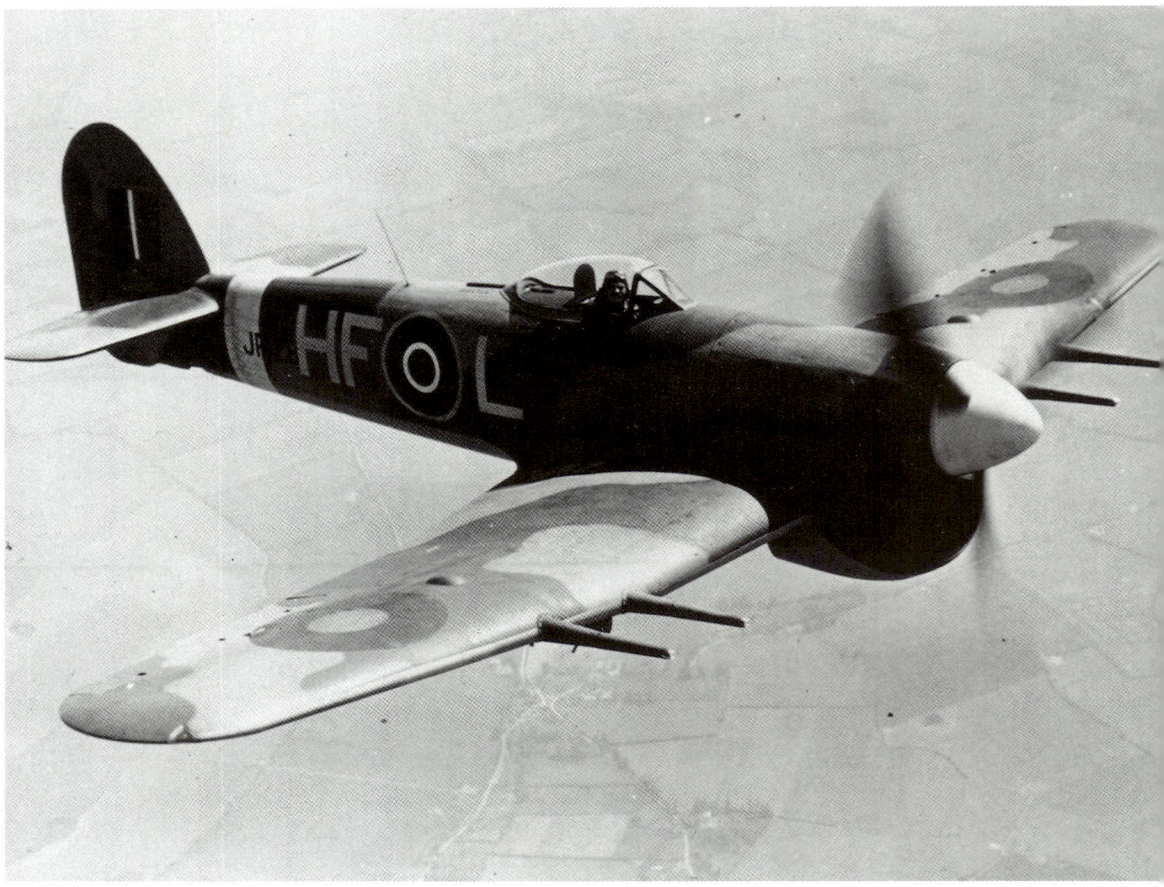

3
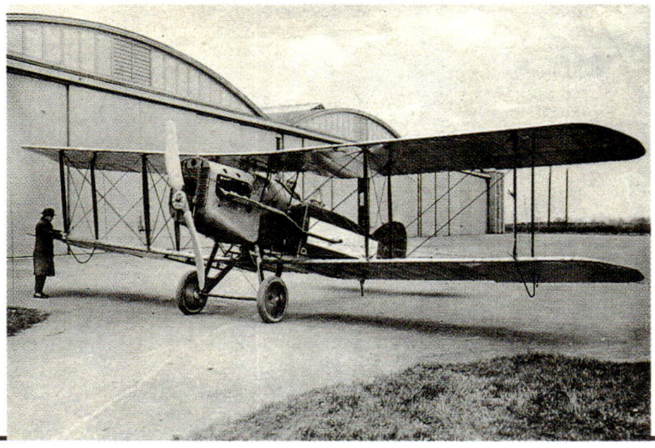

5
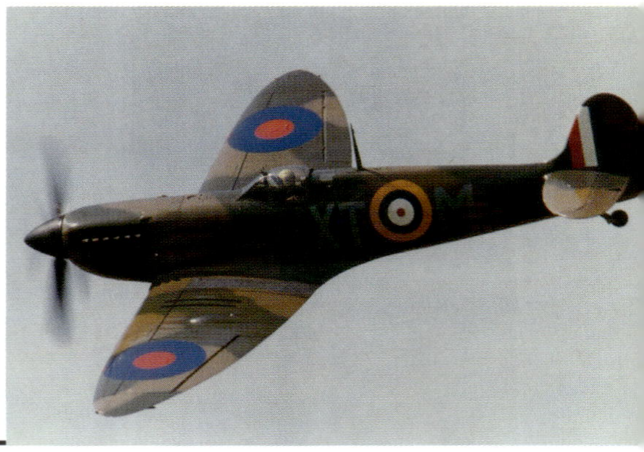

6
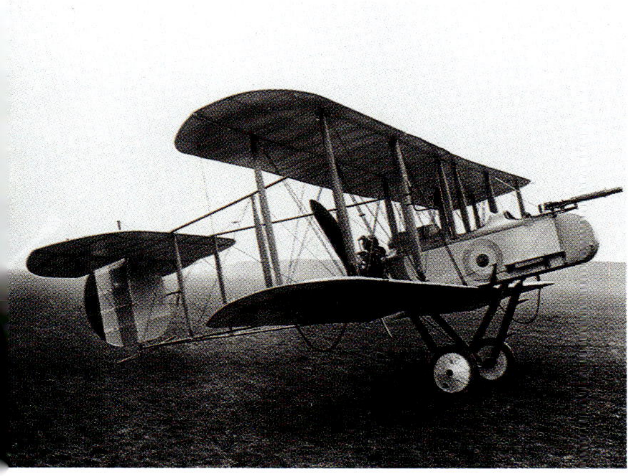

12
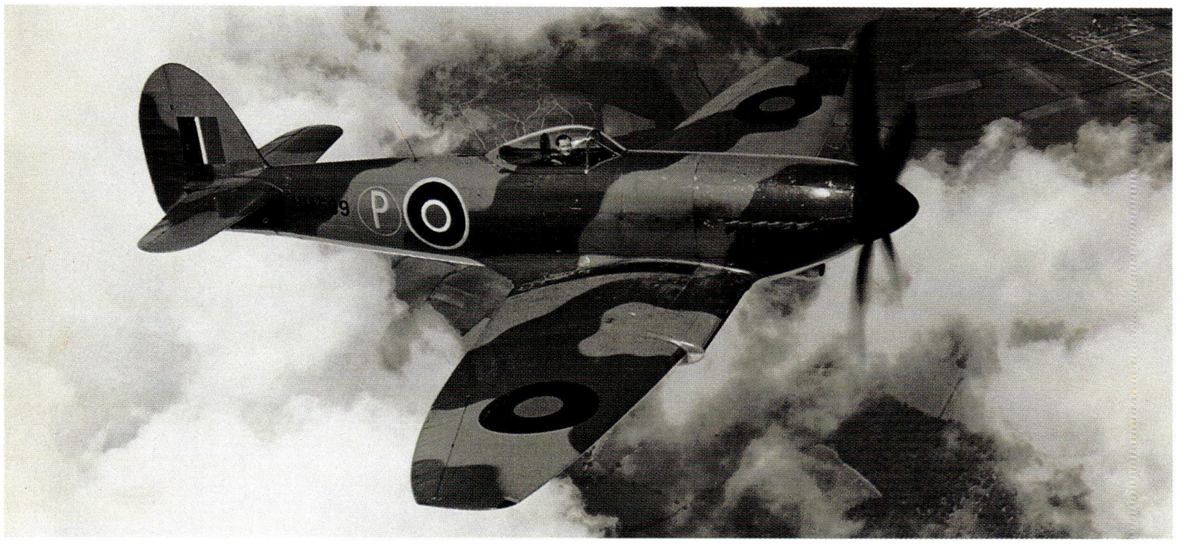

7
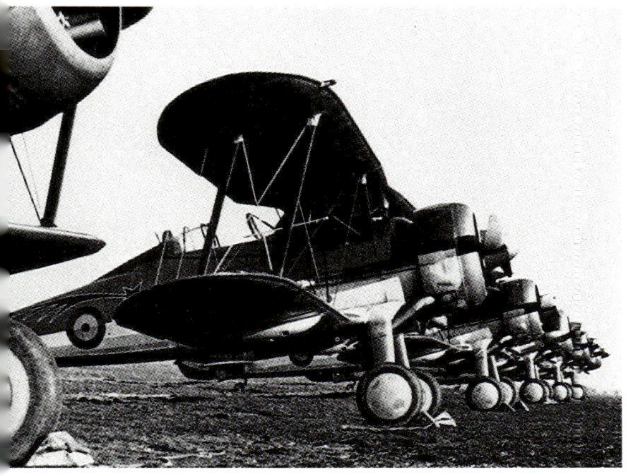

13
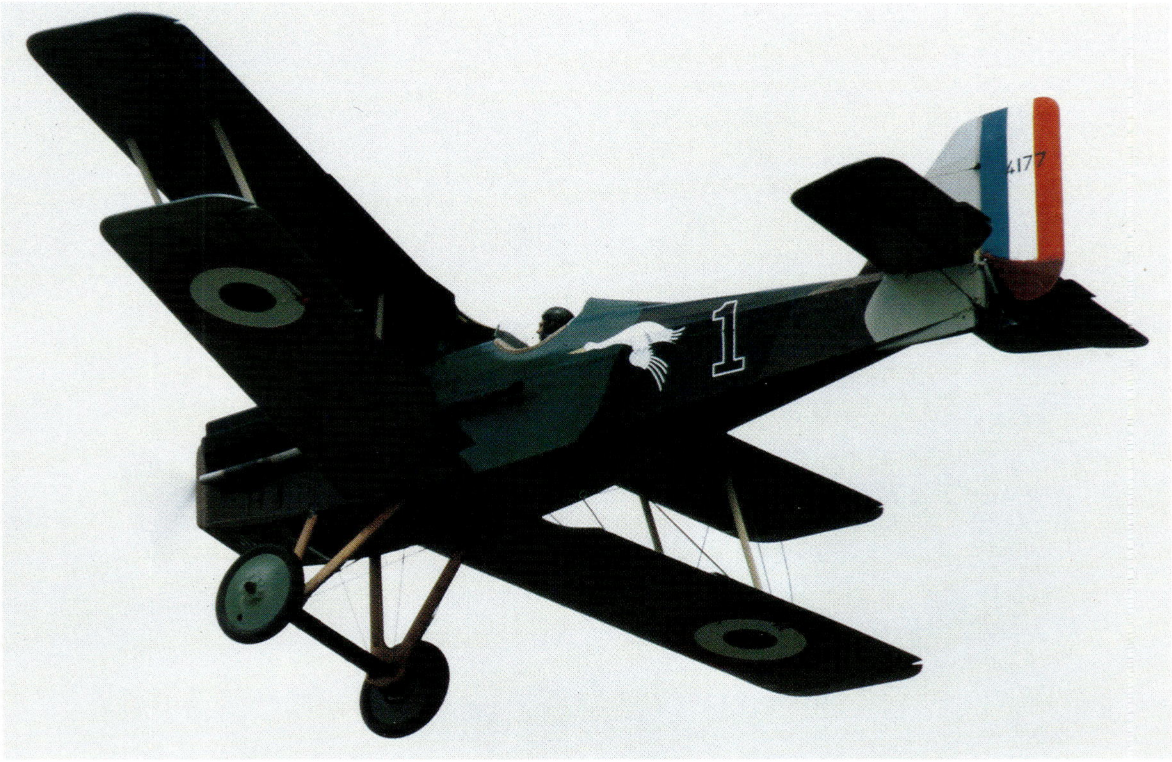

8
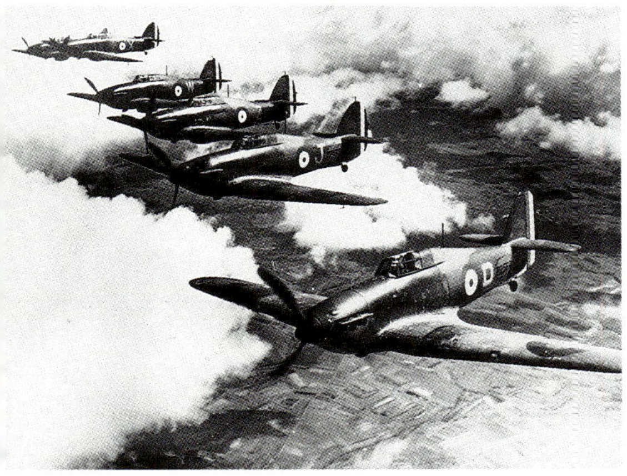

10
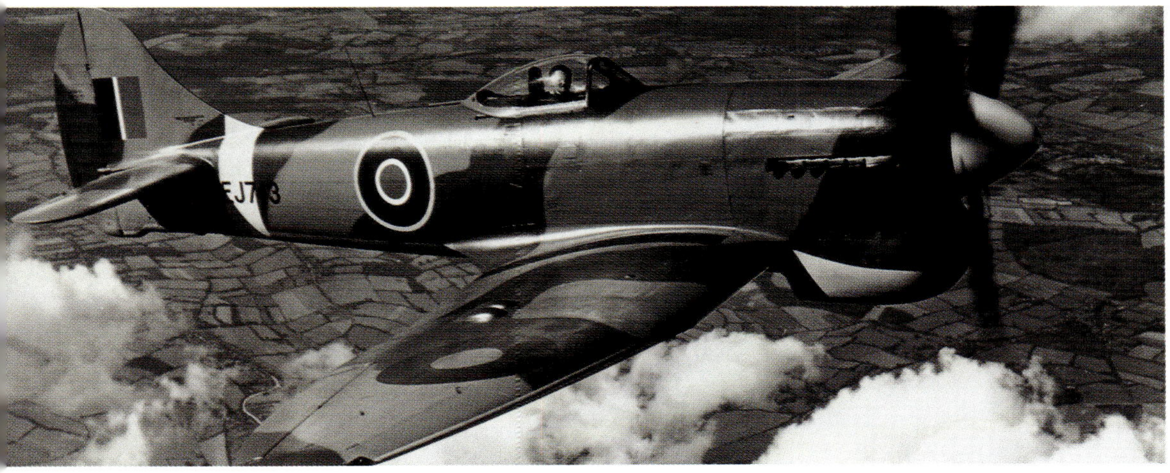

Photo Nos. 1 and 8: Hawker Hurricane
Photo No. 2: Hawker Typhoon
Photo No. 3: Bristol F.2b
Photo No. 4: Hawker F.36/34
Photo Nos. 5: Spitfire MkV
Photo No. 6: Vickers FB 5 replica
Photo No. 7: Gloster Gladiator
Photo No. 9: Sopwith F1 Camel
Photo No. 10: Hawker Tempest V
Photo No. 11: F.E.2b
Photo No. 12: Hawker Tempest I
Photo No. 13: S.E.5a replica

9
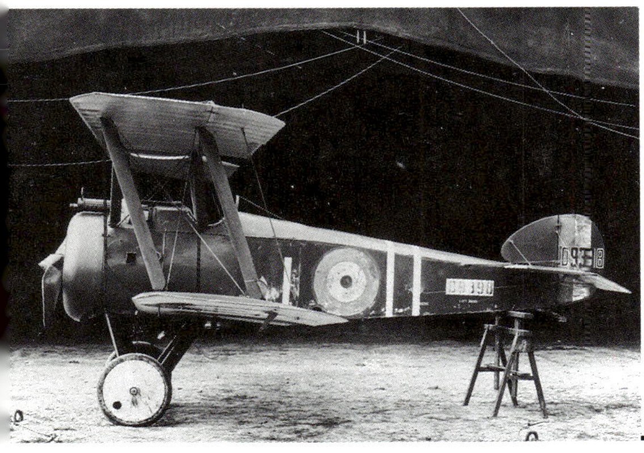

11
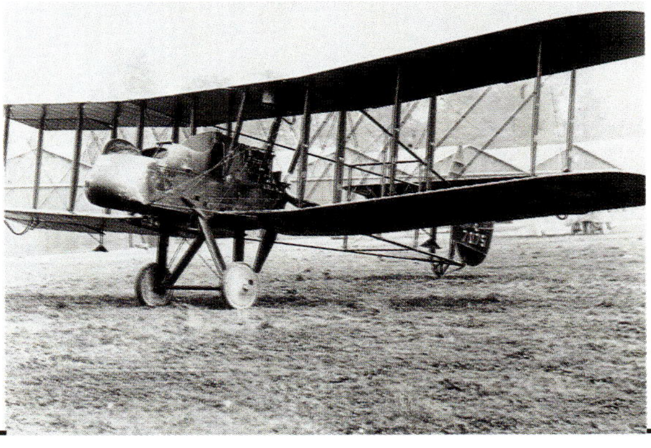

BRITISH FIGHTER AND ATTACK PLANES

4
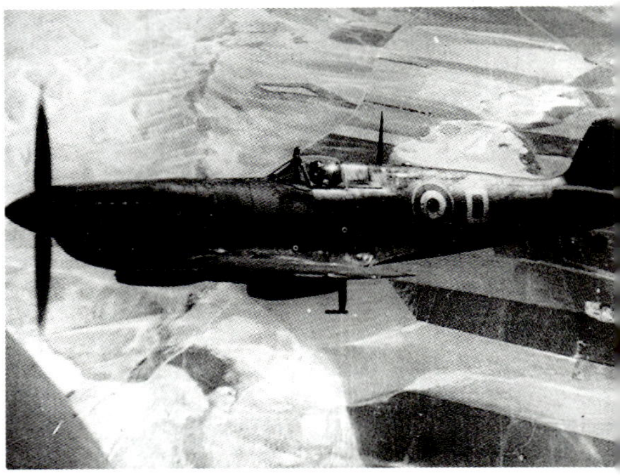

Though the chief winner of the Battle of Britain in 1940 was the Hurricane, its partner the Spitfire became more famous. First flown in March 1936, it was developed in 24 versions throughout the war. The output of its 12-cylinder Rolls-Royce engine was augmented from 1,030 to 2,050 hp, its speed from 357 mph (571 kph) to 450 mph (720 kph), and its ceiling from 33,780 ft (10,300m) to 44,600 ft (13,600 m). Originally equipped with eight machine guns, the 1944 version sported two 20-mm cannon and four machine guns, giving it formidable firepower. In all, 20,334 Spitfires were built, plus 2,556 carrier-based Seafires.

Developed during the war years, the Gloster Meteor was the RAF's first jet fighter. A twin-engined aircraft, it flew for the first time in 1943. The version commissioned in 1944 reached speeds of almost 600 mph (966 kph). For its part, the de Havilland company had designed a single-engined jet fighter, the Vampire, which also made its debut in 1943. It flew at 543 mph (870 kph) and was armed with four 20-mm cannon. In addition, it could deliver two bombs or eight rockets. The Vampire was also produced in France, by SNCASE, where it went by the name of Mistral.

In 1953, the RAF began to take delivery of two new aircraft built by Hawker Siddeley: the Hawker Hunter, a fighter-bomber which reached supersonic speeds in a shallow dive and was powerfully armed with four 30-mm cannon; and the Gloster Javelin, an all-weather fighter, in this case armed with four 30-mm cannon and four air-to-air missiles.

The RAF is at present equipped with two aircraft resulting from international cooperation. The first is the Anglo-French Jaguar, which comes in single-seater all-weather strike and two-seater trainer versions. A twin-engined supersonic jet with a maximum speed of 1,062 mph (1,700 kph), it is armed with two 30-mm cannon and can carry more than 4.5 tons of weaponry under its wings. The Jaguar is also used by the French air force. The second is the two-seater, multi-purpose Panavia Tornado, a joint venture involving Britain, Germany and Italy. This European plane has a top speed of over 1,312 mph (2,100 kph) and can fly at altitudes in excess of 49,200 ft (15,000 m). The successor to the Tornado should be the EFA (European Fighter Aircraft), for which Spain has joined the Eurofighter consortium, but Germany's withdrawal from the project in June 1992 could signal the abandonment of this 21-ton multi-role twin-engined fighter.

1
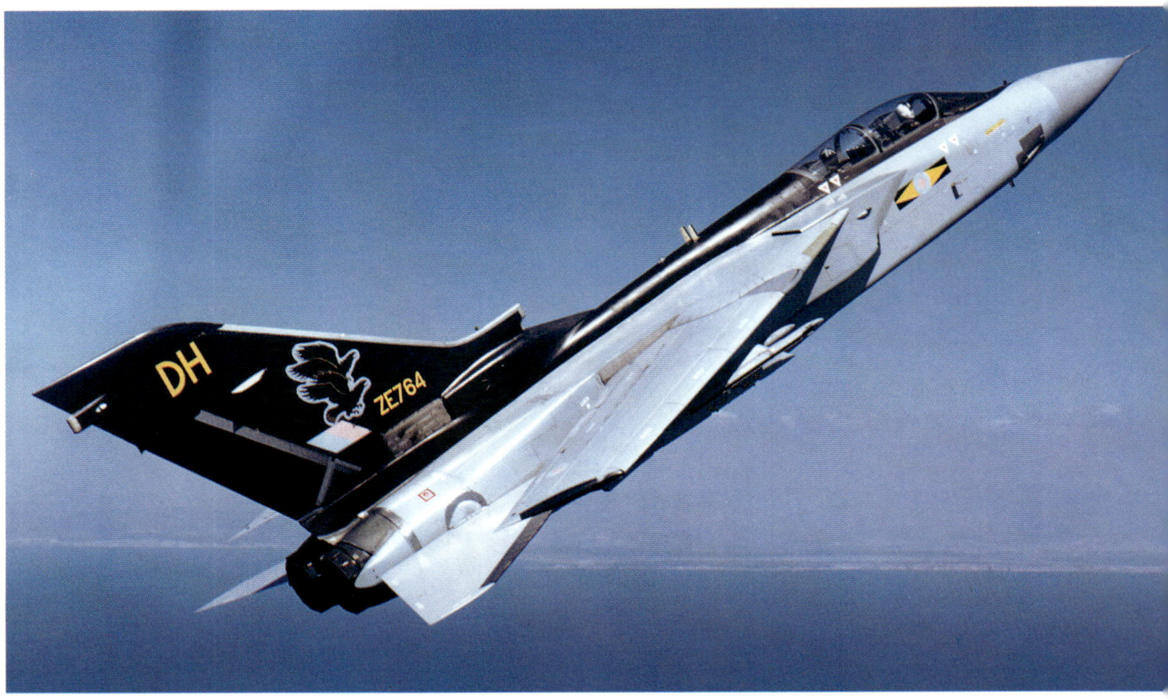

2
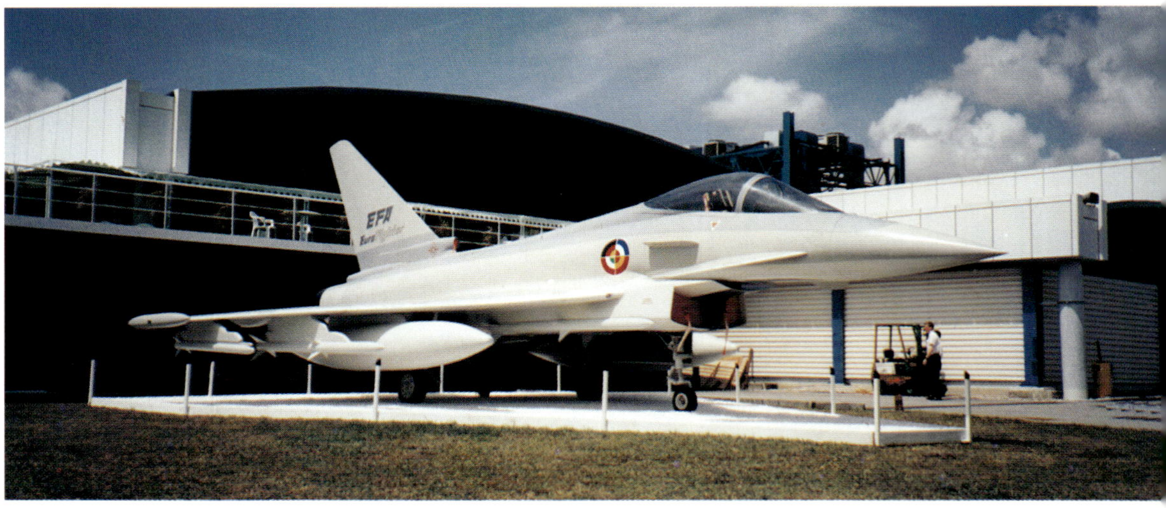

3
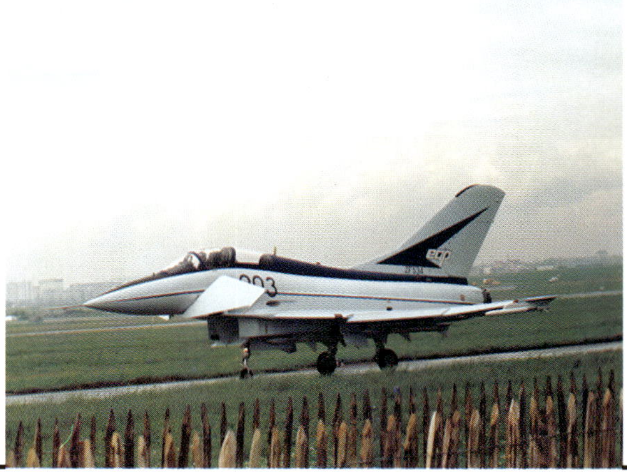

5
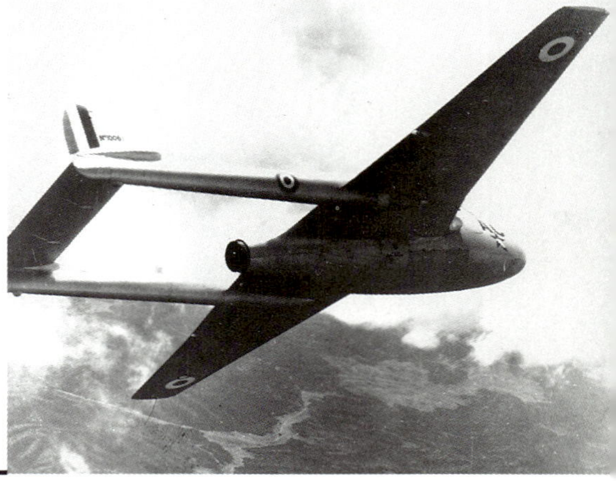

9

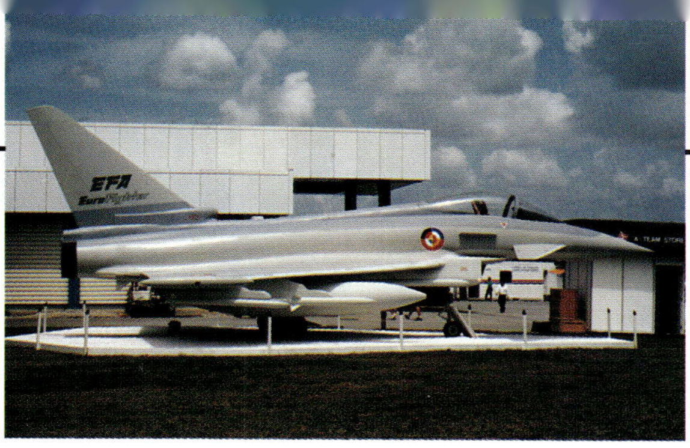

6

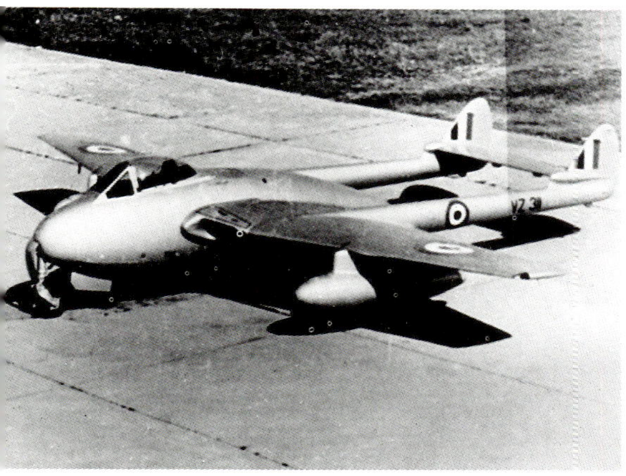

10

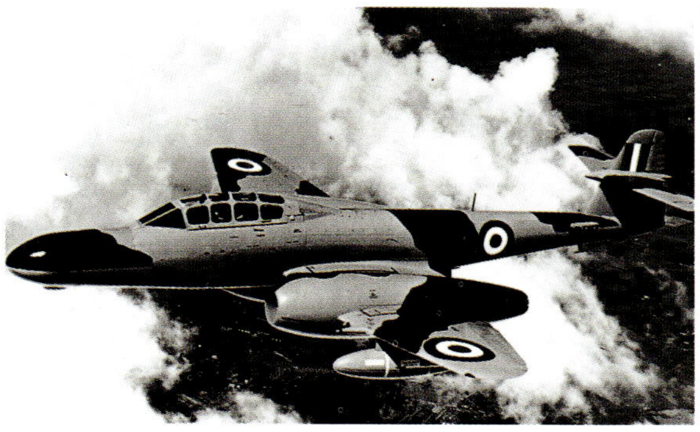

12

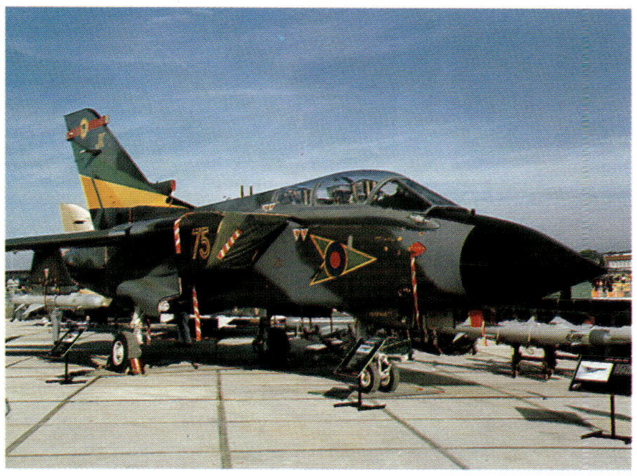

7

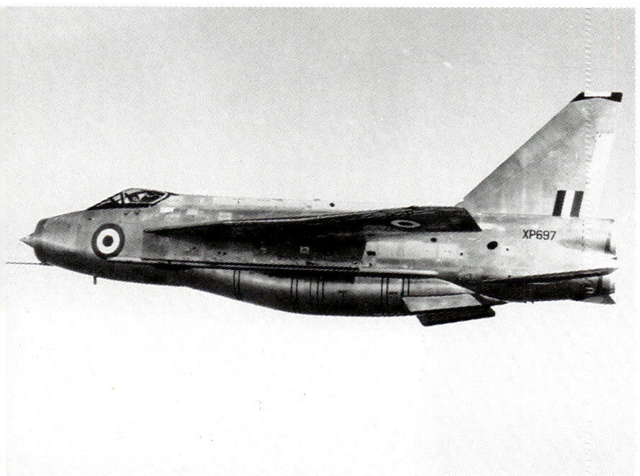

13

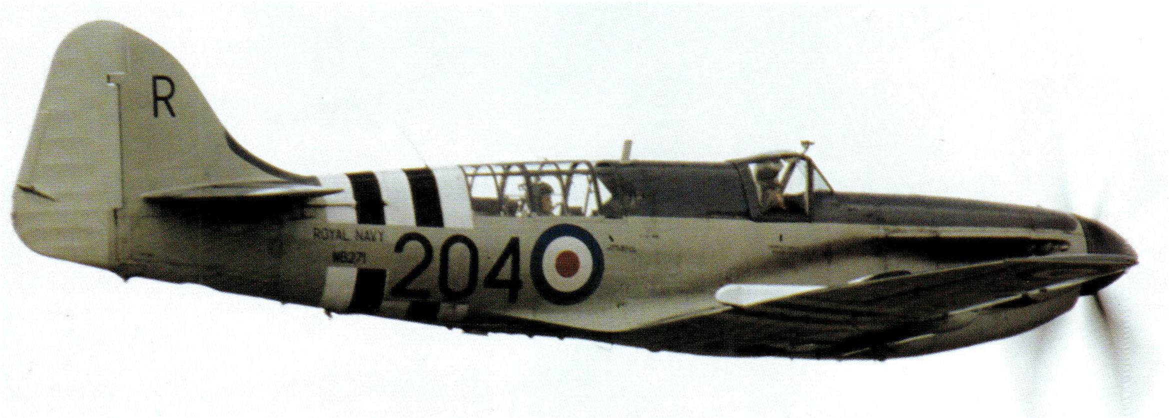

11

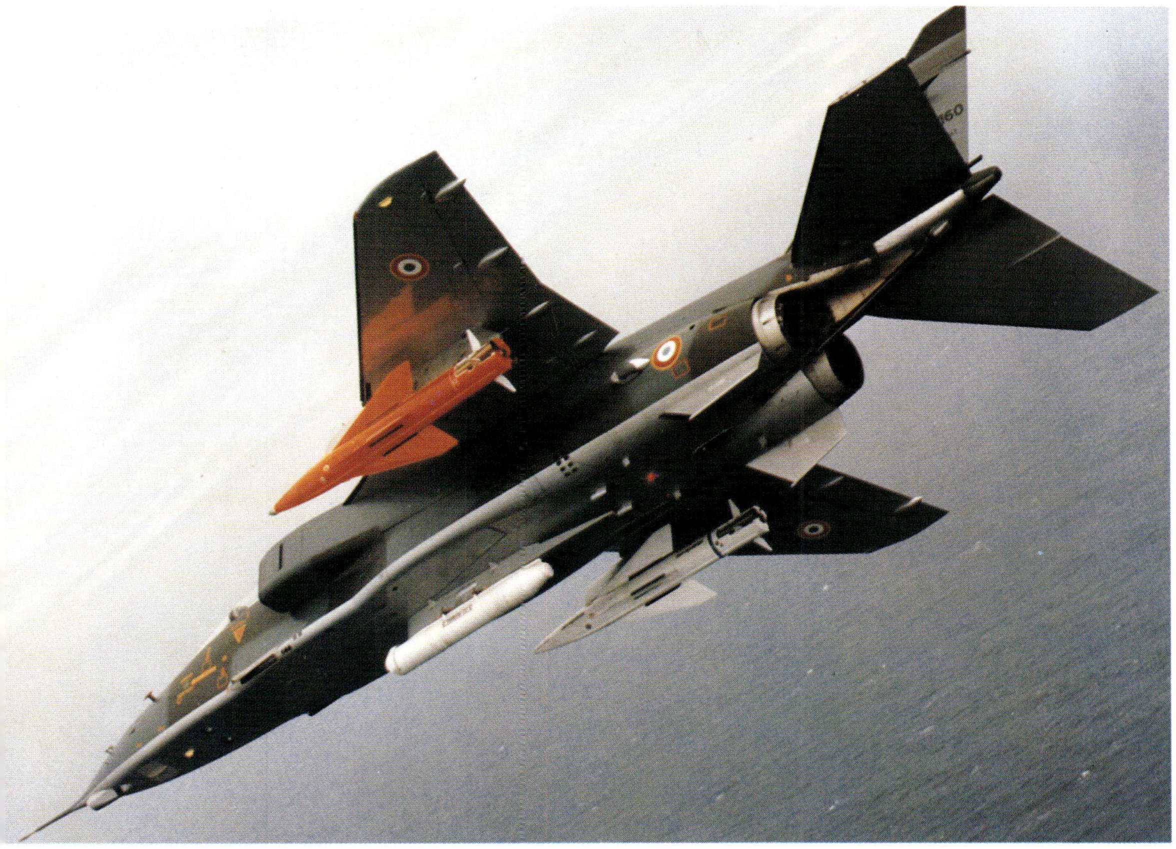

14

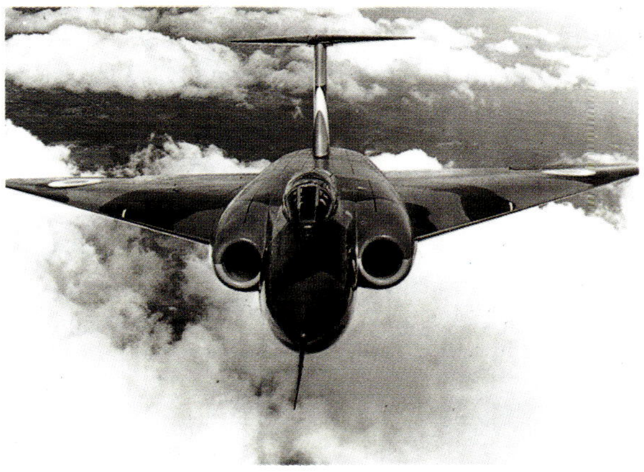

Photo Nos. 1, 12 and 15: Panavia Tornado (Britain, Germany and Italy)
Photo Nos. 2 and 9: Eurofighter (EFA)
Photo No. 3: British Aerospace EAP
Photo Nos. 4: Supermarine Spitfire
Photo Nos. 5 and 6: de Havilland Vampire
Photo No. 7: BAC Lightning
Photo Nos. 8 and 11: SEPECAT Jaguar (Britain and France)
Photo No. 10: Gloster Meteor
Photo No. 13: Fairey Firefly AS.5
Photo No. 14: Gloster Javelin

8

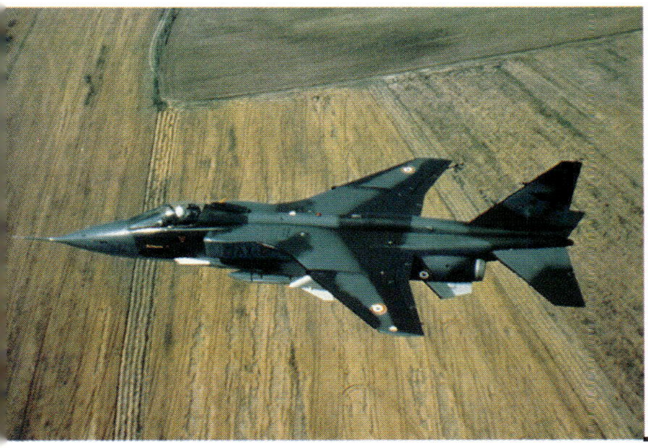

15

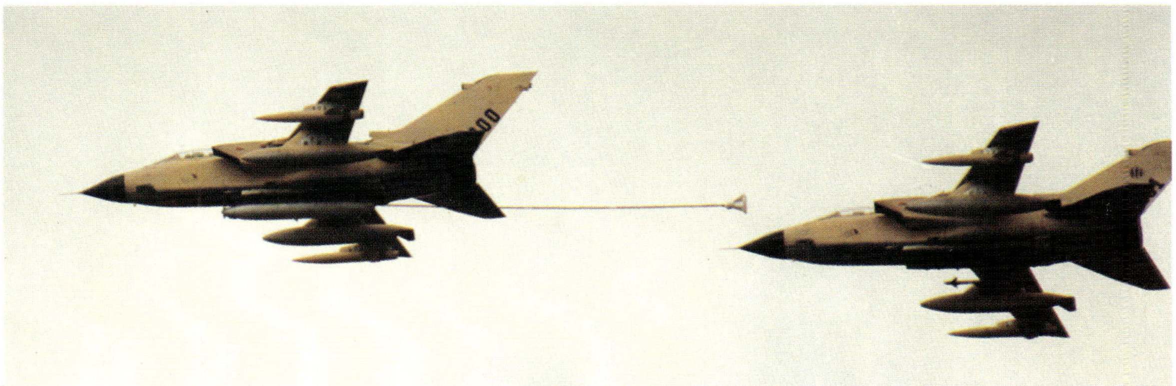

AMERICAN FIGHTER PLANES

4

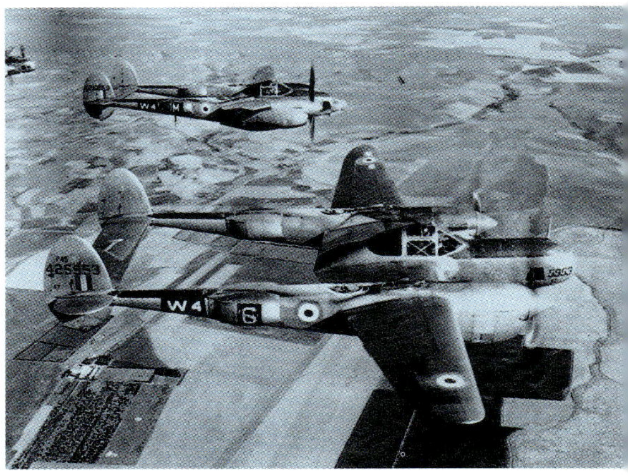

No home-grown American fighters took part in World War I. The fighter aces of the American Expeditionary Force flew French and British warplanes – and with con-siderable success, since they accounted for some 800 enemy aircraft.

Of the fighters designed during the 1930s, the Boeing P-26A was a monoplane of entirely metal construction with a top speed of 234 mph (375 kph). Equipped with two machine guns, it was adopted by the US Army Air Corps. Meanwhile, Grumman were developing their first carrier-based fighter, the FF-1, which had a retractable undercarriage. A single-engined, two-seater biplane, it was armed with three machine guns, flew at 206 mph (330 kph), and reached an altitude of 21,300 ft (6,500 m). It was succeeded, in 1935, by the F3F-1, a single-seater biplane armed with two machine guns, which flew both faster (231 mph/370 kph) and higher (28,530 ft/8,700 m).

When the Japanese made their surprise attack on Pearl Harbor in 1941, the fighters available to the Americans were outclassed by the enemy aircraft. Curtiss had begun to deliver the P-36C, which, despite its speed (312 mph/500 kph) and ceiling of over 32,800 ft (10,000 m) was soon superseded by the Curtiss P-40 Warhawk. The final version of this aircraft had a top speed in excess of 375 mph (600 kph) and could fly at altitudes of over 37,700 ft (11,500 m).

One of the most curious US aircraft of the early war years was the Bell P-39 Airacobra, a single-seater with a nose-wheel undercarriage and a 1,200-hp centrally-located engine. Despite its speed (375 mph/600 kph) and heavy armament of four or six machine guns and 37-mm cannon, it proved disappointing in combat, except on the Russian front where it was popular.

For night operations, in 1941 Northrop began work on a three-seater twin-engined aircraft equipped with nose-mounted radar, four 20-mm cannon and four machine guns. They also produced a two-seater strategic reconnaissance version. Named the Black Widow, this plane flew at up to 366 mph (589 kph) and had a range of 3,000 miles (4,800 kilometres). It served in the Pacific theatre and in Europe.

Beginning in 1942, the first generation of daylight fighters began to be replaced by higher-performance aircraft. The heaviest, weighing almost nine tons, was the Republic P-47 Thunderbolt, powered by a 2,000-hp 18-cylinder

1

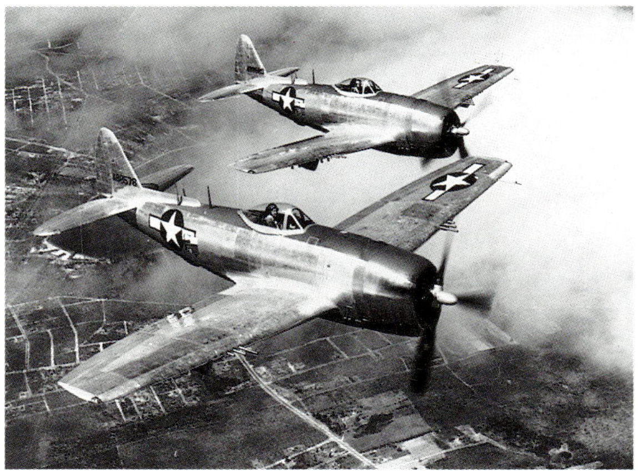

5

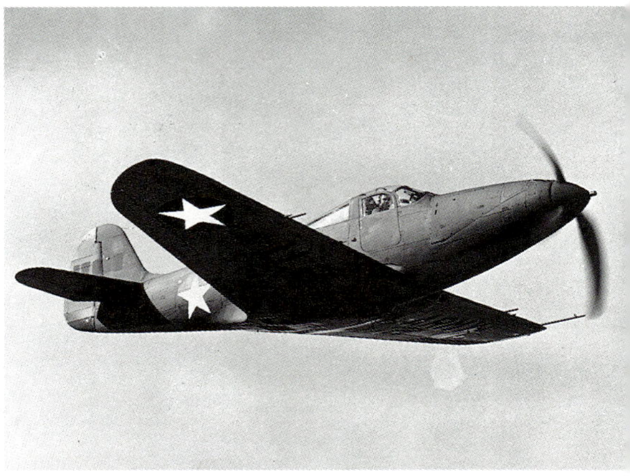

2

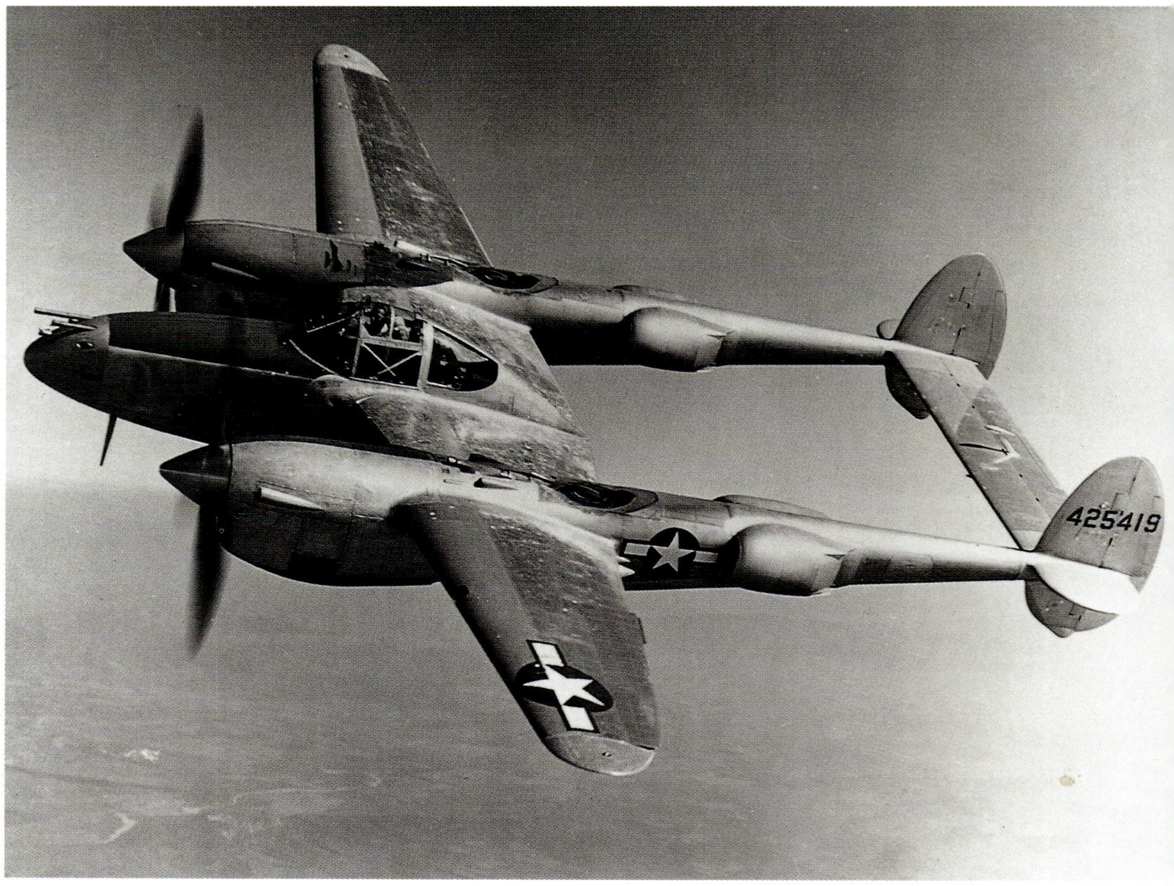

3

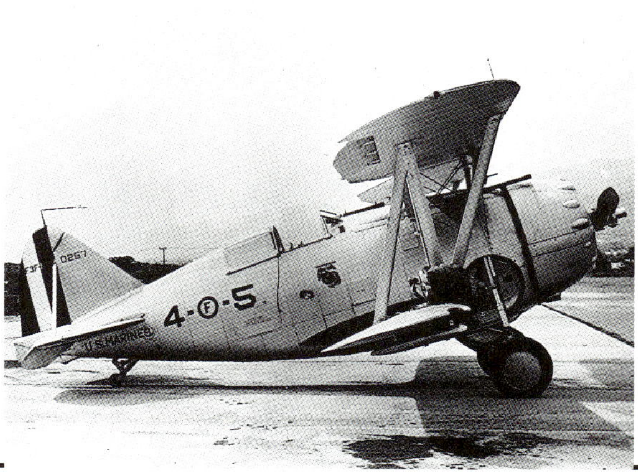

6

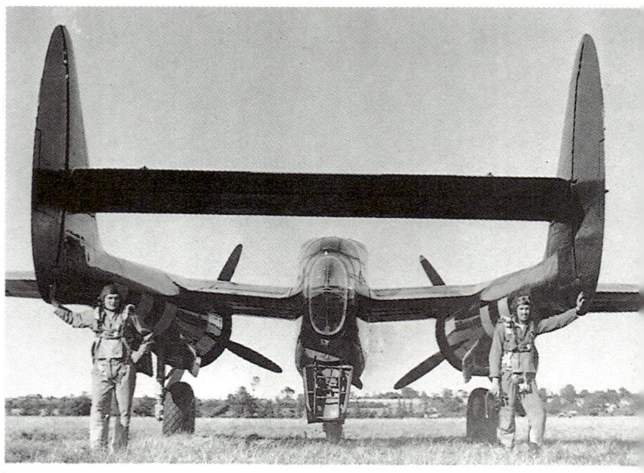

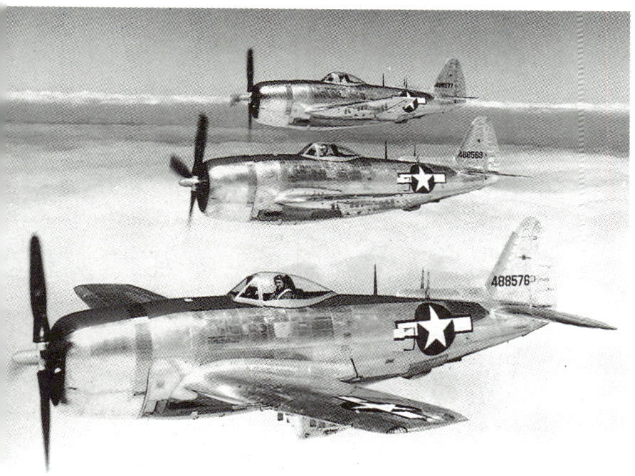

7

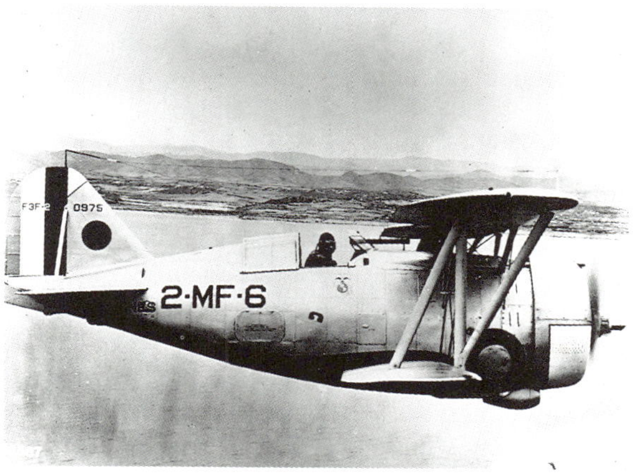

10

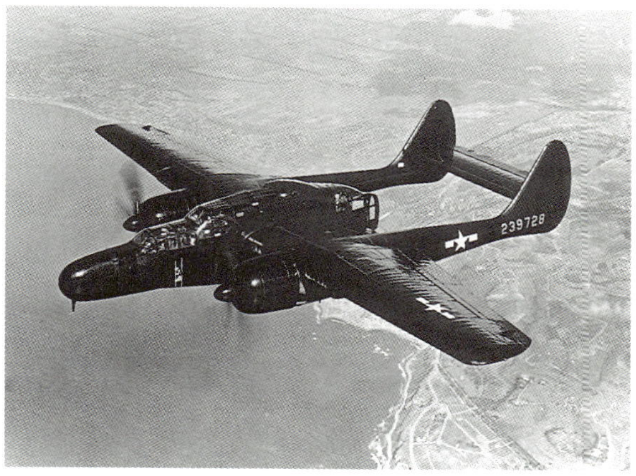

14

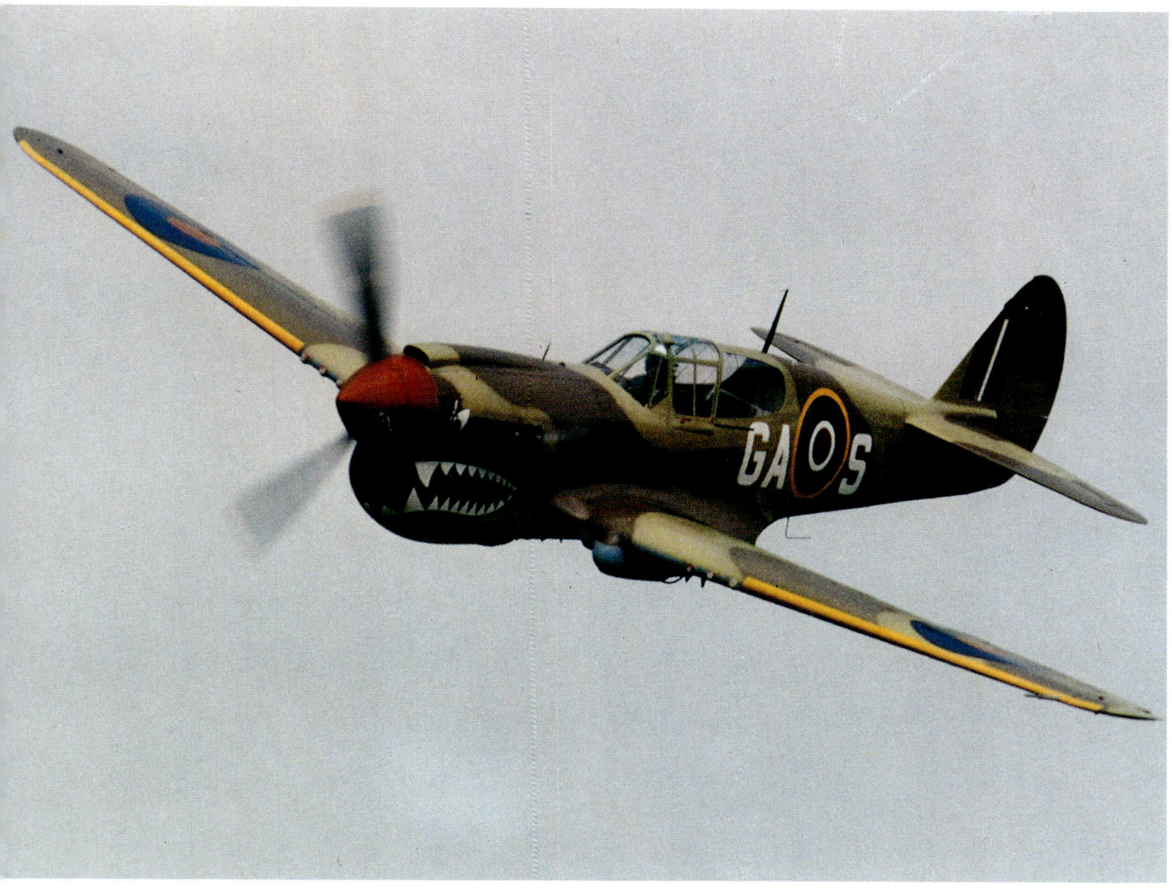

11

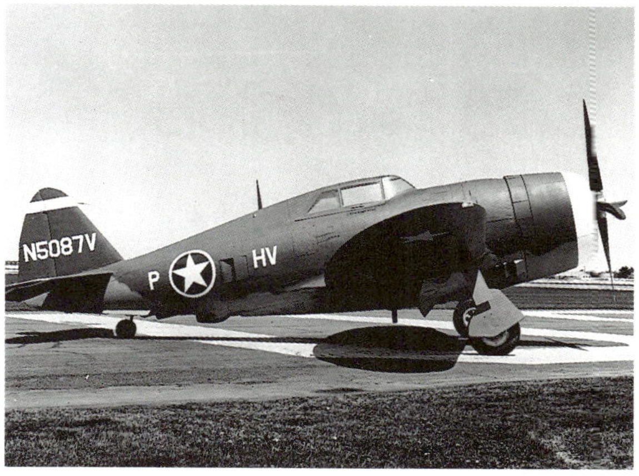

15

engine, which gave it a top speed of 430 mph (690 kph). It was armed with eight 0.5-inch machine guns and could carry 2,000 lb (900 kg) of bombs. Another American star of World War II was the Lockheed P-38 Lightning.

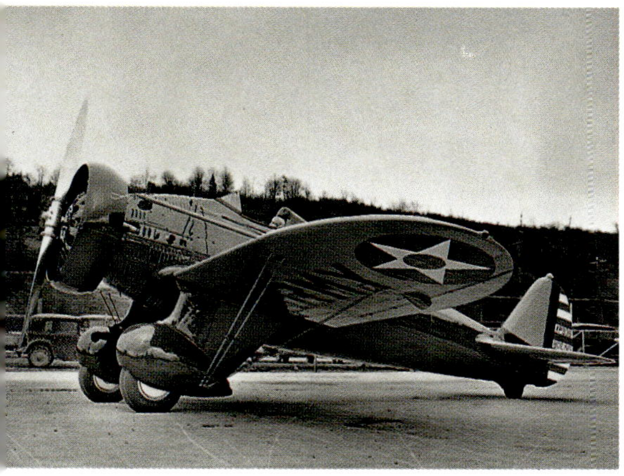

8

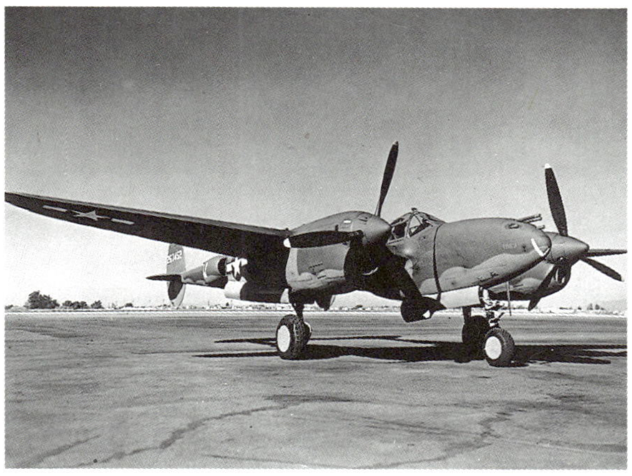

12

Photo Nos. 1, 7 and 15: Republic P-47 Thunderbolt
Photo Nos. 2, 4 and 12: Lockheed P-38 Lightning
Photo Nos. 3 and 10: Grumman F3F
Photo Nos. 5 and 9: Bell P-39 Airacobra
Photo Nos. 6 and 14: Northrop P-61 Black Widow
Photo No. 8: Boeing P-26
Photo Nos. 11 and 13: Curtiss P-40 Warhawk

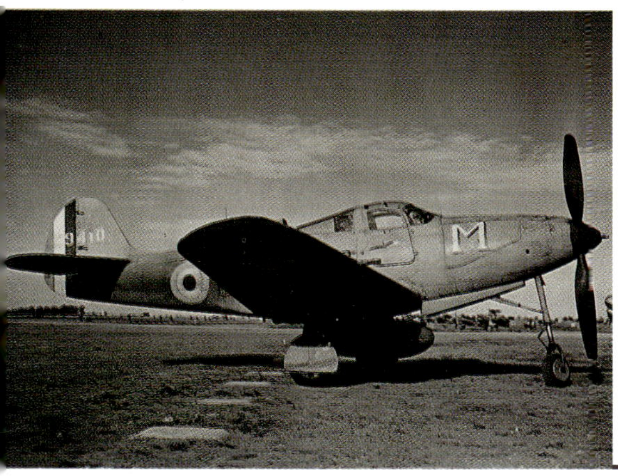

9

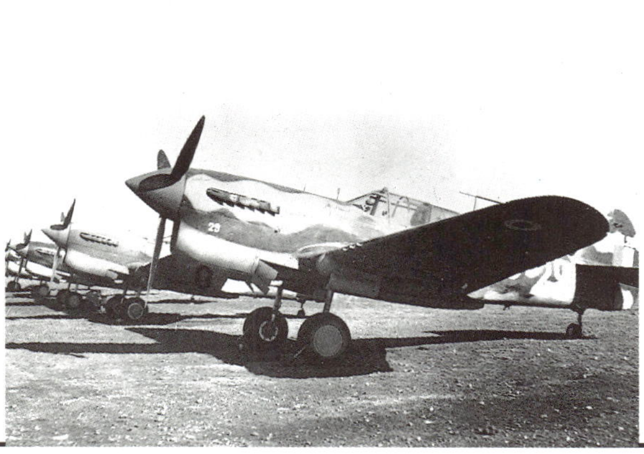

13

AMERICAN FIGHTER PLANES

4

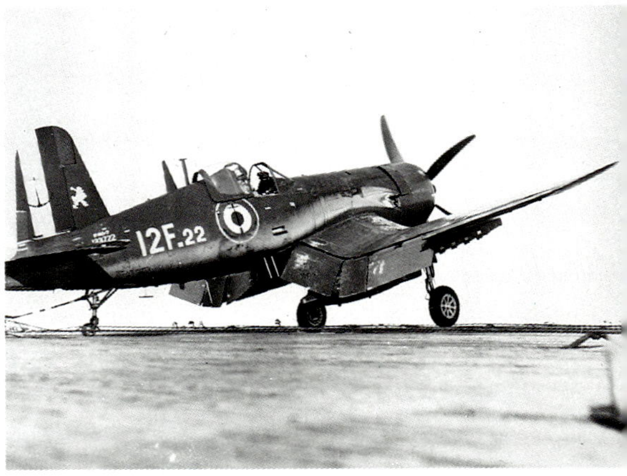

More than 10,000 Lockheed P-38 Lightnings were built. The aircraft had a particularly distinguished career in the Pacific, accounting for large numbers of Japanese planes. The P-38 was a twin-engined single-seater fighter with twin tail booms. The final version weighed almost 10 tons. Its 1,475-hp engines gave it a top speed of 412 mph (660 kph) and a ceiling of 42,600 ft (13,000 m). Armament consisted of a 20-mm cannon and four machine guns.

But the US Air Force's most popular fighter was the P-51 North American Mustang, 15,367 of which were manufactured. Its American airframe and, in later versions, British Rolls-Royce engine built under licence in the United States, proved a formidable combination. The single-seater Mustang flew at up to 437 mph (700 kph), could climb to 19,680 ft (6,000 m) in six minutes, and had an overall ceiling of 41,000 ft (12,500 m). With a range of 2,300 miles (3,700 km), it could be used as an escort on bomber raids. Its armament usually consisted of six heavy machine guns, and it could deliver a bomb load of 2,000lb (907 kg).

In the Pacific, the Americans used carrier-based aircraft in all the great battles against the Japanese. The Grumman F4F Wildcat was in action with the British from 1940, an improved version appearing in 1942. The Wildcat was a tubby single-seater powered by a 1,200-hp engine. It flew at over 312 mph (500 kph) at 19,700 ft (6,000 m) and was armed with six machine guns. Its successor, entering service in 1943, was the Grumman F6F Hellcat, 12,275 of which were produced. This aircraft had a 2,000-hp 18-cylinder engine, flew at speeds in excess of 375 mph (600 kph), and could climb to 36,000 ft (11,000 m). It had a range of 1,062 miles (1,700 km) and was armed with six heavy machine guns.

But the most redoubtable carrier-based aircraft of World War II was undoubtedly the Vought F4U Corsair, which shot down 2,140 Japanese planes in the last two years of the conflict. A single-seater fighter, the Corsair continued in production until 1952 and was still in service in certain countries in 1965. Its distinguishing feature was its 'W' wing configuration. The 18-cylinder engine developed 2,000 hp. Weighing six tons, the Corsair flew at over 425 mph (680 kph) and had a ceiling of over 36,000 ft (11,000 m). Its armament consisted of six heavy 0.5-inch machine guns.

1

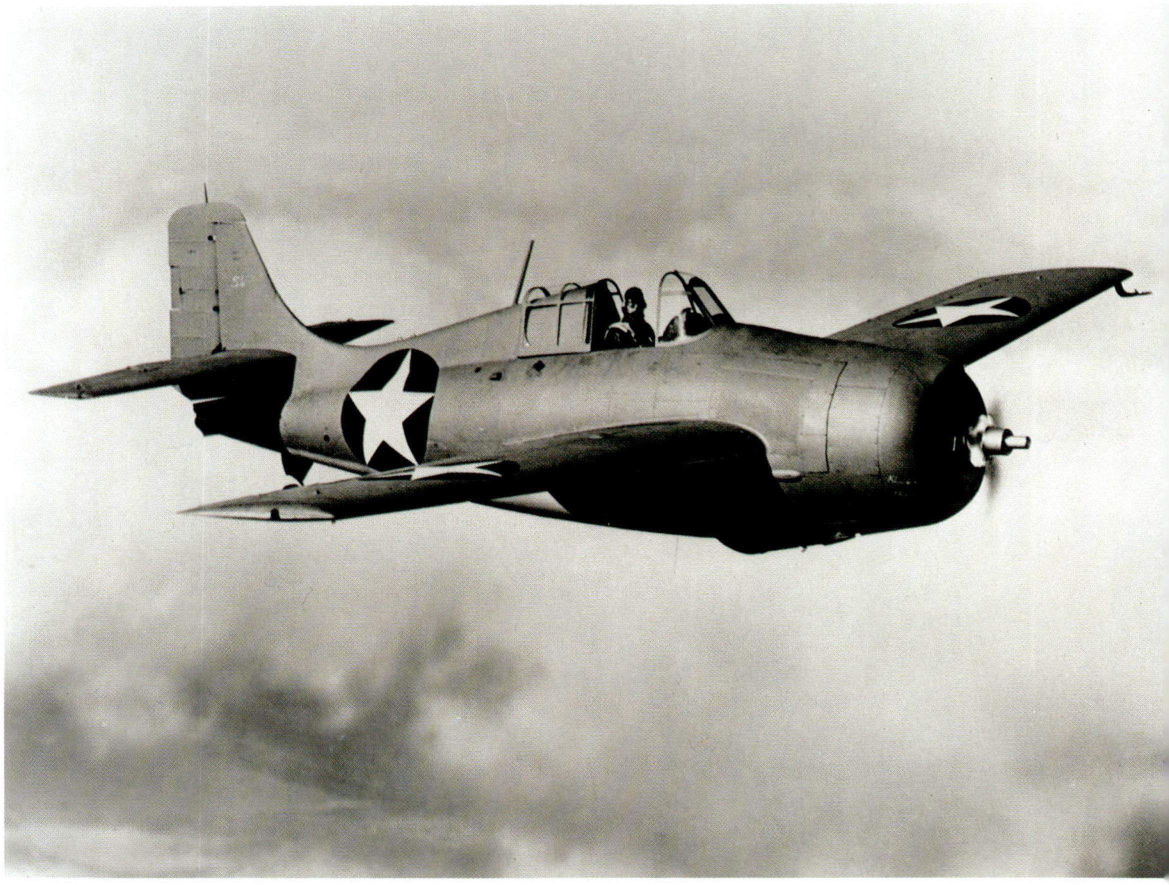

2

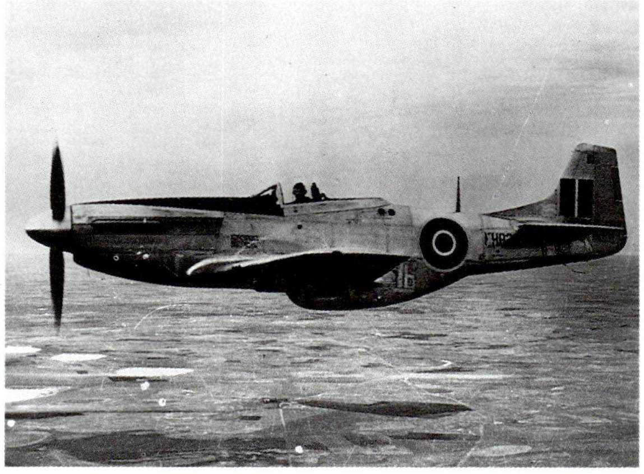

5

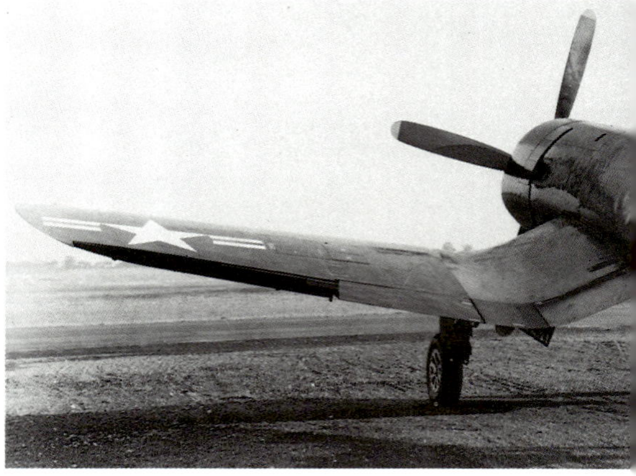

3

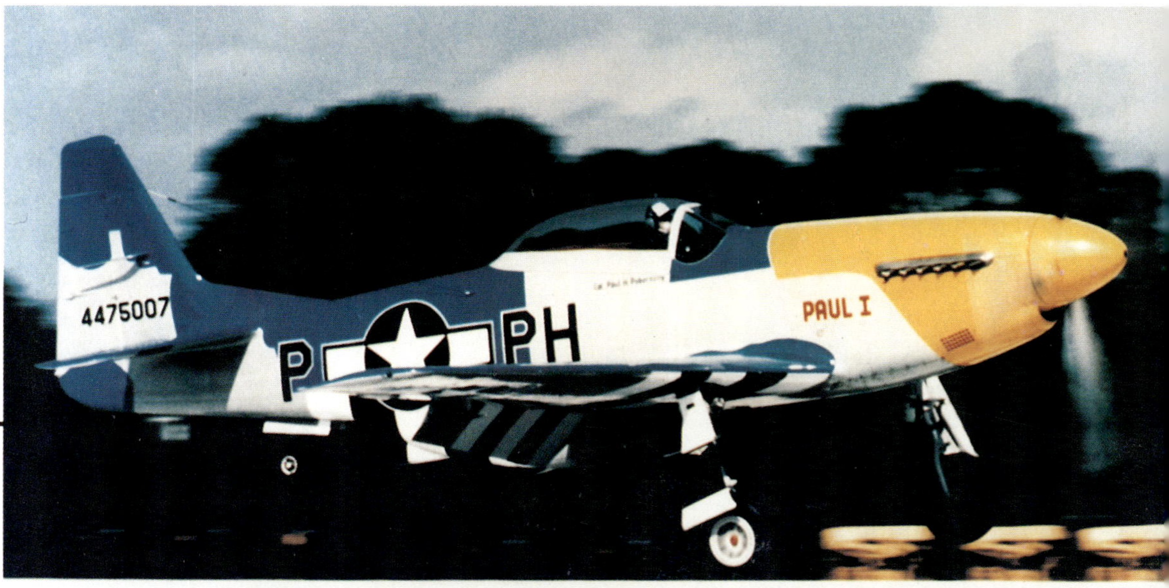

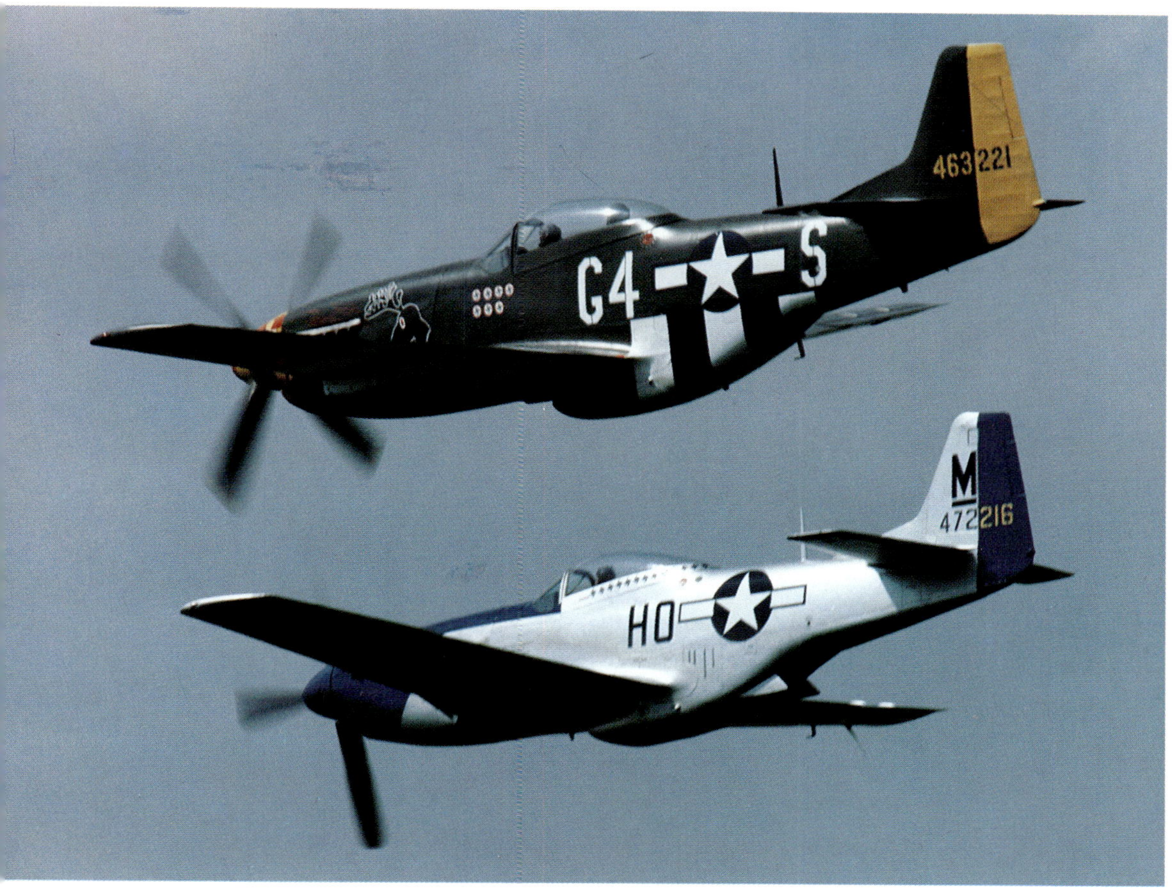

8

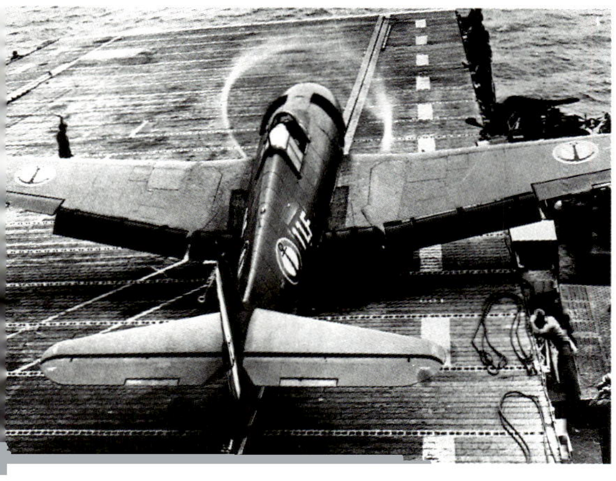

6

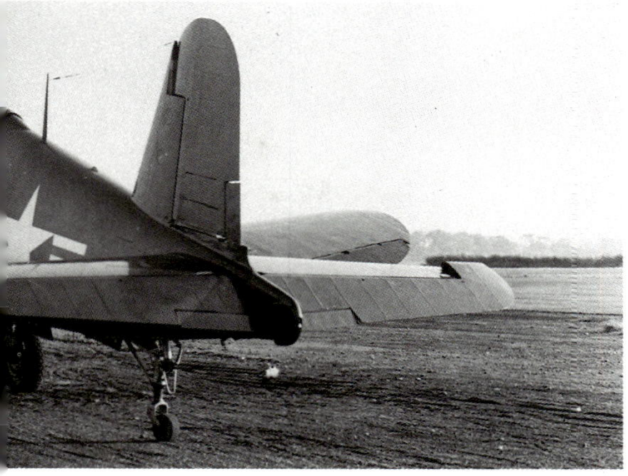

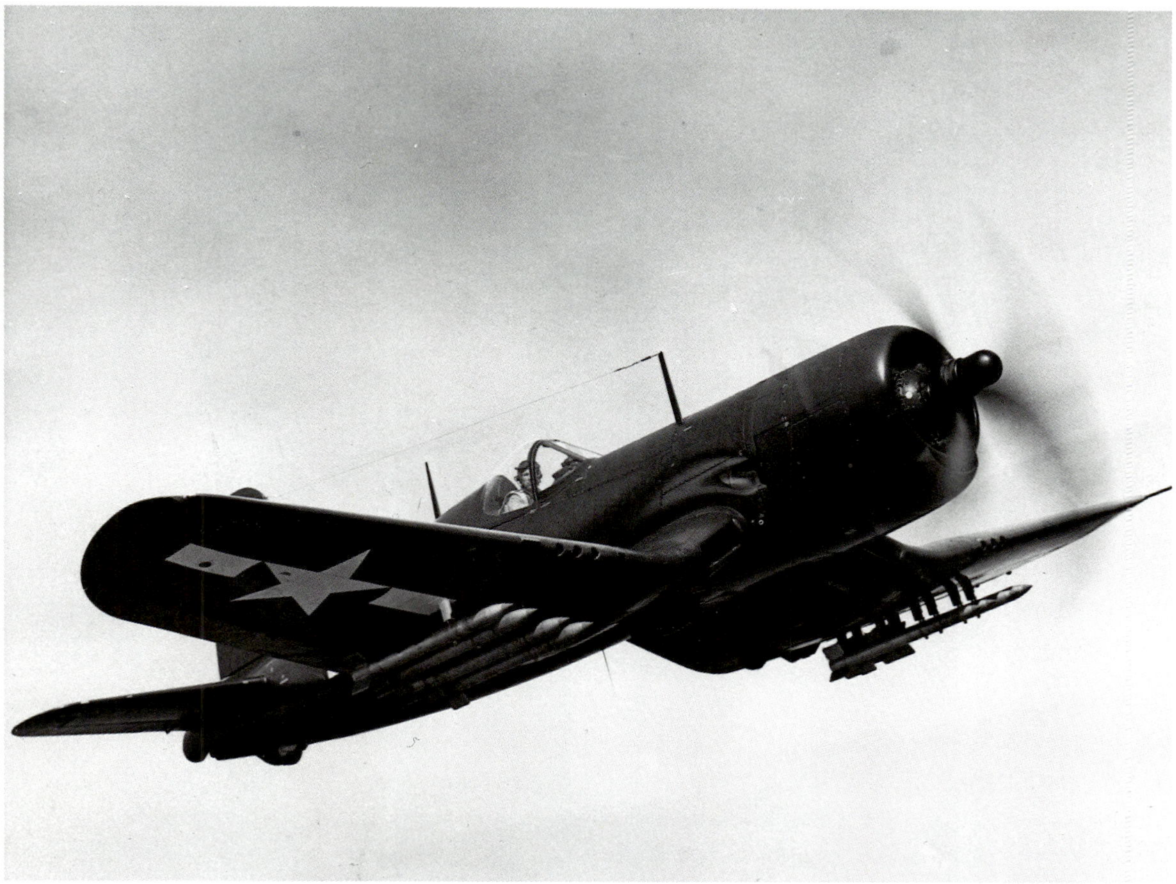

9

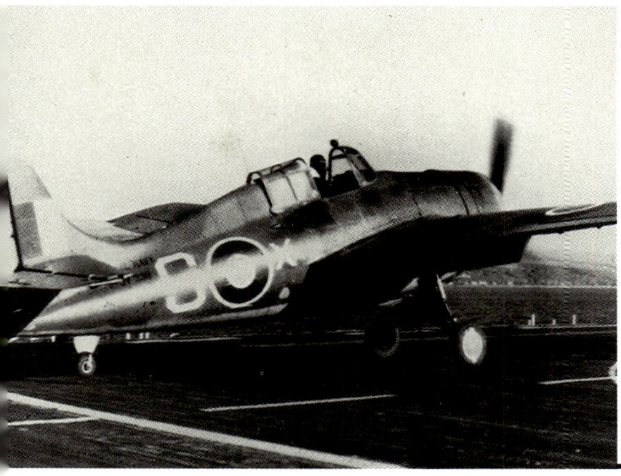

7

Photo Nos. 1 and 7: Grumman F4F Wildcat
Photo Nos. 2, 3 and 8: North American P-51 Mustang
Photo Nos. 4, 5 and 9: Vought F4U Corsair
Photo No. 6: Grumman F6 F Hellcat

AMERICAN FIGHTER PLANES

Bell, with the P-59A Airacomet fighter, was the first American firm to develop a jet aircraft, but the first jet fighter to enter service with the US Army Air Force in large numbers was the Lockheed P-80 Shooting Star. Some played a low-key role in Europe in 1945, but it was not until the Korean War in 1950 that they really showed their mettle, against the Soviet MiG-15. A single-engined aircraft, of which 1,732 were produced, the Shooting Star flew at 593 mph (950 kph), with a ceiling of 45,920 ft (14,000 m) and a range of 1,250 miles (2,000 km). Meanwhile, North American had also been designing a straight-wing jet fighter, the FJ-1, which quickly evolved into the swept-wing F-86 Sabre, the most celebrated aircraft of the Korean War. This ten-ton single-seater was capable of 692 mph (1,114 kph) and altitudes in excess of 49,000 ft (15,000 m). It had six machine guns or four 20-mm cannon located in the nose and could carry rockets or air-to-air missiles. To replace this legendary aircraft, in 1949 North American began designing a more powerful machine which would break the sound barrier in level flight. The result was the F-100 Super Sabre, a 17-ton single-seater, with a top speed of over 875 mph (1,400 kph) and a ceiling of over 42,600 ft (13,000 m). Its armament consisted of four 20-mm cannon plus bombs and rockets.

For its part, in the immediate post-war period Grumman had begun working on a new generation of carrier-based jet fighters for the US Navy. They were already in service in 1950, when the Korean War broke out. The straight-winged F9F Panther and swept-wing Cougar were both 11/12-ton single-seater fighter-bombers. They flew at around 625 mph (1,000 kph) and were armed with four 20-mm cannon.

Two other carrier-based fighter-bombers of this period, the McDonnell F2H Banshee and the Vought F7U Cutlass, were twin-engined aircraft with performance characteristics similar to the Grummans. More original in conception was the Douglas F4D Skyray, which entered service in 1956. The Skyray was a tailless single-seater capable of speeds in excess of 720 mph (1,150 kph) and with a ceiling of over 54,000 ft (16,500 m). It was armed with four 20-mm cannon and could carry 4,000 lb (1,800 kg) of bombs, rockets and other weaponry slung under the wings.

1
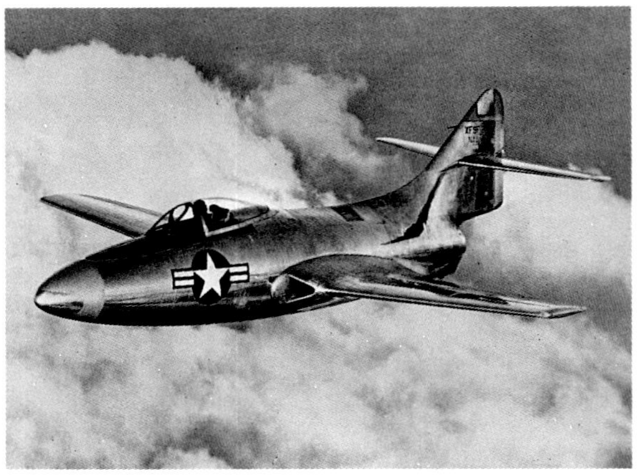

2
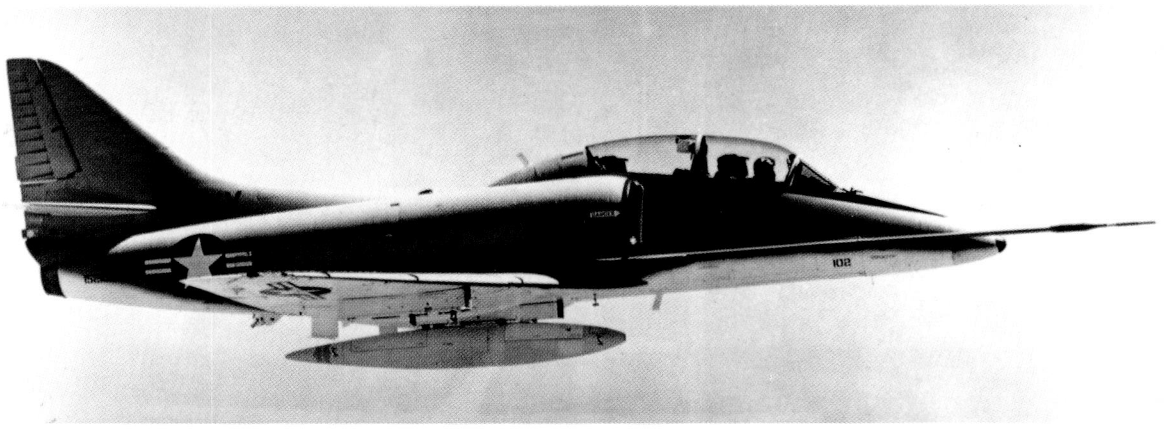

3
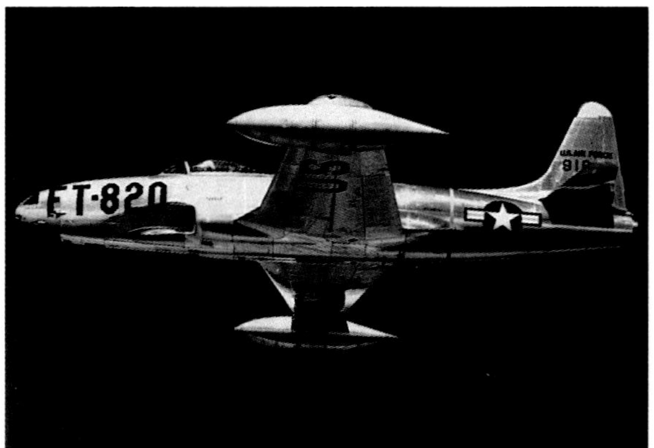

4
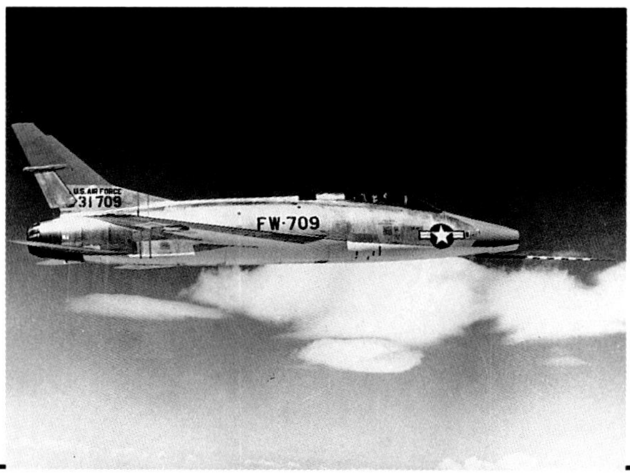

5
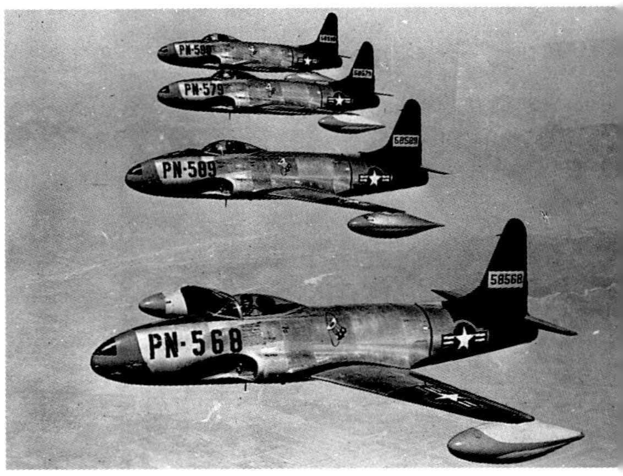

6
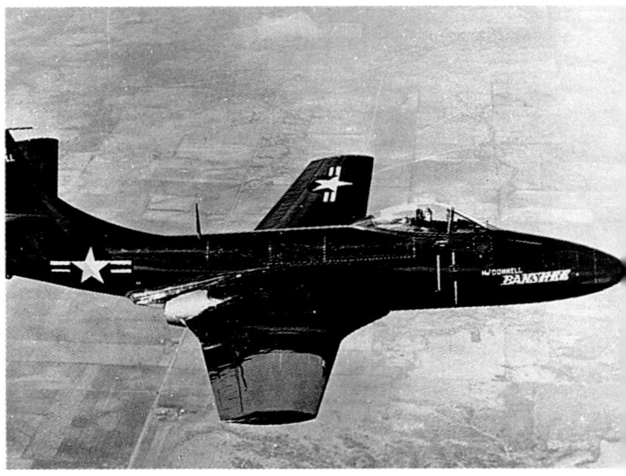

7
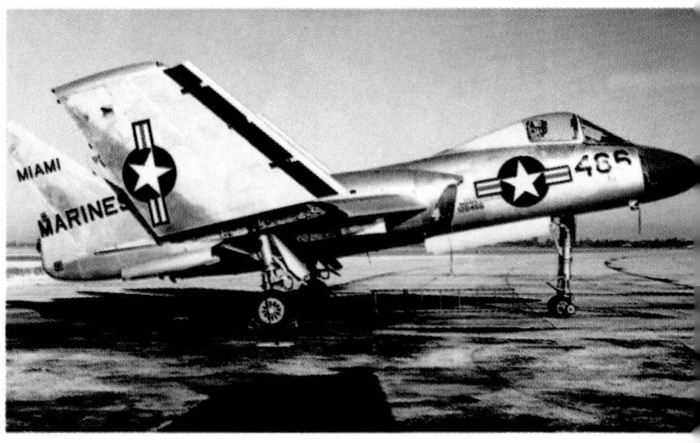

8
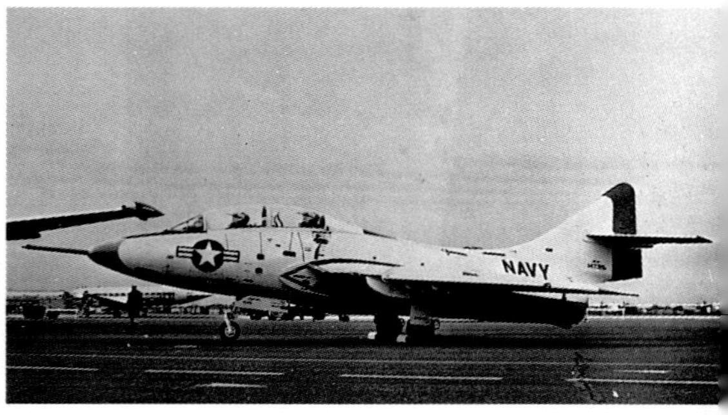

9
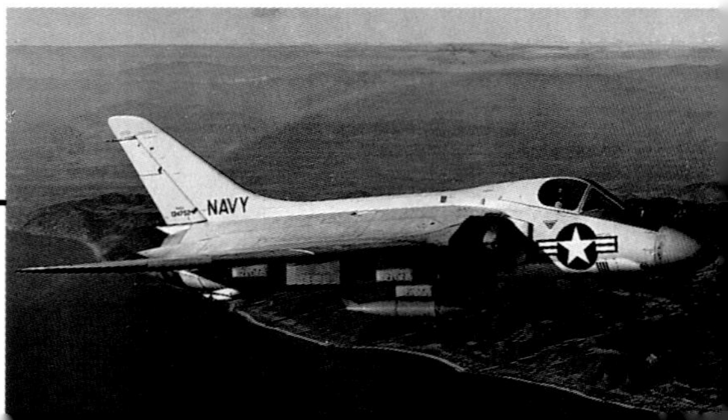

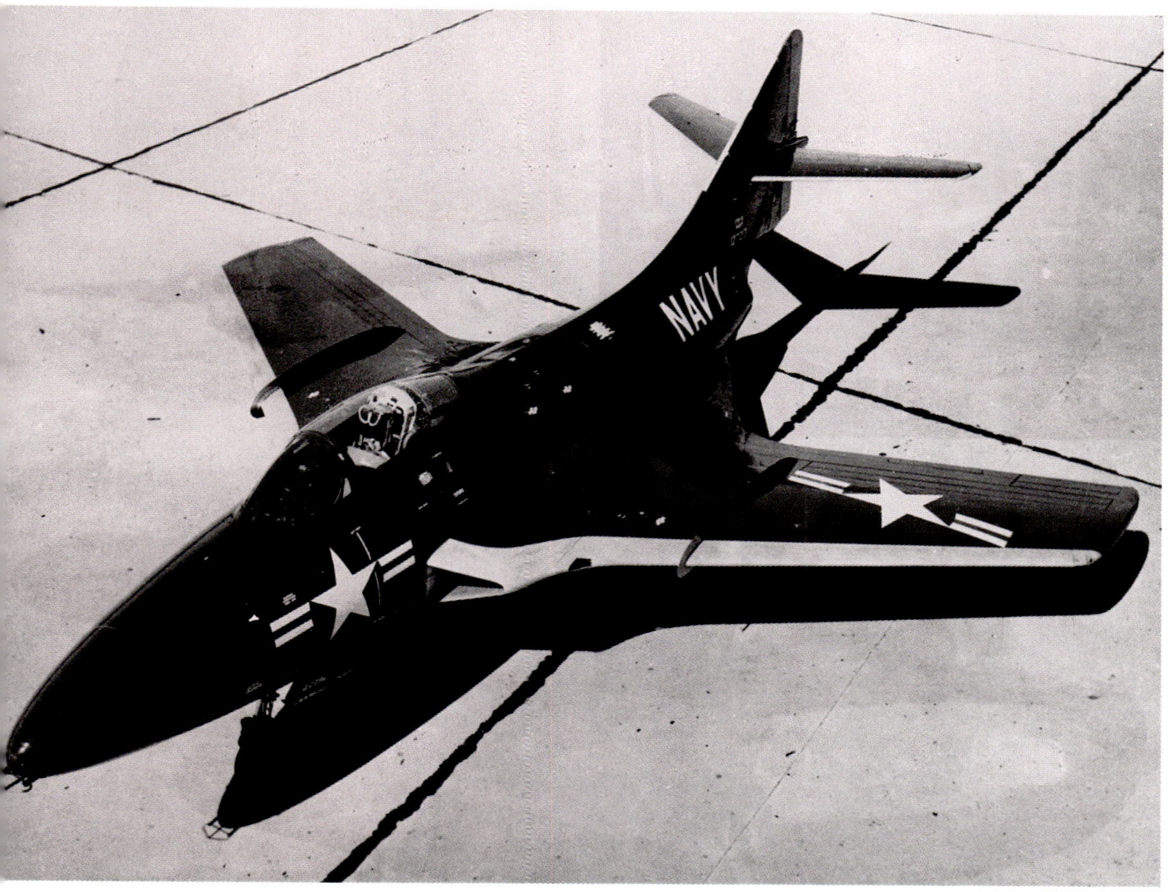

12

Photo Nos. 1: Grumman F9F Panther
Photo No. 2: Douglas A4D Skyhawk attack trainer
Photo Nos. 3 and 5: Lockheed P-80 Shooting Star
Photo Nos. 4 and 14: North American F-100 Super Sabre
Photo No. 6: McDonnell F2H Banshee
Photo Nos. 7 and 10: Vought F7U Cutlass
Photo Nos. 8 and 12: Grumman F-9 Cougar
Photo Nos. 9 and 13: Douglas F4D Skyray
Photo No. 11: North American F-86 Sabre

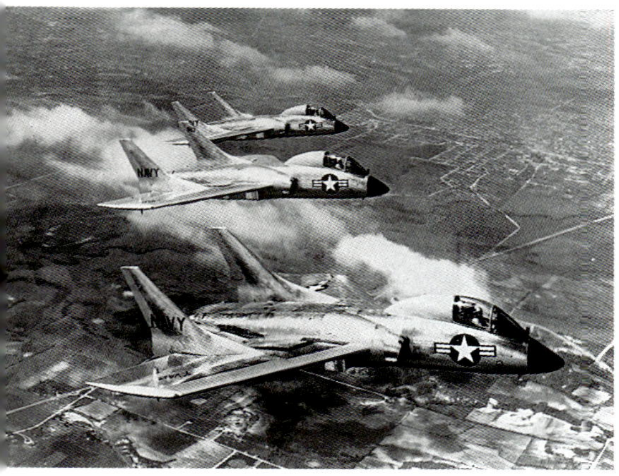
10

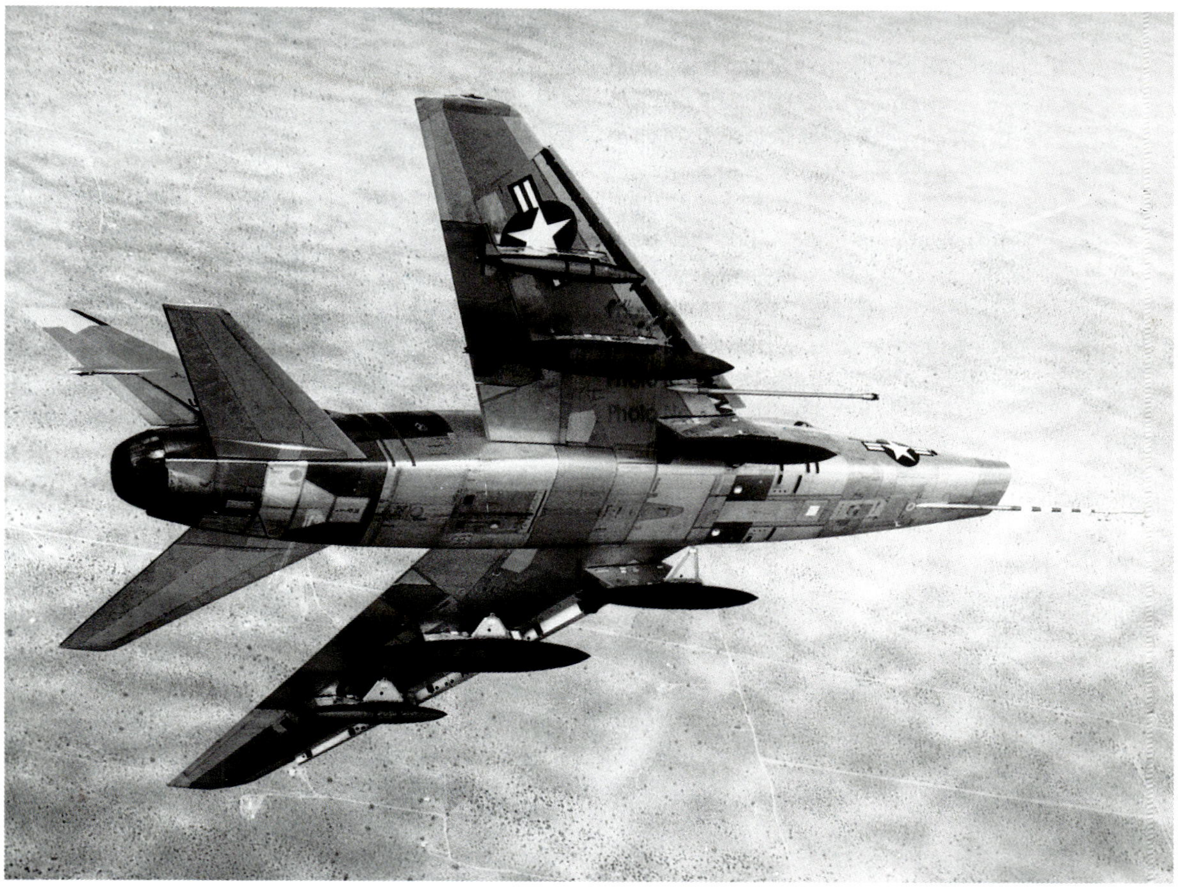
14

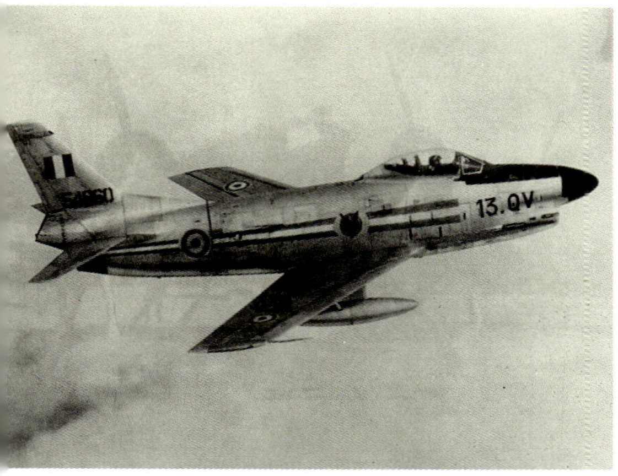

11

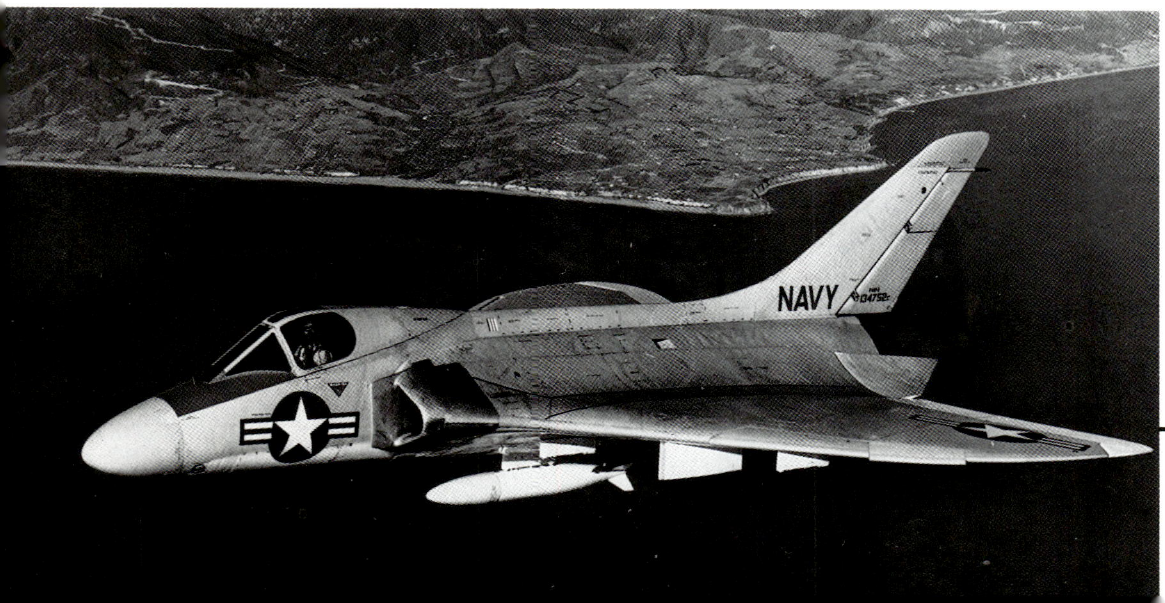

13

4

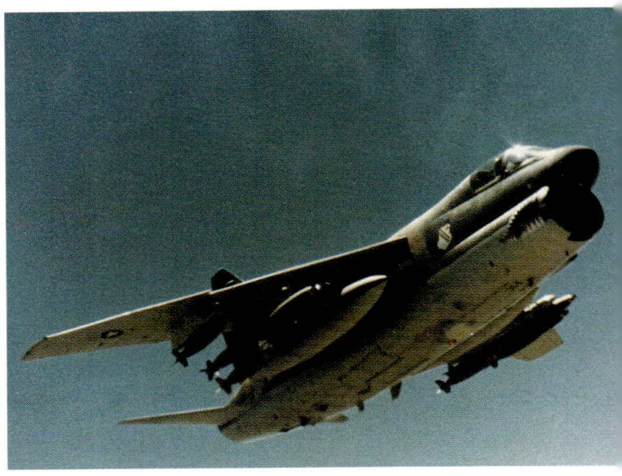

AMERICAN FIGHTER PLANES

Encouraged by its success with the P-47 Thunderbolt, Republic brought out a successor, the F-84 Thunderjet, which was later modernised to become the swept-wing F-84 F Thunderstreak. These aircraft, weighing between ten and fourteen tons, flew at speeds of around 625 mph (1,000 kph) and had ceilings of between 41,000 ft (12,500m) and 45,929 ft (14,000 m). They were armed with six 0.5-inch machine guns. The F-84 was widely used by the air forces of NATO countries. After building 7,886 F-84s, Republic followed up with the F-105 Thunderchief, a single-engined fighter-bomber weighing 26 tons. This hefty machine, whose armament consisted of a 20-mm cannon, was capable of over 1,250 mph (2,000 kph) and could carry either nuclear or conventional weapons. The Thunderchief was widely used in Vietnam.

The characteristic feature of the Lockheed F-104 Starfighter was its stumpy wings, giving it a span of less than 22 ft (6.6 m). The aircraft entered service in 1958 as a high-performance interceptor: it could fly at speeds in excesss of 1,440 mph (2,300 kph) and in 1959 broke the world zoom altitude record, climbing to over 103,389 ft (31,513m). It carried missiles or a 20-mm cannon.

It was followed a few months later by the Northrop F-5 A, a light, twin-engined fighter weighing only 4 tons. There were various versions, flying at speeds of between 937 mph (1,500 kph) and 1,062 mph (1,700 kph). Armed with two 20-mm cannon and air-to-air missiles, it was intended mainly for export. The F-4 Phantom II, a multi-role fighter manufactured by McDonnell, made history on being adopted by the Air Force ad well as the Navy. Since 1961, 5,195 Phantoms have been produced and, in its time, it was acknowledged as the best fighter in the Western camp. Weighing 31 tons, it flew at over 1,500 mph (2,400 kph), with a ceiling approaching 65,600 ft (20,000 m). It was armed with a 20-mm cannon and various air-to-air missiles, and could deliver both nuclear and conventional bombs.

In addition to the Phantom, the US Navy had selected the Vought F-8 Crusader, a single-engined single-seater aircraft, the different versions of which flew at between 1,000 mph (1,600 kph) and 1,237 mph (1,980 kph), with a ceiling of 42,640 ft (13,000 m). It was armed with four 20-mm cannon, air-to-air missiles and rockets.

From this remarkable aircraft was derived the quite different A-7 Corsair II. More bomber than fighter, it was slower in flight but, with supplementary fuel tanks fitted,

1

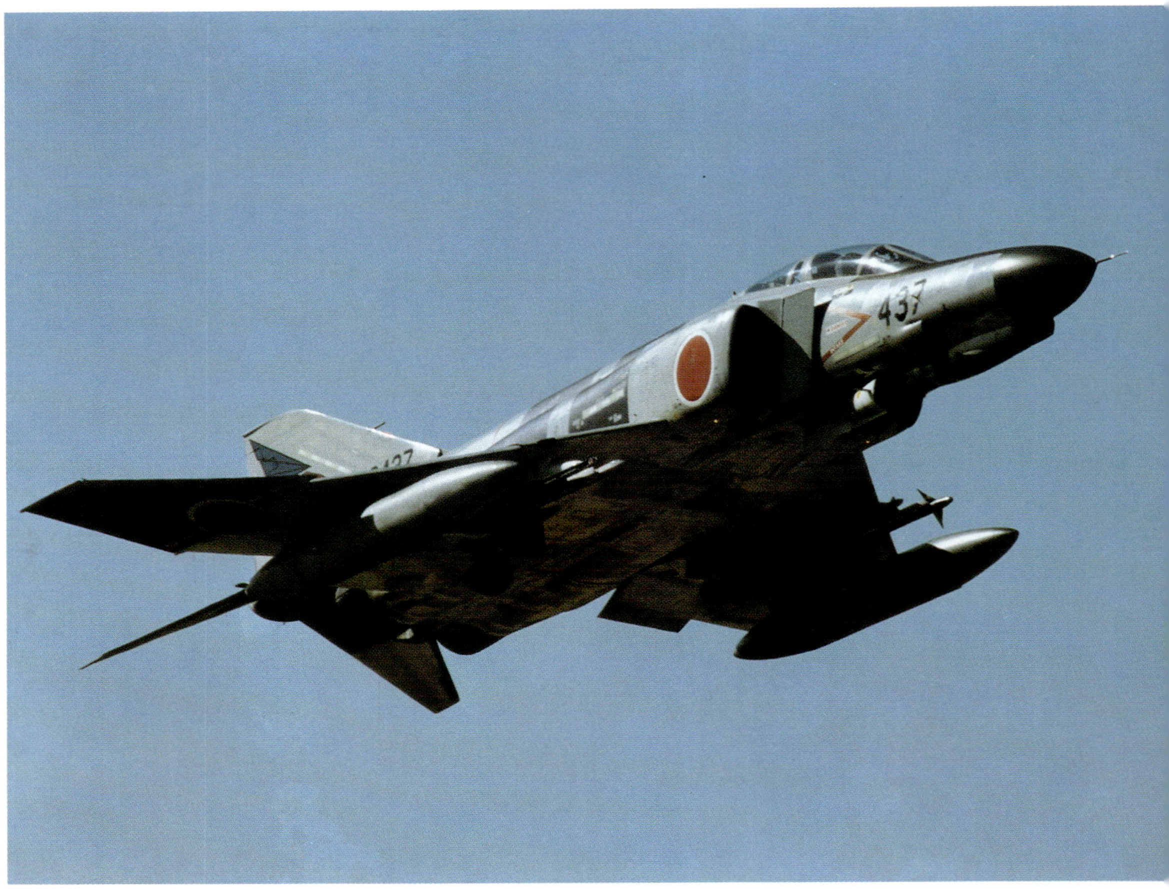

2

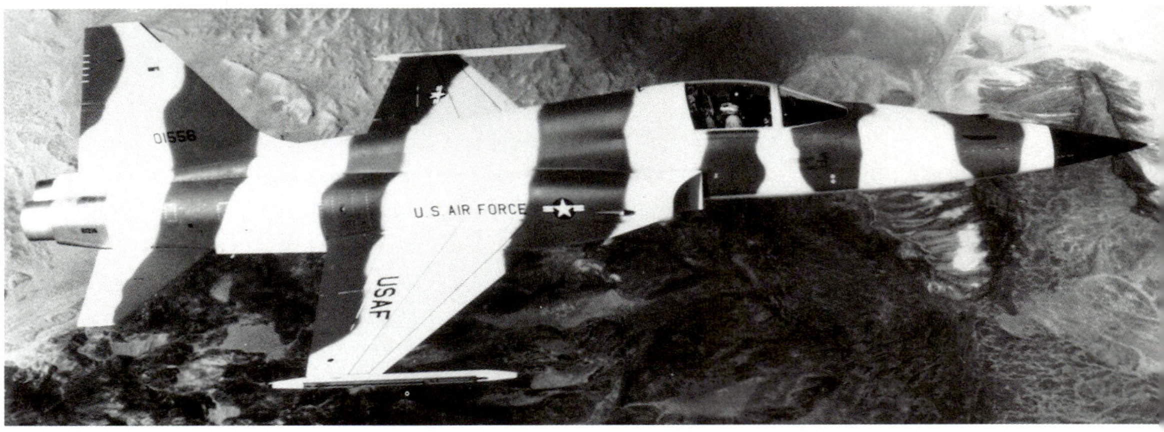

3

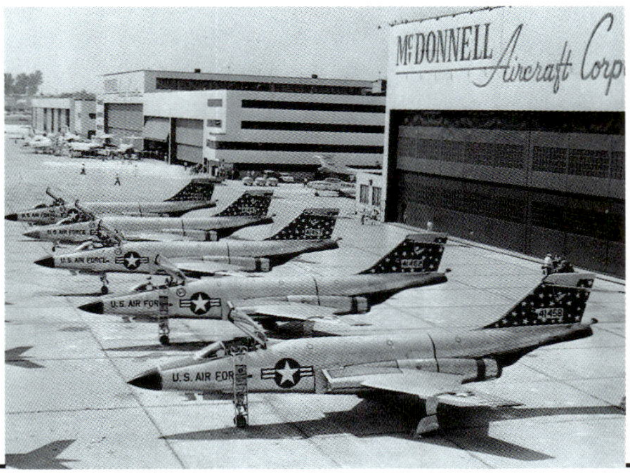

5

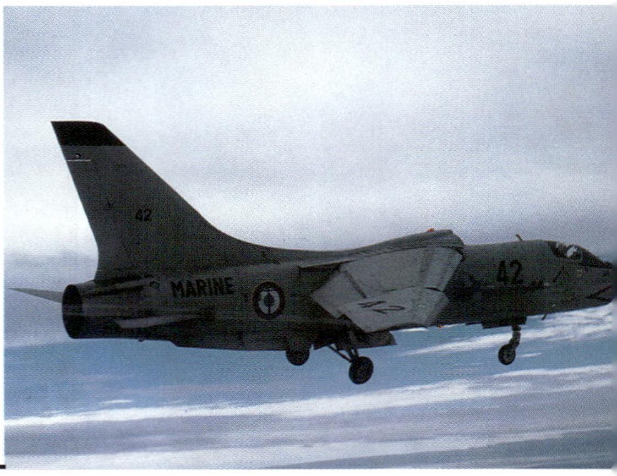

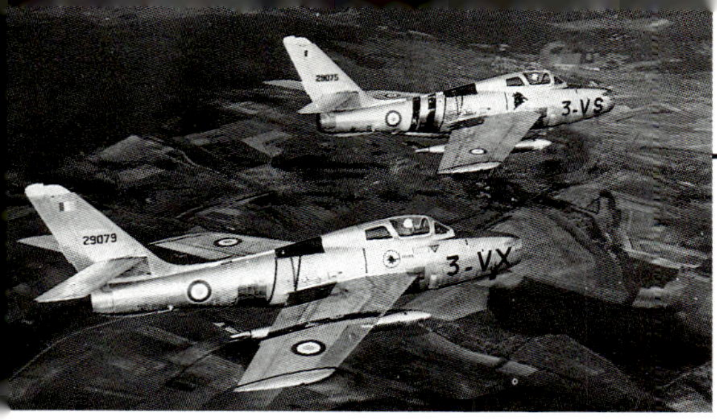

6

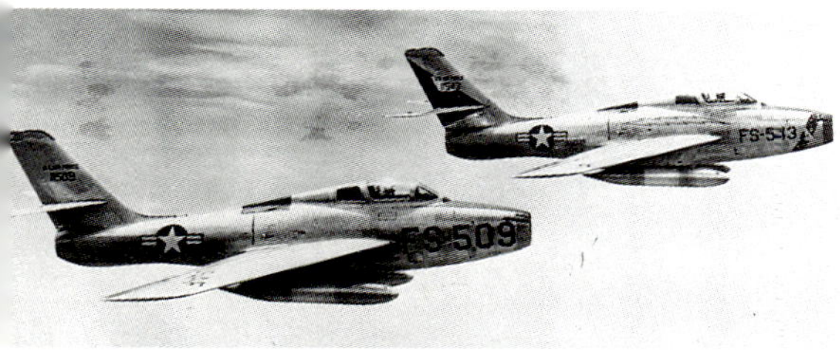

7

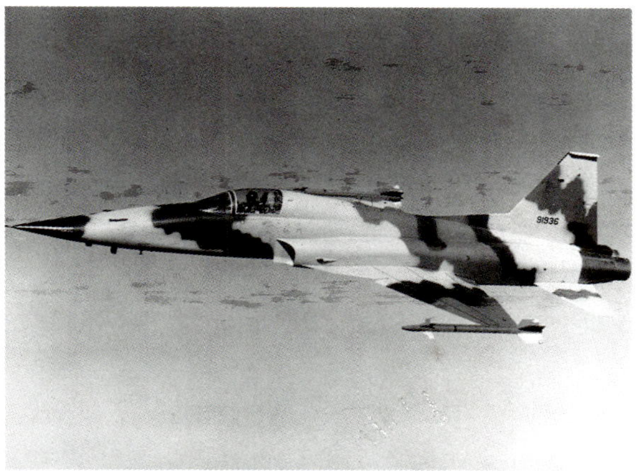
11

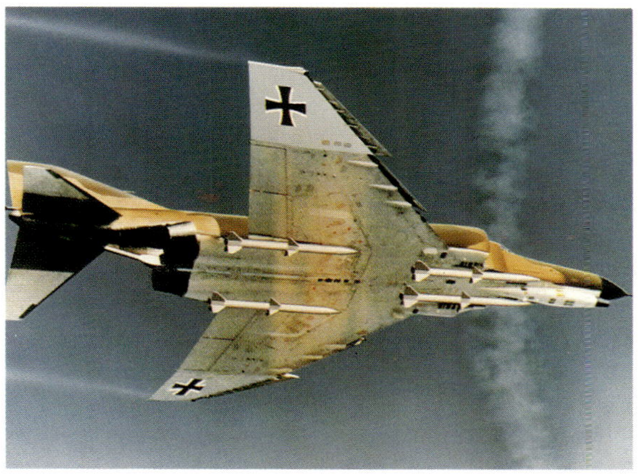
14

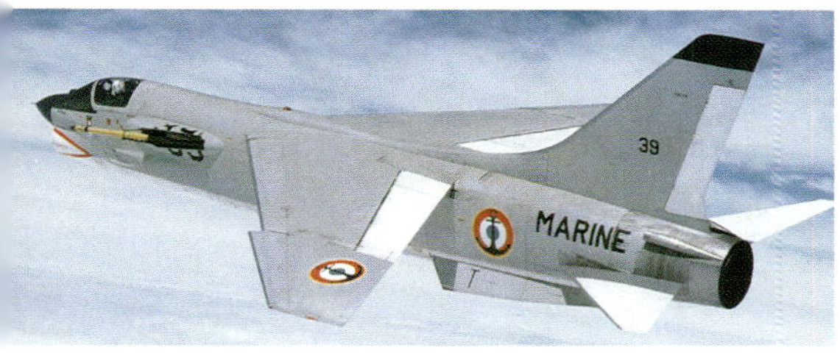

8

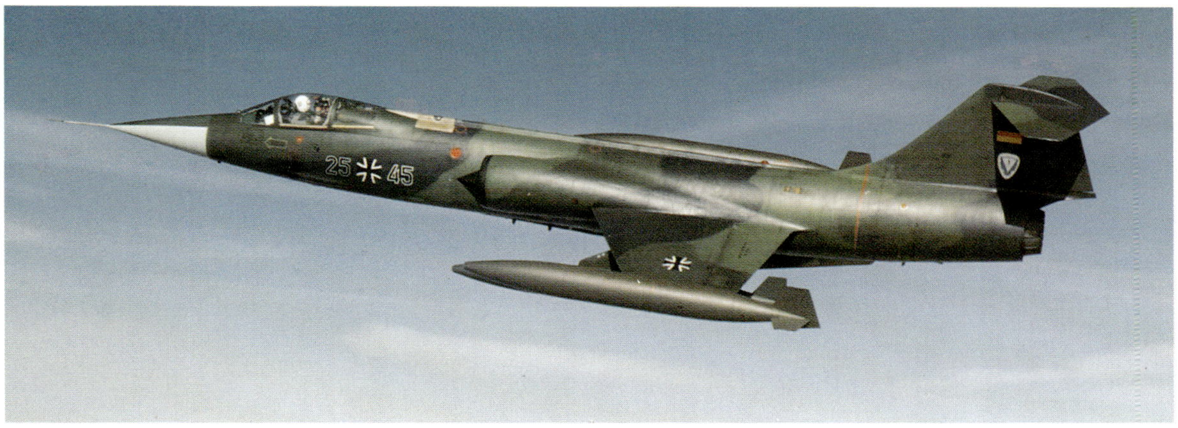

15

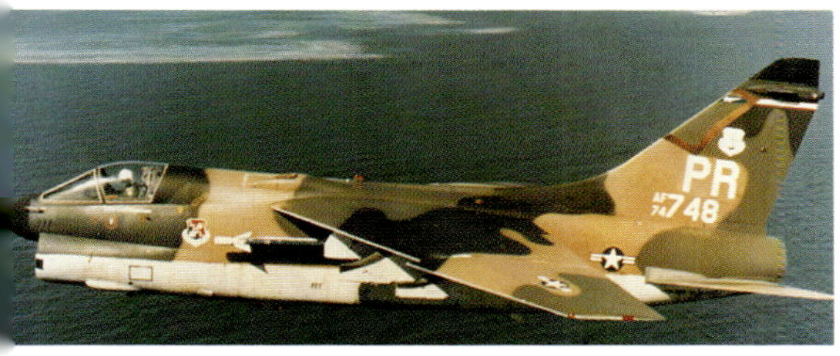

9

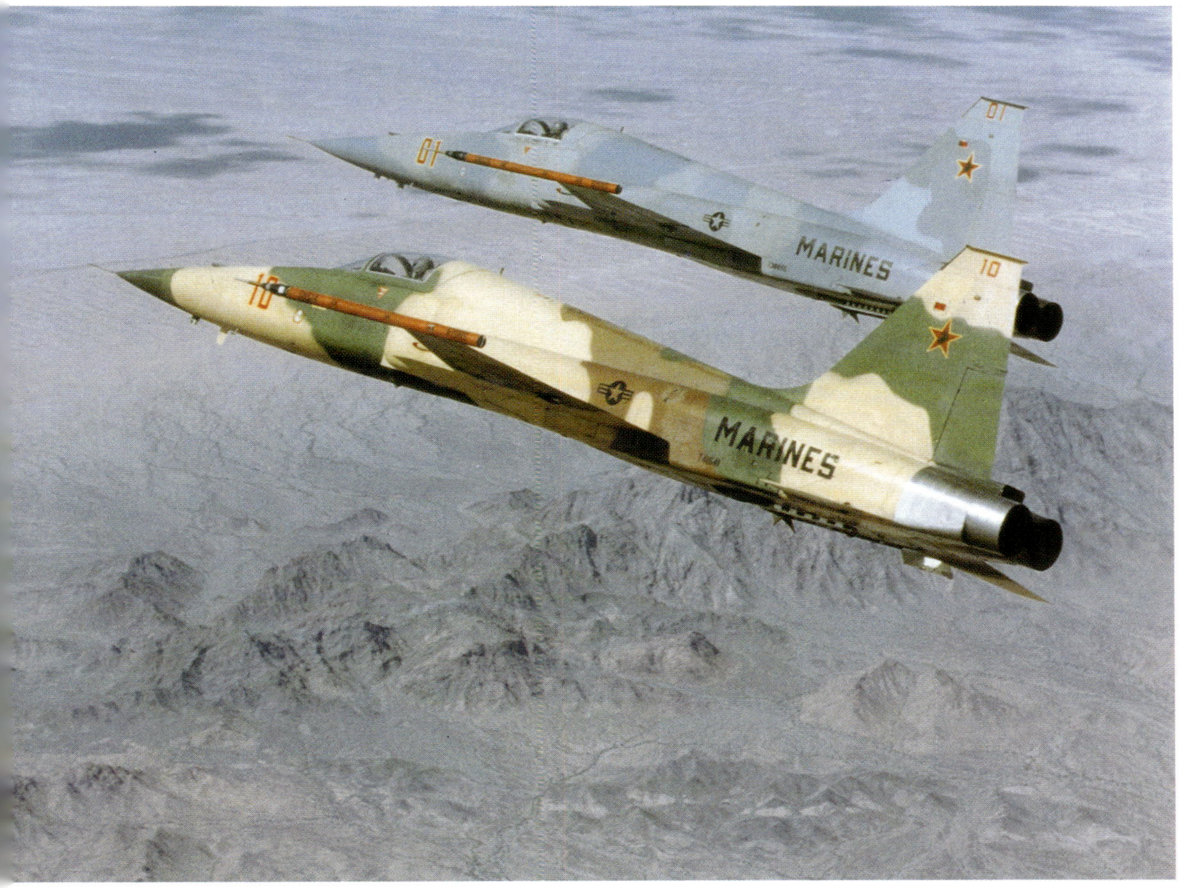

12

had a range of 3,750 miles (6,000 km). It went into service in 1966. Its basic armament consisted of one or two 20-mm cannon, but its main strength was the ability to carry nine tons of weaponry under the wings.

Photo Nos. 1 and 14: McDonnell F-4 Phantom II
Photo Nos. 2, 11, 12 and 13: Northrop F-5
Photo No. 3: McDonnell F-101 Voodoo
Photo Nos. 4 and 9: Vought A-7 Corsair II
Photo Nos. 5 and 8: Vought F-8 Crusader
Photo Nos. 6 and 7: Republic F-84 F Thunderstreak
Photo No. 10: Republic F-105 Thunderchief
Photo No. 15: Lockheed F-104 Starfighter

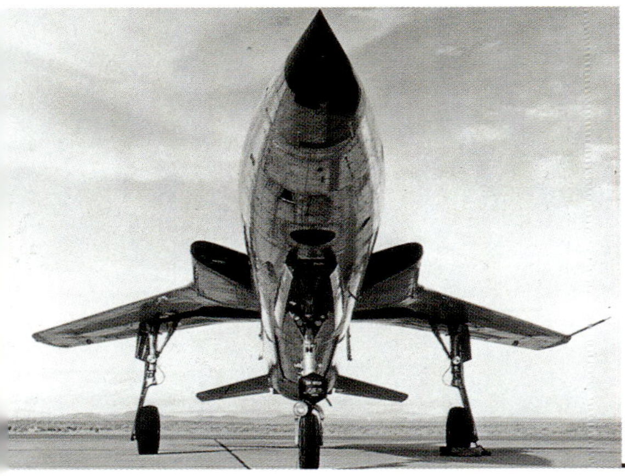
10

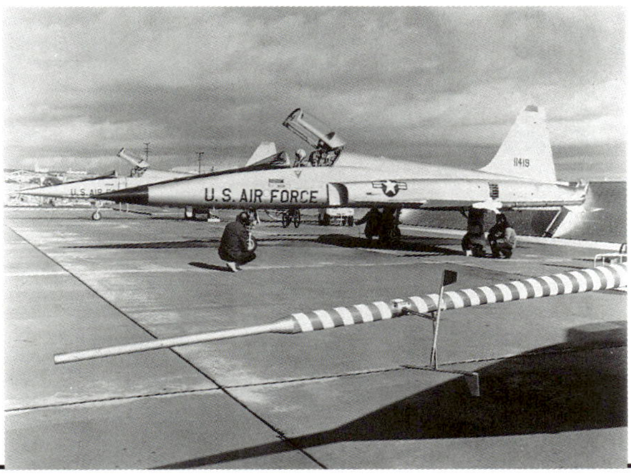

13

AMERICAN FIGHTER PLANES

5
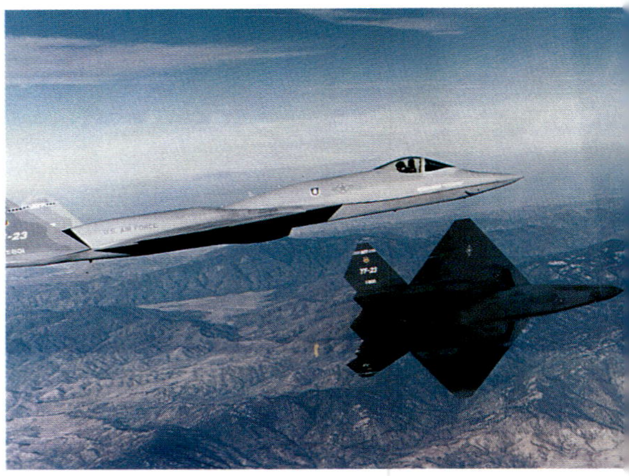

From the vast array of fighters deployed by the United States since 1950, two stand out from the crowd. The first was the McDonnell F-101 Voodoo, the most powerful fighter of its day, whose mission was to escort the bombers of Strategic Air Command on long-range sorties. After assuming the role of tactical fighter-bomber, this 26-ton twin-engined aircraft became an all-weather two-seater interceptor. It reached speeds approaching 1,250 mph (2,000 kph) and could fly at almost 52,480 ft (16,000 m). Its armament consisted of four 20-mm cannon and air-to-air missiles.

The second was the F-106 Delta Dart, developed in the 1950s by Convair, who had been responsible for the first delta-winged supersonic fighter, the F-102 Delta Dagger. The Dagger flew at 812 mph (1,300 kph) and carried a sophisticated complement of six air-to-air guided missiles. Its successor flew at almost twice the speed.

The US Air Force is currently equipped with the General Dynamics F-16 Fighting Falcon, an 18-ton lightweight fighter with a maximum speed of Mach 2 and a ceiling of 60,000 ft (18,288 m). It also boasts the McDonnell Douglas F-15 Eagle, an exceptionally powerful twin-engined fighter, currently the best of its kind. It flies at over 1,560 mph (2,500 kph), has a ceiling of 68,880 ft (21,000 m) and a range of almost 3,750 miles (6,000 km). Its armament consists of a 20-mm cannon and eight air-to-air missiles.

The Lockheed F-117 Stealth, meanwhile, is a reconnaissance and attack aircraft designed to avoid detection by enemy radar. It was deployed with success during the Gulf War. In keeping with its special role, it is a subsonic aircraft, and its missiles are carried inside the fuselage.

The US Navy, for its part, has adopted the Grumman F-14 Tomcat, commissioned in 1972. A carrier-based twin-engined two-seater fighter weighing 36 tons, it can fly at speeds in excess of 1,560 mph (2,500 kph) and has a ceiling of over 55,760 ft (17,000 m). Its armament consists of a 20-mm cannon and eight air-to-air missiles. The Navy also uses the McDonnell Douglas F/A-18 Hornet, a single-seater twin-engined attack fighter with a maximum speed of over 1,250 mph (2,000 kph). It can fly at altitudes in excess of 59,000 ft (18,000 m).

1
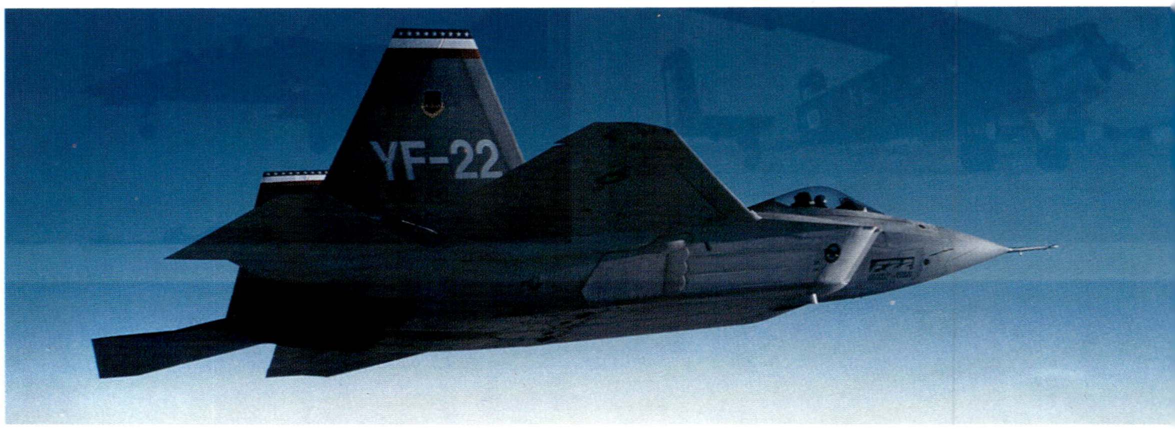

2
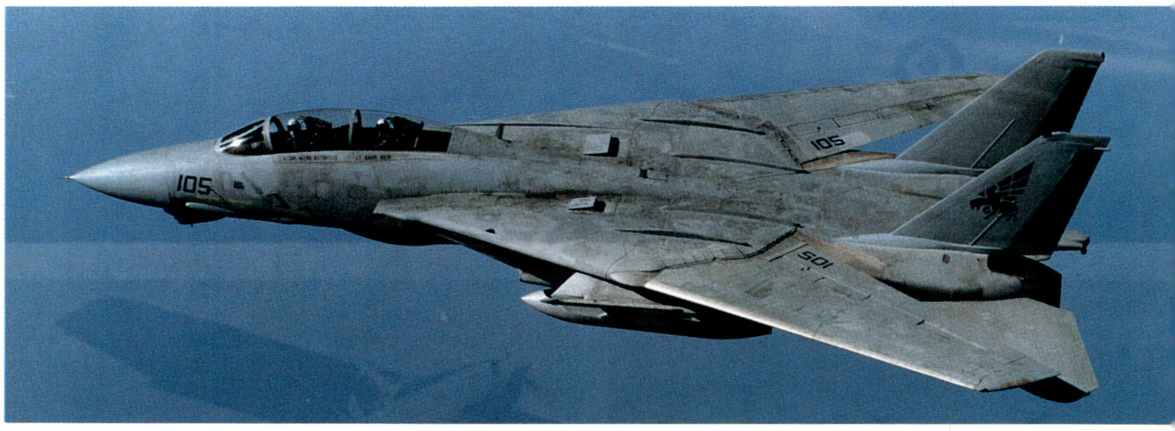

3
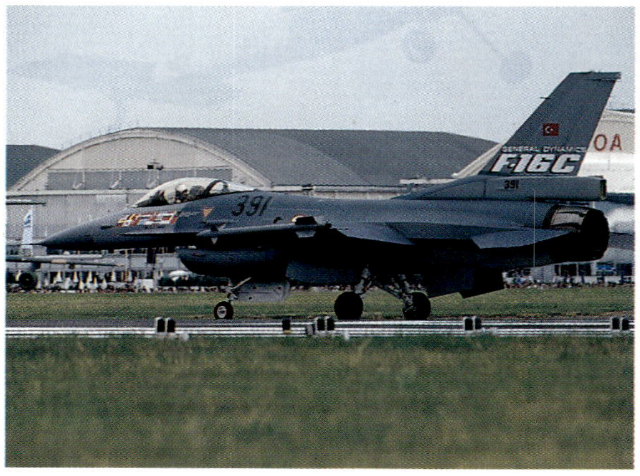

6
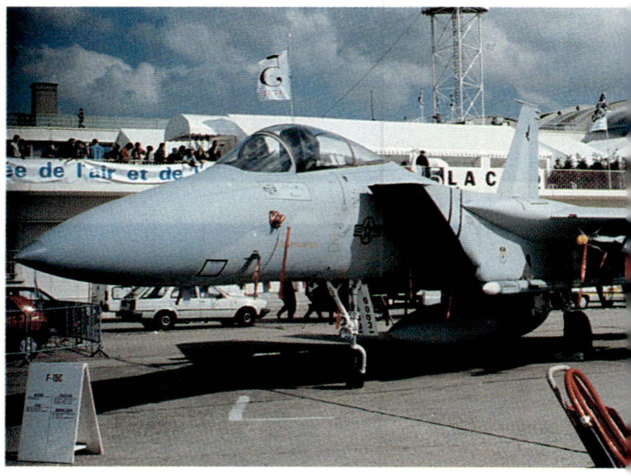

4
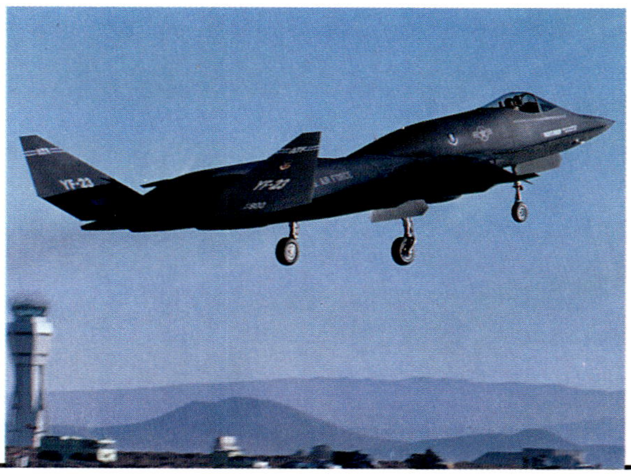

7
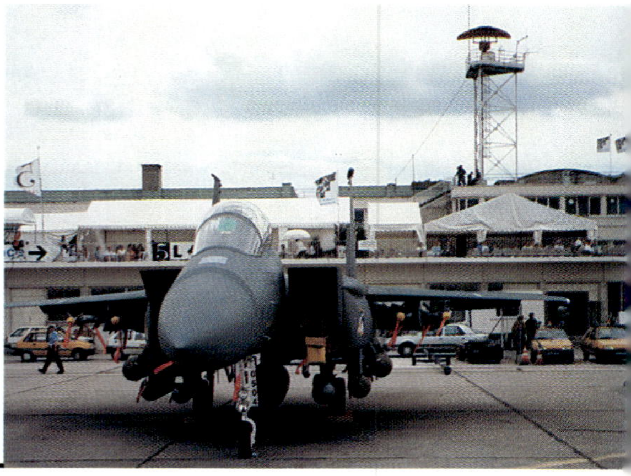

14
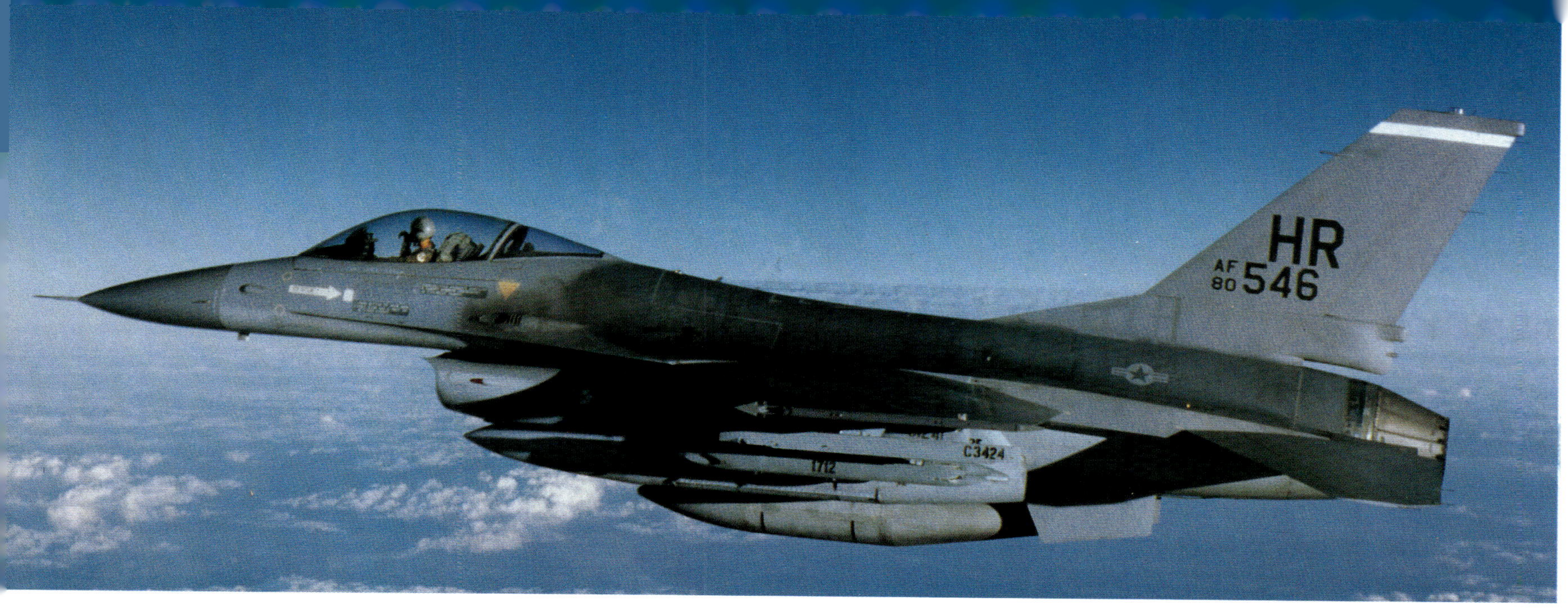

11
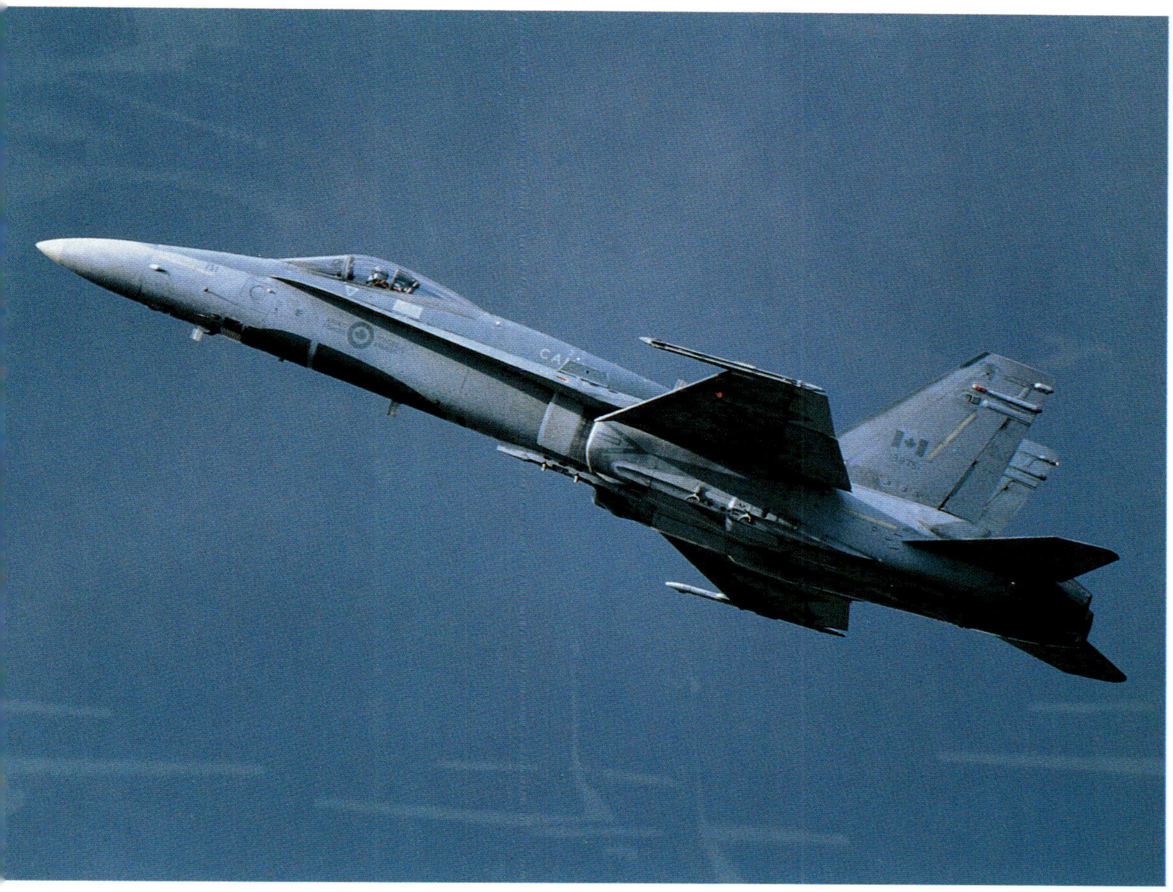

15
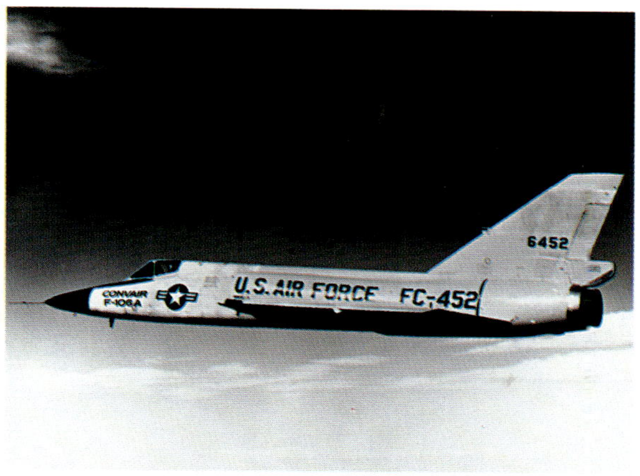

16
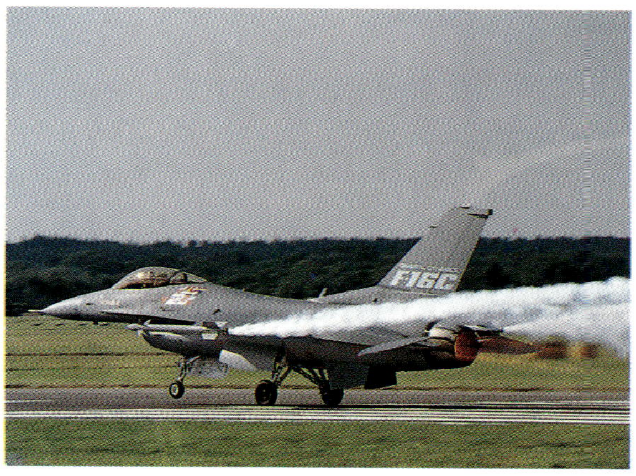

8
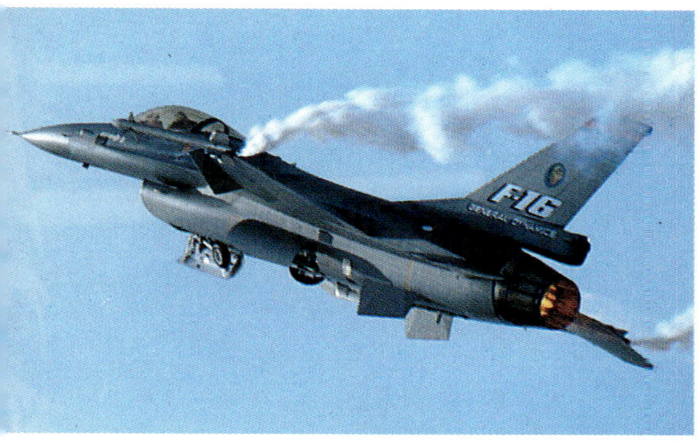

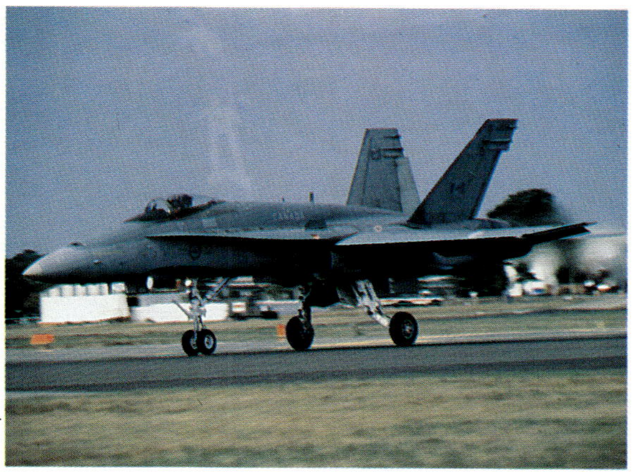

9
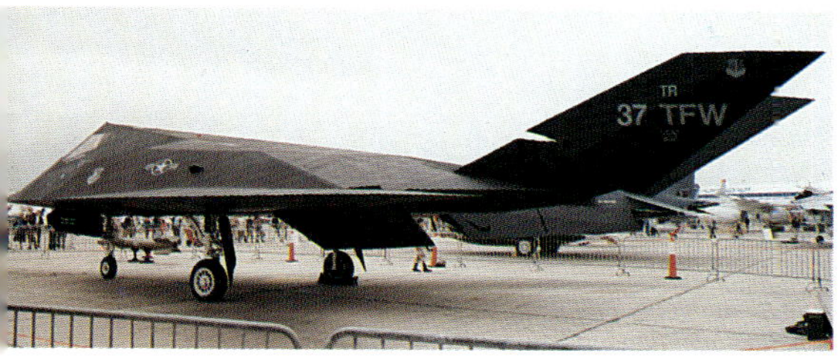

10
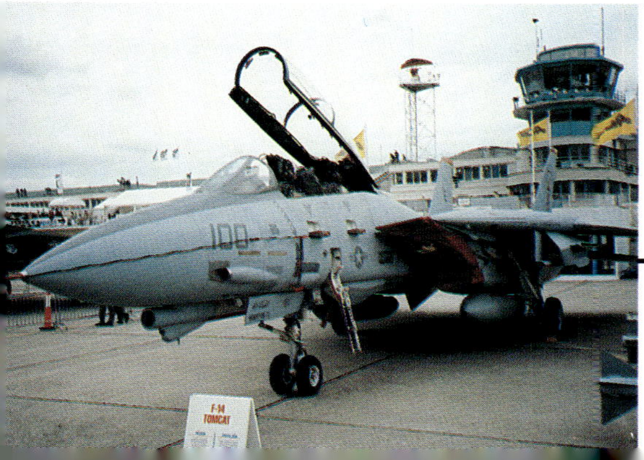

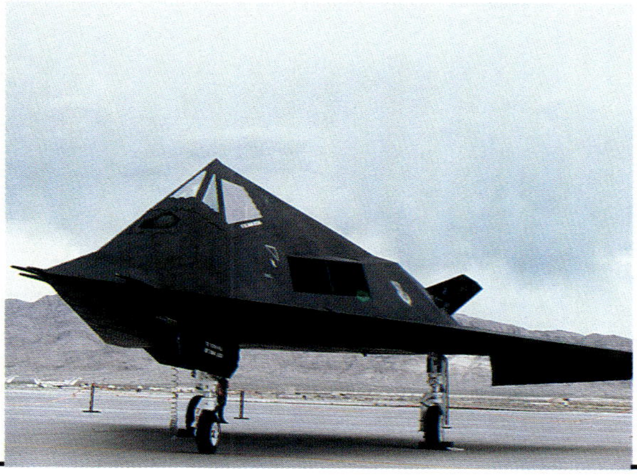

12 The US Air Force recently staged a competition for a new fighter aircraft. The contenders were the YF-23, developed by Northrop/McDonnell Douglas, and the YF-22, built by Lockheed/Boeing/General Dynamics, which was eventually adopted. The YF-22 is a 15-ton twin-engined fighter designed to fly at Mach 1.8, with a ceiling of 65,600 ft (20,000 m). Its armament will consist of a 20-mm cannon and nine missiles.

13 **Photo No. 1:** Lockheed YF-22
Photo Nos. 2 and 10: Grumman F-14
Photo Nos. 3, 8, 14 and 16: General Dynamics F-16
Photo Nos. 4 and 5: Northrop/McDonnell Douglas YF-23
Photo Nos. 6 and 7: McDonnell Douglas F-15
Photo Nos. 9 and 13: Lockheed F-117 Stealth
Photo Nos. 11 and 12: McDonnell Douglas F/A-18
Photo No. 15: Convair F-106A Delta Dart

RUSSIAN AND SOVIET FIGHTER PLANES

In the years before World War II, the Russians built a series of high-performance fighters, culminating in the Polikarpov I-16, which weighed less than two tons and had a top speed of around 312 mph (500 kph). It made its debut in 1934 and was used by the Republican air force during the Spanish Civil War. More than 7,000 came off the production lines, armed with four 7.62-mm machine guns or two machine guns and two 20-mm cannon.

In the late 1930s, the Soviet aircraft constructors Lavochkin, Mikoyan-Gurevich and Yakovlev brought out a number of prototype fighters, which were subsequently mass-produced and constantly modernised throughout the war. Lavochkin developed a single-seater, the LaGG-1, which was followed by the LaGG-3. Of wooden construction, weighing almost three tons, these aircraft flew at around 375 mph (600 kph) and had a ceiling of 29,520 ft (9,000 m). Sturdy and manoeuvrable, their armament of machine guns and cannon varied from one version to the next. In 1942, the LaGG-3 was replaced by the faster La-5, of which thousands were produced. This fighter was armed with two 20-mm cannon. After the War, an updated version, the La-11, saw service in Korea. At the same time, the partnership of Mikoyan-Gurevich began producing their first series of MiG-1 fighters, followed by the MiG-3. The MiG-3 was of metal construction throughout, weighed around 6,600 lb (3,000 kg), and had a top speed well in excess of 375 mph (600 kph). It carried one 12.7-mm and two 7.62-mm machine guns.

But credit for designing the best Soviet fighters of World War II must go to engineer Aleksandr Yakovlev. His single-seater Yak-1 had wooden wings and weighed 2.4 tons. It flew at 375 mph (600 kph) and was armed with a 20-mm cannon and one or two 12.7-mm machine guns. First produced in 1941, the Yak-1 was superseded in 1942 by the Yak-7 and then by the Yak-9. In 1944 they were joined by the Yak-3, one of the most agile fighters of the entire war. The Yak-3 was a single-seater weighing only 2.2 tons. It flew at around 437 mph (700 kph) and could climb to over 32,800 ft (10,000 m). Its armament consisted of one 20-mm cannon and two 12.7-mm machine guns. Eventually, more than 35,000 Yak fighters were built, breaking all records.

4

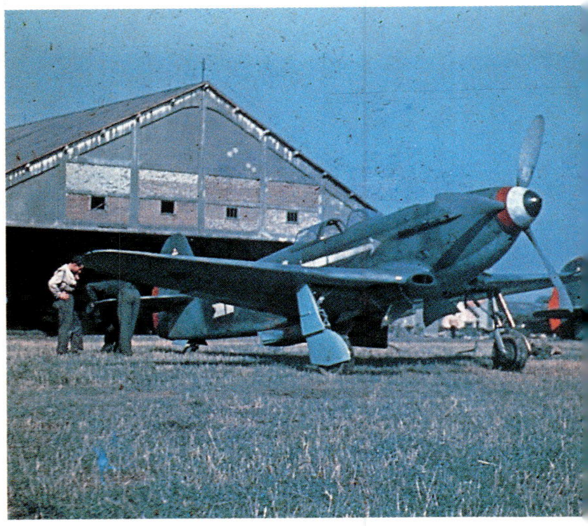

1

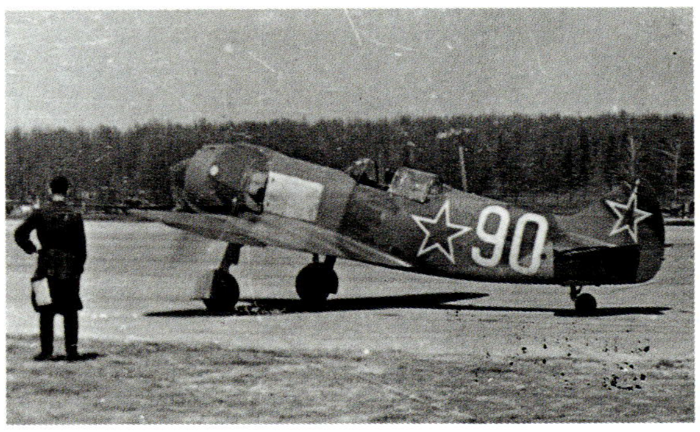

5

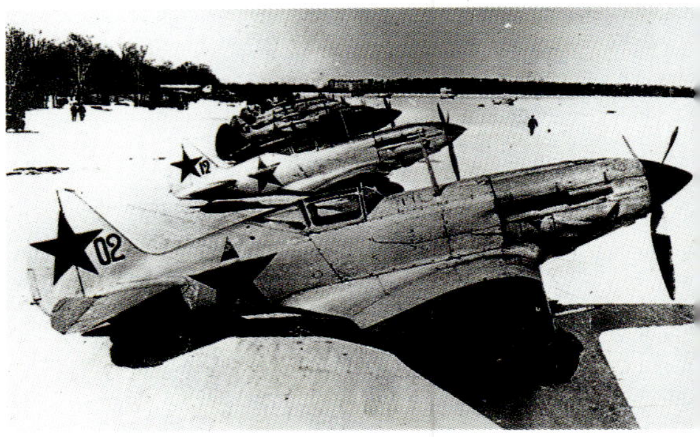

2

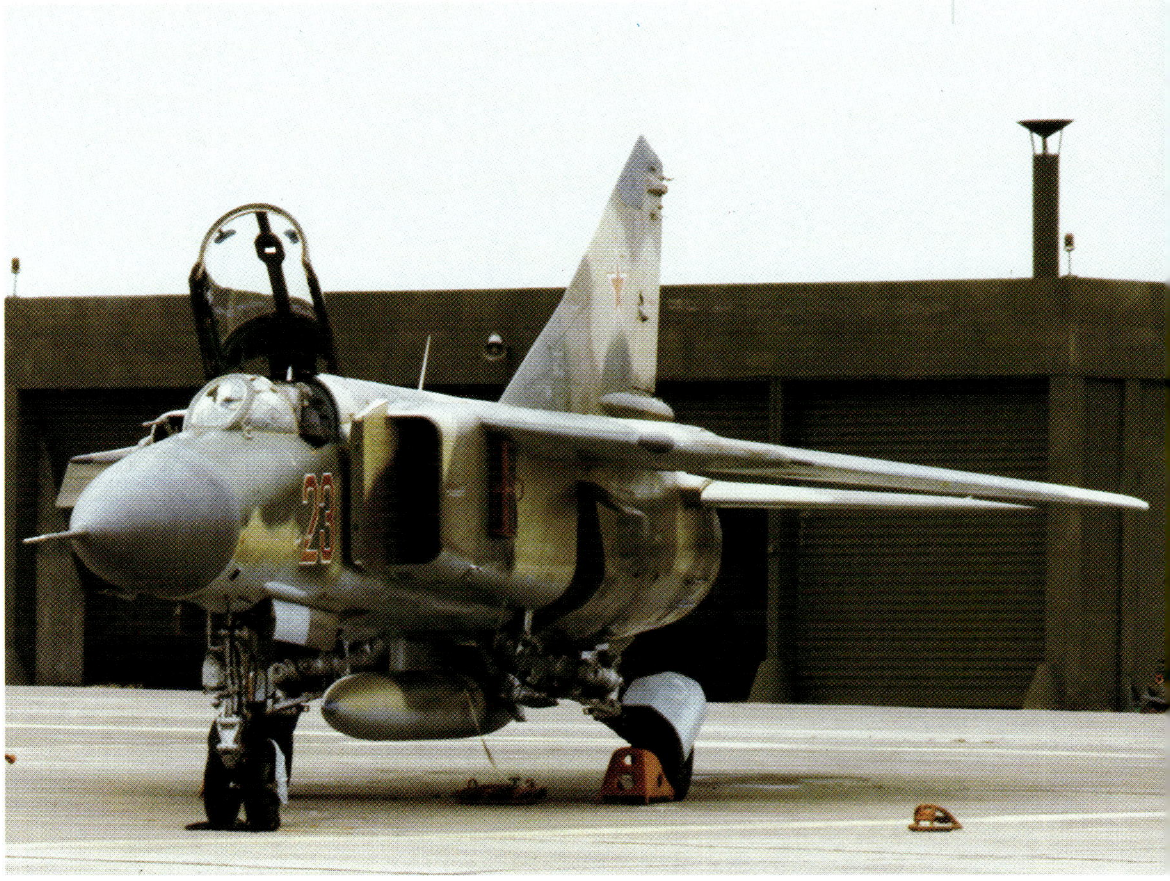

3

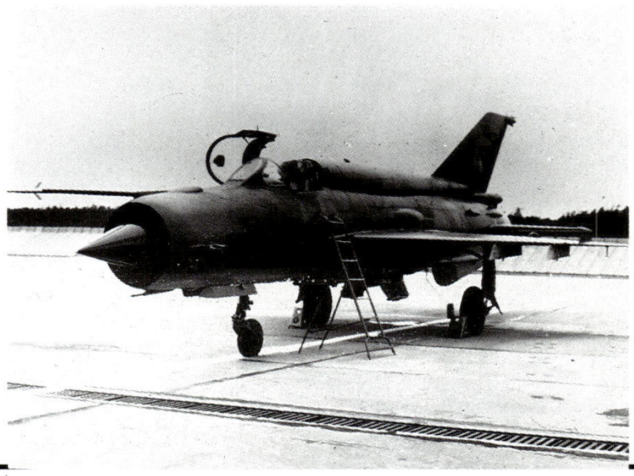

6

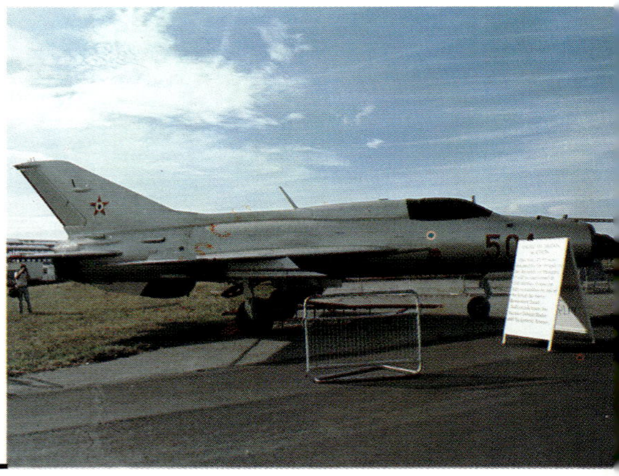

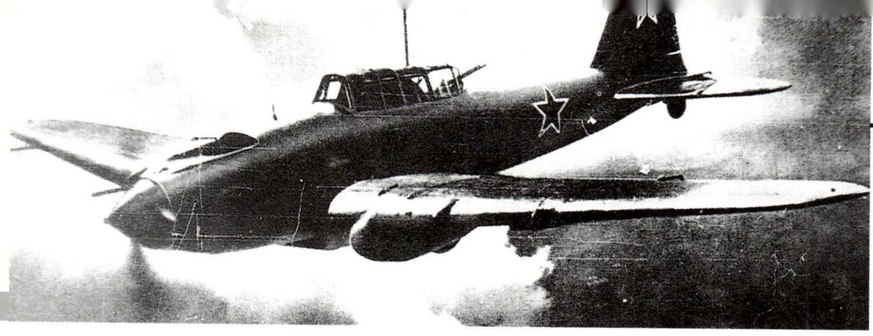

9

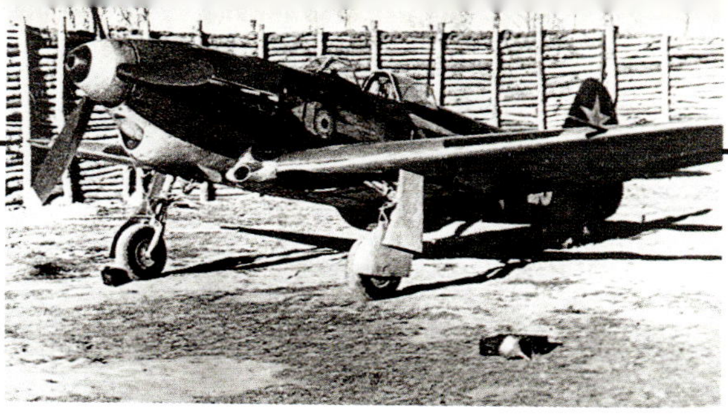

14

10

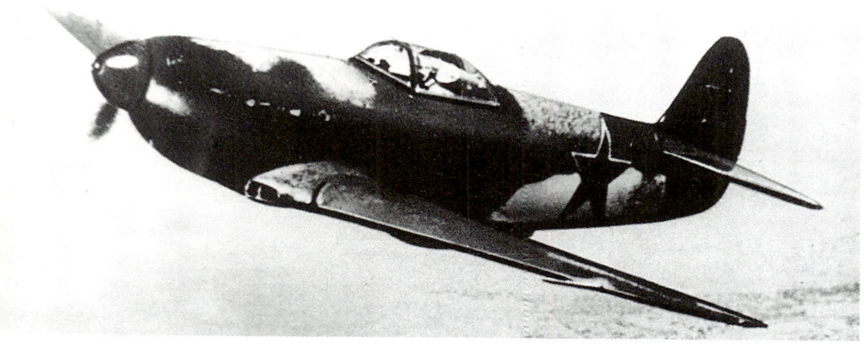

15

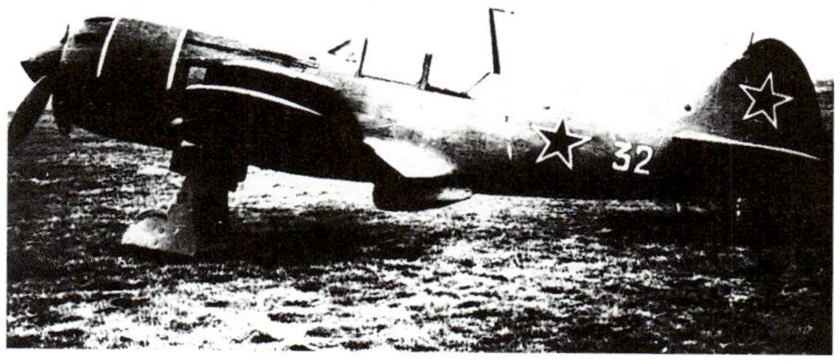

7

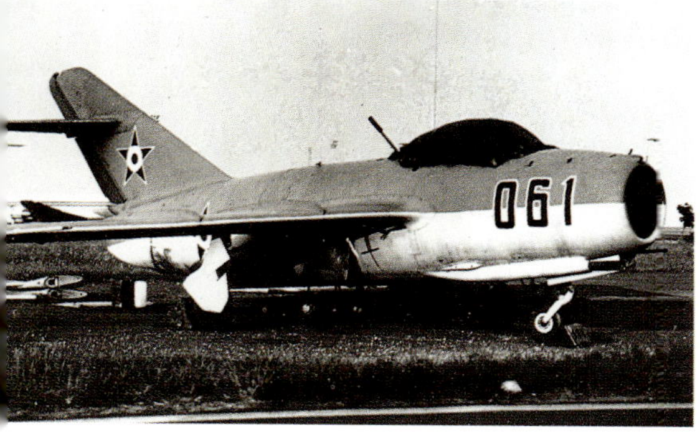

11

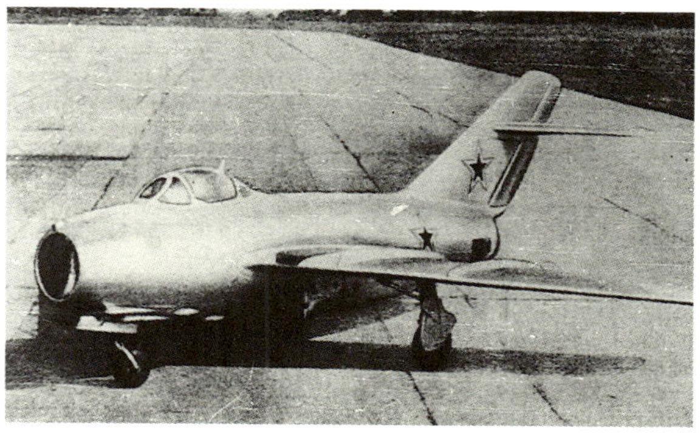

16

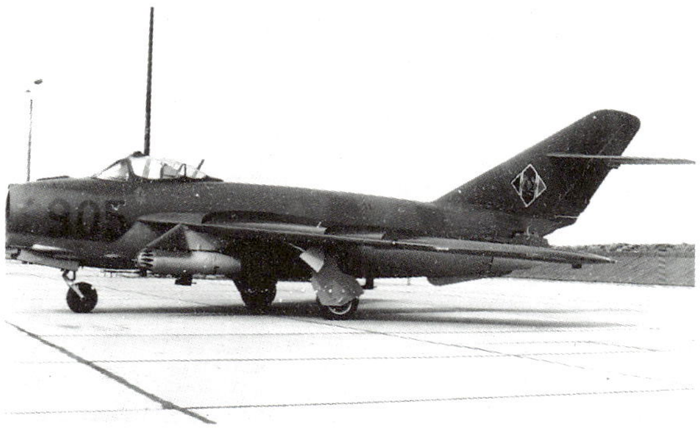

8

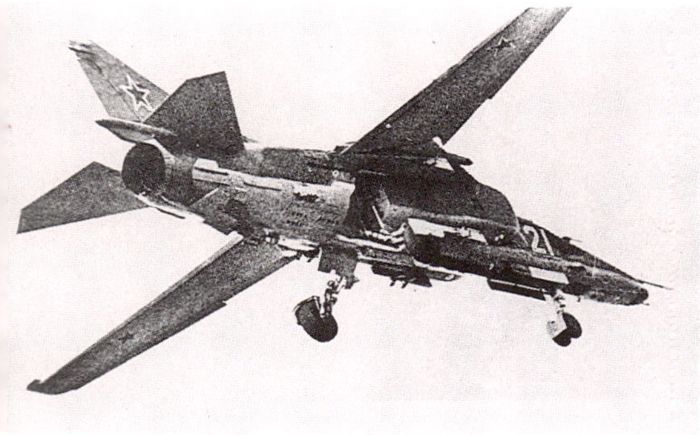

17

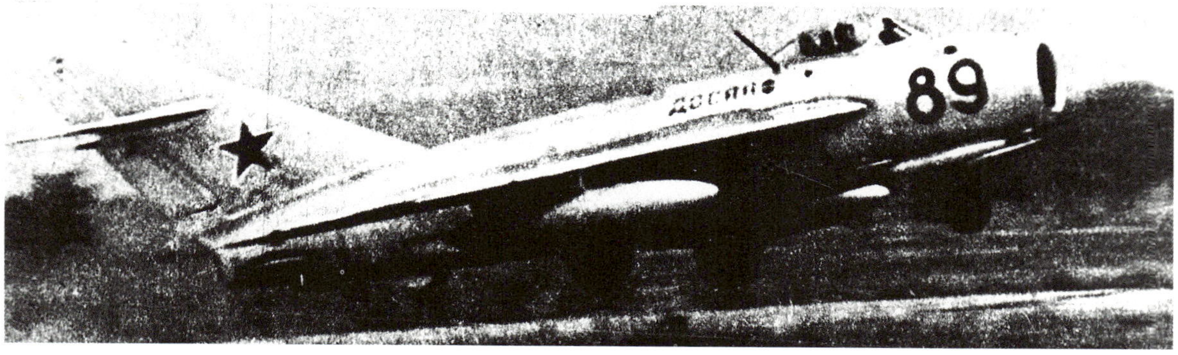

12

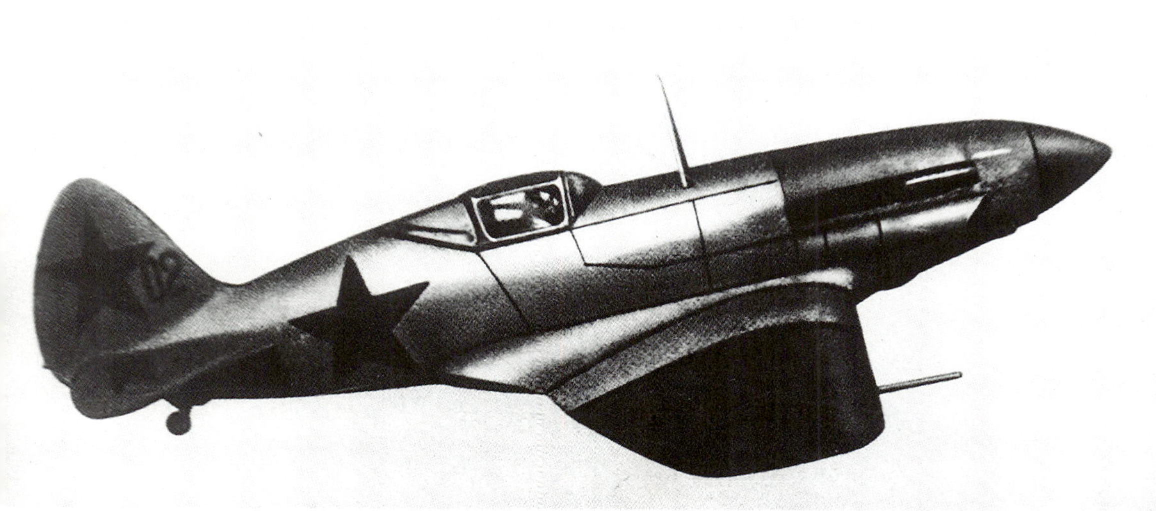

Photo No. 1: Lavochkin La-5
Photo Nos. 2: MiG-23
Photo Nos. 3, 6 and 13: MiG-21
Photo Nos. 4 and 10: Yakovlev Yak-3
Photo No. 5 and 12: MiG-3
Photo Nos. 7 and 11: MiG-15
Photo No. 8: MiG-27
Photo No. 9: Ilyushin Il-2M3
Photo Nos. 14: Yakovlev Yak-9
Photo No. 15: Lavochkin La-9
Photo Nos. 16 and 17: MiG-17

13

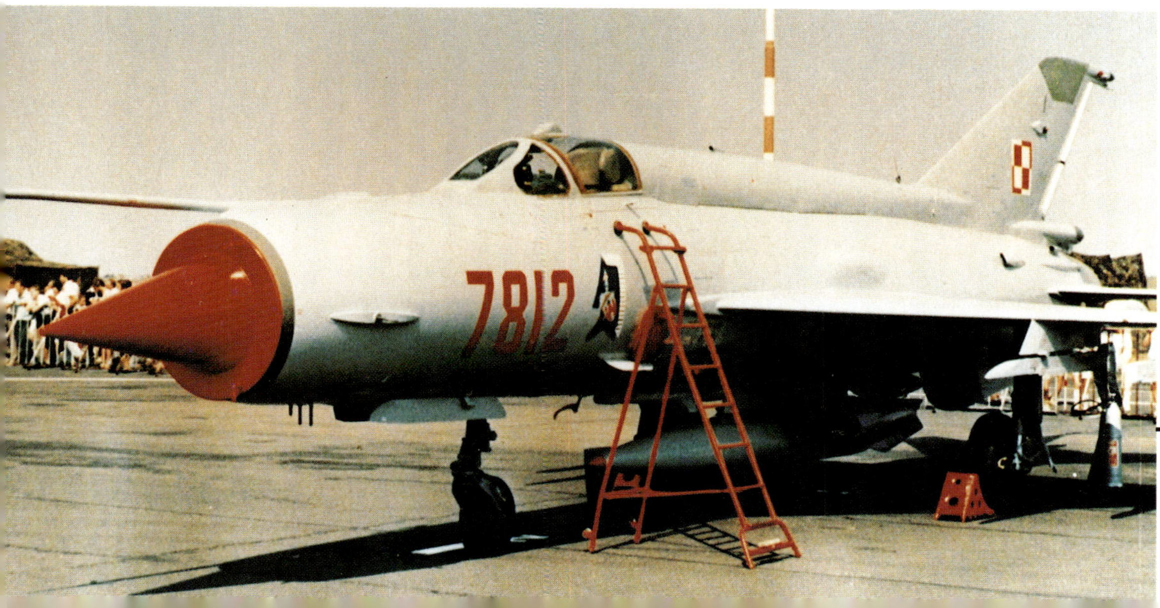

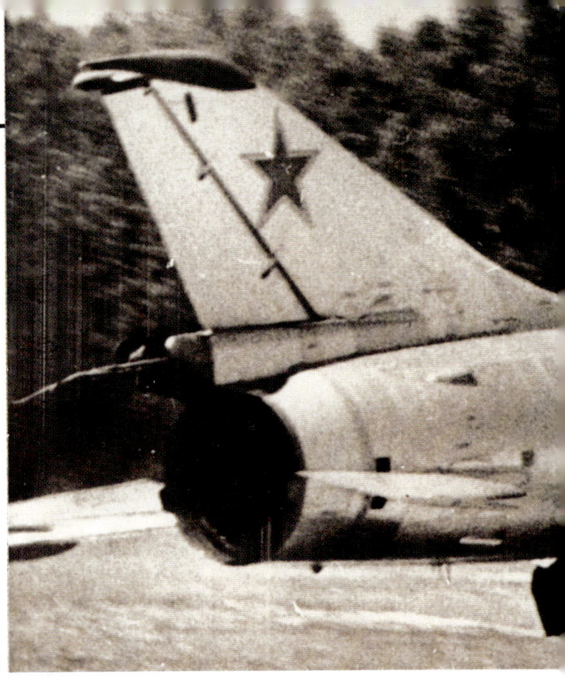

3

RUSSIAN AND SOVIET FIGHTER PLANES

When hostilities ended, the Soviet constructors all began to develop jet-propelled aircraft, drawing inspiration from the jet fighters pioneered by the Germans. The Yak-15 (later to become the 17), a three-ton single-engined single-seater armed with two 23-mm cannon and capable of 500 mph (800 kph), made its debut in 1946, together with the MiG-9.

The MiG-9 was a twin-engined aircraft weighing six tons. It could fly at 562 mph (900 kph) and had a ceiling of 42,600 ft (13,000 m). It was heavily armed with one 37-mm and two 23-mm cannon.

Its successor, the MiG-15, appeared in 1947 and made a name for itself in the Korean War. It was used by the air forces of a dozen or more countries, as well as the Soviet Union. The MiG-15 was a single-engined single-seater fighter weighing five tons. Armed with one 37-mm and two 23-mm cannon, it flew at 652 mph (1,050 kph) and had a ceiling of 49,200 ft (15,000 m). The MiG-15 was the first in a new generation of combat aircraft with completely swept-back wings and tail. It quickly evolved into the much-improved MiG-17. Weighing six tons, the MiG-17 flew at 690 mph (1,100 kph) and could reach altitudes of 55,700 ft (17,000 m). Its armament consisted of three 23-mm cannon, replaced in later versions by missiles.

The MiG-19, which first appeared on the scene in 1955, was a twin-engined interceptor weighing nine tons. It could reach speeds of almost 900 mph (1,450 kph) and had a ceiling of 59,000 ft (18,000 m).

It was soon followed by the MiG-21, more than 10,000 of which were built. A single-engined single-seater weighing up to ten tons, the MiG-21 flew at more than 1,250 mph (2,000 kph) and could climb to 59,000 ft (18,000 m). Early versions were armed with two 30-mm cannon and two air-to-air missiles. In the early 1970s, in response to developments in the American camp, the Soviets commissioned the MiG-23, an all-weather single-engined swing-wing interceptor weighing 20 tons. At altitude, it could fly at over 1,500 mph (2,400 kph), with a ceiling of 59,000 ft (18,000 m). Next in line was the MiG-25, an extremely fast, twin-engined interceptor weighing 37 tons. This powerful aircraft has a maximum speed of 1,864 mph (3,000 kph) and a ceiling of 75,400 ft (23,000 m). Its armament consists of four air-to-air missiles.

The MiG-31 is a completely redesigned version of the 25, designed to fly supersonic at all altitudes. A two-seater, it carries nine air-to-air missiles.

1

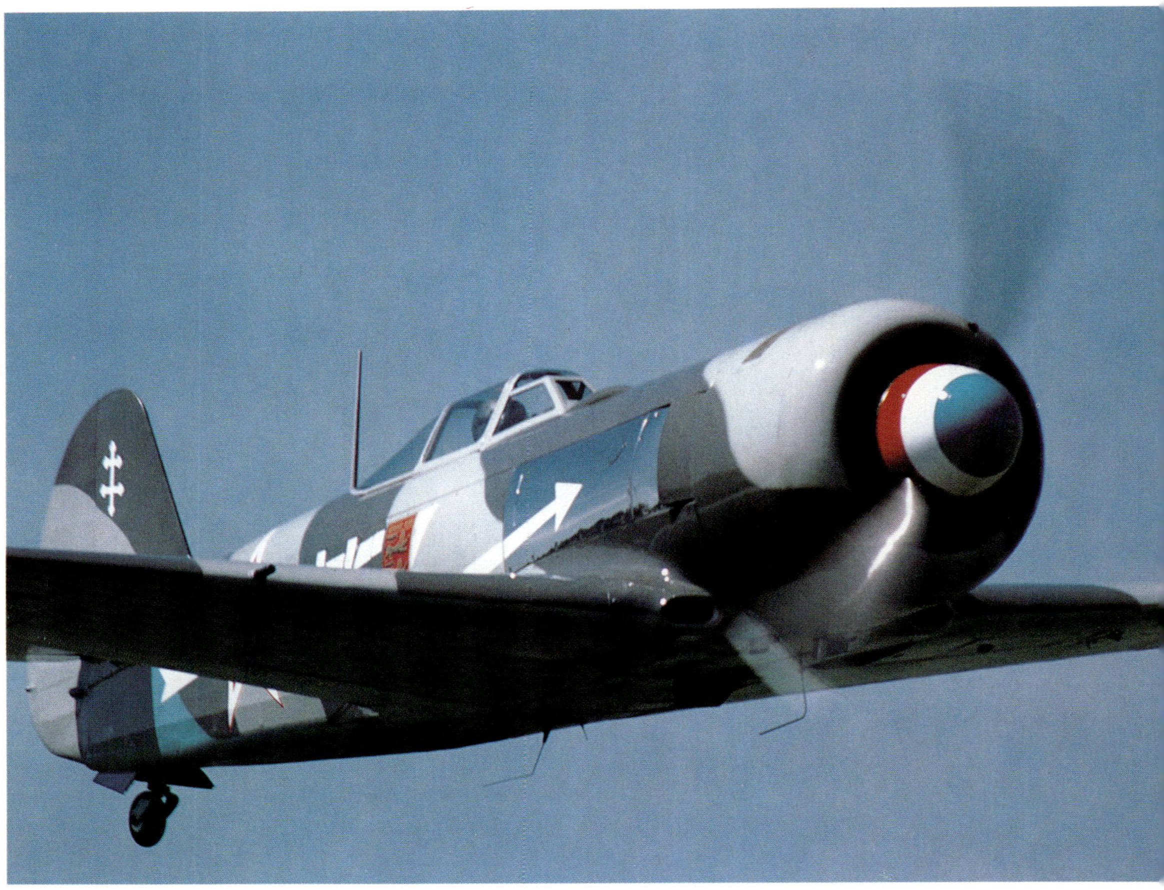

4

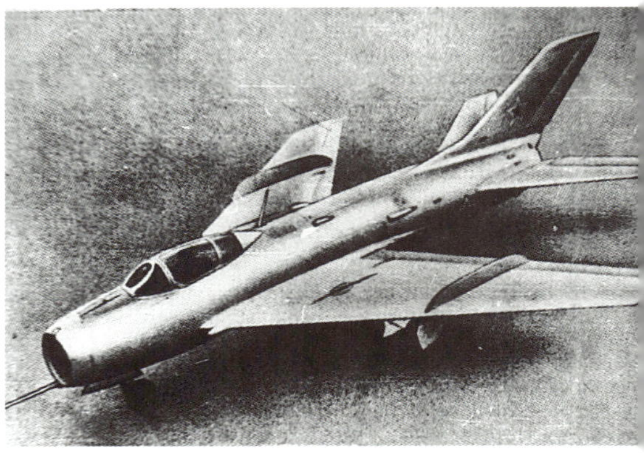

2

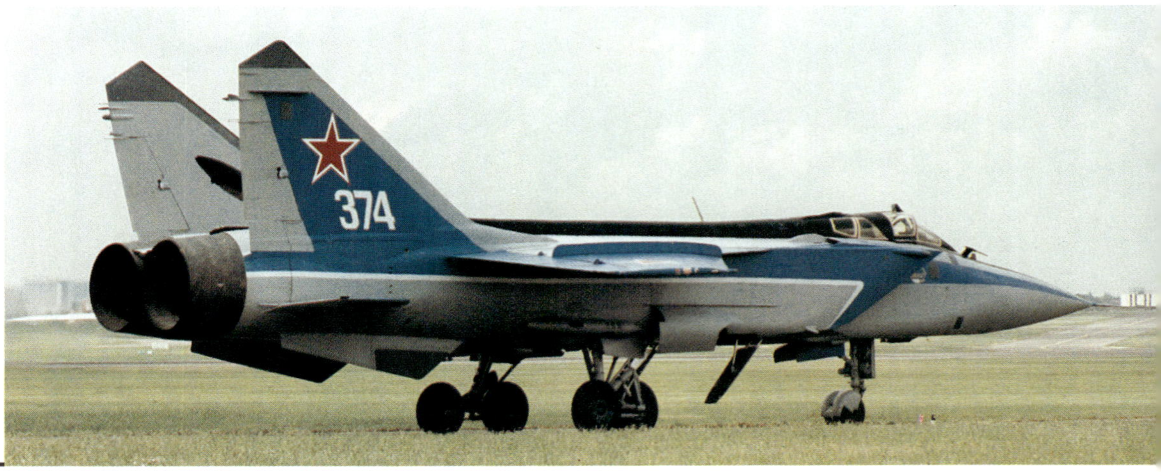

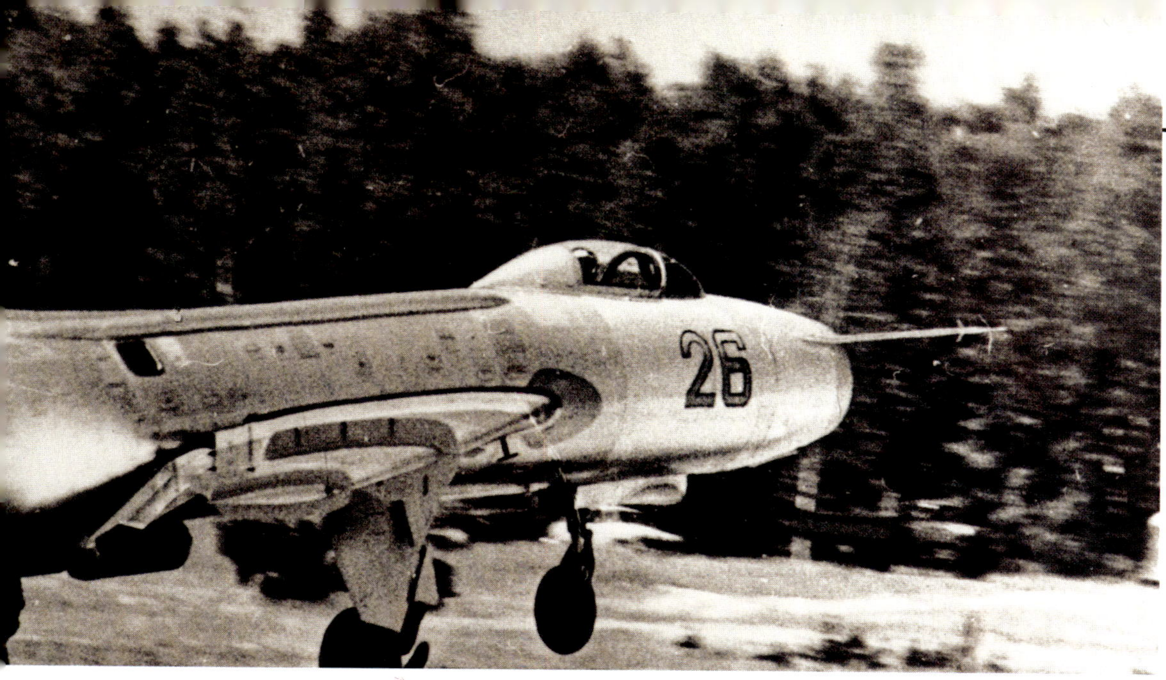

5

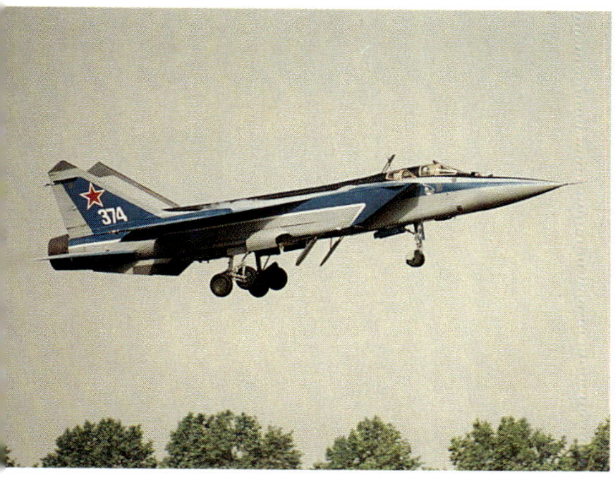

11

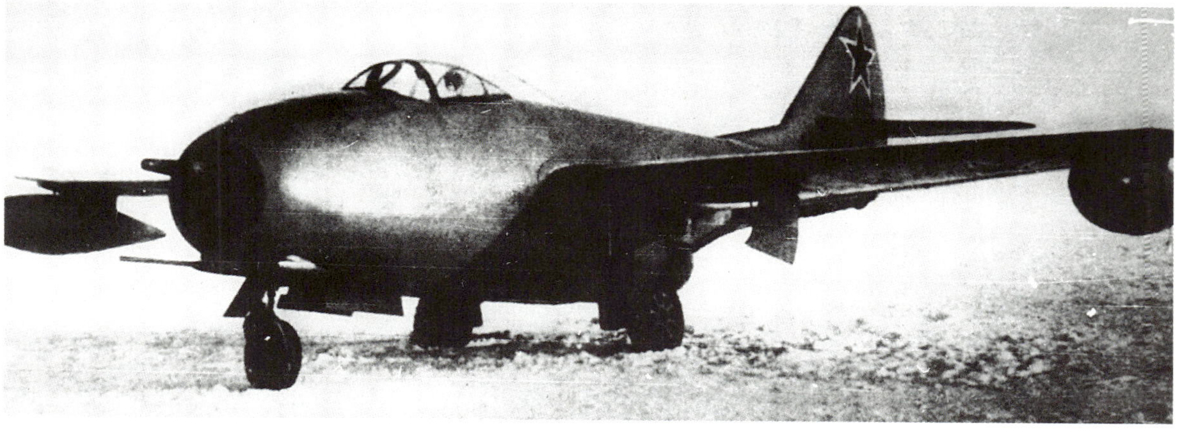

6

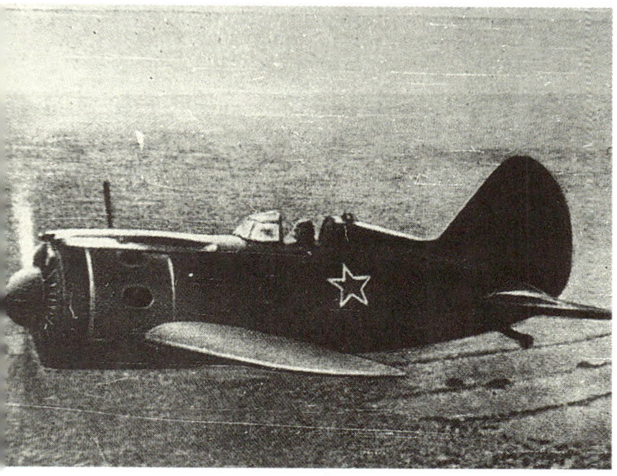

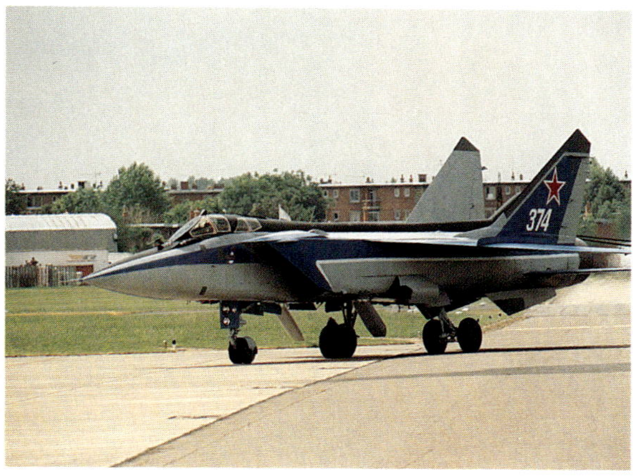

8 Since 1985, the Soviet air force has commissioned the MiG-29 "Fulcrum", an 18.5-ton twin-engined fighter able to fly at over 1,500 mph (2,400 kph) and climb to 65,500 ft (20,000 m). This high-performance aircraft carries various types of air-to-air missile.

7

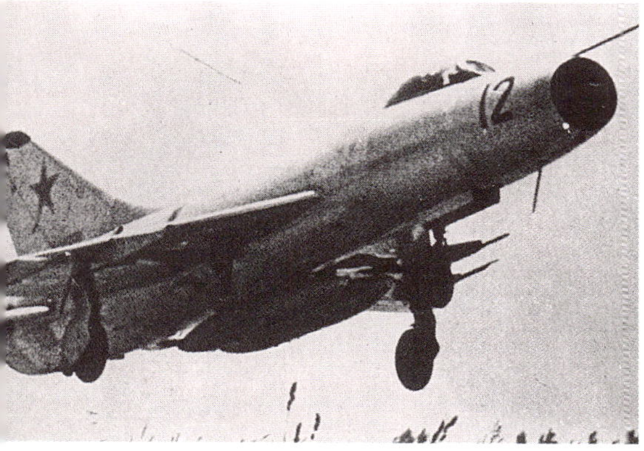

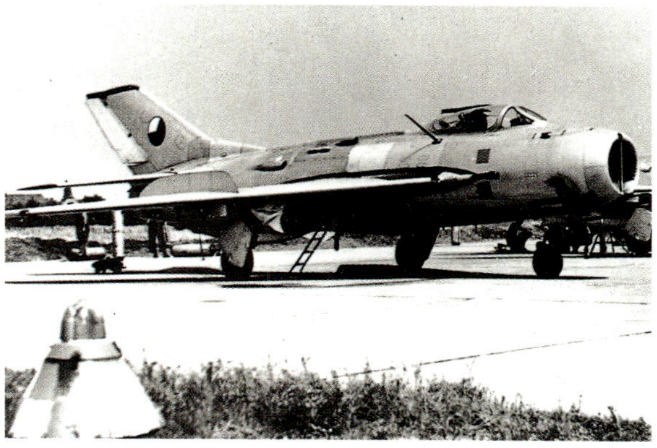

9 **Photo No. 1:** Yak-11 trainer
Photo Nos. 2, 5 and 8: MiG-31
Photo No. 3: Sukhoi Su-7B
Photo Nos. 4 and 9: MiG-19
Photo No. 6: Polikarpov I-16
Photo No. 7: Sukhoi Su-9
Photo No. 10: Yakovlev Yak-28PM
Photo No. 11: MiG-9

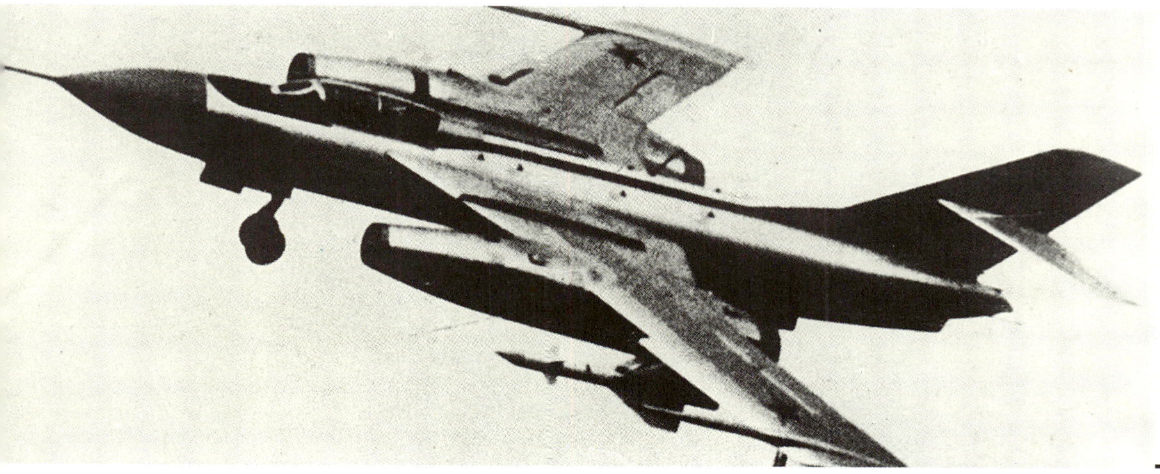

10

RUSSIAN AND SOVIET FIGHTER PLANES

Another major family of Soviet fighter planes was designed by Sukhoi, an engineer in the Tupolev design bureau until 1938. Having gained experience with a number of World War II warplanes, Sukhoi produced supersonic attack aircraft and interceptors from 1955. These included the Su-9 a 12-ton all-weather single-engined interceptor, which could fly at over 1,180 mph (1,900 kph) and at altitudes of 55,700 ft (17,000 m). Its armament consisted of two, later four, air-to-air missiles.

In 1965 came the Su-15, a twin-engined all-weather interceptor weighing 19.2 tons, and capable of speeds in excess of 1,500 mph (2,400 kph). It was armed with two air-to-air missiles, later adding a gun. For his next series of aircraft, Sukhoi adopted variable-geometry technology, designing the Su-17, Su-20 and Su-22 models. These were multi-role attack fighters capable of speeds in excess of Mach-2 and armed with various types of missile.

After the Su-24 – a 40-ton two-seater swing-wing attack aircraft – the latest in the Sukhoi family is the Su-27. This outstanding fighter came into production in 1981. A single-seater armed with a 30-mm cannon and ten air-to-air missiles, the Su-27 reaches speeds of 1,560 mph (2,500 kph) and can operate up to 59,000 ft (18,000 m).

Tupolev specialize mainly in heavy aircraft and bombers, but in the late 1960s the company brought out the Tupolev Tu-28P, which must be the biggest fighter plane ever produced. A long-range interceptor weighing 40 tons, the Tu-28P flew at 1,180 mph (1,900 kph) and could climb to 65,600 ft (20,000 m). Its armament consisted of four air-to-air missiles.

After the War, Yakovlev first produced the Yak-25, an all-weather twin-engined interceptor with tandem seats for the two crew. This was followed in the 1960s by another all-weather interceptor, the Yak-28, of which there were many versions. Armed with two air-to-air missiles, the Yak-28PM fighter could fly at 1,280 mph (2,060 kph) and had a ceiling of 52,500 ft (16,000 m).

5

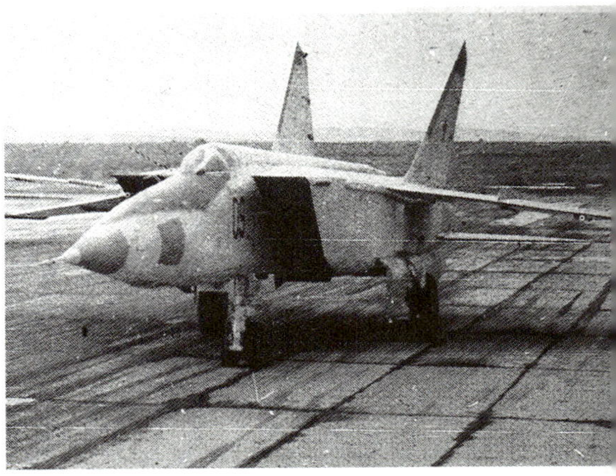

1

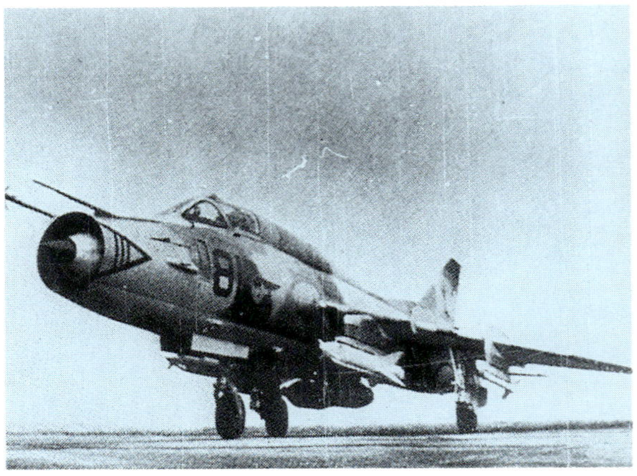

6

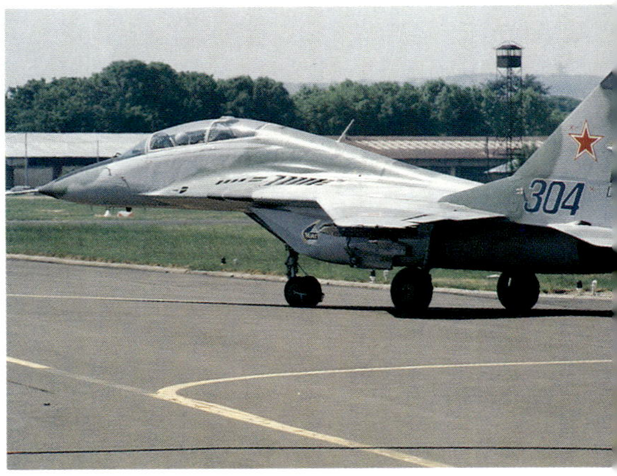

2

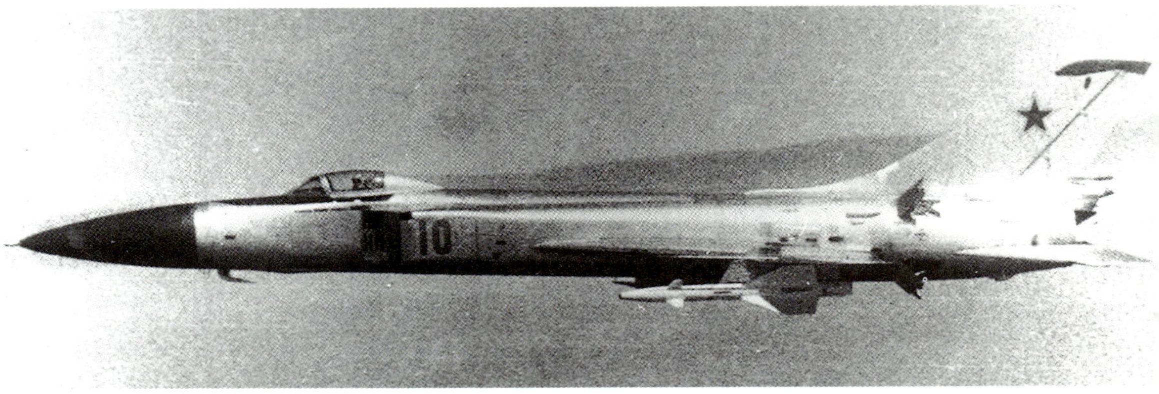

3

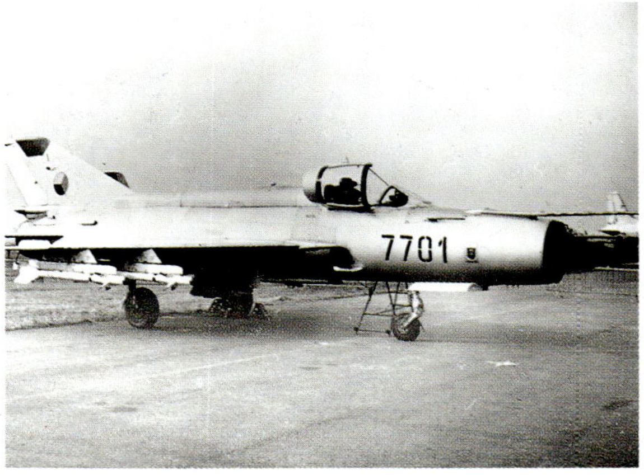

7

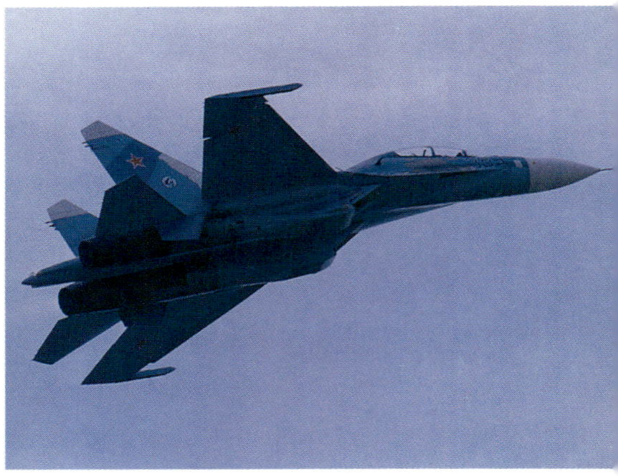

4

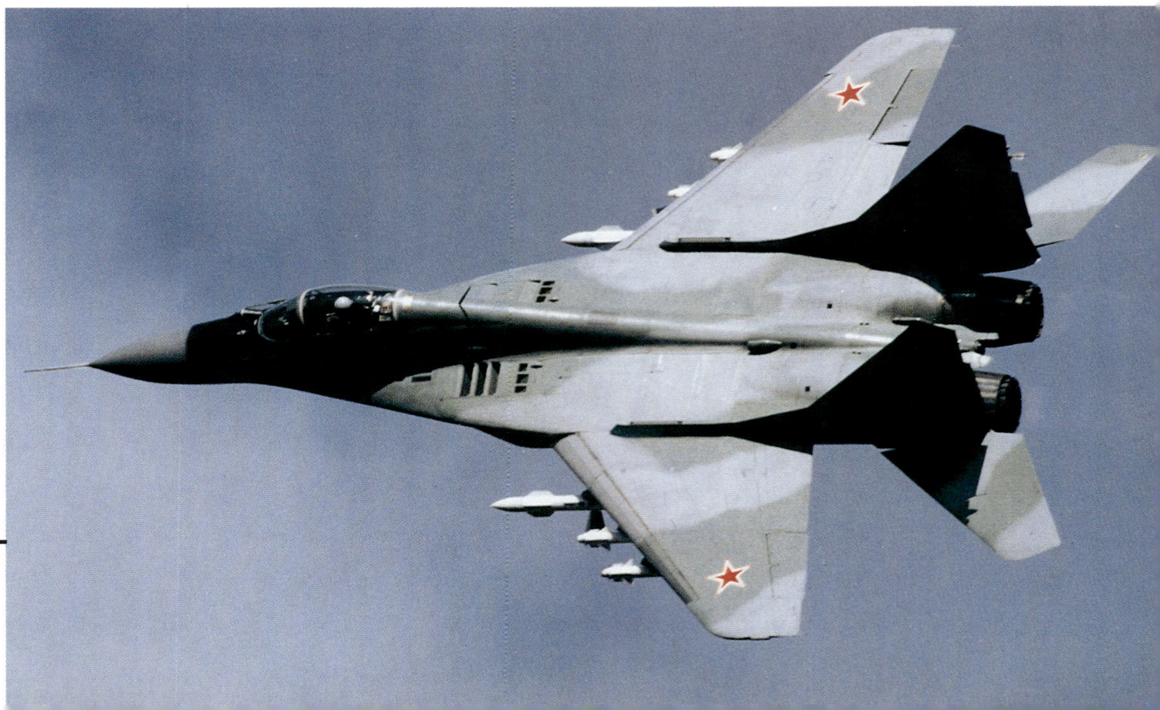

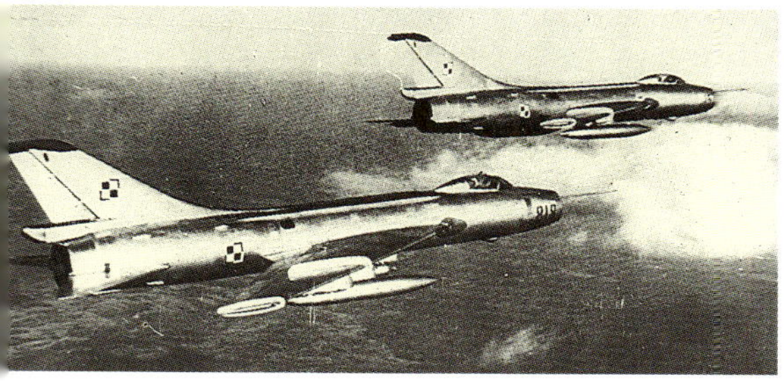

8

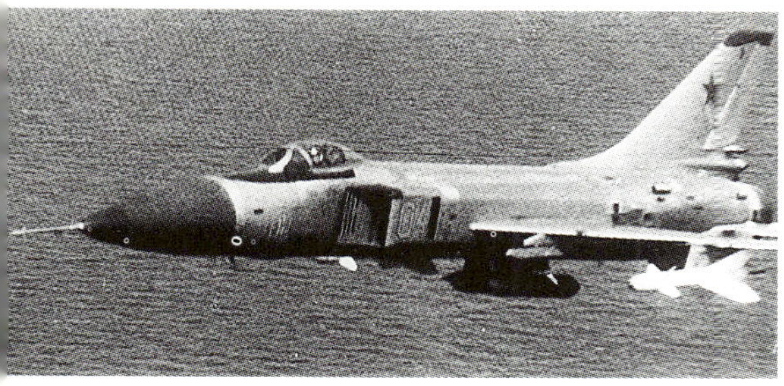

9

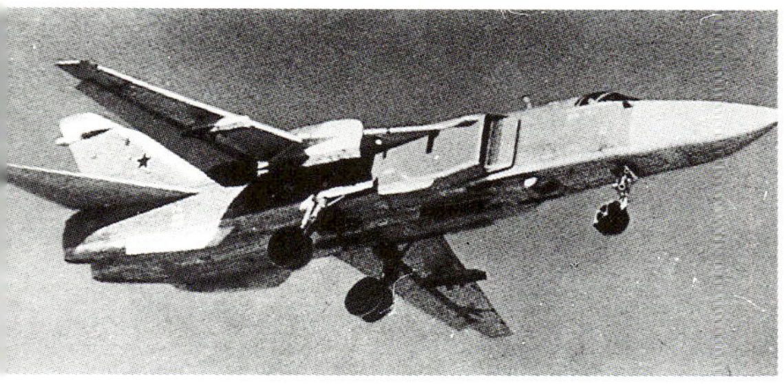

10

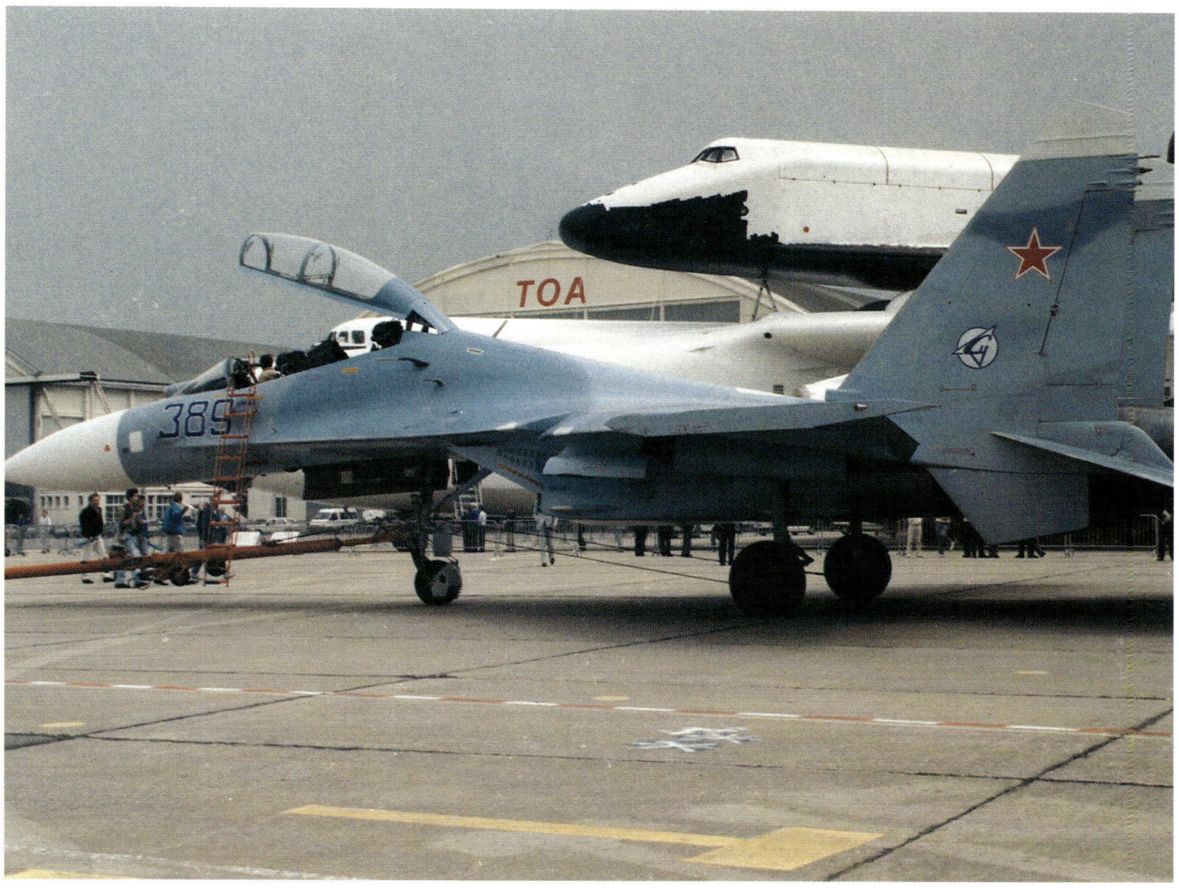

14

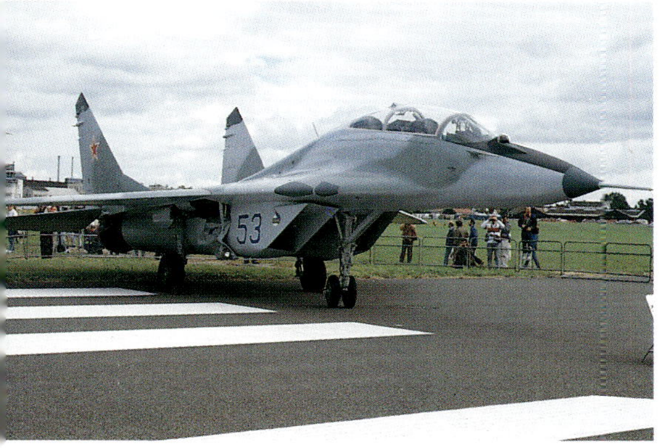

11

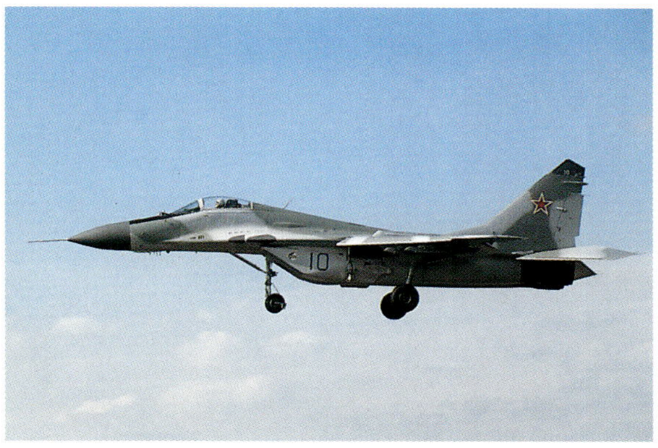

12

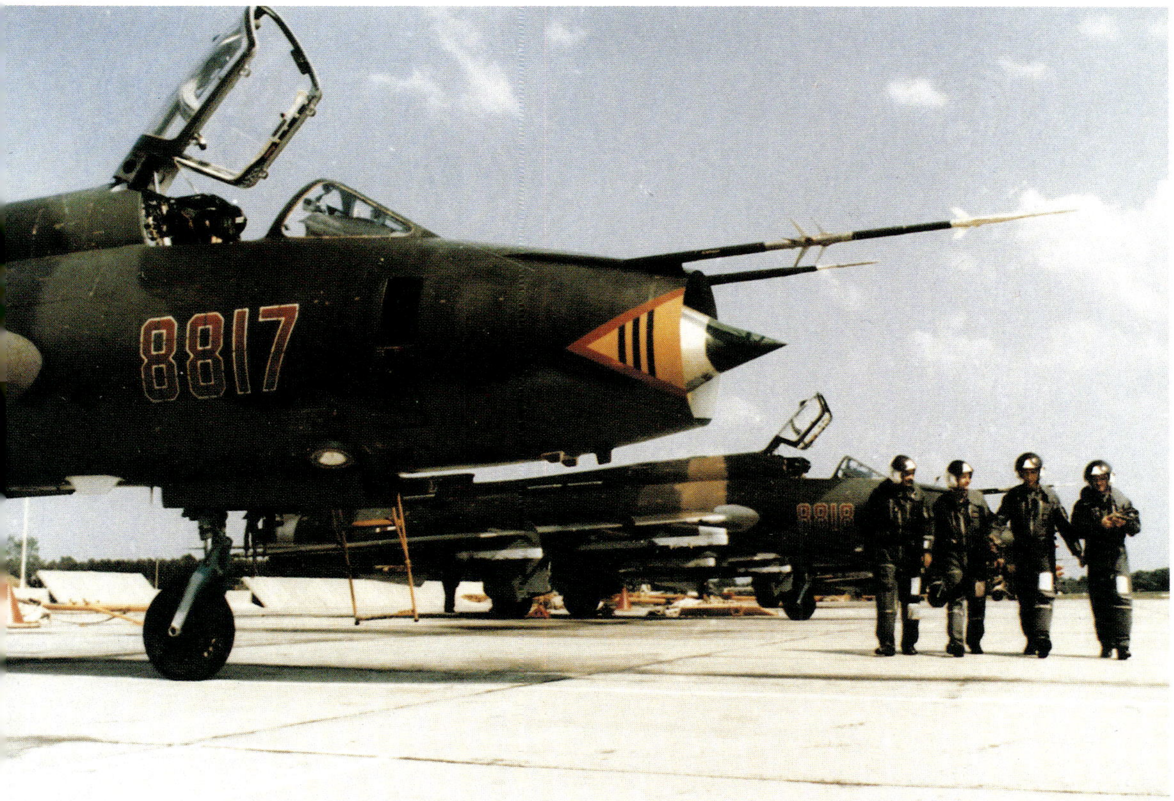

13

Photo Nos. 1: Sukhoi Su-17
Photo Nos. 2 and 9: Sukhoi Su-15
Photo Nos. 3: MiG-21
Photo Nos. 4, 6, 11 and 12: MiG-29
Photo No. 5: MiG-25
Photo Nos. 7, 14 and 15: Sukhoi Su-27
Photo No. 8: Sukhoi Su-7B
Photo No. 10: Sukhoi Su-24
Photo No. 13: Sukhoi Su-22

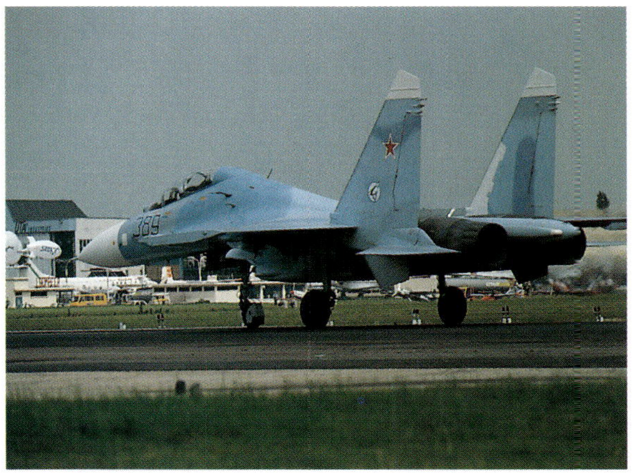

15

4
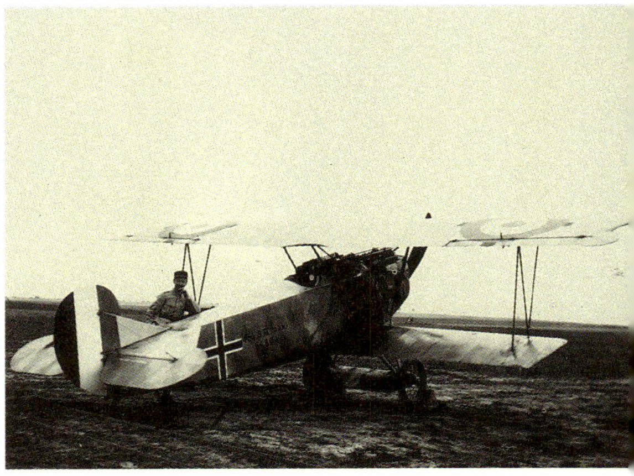

GERMAN FIGHTER PLANES

The first fighter plane in German aviation history was in fact of Austrian descent. The Taube, or "Dove", was built in 1910 by a Dr Etrich, who then sold the patents to various German constructors. The two-seater machine was powered by a 100-hp engine and weighed 1,320 lb (600 kg). It could fly at just over 62 mph (100 kph) and reached altitudes of 9,850 ft (3,000 m). The observer was armed with a rifle, or just a pistol.

Before World War I, the Dutch Fokker company had already built a number of aircraft, including the E III, which was fitted with a synchronising gear enabling machine-guns bullets to pass between the blades of the propeller. In 1915 Fokker began producing his D series. The D VII was a fighter capable of 120 mph (190 kph), with a ceiling of around 16,400 ft (5,000 m). Its armament consisted of two 7.92-mm machine guns. The Fokker Dr I triplane, whose most famous pilot was the "Red Baron" Manfred von Richthofen, made its appearance in 1917. Armed with two 7.92-mm machine guns, it flew at 103 mph (165 kph) and could climb to altitudes of over 19,600 ft (6,000 m). The Pfalz D III was another single-seater fighter, weighing 1,650 lb (750 kg). Armed with two 7.92-mm machine guns, it was capable of similar speeds to the Dr I and had a ceiling of 16,400 ft (5,000 m).

One of the best German fighters of the 1914-18 war was undoubtedly the Albatros D III. Powered by a 175-hp engine, it could fly at 110 mph (175 kph).

Although forbidden to do so by international treaty, Germany recommenced building combat aircraft during the 1930s. In 1935, Willy Messerschmitt designed the Bf 109, more than 35,000 of which were eventually built – the longest production run of any World War II aircraft. The Bf 109 had a 1,500-hp V12 engine, enabling later versions to fly at over 440 mph (700 kph) and reach altitudes of 39,400 ft (12,000m). The fighter was armed with two 13-mm machine guns and two 20-mm cannon.

The Messerschmitt Bf 110, on the other hand, was a twin-engined two-seater, used for both day and night-time operations. It had a top speed of 350 mph (560 kph) and a ceiling of 32,800 ft (10,000 m). Its armament consisted of two 20-mm cannon and five 7.92-mm machine guns. But the best German fighter of the War was the Focke-Wulf Fw 190, whose engine developed more than 2,000 hp. Armed with 13-mm machine guns and 20-or 30-mm cannon, it attained speeds of 440 mph (700 kph) and could climb to over 32,800 ft (10,000 m).

1
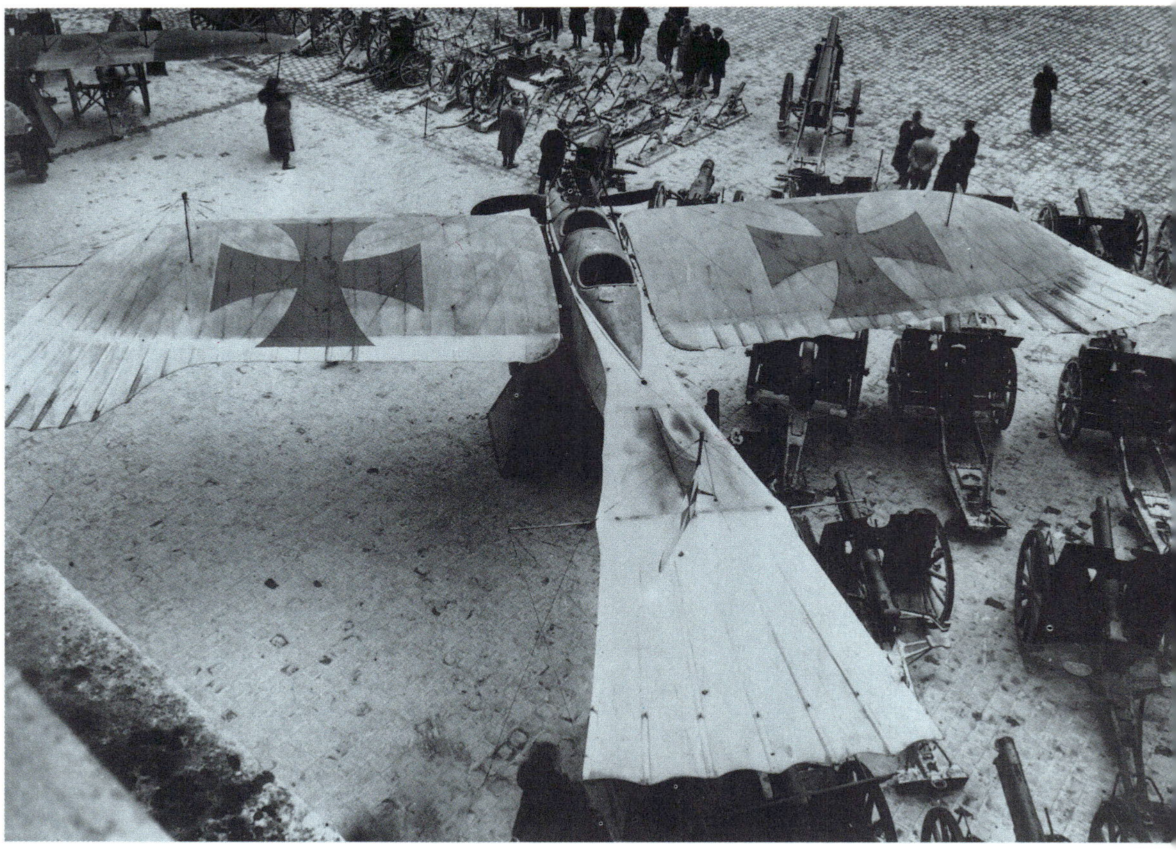

2
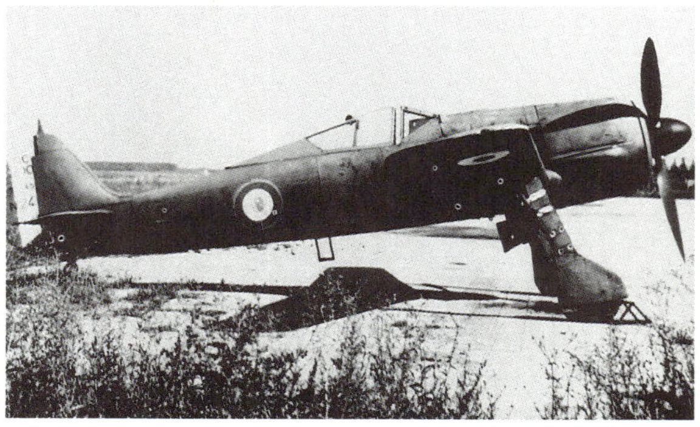

5
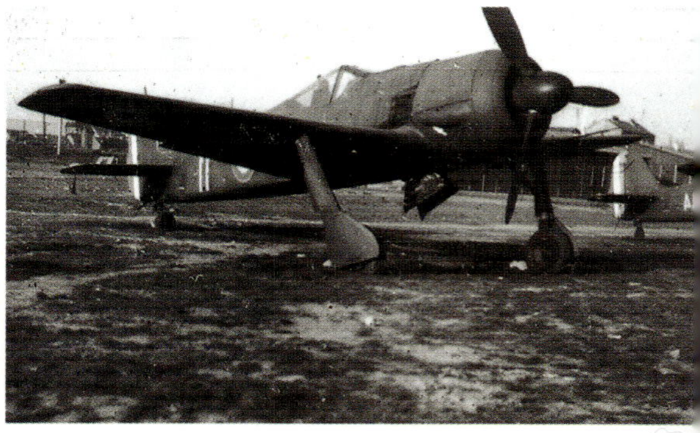

3
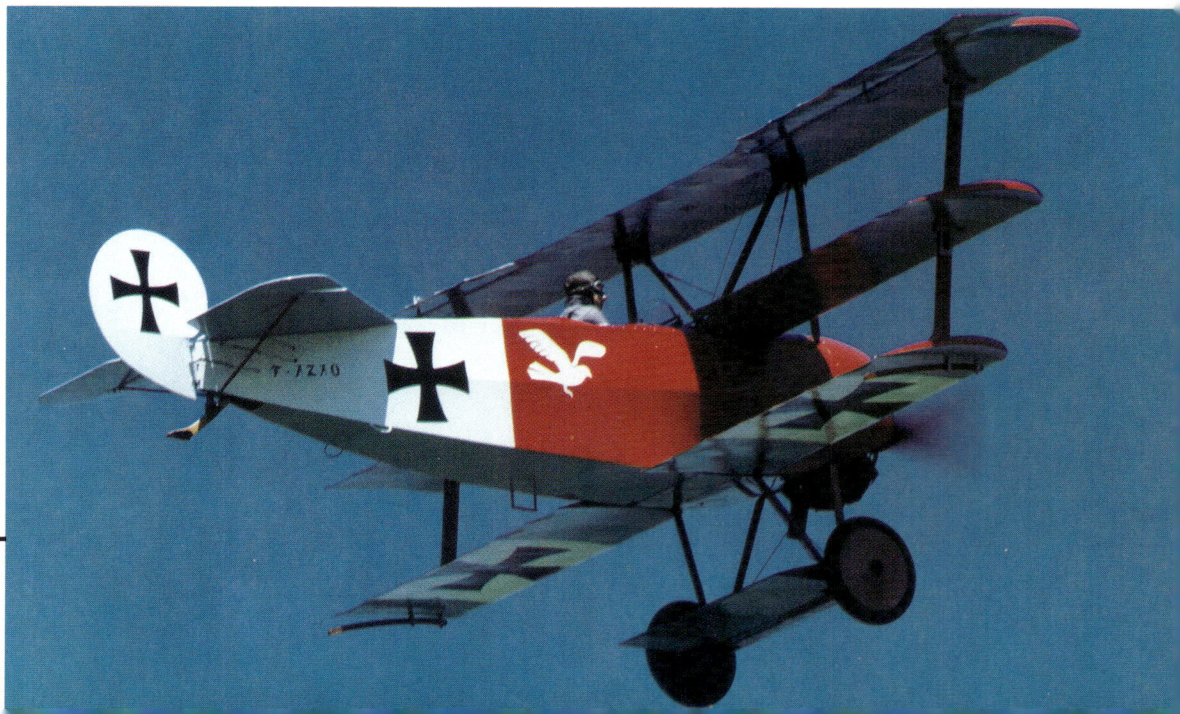

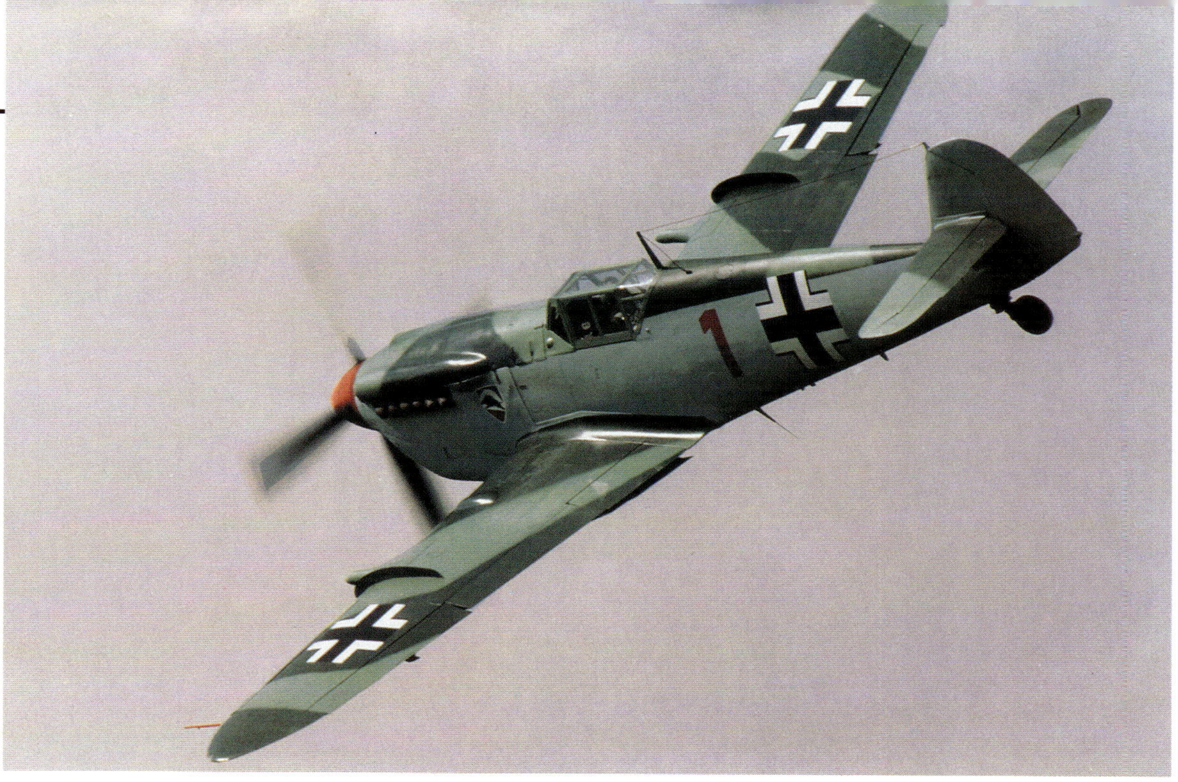

16

6

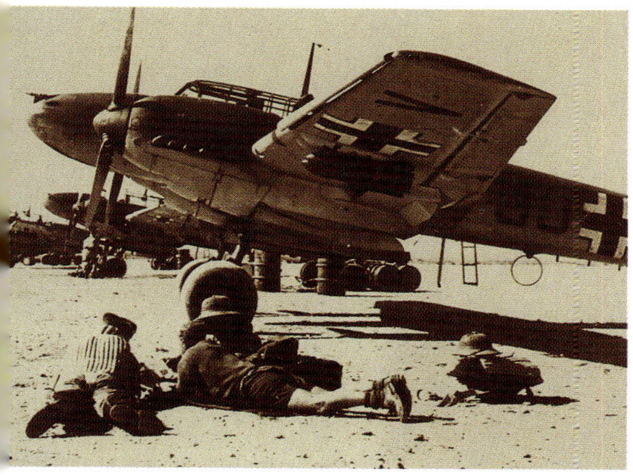

7

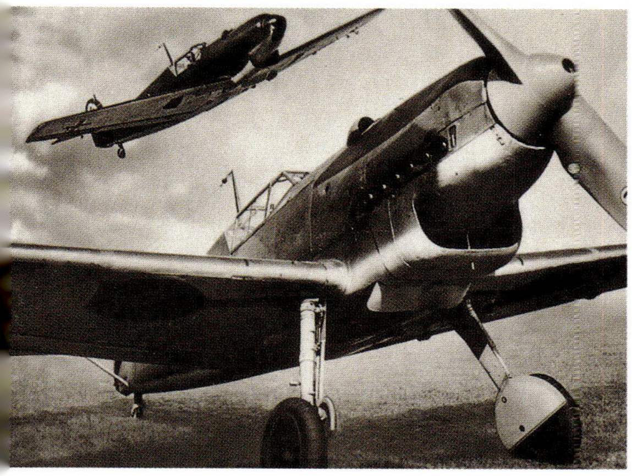

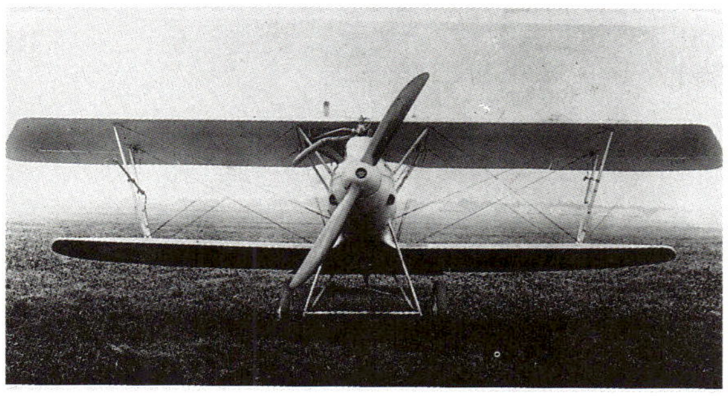

12

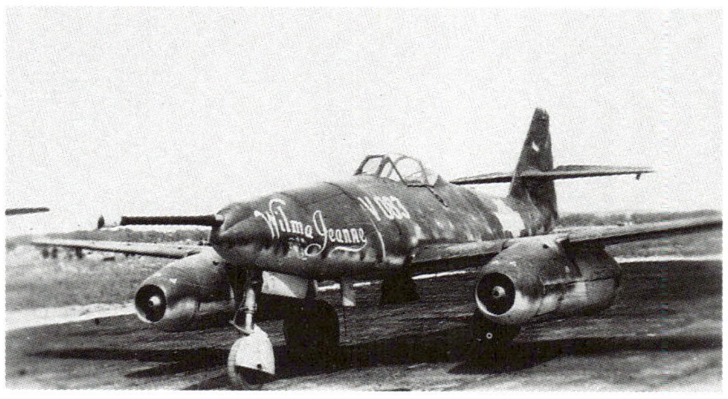

17

8

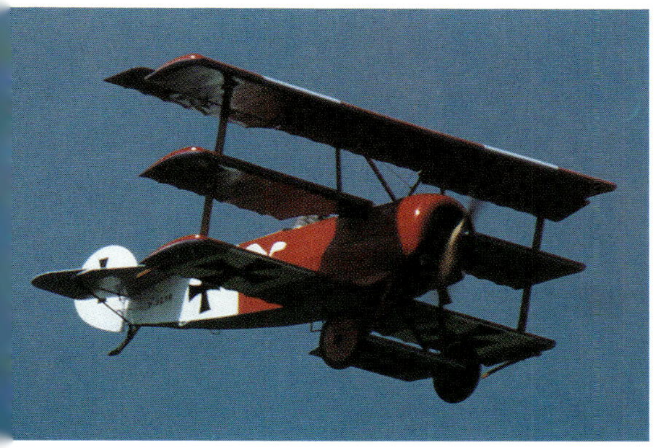

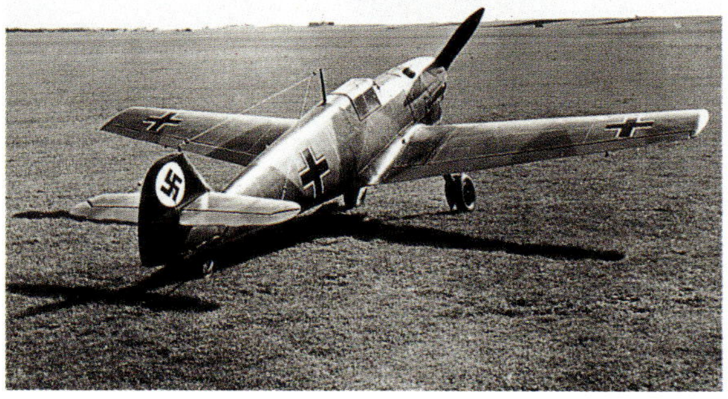

13 In the final years of the War, the Germans developed several jet-propelled interceptors, such as the Messerschmitt Me 262 – capable of 500 mph (800 kph) – and the Heinkel He 162, which could fly at over 525 mph (840 kph). There was also the diminutive Messerschmitt Me 163: a rocket-powered interceptor which could climb to 32,800 ft (10,000 m) in two minutes 30 seconds and fly at speeds of almost 625 mph (1,000 kph). Its armament consisted of two 30-mm cannon.

9

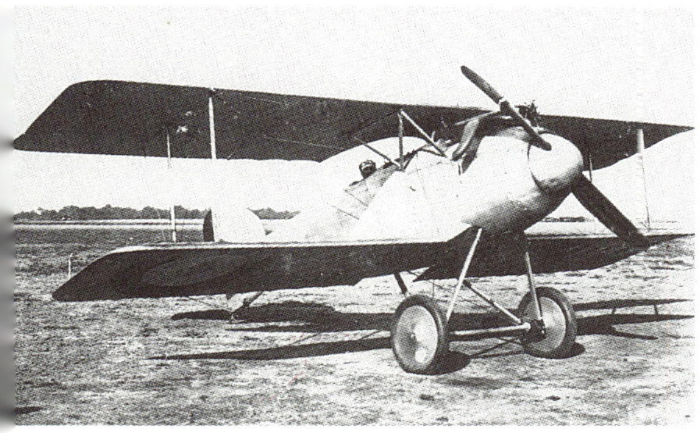

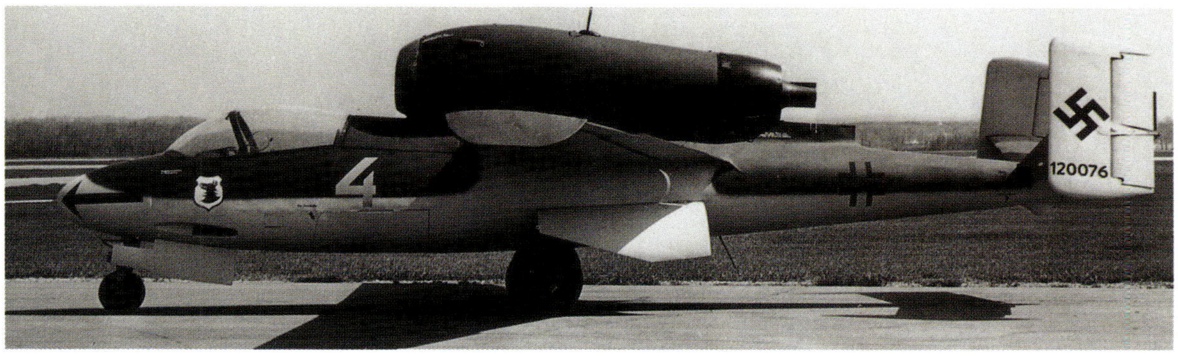

18

10

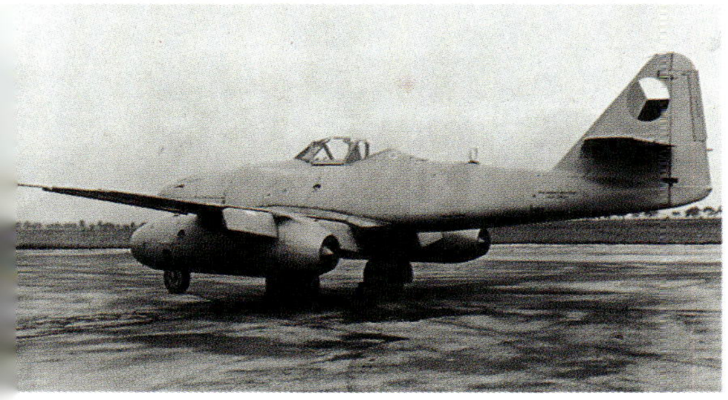

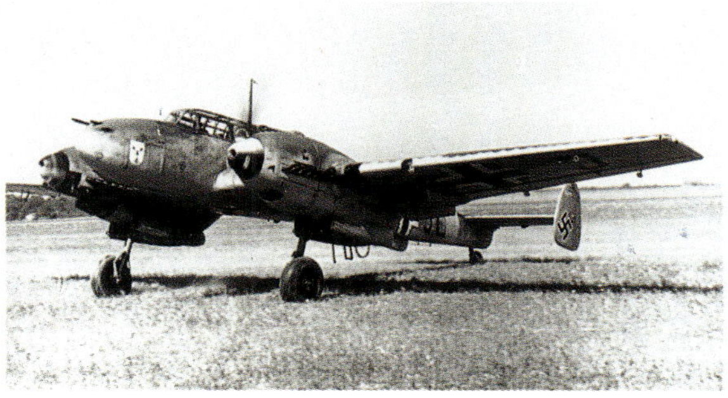

14 **Photo No. 1:** Etrich Taube
Photo Nos. 2 and 5: Focke-Wulf Fw 190
Photo Nos. 3 and 8: Fokker Dr I Triplane (replica)
Photo No. 4: Fokker D VII
Photo Nos. 6 and 14: Messerschmitt Bf 110
Photo Nos. 7 and 13: Messerschmitt Bf 109
Photo No. 9: Albatros D II
Photo Nos. 10 and 17: Messerschmitt Me 262
Photo No. 11: Messerschmitt Me 163
Photo No. 12: Pfalz D III
15 **Photo Nos. 15 and 16:** Hispano-built Spanish Bf 109
Photo No. 18: Heinkel He 162A

11

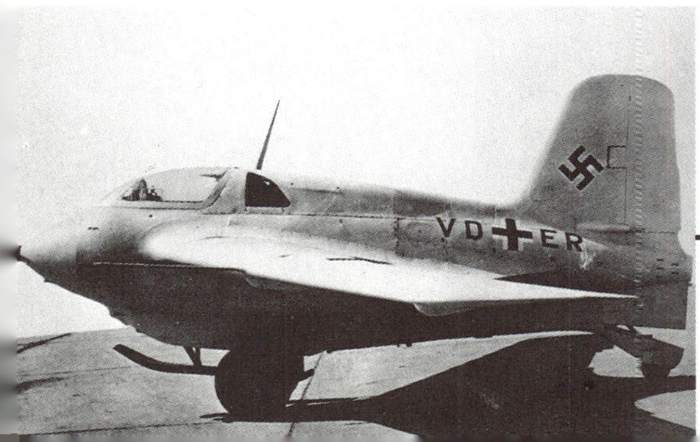

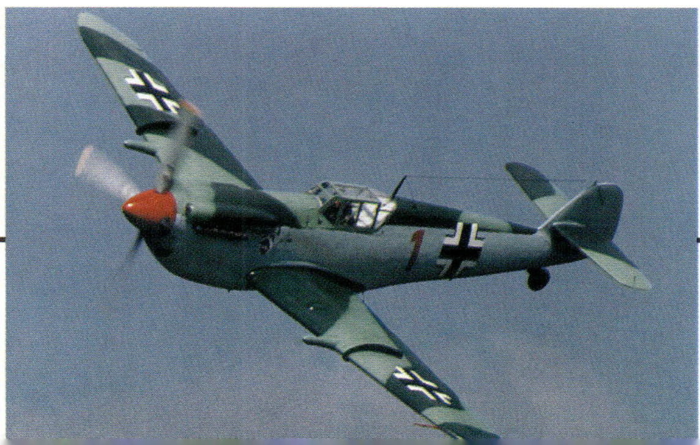

4

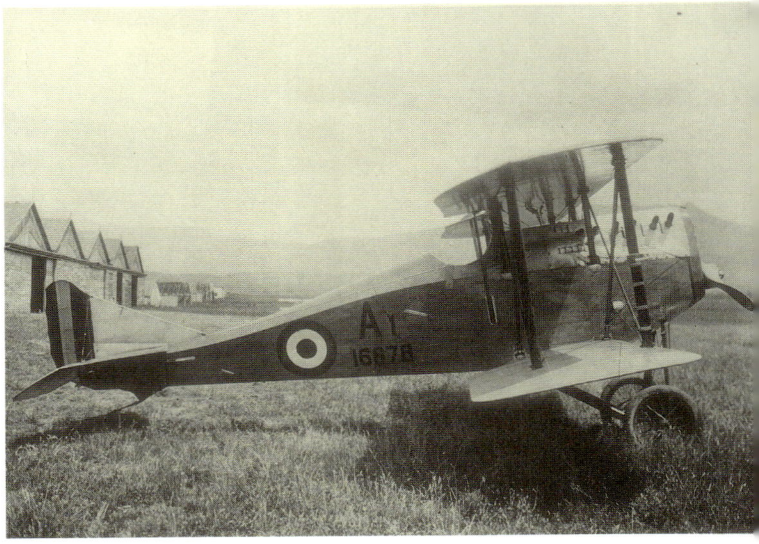

ITALIAN AND POLISH FIGHTER PLANES

Built in 1917, the Italian air force's first fighter plane was too late to play any significant role in World War I. Powered by a 220-hp 6-cylinder engine, the Ansaldo A-1 Balilla was fast (140 mph/220 kph), and could climb to 16,400 ft (5,000 m). It had an armament of two machine guns.

During the 1920s, Italian industrialists planned a new generation of fighters for their country's air force, the Regia Aeronautica. The Fiat CR.30, which made its appearance in 1932, was a single-seater biplane, powered by a 600-hp engine and armed with two machine guns. It flew at 220 mph (350 kph). It was followed by the more powerful CR.32, then the CR.42, another biplane, which came into production on the eve of World War II. The CR.42 flew at speeds in excess of 250 mph (400 kph), with a ceiling of 32,800 ft (10,000 m), and was armed with two 0.5-inch machine guns.

Next came the more modern, all-metal, Fiat G.50 Freccia and G.55 Centauro. Powered by a 1,475-hp engine, the G.55 was capable of over 375 mph (600 kph) and could climb to 42,600 ft (13,000 m). Its armament consisted of two 0.5-inch machine guns and three 20-mm cannon.

The Macchi company began delivering its C.200 Saetta in 1939. A single-engined monoplane armed with two 0.5-inch machine guns, it was powered by an 870-hp engine, which gave it a top speed of around 310 mph (500 kph) and a ceiling of 29,500 ft (9,000 m). Distinctly superior in performance was the C.205 Veltro, whose 1,500-hp engine enabled it to fly at over 400 mph (650 kph) and at altitudes of 36,000 ft (11,000 m). Its armament consisted of two 20-mm cannon and two 0.5-inch machine guns.

On the eve of the war, a subsidiary of Caproni Reggiane had developed an excellent light fighter with a 1,000-hp 14-cylinder engine – the Re.2001 Falco – which flew at 330 mph (530 kph) and could climb to over 36,000 ft (11,000 m). The Falco was followed in 1942 by the more powerful, better armed and slightly faster Re.2002 Ariete, which carried two 0.5-inch and two 7.7-mm machine guns. In 1943 appeared the Re.2005 Sagittario, whose 1,500-hp engine gave it a top speed of over 375 mph (600 kph) and a ceiling of 39,400 ft (12,000 m). It packed a powerful punch, with three 20-mm cannon as well as two 0.5-inch machine guns.

1

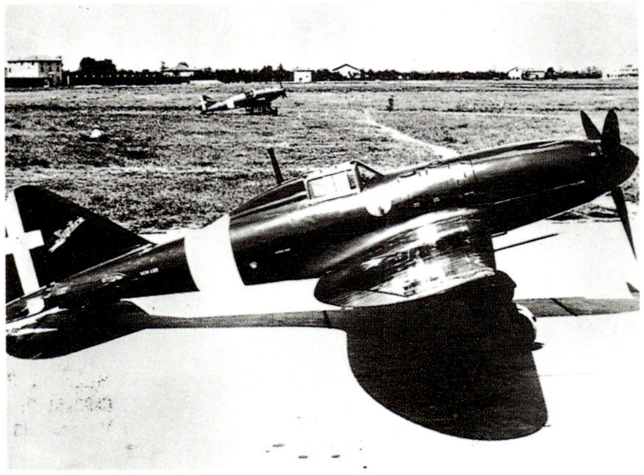

5

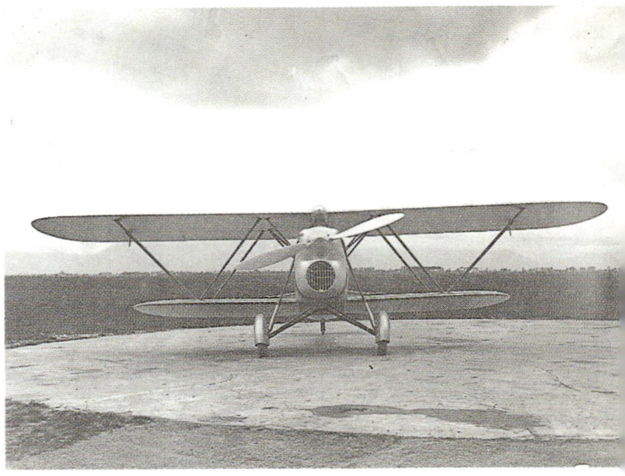

2

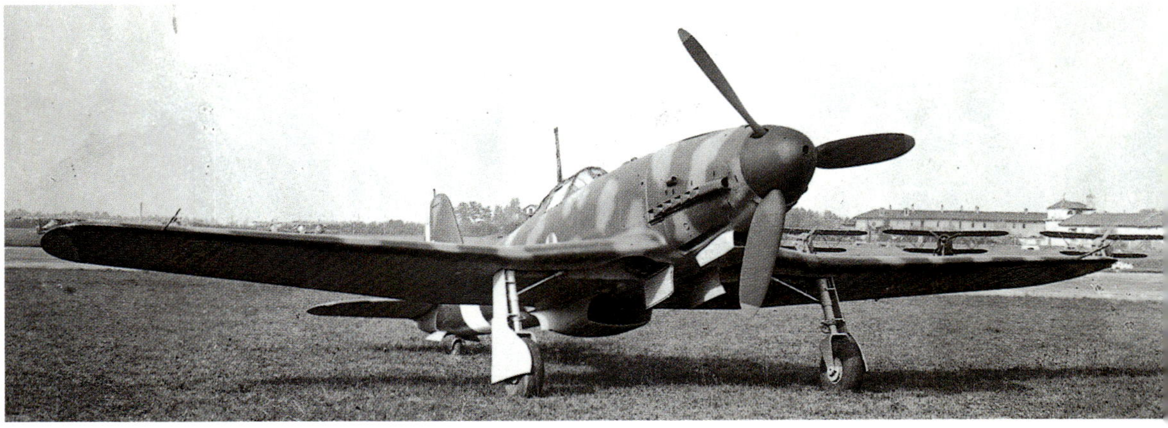

3

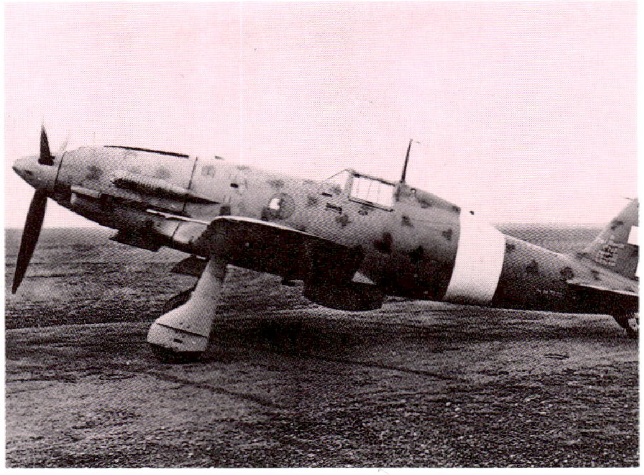

6

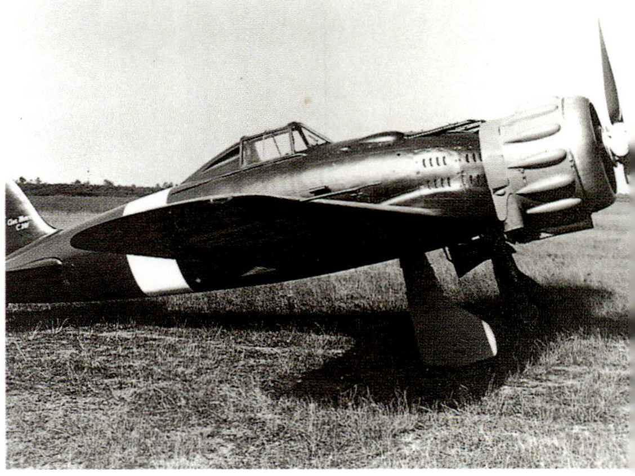

7

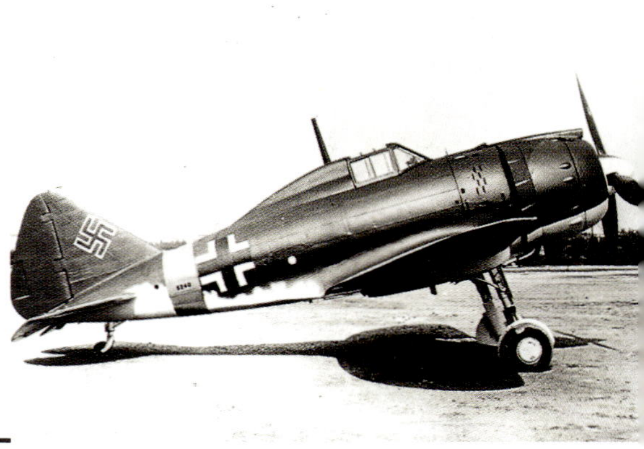

8
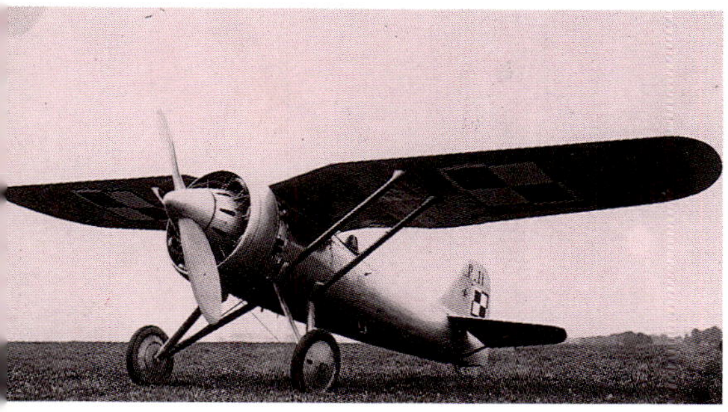

9
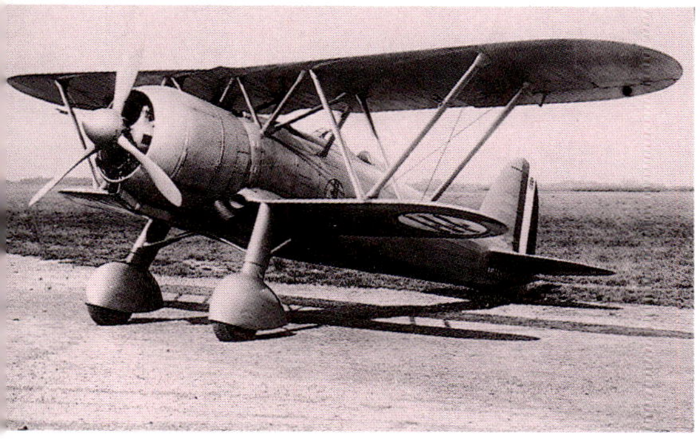

14
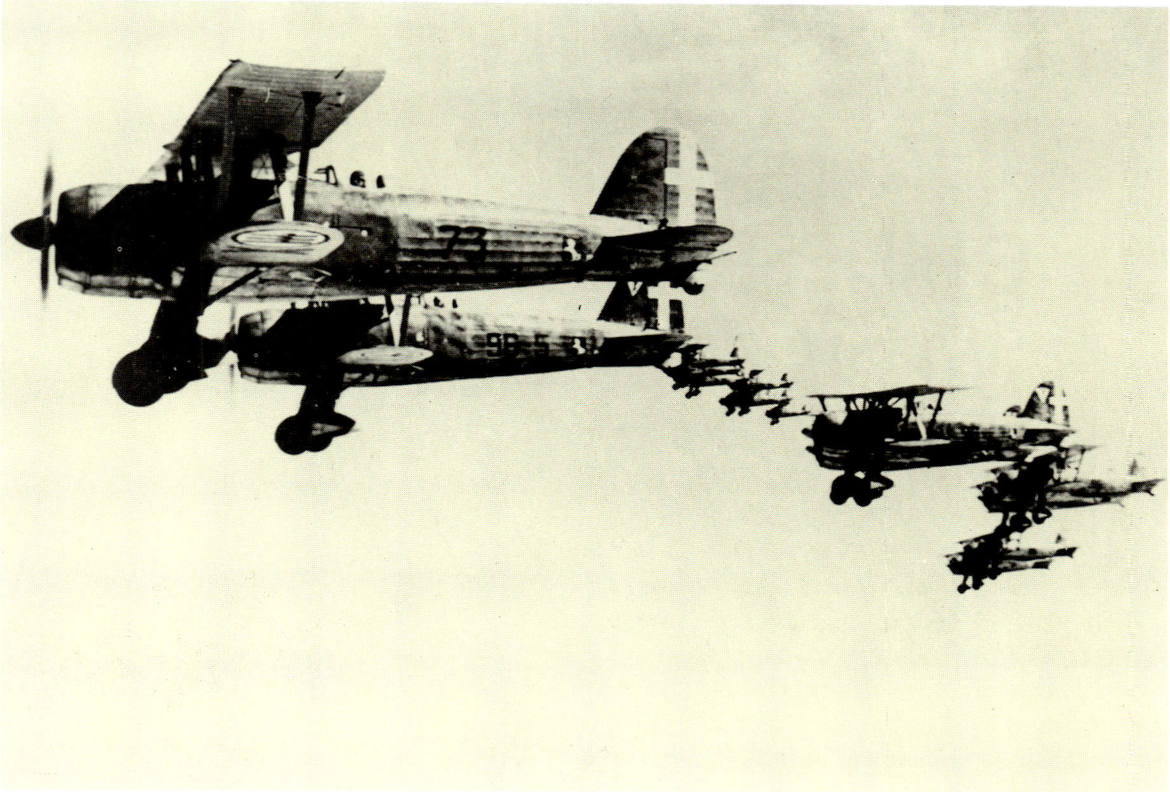

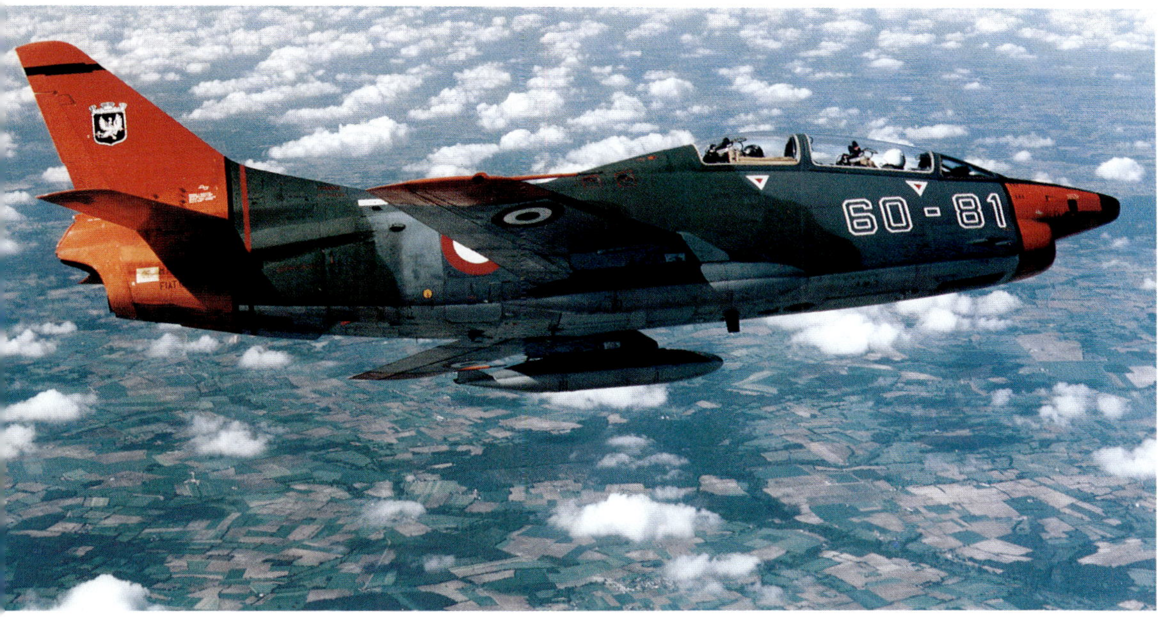

11 After the war, Fiat continued its involvement in military aviation, in the late 1950s building a six-ton jet fighter, the G.91, which could fly at 690 mph (1,100 kph) and climb to 41,000 ft (12,500 m). It was armed with two 30-mm cannon.

The Polish aviation industry built a series of combat aircraft in the inter-war years. The PZL 11, for instance, which appeared in the early 1930s, was a monoplane capable of 250 mph (400 kph) and armed with four 7.7-mm machine guns.

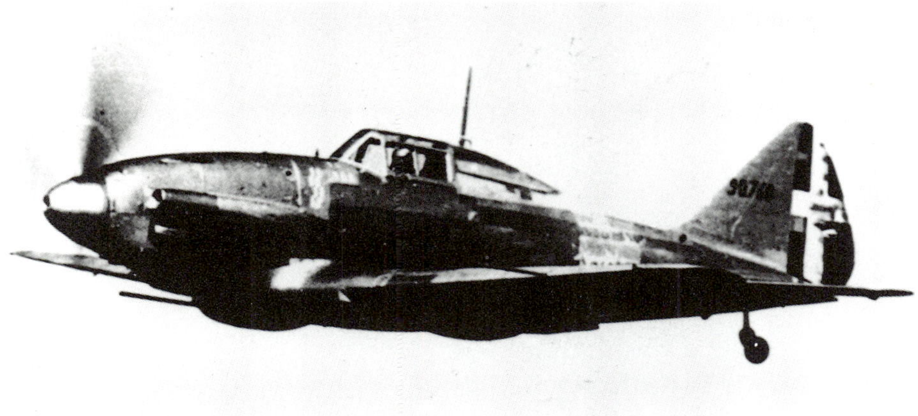

12 **Photo No. 1:** Reggiane Re.2005 Sagittario (Italy)
Photo No. 2: Fiat G.55 Centauro (Italy)
Photo No. 3: Macchi MC 202 Folgore (Italy)
Photo No. 4: Ansaldo A300 (Italy)
Photo No. 5: Fiat CR.30 (Italy)
Photo No. 6: Macchi MC 201 (Italy)
Photo No. 7: Reggiane Re.2002 Ariete (Italy)
Photo No. 8: PZL P 11c (Poland)
Photo Nos. 9 and 14: Fiat CR 42 Falco (Italy)
Photo No. 10: Fiat G 50 Freccia (Italy)
Photo No. 11: Fiat G 91 (Italy)
Photo No. 12: Reggiane Re.2001 Falco II (Italy)
Photo No. 13: Macchi MC 200 Saetta (Italy)

10
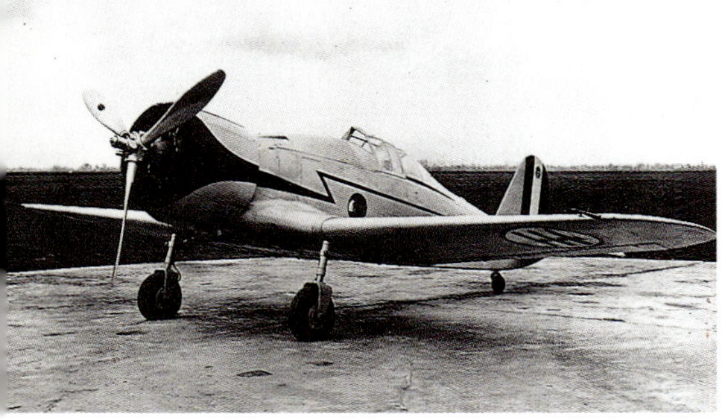

13
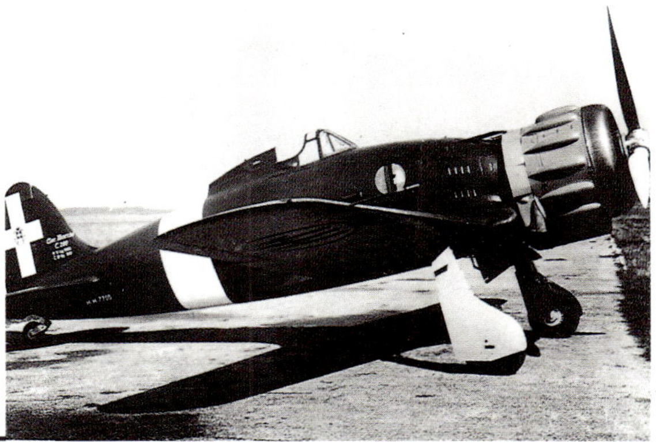

4

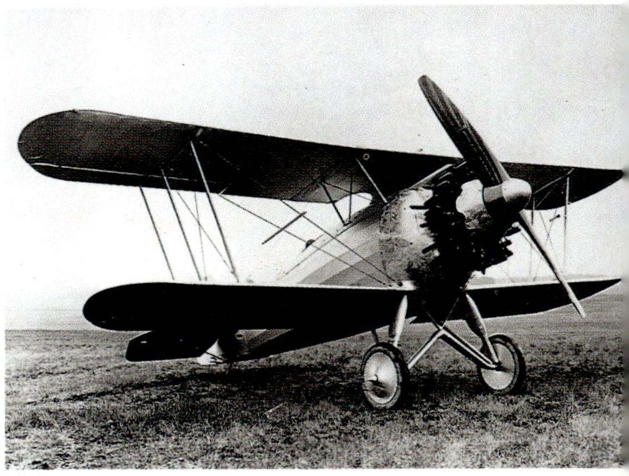

CHINESE, JAPANESE AND SWEDISH FIGHTER PLANES

Sweden joined the ranks of combat aircraft designers in the early 1930s, when the Svenska Aero company developed the J6A Jaktfalk. It was a handy plane with an armament of two machine guns, but only 17 were produced. Its 500-hp engine gave it a maximum speed of over 185 mph (300 kph) and a ceiling of 26,250 ft (8,000 m).

Saab began building aircraft in 1937, starting with piston-engined models, such as the excellent Saab 21, and progressing to jet propulsion. The Saab 29, which made its debut in 1950, was a single-engined, single-seater fighter-bomber with swept-back wings. It could fly at slightly over 625 mph (1,000 kph) and climbed to 49,200 ft (15,000 m). Armament consisted of four 20-mm cannon.

Very modern for its time was the Saab 35 Draken, an all-weather fighter-bomber weighing up to 16 tons, which went into service in 1958. Its maximum speed was in excess of 1,250 mph (2,000 kph) and it could operate at 65,600 ft (20,000 m). It was armed with two 30-mm cannon and four air-to-air missiles. The Saab 37 Viggen, which made its debut in 1970, is even more sophisticated. The all-weather fighter version is capable of over 1,310 mph (2,100 kph) and it has a ceiling of 59,040 ft (18,000 m). It carries two 30-mm cannon and a variety of missiles.

At the present time, the Swedish constructor is developing the JAS 39 Gripen, similar in shape to the Viggen but lighter in weight. Armed with missiles and a 27-mm cannon, it is supersonic at all altitudes.

The Japanese built thousands of aircraft during World War II, but the symbol of that nation's wartime air power remains the so-called Zero fighter, more properly known as the Mitsubishi A6M Reisen. Fast and manoeuvrable, the Zero was powered by a 950-hp engine, which gave it a maximum speed of over 312 mph (500 kph) and a ceiling of 32,800 ft (10,000 m). It was armed with two 20-mm cannon and two 7.7-mm machine guns. The attack on Pearl Harbor was carried out mainly by Zeros, with the support of the Aichi D3A1. Powered by a 1,000-hp engine, this dive bomber, could fly at almost 245 mph (390 kph) and had a ceiling of over 29,500 ft (9,000 m). It carried three 7.7-mm machine guns and heavy bombs.

The Nakajima Ki-43 was manufactured in large numbers from 1940. With an output of almost 1,000 hp, its engine gave it a top speed of 312 mph (500 kph), and it could climb to over 36,000 ft (11,000 m). Its armament consisted of two 0.5-inch machine guns. The Mitsubishi J2M Raiden

1

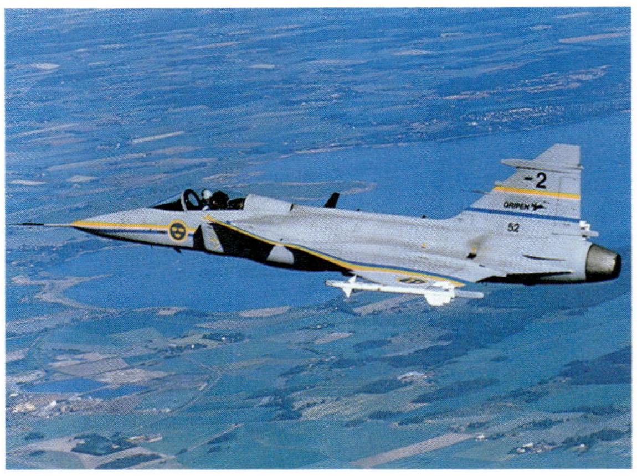

5

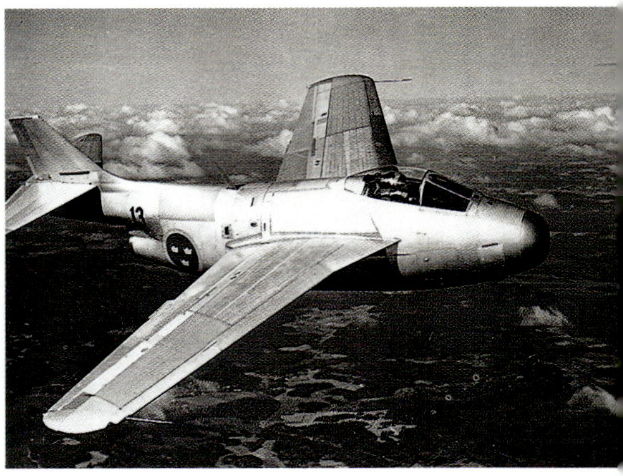

2

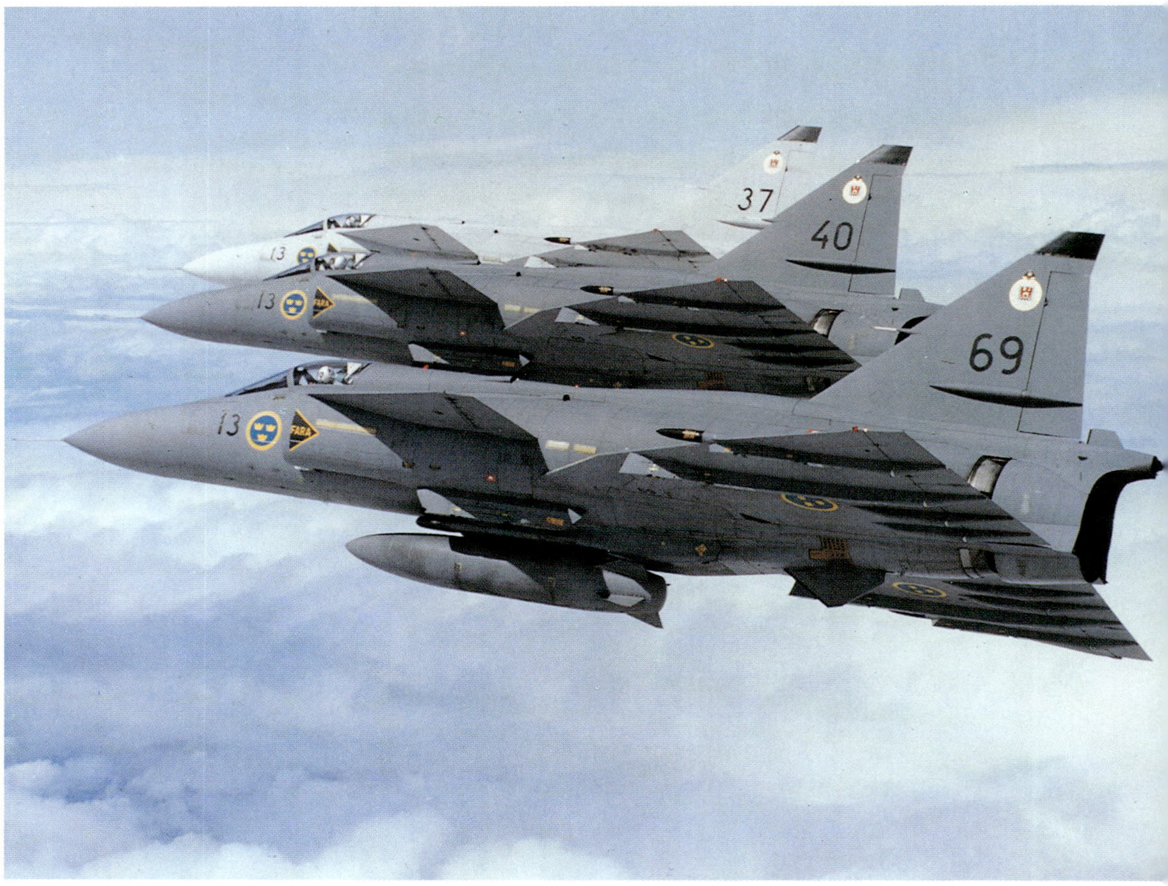

3

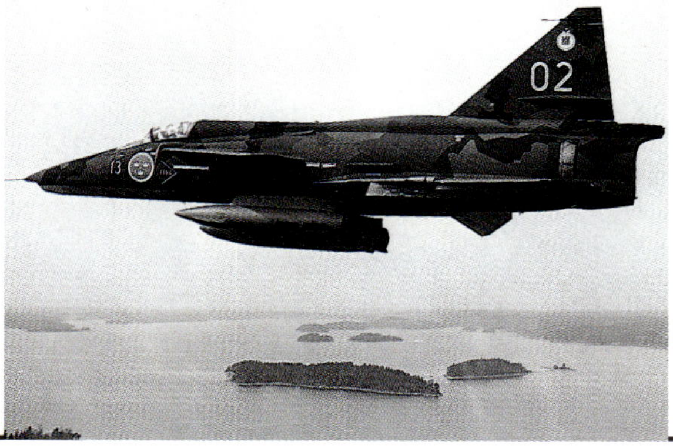

6

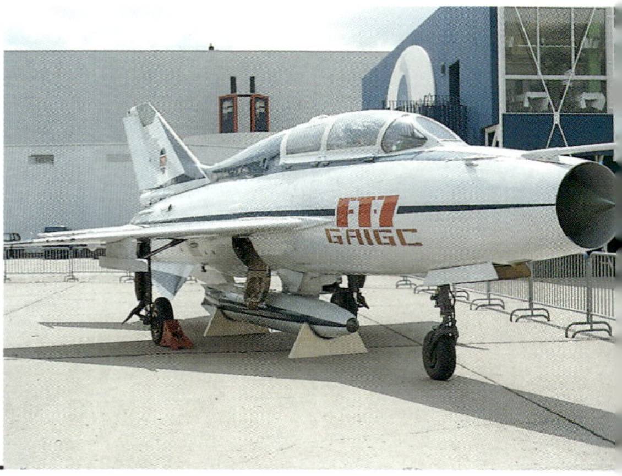

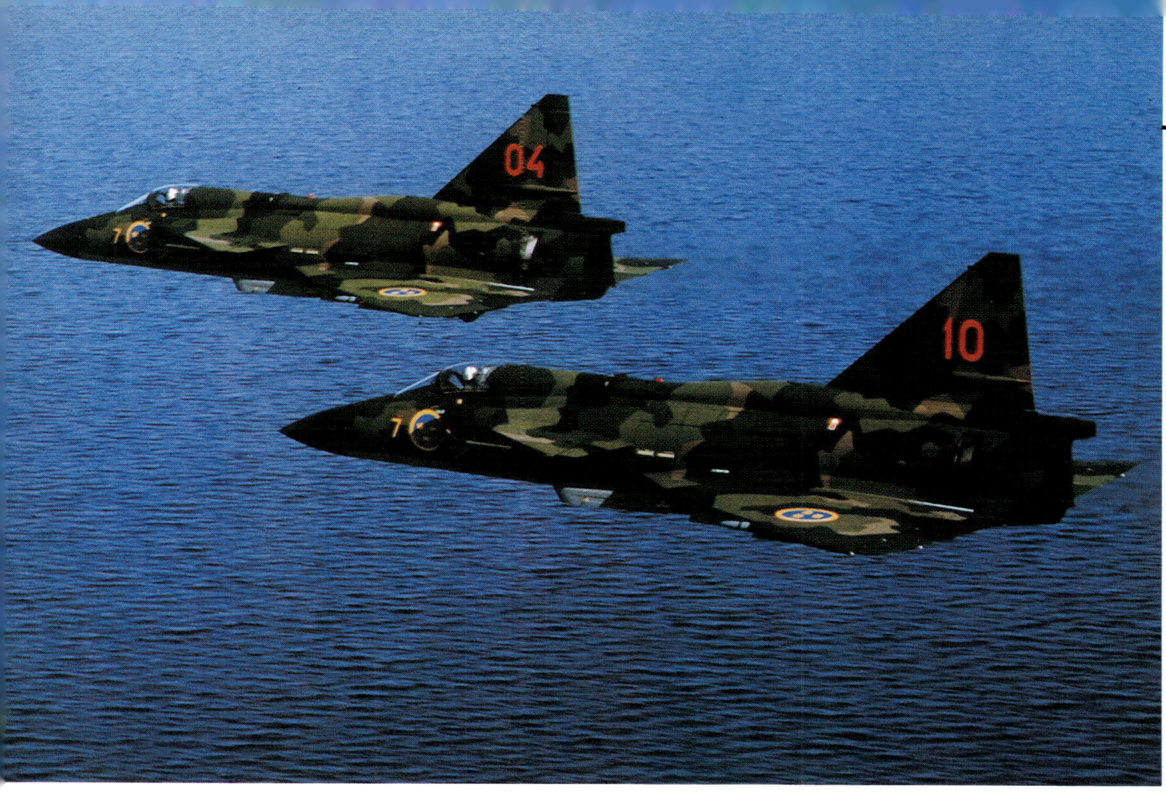

11

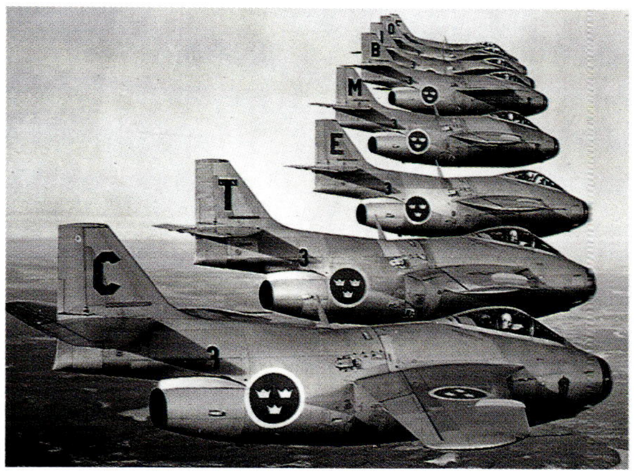

16

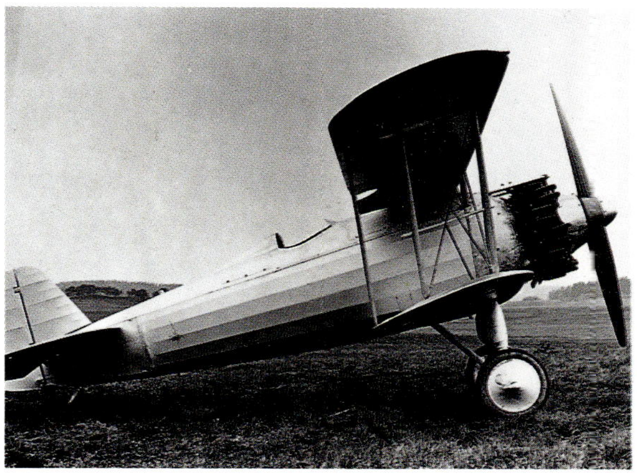

17

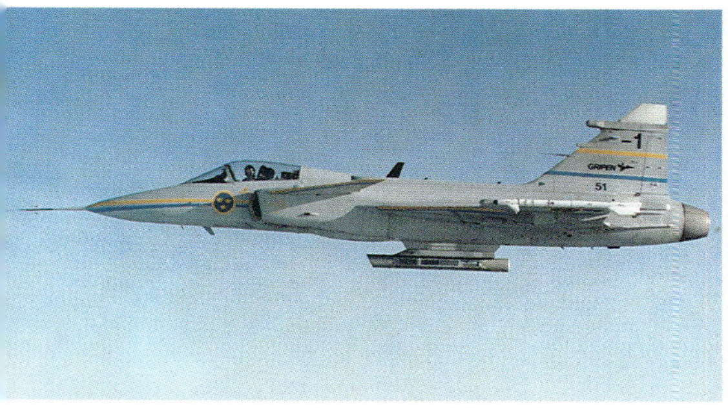

7

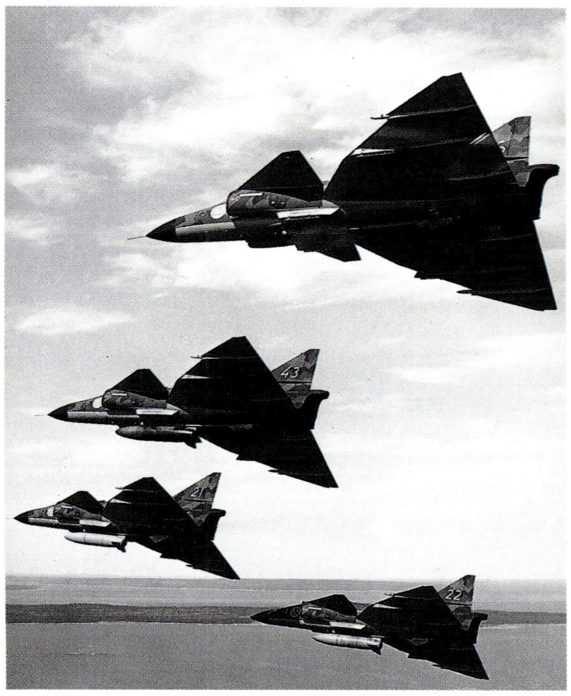

12

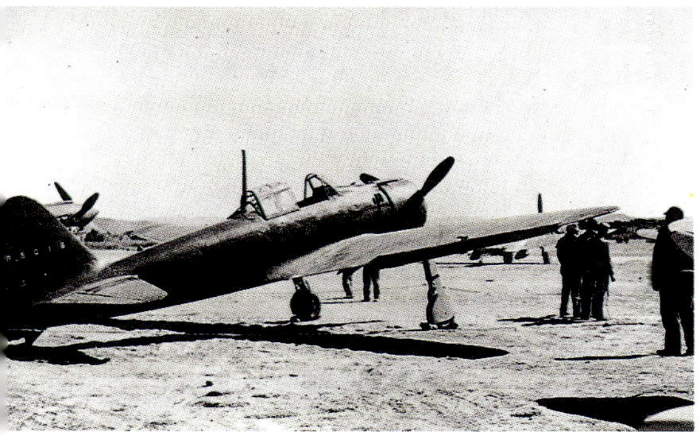

8

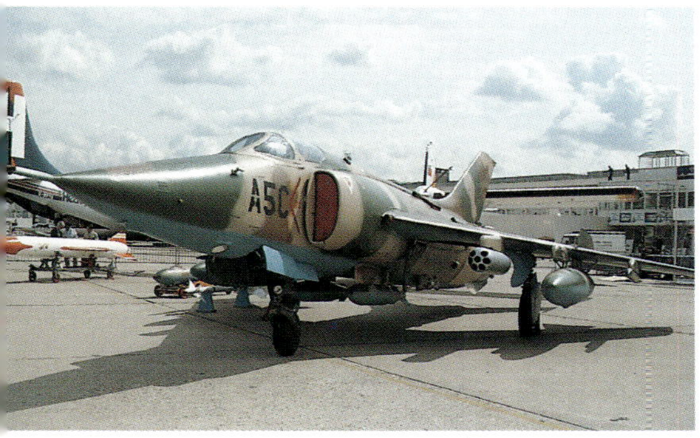

9

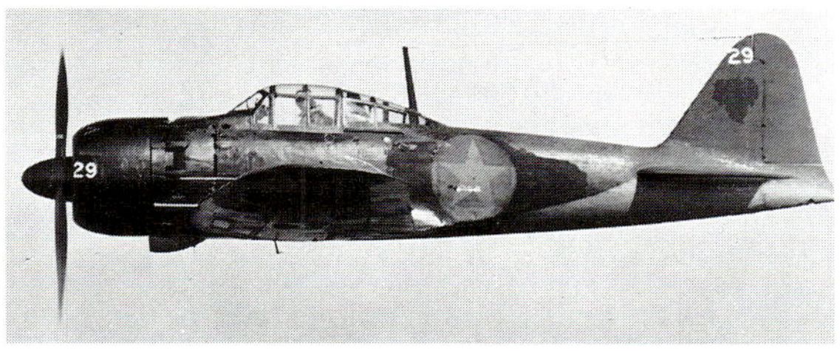

13

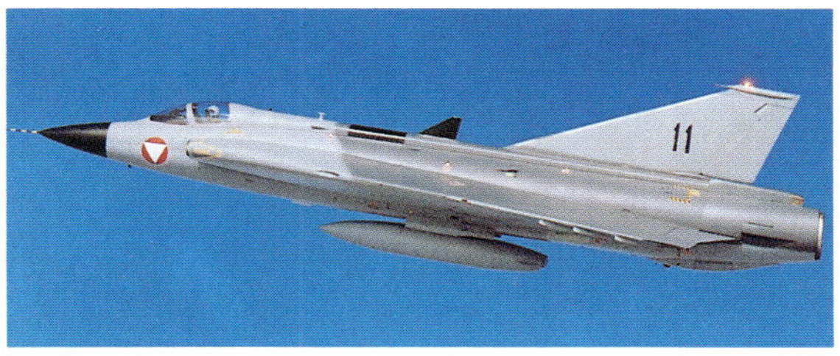

14

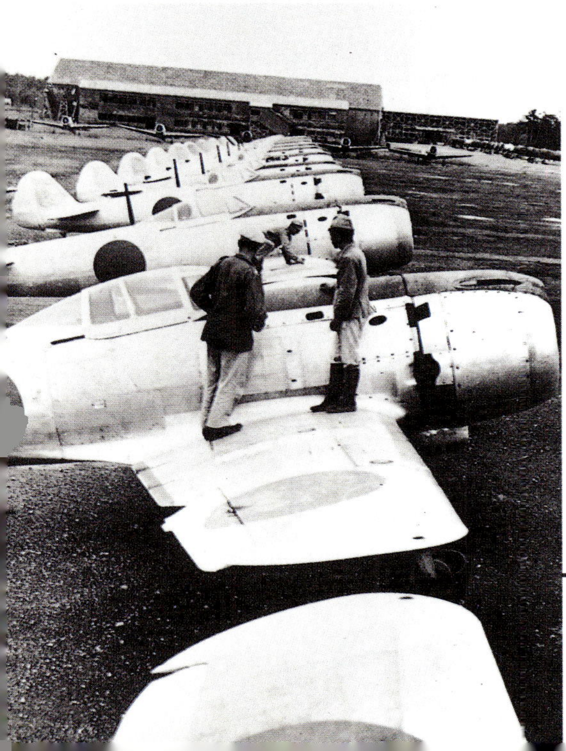

10

came into service in 1943. A single-seater interceptor, it was powered by a 1,800-hp engine, which gave it a maximum speed of over 375 mph (600 kph). It carried two 20-mm cannon and two 7.7-mm machine guns.

The Chinese also manufacture combat aircraft: starting with versions of Soviet fighters. The 1965 NAMC A-5C, for instance, was based on the MiG-19, while the 1966 CAC J-7 corresponds to the MiG-21. There is also a two-seater trainer version of this latter aircraft, the JJ-7.

Photo Nos. 1 and 7: JAS 39 Gripen (Sweden)
Photo Nos. 2, 3, 11 and 12: Saab 37 Viggen (Sweden)
Photo Nos. 4 and 17: Svenska J6 Jaktfalk (Sweden)
Photo Nos. 5 and 16: Saab J 29 (Sweden)
Photo No. 6: GAIGC JJ (FT)-7 (China)
Photo Nos. 8, 13 and 15: Mitsubishi A6M Reisen (Japan)
Photo No. 9: NAMC A-5C (China)
Photo No. 10: Nakajima Ki-84 (Japan)
Photo No. 14: Saab 35 Draken (Sweden)
Photo No. 18: Mitsubishi J2M (Japan)

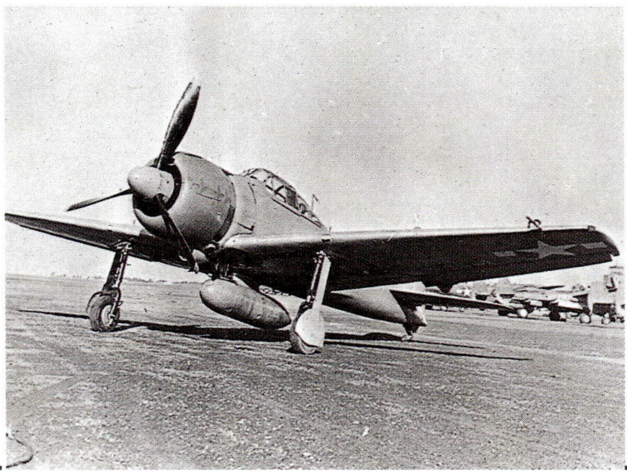

15

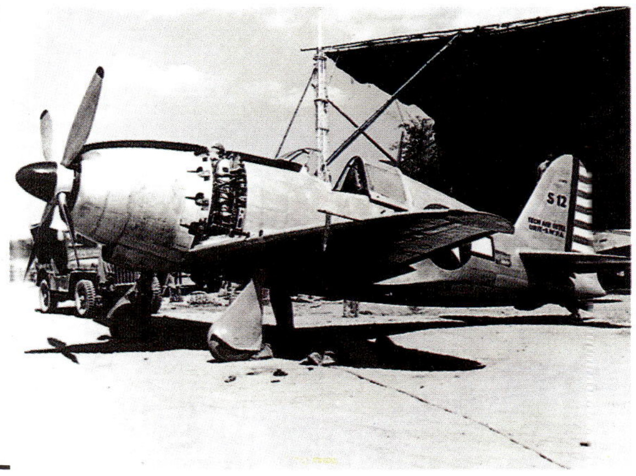

18

FRENCH BOMBERS

Even before World War I, the Voisin brothers had supplied the French army with two-seater aircraft for artillery observation purposes. In 1914 these were converted to light bombing duties. The Voisin Type 3, and slightly improved Voisin 5, were powered by pusher engines. The Type 5 had a maximum speed of 75 mph (120 kph) and could deliver 130 lb (60 kg) of bombs to a distance of 156 miles (250 km).

In 1917 the Voisins were joined by the Breguet Br 14, more than 5,000 of which were built during the war. It was a two-seater biplane, capable of carrying a bomb load of 32 20-lb bombs and with a radius of action of 156 miles (250 km). In the years 1928 to 1939 the French air force was equipped with a real medieval fortress of a plane – the Lioré et Olivier LeO 20 – carrying five machine guns in open turrets. A twin-engined biplane, it carried 1,100 lb (500 kg) of bombs at 125 mph (200 kph), with a radius of action of 312 miles (500 km). Another aircraft of this period was the Amiot 143, a twin-engined monoplane with a fixed undercarriage. It flew at 185 mph (300 kph), dropping its bomb load of 2,800 lb (1,300 kg) on targets up to 375 miles (600 km) distant.

In 1936, Farman brought out the F.222, a four-engined bomber carrying a crew of five and armed with three machine guns. Its maximum speed was 199 mph (320 kph) and it could haul a four-ton load of bombs a distance of 625 miles (1,000 km). One of the best French bombers of World War II was the Lioré et Olivier LeO 45, a modern, twin-engined aircraft with a maximum speed of almost 315 mph (500 kph). It had a crew of four and was able to deliver two tons of bombs to a distance of 750 miles (1,200 km). The Breguet 691 also performed to a high specification. A light, twin-engined bomber with a two-man crew, it was capable of 300 mph (480 kph). Its armament consisted of a 20-mm cannon and four 7.5-mm machine guns and, carrying 880 lb (400 kg) of bombs, it had a radius of action of 440 miles (700 km).

The Bloch 174 was a fast, highly manoeuvrable light bomber with a maximum speed of over 310 mph (500 kph). A twin-engined three-seater aircraft, it was armed with seven 7.5-mm machine guns and delivered a bomb load of 880 lb (400 kg) to over 440 miles (700 km).

The SNCASE SE 2415 Grognard – a twin-engined jet with swept-back wings – made its appearance in 1950, but did

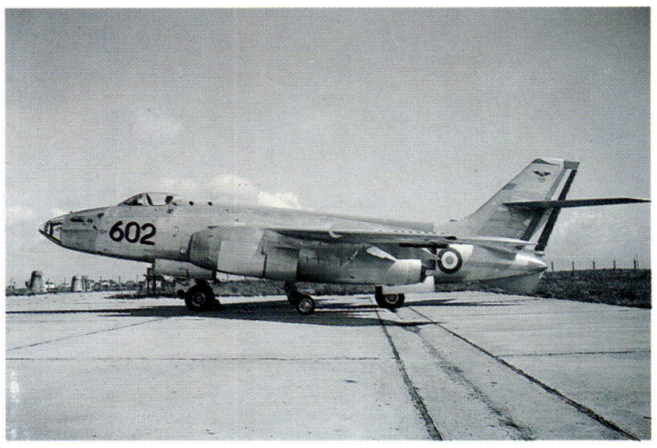

1

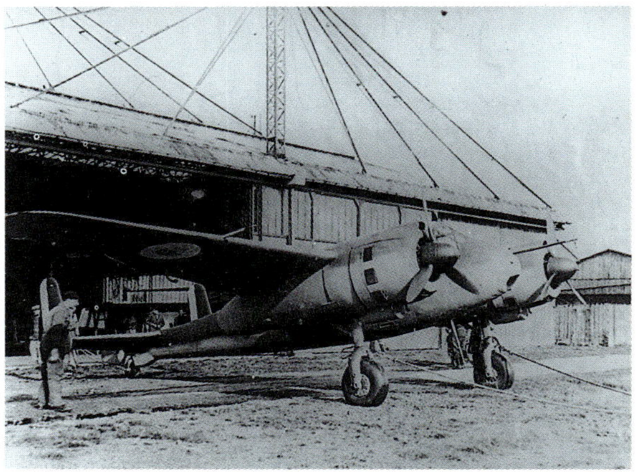
2

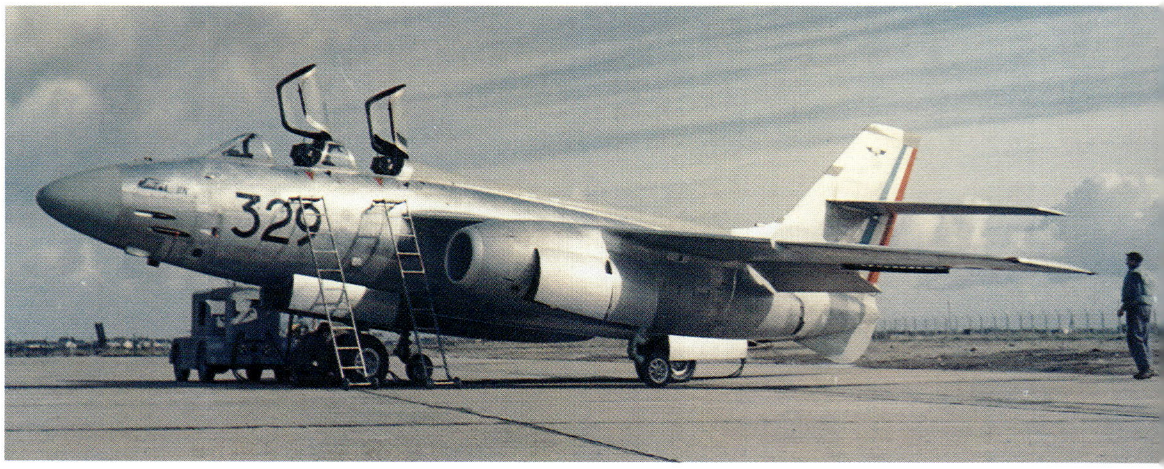

3

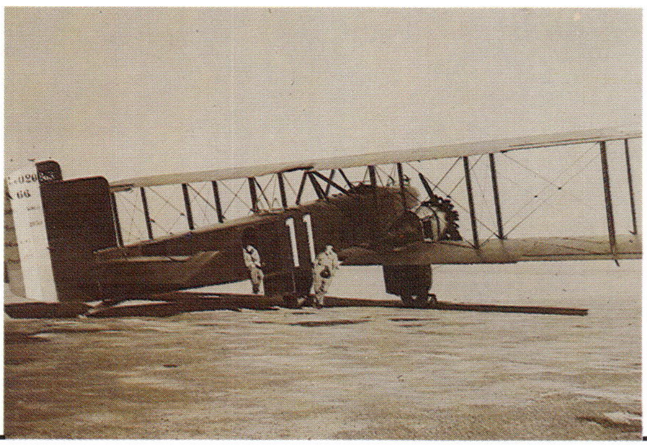
4

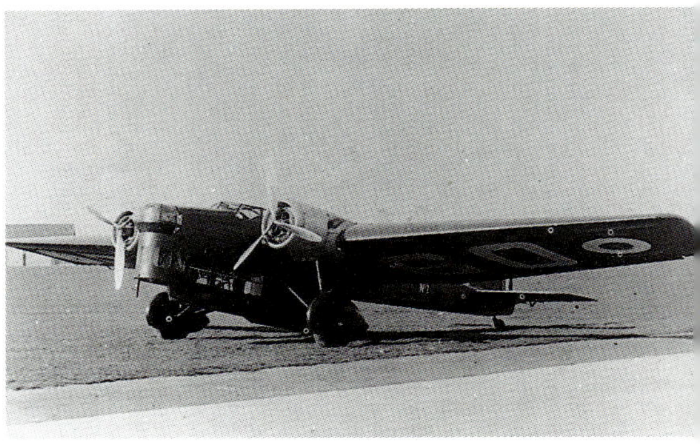
5

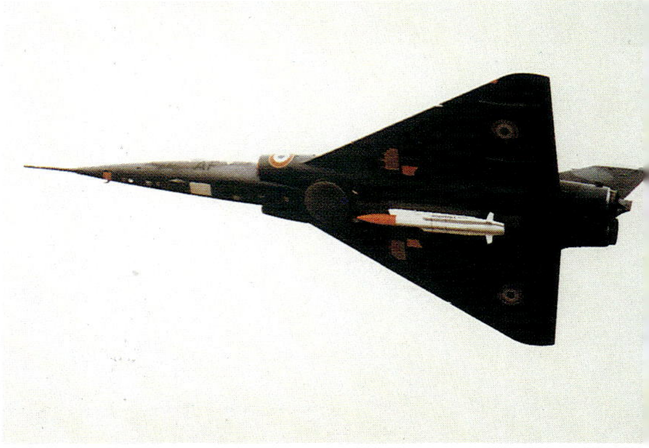
6

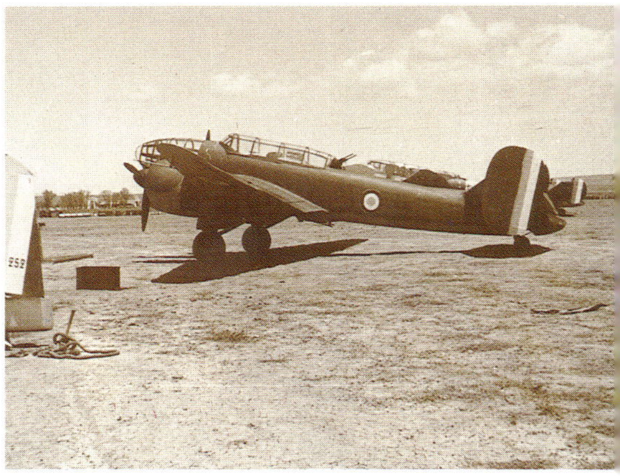
7

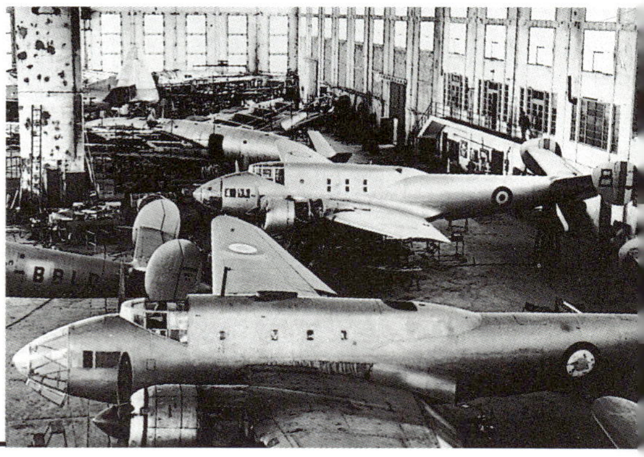
8

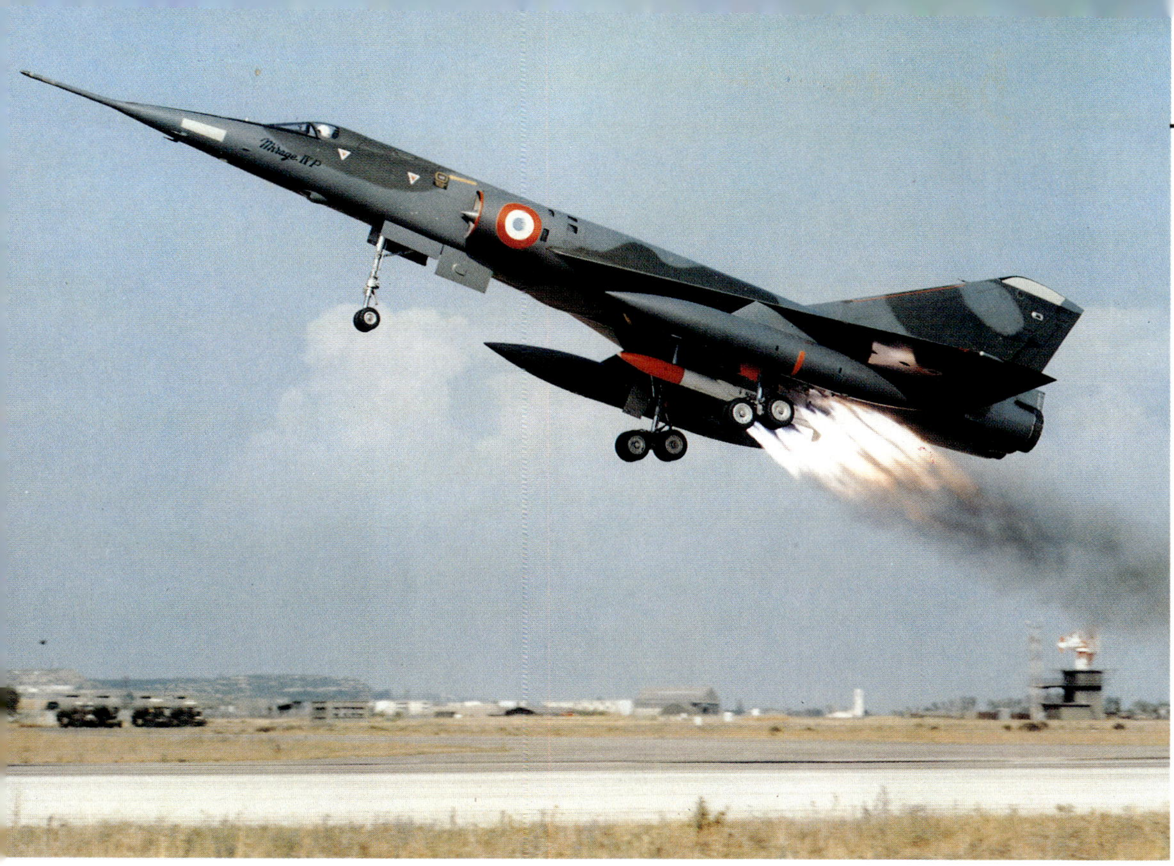

11

15

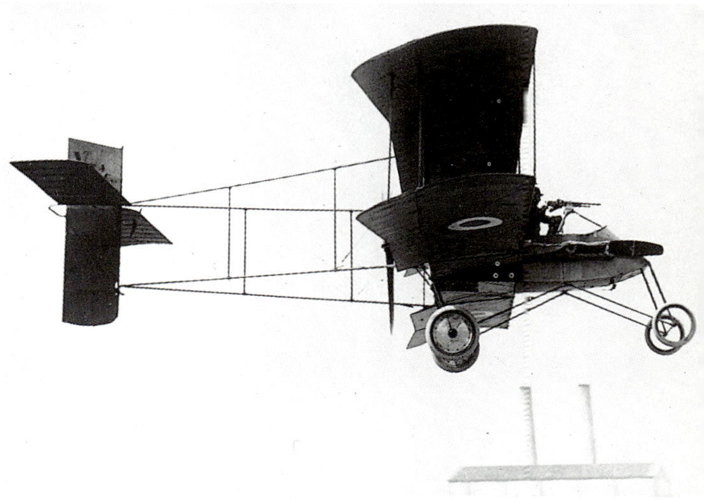

16

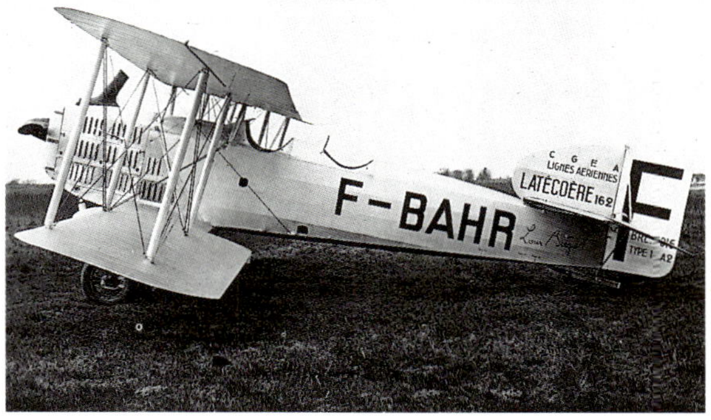

9

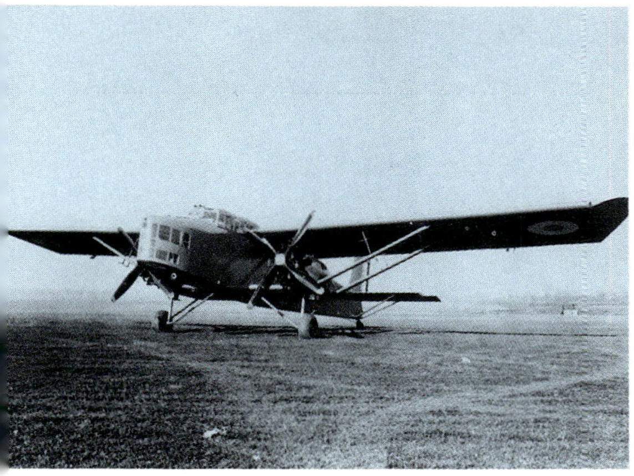

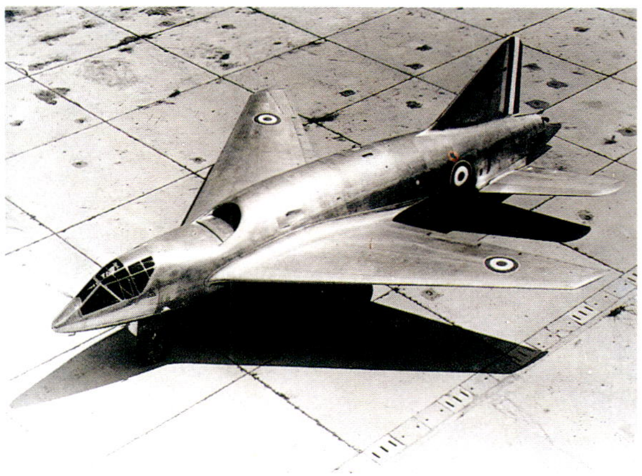

12

not get beyond the prototype stage. Its successful rival was another twin-engined jet, the SNCASO SO 4050 Vautour. This aircraft flew at 687 mph (1,100 kph) and could deliver 5,300 lb (2,400 kg) of bombs to targets 940 miles (1,500 km) distant.

13

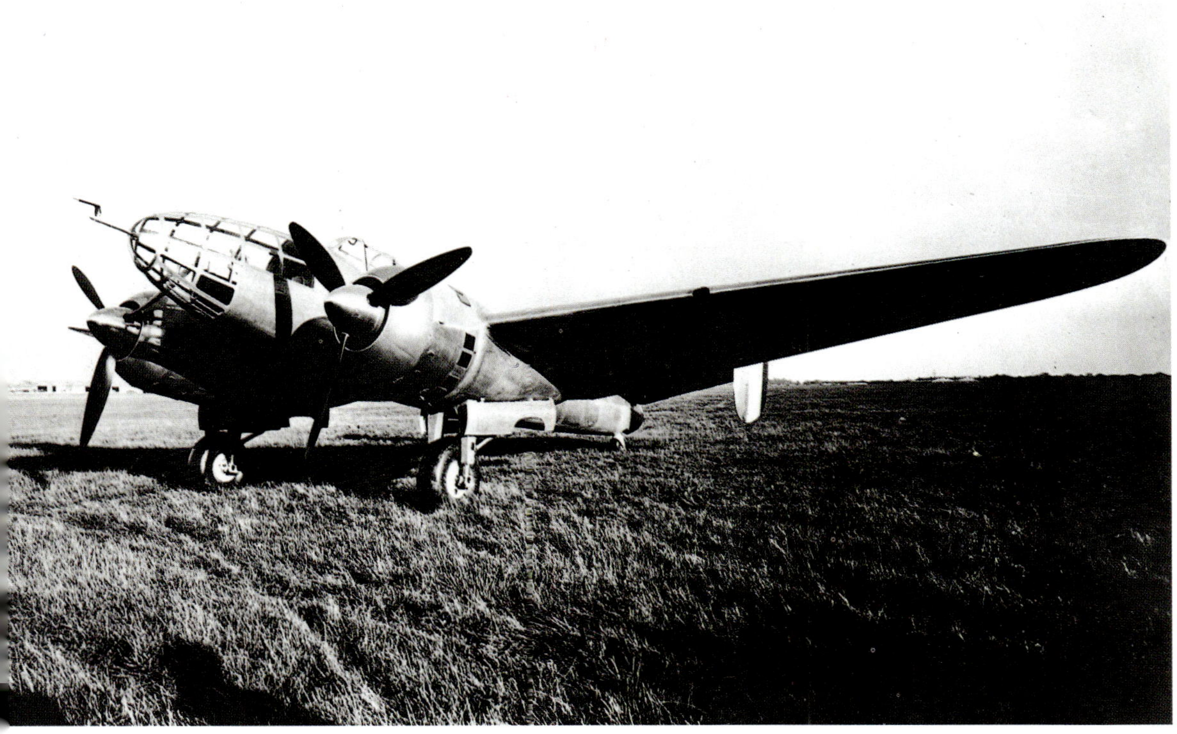

As part of its nuclear strike deterrent force, France commissioned the Dassault Mirage IVA strategic bomber, which can be refuelled in flight. Its original purpose was to deliver an atomic bomb to targets in the Soviet Union. Able to carry a bomb load of over seven tons and fly at 1,460 mph (2,340 kph), the two-man Mirage IV has a radius of action of 750 miles (1,200 km).

Photo Nos. 1 and 3: Sud-Ouest SO 4050 Vautour
Photo No. 2: Breguet Br 691
Photo No. 4: LeO 20
Photo No. 5: Amiot 143
Photo Nos. 6 and 11: Dassault Mirage IV
Photo No. 7: Bloch 175
Photo No. 8: LeO 45
Photo No. 9: Farman F.470
Photo Nos. 10 and 16: Breguet Br 14 B2 and A2
Photo No. 12: SNCASE SE 2415 Grognard
Photo No. 13: Bloch 174
Photo Nos. 14 and 15: Voisin Type 5 LA5

10

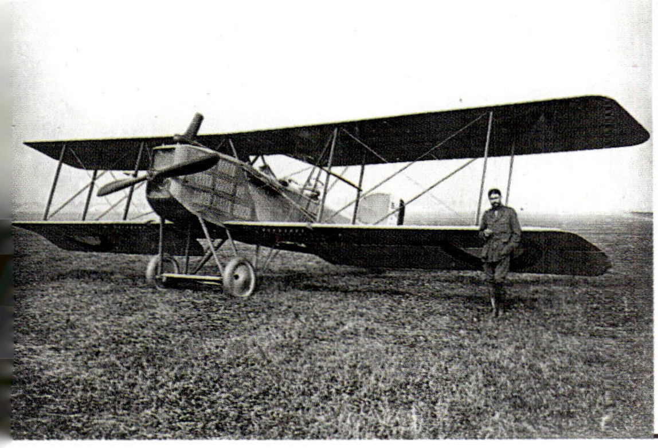

14

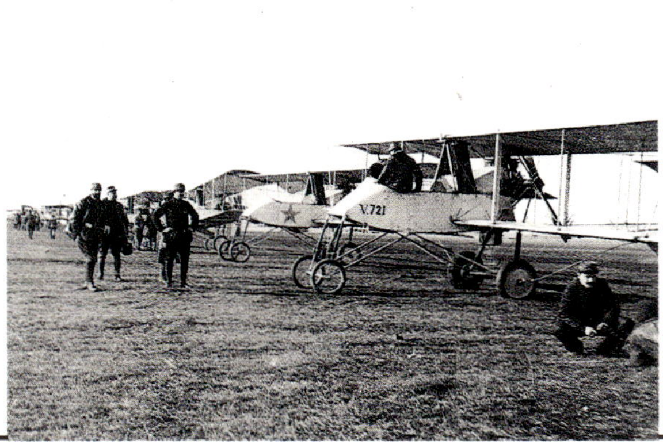

BRITISH BOMBERS

5

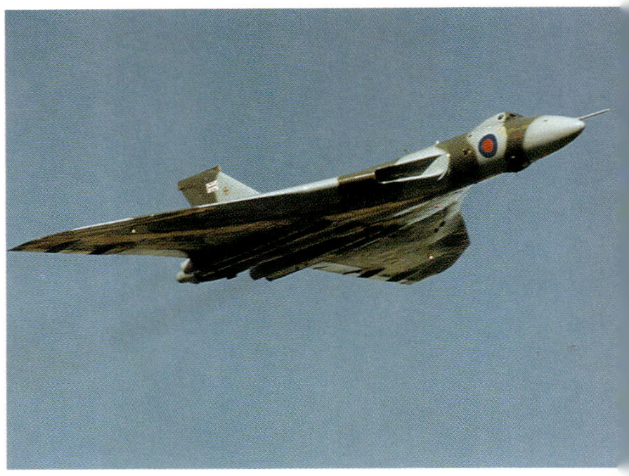

Britain's first heavy aircraft of this type was the Short Bomber, first engaged on the Western Front in 1915. A single-engined plane with a maximum speed of 78 mph (125 kph), it could deliver four 220-lb (100-kg) or eight 110-lb (50-kg) bombs to targets at a distance of 220 miles (350 km). Derived from the Handley Page O/100, the twin-engined O/400 biplane came into service in 1917 and was used for bombing the Saar and Ruhr regions. It had a four-man crew and could deliver six tons of bombs – including 1,650-lb (750-kg) blockbusters. Its radius of action was 375 miles (600 km) and maximum speed 100 mph (160 kph). The V/1500 was a bigger, four-engined aircraft designed to drop bombs on Berlin. It could carry its load of two 1,500-kg bombs to a target 625 miles (1,000 km) from base.

The Bristol Blenheim was developed from a fast business aircraft first produced in 1935. A three-seater twin-engined bomber, it flew at around 280 mph (450 kph). With a load of 1,000 lb (450 kg), its bombing range was 625 miles (1,000 km). During World War II, the Blenheim was replaced by the formidable de Havilland Mosquito.

In 1938 appeared the Vickers Wellington, a twin-engined bomber with a maximum speed of over 250 mph (400 kph). Its bomb load exceeded two tons, delivered to a range of 940 miles (1,500 km). Another twin-engined bomber of this period, carrying a four-man crew, was the Handley Page Hampden, which flew at over 250 mph (400 kph) with a bomb load of 4,000 lb (1,800 kg). The Royal Air Force's first four-engined bomber was the Short Stirling, which came into service in 1940. It had an eight-man crew and was armed with ten machine guns. It could fly at over 250 mph (400 kph) and delivered more than 8,000 lb (3,630 kg) of bombs to a distance of 1,000 miles (1,600 km).

In the course of the war, four-engined Handley Page Halifax bombers dropped over 200,000 tons of bombs on Germany. Carrying a load of six tons, the Halifax flew at almost 315 mph (500 kph) and had a radius of action of 625 miles (1,000 km).

But the most celebrated of World War II strategic bombers was the Avro Lancaster, another four-engined aircraft, which flew at over 280 mph (450 kph). Its bomb load was in excess of six tons, delivered to targets 875 miles (1,400 km) distant. Immediately after the war, the R.A.F. took delivery of the English Electric Canberra, a twin-jet bomber with a three-man crew. It had a maximum speed of 580 mph (930 kph). Carrying a bomb load of up to 6,000 lb (2,722 kg), its radius of action was 405 miles (650 km).

In 1955, Great Britain acquired a nuclear strike capability. The aircraft designed to carry its atomic bombs were the Handley Page Victor and the Hawker Siddeley Vulcan. To escape the unwelcome attention of fighters, they had to fly fast and high. The Victor had a maximum speed of

1

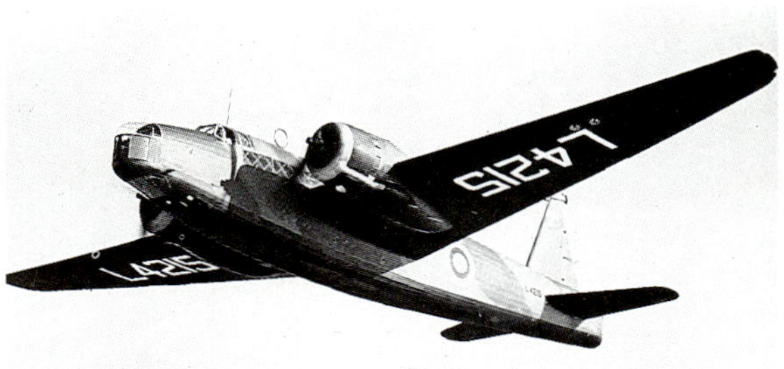

6

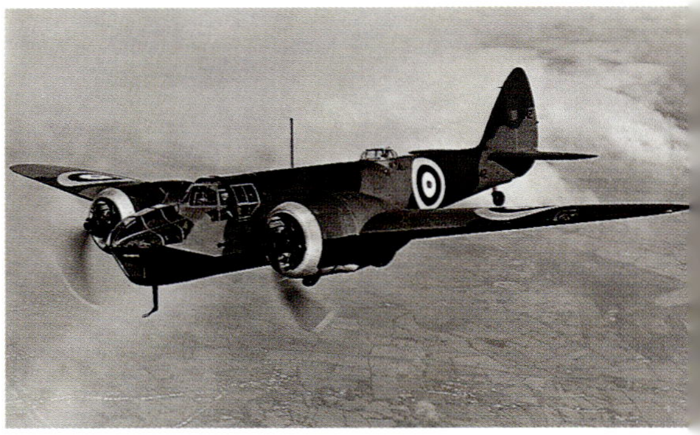

2

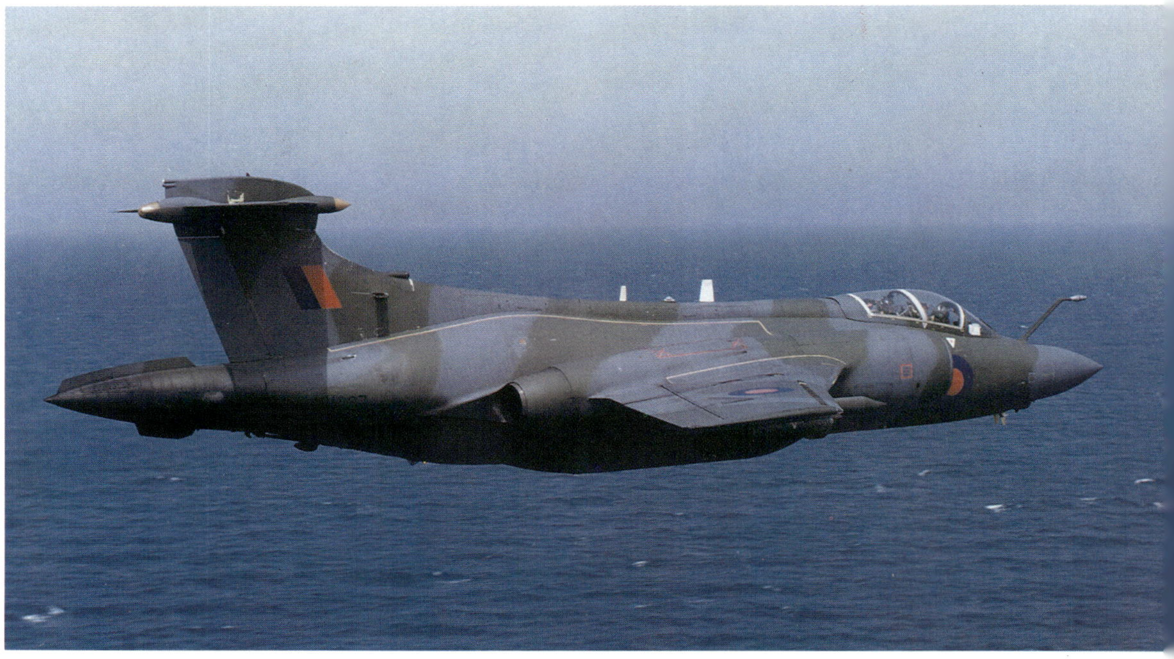

3

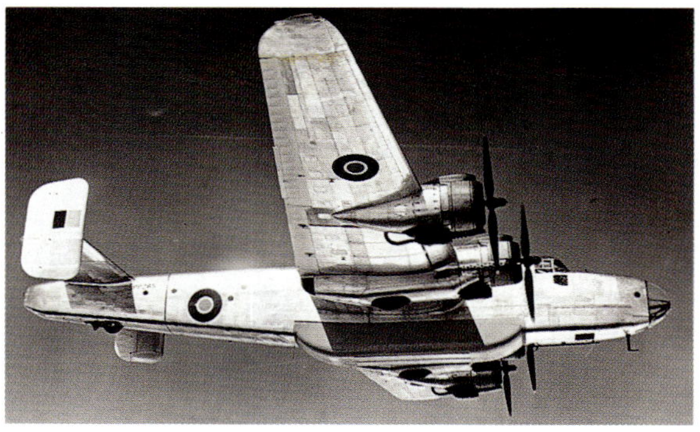

7

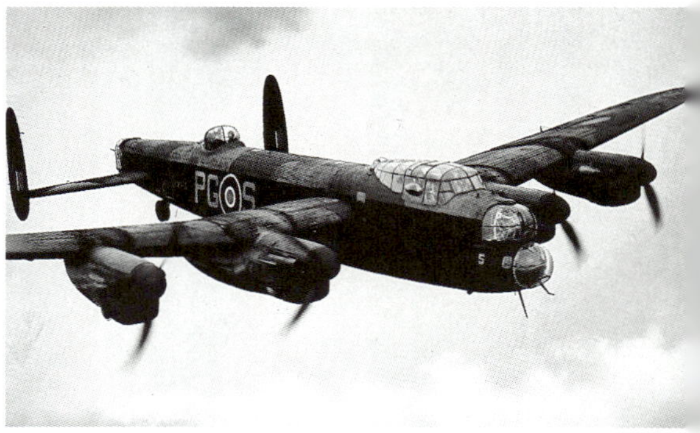

4

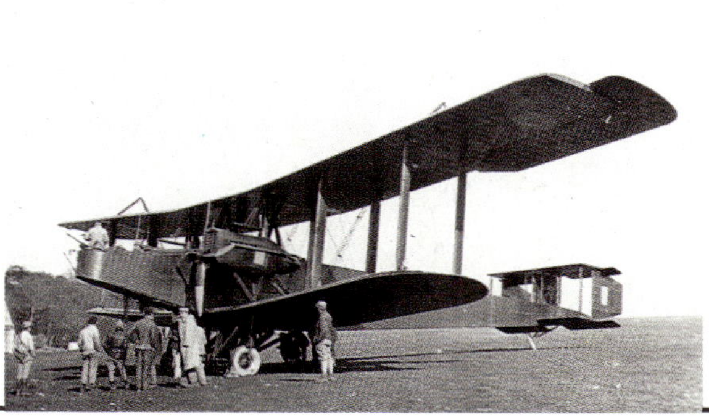

8

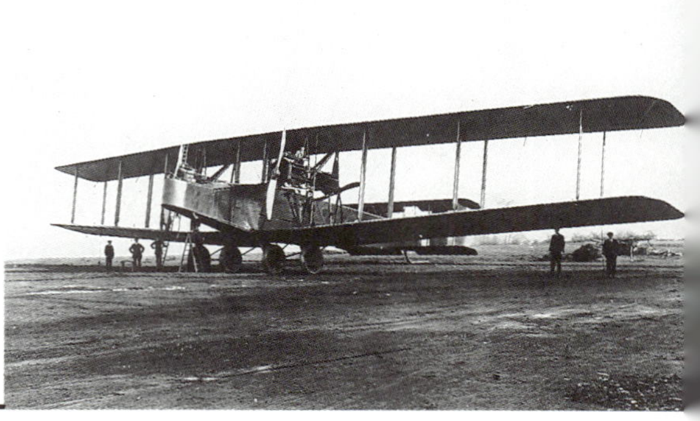

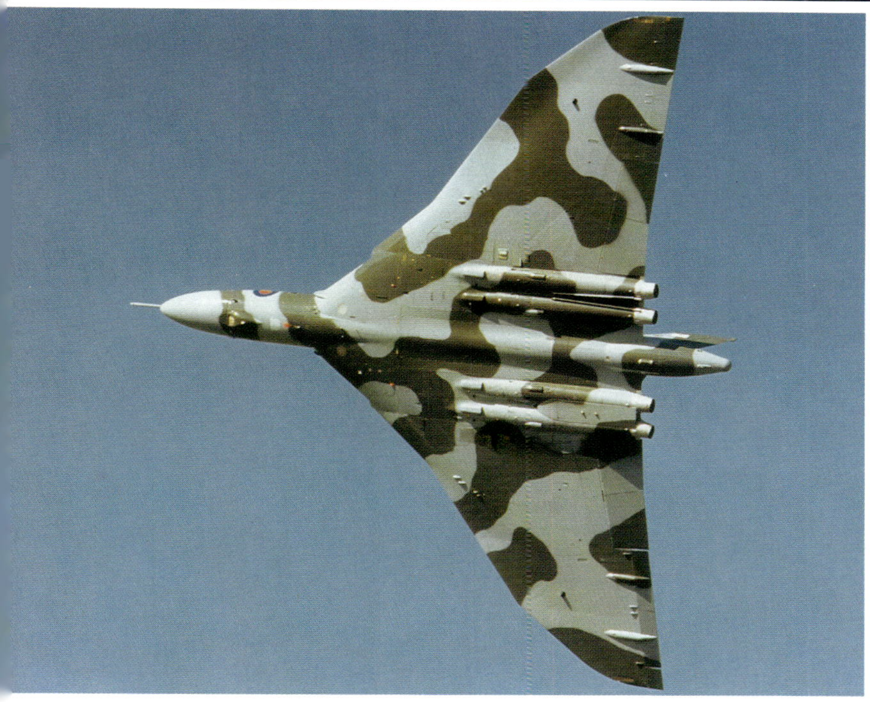
11

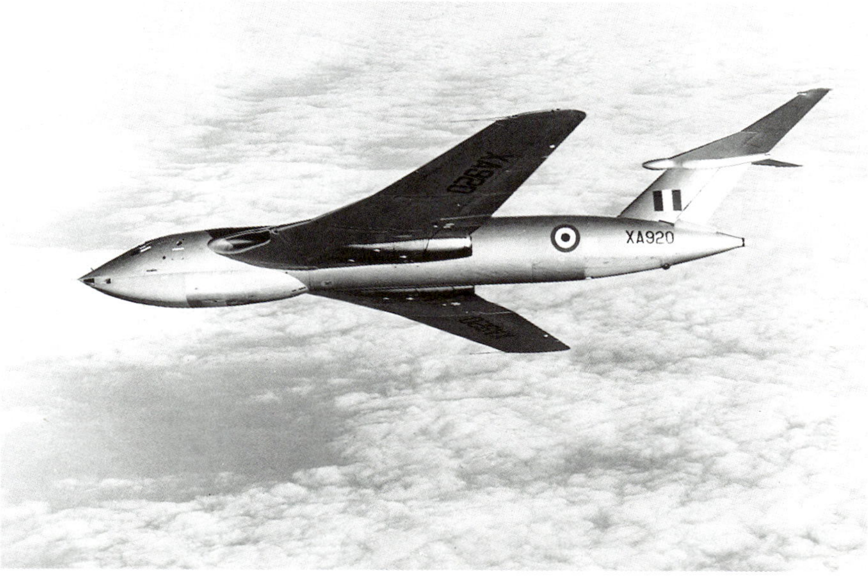

15

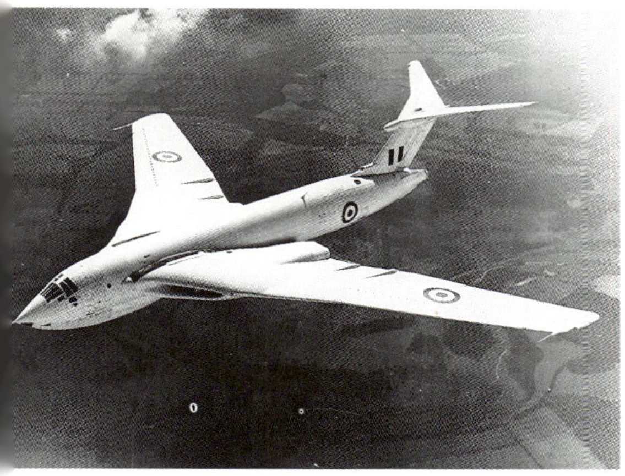
9

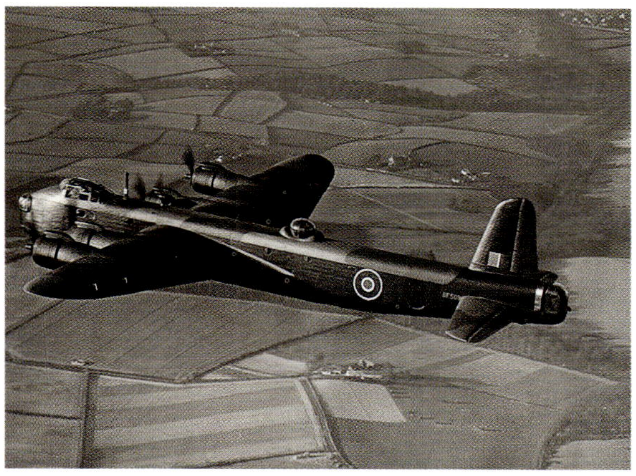
12

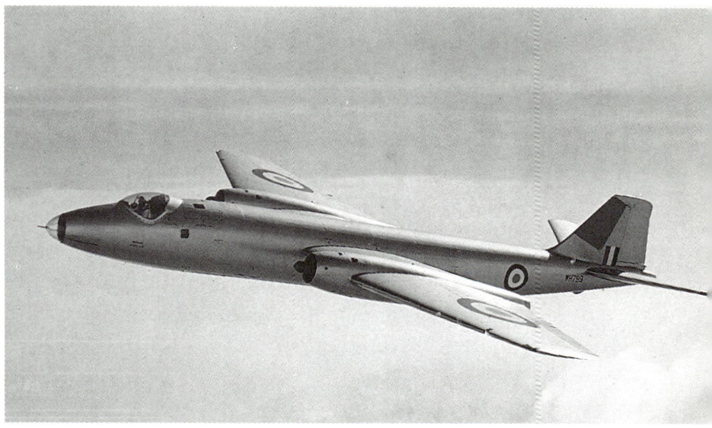
16

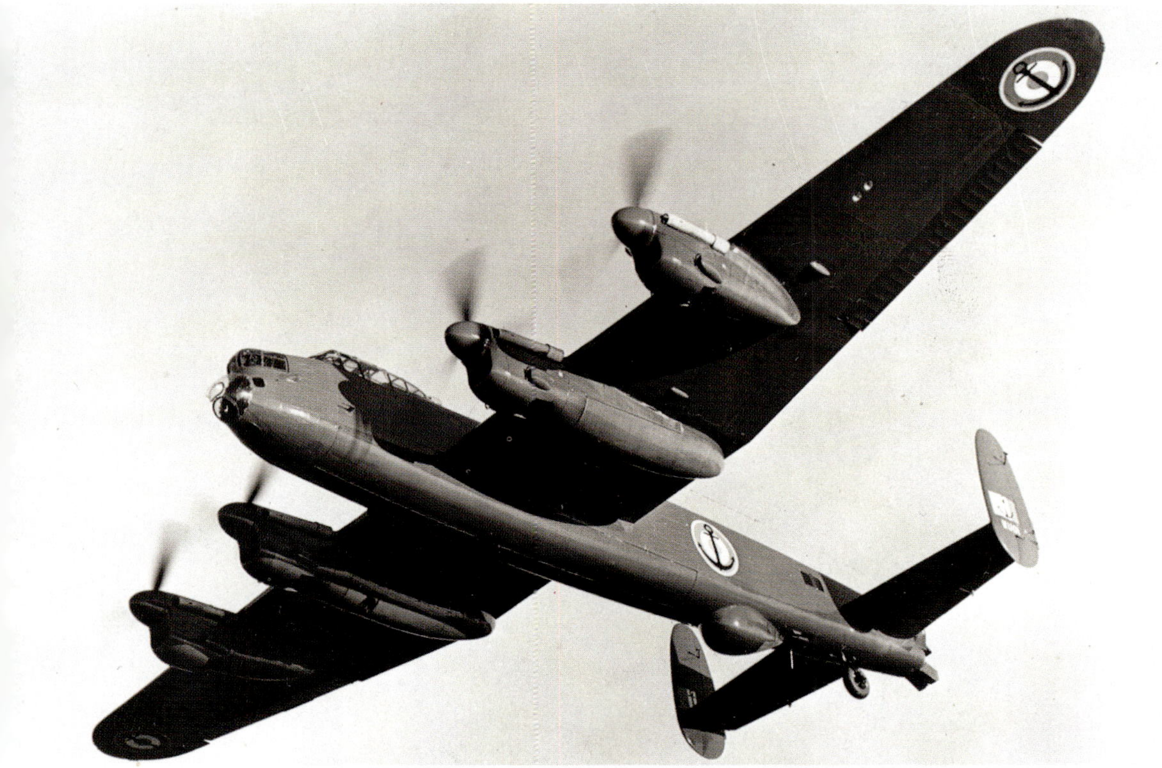
13

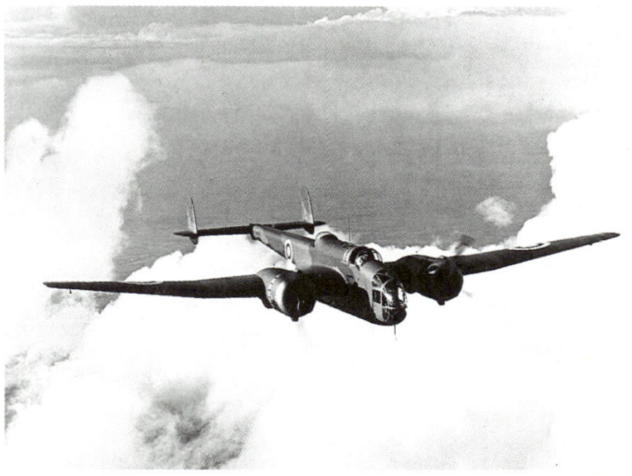
17

over 625 mph (1,000 kph) and a ceiling of 59,000 ft. Its radius of action was 2,500 miles (4,000 km). Also a four-engined jet aircraft, the delta-winged Vulcan – used in the Falklands before its eventual retirement – achieved similar performance figures. The Hawker Siddeley Buccaneer, which came into service in 1962, was a twin-engined strike and reconnaissance aircraft capable of over 650 mph (1,050 kph). Carrying a bombload of up to seven tons it had a radius of action of 1,190 miles (1,900 km).

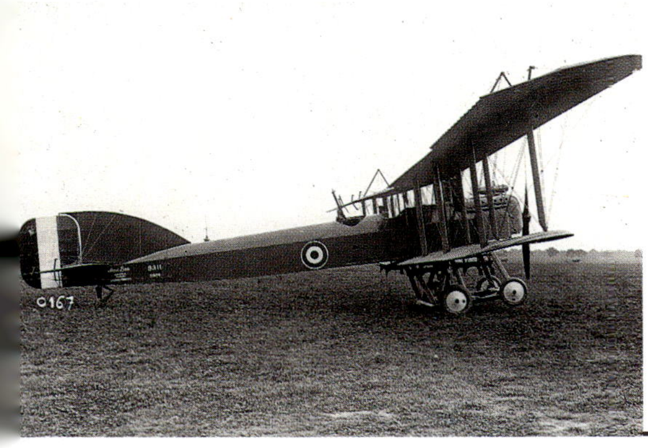

10

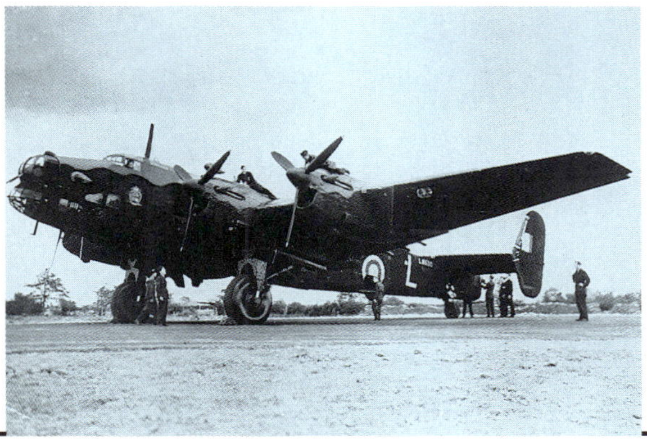
14

Photo No. 1: Vickers Wellington
Photo No. 2: Hawker Siddeley Buccaneer
Photo Nos. 3 and 14: Handley Page Halifax
Photo No. 4: Handley Page O/400
Photo Nos. 5 and 11: Hawker Siddeley Vulcan
Photo No. 6: Bristol Blenheim
Photo Nos. 7 and 13: Avro Lancaster
Photo No. 8: Handley Page V/1500
Photo Nos. 9 and 15: Handley Page Victor
Photo No. 10: Short Bomber
Photo No. 12: Short Stirling
Photo No. 16: English Electric Canberra
Photo No. 17: Handley Page Hampden

5

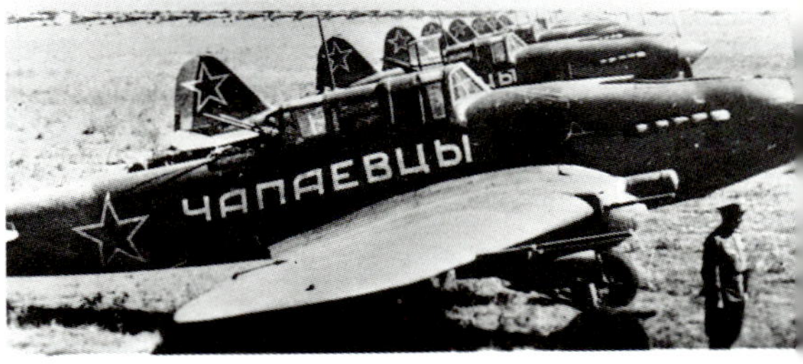

RUSSIAN AND SOVIET BOMBERS

The world's first four-engined bomber was designed for the Russian armed forces by Igor Sikorsky before the outbreak of World War I. With a maximum speed of 75 mph (120 kph), his Ilya Mourometz bombers took part in over 400 air raids. The aircraft carried 1,100 lb (500 kg) of bombs and had a radius of action of 187 miles (300 km).

In the 1930s, Tupolev developed a quite revolutionary four-engined bomber. The TB-3 was a monoplane of all-metal construction. Carrying a payload of two tons at over 125 mph (200 kph), it could bomb targets within a radius of 690 miles (1,100 km). During World War II, Tupolev built a number of aircraft, including the outstanding Tu-2, a twin-engined bomber capable of delivering a bomb load of 3,300 lb (1,500 kg) to a distance of 810 miles at 340 mph (550 kph). Also introduced during the war was the single-engined Ilyushin Il-2 "Sturmovik" ground attack aircraft. It could carry 1,300 lb (600 kg) of bombs as well as armour-piercing rockets and cannon, with a top speed in excess of 220 mph (350 kph) and a range of action of 190 miles (300 km). Though fast (356 mph/570 kph), the twin-engined Yak-4 proved too vulnerable and had only a brief career. It delivered 1,300 lb (600 kg) of bombs to targets up to 500 miles (800 km) from its base.

Among the Soviet heavy bombers was the four-engined Petlyakov Pe-8 – bomb load four tons, maximum speed 280 mph (450 kph), radius of action 1,500 miles (2,400 km) – and the Ilyushin Il-4 – bomb load 4,400 lb (2,000 kg), maximum speed 265 mph (425 kph), radius of action 812 miles (1,300 km).

But the most prolific Soviet bomber manufacturer has undoubtedly been Tupolev. After the war, his Tu-2 was followed by the Tu-4, a faithful copy of the American B-29, three of which had made forced landings in the USSR. The jet-powered Tu-16, which appeared in 1954, was a twin-engined strategic bomber, with a payload of nine tons and a radius of action of 1,500 miles (2,400 km). Even larger was the Tu-20, a four-engined turboprop with a top speed of 560 mph (900 kph), able to deliver 12 tons of bombs to distances of over 3,750 miles (6,000 km). The Tu-22, which followed, was a supersonic tactical bomber. Twin-engined, it flew at 940 mph (1,500 kph), with a payload of eight tons and a radius of action of over 940 miles (1,500 km).

1

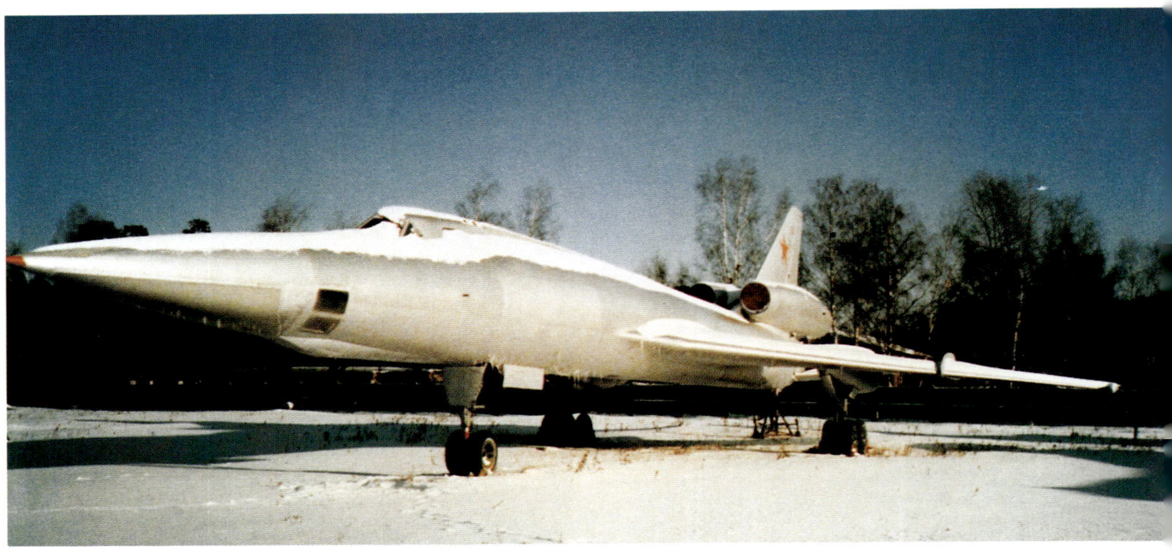

2

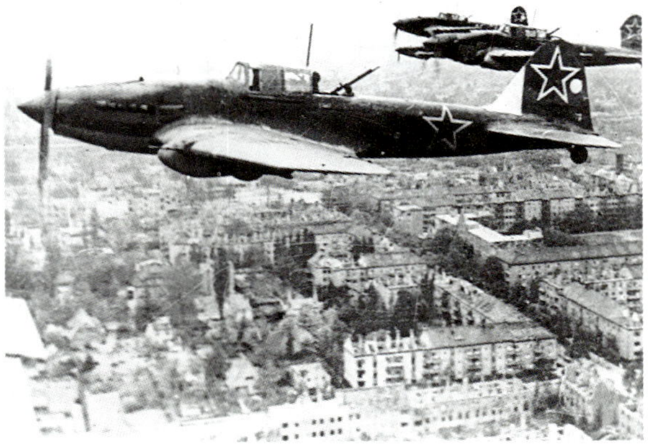

6

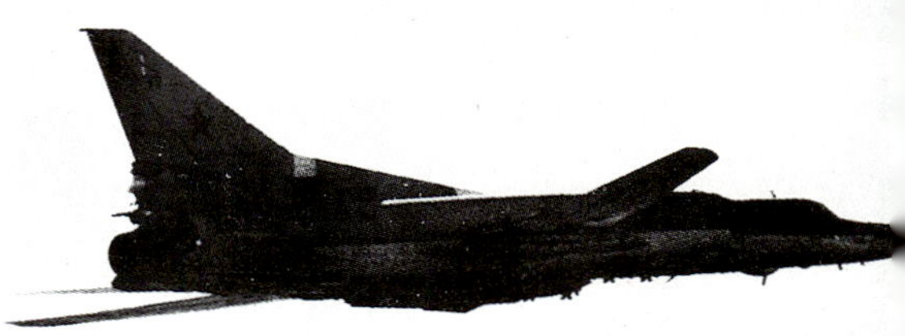

3

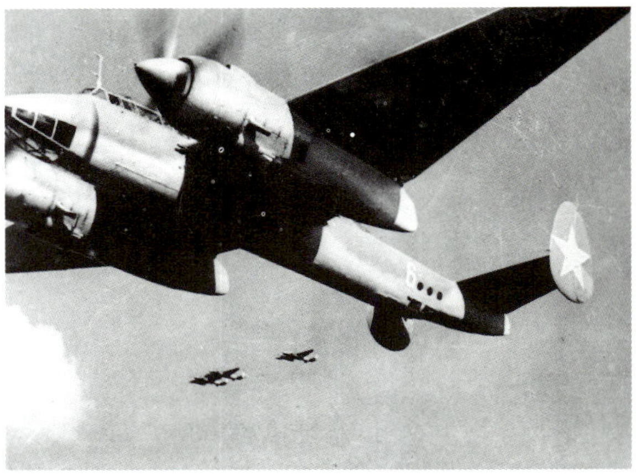

7

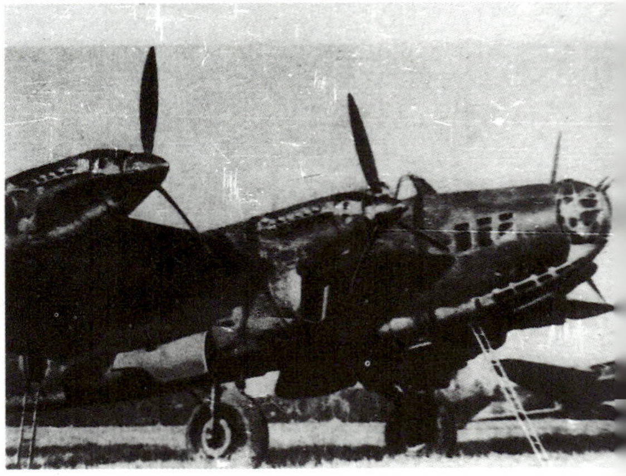

4

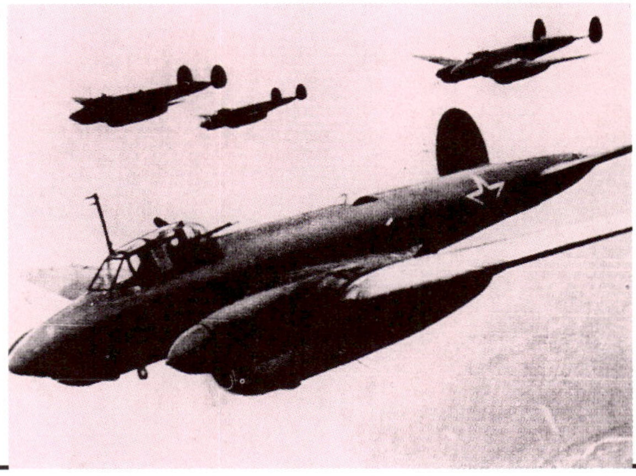

8

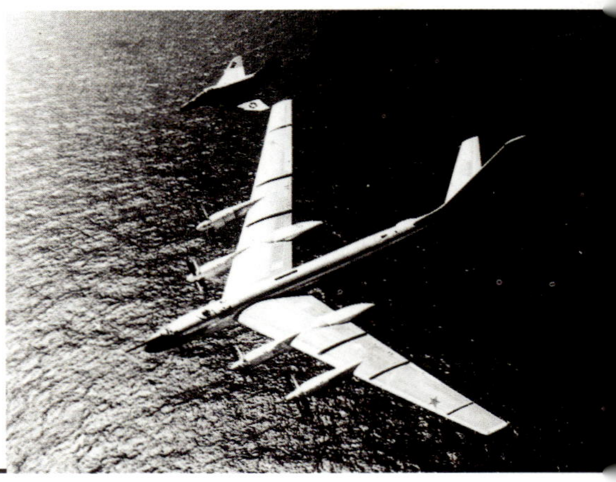

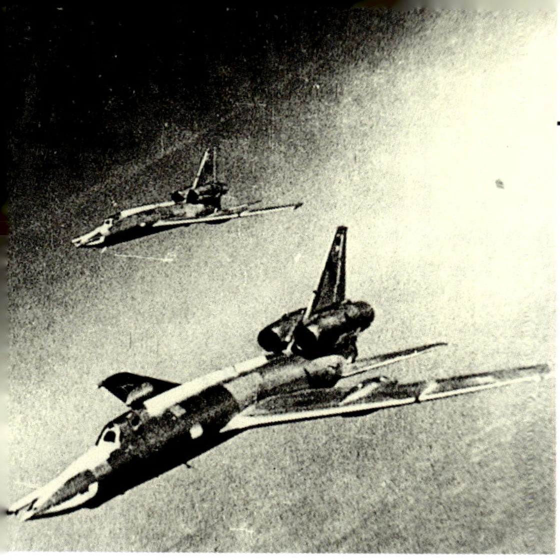
9

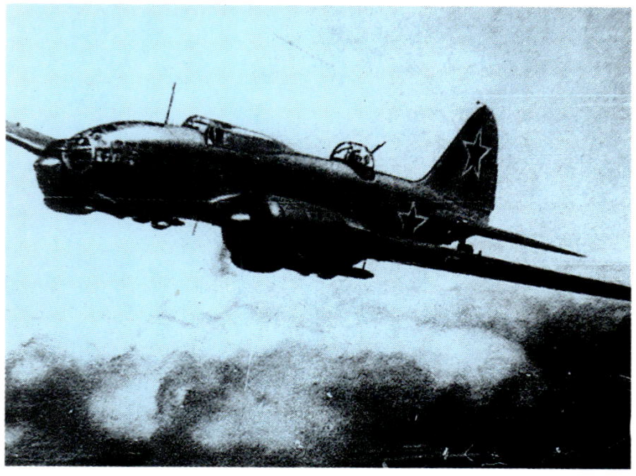
14

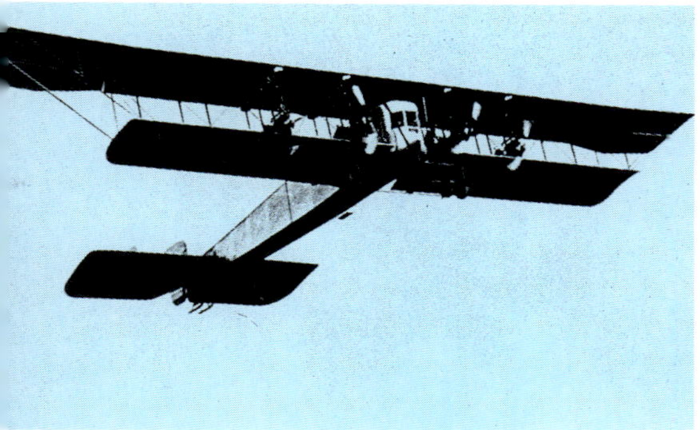
10

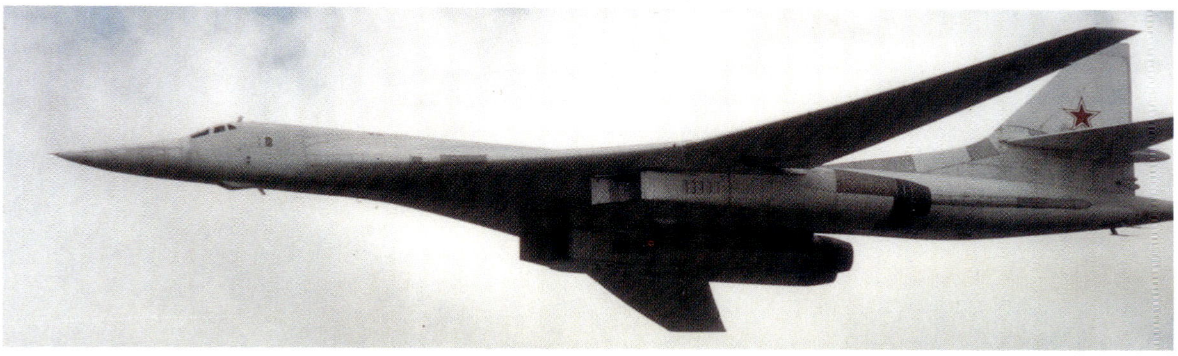
18

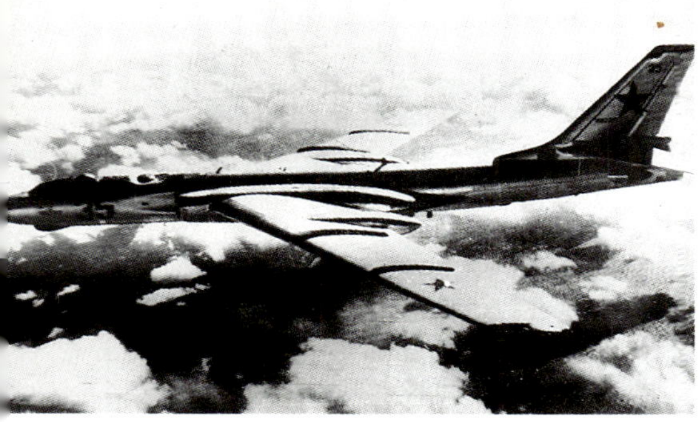
11

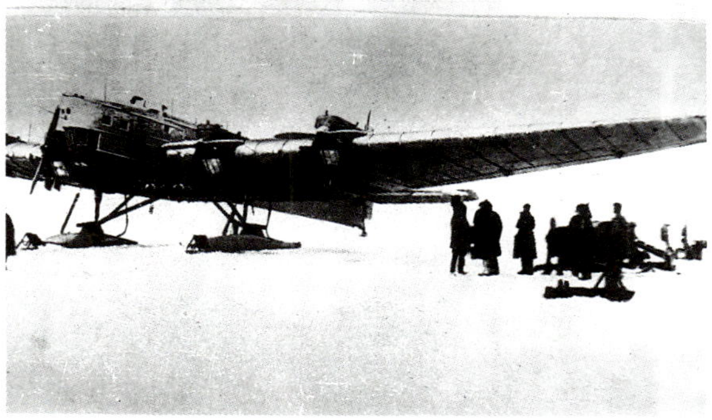
15

In the 1970s, the Soviets developed a twin-engined medium-range bomber with swing wings, the Tupolev Tu-22M family, which carry 12 tons of bombs and cruise missiles of various kinds and can strike a target 1,250 miles (2,000 km) from base without refuelling, at speeds up to Mach 2. The latest addition to the Tupolev family is the Tu-160 strategic bomber, which reaches Mach 2.3 and can deliver 16 tons of bombs or missiles to a distance of 2,250 miles (3,600 km).

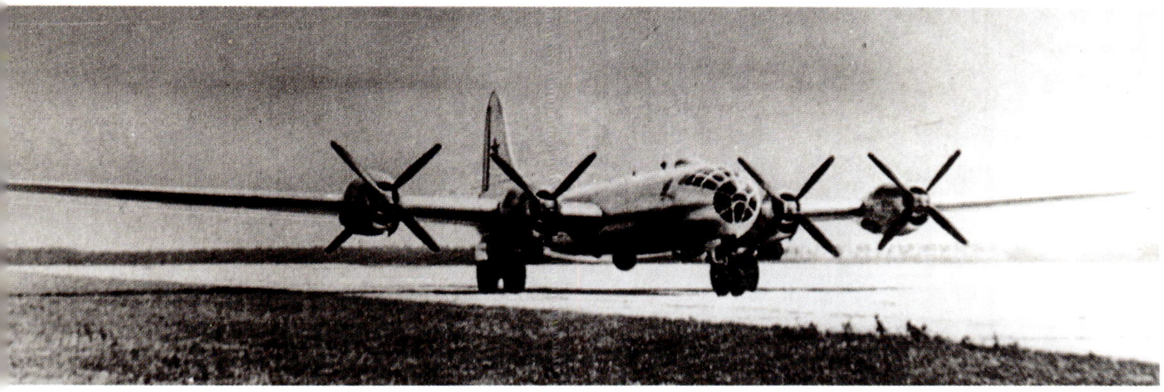
16

Photo Nos. 1, 6 and 9: Tupolev Tu-22
Photo Nos. 2 and 5: Ilyushin Il-2 Sturmovik
Photo Nos. 3 and 17: Tupolev Tu-2
Photo No. 4: Petlyakov Pe-2
Photo No. 7: Petlyakov Pe-8
Photo Nos. 8 and 19: Tupolev Tu-20
Photo No. 10: Ilya Mourometz
Photo Nos. 11 and 13: Tupolev Tu-16
Photo No. 12: Tupolev Tu-22M2
Photo No. 14: Ilyushin Il-4
Photo No. 15: Tupolev TB-3
Photo No. 16: Tupolev Tu-4
Photo No. 18: Tupolev Tu-160

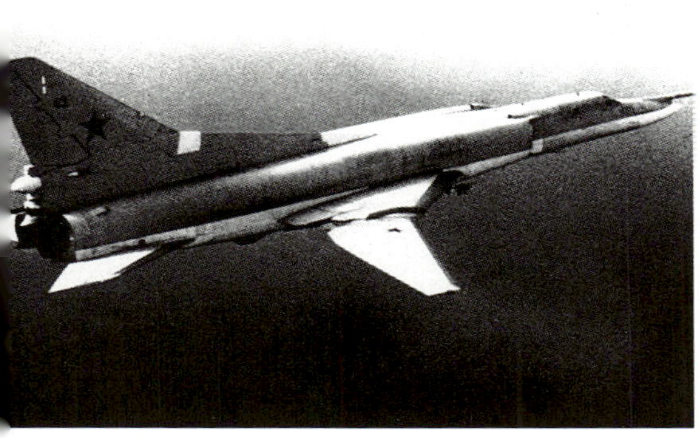
12

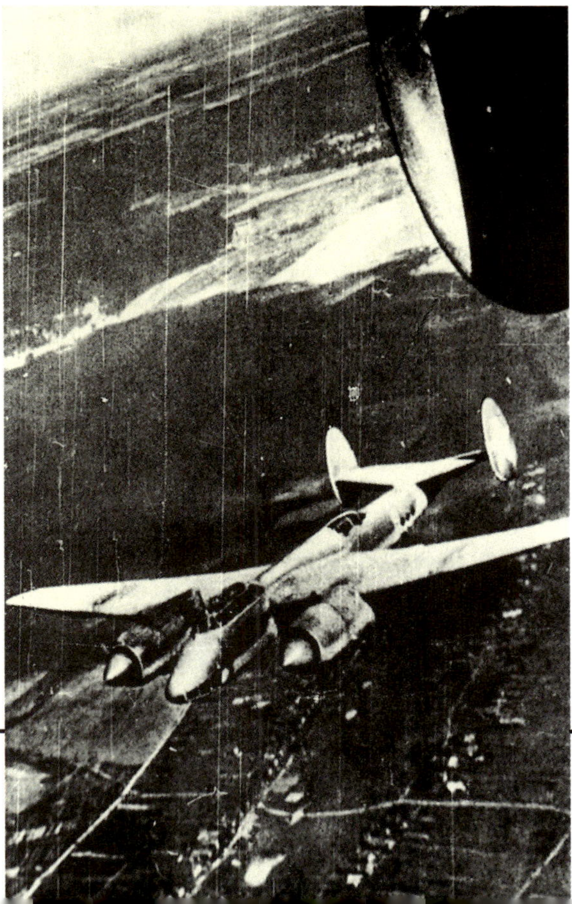
17

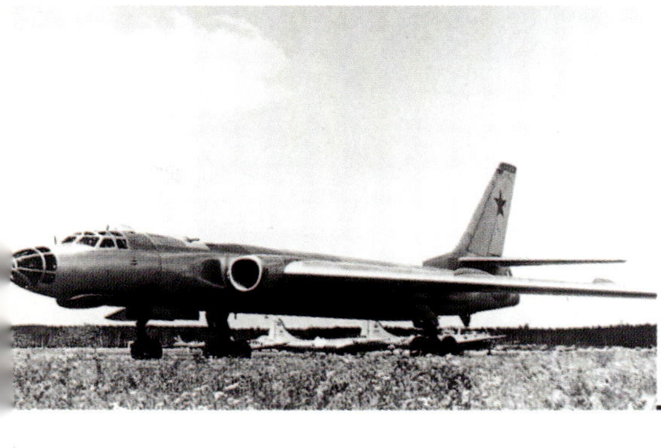
13

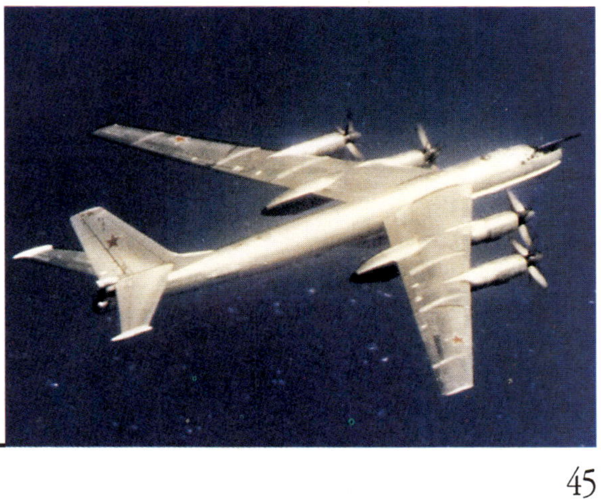
19

5

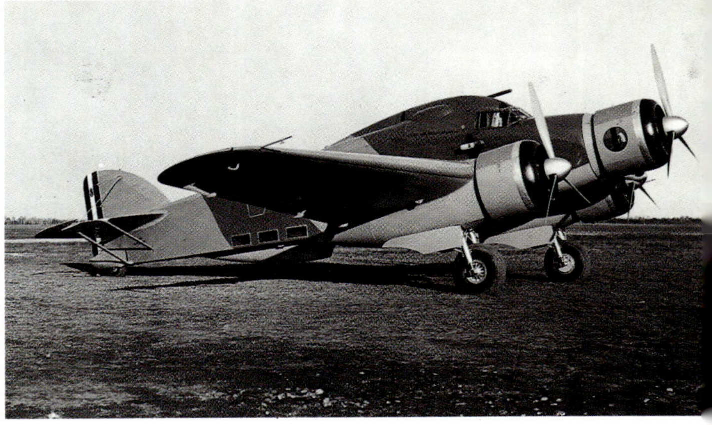

ITALIAN AND GERMAN BOMBERS

In 1936, when it entered service with the Italian Regia Aeronautica, the Fiat BR.20M Cicogna (Stork) was among the most advanced bombers in the world. A twin-engined monoplane, it could fly at speeds well in excess of 250 mph (400 kph), and carried a bomb load of 5,500 lb (2,500 kg). Its radius of action was 625 miles (1,000 km). At the same time, the Italian air force took delivery of the Savoia-Marchetti SM.79 Sparviero (Sparrowhawk), a three-engined aircraft which carried 2,600 lb (1,200 kg) of bombs at 270 mph (430 kph) and could also strike at targets within a 625-mile (1,000-kilometre) radius. Aerodynamic, with retractable undercarriage, it saw action in the Spanish Civil War. The CRDA Cant Z.1007 Alcione (Kingfisher), which appeared in 1937, was a three-engined medium range bomber with a maximum speed approaching 300 mph (475 kph). It could deliver two tons of bombs within a radius of 400 miles (650 km). Its sister, the Cant Z.506 Airone (Heron), was a seaplane used for torpedo bombing. With a radius of action of 875 miles (1,400 km), it could carry a bomb load of 2,600 lb (1,200 kg) at 230 mph (365 kph). The Piaggio P.108 B, Italy's equivalent of the Flying Fortress, was a four-engined bomber, capable of transporting a 7,700-lb (3,500-kg) bomb load at over 250 mph (400 kph) on sorties of up to 1,000 miles (1,600 km).

Germany's Gotha G V was a twin-engined biplane used extensively for night-time bombing of London in 1917 and 1918. It reached speeds of 90 mph (140 kph) and carried 1,300 lb (600 kg) of bombs. On raids of over 250 miles (400 km), the bomb load was reduced. During the same period, London received the attentions of the Zeppelin Staaken R.VI, an aircraft which could carry 2,200-lb (1,000-kg) blockbusters and flew at 85 mph (135 kph). Its maximum bomb load was two tons, and it had a radius of action of 440 miles (700 km). During World War I, the Germans also used the Friedrichshafen G III, a twin-engined aircraft capable of carrying a 2,200-lb (1,000-kg) bomb load at 90 mph (140 kph) on sorties of 250 miles (400 km).

During World War II, London was again a prime target. The main German bomber in the early stages was the Heinkel He 111, whose top speed was 250 mph (400 kph). It could carry two tons of bombs and had a bombing radius of 375 miles (600 km). The He 111 was accompanied by the Dornier Do 17 and the Junkers Ju 88. The Do 17, nicknamed the "flying pencil", flew at over 220 mph (350 kph) to deliver its 2,200-lb (1,000-kg) load, while the Ju 88 was superior all round: maximum speed 280 mph (450 kph), bomb load three tons, radius of action 625 miles (1,000 km). The Dornier Do 217 was a remarkable twin-engined heavy bomber, capable of carrying a four-ton load. Entering service in 1939, it flew at over 315 mph (500

1

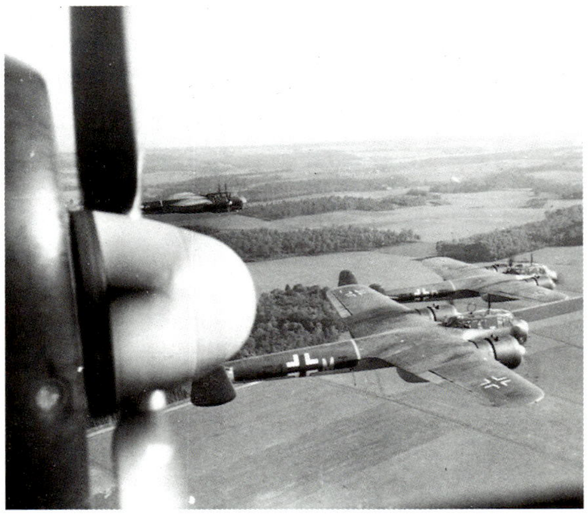

6

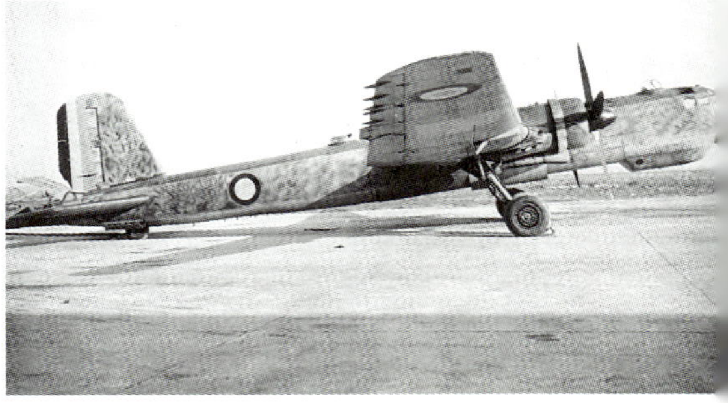

7

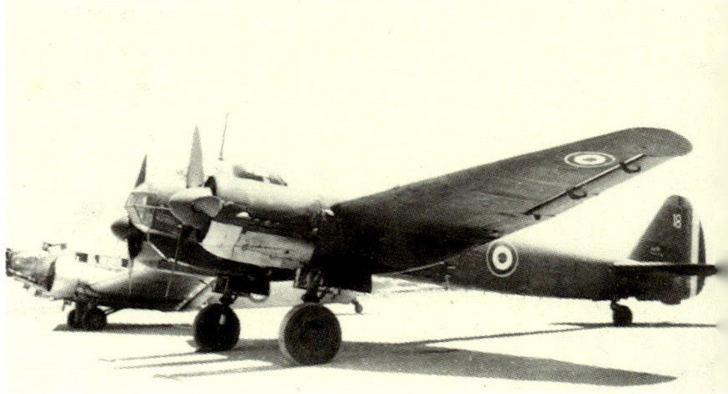

2

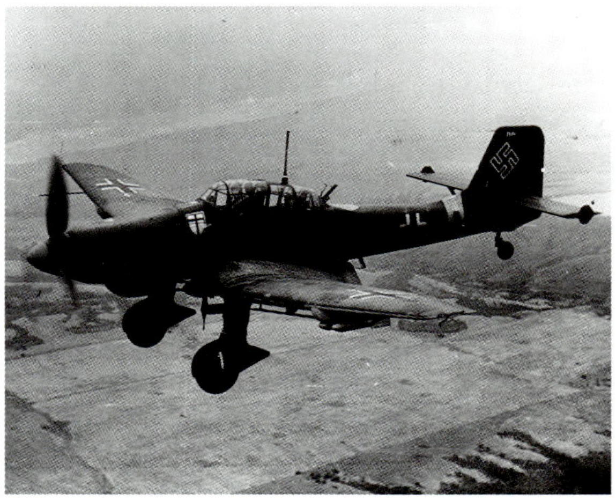

8

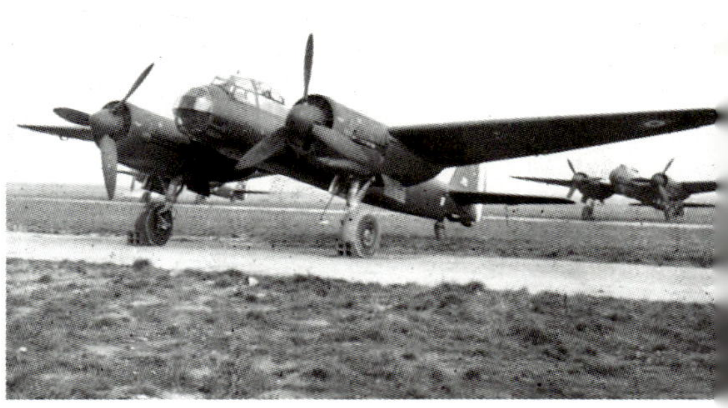

3

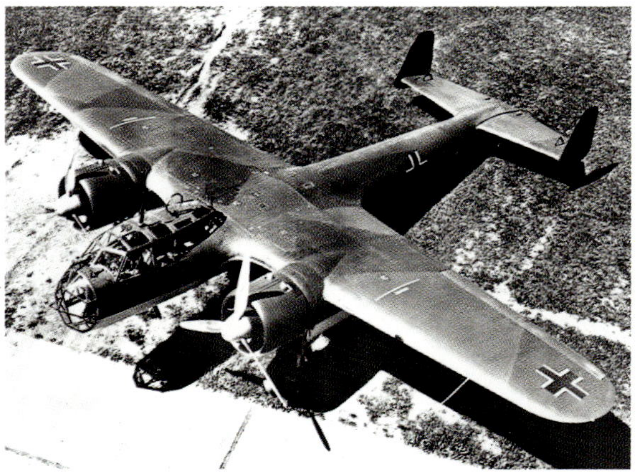

9

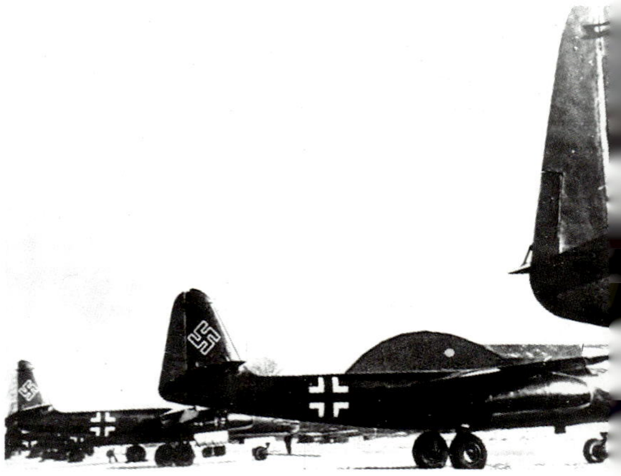

4

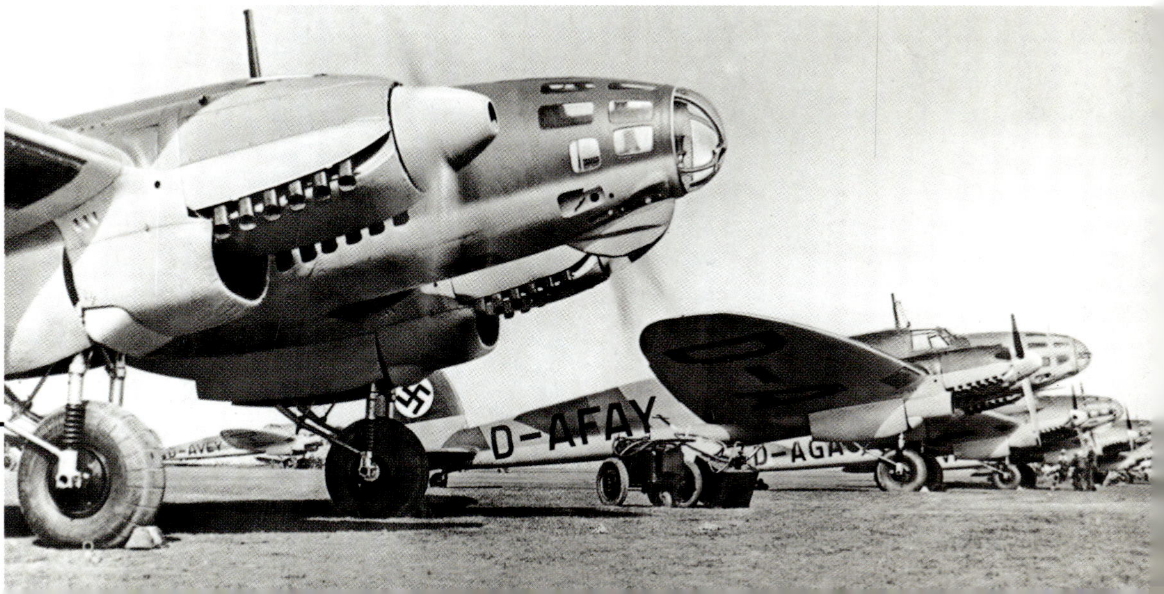

10

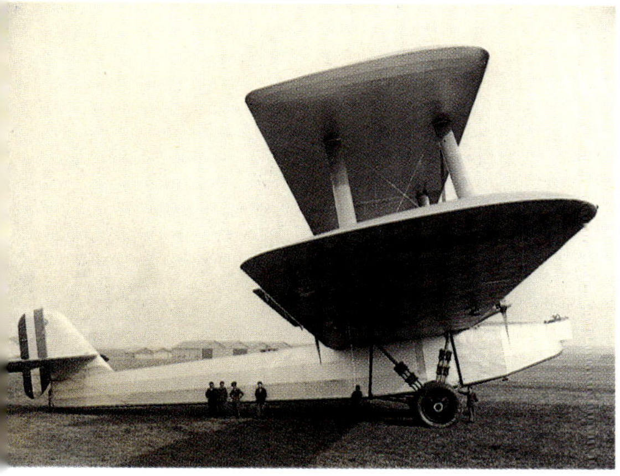

13

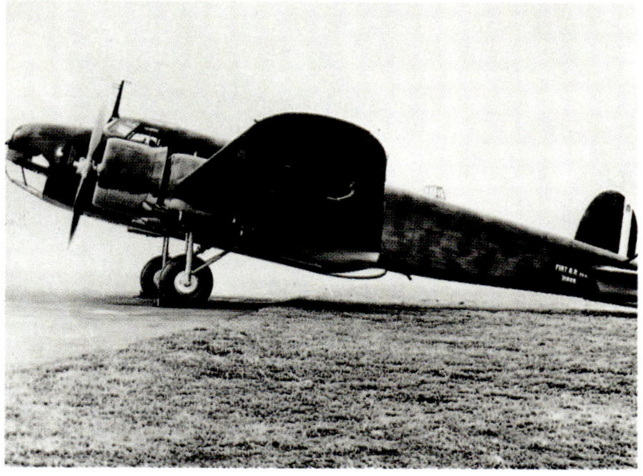

kph) and had an effective range of 625 miles (1,000 km). It was followed in 1942 by the 295-mph (470-kph) Heinkel He 177, which could deliver six tons of bombs or launch remote-controlled missiles. Its radius of action was 1,250 miles (2,000 km).

The twin-engined single-seater Arado Ar 234 Blitz was the world's first jet bomber, though it came too late to make any effective contribution to the German war effort. With a bombing range of 400 miles (650 km), it carried a bomb load of 3,300 lb (1,500 kg) at 460 mph (740 kph).

14

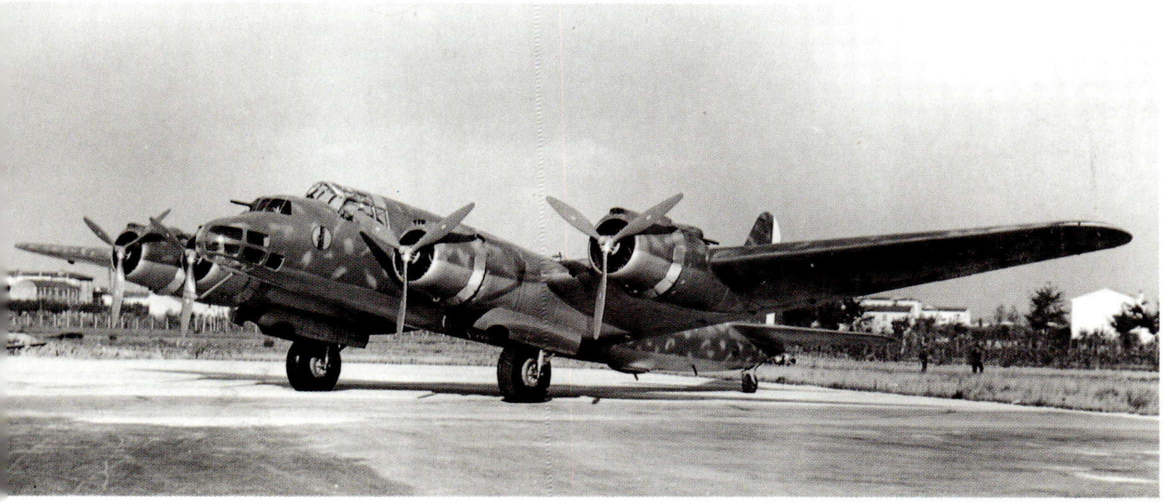

20

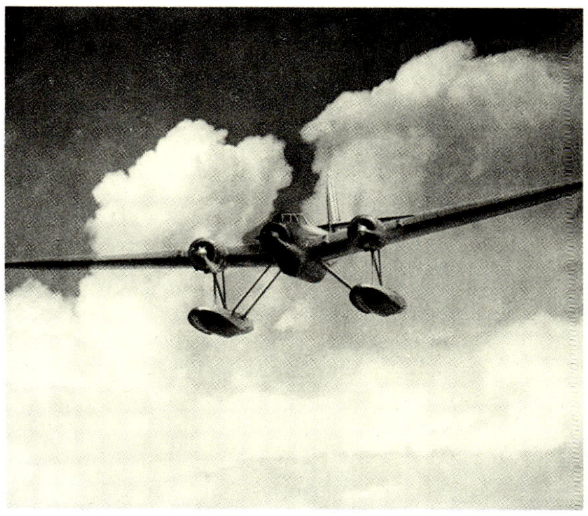

15

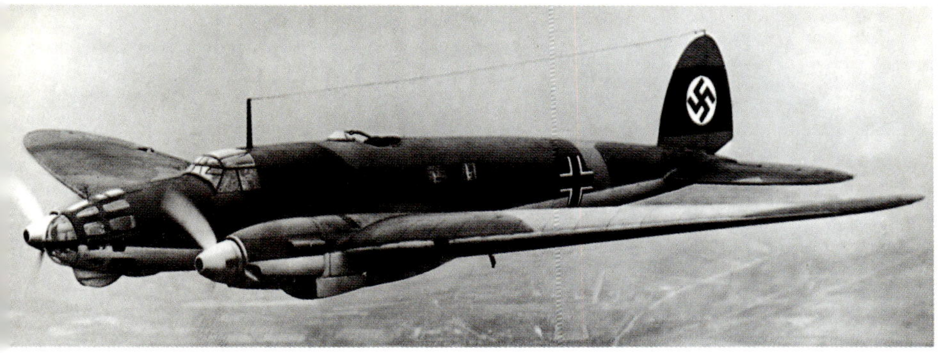

21

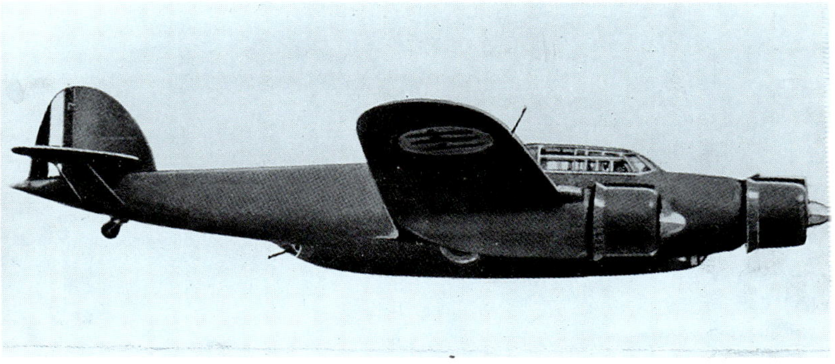

11

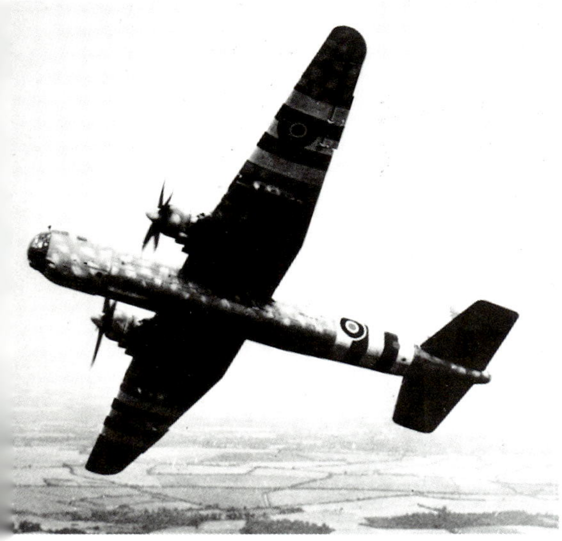

16

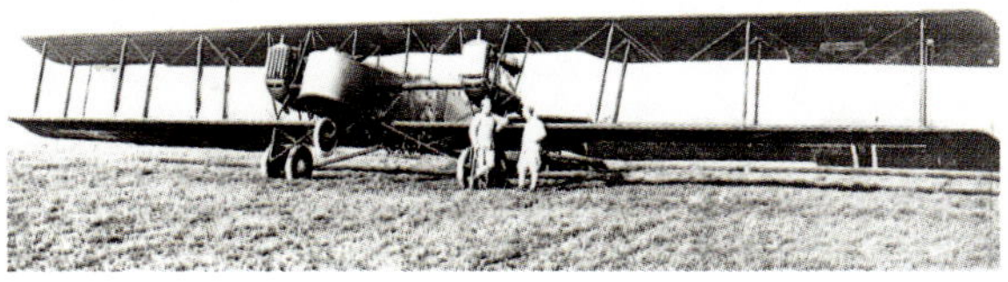

Throughout the war, the Luftwaffe made highly effective use of the Junkers Ju 87 Stuka dive bomber. Flying at 250 mph (400 kph), it delivered a load of up to 4,000-lb (1,800-kg) bomb within 310 miles (500 km).

Photo No. 5: Savoia Marchetti SM.79 Sparviero
Photo No. 10: Caproni Ca.90
Photo No. 13: Fiat BR.20 M Cicogna
Photo No. 14: Piaggio P.108B
Photo No. 20: Cant Z.506B Airone
Photo No. 21: Cant Z.1007 bis Alcione
Photo Nos. 1 and 3: Dornier Do 17Z

Photo No. 2: Junkers Ju 87 Stuka
Photo Nos. 4, 12 and 15: Heinkel He 111
Photo Nos. 6 and 11: Heinkel He 177
Photo Nos. 7 and 8: Junkers Ju 88
Photo No. 9: Arado Ar 234 Blitz
Photo No. 16: Friedrichshafen G III
Photo No. 17: Dornier Do 217
Photo No. 18: Gotha G V
Photo No. 19: Zeppelin Staaken R IV

17

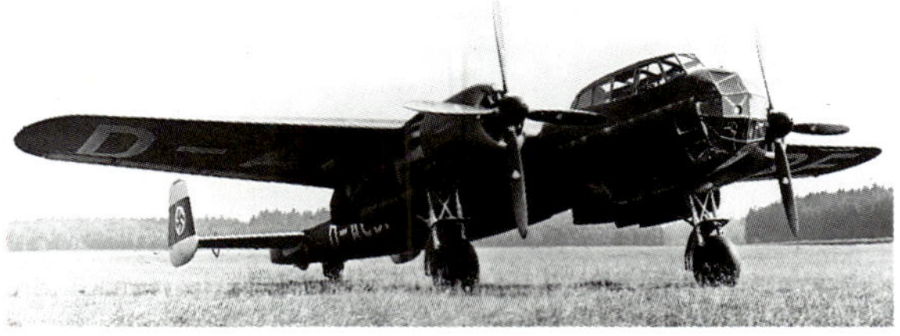

12

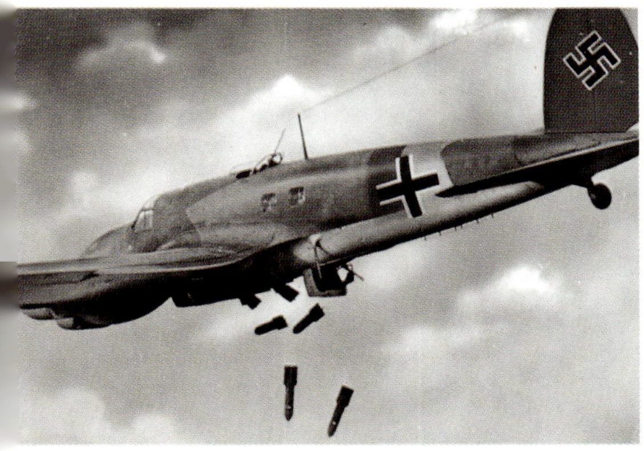

18

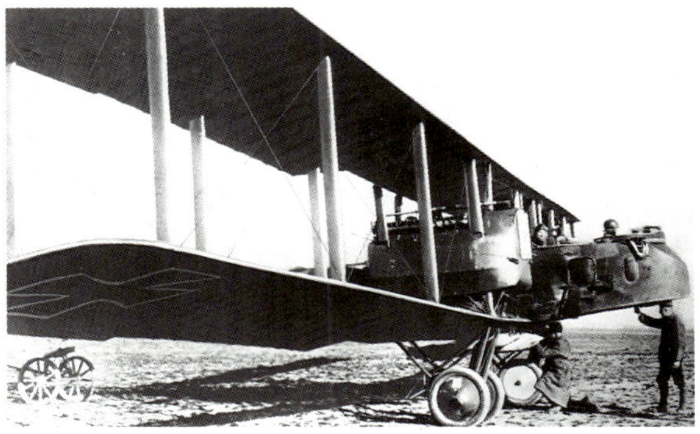

19

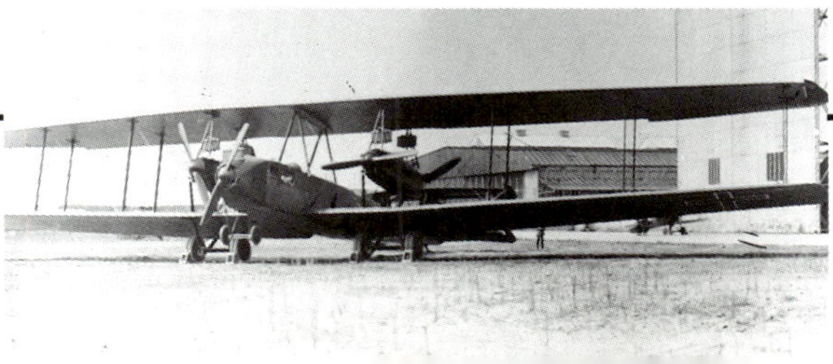

5

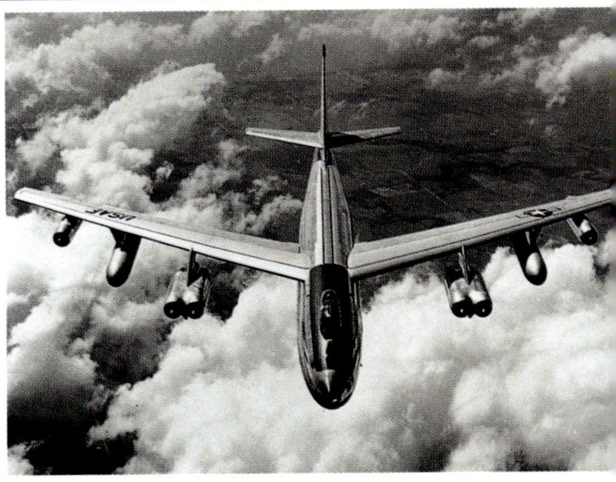

AMERICAN BOMBERS

The first bombing raid on Japan was made in 1942 by North American B-25 Mitchell aircraft launched from the carrier USS *Hornet*. Flying at over 310 mph (500 kph), the B-25 could carry a bomb load of 3,000 lb (1,360 kg), with a radius of action of 625 miles (1,000 km).

From 1941, the US Air Force also deployed the Martin B-26 Marauder – maximum speed 280 mph (450 kph), bomb load 3,000 lb (1,350 kg), radius of action 560 miles (900 km) – and, after 1943, the remarkable Douglas A-26 Invader – maximum speed 375 mph (600 kph), bomb load 7,700 lb (3,500 kg) – a light, twin-engined bomber, which could fly missions of 750 miles (1,200 km).

By 1941, the US also had two heavy four-engined bombers. Defended by thirteen machine guns, the celebrated Boeing B-17 Flying Fortress flew at 220 mph (350 kph), carrying a bomb load of four tons to targets more than 1,000 miles (1,600 km) from base. The Consolidated B-24 Liberator could fly even further (1,250 miles/2,000 km), transporting four tons of bombs at nearly 300 mph (480 kph).

The task of dropping the first atomic bomb on Hiroshima fell to the Boeing B-29 Superfortress *Enola Gay*. The B-29 had a maximum speed of 357 mph (575 kph) and could drop its 10,000-lb (4,500-kg) bomb load at distances of over 1,875 miles (3,000 km).

In the Pacific theatre, the US used a number of carrier-based torpedo bombers, including the Douglas SBD Dauntless (1941), the Grumman TBF Avenger (1942) and the Curtiss SB2C Helldiver (1943). The mighty Convair B-36 (1947) did not see wartime service. Powered by six pusher propeller engines and four turbojets, it flew at 435 mph (700 kph), carrying 40 tons of bombs for distances of up to 4,375 miles (7,000 km).

The Boeing B-47 Stratojet, a six-engined bomber with swept-back wings, entered service in 1950. It reached almost 625 mph (1,000 kph) with a 10-ton bomb load, and had a radius of action of 1,875 miles (3,000 km). The B-47 was succeeded in 1955 by the famous Boeing B-52 Stratofortress. An eight-engined aircraft, it flew at 650 mph (1,050 kph), while carrying 32 tons of conventional bombs or nuclear weapons. Its range was 6,500 to 10,000 miles (10,000-16,000 km), or more if refuelled in flight.

In 1959, Convair began supplying Strategic Air Command with the four-engined B-58 Hustler, a three-man supersonic bomber capable of 1,300 mph (2,100 kph). It could carry nearly nine tons of bombs or nuclear weapons on missions of 4,500 miles (7,200 km) without refuelling.

1

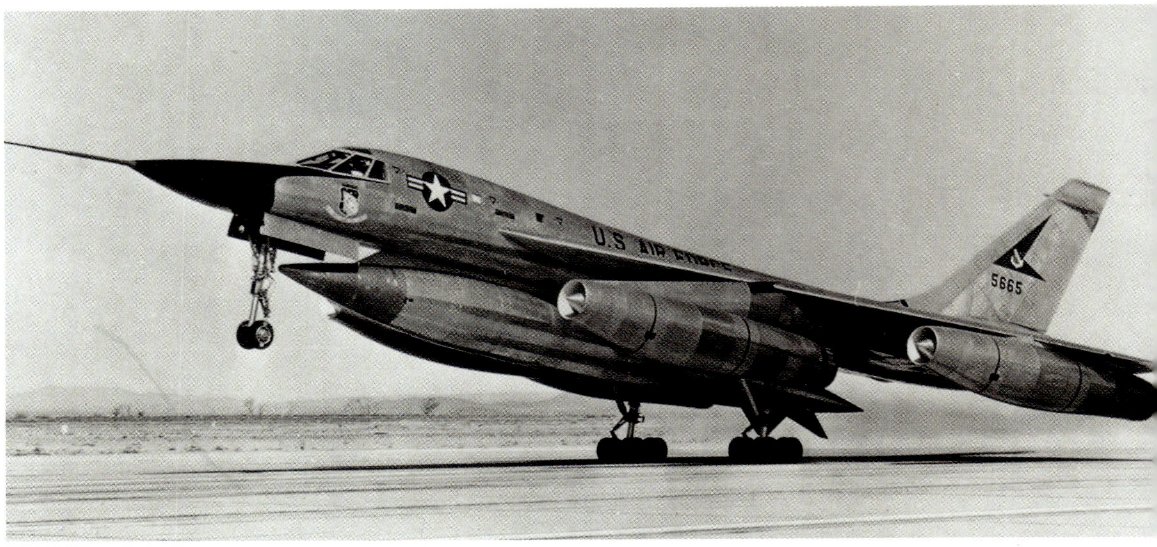

2

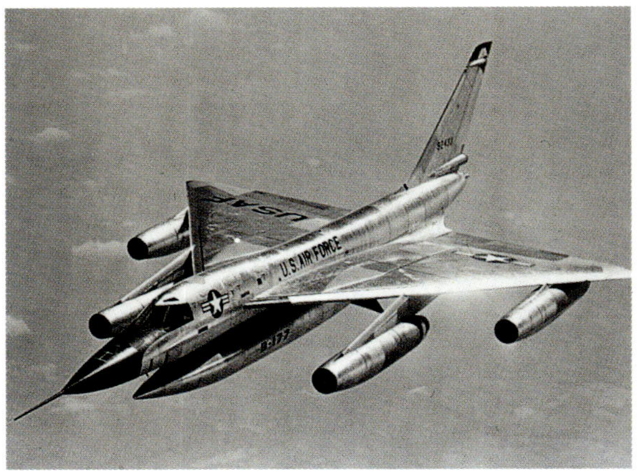

6

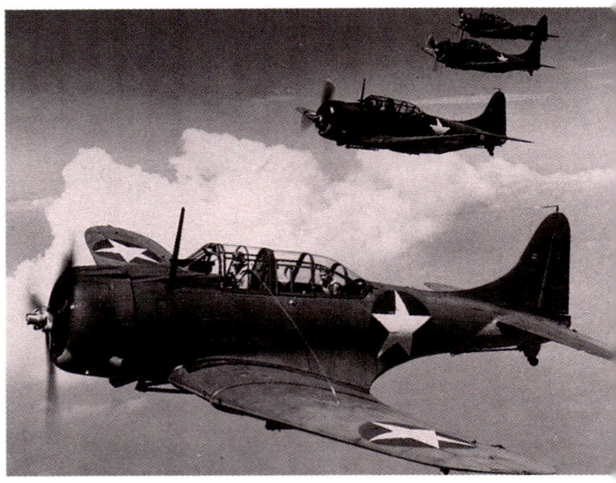

3

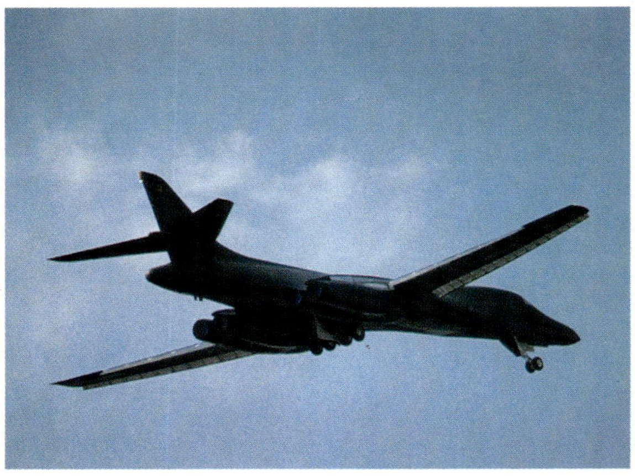

7

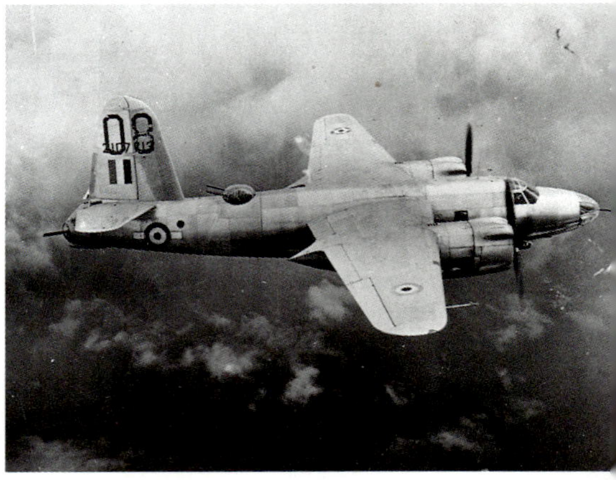

4

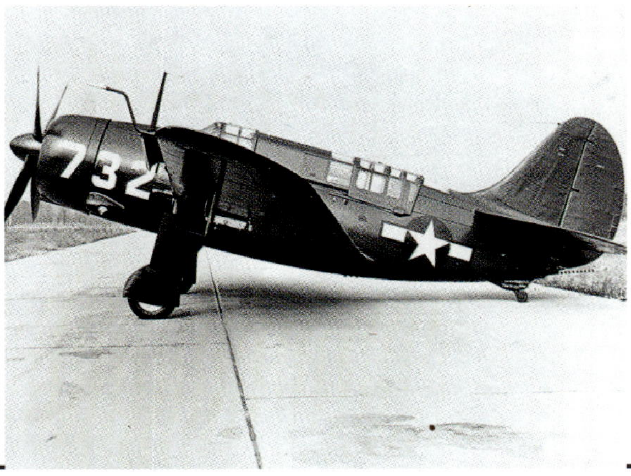

8

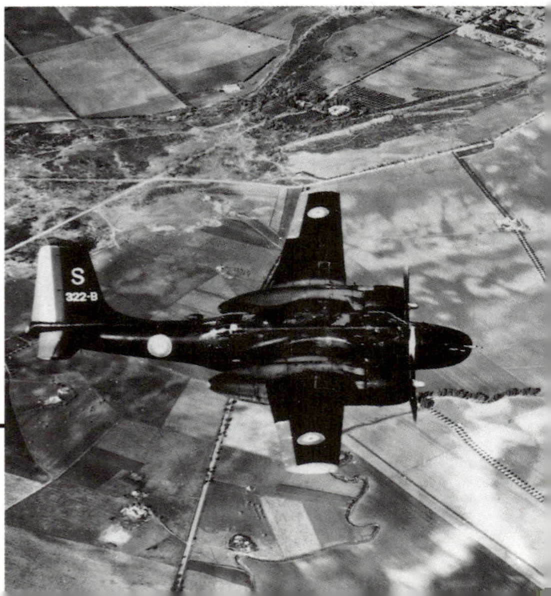

9

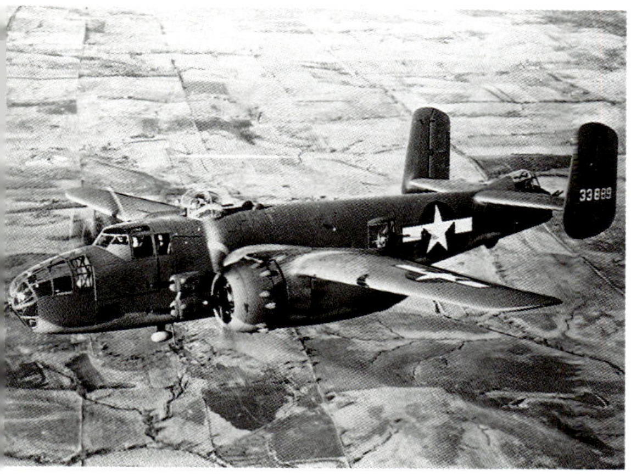

13

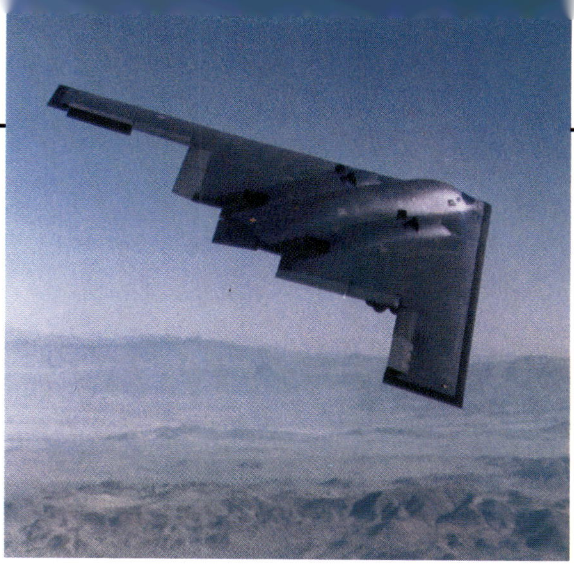

18

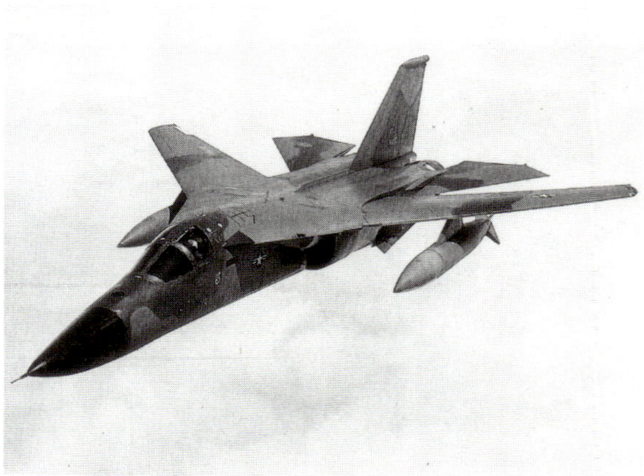

10

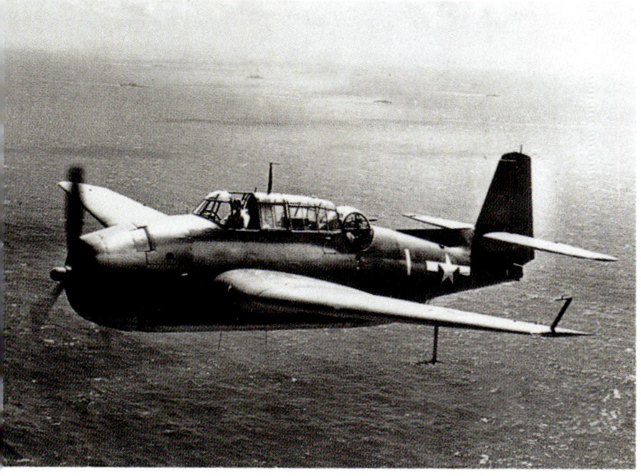

14

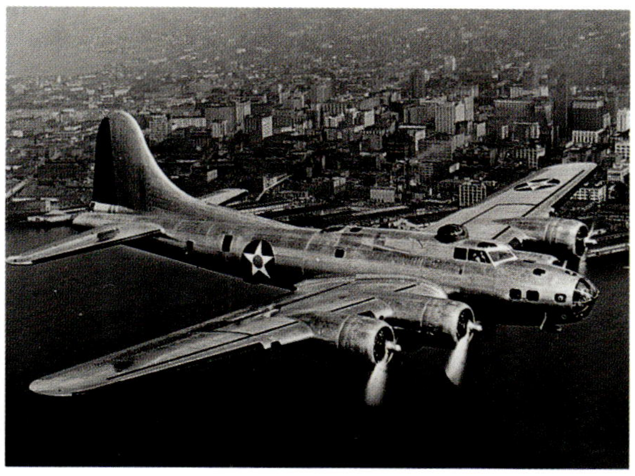

The General Dynamics F-111, which entered service in 1967 and was used in Vietnam, is a twin-engined, all-weather attack bomber with a two-man crew. A swing-wing aircraft, it can deliver 15 tons of bombs to targets within a 1,560-mile (2,500-km) radius, and flies at over 1,440 mph (2,300 kph). A more recent addition to the US arsenal is the Rockwell International B-1B Lancer, a variable-geometry strategic bomber which has been in service since the late 1980s. The latest recruit is the formidable Northrop B-2, whose unusual wing configuration is designed for maximum stealth. Its performance details are still largely secret.

11

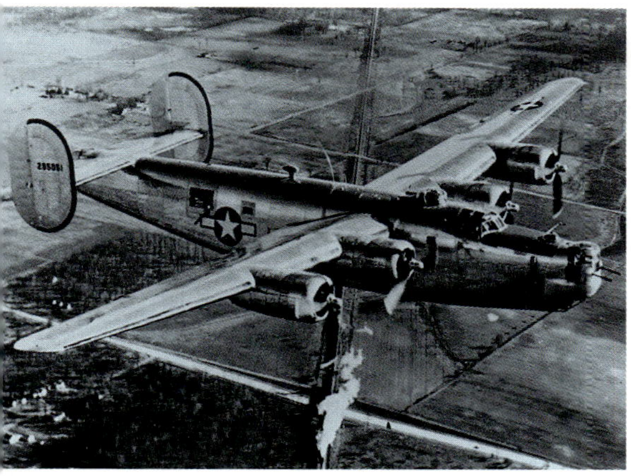

15

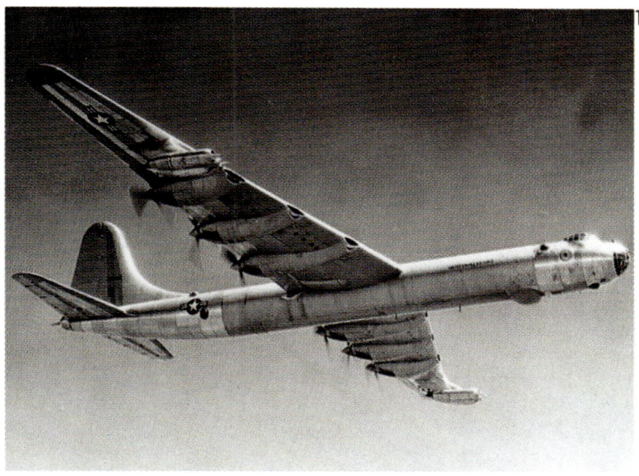

16

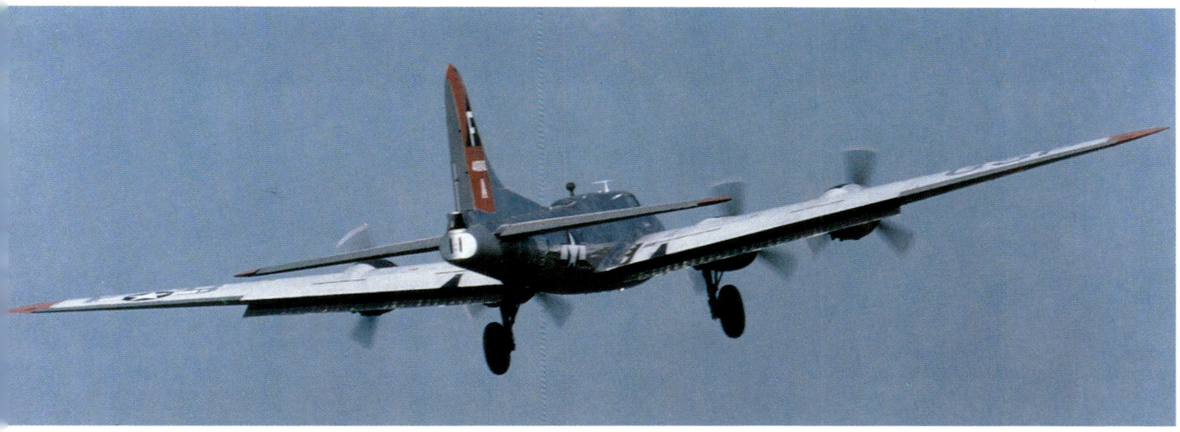

Photo Nos. 1 and 2: Convair B-58 Hustler
Photo No. 3: Rockwell B-1B Lancer
Photo No. 4: Curtiss SB2C Helldiver
Photo No. 5: Boeing B-47 Stratojet
Photo No. 6: Douglas SBD Dauntless
Photo Nos. 7 and 19: Martin B-26 Marauder
Photo No. 8: Douglas A-26 Invader
Photo No. 9: North American B-25 Mitchell
Photo No. 10: Grumman TBF Avenger
Photo No. 11: Consolidated B-24 Liberator
Photo No. 12: Boeing B-52 Stratofortress prototype
Photo No. 13: Northrop B-2
Photo Nos. 14 and 16: Boeing B-17 Flying Fortress
Photo No. 15: Convair B-36
Photo No. 17: Boeing B-29 Superfortress
Photo No. 18: General Dynamics FB-111

12

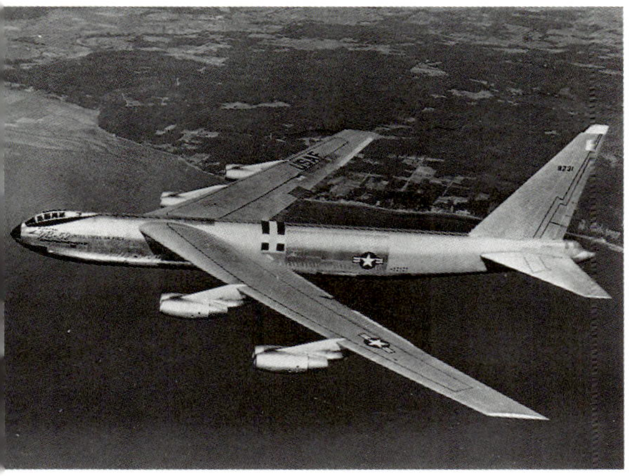

17

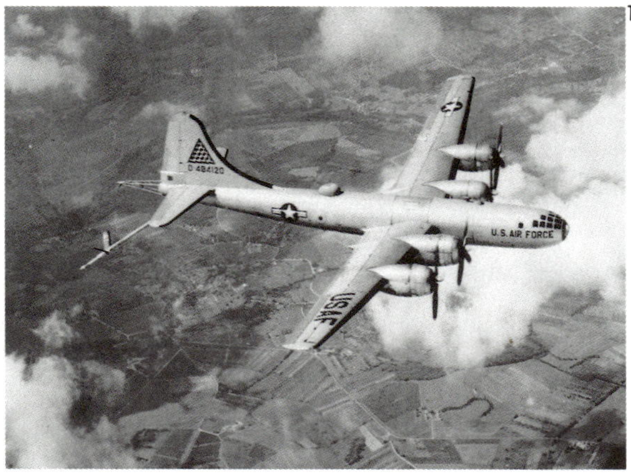

19

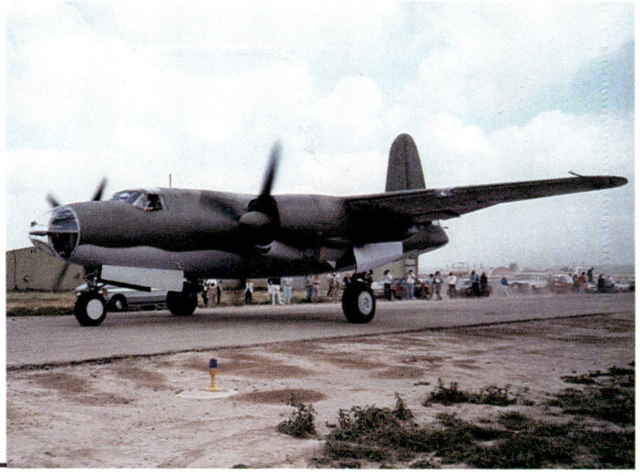

RECONNAISSANCE AND OBSERVATION AIRCRAFT

When war broke out in 1914, aircraft were initially used for observation and reconnaissance duties. In the French camp, the 1915 Farman HF.40, which flew at 85 mph (135 kph) and could climb to 6,500 ft (2,000 m), was replaced in 1917 by the Dorand AR 1 biplane. This aircraft flew at 95 mph (150 kph) and could remain aloft for up to three hours. The AR 1 was in turn superseded by the Salmson 2, capable of 115 mph (185 kph) and altitudes of over 19,600 ft (6,000 m).

The scout most widely used by the British was the Royal Aircraft Factory's R.E.8, of which more than 4,000 were eventually built. It could remain airborne for four hours, at speeds of around 100 mph (165 kph). In Italy, the Pomilio PE biplane was capable of 120 mph (195 kph) and could fly for three hours 30 minutes, climbing to altitudes of 16,000 ft (5,000 m). From 1918, the Italians also used a small single-engined seaplane, the single-seater Macchi M.5. It flew at 125 mph (200 kph) and had an endurance of three hours 40 minutes.

The first German reconnaissance aircraft was the Aviatik B. Although its performance was modest – maximum speed 65 mph (105 kph), ceiling 8,200 ft (2,500 m) – it could remain in flight for up to four hours. It was followed, in 1915, by the Albatros C, an aircraft able to fly at 80 mph (130 kph) for two hours 30 minutes and climb to 10,000 ft (3,000 m). In 1916, Deutsche Flugzeug Werke brought out the DFW CV, which could fly at 95 mph (155 kph) for four hours 30 minutes, with a ceiling of 16,400 ft (5,000 m).

During World War II, the Germans made extensive use of the amazing Fieseler Fi 156 Storch, an aircraft which could take off over 65 metres and land in just 20. It was a high-winged three seater, flying at speeds of between 30 (50) and 110 mph (175 kph) and operating within a radius of 250 miles (400 km). After the war, it was given a new power plant and produced in France as the Morane 500. Another German spotter aircraft was the Focke-Wulf Fw 189, which flew at 220 mph and had a ceiling of 24,000 ft (7,300 m).

Though widely used by the British as a light bomber, the de Havilland Mosquito (pp 52/53) was originally intended (in 1941) as a reconnaissance aircraft. In this role it used its speed (375 mph/600 kph) to escape the unwelcome attentions of enemy fighters. The main task of the Westland Lysander was to ferry secret agents to and from enemy-occupied territory in the years 1941 to 1944. A single-engined aircraft with high, braced wings, it flew at 190 mph (300 kph) and had a quite exceptional radius of action: 1,400 miles (2,260 km).

1

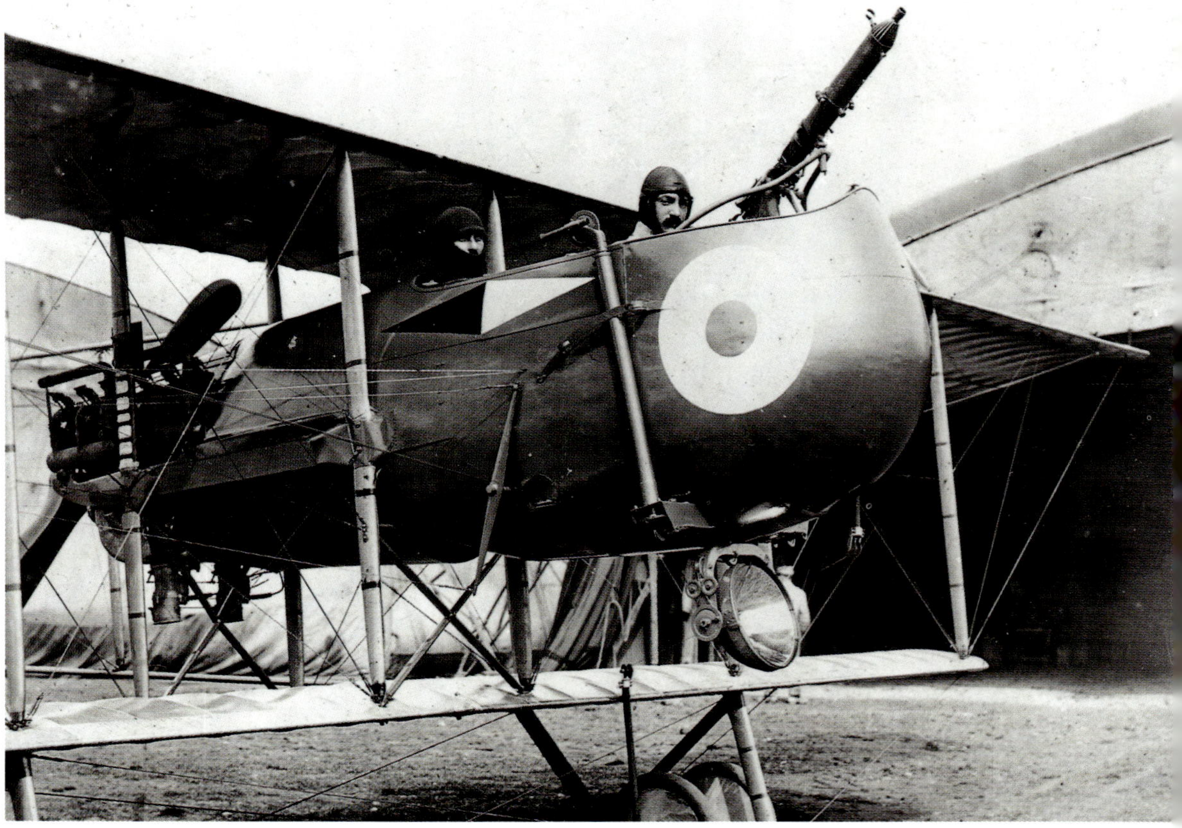

2

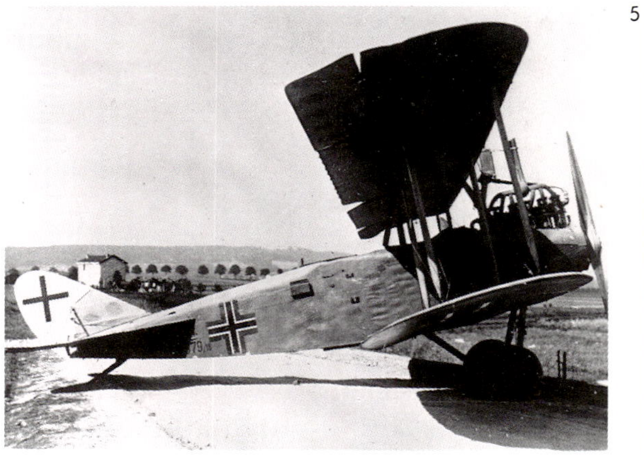

3

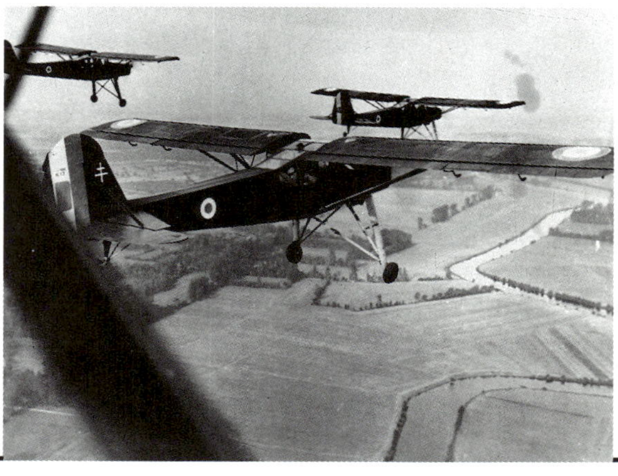

4

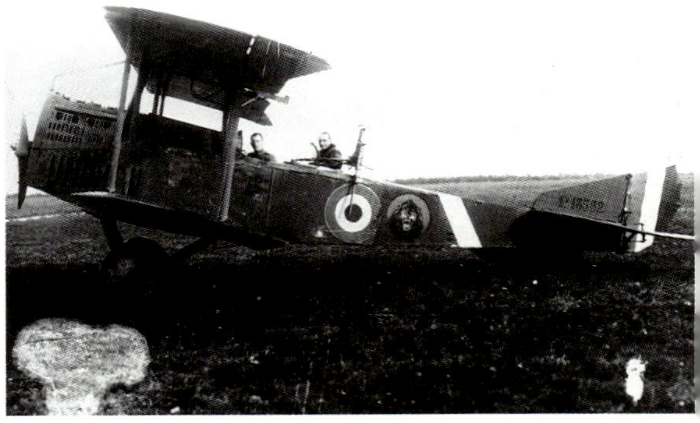

5

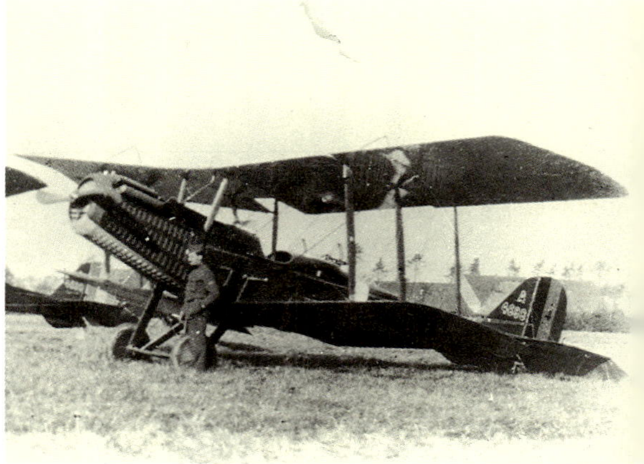

6

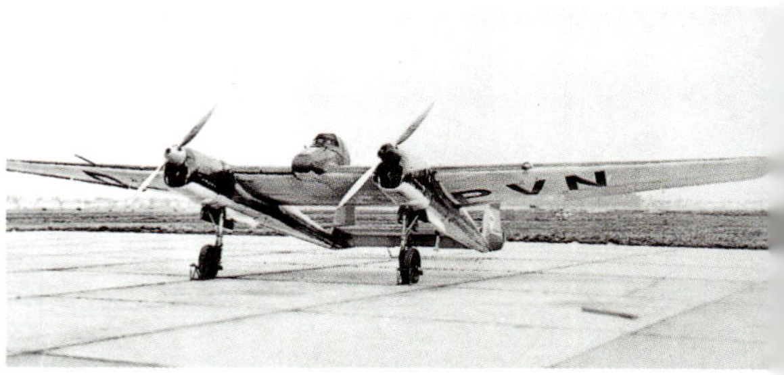

7

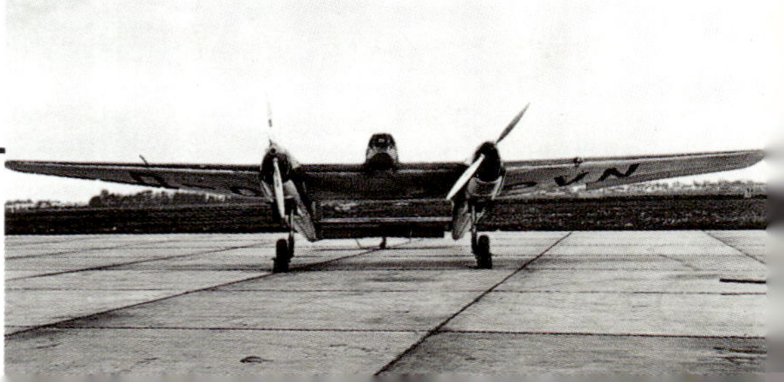

9

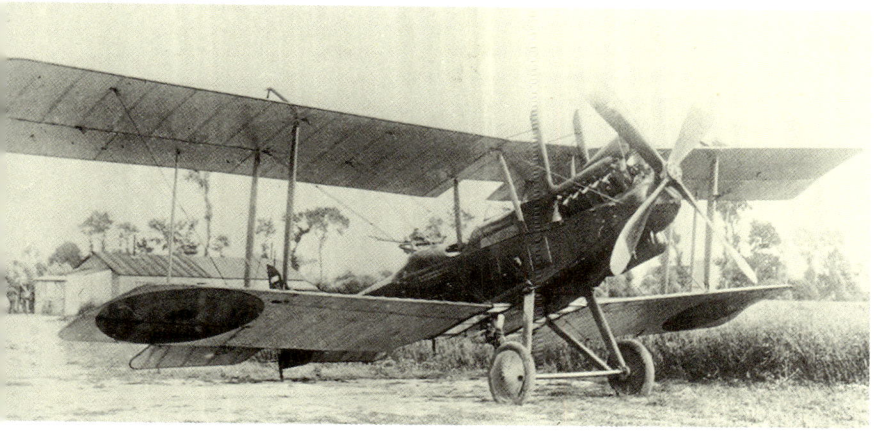

13

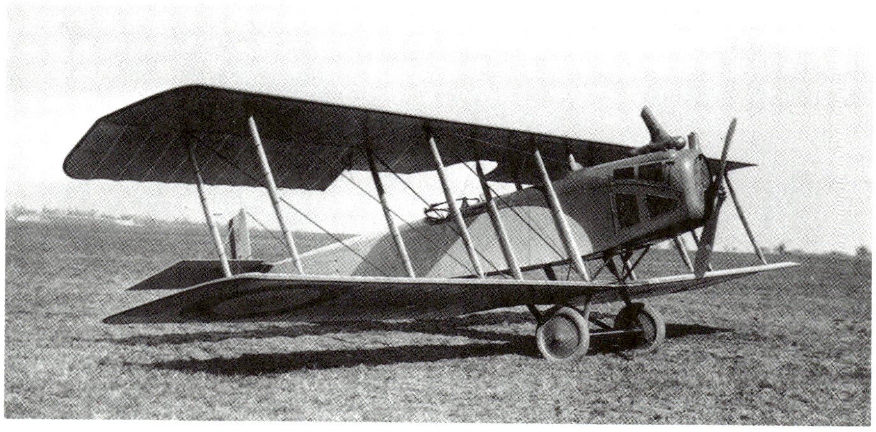

8

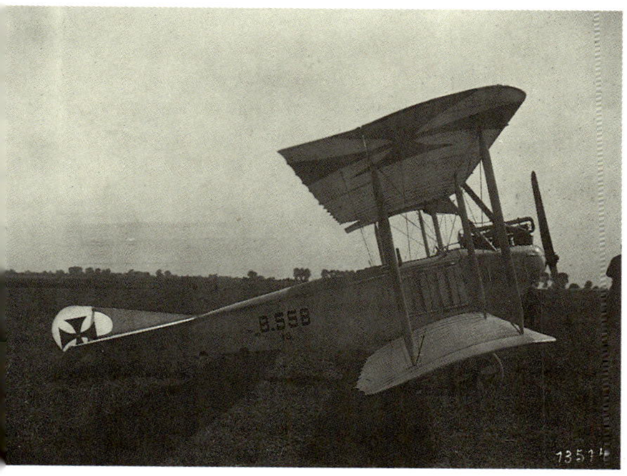

10

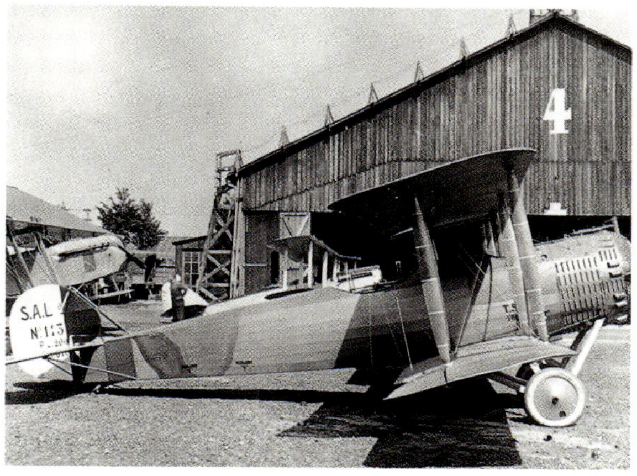

14

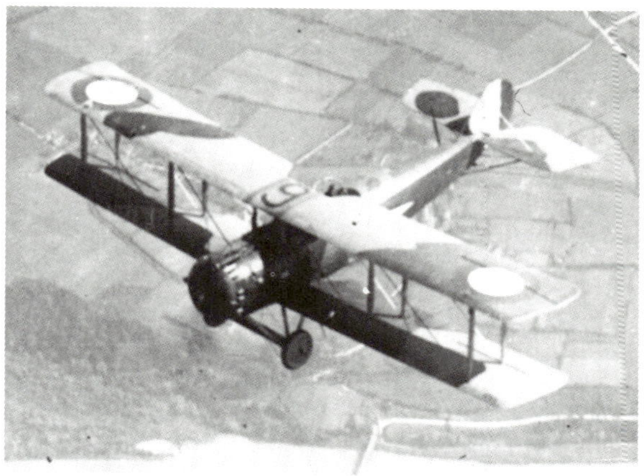

11

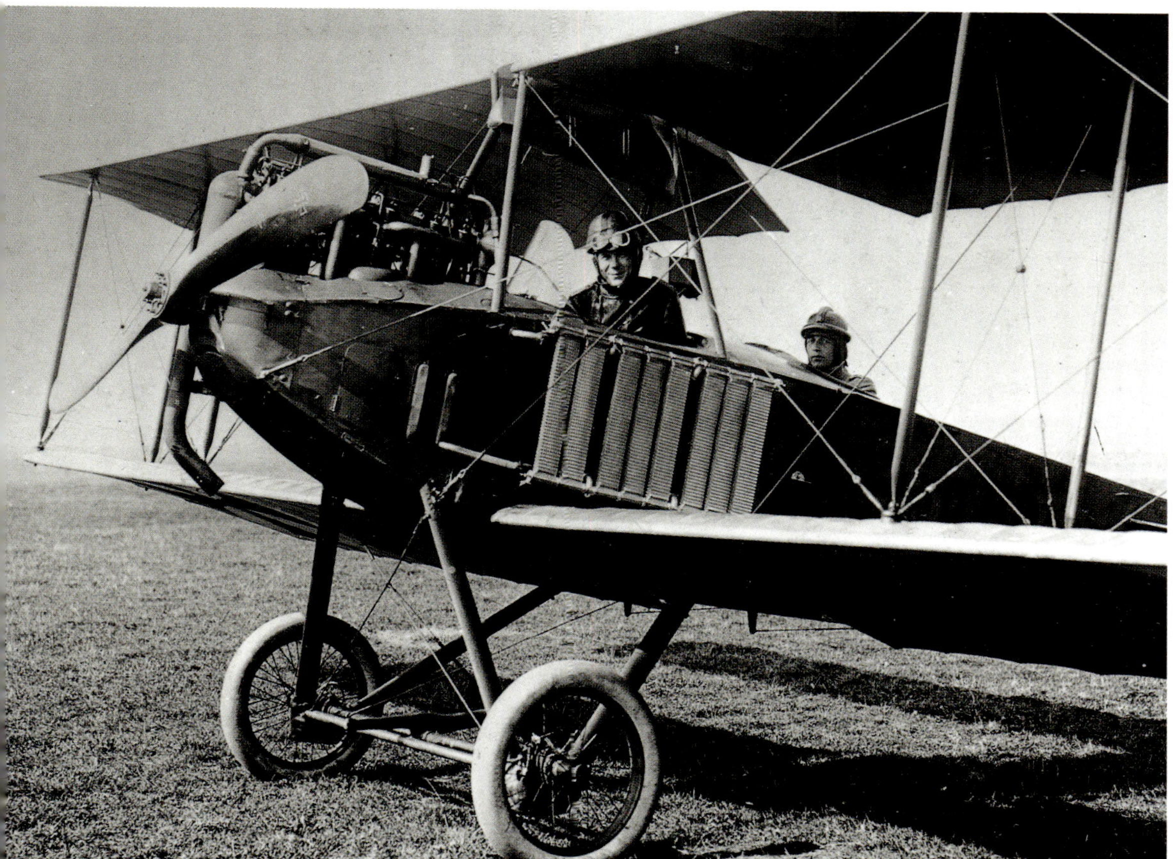

15

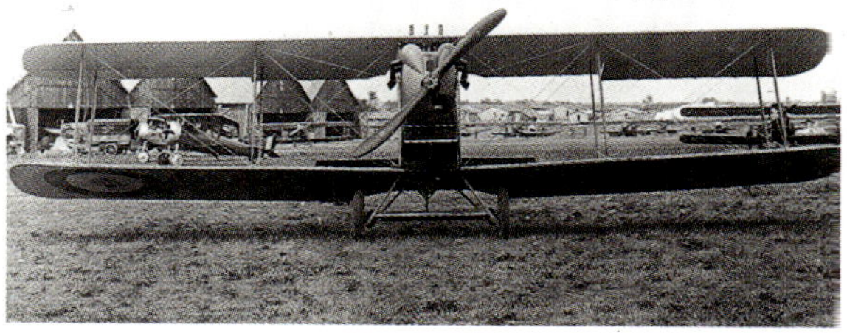

Photo No. 1: Farman HF.40 (France)
Photo Nos. 2 and 12: DFW CV (Germany)
Photo No. 3: Fieseler Fi 156 Storch (Germany)
Photo No. 4: Pomilio PE (Italy)
Photo Nos. 5 and 9: Royal Aircraft Factory R.E.8 (Great Britain)
Photo Nos. 6 and 7: Focke-Wulf Fw 189 Uhu prototype (Germany)
Photo No. 8: Aviatik B II (Germany)
Photo Nos. 10 and 14: Salmson 2 (France)
Photo No. 11: Albatros C (Germany)
Photo Nos. 13 and 15: Dorand AR I (France)

12

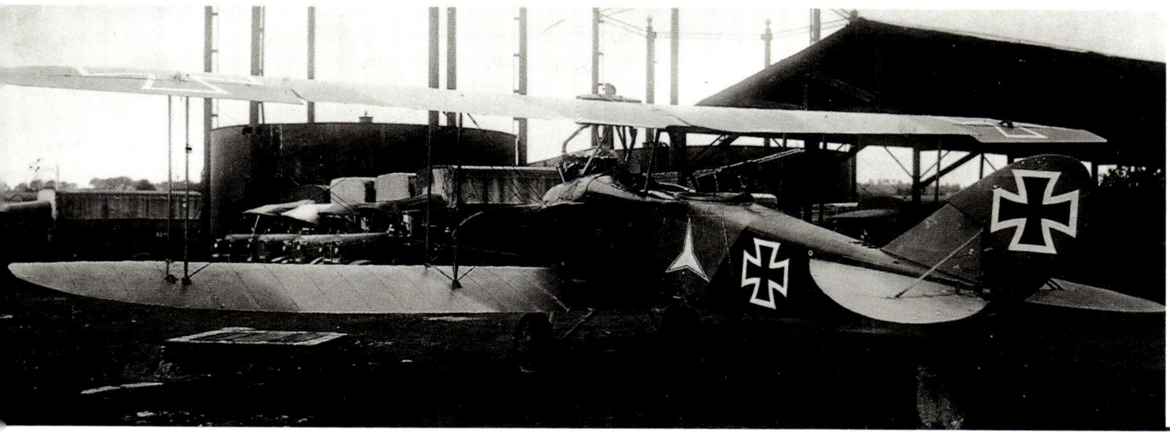

4

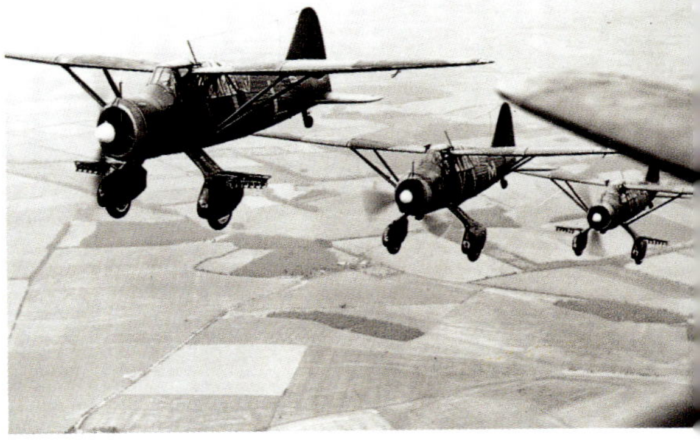

MARITIME PATROL AND RECONNAISSANCE AIRCRAFT

In the years following World War II, the British made improvements to their four-engined Avro Lancaster bomber, renaming it the Lincoln. From this aircraft was derived a maritime reconnaissance plane, the Avro 696 Shackleton. Flying at 275 mph (440 kph), it was equipped for anti-submarine warfare and had a range of 4,250 miles (6,800 km). In 1946, the United States brought out the Lockheed P2V Neptune, a maritime patrol and anti-submarine aircraft with a maximum speed of 360 mph (757 kph) and a range of 4,000 miles (6,500 km). It began its career with a record-breaking flight of 11,250 miles (18,000 km) between Australia and the USA. Two years later, SNCASE of France developed the SE.1010, a four-engined photographic reconnaissance aircraft, but it was not taken beyond the prototype stage.

The highly specialised Lockheed U-2 single-seater spy plane entered service in 1956. Its exaggeratedly-long wings enabled it to fly at extremely high altitudes (over 82,000 ft/25,000 m) in order to take photographs of unfriendly territory. It flew at over 500 mph (800 kph). With a range of 4,000 miles (6,400 km), it could overfly Soviet air space, from Pakistan to Norway. Grumman has specialized in reconnaissance aircraft of all kinds. In 1959, the company began delivering a twin-engined reconnaissance and battlefield monitoring plane, the G-134 Mohawk, which flew at 310 mph (500 kph), had a range of 1,250 miles (2,000 km), and could be fitted with photographic equipment or radar. More specialised was Grumman's G-89 Tracker, a carrier-borne four-seater designed for anti-submarine warfare. Brought out in 1954, the G-89 was powered by two piston engines and flew at 290 mph (470 kph). It had a range of 935 miles (1,500 km) and carried depth charges and two torpedoes. This aircraft and its derivatives (the Trader and Tracer) are now used in fighting forest fires.

The Tracer was succeeded, in 1974, by the Lockheed S-3 Viking. Designed for anti-submarine warfare, this carrier-based aircraft is powered by twin jet engines and has a crew of four. It can fly at 500 mph (800 kph) and has a range of 2,300 miles (3,700 km). The Viking's armament consists of depth charges, mines or four torpedoes.

1

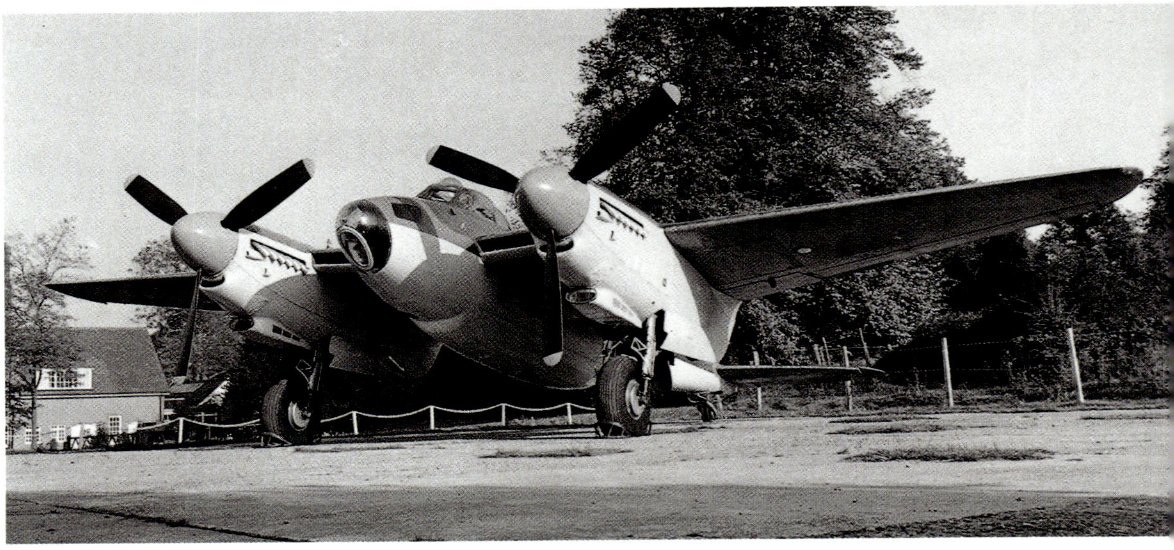

2

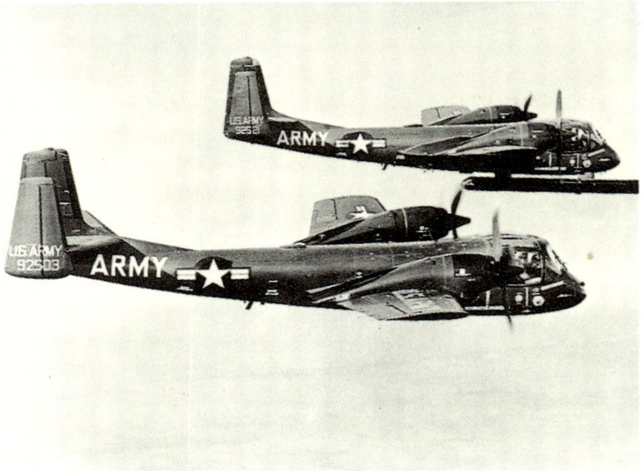

5

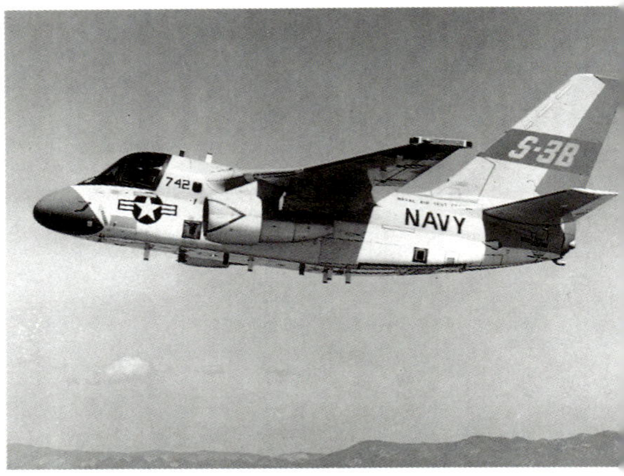

3

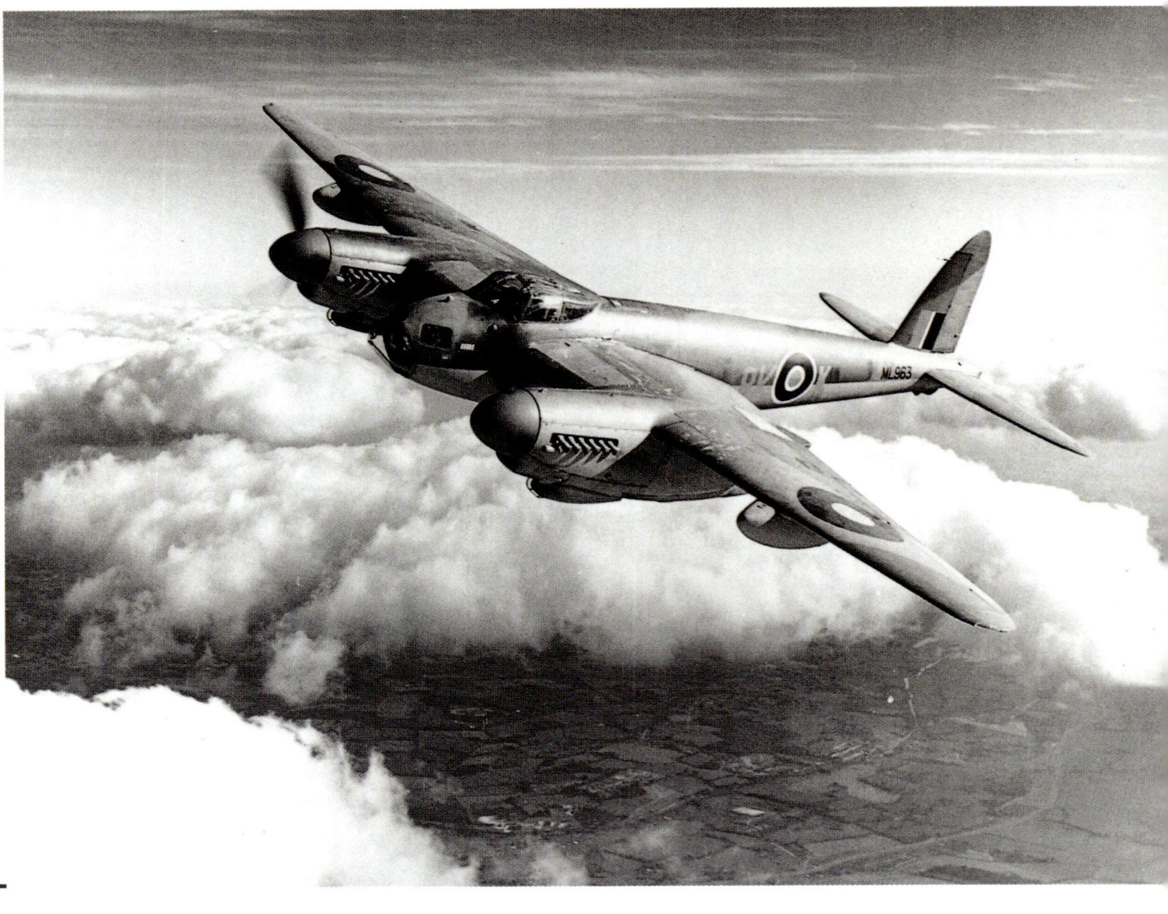

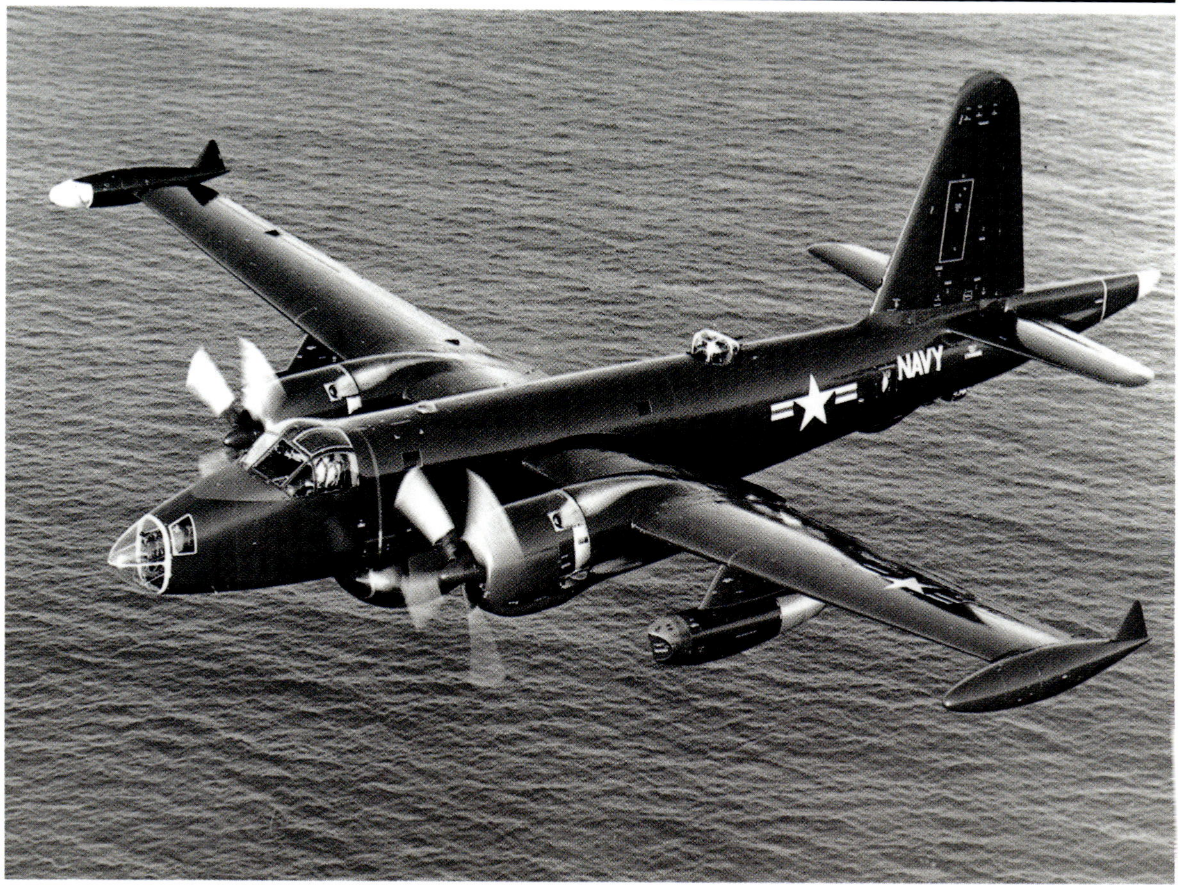

11

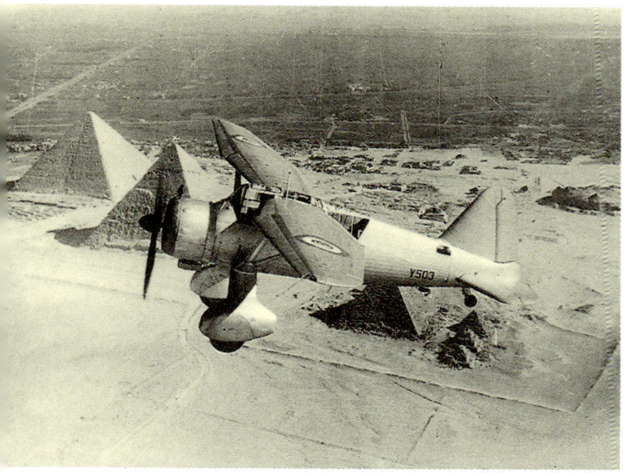
6

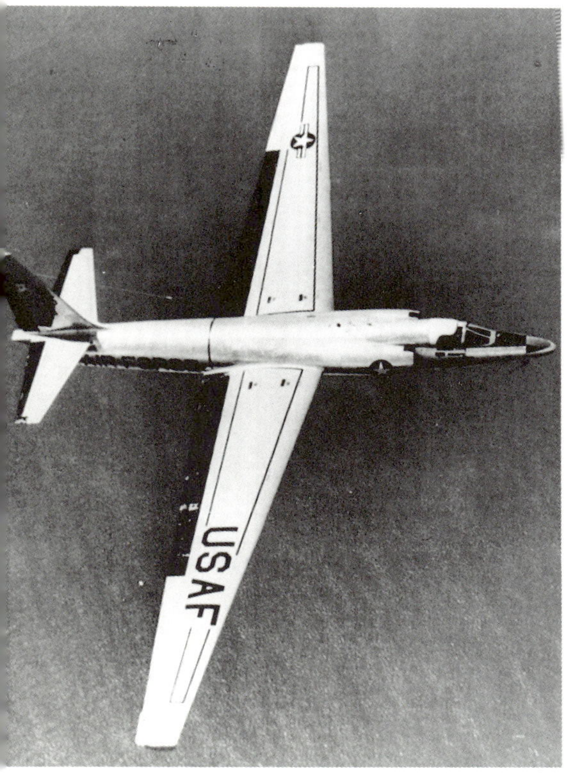

7

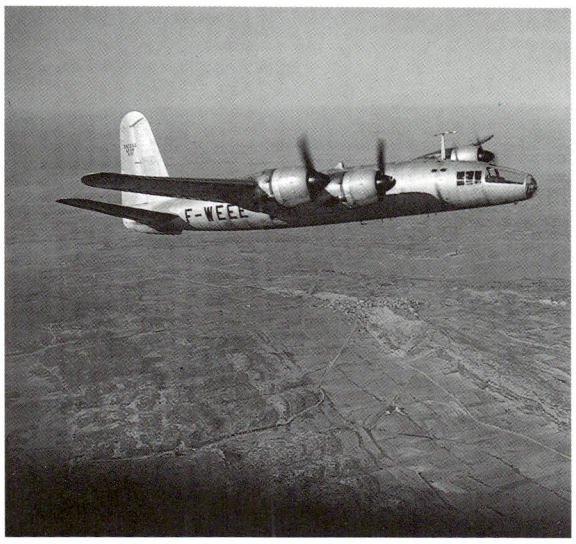

9

Photo Nos. 1 and 3: de Havilland Mosquito (Great Britain)
Photo No. 2: Grumman OV-1 Mohawk (USA)
Photo Nos. 4 and 6: Westland Lysander (Great Britain)
Photo No. 5: Lockheed S-3 (USA)
Photo No. 7: Lockheed U-2 (USA)
Photo No. 8: Grumman S-2 Tracker (USA)
Photo No. 9: SE.1010 (France)
Photo No. 10: Avro Shackleton (Great Britain)
Photo No. 11: Lockheed P-2H (previously P2V) Neptune (USA)

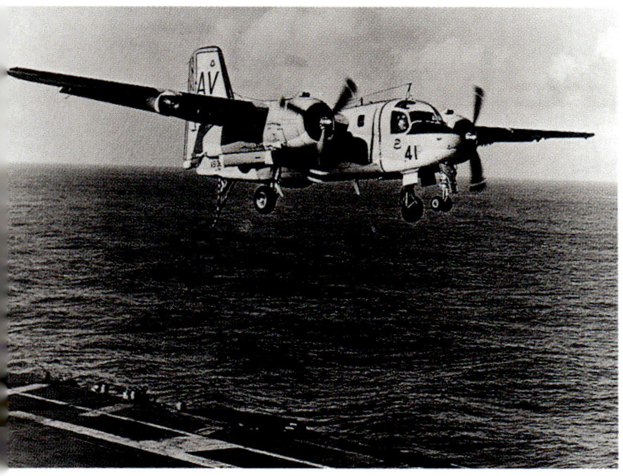
8

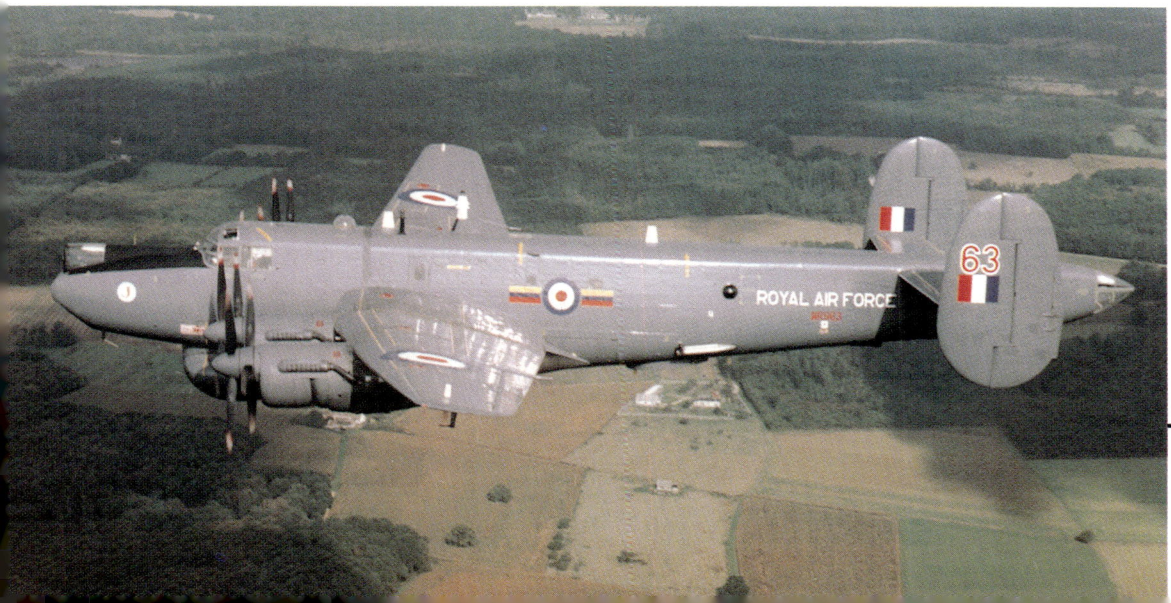

10

3

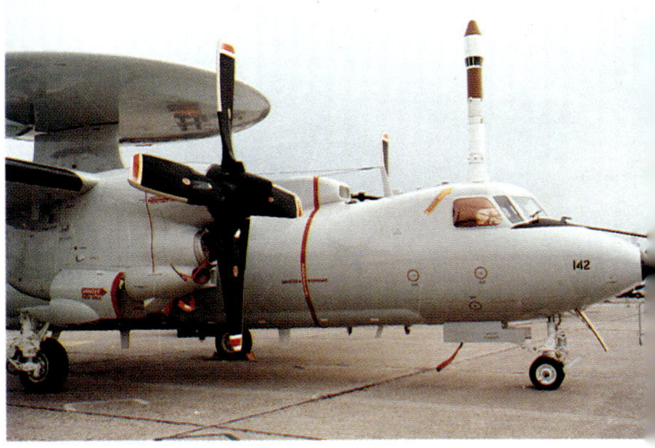

RECONNAISSANCE, OBSERVATION AND MARITIME PATROL AIRCRAFT

In 1959, French carriers were equipped with a three-man aircraft designed for anti-submarine warfare, the Breguet Br 1050 Alizé, which is still in service. Powered by a single turboprop engine, the Alizé can fly at over 285 mph (460 kph) and remain airborne for more than five hours. It carries missiles, depth charges or a torpedo.

Meanwhile, in the early 1960s Grumman developed the carrier-based E-2 Hawkeye, the first advanced airborne early warning aircraft equipped with a rotating radar dish. Powered by twin turboprop engines, the Hawkeye flies at 375 mph (600 kph) and has a range of over 1,680 miles (2,700 km). More sophisticated is the Boeing E-3 Sentry, an airborne warning and control system (AWACS) aircraft. The Sentry is simply a 707 fitted with an enormous, long-range (190 miles/300 km) radar dish. It flies at 400 mph (644 kph) and can remain aloft for up to 12 hours. It is also in service with the British and French. To replace the Neptune, in 1960 the US Navy took delivery of the Lockheed P-3 Orion, a maritime patrol and anti-submarine aircraft. Powered by four turboprop engines, the Orion flies at speeds in excess of 400 mph (644 kph) and has a range of over 4,800 miles (7,700 km). Its armament consists of depth charges and other weaponry, or it can carry four torpedoes. The Orion has been modernised four times – in 1975, 1976, 1984 and 1990 – in order to accommodate new detection systems and weapons.

In 1965, the French navy replaced its Neptunes with the Breguet Br 1150 Atlantic, a twin-engined turboprop with a maximum speed of over 400 mph (650 kph), able to stay on patrol for 18 hours. The Atlantic carries an armament of torpedoes, bombs or missiles.

The British used the airframe of the Comet to create their maritime patrol aircraft, the Hawker Siddeley Nimrod. Commissioned in 1967, the four-engined Nimrod has a maximum speed of over 560 mph (900 kph) and can remain airborne for up to 15 hours. It carries torpedoes, mines and depth charges.

Successor to the U-2, the Lockheed SR-71 Blackbird is a two-seater with twin jet engines. Constructed of a special alloy, this strategic reconnaissance aircraft is extraordinarily fast (over 2,000 mph/3,200 kph). It has a ceiling of 82,000

1

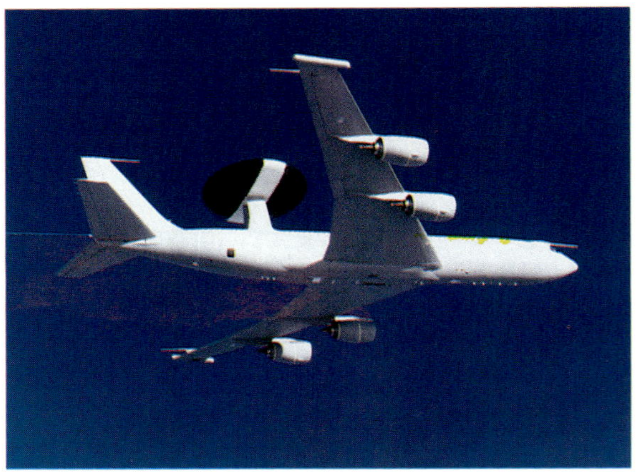

4

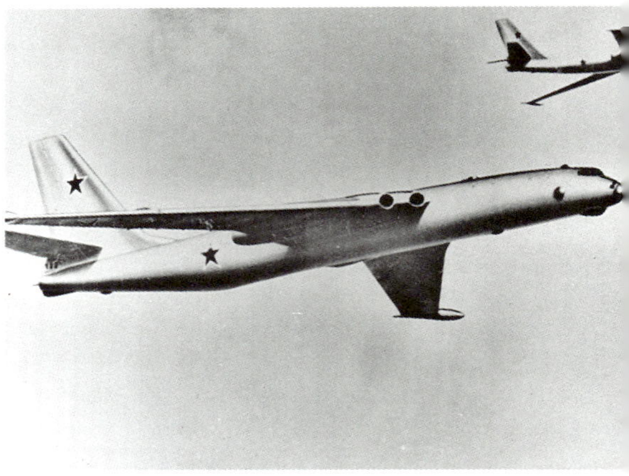

2

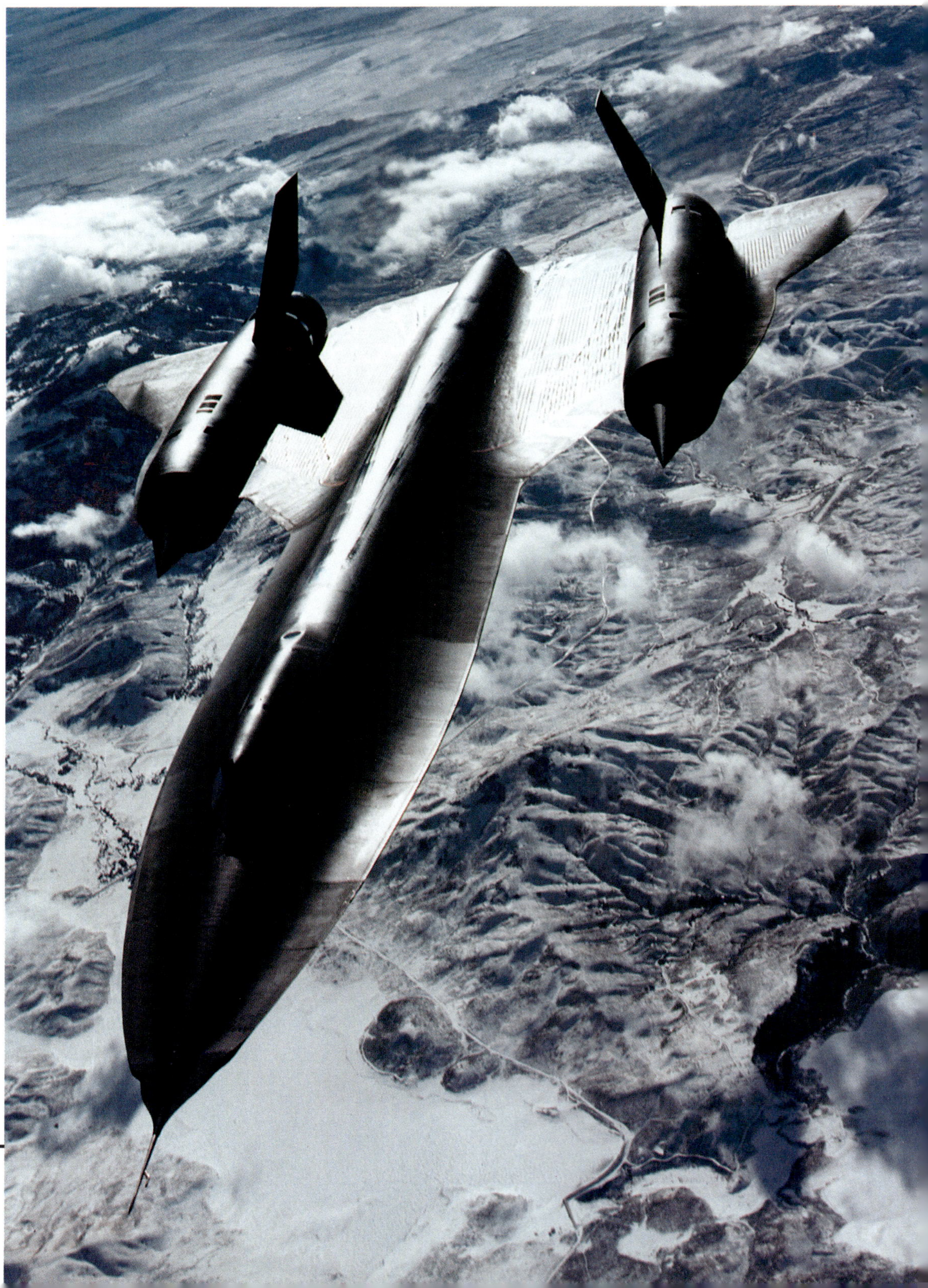

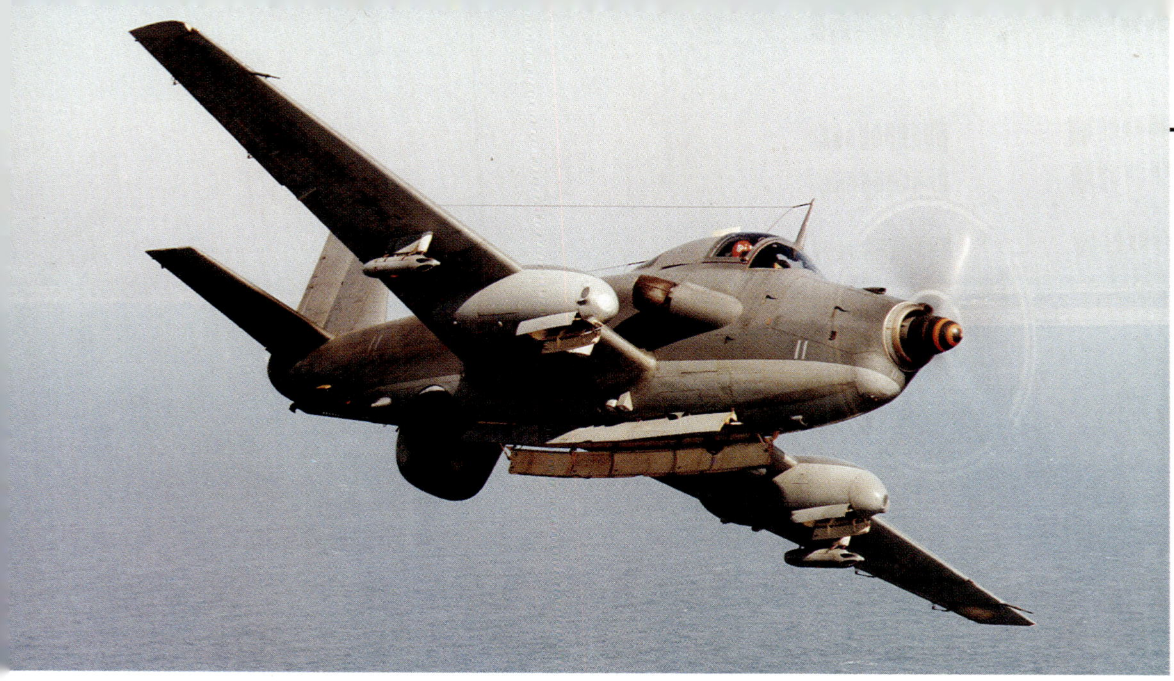

9

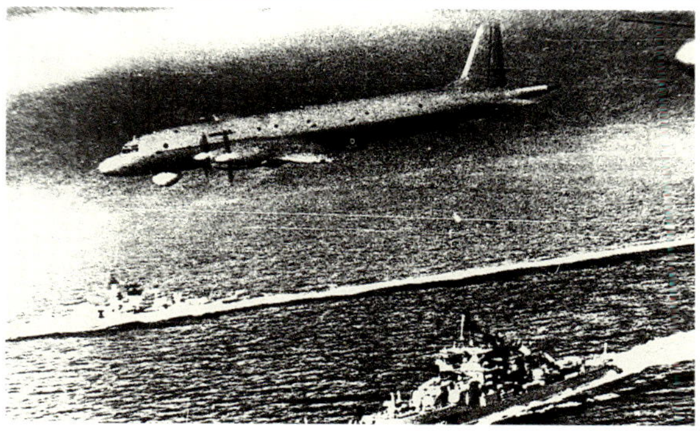

13

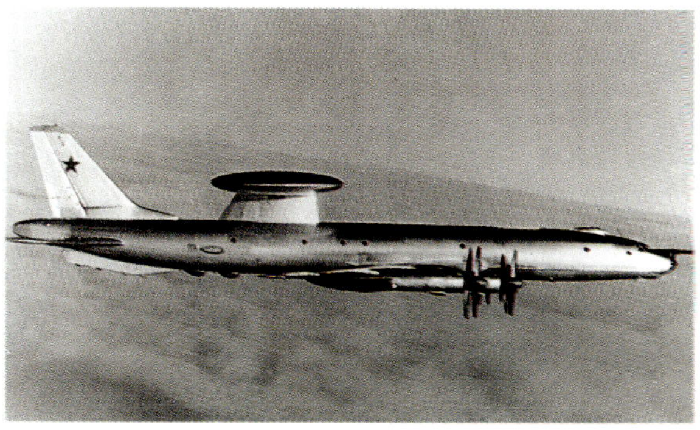

14

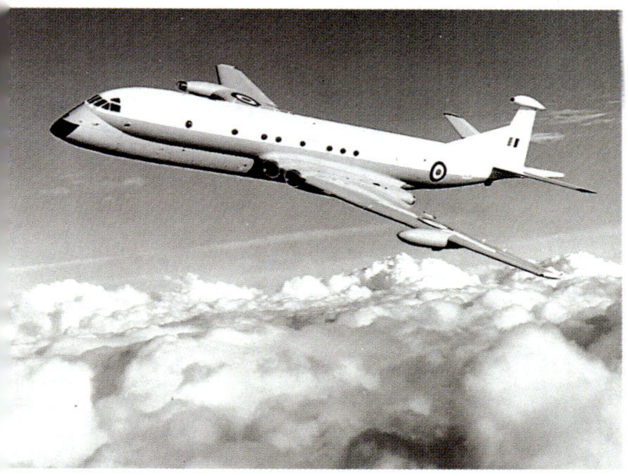

5

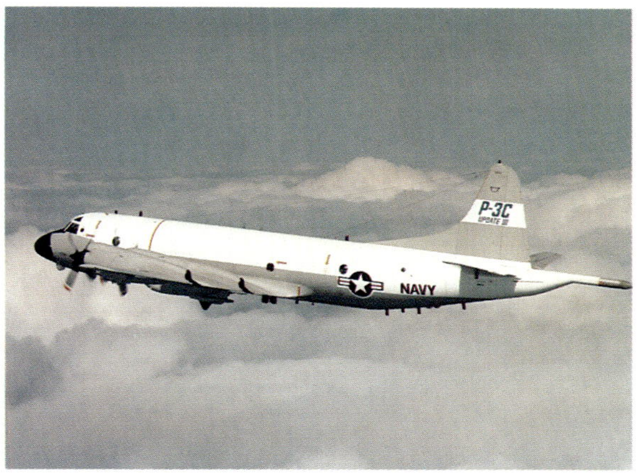

10

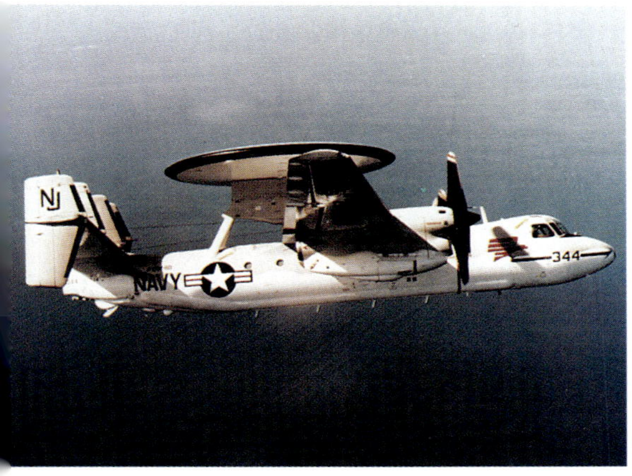

6

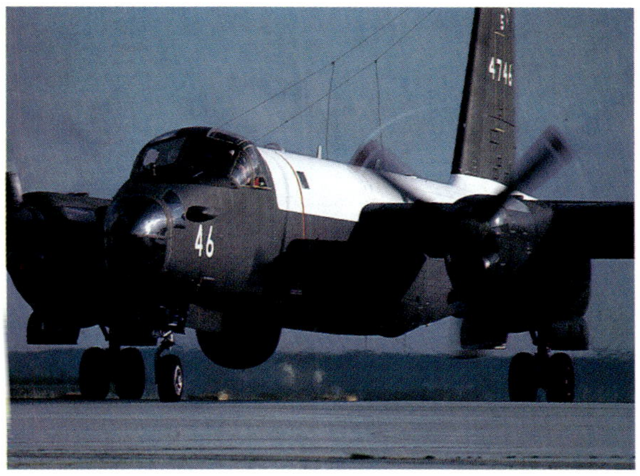

11

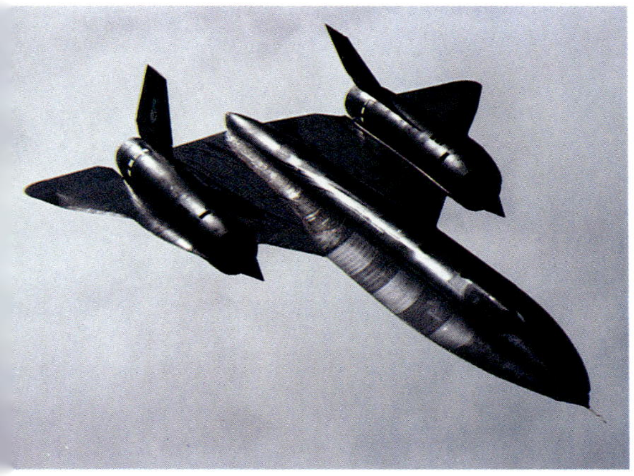

7

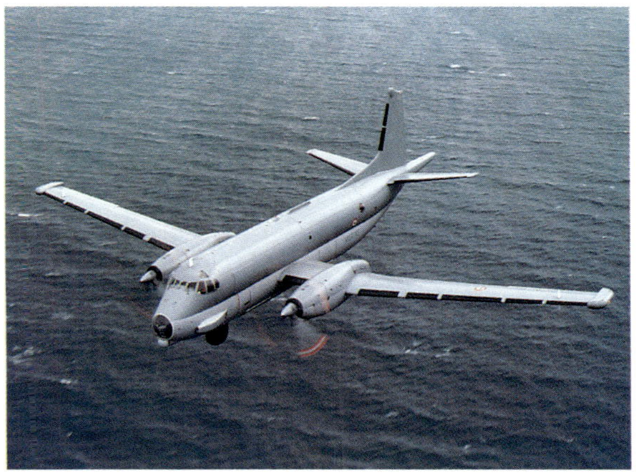

12

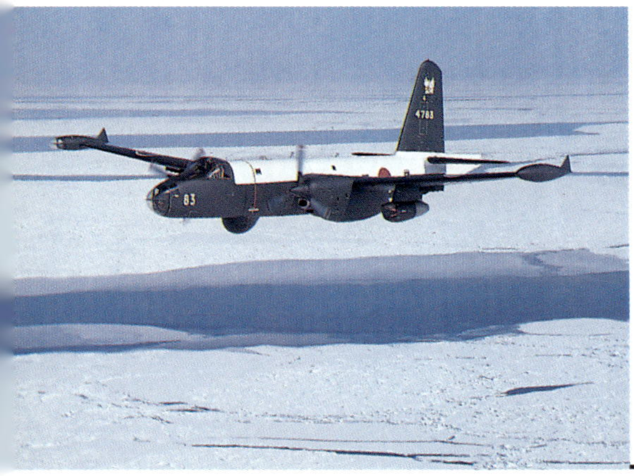

8

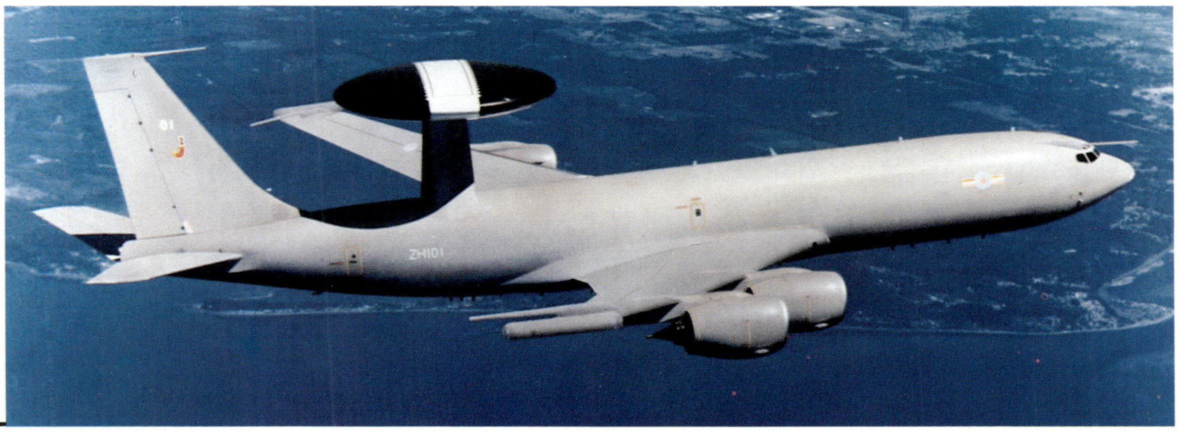

15

ft (25,000 m) and a range of 3,000 miles (4,800 km). On the Soviet side, the Myasishchev M-4 is an enormous bomber, originally commissioned in 1953, con-verted for strategic reconnaissance purposes. Powered by four jet engines, it flies at 560 mph (900 kph) and has a range of 6,900 miles (11,000 km). The more recent (1970) Ilyushin Il-38, is a reconnaissance aircraft derived from the Il-18 transport plane. It flies at over 430 mph (700 kph), patrolling the seas with an armament of torpedoes, mines and depth charges.

Meanwhile, the AWACS-type Tupolev Tu-126 (shown on page 45) appeared in 1967. It carries a large rotating radar dish above the fuselage. Powered by four turboprop engines, the Tu-126 flies at up to 400 mph (644 kph) and can stay on patrol for up to 18 hours.

Photo Nos. 1 and 15: Boeing E-3A Sentry (USA)
Photo Nos. 2 and 7: Lockheed SR-71A Blackbird (USA)
Photo Nos. 3 and 6: Grumman E-2 Hawkeye (USA)
Photo No. 4: Myasishchev M-4 (USSR)
Photo No. 5: Hawker Siddeley Nimrod (Great Britain)
Photo Nos. 8 and 11: Kawasaki P-2J, the Japanese version of the Lockheed Neptune
Photo No. 9: Breguet Br 1050 Alizé (France)
Photo No. 10: Lockheed P-3C Orion (USA)
Photo No. 12: Breguet Br 1150 Atlantic (France)
Photo No. 13: Ilyushin Il-38 (USSR)
Photo No. 14: Tupolev Tu-126 (USSR)

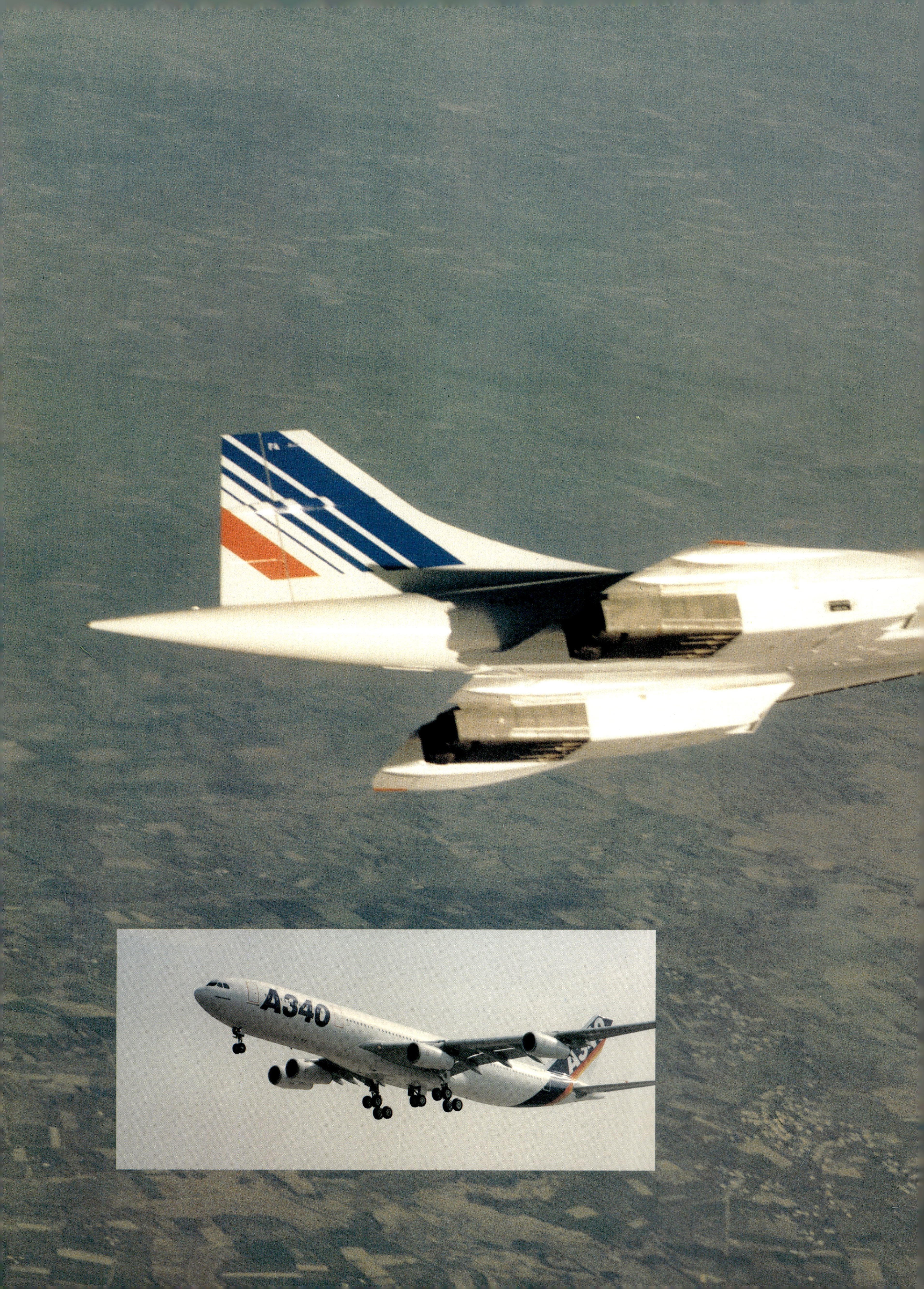
A340

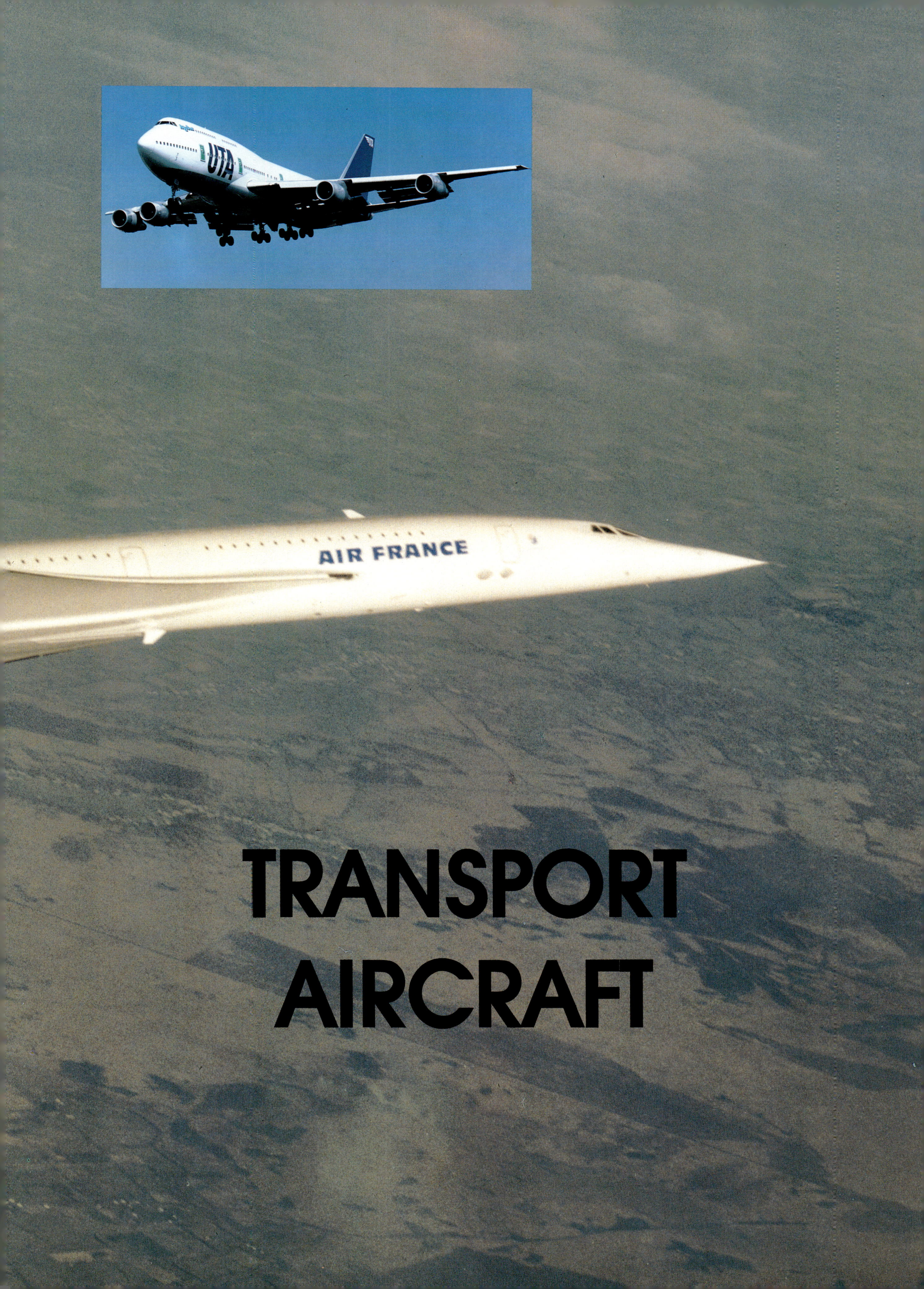

TRANSPORT AIRCRAFT

4
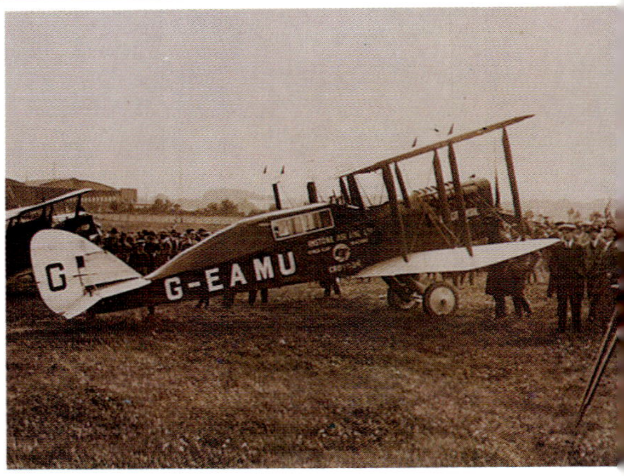

COMMERCIAL AIRLINERS

Commercial aviation began in 1919, when former bombers were converted for passenger transport. In France, for instance, the Breguet Br 14T, with a range of 290 miles (460 km), could carry two passengers at speeds of 80 mph (125 kph). The Airco DH.4A also had space for two passengers, but could fly slightly faster, at 120 mph (195 kph). The Farman F.60 Goliath biplane was more what one would expect of an airliner. Powered by two engines, it carried 12 passengers at 75 mph (120 kph) over distances of 250 miles (400 km). In 1920, the former Spad fighter was adapted to transport six passengers up to 250 miles (400 km), becoming the Blériot Spad 33. It was followed in 1921 by the more powerful Spad 46 and, in 1923, the Spad 56.

In Germany, the first air transport companies used the A.E.G. J II, a former combat aircraft with space for two passengers and a range of 350 miles (565 km). But already constructors were working on specially designed aircraft, and the new airlines soon had a range of planes to choose from. Fokker sold his F.II to the newly established KLM, then in 1921 brought out the F.III, which could carry five passengers for distances of 425 miles (680 km) and at speeds of 85 mph (135 kph). His T-2, built in the USA, was less successful, though it could transport 10 passengers at nearly 100 mph (155 kph). Three years later, Fokker unveiled the F.VII, which was used to link Amsterdam with the Dutch East Indies. A three-engined high-wing aircraft, the F.VII/3m flew at 100 mph (155 kph) and carried its eight passengers in stages of over 690 miles (1,100 km).

The French constructor Blériot had opted for a four-engined biplane design, the 135, which Air Union operated on the Paris-London route from 1924 to 1926. It carried 10 passengers at 85 mph (135 kph) and had a range of 375 miles (600 km). The Potez 25, commissioned in 1925, was used by Aéropostale for ferrying mail. With a two-man crew, it carried 660 lb (300 kg) of cargo at 105 mph (170 kph) over distances of 310 miles (500 km).

The Dewoitine D.33, a single-engined low-wing monoplane with a fixed undercarriage, which first flew in 1930 as a long-range record-breaker, led to the later development of the three-engined D.332.

In Germany, Hugo Junkers was one of the apostles of "all-metal" construction. In 1919, he built a revolutionary low-wing monoplane, the Junkers F 13. It flew distances of over 340 miles (550 miles) at 90 mph (140 kph), and the four passengers were accommodated in an enclosed cabin. From the F 13 was derived a three-engined aircraft of similar design, the G 24, which could carry nine passengers on journeys of 800 miles (1,300 km) at over 110 mph (180 kph).

1
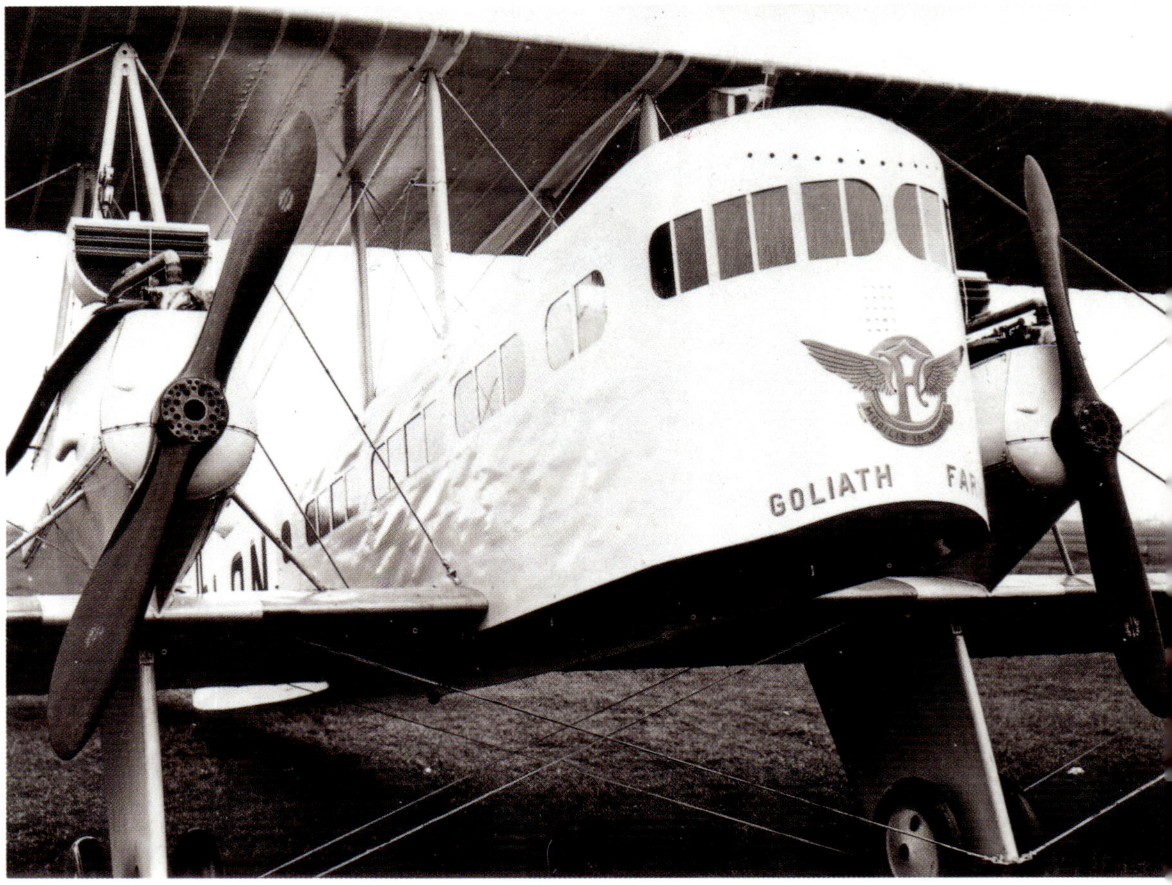

2
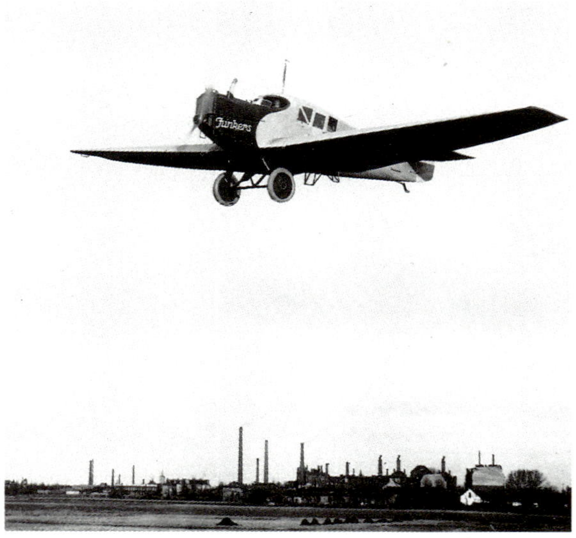

5
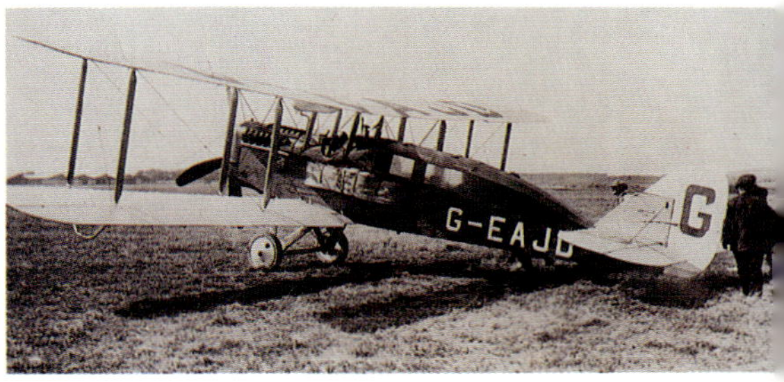

6
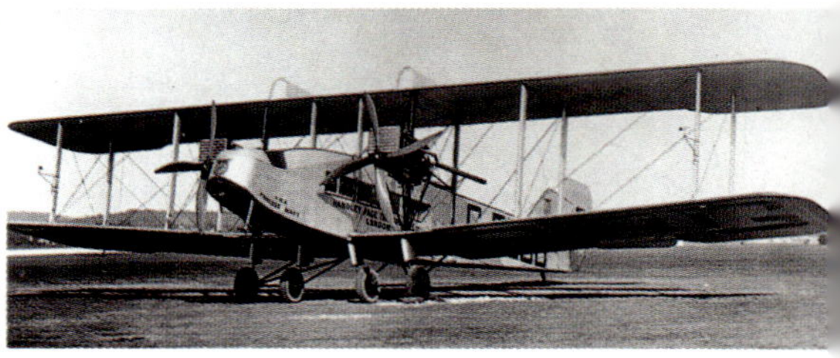

3
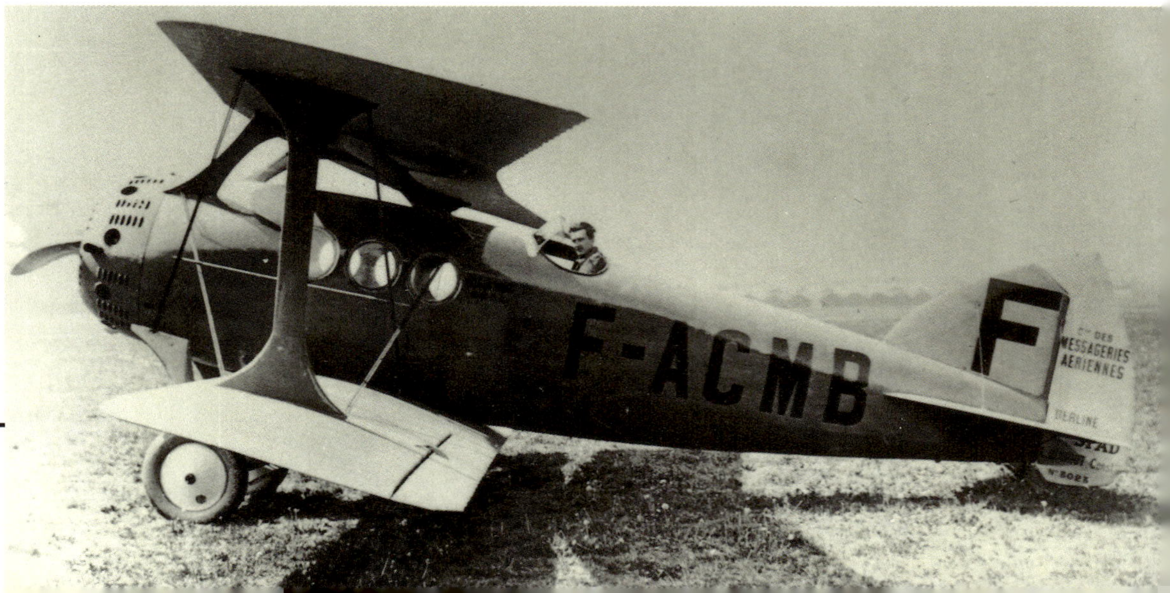

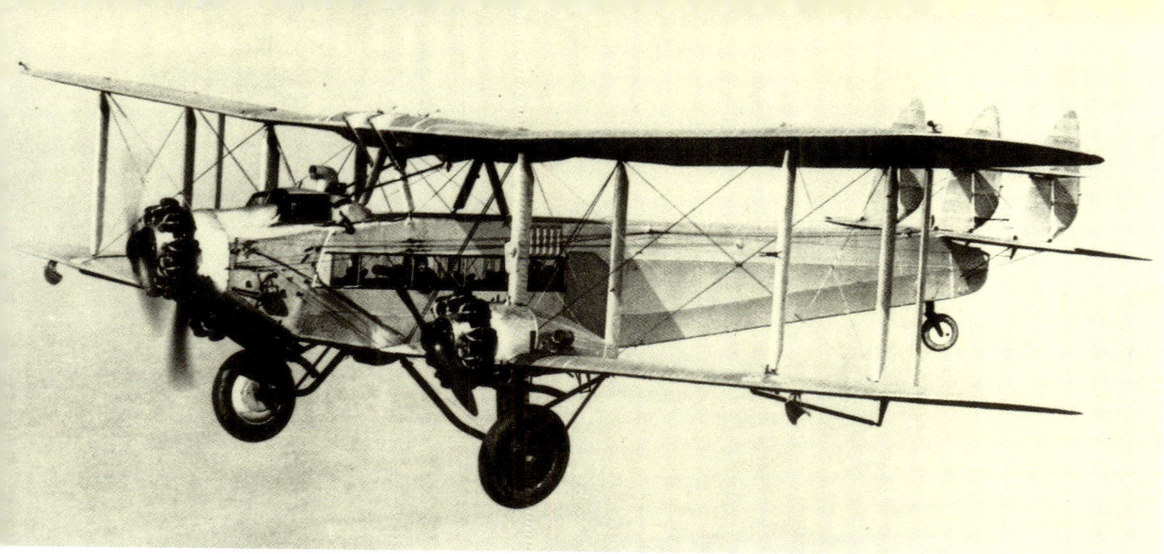

11

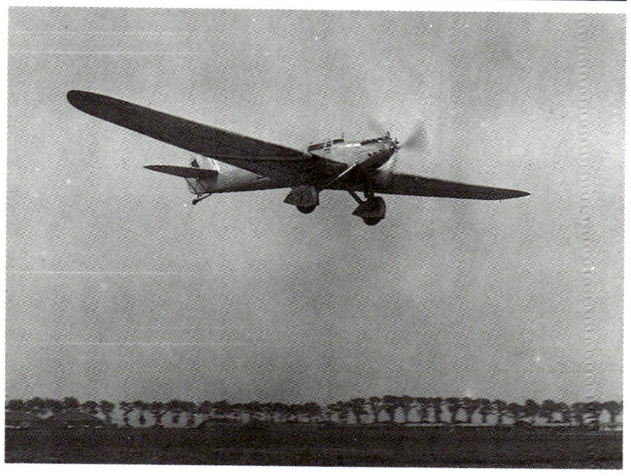

16

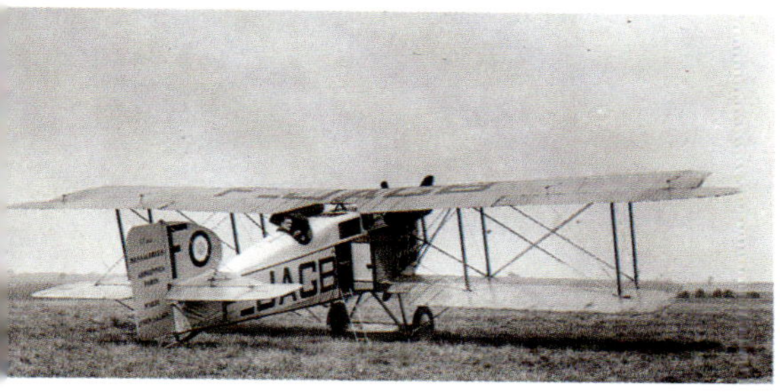

7

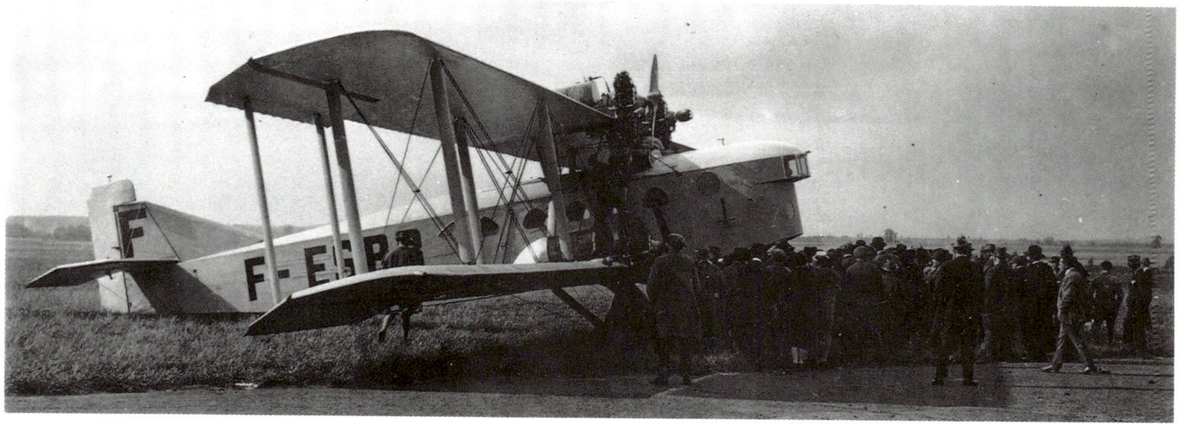

17

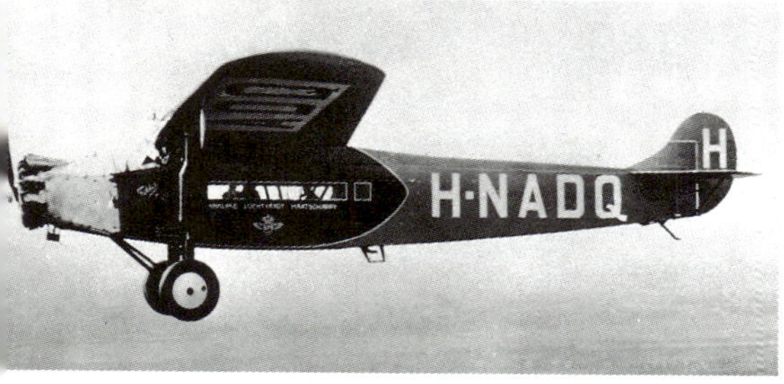

8

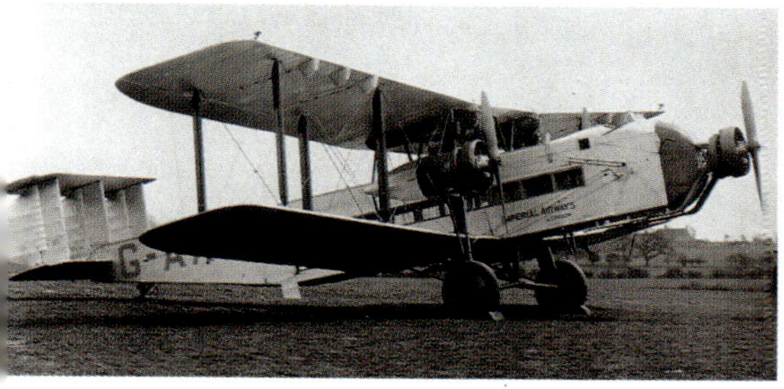

9

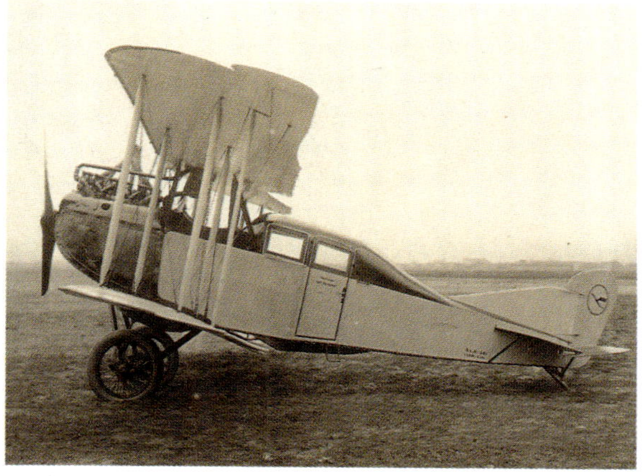

12

In 1922, the British constructor Handley Page brought out the W8b, a powerful twin-engined biplane, which was used to ferry 12 passengers to the continent. It flew at 90 mph (145 kph) and had a range of 400 miles (640 km). In 1926, the newly formed Imperial Airways took delivery of two three-engined biplanes. The Armstrong Whitworth Argosy (20 passengers, 90 mph/145 kph, 400 miles/659 km) was used on its shorter European routes, while the de Havilland D.H.66 Hercules (seven passengers, 110 mph/180 kph), made the long haul to India.

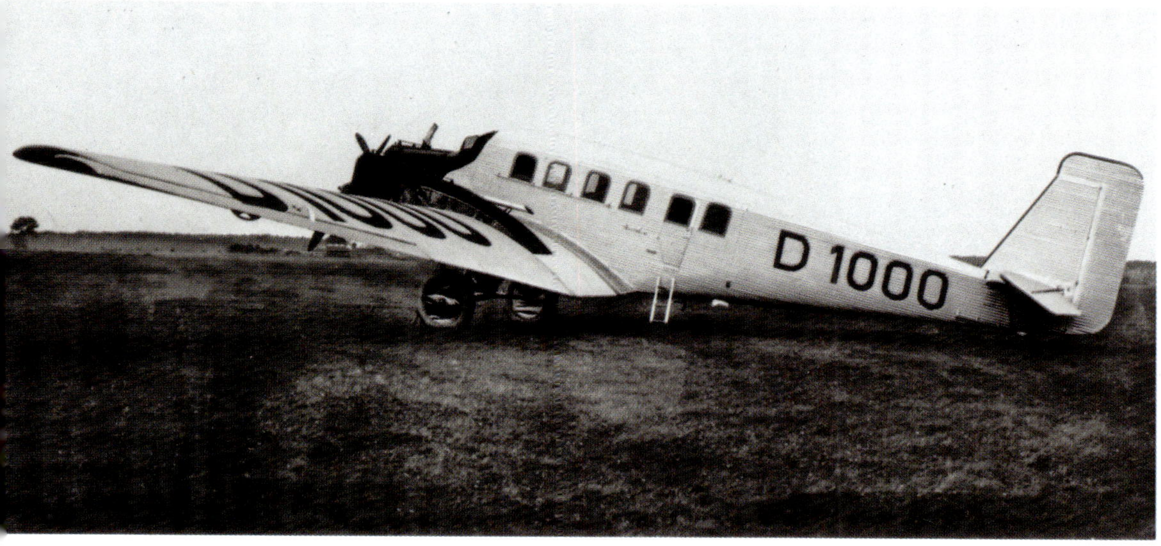

13

Photo Nos. 1, 10 and 15: Farman F.60 Goliath (France)
Photo No. 2: Junkers F 13 (Germany)
Photo No. 3: Blériot Spad 33 (France)
Photo Nos. 4 and 5: Airco DH.4A (Great Britain)
Photo No. 6: Handley Page W8b (Great Britain)
Photo No. 7: Breguet Br 14 T (France)
Photo No. 8: Fokker F.VIIa (Netherlands)
Photo No. 9: Armstrong Whitworth Argosy (Great Britain)
Photo No. 11: de Havilland D.H.66 Hercules (Great Britain)
Photo No. 12: A.E.G. J II (Germany)
Photo No. 13: Junkers G 24 (Germany)
Photo No. 14: Fokker F.III (Netherlands)
Photo No. 16: Dewoitine D.33 (France)
Photo No. 17: Blériot 135 (France)
Photo No. 18: Fokker F.II prototype (Netherlands)

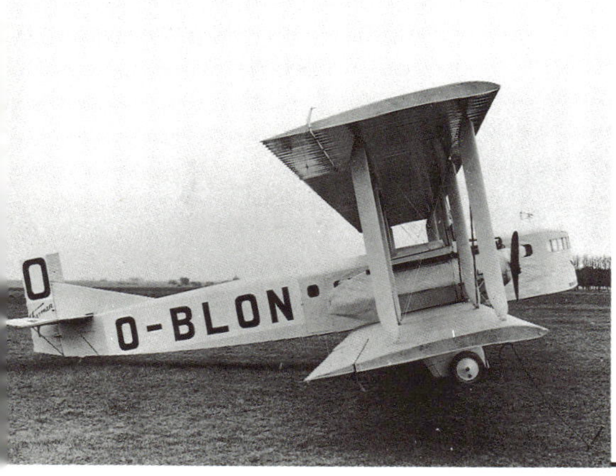

10

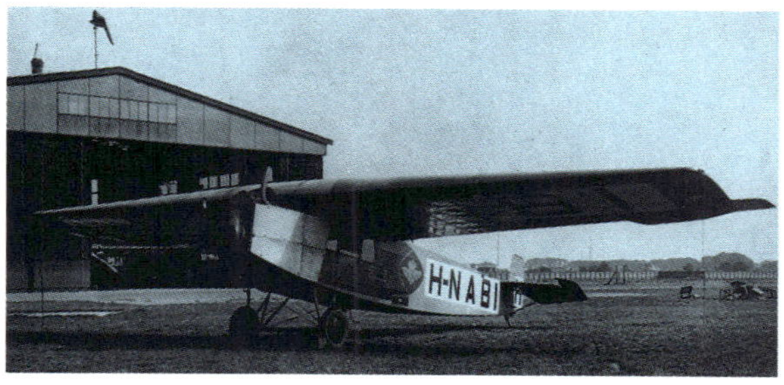

14

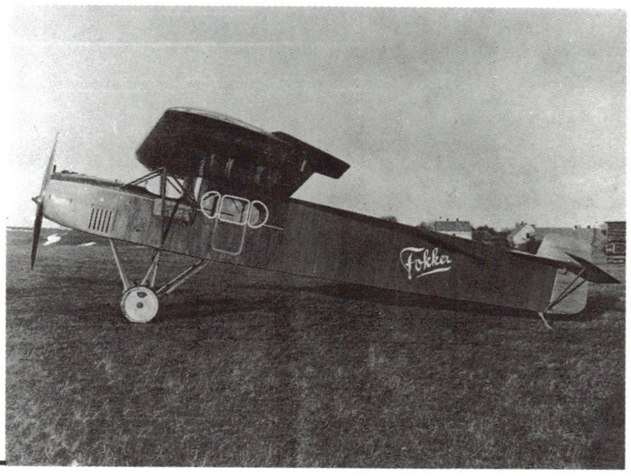

18

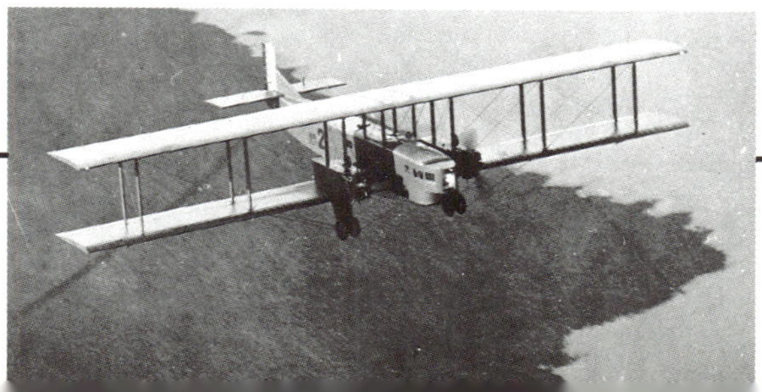

15

5
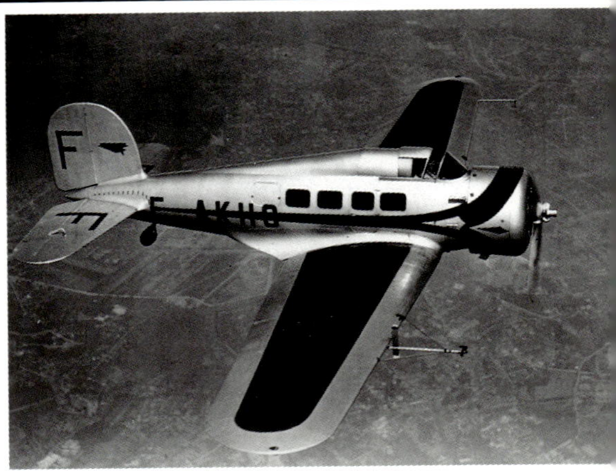

COMMERCIAL AIRLINERS

The 1920s were a fertile period for civil aviation as the race to set up worldwide services began. On European routes, comfort began to be a consideration. For instance, meals were served on the luxurious Lioré et Olivier LeO 213 "Rayon d'or", a twin-engined French biplane which cruised at 110 mph (175 kph) and carried 12 passengers on journeys of up to 350 miles (560 km). In 1929, Aéropostale brought into service the Latécoère 28, a high-winged monoplane whose single engine enabled it to transport 660 lb (300 kg) of cargo over distances of 2,000 miles (3,200 km).

1
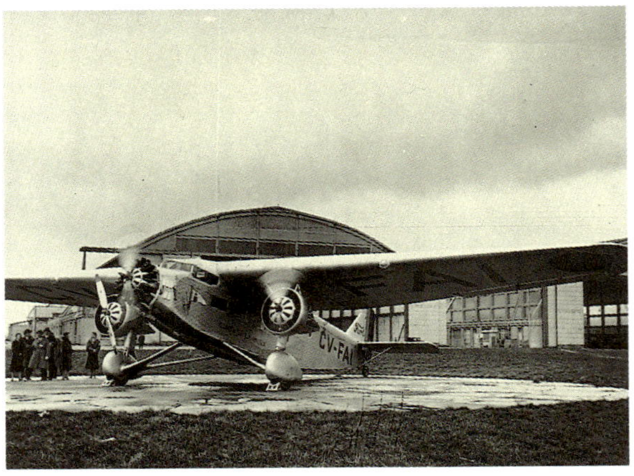

6
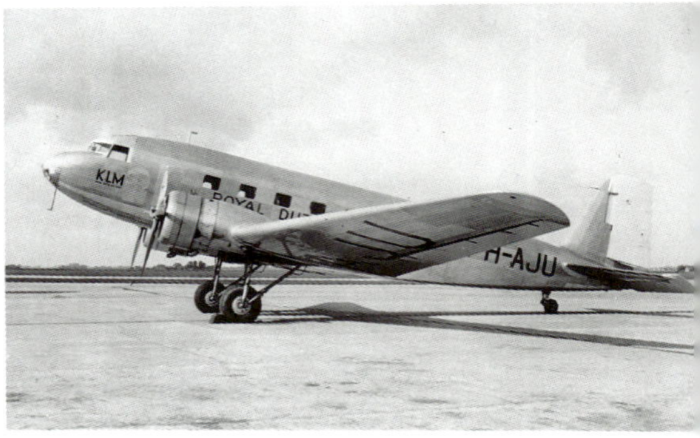

In 1928, the Dutch constructor Anthony Fokker produced a new version of his three-engined F.VII/3m. Commercially, the F.VIIb was a great success, transporting 10 passengers at a cruising speed of 125 mph (200 kph), with a range of 750 miles (1,200 km).

2
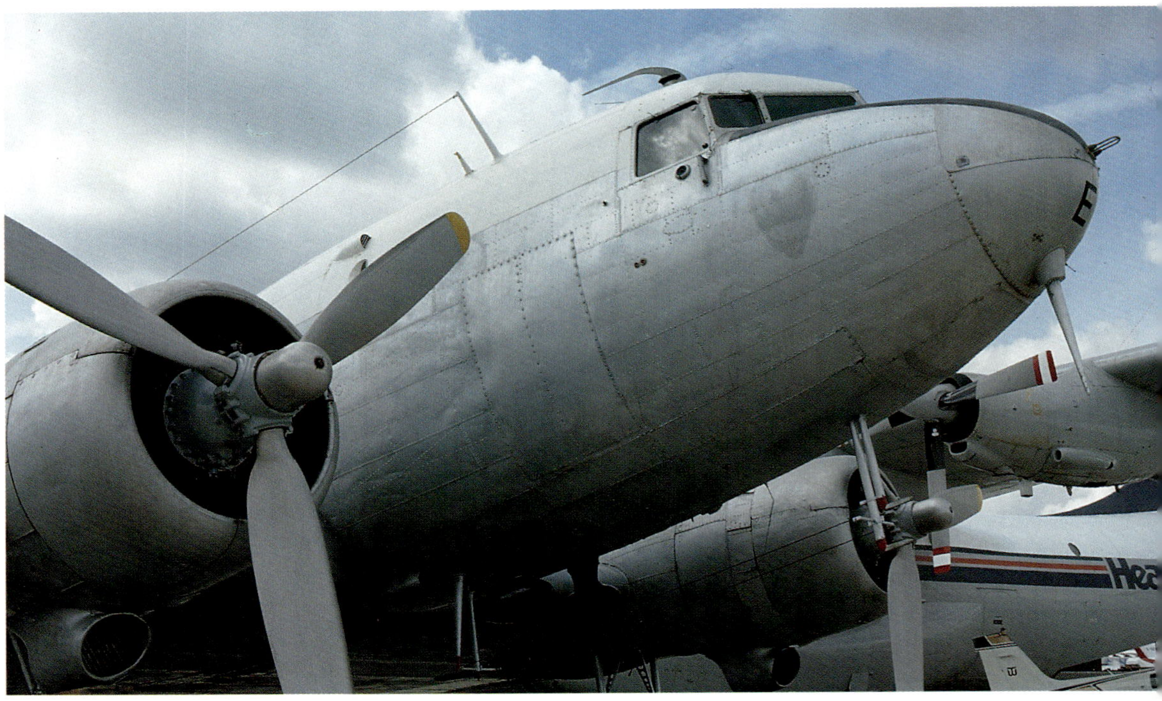

In Germany, one of the first planes manufactured by Focke-Wulf, the A 16, made its debut in 1927. Propelled by a single engine, this high-wing monoplane flew at 104 mph (165 kph), carrying eight passengers on journeys of up to 500 miles (800 km). In 1932, Hugo Junkers unveiled his celebrated Ju 52/3m. A three-engined, all-metal aircraft with a range of 568 miles (900 km), it cruised at 152 mph (250 kph) with 17 passengers on board.

In Britain, Imperial Airways updated its fleet in 1931, taking delivery of eight Handley Page H.P.42 biplanes. Powered by four engines, they could carry between 24 and 40 passengers at 100 mph (160 kph) on routes in Europe and the Middle East. In 1933, de Havilland began marketing a small, twin-engined biplane, the D.H. 84 Dragon, followed by a four-engined version, the D.H. 86 Express. Cruising at 143 mph (233 kph), the D.H. 86 carried 10 passengers over distances of 760 miles (1,220 km).

3
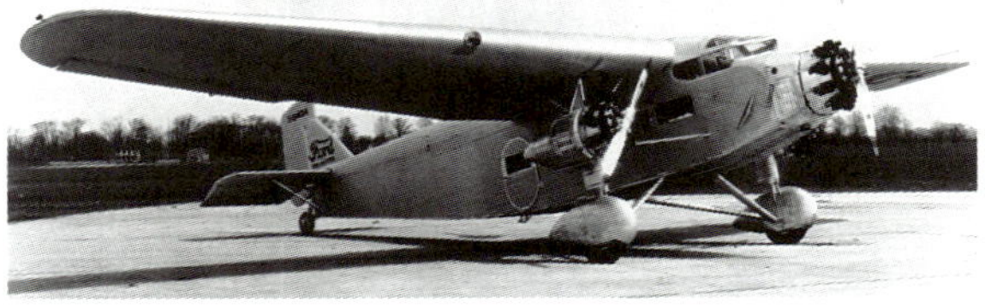

7
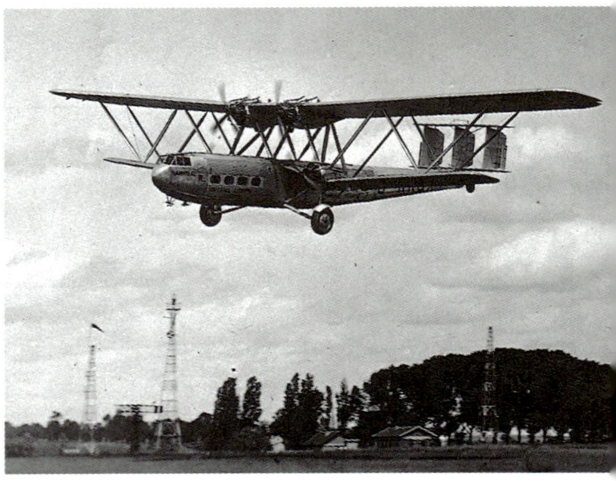

In the United States, Ford entered the aviation field in 1926 and later built the 4AT Trimotor. A high-wing monoplane of metal construction, it became famous as the "Tin Goose". Powered by its three engines, it carried 14 passengers at 107 mph (170 kph) and had a range of 570 miles (900 km).

4
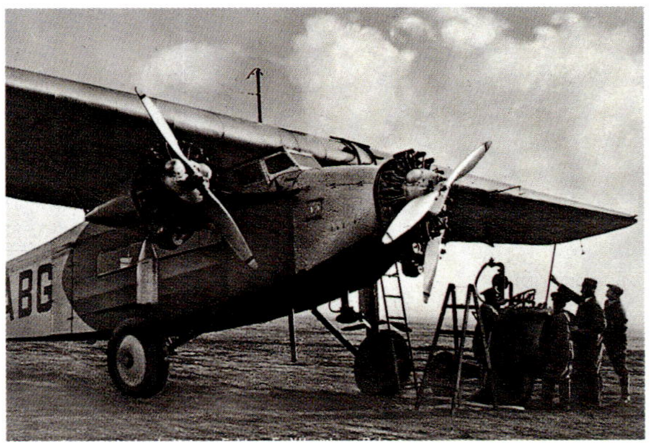

The Lockheed company produced a high-speed aircraft, the Vega, in 1927. Their next effort was the Orion, a single-engined monoplane with retractable undercarriage, which made its debut in 1931. Carrying four passengers, it could cover a distance of 560 miles (900 km) at 191 mph (300 kph).

8
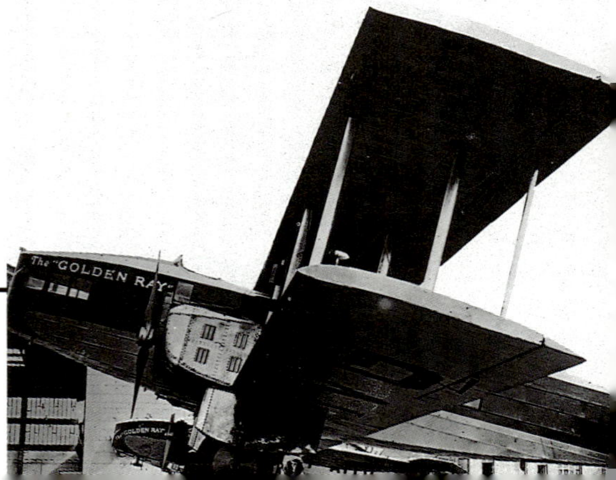

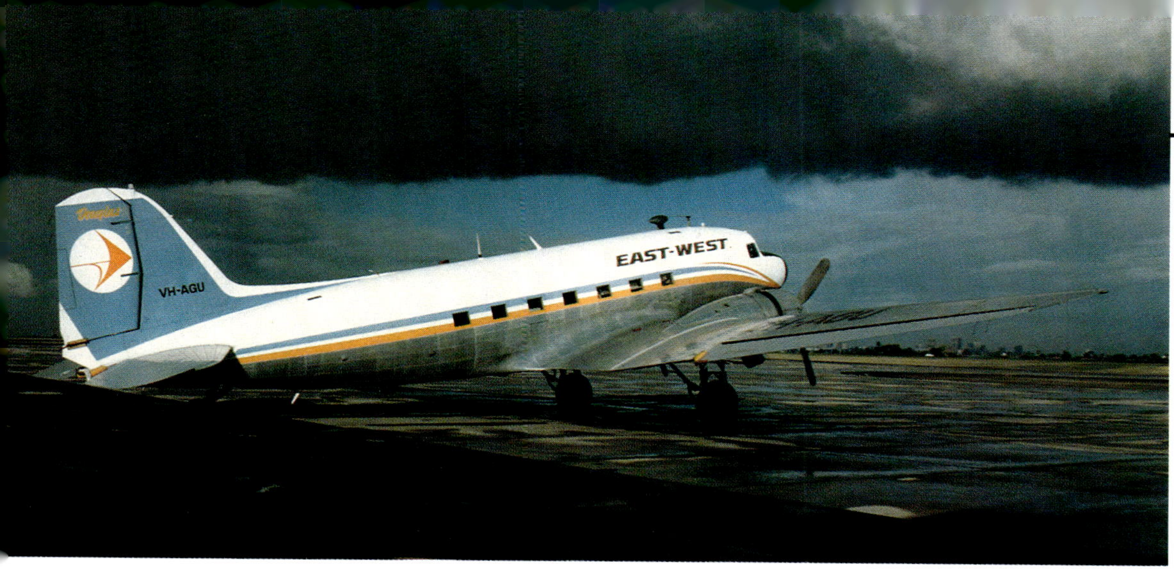

12

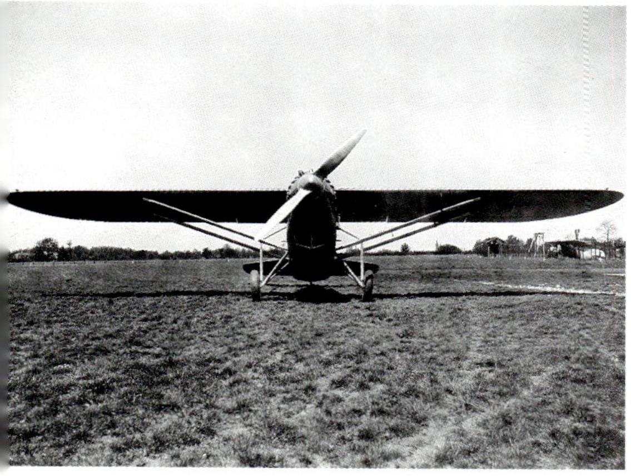

9

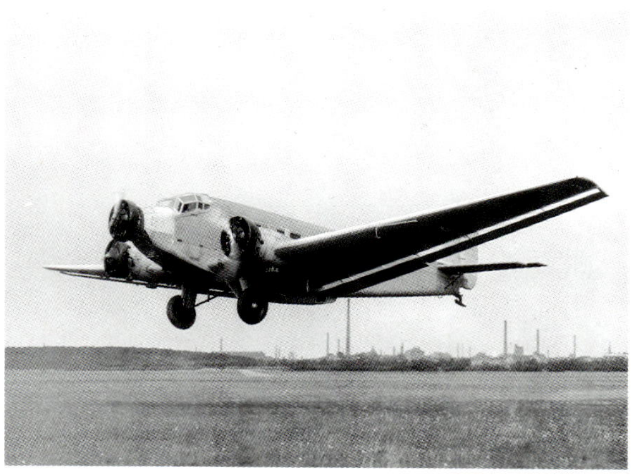

13 Soon came the famous Douglases. Following the prototype DC-1, the DC-2 was built for TWA in 1934. A low-wing, twin-engined aircraft with retractable undercarriage, the DC-2 had a range of 1,200 miles (1,930 km), carrying 14 passengers at a cruising speed of 170 mph (270 kph). The bigger and more powerful DC-3 was introduced two years later. It cruised at 180 mph (290 kph) over distances of 1,300 miles (2,100 km) with 21 (later up to 32) passengers aboard. Eventually, over 10,000 DC-3s were built, some of which are still in airline service.

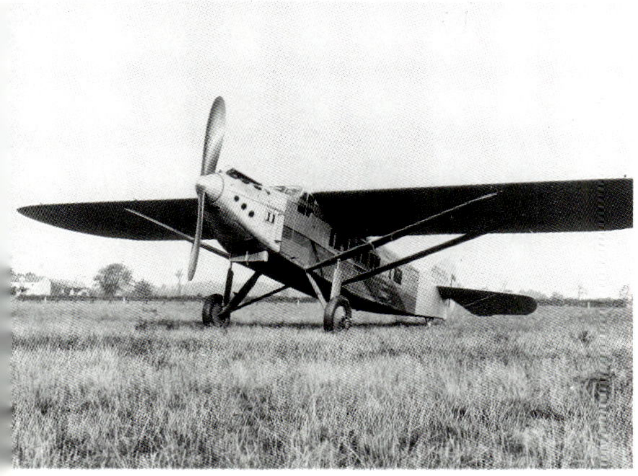

10

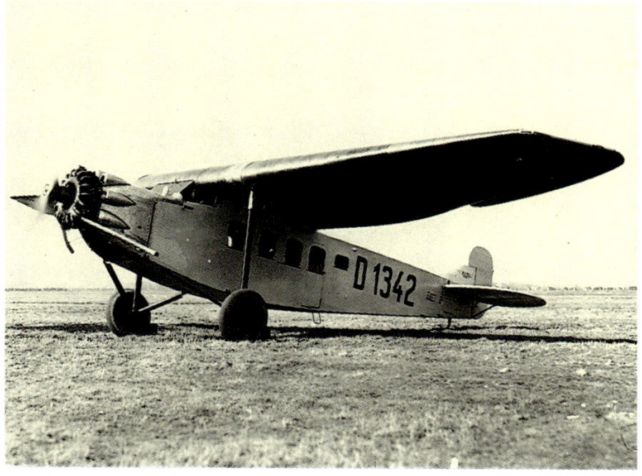

14

Photo Nos. 1 and 3: Ford Trimotor "Tin Goose" (USA)
Photo Nos. 2, 12 and 15: Douglas DC-3 (USA)
Photo No. 4: Fokker F.VII/3m (Netherlands)
Photo No. 5: Lockheed Orion (USA)
Photo Nos. 6 and 11: Douglas DC-2 (USA)
Photo Nos. 7 and 17: Handley Page H.P. 42 (Great Britain)
Photo No. 8: Lioré et Olivier LeO 213 (France)
Photo Nos. 9 and 10: Latécoère 28 (France)
Photo No. 13: Junkers Ju 52/3m (Germany)
Photo No. 14: Focke-Wulf A 17A (Germany)
Photo No. 16: de Havilland D.H. 86A (Great Britain)

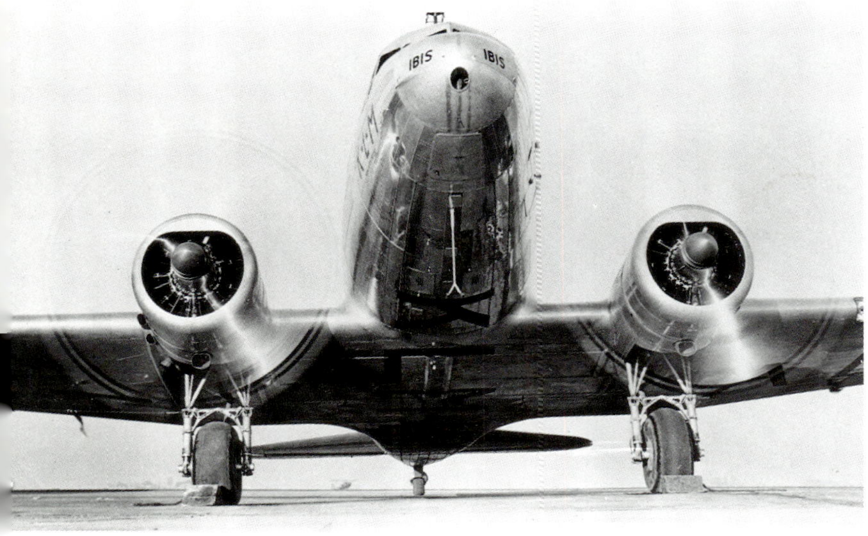

15

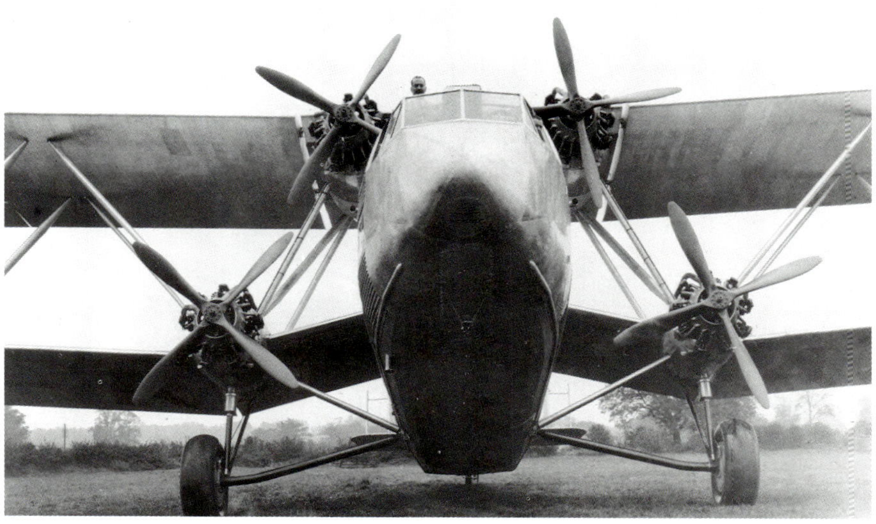

17

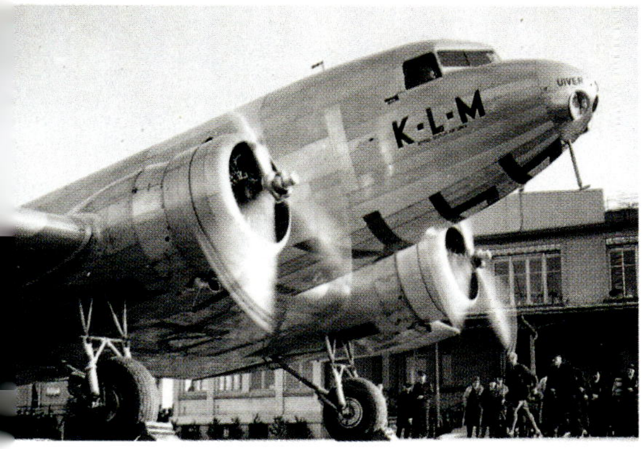

11

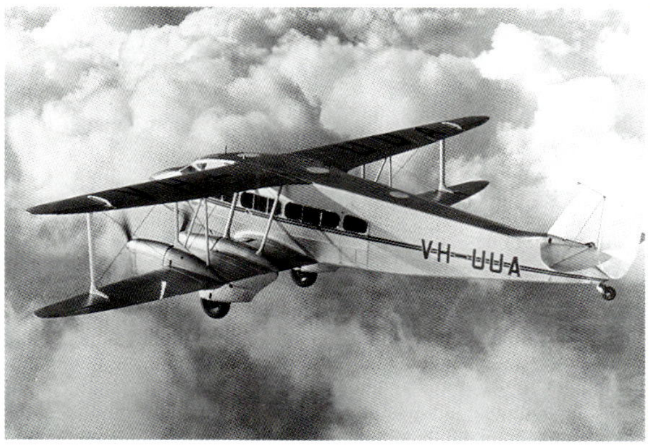

16

COMMERCIAL AIRLINERS

In 1931 – before the DC-3 began its long and illustrious career – Douglas's closest competitor, Boeing, had launched a single-engined, low-wing monoplane with retractable undercarriage. The 221 Monomail, which could carry eight passengers over 540 miles (870 km) at 137 mph (220 kph), was the aircraft which spurred Douglas to build the DC-1, the Boeing 247. This twin-engined monoplane, also with retractable undercarriage, made its debut in 1933, commissioned by United Airlines. With 10 passengers on board, it cruised at 155 mph (250 kph) and had a range of 485 miles (780 km).

Lockheed made the switch from single to twin-engined aircraft in 1934. The retractable-undercarriage 10A Electra had a range of 850 miles (1,370 km) and could carry 12 passengers at speeds of 200 mph (330 kph). It developed into the Model 14 and, in 1940, the Lodestar. The Lodestar flew at 250 mph (400 kph), carrying 17 passengers on journeys of up to 1,600 miles (2,550 km).

Meanwhile, Northrop had built its last single-engined airliner, the Delta, which cruised at 200 mph (320 kph) and could carry seven passengers up to 1,900 miles (3,100 km). In Italy, after specializing in seaplanes, in 1932 SIAI-Marchetti produced a land-based aircraft. The three-engined, high-wing S.M.71 cruised at 142 mph (230 kph), flying up to 750 miles (1,200 km) with 10 passengers on board.

France was also making progress in commercial aviation. In 1928 Farman had designed the F.180 Oiseau Bleu, a quaint twin-engined biplane with space for 24 passengers, which could cover 620 miles (1,000 km) at 106 mph (170 kph). The lighter F.190, which also made its debut in 1928, was a single-engined, high-wing monoplane designed for shorter hauls of up to 530 miles (850 km). It carried four passengers and cruised at 100 mph (160 kph). For long-distance routes, Farman brought out the four-engined F.220 monoplane, which in 1935 crossed the South Atlantic in just under 15 hours. Other planes of this period were the three-engined F.300 monoplane, which could carry eight passengers for distances of up to 530 miles (850 km) at 118 mph (190 kph), and, on colonial routes, the Bloch 120. This metal-construction high-wing aircraft entered service in 1934. Powered by three engines, it carried four passengers at 143 mph (230 kph).

Derived from the single-engined low-wing Dewoitine D.33, the three-engined D.332 Emeraude appeared in 1933. An all-metal aircraft with a fixed undercarriage in

1
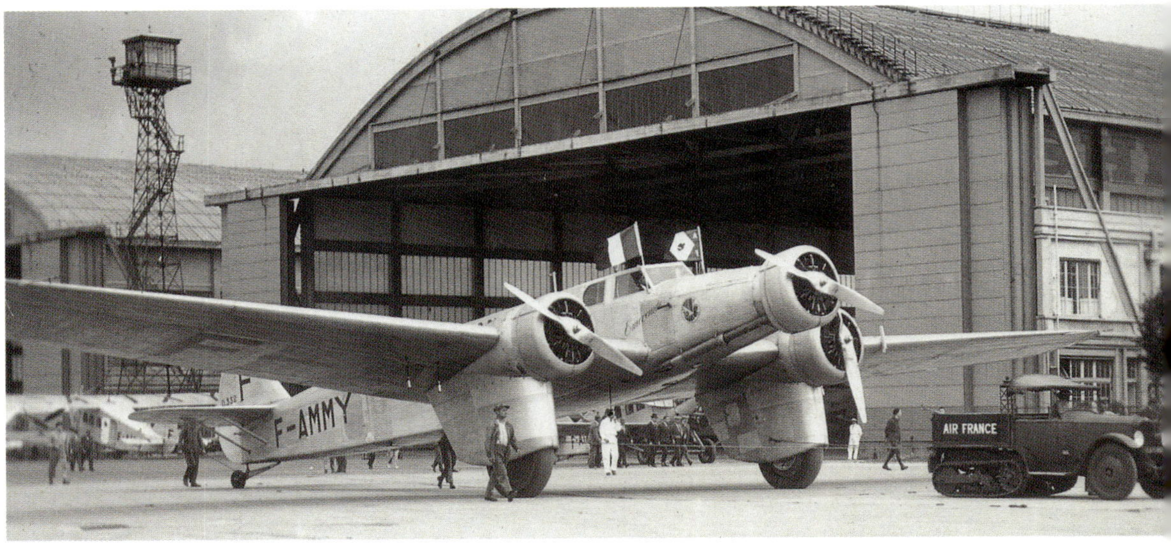

2
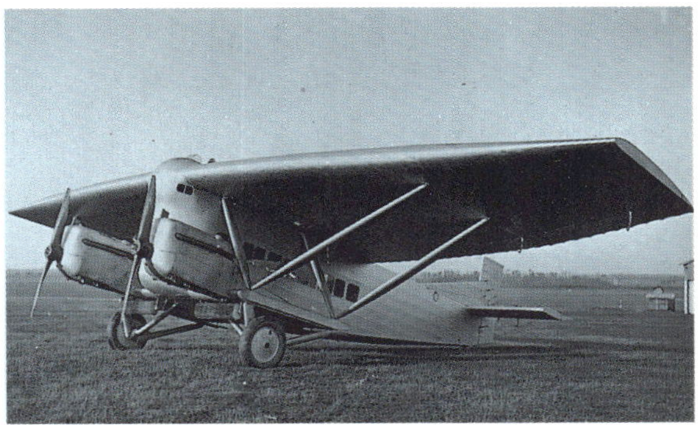

3
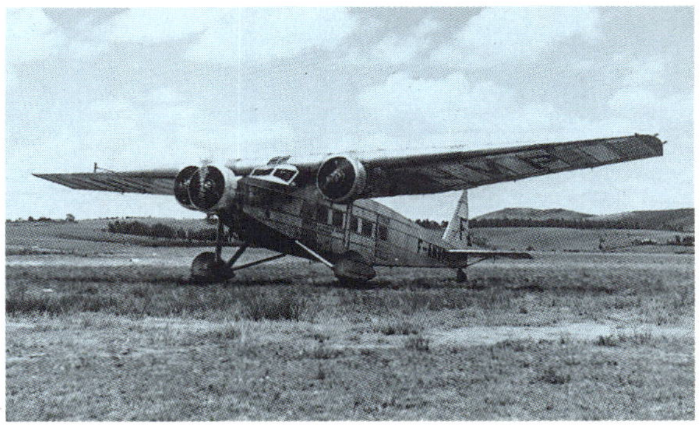

4
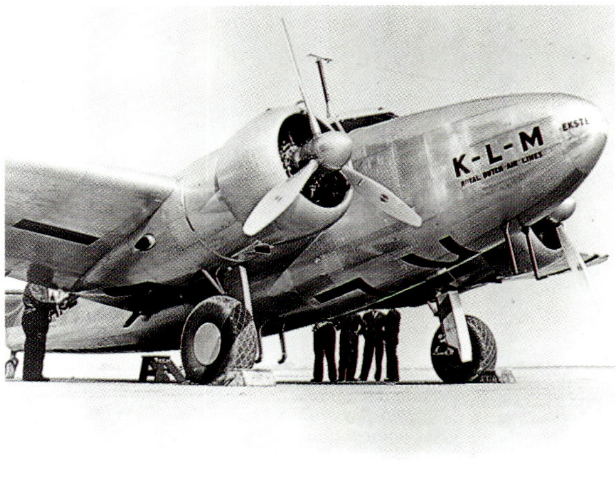

5
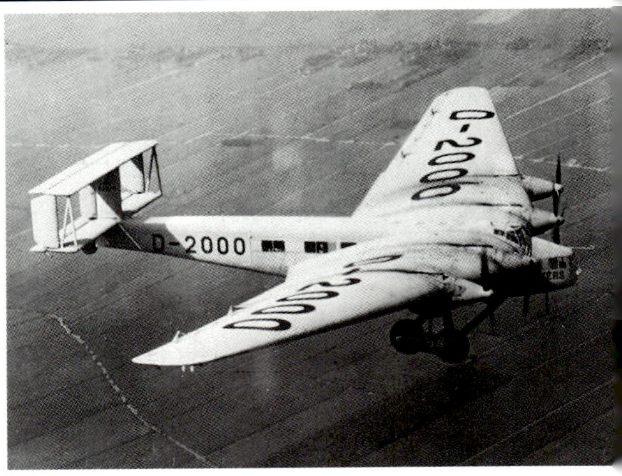

6
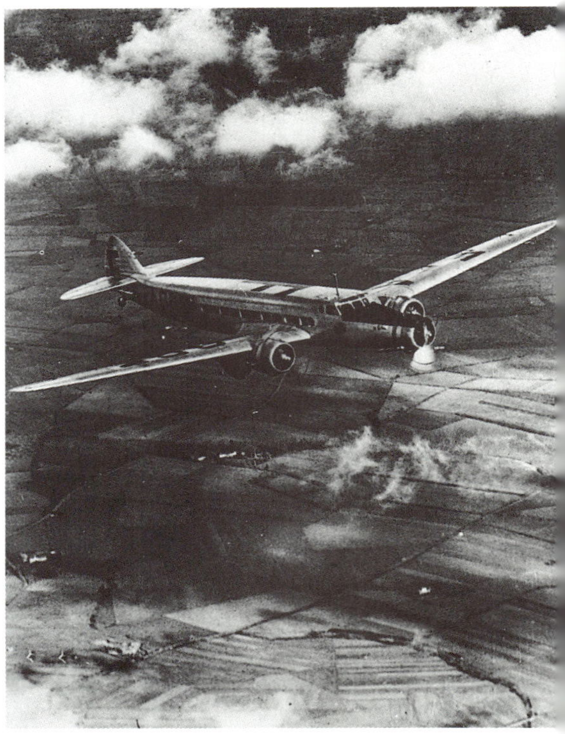

7
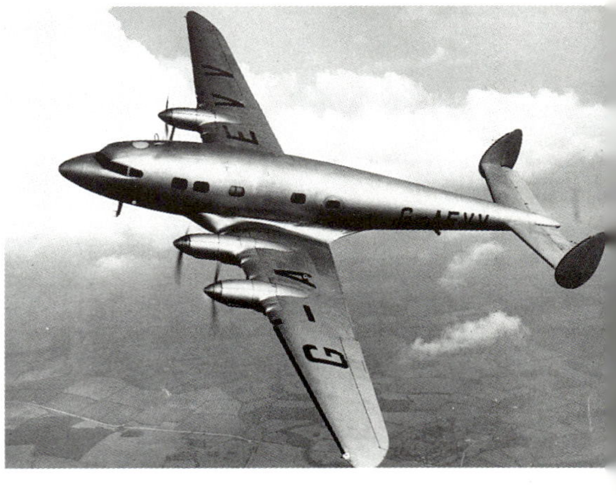

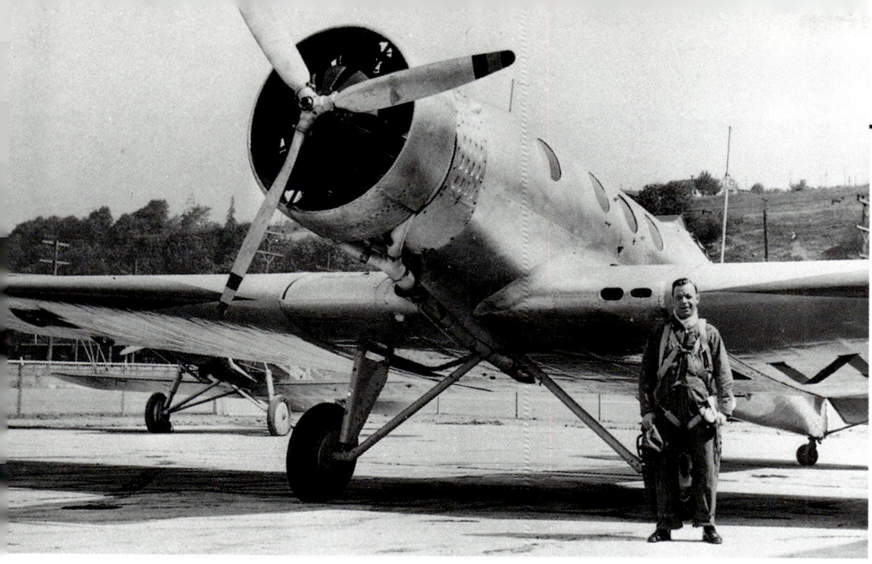
12

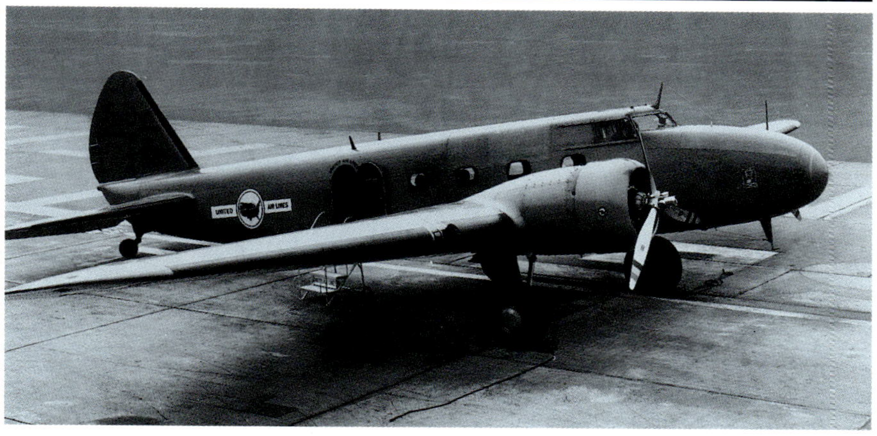
17

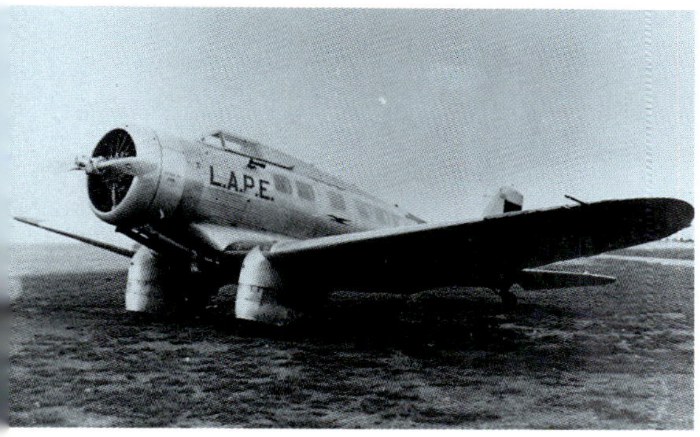
8

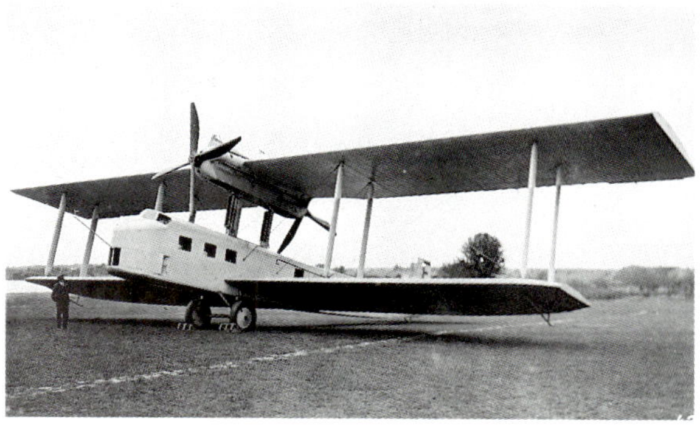
13

aerodynamic fairings, it carried eight passengers. Two years later, it was replaced by the retractable-undercarriage D.338. Capable of carrying 22 passengers on journeys of 1,200 miles (1,950 km), this long-range aircraft was used by Air France in conjunction with the medium-distance Wibault 283.T, which cruised at 143 mph (230 kph) with 10 passengers on board and had a range of 620 miles (1,000 km).

In 1937, de Havilland of Hatfield began delivering the elegant low-wing D.H. 91 Albatross. Powered by four engines, it carried 22 passengers at 210 mph (340 kph). The mail version had a range of 3,100 miles (5,000 km).

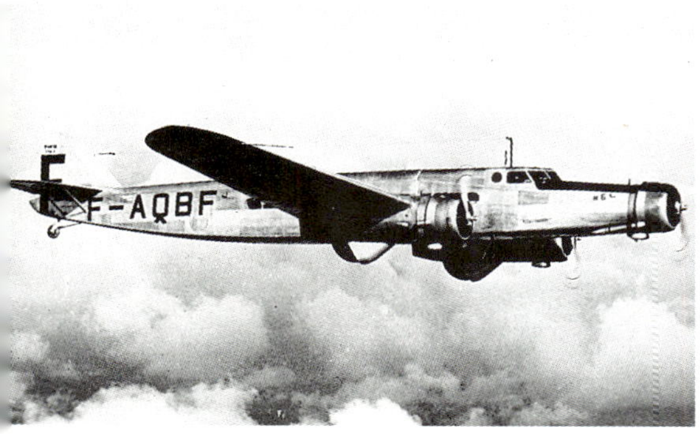

9

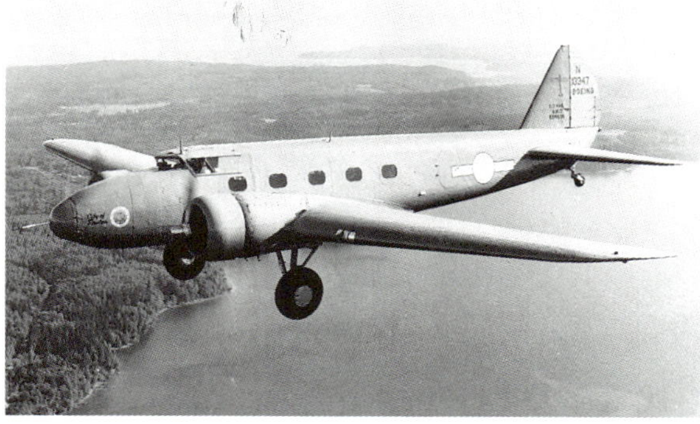
14

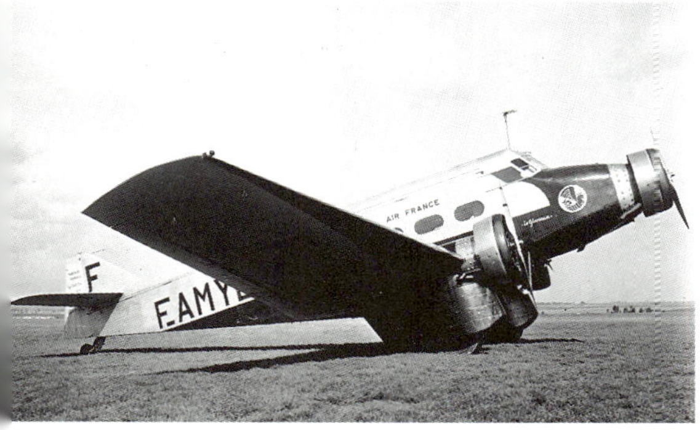

10

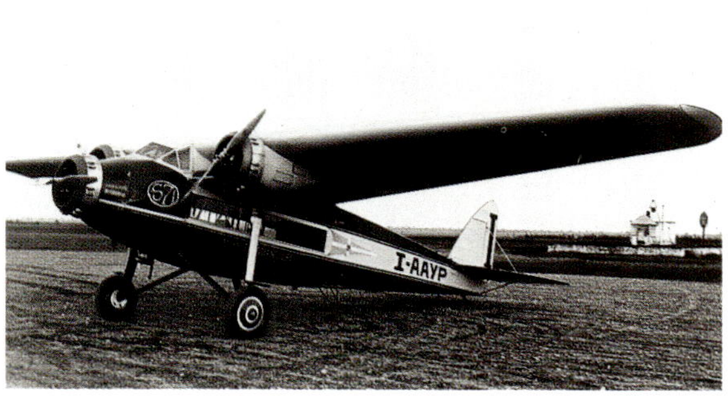

15

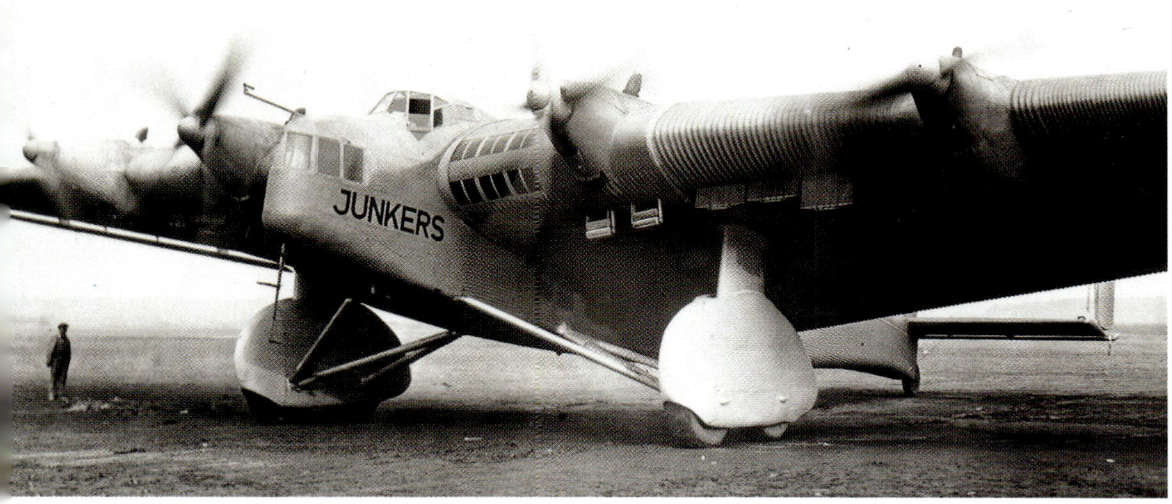

16

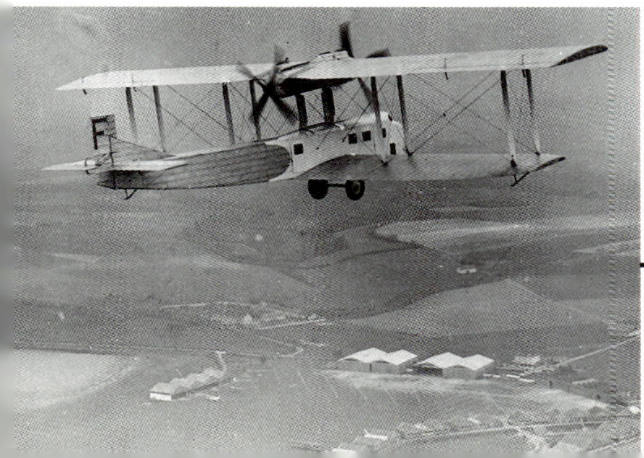
11

Photo No. 1: Dewoitine D.332 Emeraude (France)
Photo No. 2: Farman Jabiru (France)
Photo No. 3: Bloch 120 T (France)
Photo No. 4: Lockheed 14 (USA)
Photo Nos. 5 and 16: Junkers G 38 (Germany)
Photo Nos. 6 and 9: Dewoitine D.338 (France)
Photo No. 7: de Havilland D.H. 91 Albatross (Great Britain)
Photo No. 8: Northrop Delta (USA)
Photo No. 10: Wibault 283 T (France)
Photo Nos. 11 and 13: Farman F.180 (France)
Photo No. 12: Boeing Monomail 200 (USA)
Photo Nos. 14 and 17: Boeing 247 (17 shows 247B)(USA)
Photo No. 15: Savoia-Marchetti S.M.71 (Italy)

COMMERCIAL AIRLINERS

The Potez 62, a high-wing twin-engined monoplane with retractable undercarriage, came into service with Air France in 1935. Carrying 16 passengers, it had a cruising speed of 170 mph (270 kph) and a range of 620 miles (1,000 km).

Before coming up with his durable workhorse, the Ju 52, in 1932, the German constructor Hugo Junkers had produced a single-engined monoplane, the W 33, which in 1928 made the first east-west crossing of the Atlantic. In its passenger version it carried six passengers over distances of 620 miles (1,000 km) at a speed of 93 mph (150 kph). After this first attempt at long-distance flight, Junkers developed an enormous four-engined aircraft, the G 38. Weighing 24 tons on take-off, it had space for 39 passengers, a range of 2,100 miles (2,500 km) and a cruising speed of 112 mph (180 kph). In 1935, to replace the Ju 52, Junkers introduced the Ju 86, a low-wing aircraft with twin diesel engines and a retractable undercarriage. It was fast (160 mph/255 kph) and could carry 10 passengers on journeys of up to 680 miles (1,100 km). The last pre-war Junkers was the Ju 90, which came into service in 1938. A four-engined aircraft with a range of 780 miles (1,250 km), it carried 40 passengers at 210 mph (340 kph).

The fastest commercial aircraft of this period was the Heinkel He 70, a low-wing monoplane whose single engine gave it a maximum speed of over 220 mph (350 kph). It had space for four passengers and a range of 620 miles (1,000 km). In 1938, Focke-Wulf brought out the Fw 200 Condor, which was operated briefly by Lufthansa, before becoming a maritime reconnaissance aircraft. With 26 passengers on board, it flew at 245 mph (390 kph) and had a range of 1,440 miles (2,300 km).

In 1935, the Italian airline Ala Littoria introduced the SIAI-Marchietti S.M.74 on its Rome-Paris run. A big, four-engined aircraft with high wing and fixed undercarriage, it cruised at 186 mph (300 kph) with up to 27 passengers. With a full load, the S.M.74 had a range of 620 miles (1,000 km); with only 16 passengers it could fly double the distance.

Until 1939, Imperial Airways used the Armstrong Whitworth A.W.15 Atalanta on its Egypt-India service. A four-engined high-wing aircraft with fixed undercarriage, the A.W.15 cruised at little more than 125 mph (200 kph), carrying 17 passengers on stages of up to 400 miles (640 km). Its successor, the Armstrong Whitworth A.W.27 Ensign, was the largest British plane of the period. It carried 40 passengers on journeys of up to 810 miles (1,300 km) at a cruising speed of 170 mph (275 kph).

5
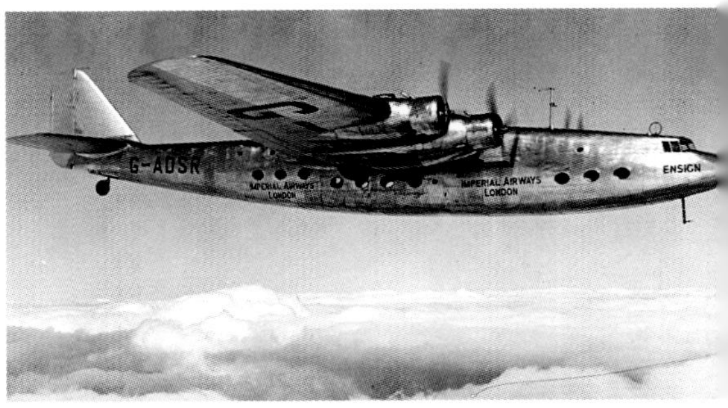

1
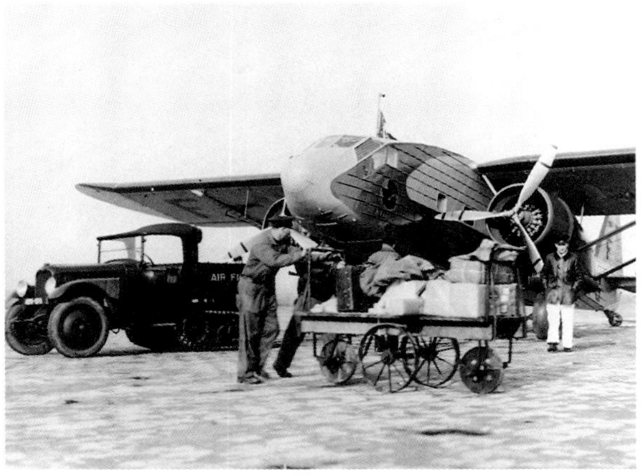

6
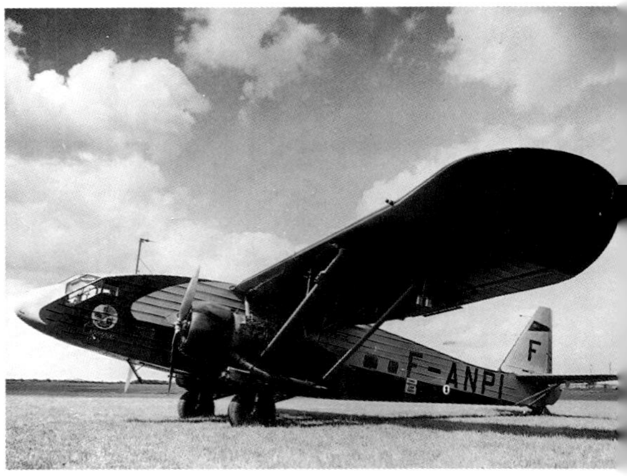

2
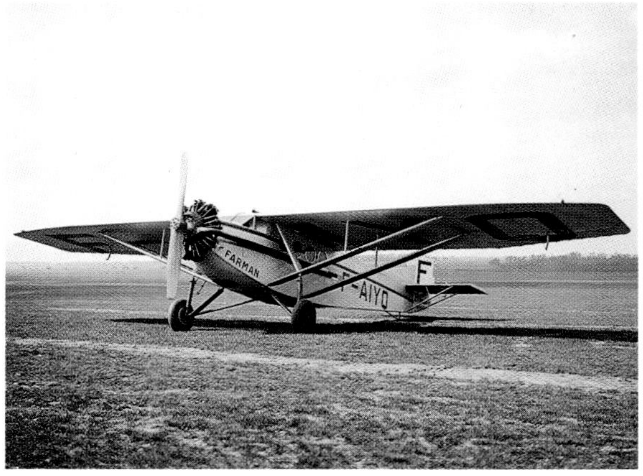

7
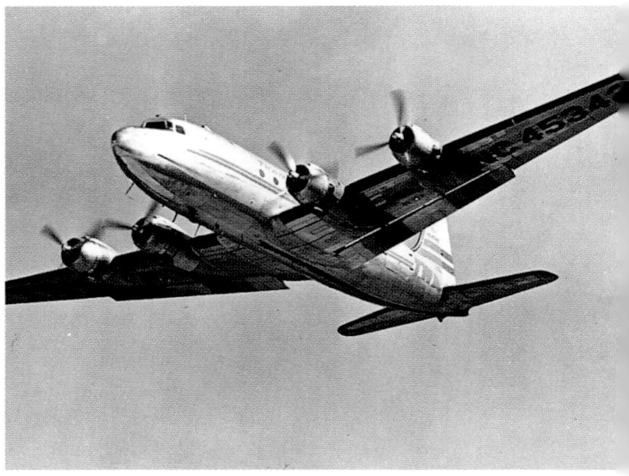

3
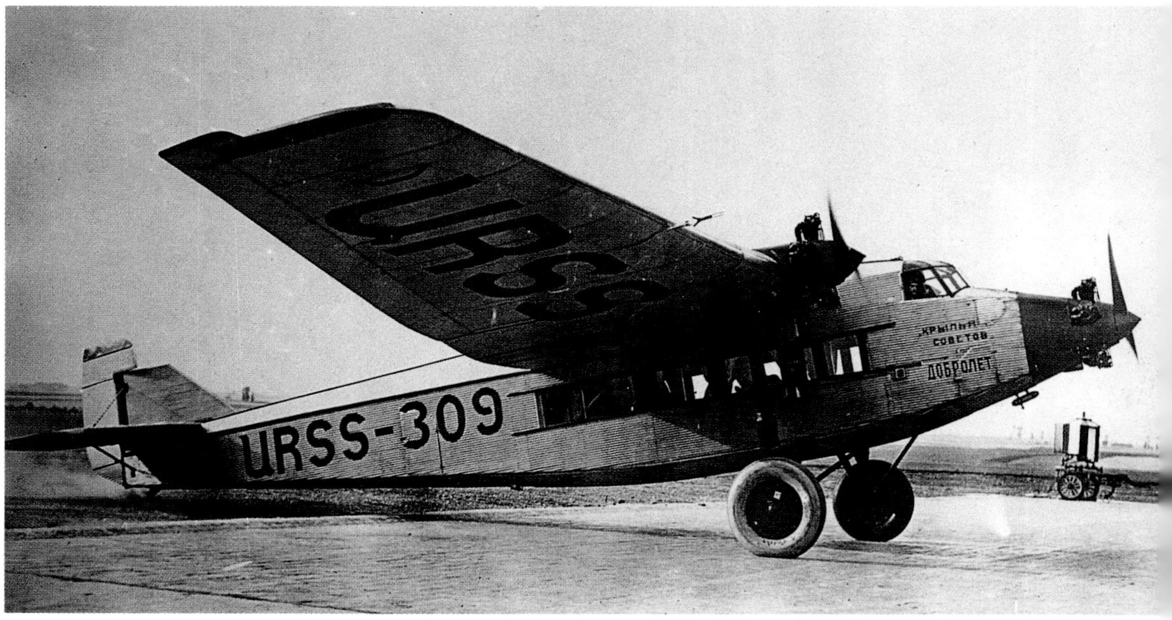

4
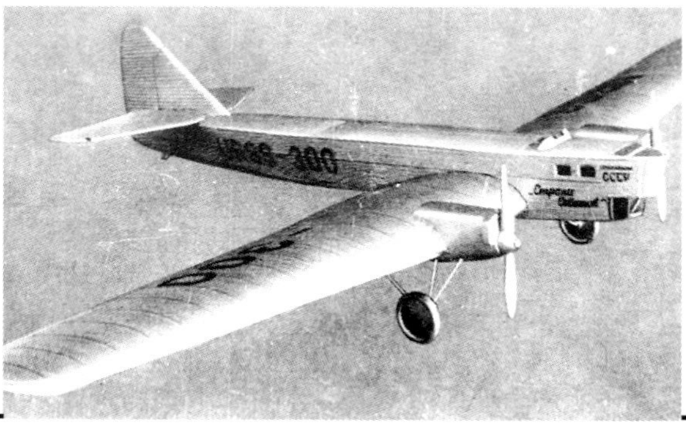

8
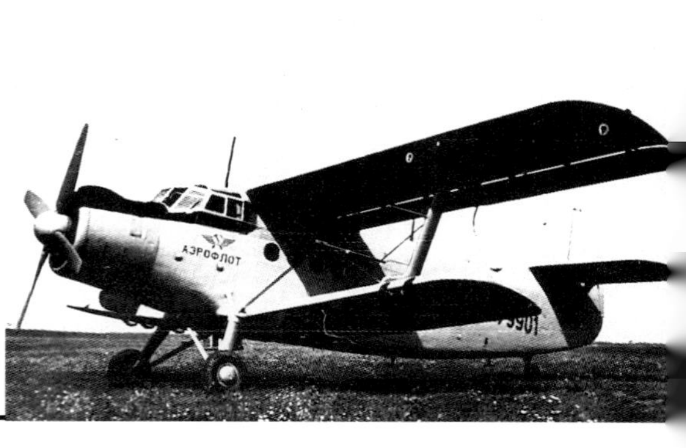

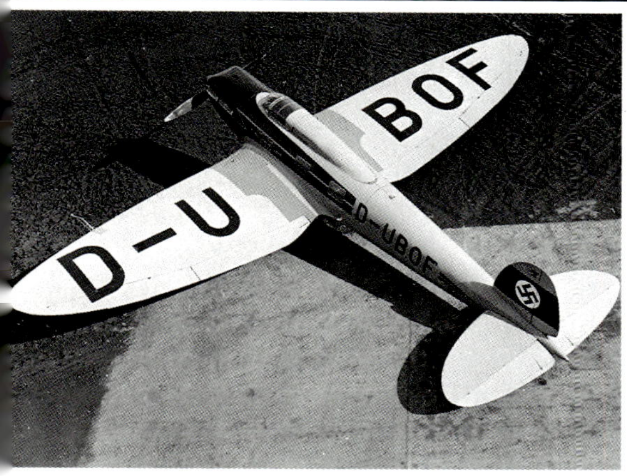

9

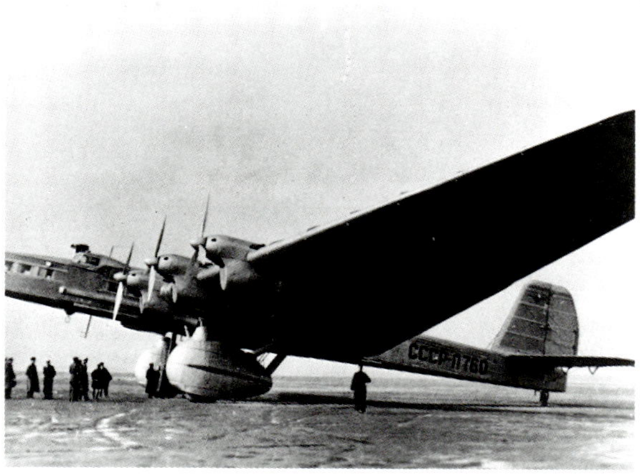

12

Photo Nos. 1 and 6: Potez 62 (France)
Photo Nos. 2 and 16: Farman F.190 (France)
Photo No. 3: Tupolev ANT-9 (USSR)
Photo No. 4: Tupolev ANT-4 (USSR)
Photo No. 5: Armstrong Whitworth A.W. 27 Ensign (Great Britain)
Photo No. 7: Douglas DC-4 (USA)
Photo Nos. 8 and 15: Antonov An-2 (USSR)
Photo Nos. 9 and 18: Heinkel He 70 (Germany)
Photo No. 10: Armstrong Whitworth A.W. 15 Atalanta (Great Britain)
Photo No. 11: Junkers W 33 (Germany)
Photo No. 12: Tupolev ANT-20 bis (USSR)
Photo No. 13: Junkers Ju 90 (Germany)
Photo No. 14: Focke-Wulf Fw 200 Condor (Germany)
Photo No. 17: Savoia-Marchetti S.M.74 (Italy)

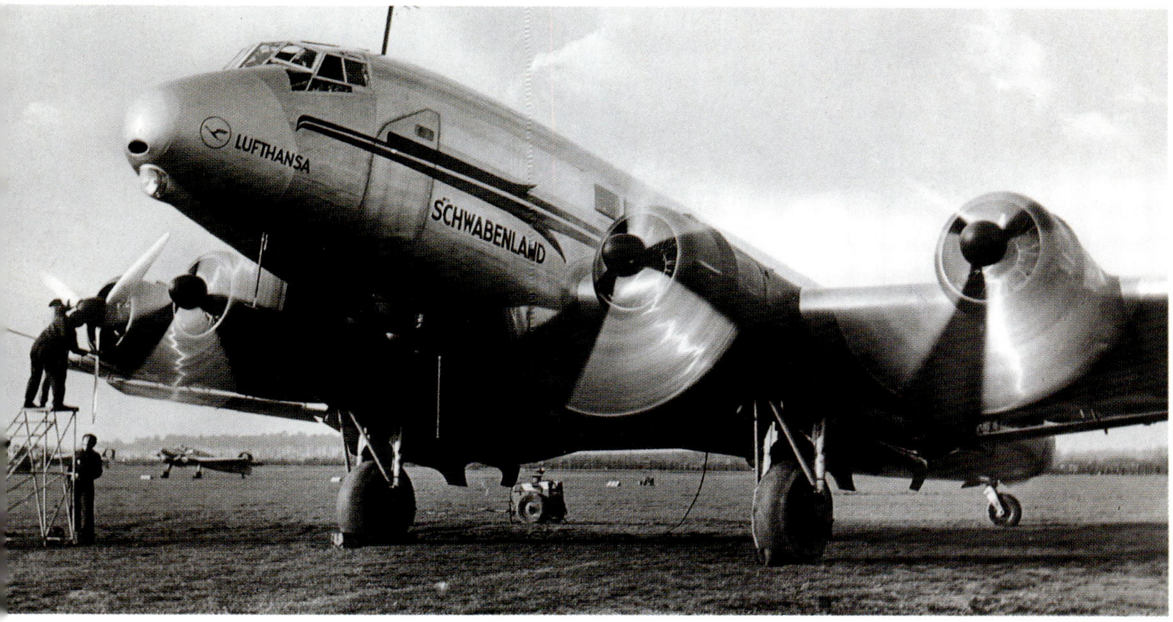

13

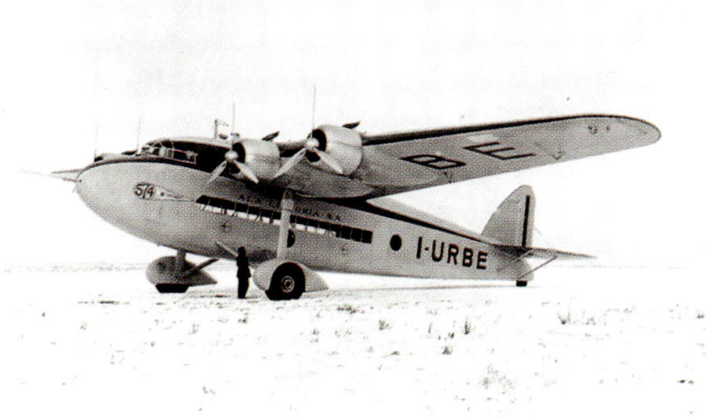

17

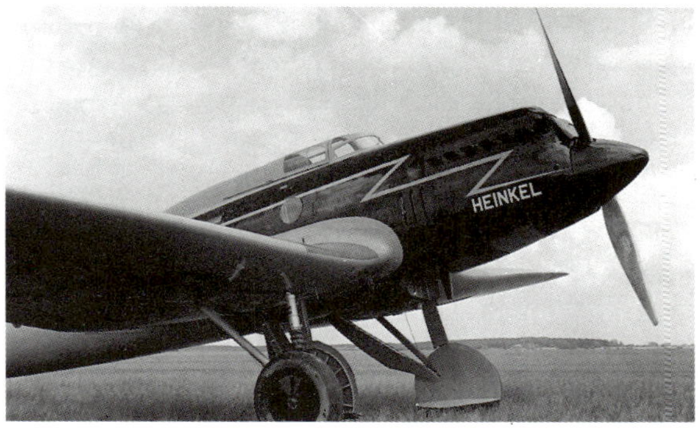

18

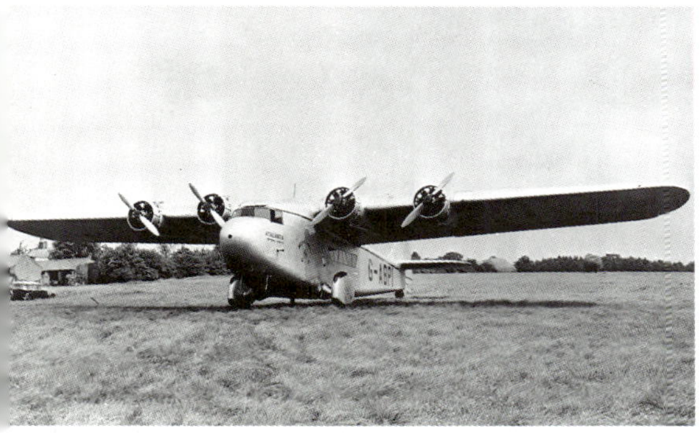

10

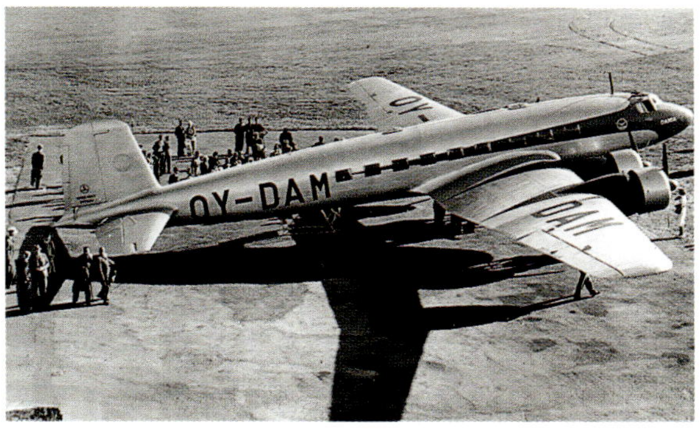

14

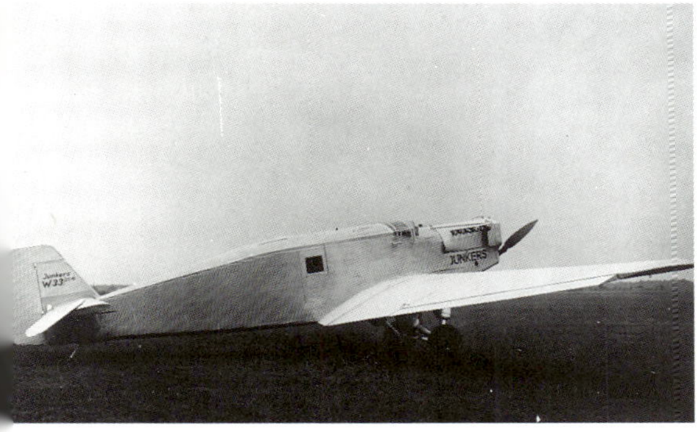

11

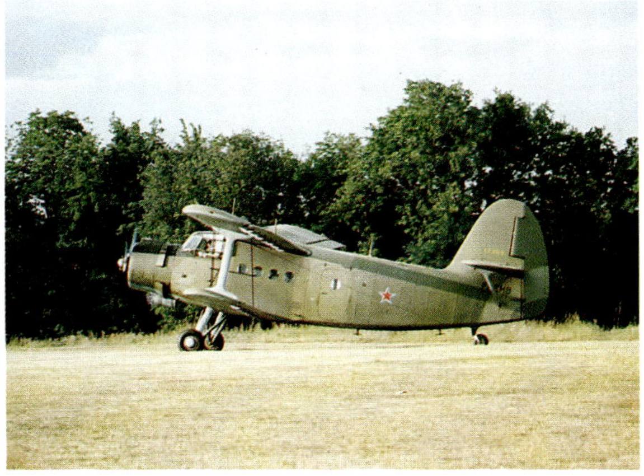

15

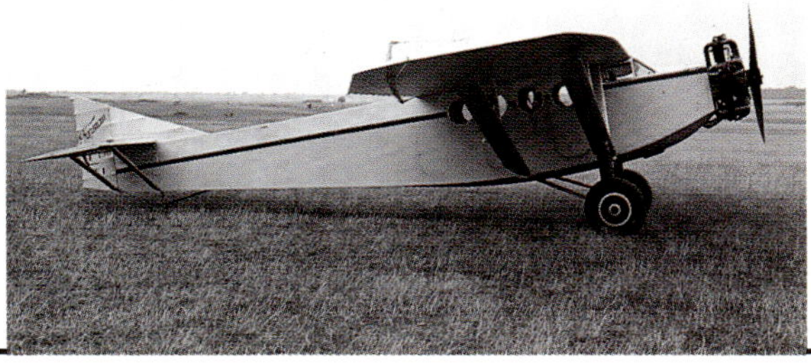

16

After early experience with the ANT-2 and ANT-4, in 1932 the Russian designer Andrei Nikolaevich Tupolev brought out a high-wing aircraft of all-metal construction, the ANT-9. Carrying nine passengers at 108 mph (175 kph) over distances of 620 miles (1,000 km), it was widely used during the 1930s with two or three engines. In 1934, Tupolev went on to produce the biggest land-based aircraft in the world, the ANT-20 Maxim Gorki. A monoplane powered by eight engines, this monster could carry 80 passengers in addition to its eight-man crew. Cruising at 137 mph (220 kph), it had a range of 1,200 miles (2,000 km). It was developed into the ANT-20 bis.

In the pre-war years, Douglas were already developing a successor to the DC-3: a modern four-engined aircraft capable of transporting 40 passengers at 220 mph (350 kph) over distances of 2,200 miles (3,500 km). Though, as the C-54 Skymaster, it served as a military transport during the War, the DC-4 was not used as a commercial airliner until 1945.

COMMERCIAL AIRLINERS

The War proved an extraordinary stimulus to aeronautical development in the United States. As early as 1938, Boeing built an aircraft with a pressurized cabin – the four-engined 307 Stratoliner, derived from the B-17 bomber – which carried 33 passengers. Cruising at 225 mph (360 kph), it had a range of 2,375 miles (3,800 km). And 1948 saw the introduction of Boeing's 377 Stratocruiser, developed from the B-29 Superfortress bomber. A four-engined aircraft with a double-decker pressurised cabin, it could fly the Atlantic at 375 mph (600 kph) carrying 100 passengers.

By way of contrast, the Lockheed Constellation was designed as a civilian aircraft, but used for military transport as the C-69 before entering airline service in 1946. Powered by four piston engines, it carried 80 passengers at 330 mph (530 kph) over distances of nearly 2,500 miles (4,000 km). It was followed in 1951 by the 102-seater L-1049 Super Constellation – cruising speed 327 mph (526 kph), range 4,375 to 5,000 miles (7,000 to 8,000 km) – and, in 1956, by the L-1649 Starliner.

Meanwhile, Douglas had been developing the four-engined DC-6, a pressurised and enlarged version of the DC-4. Introduced in 1946, it could traverse the United States from coast to coast in 10 or 11 hours. Carrying 52 passengers, it cruised at over 310 mph (500 kph) and had a range of 3,100 miles (5,000 km). It was followed, in 1953, by the bigger and more powerful DC-7, which carried 95 passengers and cruised at 350 mph (560 kph). Its range of 3,750 miles (6,000 km) meant that it could cross the North Atlantic in one hop.

In the medium-range category, in 1946 Convair began producing a twin-engined aircraft for American Airlines, the 240, with capacity for 40 passengers and a cruising speed of 290 mph (470 kph). It was used for journeys of up to 1,875 miles (3,000 km). The 240 was followed, in 1951, by the 44-passenger 340 and, in 1955, by the higher-performance 440-Metropolitan, which had seating for 52. In France, SNCASO developed the twin-engined SO.95 Corse (1948) and the SO.30P Bretagne (1949). The Bretagne seated from 30 to 37 passengers on journeys of up to 900 miles (1,450 km).

The British aircraft industry was meanwhile producing a succession of new planes. In 1946 appeared the twin-engined Vickers Viking, which carried 36 passengers over distances of 1,680 miles (2,700 km) at 250 mph (400 kph), and, in 1949, the ill-fated Bristol 167 Brabazon, a gigantic aircraft powered by eight engines mounted in pairs.

1
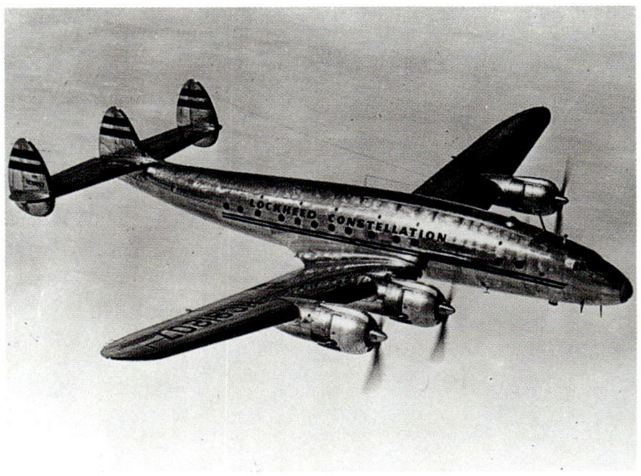

2
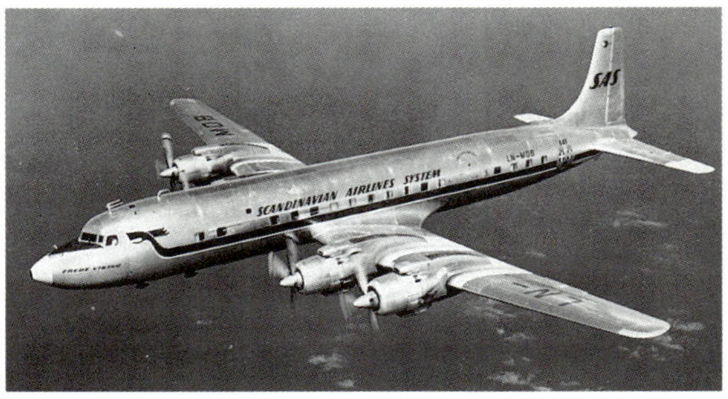

3
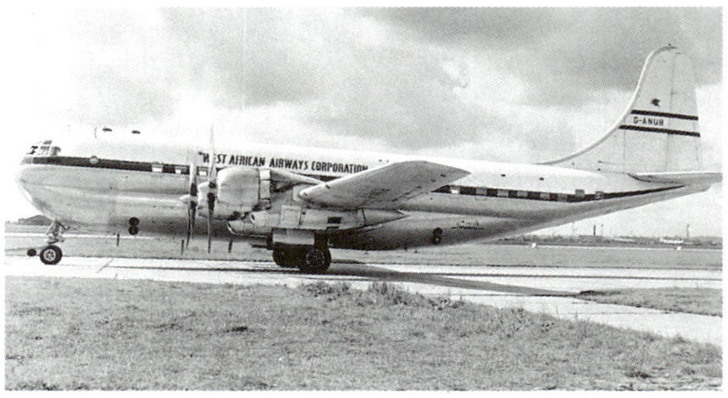

4
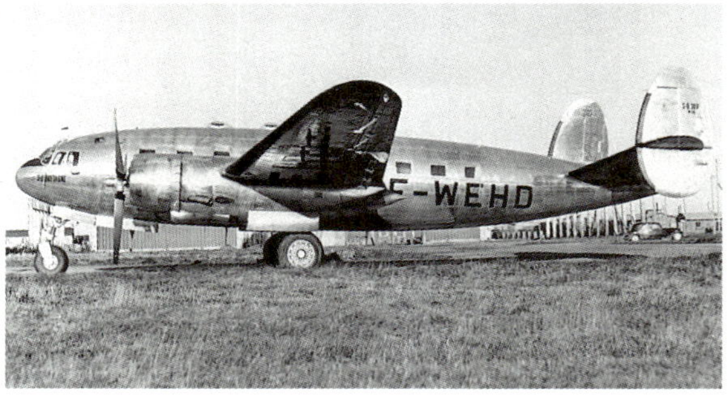

5
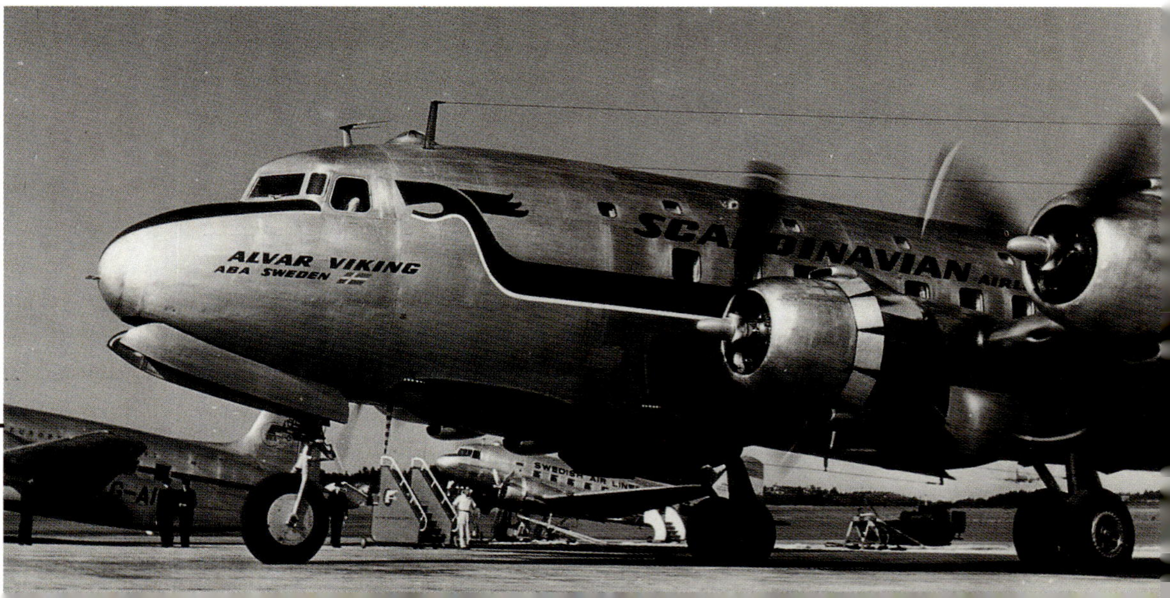

6
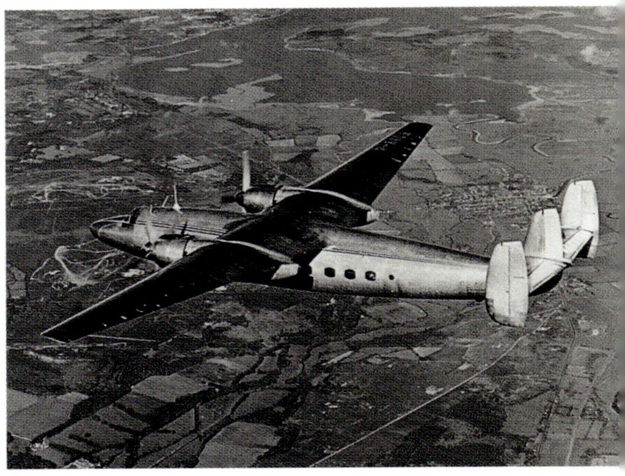

7
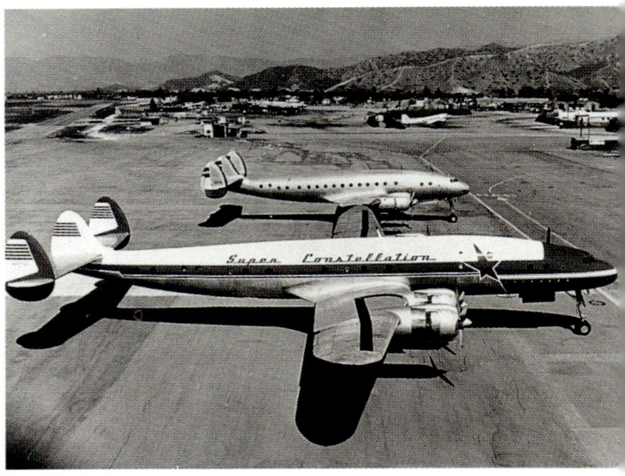

8
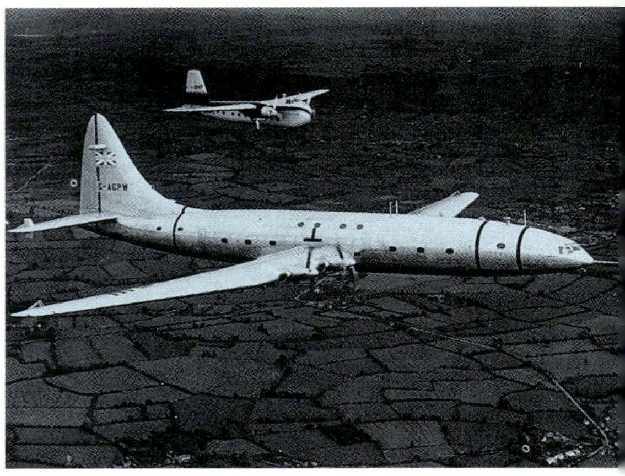

9
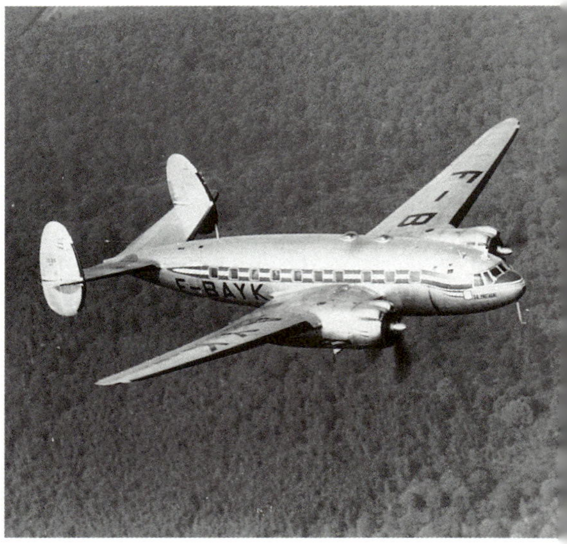

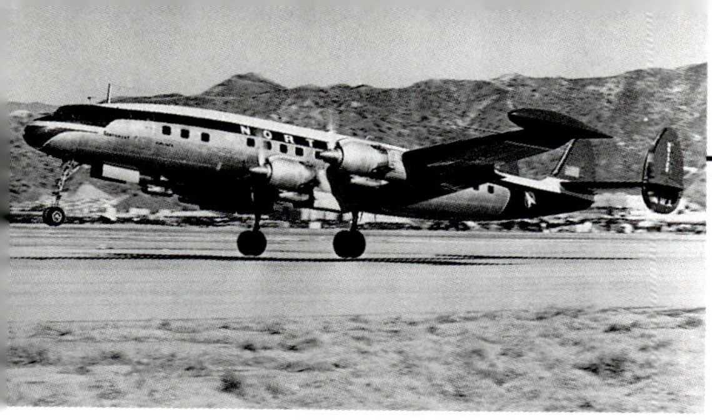
10

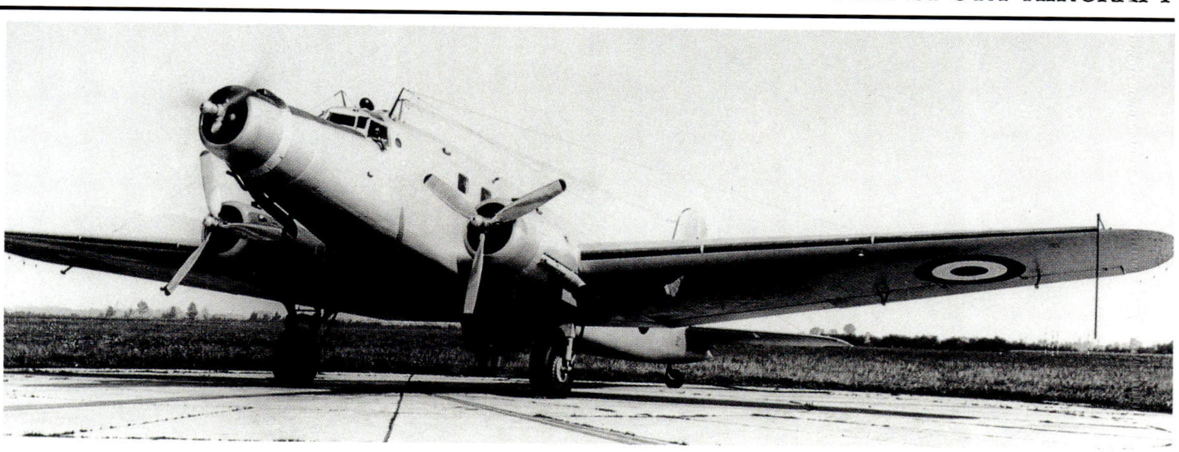
16

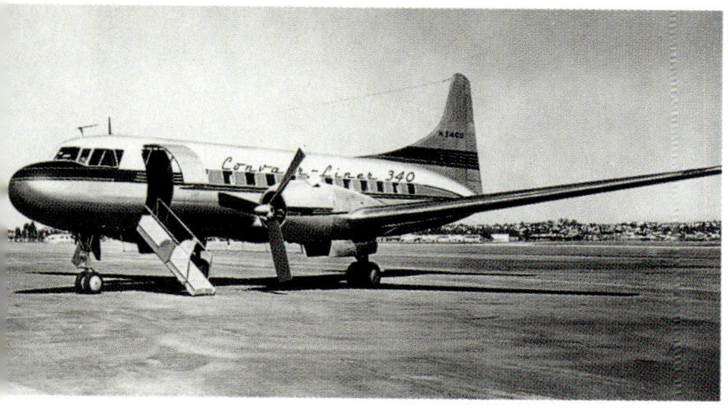
11

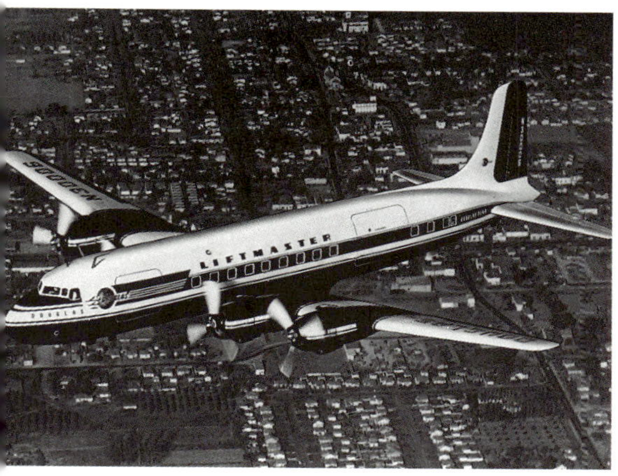
12

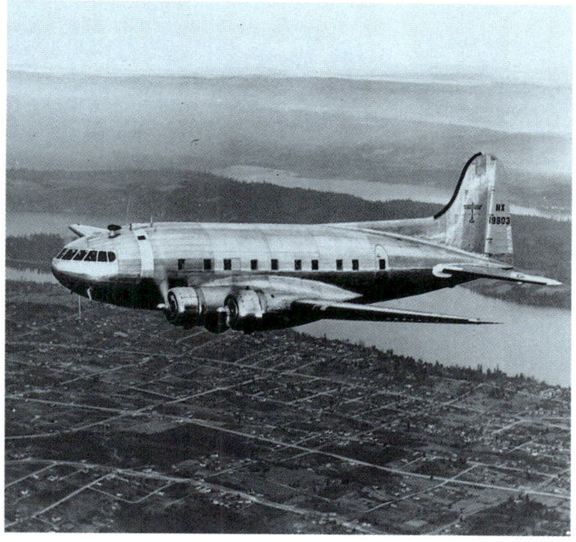

14 Designed to carry 80 passengers at 250 mph (400 kph) with a range of 5,530 miles (8,850 km), it never got beyond the prototype stage. The four-engined Avro 685 York, derived from the Lancaster bomber – capacity 18 to 40 passengers, cruising speed 235 mph (375 kph), range 2,680 miles (4,300 km) – made its debut in 1945, and the twin-engined short-range Airspeed A.S.57 Ambassador – capacity 55 passengers, cruising speed 260 mph (420 kph), range 550 miles (880 km) – in 1952.

Photo No. 1: Lockheed Constellation (USA)
Photo No. 2: Douglas DC-7 (USA)
Photo Nos. 3 and 15: Boeing 377 Stratocruiser (USA)
Photo Nos. 4 and 9: SNCASO SO.30 P Bretagne (France)
Photo Nos. 5 and 12: Douglas DC-6 (USA)
Photo No. 6: Airspeed A.S. 57 Ambassador (Great Britain)
Photo Nos. 7 and 10: Lockheed L-1049 Super Constellation (USA)
Photo No. 8: Bristol 167 Brabazon (Great Britain)
Photo Nos. 11 and 13: Convair 340/440/580 (USA)
Photo No. 14: Boeing 307 Stratoliner (USA)
Photo No. 16: Fiat G.212 (Italy)
Photo No. 17: Vickers Viking (Great Britain)

15

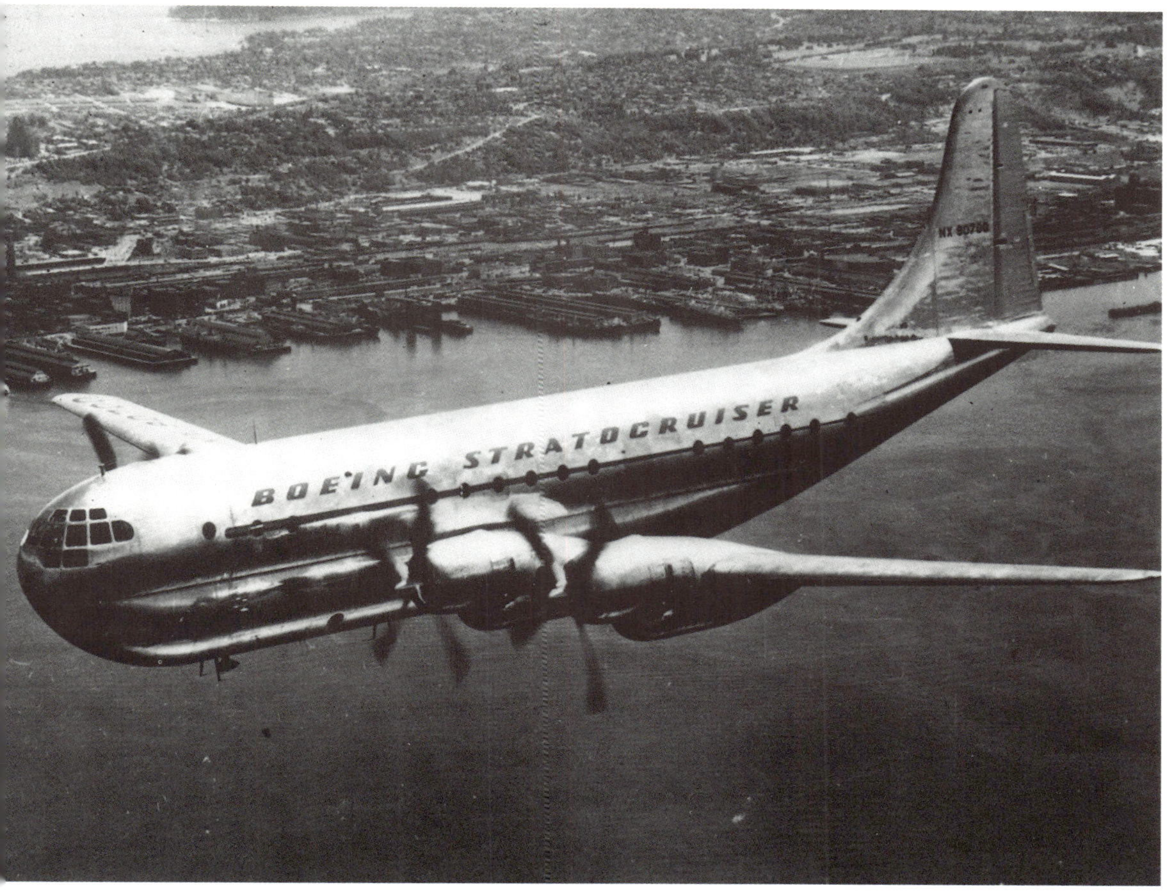

13

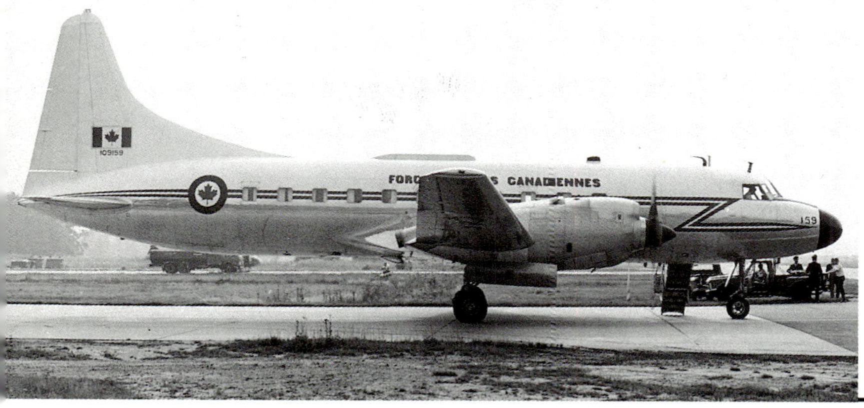
17

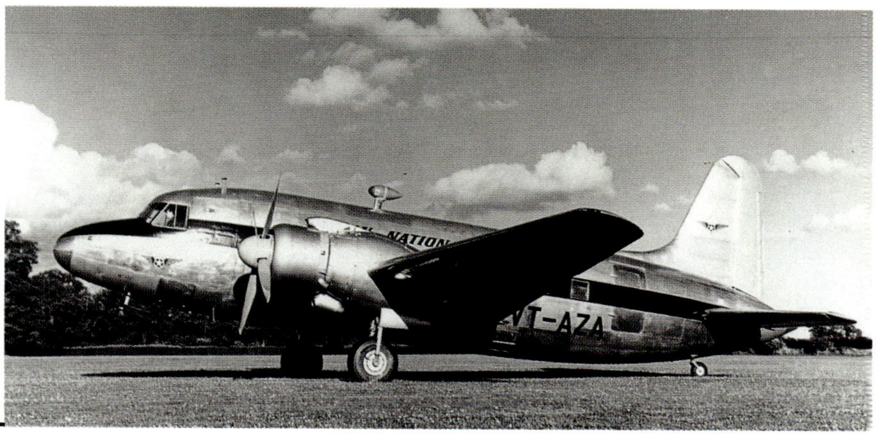

5
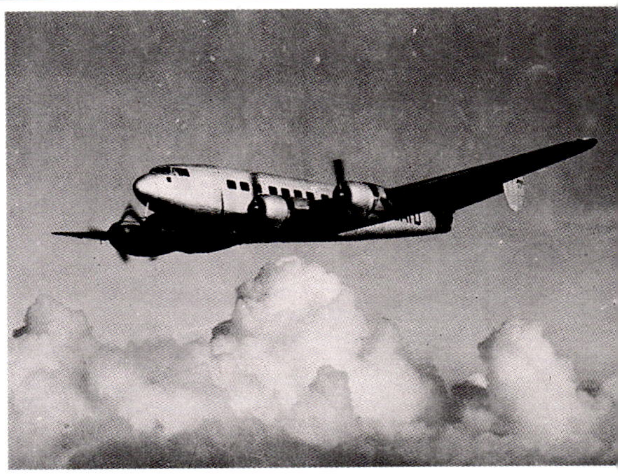

COMMERCIAL AIRLINERS

Piston-engined aircraft continued to dominate for some years after the war. In 1946, the French company SNCASE brought out the four-engined 33-seater SE.161 Languedoc (range 625 miles/1,000 km, cruising speed 210 mph/340 kph) and, in 1950, the 160-seater SE.2010 Armagnac (3,125 miles/5,000 km at over 280 mph/450 kph). Then, in 1953, Breguet unveiled the 763 Provence, a four-engined double-decker with capacity for 110 passengers (1,440 miles/2,300 km at 210 mph/335 kph).

Italian airlines used the Fiat G.212 (1947), a three-engined aircraft with seating for 34 (1,875 miles/3,000 km at 187 mph/300 kph) and the Savoia-Marchetti S.M.95 (1948), which was powered by four engines and accommodated 38 passengers.

The world's first passenger turboprop, the British Vickers Viscount 701 went into service in 1952. Highly successful, it flew at 350 mph (570 kph) over distances of 1,750 miles (2,800 km), carrying from 40 to 70 passengers. Similar in conception was the 139-seater Vickers Vanguard (1959), which had a cruising speed of 425 mph (680 kph) and a range of over 1,800 miles (2,900 km).

Other four-engined turboprops were the Bristol Britannia (139 passengers, cruising speed 375 mph/680 kph, range 3,125 miles/5,000 km) and the medium-range Lockheed Electra of 1959 (100 passengers, cruising speed 375 mph/680 kph, range 2,190 miles/3,500 km).

The first passenger flight (London-Johannesburg) using a jet aircraft was made in 1952 by the de Havilland D.H. 106 Comet. But the Comet had a chequered history, and the first great commercial success of the jet age was the four-engined Boeing 707, introduced in 1958. The 707-Intercontinental version flew at over 590 mph (950 kph) and had a range of 4,375 miles (7,000 km).

The BAC VC-10 entered service in 1964, its four engines mounted in paired nacelles at the rear. Carrying 135 passengers, it cruised at 560 mph (900 kph) and had a range of 5,000 miles (8,000 km). A bigger version, the Super VC-10 – with capacity for 174 passengers and a range of 4,750 miles (7,600 km) – made its debut the following year.

In France, SNCASE (Aérospatiale) tested a medium-range twin-engined jet in 1955: the SE.210 Caravelle. In airline service from 1959, the Caravelle flew at 500 mph (800 kph), carrying 100 passengers on journeys of up to 1,430 miles (2,300 km).

1
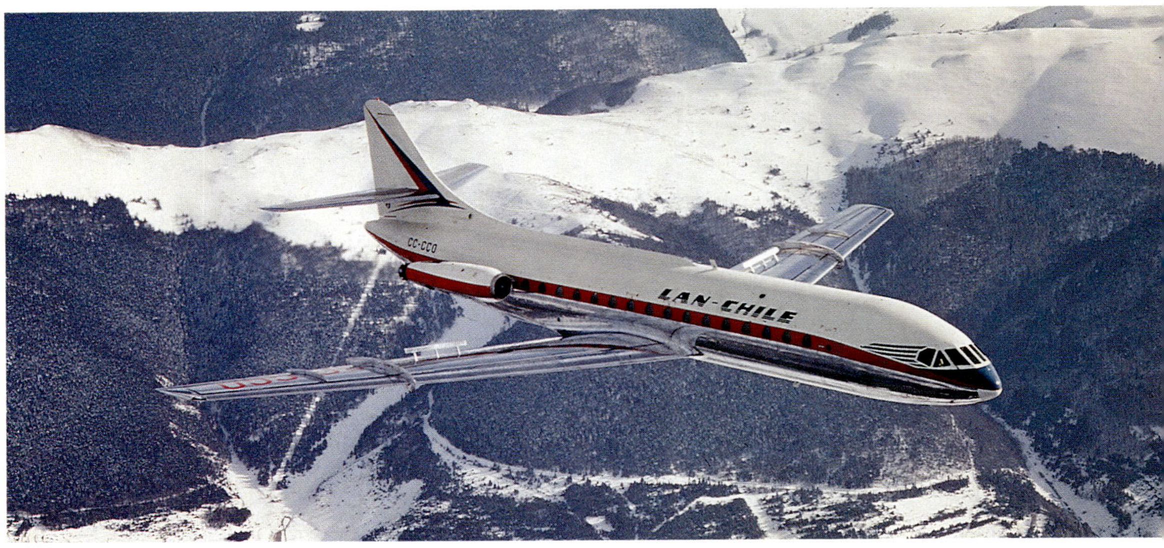

2
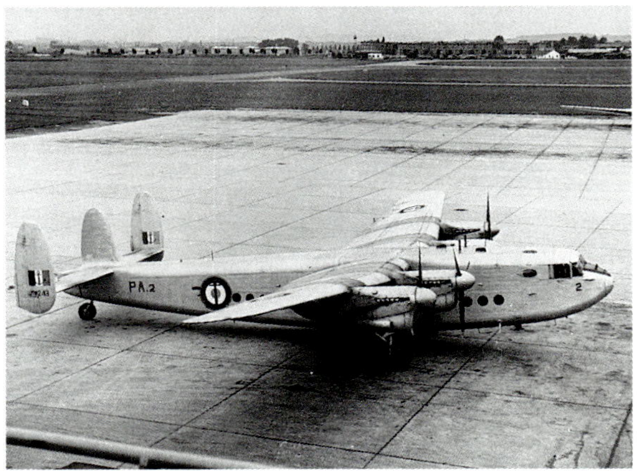

6
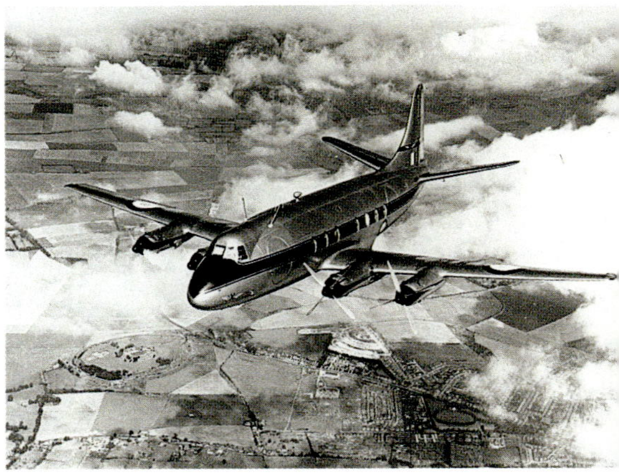

3
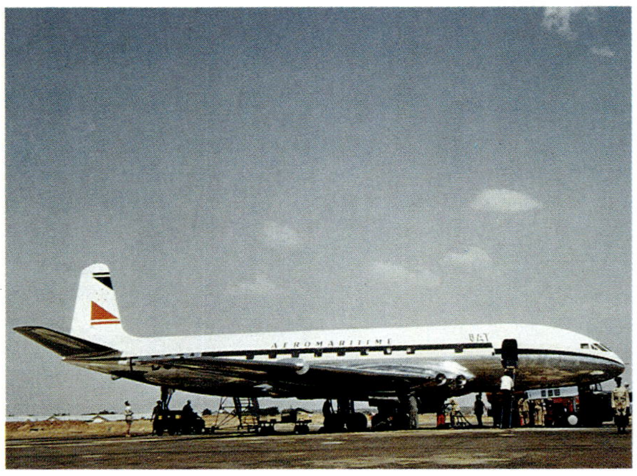

7
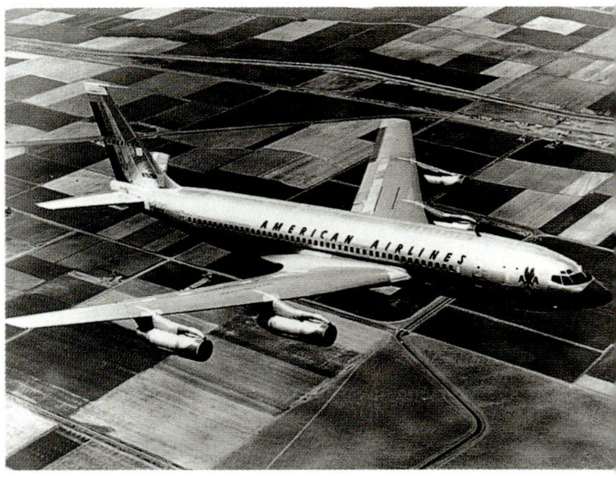

4
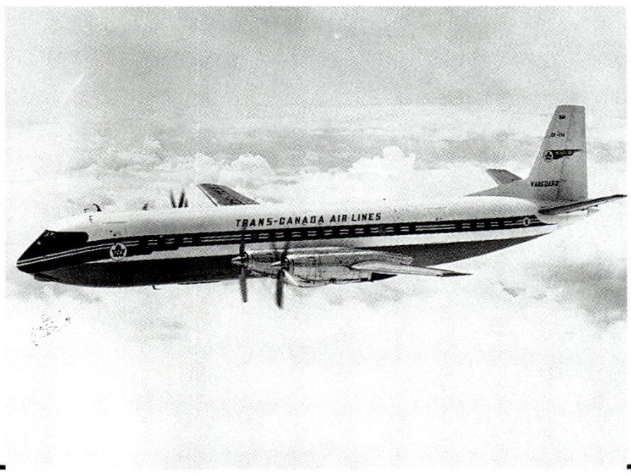

8
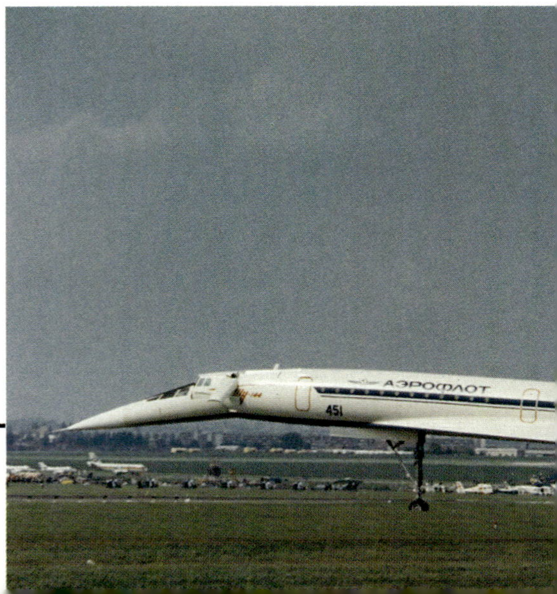

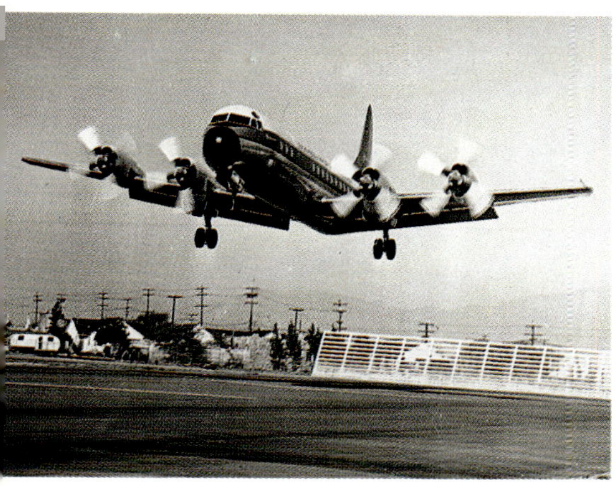
9

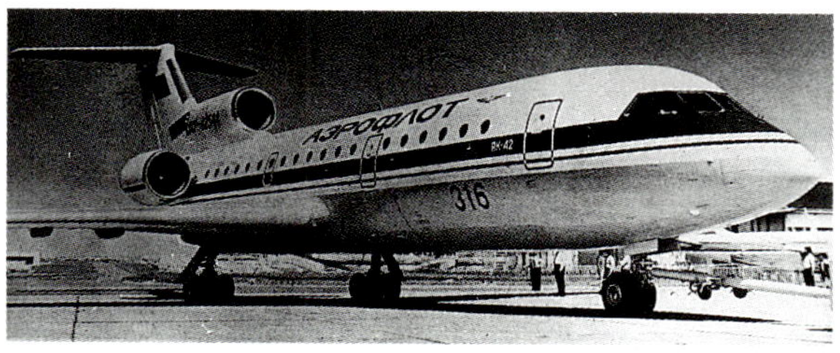

13 The Anglo-French supersonic airliner, Concorde, was a joint effort involving BAC and Aérospatiale, Rolls-Royce and SNECMA. The aircraft were assembled at Toulouse and Bristol. A four-engined delta-wing jet, Concorde flies at speeds of 1,450 mph (2,330 kph), carrying 100 passengers up to 4,375 miles (7,000 km). Its only rival, the Tupolev Tu-144, has reached 1,560 mph (2,500 kph). It can carry 140 passengers over stages of 4,060 miles (6,500 km).

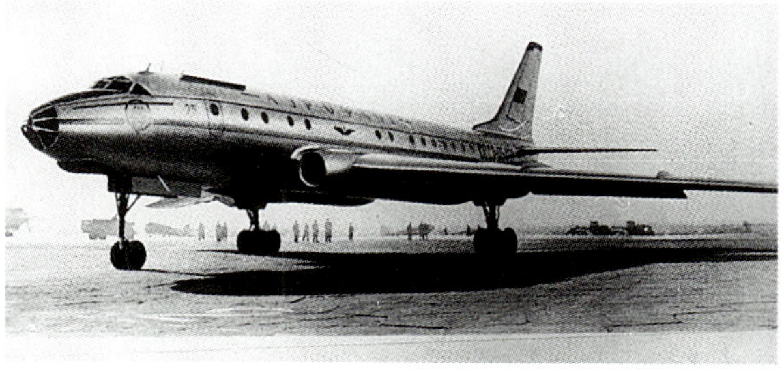
14

The Soviets began producing civil jets in 1956, with the medium-range Tupolev Tu-104. A twin-engined aircraft, the Tu-104 carried from 50 to 100 passengers, cruising at 500 mph (800 kph) on stages of around 1,875 miles (3,000 km). Its successor, the Tu-204, appeared in 1990 (200 passengers, cruising speed 530 mph/850 kph, range from 1,560 to 2,500 miles/2,500 to 4,000 km).

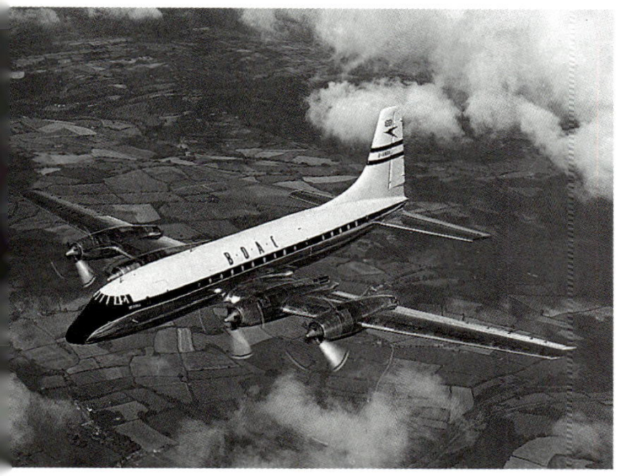
10

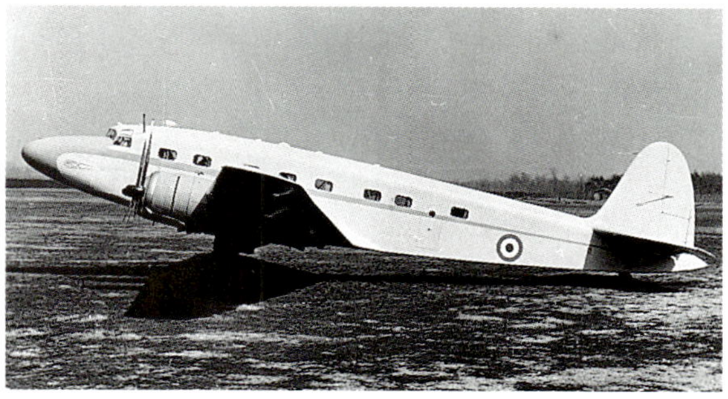
15

The three-engined Yakovlev Yak-42 has been in service since 1975. A medium-range aircraft, it carries between 100 and 120 passengers, covering up to 1,250 miles (2,000 km) at around 500 mph (800 kph).

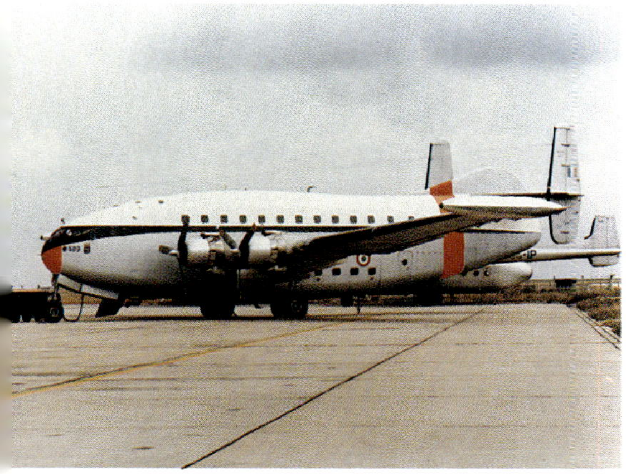
11

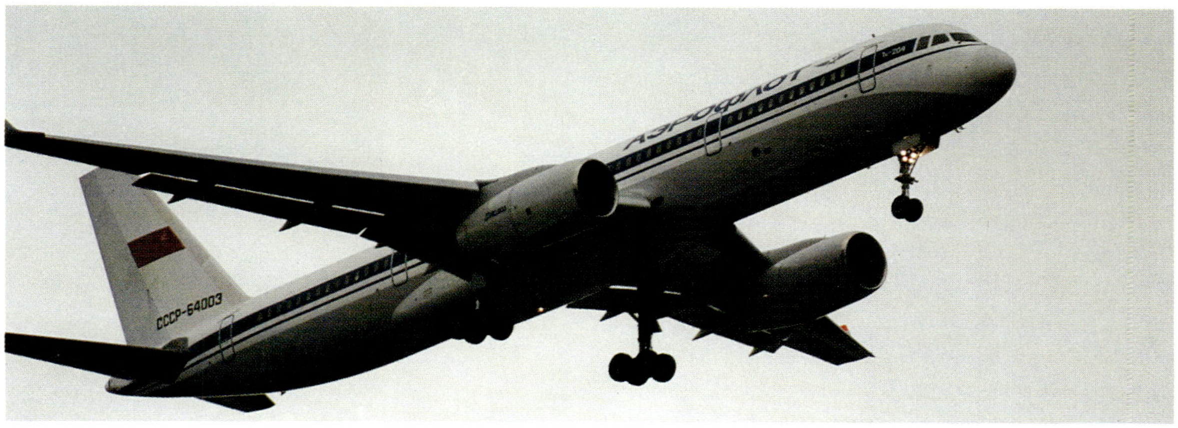

18

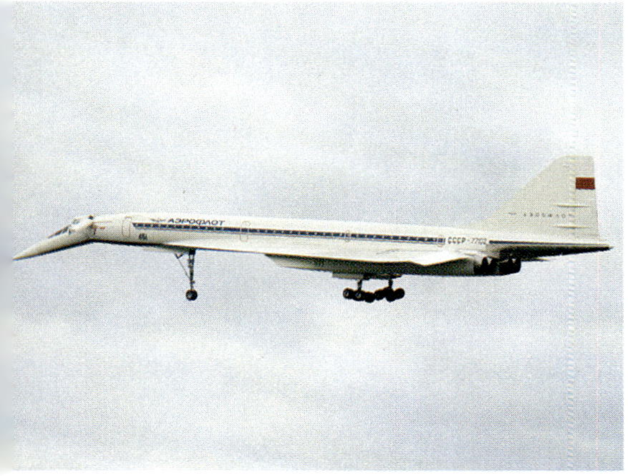
12

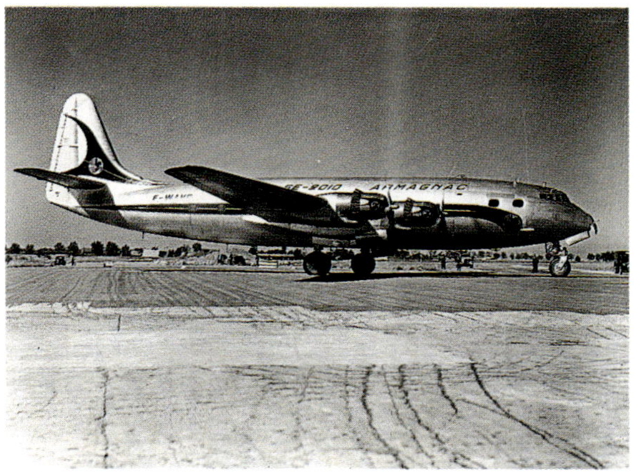
16

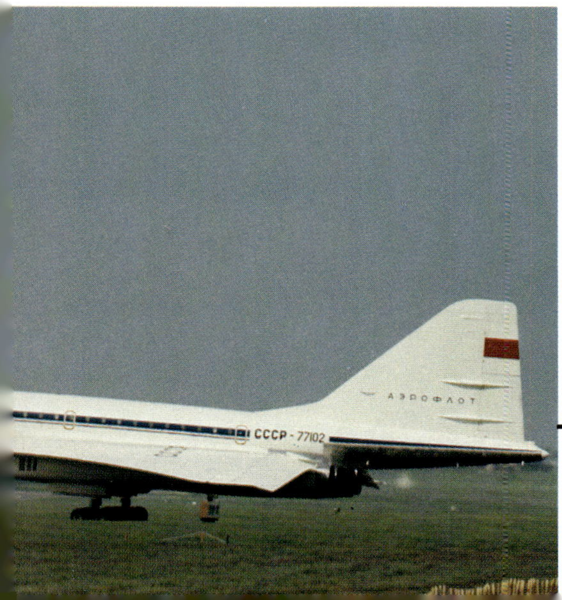

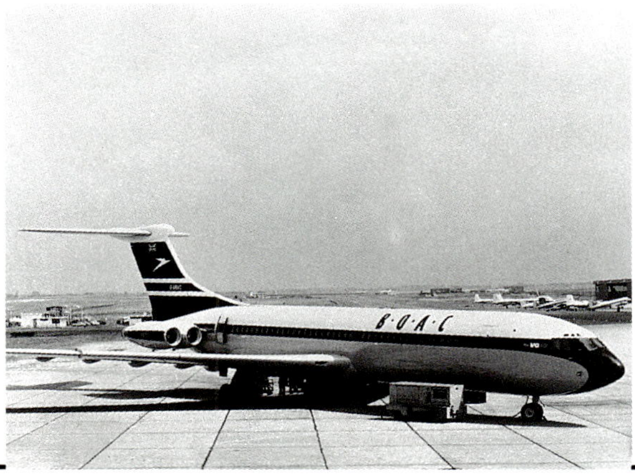
17

Photo No. 1: Sud Aviation SE.210 Caravelle (France)
Photo No. 2: Avro 685 York (Great Britain)
Photo No. 3: de Havilland Comet (Great Britain)
Photo No. 4: Vickers Vanguard (Great Britain)
Photo No. 5: SNCASE SE.161 Languedoc (France)
Photo No. 6: Vickers Viscount (Great Britain)
Photo No. 7: Boeing 707 (USA)
Photo Nos. 8 and 12: Tupolev Tu-144 (USSR)
Photo No. 9: Lockheed L-188 Electra (USA)
Photo No. 10: Bristol 175 Britannia (Great Britain)
Photo No. 11: Breguet 763 Provence (France)
Photo No. 13: Yakovlev Yak-42 (USSR)
Photo No. 14: Tupolev Tu-104 (USSR)
Photo No. 15: Savoia-Marchetti S.M.95 (Italy)
Photo No. 16: SNCASE SE.2010 Armagnac (France)
Photo No. 17: BAC VC-10 (Great Britain)
Photo No. 18: Tupolev Tu-204 (USSR)

5
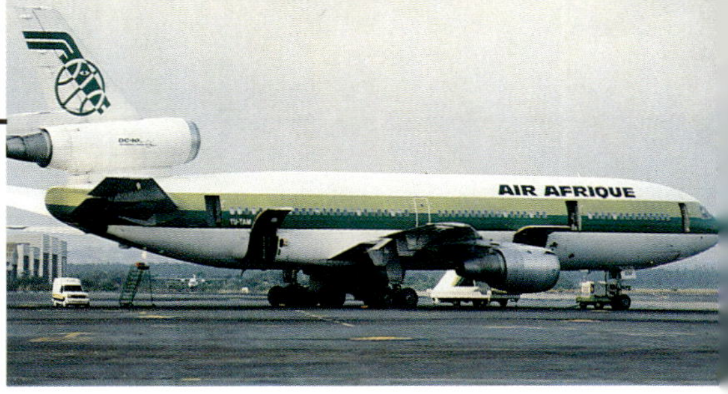

COMMERCIAL AIRLINERS

6
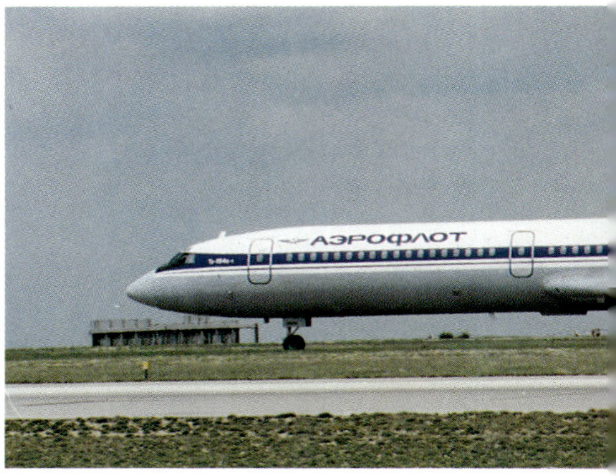

The most obvious American rival to the Boeing 707 was the Douglas DC-8, which made its debut in 1959. The DC-8-50, introduced in 1960, was a four-engined swept-wing jet with a cruising speed of 580 mph (930 kph) and a range of 5,600 miles (9,000 km). Its carrying capacity was 189 passengers, eventually increased to 259 in the stretched Super Sixty series of 1965.

1
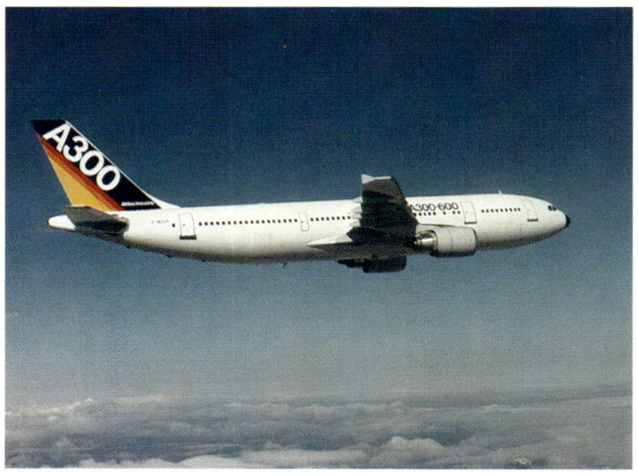

As passenger traffic increased, the concept of the jumbo-jet was born. The Boeing 747 made its first commercial flight in 1970, flying the North Atlantic in the colours of PanAm. Carrying from 350 to 498 passengers, the 200 version has a take-off weight of 356 tons, and can fly stages of 5,000 miles (8,000 km) at over 580 mph (930 kph). Many versions now exist: cargo, convertible, and the short-bodied 747SP, which has a longer range for reduced capacity of 288 seats. In response, in 1966 Lockheed began developing the three-engined L-1011 TriStar, a wide-bodied jet with of capacity of up to 345 passengers, which would cruise at 560 mph (900 kph) on stages of between 3,100 and 4,000 miles (5,000 and 6,500 km).

7
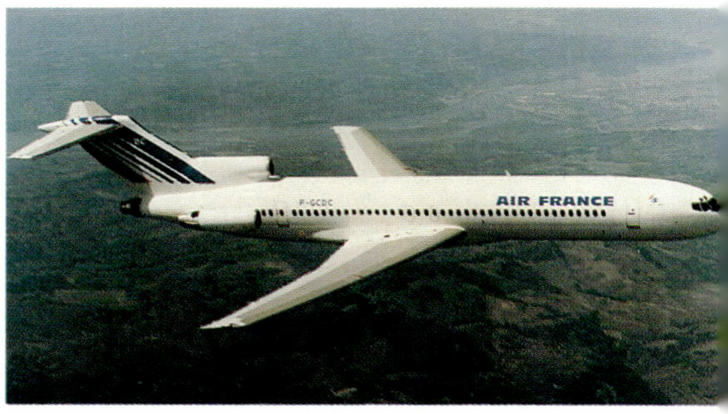

2
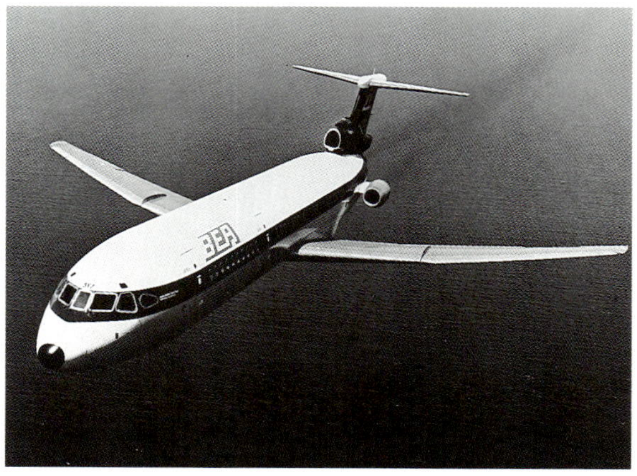

8
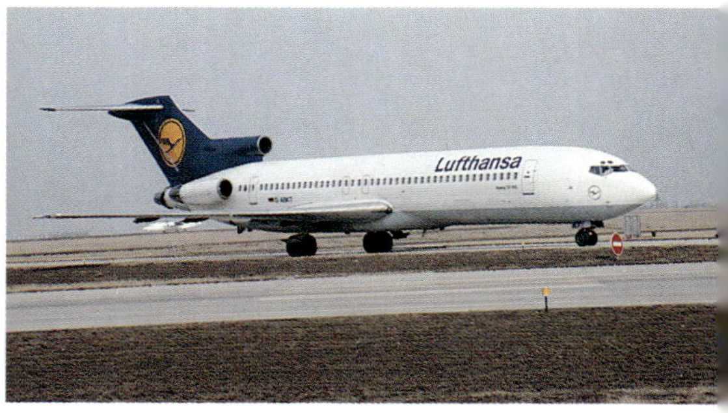

McDonnell Douglas also opted for a three-engined design, bringing its DC-10 into service in 1971. The DC-10/30 cruises at 560 mph (900 kph) and can fly distances of 4,375 miles (7,000 km) with between 270 and 380 passengers on board. The modernized MD-11, introduced in 1990, has a capacity of 350 passengers and a range of over 5,000 miles (8,000 km). In the medium-distance category, McDonnell Douglas's contribution has been the DC-9, with twin jet engines mounted at the rear. First operated in 1965 by Delta Airlines, it carries from 72 to 130 passengers at 560 mph (900 kph) on stages of up to 1,125 miles (1,800 km).

3
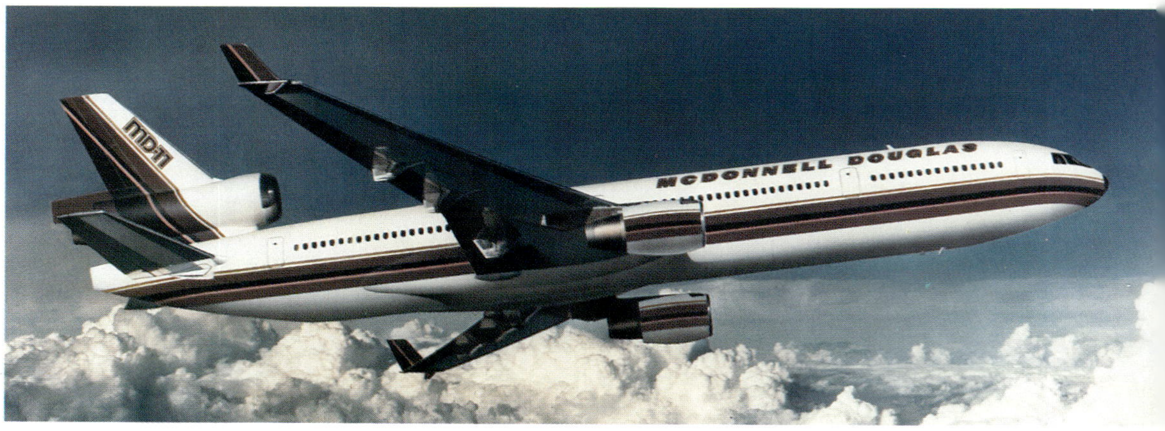

In 1963, United Airlines introduced the three-engined Boeing 727, a 125-seater jet with a range of 1,690 miles (2,700 km) and a cruising speed of 560 mph (900 kph). Stretched versions can accommodate up to 189 passengers. Boeing made 1,832.

Another three-engined jet of this vintage was the Hawker Siddeley HS.121 Trident, which made its first commercial flight in 1964. It could fly at speeds of 600 mph (960 kph), carrying 149 passengers up to 3,100 miles (5,000 km).

4
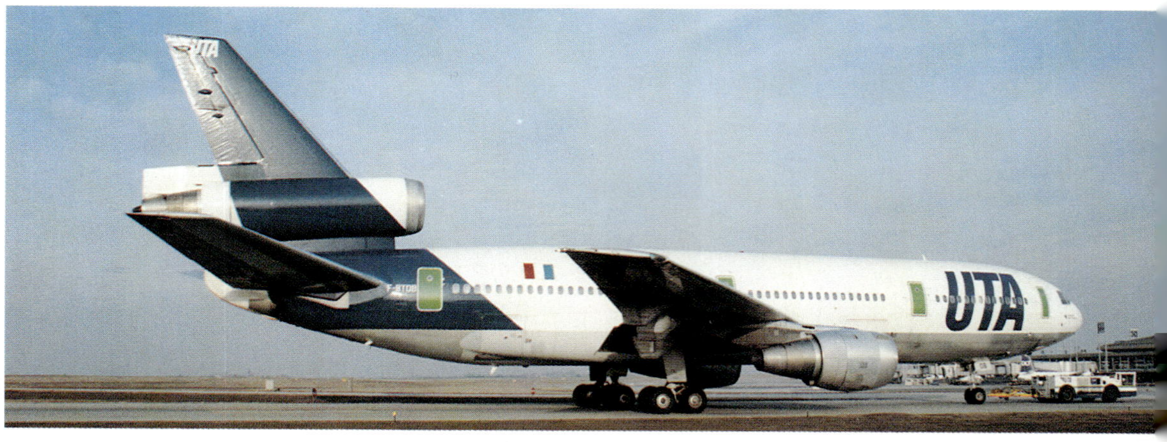

In 1972, the European Airbus consortium (Aérospatiale, DA, British Aerospace and CASA) began work on the wide-bodied Airbus A300B2 – 250 passengers, 560 mph/900 kph, 2,350 miles/3,750 km – and the longer-range (3,750-mile/6,000-km) A300B4. Later variants include the higher-performance A300-600 (1984) and the smaller

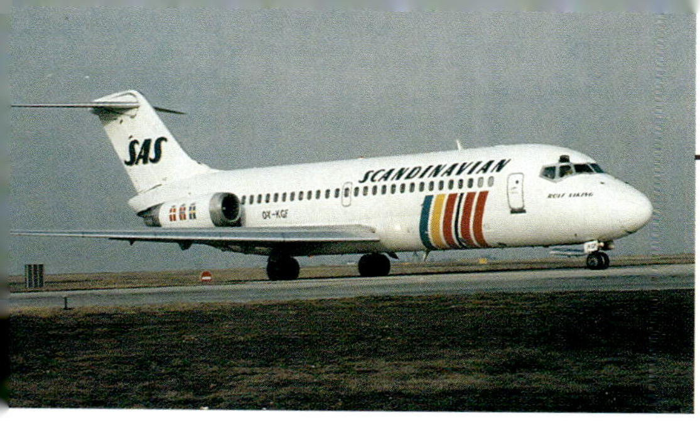
9

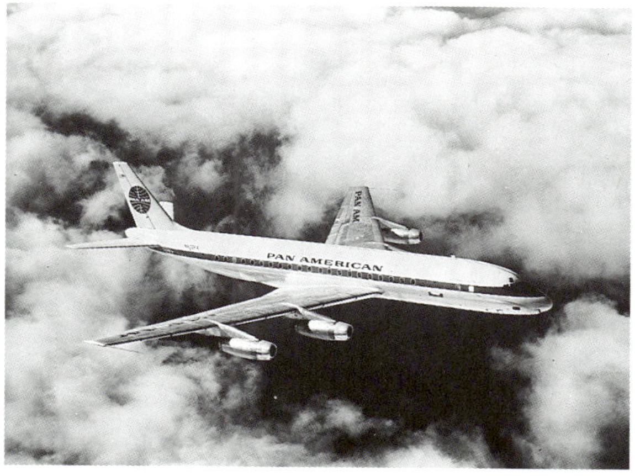
12

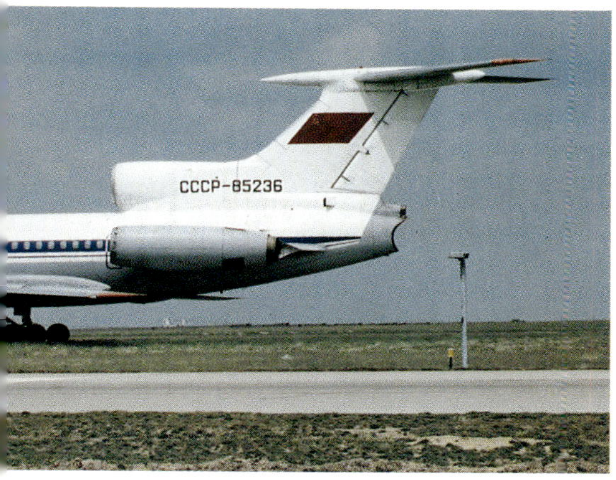

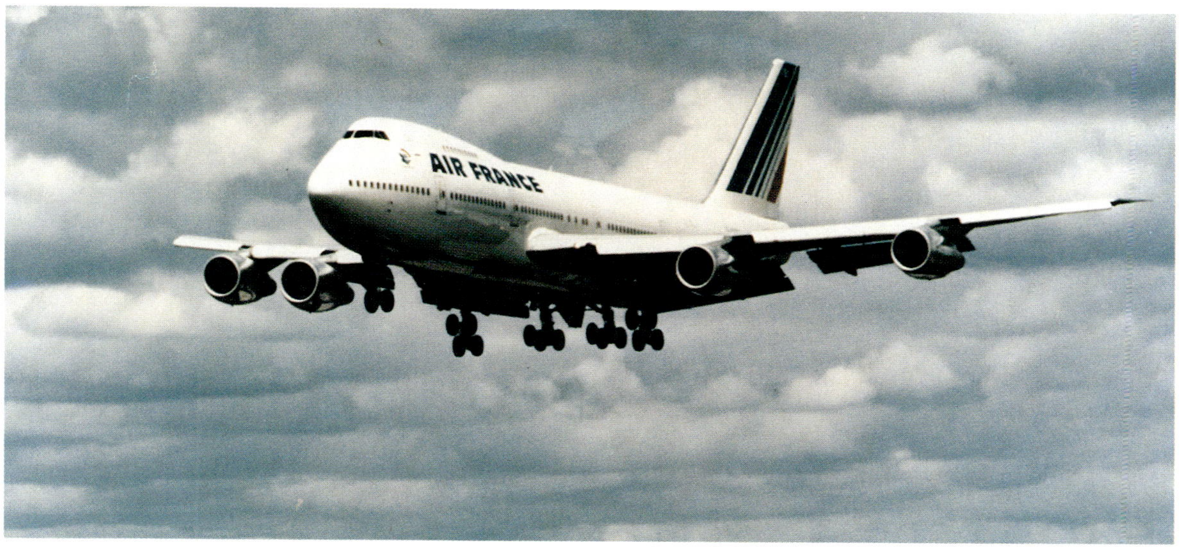
17

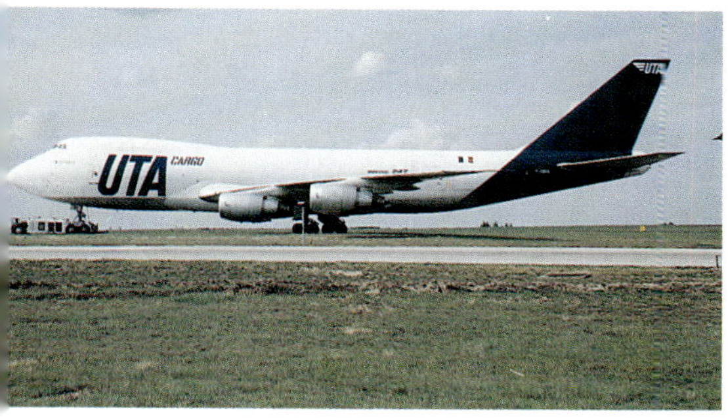
10

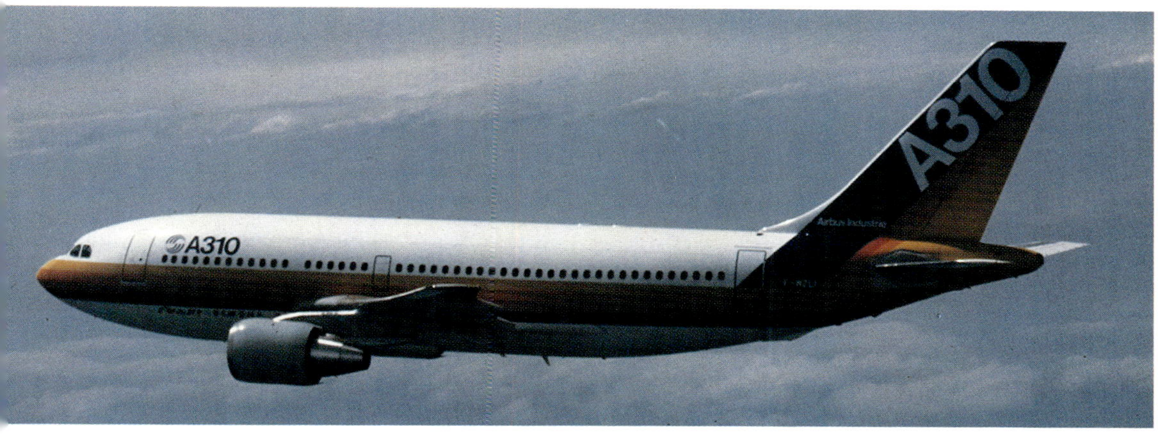
13

A310 (1982), which carries 210 to 265 passengers at 560 mph (900 kph) on hauls of between 4,000 and 6,000 miles (6,500 and 9,600 km).

In 1964, the Soviets unveiled the short-range Tupolev Tu-134, a twin-engined jet designed to carry 72 passengers over distances of 1,560 miles (2,500 km), and the three-engined Tupolev Tu-154, which carries 165 passengers at over 590 mph (950 kph) on hauls of 2,180 miles (3,500 km).

For cargo transport, the Antonov An-12 came into service in 1960. Cruising at 375 mph (600 kph), it has a payload of 10 tons and a range of 2,125 miles (3,400 km). It was followed by the An-22: payload 45 tons, cruising speed 440 mph (700 kph), range 6,900 miles (11,000 km).

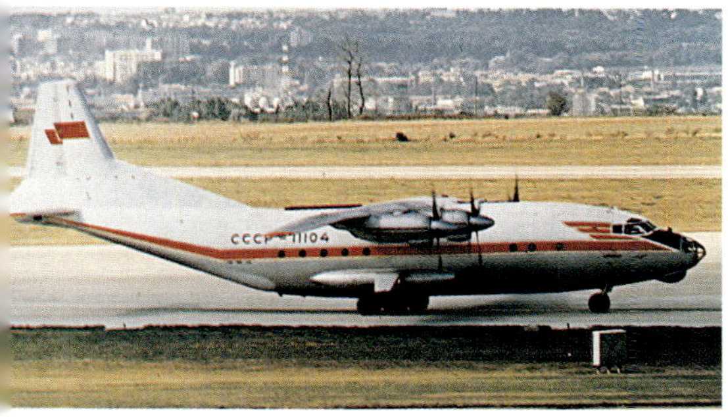
11

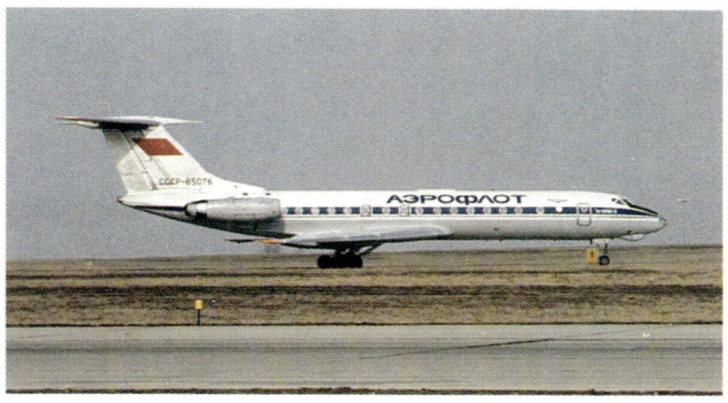
14

Photo No. 1: Airbus A300 (European consortium)
Photo No. 2: Hawker Siddeley Trident (Great Britain)
Photo No. 3: McDonnell Douglas MD-11 (USA)
Photo Nos. 4 and 5: McDonnell Douglas DC-10 (USA)
Photo No. 6: Tupolev Tu-154 (USSR)
Photo Nos. 7 and 8: Boeing 727 (USA)
Photo Nos. 9 and 15: Douglas DC-9 (USA)
Photo Nos. 10 and 17: Boeing 747 (USA)
Photo No. 11: Antonov An-12 (USSR)
Photo No. 12: Douglas DC-8 (USA)
Photo No. 13: Airbus A310 (European consortium)
Photo No. 14: Tupolev Tu-134 (USSR)
Photo No. 16: Lockheed L-1011 TriStar (USA)

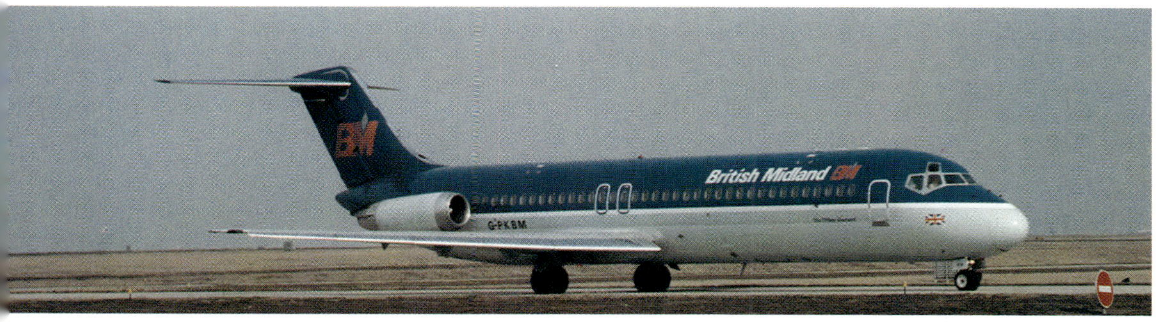
15

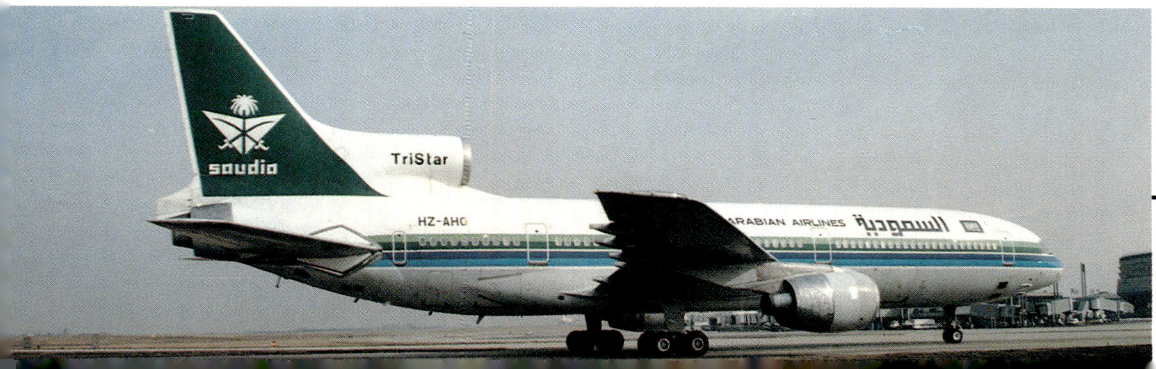
16

COMMERCIAL AIRLINERS

5
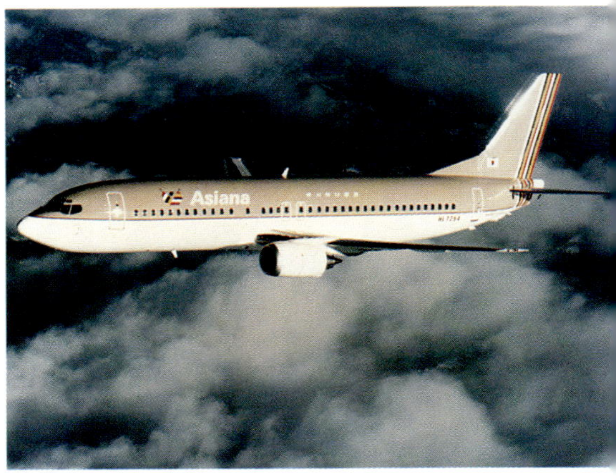

In the early 1960s the British marketed a medium-range aircraft to compete with American products: the BAC One-Eleven, which had twin jet engines mounted at the rear. It cruised at over 540 mph (870 kph), carrying 65 passengers on stages of up to 1,680 miles (2,700 km). The later 500 version had seating for 119.

In 1967, following the successes of the 707 and 727, Boeing added a short-haul jet to its family of aircraft. The twin-engined 737 then had a range of 700 miles (1,130 km) and cruised at 560 mph (900 kph) with 110 passengers aboard. Enlarged and equipped with more modern engines, the 737 still continues to sell. More recently, Boeing has brought out its twin-engined 757 and 767 models. The smaller 757 carries up to 239 passengers on flights of between 3,125 and 4,375 miles (5,000 and 7,000 km), depending on the version. Its bigger brother, which cruises at 560 mph (900 kph), has a carrying capacity of up to 261 passengers. The range varies from 3,750 to 6,875 miles (6,000 to 11,000 km).

As a rival to the 737, in 1969 the French constructor Dassault decided to build the Mercure, a fast 150-seater twin-engined jet with a cruising speed of over 560 mph (900 kph) and range of 940 miles (1,500 km). It came into service with Air Inter in 1974. Not for almost ten years was there room for another twin-engined aircraft in the 150-seater category. Finally, in 1988, airlines began to take delivery of the Airbus A320. Flying at 560 mph (900 kph), it has a range of between 2,000 and 3,330 miles (3,250 and 5,300 km) and a carrying capacity of 150 to 164 passengers. A stretched 186/200-seat version, the A321, is due out in 1993. Meanwhile, in the United States, existing models have been improved and uprated to meet new airline requirements. For instance, in 1980 the Boeing 747 was offered in a 400-seat version (the 747-300), and in 1985 appeared the 747-400, which has a carrying capacity of 412 and a range of 8,125 miles (13,000 km).

For its part, McDonnell Douglas has modernized the DC-9, bringing out the stretched, more powerful versions of the MD-80 series, and the MD-91 and 92.

In France, 1972 saw the advent of a Super-12 version of the Caravelle with a range of 1,000 miles (1,600 km), able to carry 128 passengers at 500 mph (810 kph).

In the ranks of smaller aircraft, in 1962 Nord Aviation (now part of Aérospatiale) began producing a twin-engined high-wing turboprop, the 262 Frégate, which carries 25 passengers at 240 mph (380 kph) on journeys of up to 625

1
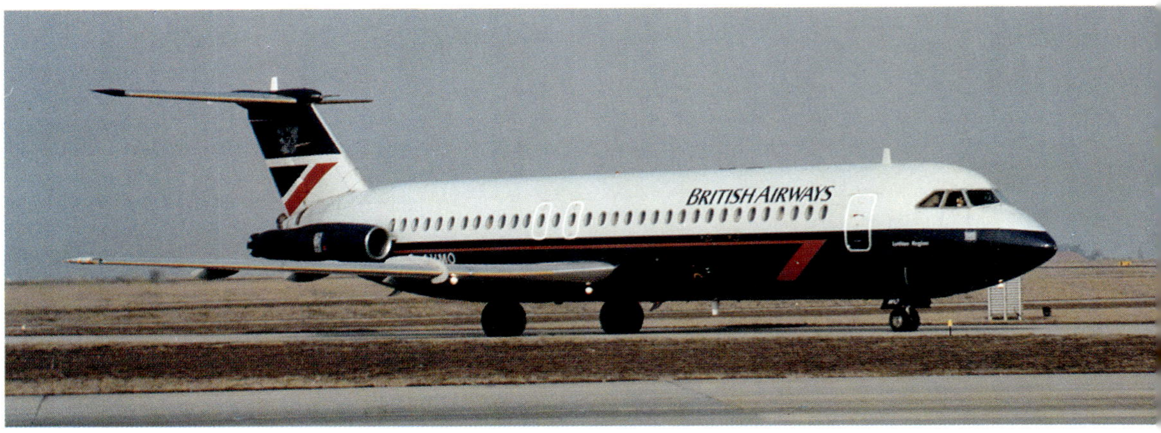

2
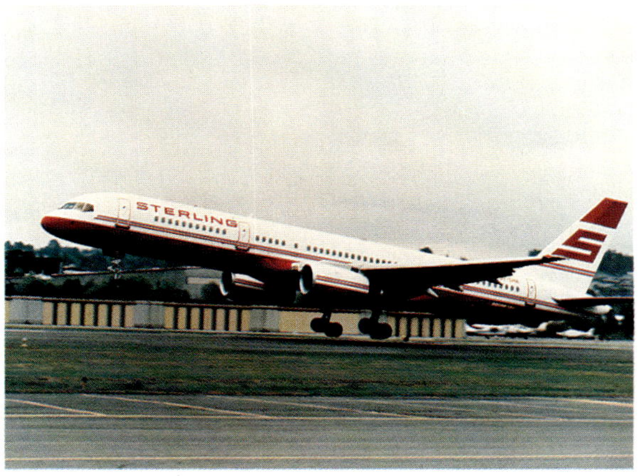

6
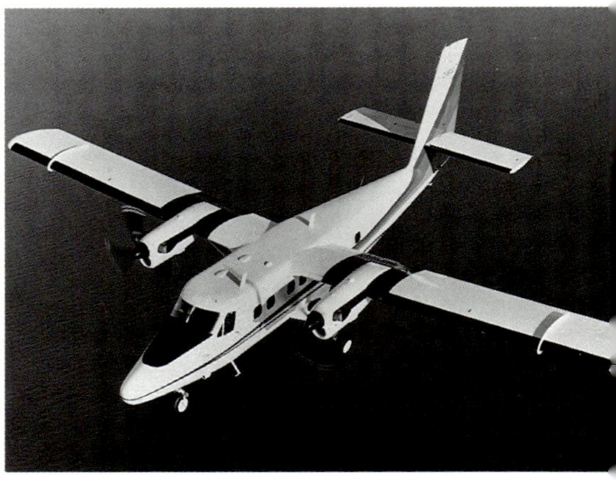

3
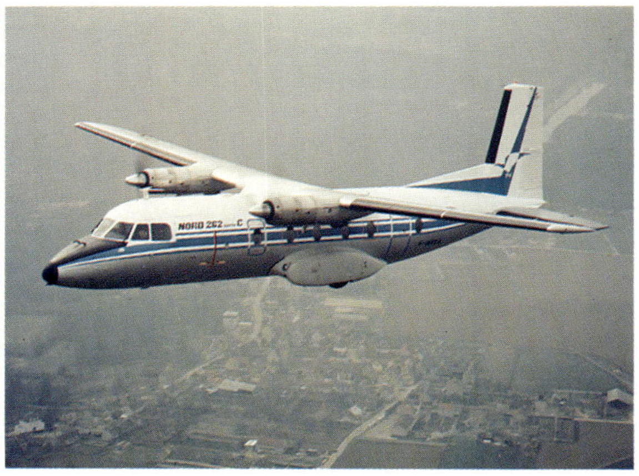

7
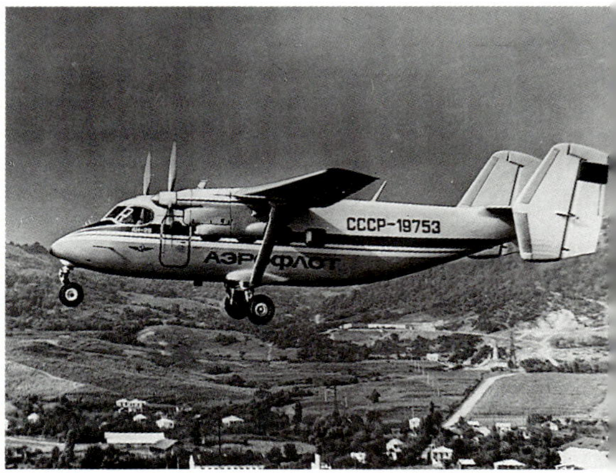

4
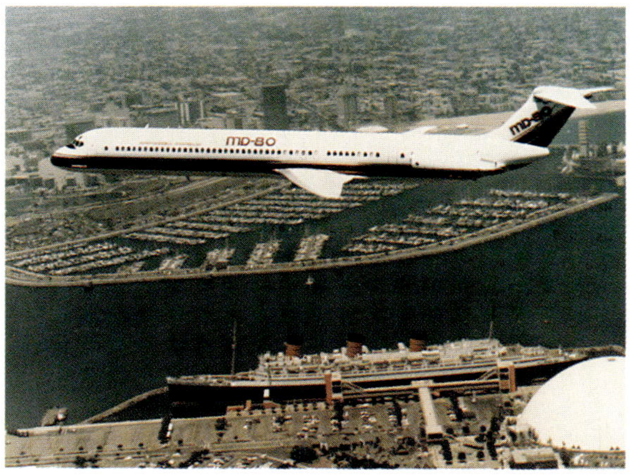

8
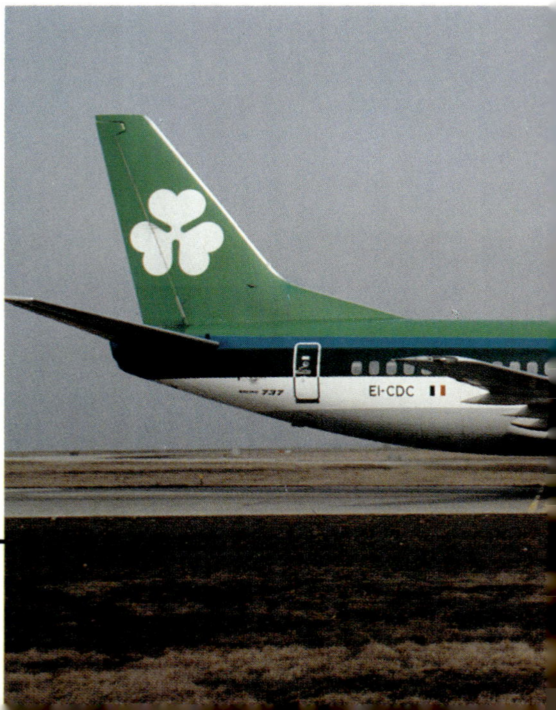

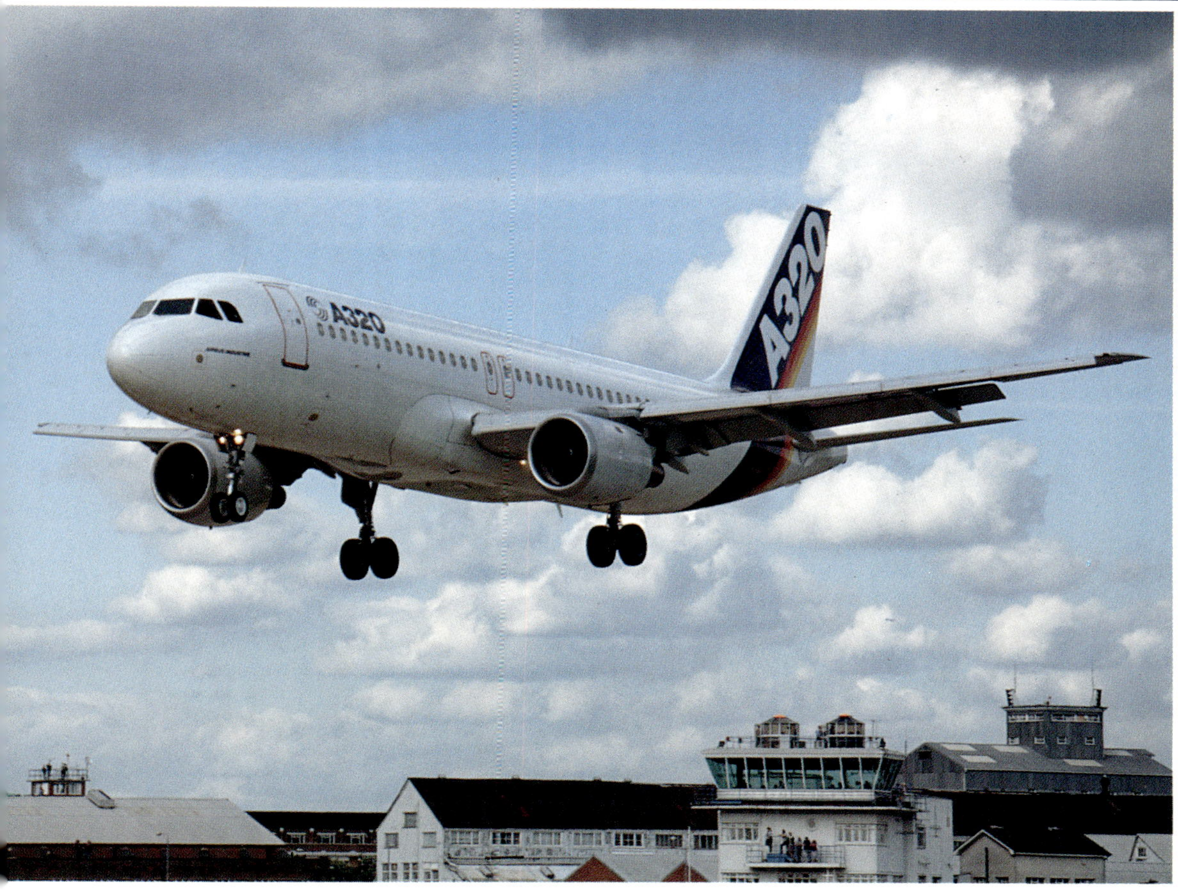

11

miles (1,000 km). A similar aircraft was brought out in 1965 by de Havilland of Canada. The DHC-6 Twin Otter, with twin turboprop engines and a fixed undercarriage, is ideal for short, unsophisticated runways. It carries 20 passengers, flying stages of around 625 miles (1,000 km) at 210 mph (340 kph). In the USSR, the same sort of need gave rise, in 1958, to the Antonov An-14 and, in 1970, to the larger An-28. A twin-engined high-wing 15-seater, the An-28 flies at 155 mph (250 kph) and has a range of 440 miles (700 km).

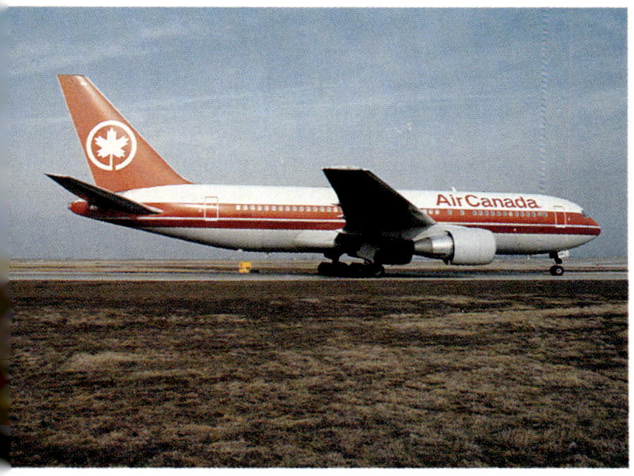

9

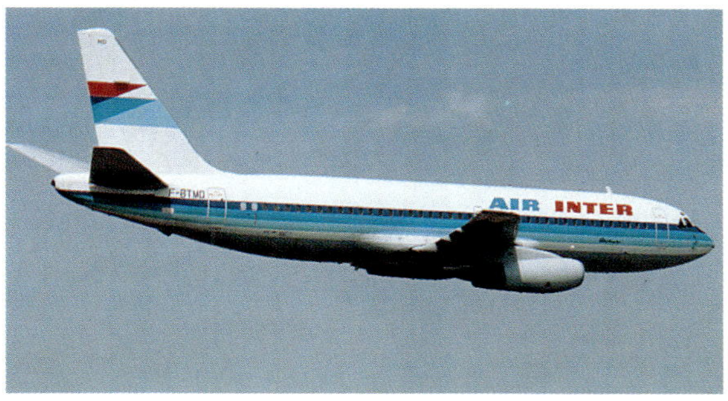

12

Photo No. 1: BAC One-Eleven (Great Britain)
Photo No. 2: Boeing 757 (USA)
Photo No. 3: Nord Aviation N.262 Frégate (France)
Photo No. 4: McDonnell Douglas MD-80 (USA)
Photo Nos. 5 and 8: Boeing 737 (USA)
Photo No. 6: DHC-6 Twin Otter (Canada)
Photo No. 7: Antonov An-28 (USSR)
Photo Nos. 9 and 10: Boeing 767 (USA)
Photo Nos. 11 and 15: Airbus A320 (European consortium)
Photo Nos. 12 and 16: Dassault Mercure (France)
Photo No. 13: Boeing 747-400 (USA)
Photo No. 14: Aérospatiale Super Caravelle 12 (France)

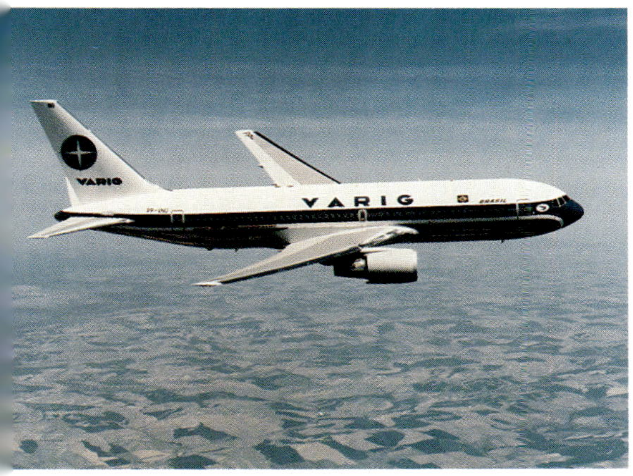

10

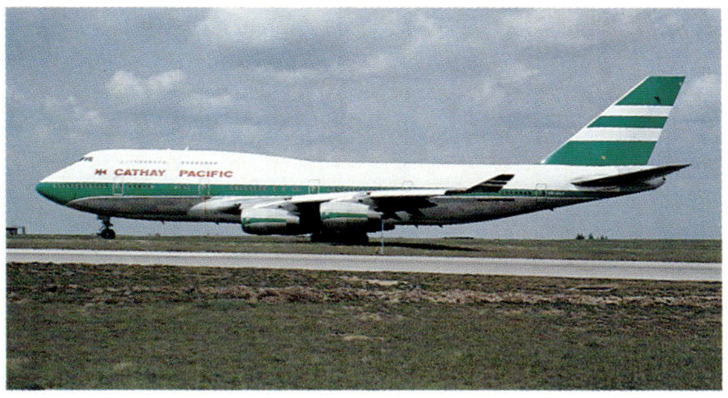

13

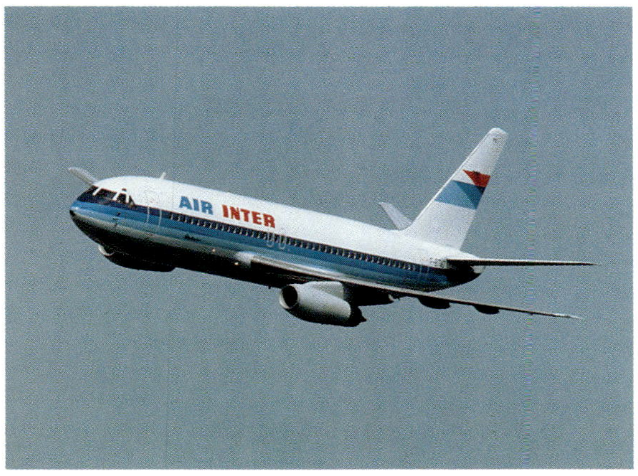

16

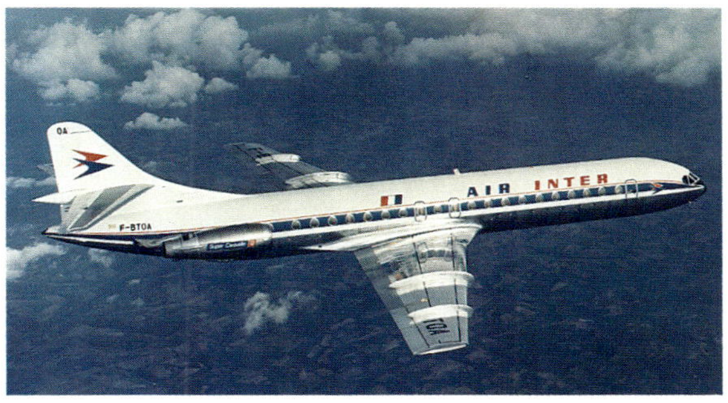

14

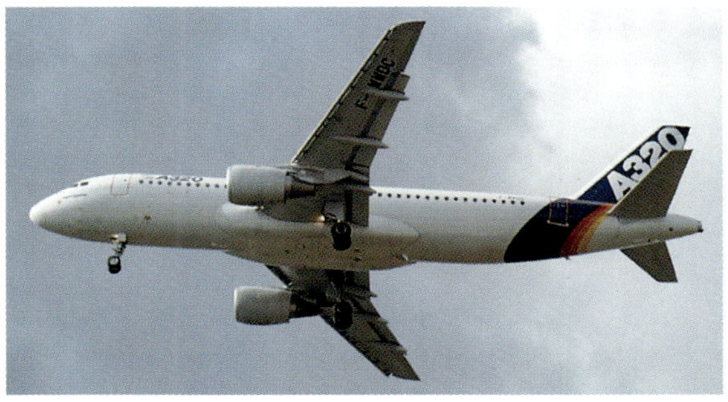

15

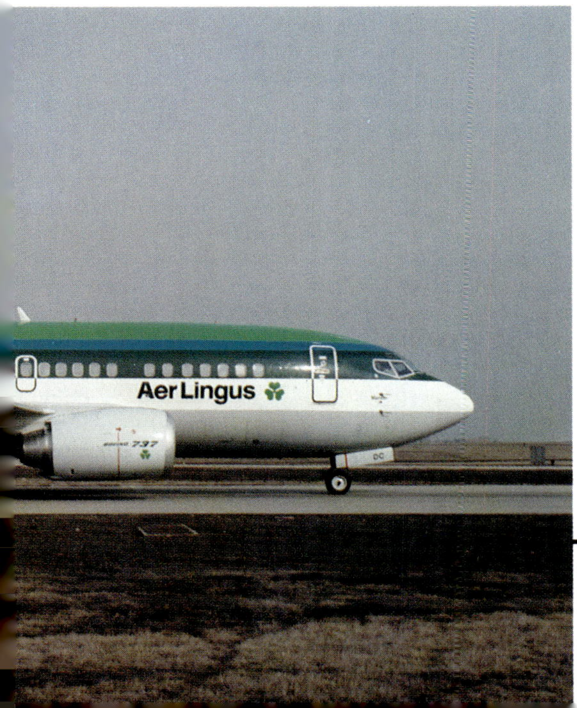

COMMERCIAL AIRLINERS

5

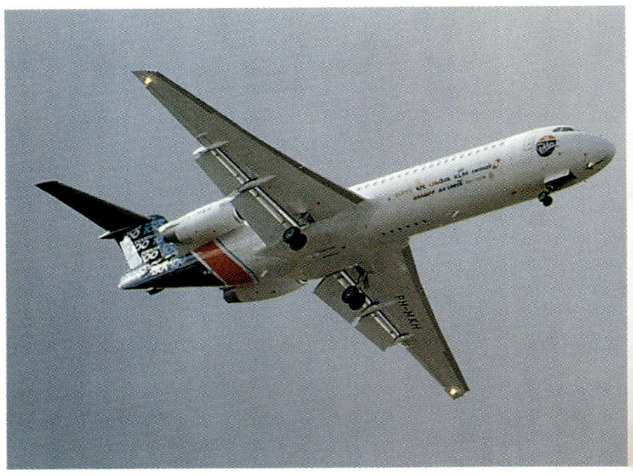

Regional air services have come to assume an increasingly important role, particularly in vast countries such as the former USSR, whose special needs have spawned a large number of aircraft. The Antonov An-24, for instance, is a high-wing twin-engined turboprop with seating capacity for 50 passengers (bigger than the An-28). It cruises at 310 mph (500 kph) and has a range of between 625 and 1,250 miles (1,000 and 2,000 km).

Its Western equivalent is the Fokker F-27 Friendship, which first saw service in 1958. A high-wing aircraft powered by twin turboprop engines, it has a range of around 1,350 miles (2,000 km), transporting 40 passengers at 310 mph (500 kph). The Fokker's main rival has been the British Hawker Siddeley HS.748, a low-wing aircraft, also powered by twin turboprop engines. Its range is up to 1,875 miles (3,000 km), and it cruises at 280 mph (450 kph) with a complement of 36 passengers.

A more recent arrival in this category is the Franco-Italian (Aérospatiale/Aeritalia) regional transport aircraft, the ATR 42, which came into service in 1985. It cruises at 306 mph (490 kph) and can carry from 42 to 50 passengers over distances of 1,250 miles (2,000 km). Its stretched version, the ATR 72, is fitted with from 64 to 74 seats and has a range of over 1,625 miles (2,600 km).

The British Aerospace ATP, a low-wing two-engined turboprop, made its maiden flight in 1986. With a range of between 1,250 and 2,150 miles (2,000 and 3,450 km), it has a cruising speed of almost 315 mph (500 kph) and can be fitted out for between 64 and 72 passengers. The de Havilland (Boeing) Canada Dash 8 came out in 1983. It is a high-wing two-engined turboprop with seating for 36. Flying at 310 mph (500 kph), it has a range of around 1,250 miles (2,000 km). Other turboprop best-sellers are the British Aerospace Jetstream 31 and 41 and Spain's CASA Aviocar.

The Germans also have an interest in this market segment. Their first venture was the Dornier Do 28 Skyservant, a small, twin-engined aircraft with high wing and fixed undercarriage, which flies at 187 mph over distances of 1,560 miles (2,500 km) carrying eight passengers. From it was derived, in 1981, the Do 228, stretched and modified to carry 15 to 19 passengers at speeds of 250 mph (400 kph), with a reduced range of between 810 and 1,250 miles (1,300 and 2,000 km). Dornier's latest creation – as part of the DASA group – is the Do 328. It has a capacity of 30 or 48 passengers and a range of 810 miles (1,300 km). Brazil's first light passenger transport was the Embraer EMB-110 Bandeirante, a low-wing twin-engined turboprop unveiled in 1973. It flies at speeds up to 285 mph and can carry 18 passengers over distances of 1,250 miles (2,000 km).

1

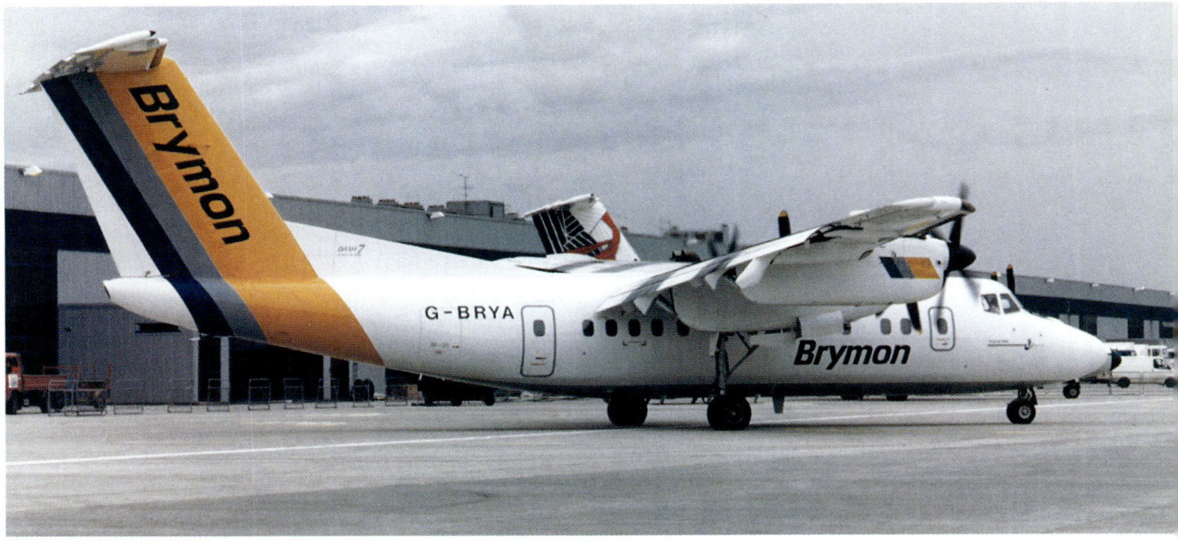

2

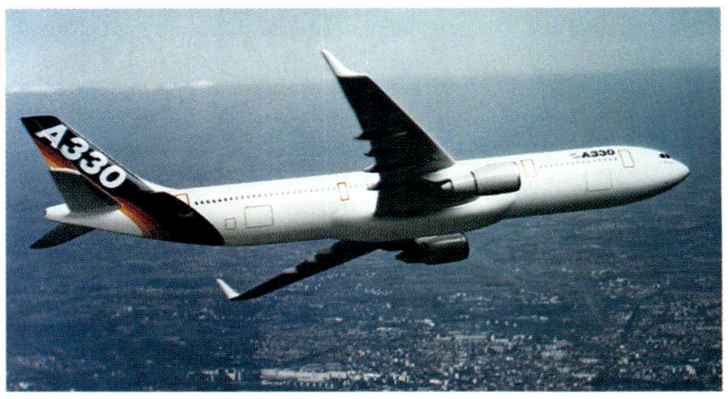

6

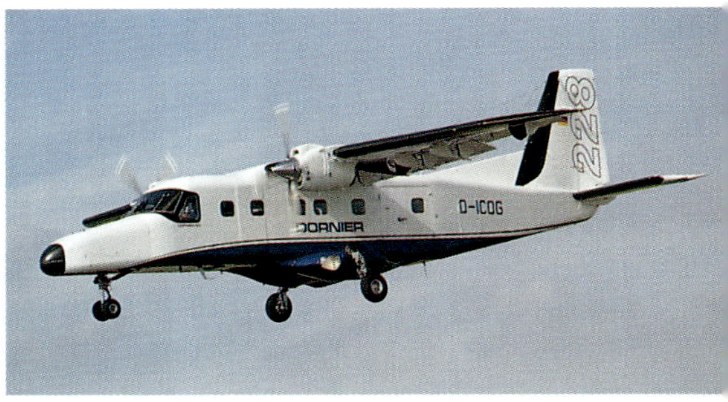

3

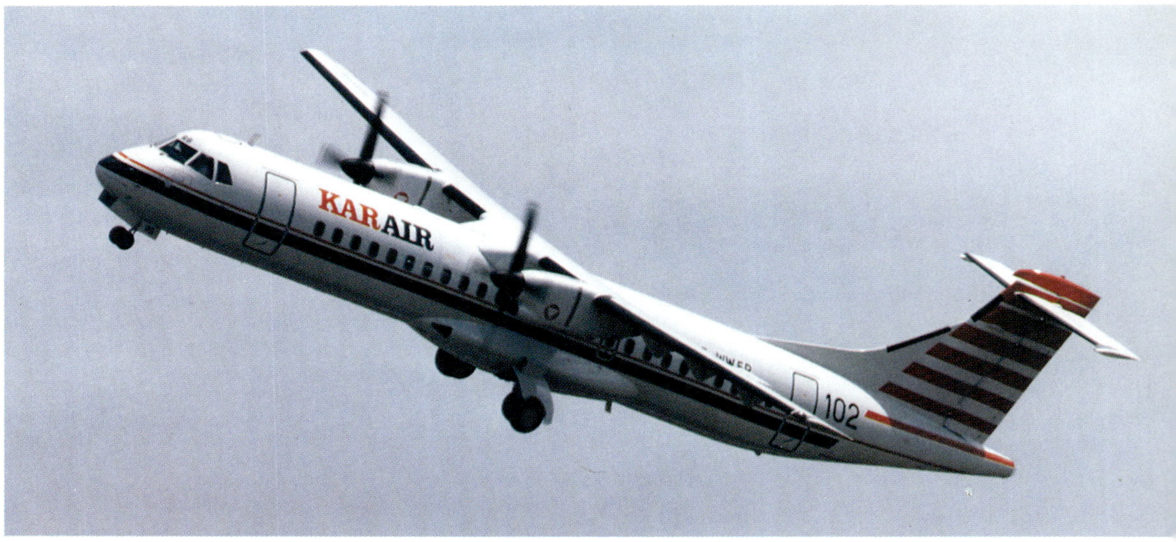

4

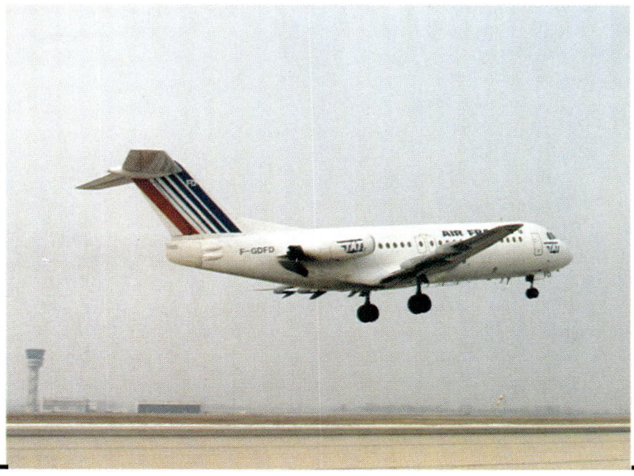

7

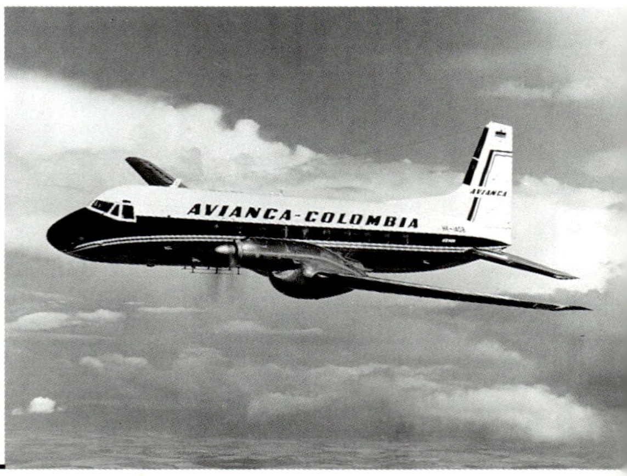

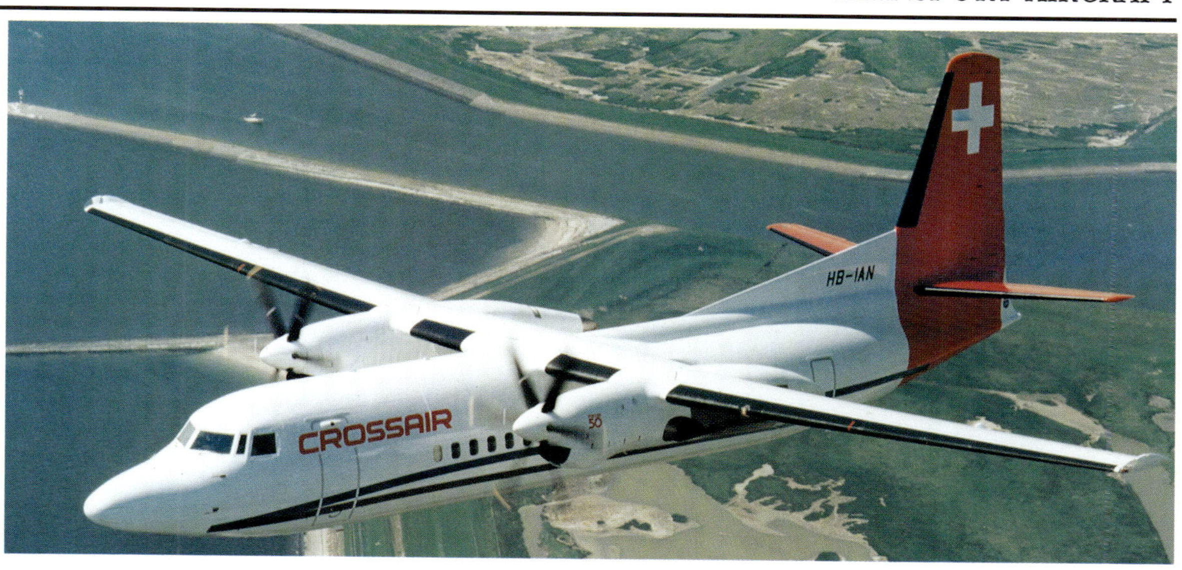
18

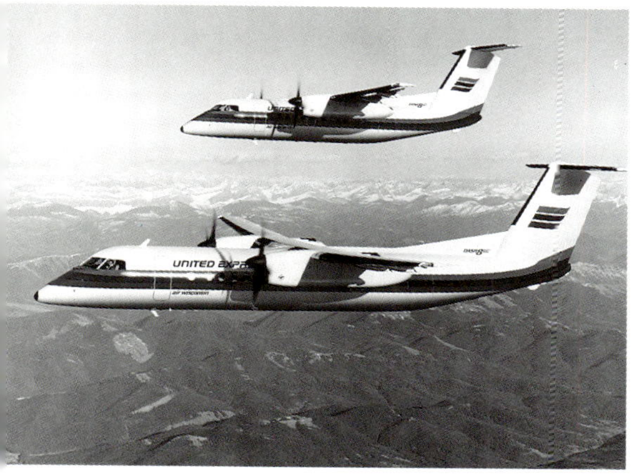
8

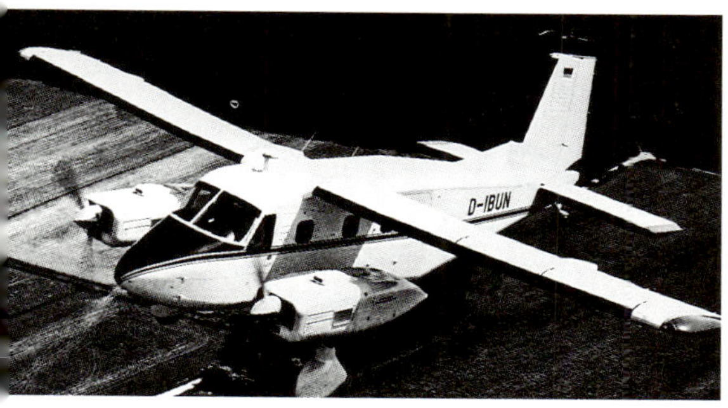
9

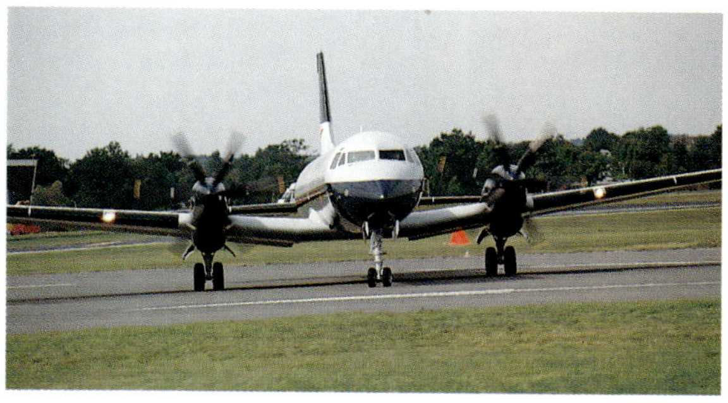
13

Fokker had meanwhile turned its attentions to jet propulsion, bringing out the F28 Fellowship in 1967. This twin-engined aircraft flies at 530 mph (850 kph). With between 50 and 80 passengers aboard, it has a range of 1,060 miles (1,700 km). The F28 eventually led to the 100, another twin-engined jet with a capacity of between 107 and 122 passengers, which first flew in 1987. Its cruising speed is in excess of 500 mph (800 kph) and it has a range of some 1,560 miles (2,500 km).

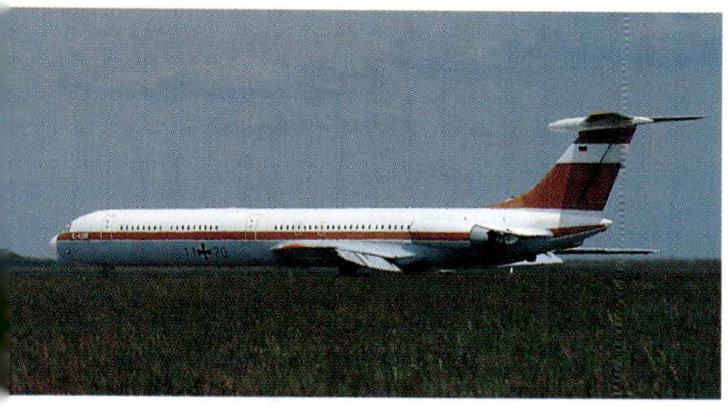
10

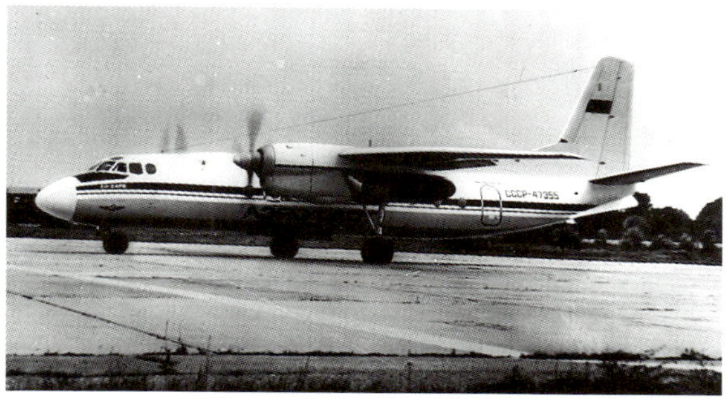
14

During these years the Airbus consortium launched into the long-haul market with two closely-related aircraft, the four-engined A340 and the twin-engined A330. The first of these two is designed to carry 262 passengers on journeys of up to 8,750 miles (14,000 km), while the A330 has a capacity of 330 and a reduced range of 5,625 miles (9,000 km). Their cruising speeds are in excess of 560 mph (900 kph).

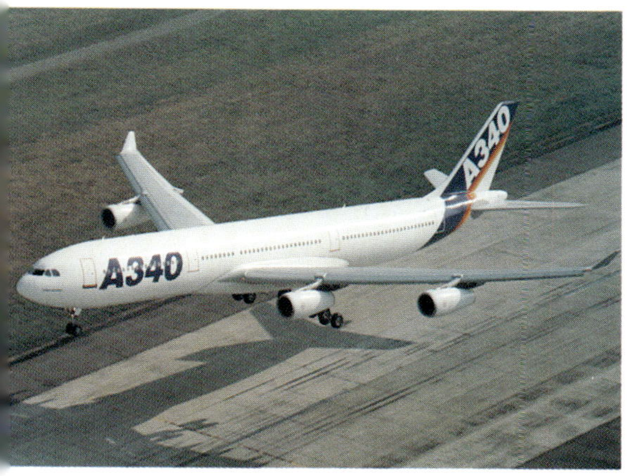
11

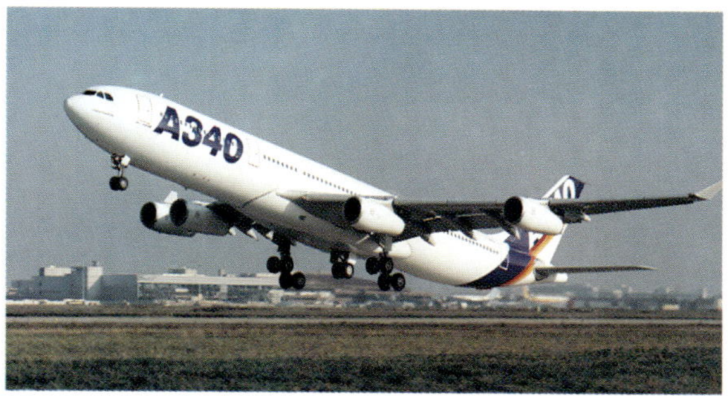
15

Photo No. 1: de Havilland Canada Dash 7 (Canada)
Photo No. 2: Airbus A330 (European consortium)
Photo No. 3: ATR 72 (France/Italy)
Photo No. 4: Fokker F28 Fellowship (Netherlands)
Photo No. 5: Fokker 100 (Netherlands)
Photo Nos. 6, 16 and 19: Dornier Do 228 (Germany)
Photo No. 7: Hawker Siddeley HS 748 (Great Britain)
Photo No. 8: de Havilland Canada Dash 8 (Canada)
Photo No. 9: Dornier Do 28 Skyservant (Germany)
Photo No. 10: Ilyushin Il-62M (USSR)
Photo Nos. 11 and 15: Airbus A340 (European consortium)
Photo No. 12: ATR 42 (France/Italy)
Photo No. 13: British Aerospace ATP (Jetstream 61) (Great Britain)
Photo No. 14: Antonov An-24 (USSR)
Photo No. 17: Embraer EMB-110 Bandeirante (Brazil)
Photo No. 18: Fokker 50 (Netherlands)

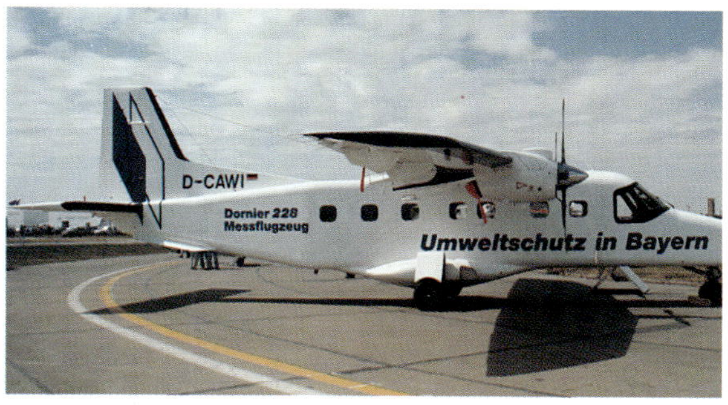

16

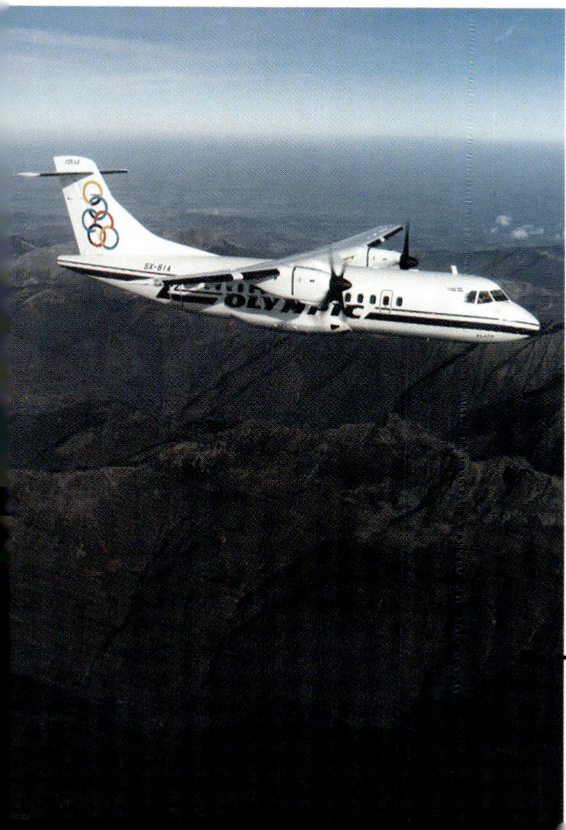
12

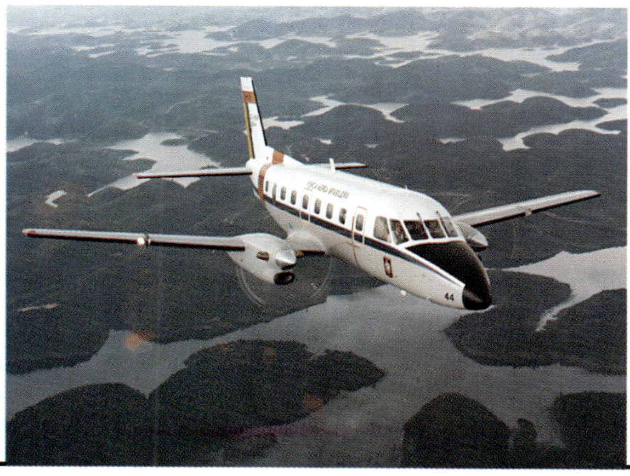
17

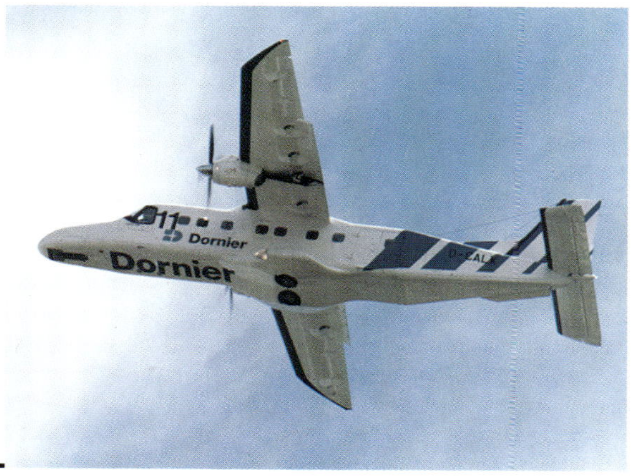

19

COMMERCIAL AIRLINERS

4

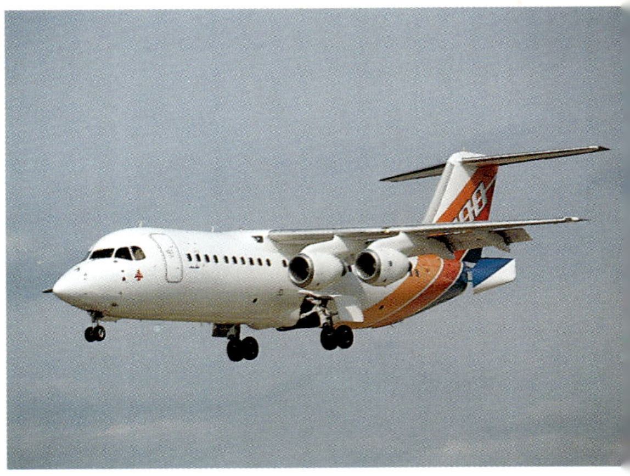

Regional airlines' quest for the transport best suited to their requirements has led to aircraft of all shapes and sizes. In the United States, for instance, the Fairchild Metro, dating from 1971, is a small 20-seater. A twin-engined turboprop, it flies at around 280 mph (450 kph) and has a range of 1,300 miles (2,100 km). The 1983 Saab 340 is of similar conception, carrying 35 passengers at 310 mph (500 kph) on flights of up to 1,123miles (1,807 km).

In 1972 appeared the Czech-manufactured Let L-410 Turbolet. A high-wing twin-engined turboprop, it cruises at 230 mph (370 kph) over distances of 625 miles (1,000 km) with 19 passengers on board.

In 1966, the Soviet constructor Yakovlev began producing a short-range three-engined jet. With capacity for 30 passengers, the Yak-40 flies at 375 mph (600 kph) and has a range of 625 miles (1,000 km).

Designed for STOL (short take-off and landing) on 600-metre runways, the de Havilland Canada Dash 7 made its debut in 1975. Powered by four turboprop engines, it carries 50 passengers at 280 mph (450 kph) on stages of between 940 and 1,250 miles (1,500 and 2,000 km).

The British Aerospace BAe 146, introduced in 1981, is a four-engined jet intended for use on short and unpaved landing strips. Depending on the version, the 146 has seating for between 82 and 128 passengers, cruises at 375 to 491 mph (600 to 789 kph) and can fly stages of between 1,250 and 1,875 miles (2,000 and 3,000 km).

Since the war, Soviet airliner design has been shared among four bureaux: Antonov, Yakovlev, Tupolev and Ilyushin. In 1950, Ilyushin designed the medium-range Il-14, a twin-engined aircraft with seating for 24 to 28 passengers, a range of between 625 and 1,250 miles (1,000 and 2,000 km), and a cruising speed of 250 mph (400 kph). In 1957, based on the Tu-20, Tupolev designed the enormous Tu-114 Rossiya, with capacity of between 170 and 200 passengers. The Tu-114 flew at 500 mph (800 kph) on stages of up to 6,250 miles (10,000 km). In 1959 came the Il-18, an 80-seater four-engined turboprop which cruised at 420 mph (675 kph) and could fly for between 2,500 and 3,750 miles (4,000 and 6,000 km) without refuelling.

1

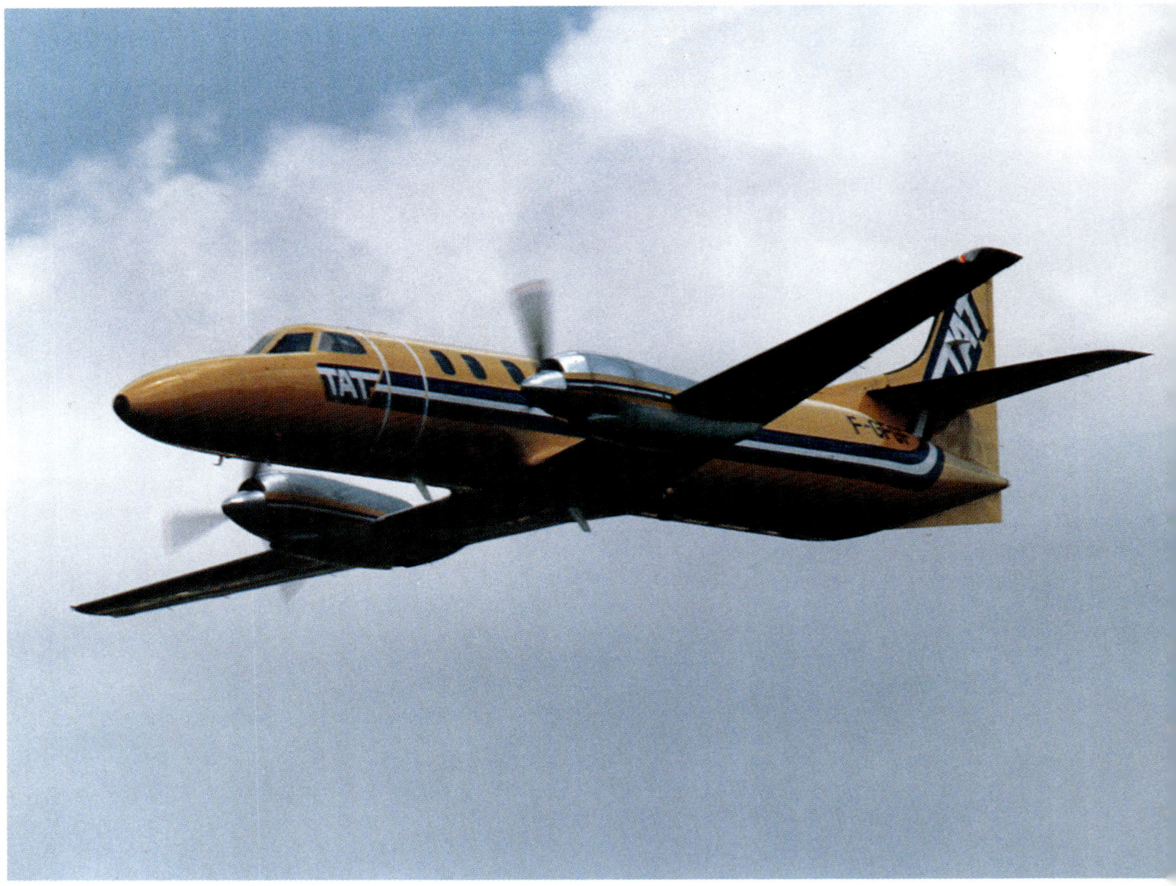

2

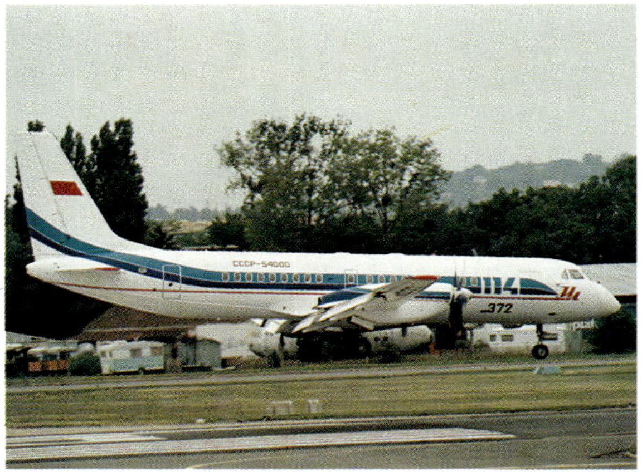

5

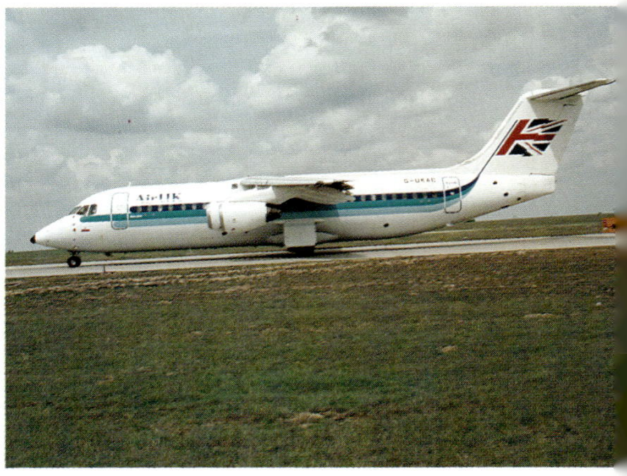

3

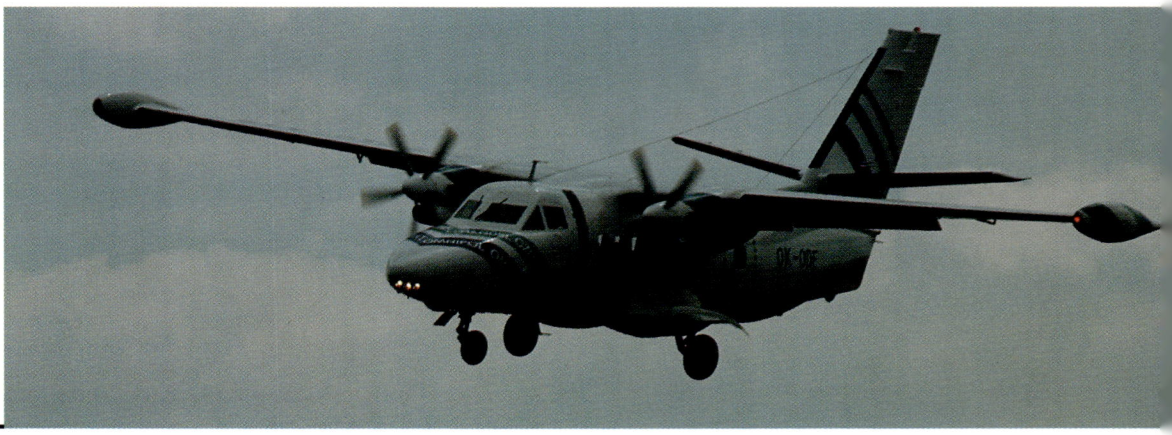

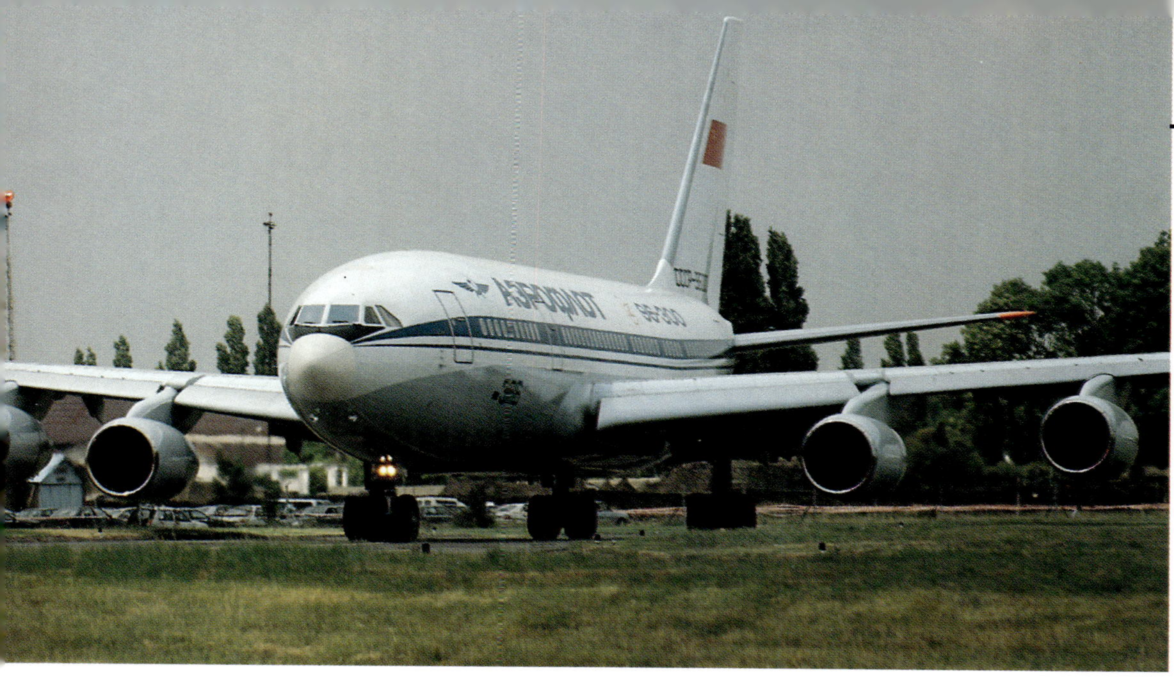

8

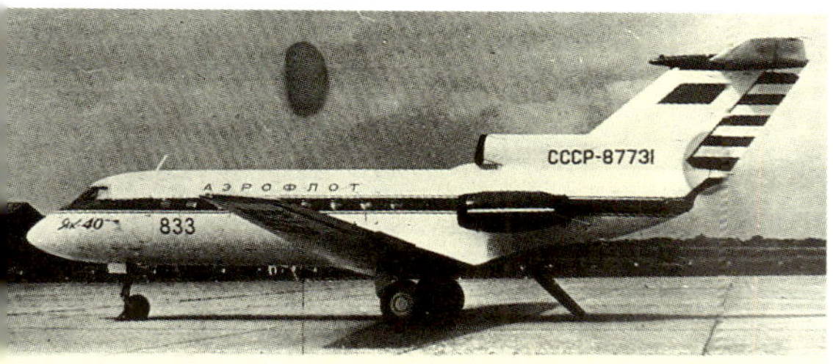

6

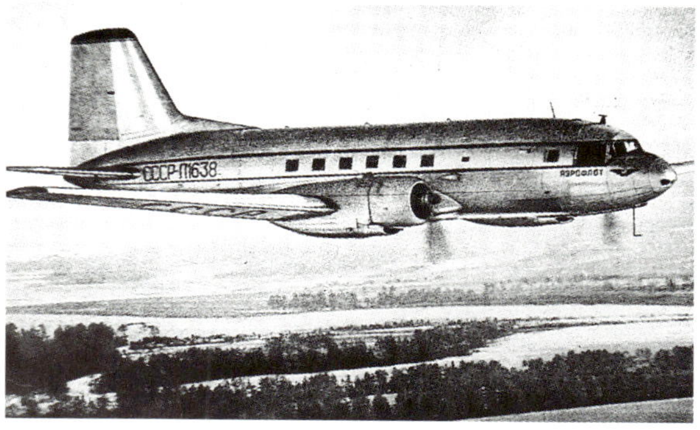

9

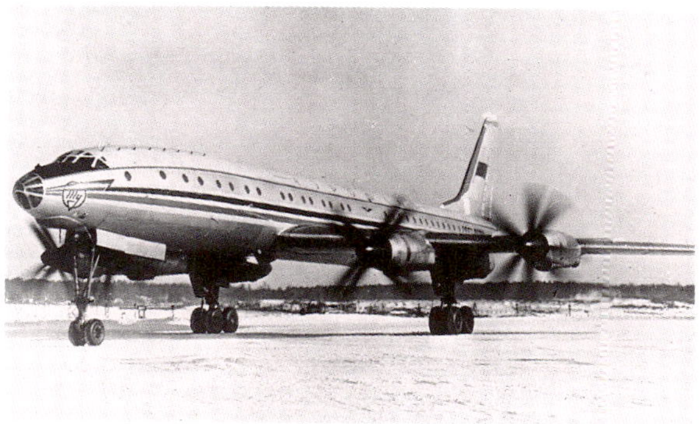

12

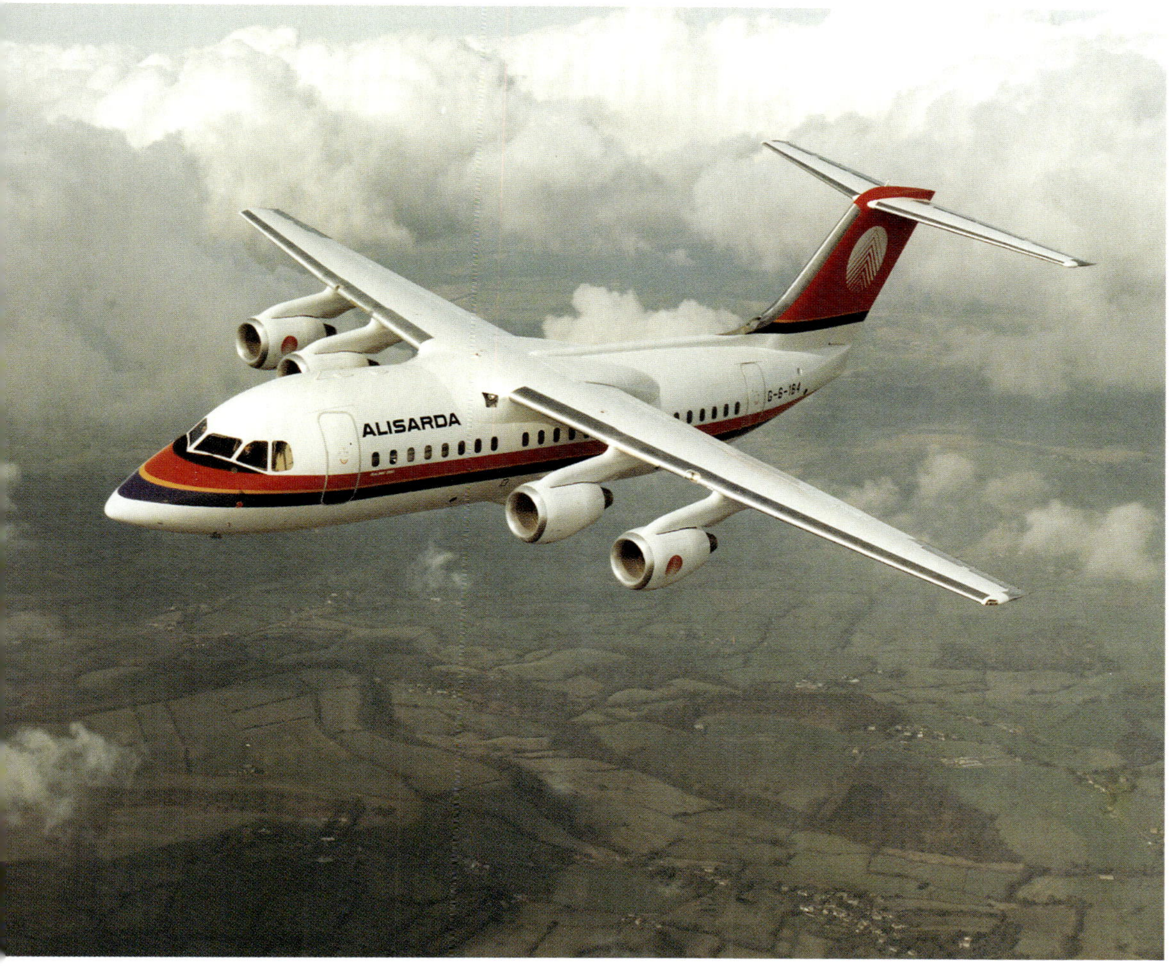

10

The first Soviet long-haul jet was the Il-62, which entered service in 1963. Powered by four rear-mounted engines, it flew stages of around 4,375 miles (7,000 km) at 560 mph (900 kph) carrying up to 186 passengers.

More recent Russian airliners include the Il-86 (1976), a wide-bodied jet with capacity for 350 passengers (cruising speed 590 mph/950 kph, range 2,375 miles/3,800 km), and the Il-96 (1988), which has seating for between 235 and 300 passengers and flies stages of up to 5,600 miles (9,000 km). The Ilyushin Il-114 twin-turboprop seats 60 to 75, and 1,000 may be built by 2005.

Photo Nos. 1 and 7: Fairchild Metro (USA)
Photo No. 2: Ilyushin Il-114 (Russia)
Photo No. 3: Let L-410 Turbolet (Czechoslovakia)
Photo Nos. 4, 5 and 10: BAe 146 (Great Britain)
Photo No. 6: Yakovlev Yak-40 (Russia)
Photo No. 8: Ilyushin Il-96 (Russia)
Photo No. 9: Ilyushin Il-14 (USSR)
Photo No. 11: Ilyushin Il-86 (Russia)
Photo No. 12: Tupolev Tu-114 (USSR)

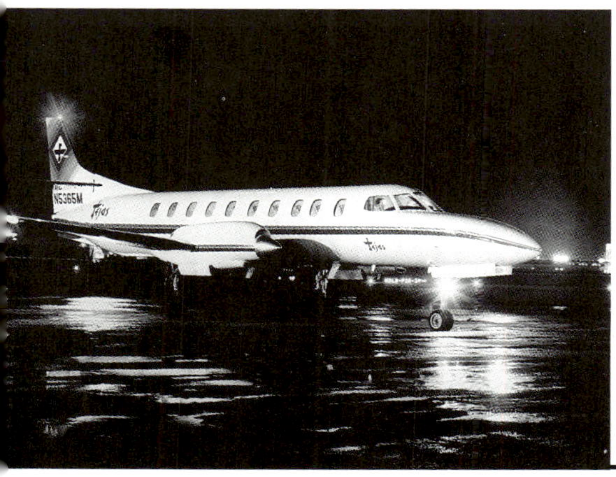

7

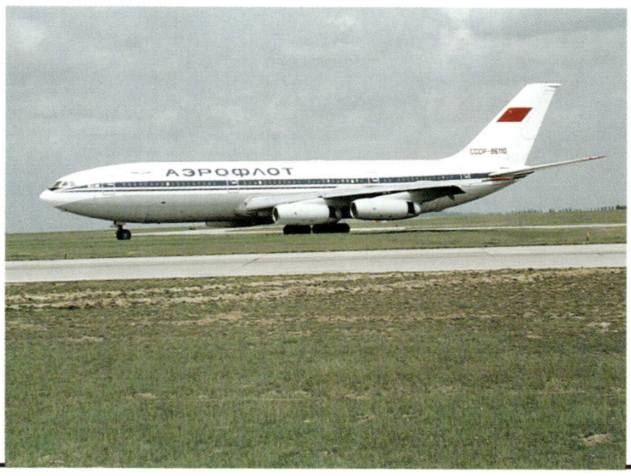

11

4
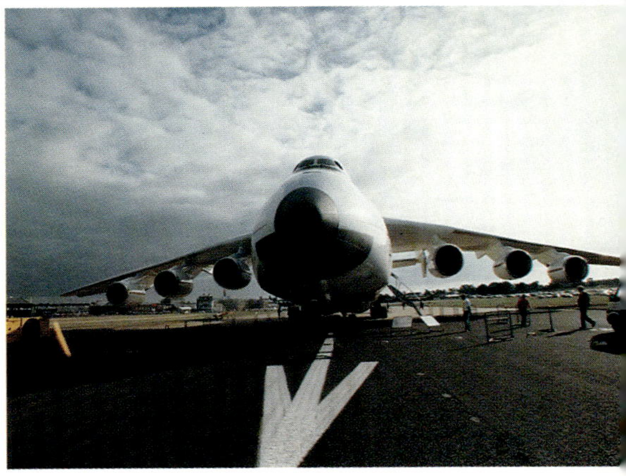

MILITARY TRANSPORT AIRCRAFT

The first military transport aircraft to be used from the beginning of World War II for dropping paratroops was the Junkers Ju 52/3m. Originally designed for civilian use, it was adapted to carry 18 men and their equipment, or twelve stretcher cases. The Germans also built the biggest transport aircraft of the war, the six-engined Messerschmitt Me 323 Gigant. Flying at 140 mph (230 kph) over distances of 750 miles (1,200 km), it could carry an infantry company, 60 stretcher cases or a number of vehicles and guns.

On the Allied side, the most widely-used transports were the military versions of the Douglas DC-3, the C-47 Skytrain and the C-53 Skytrooper, known as the Dakota. More than 10,000 of these were eventually produced.

Bigger and faster was the Curtiss C-46 Commando, another twin-engined transport, which came into service in 1941. Its range was 1,190 miles (1,900 km) and, flying at 280 mph (450 kph), it could carry 50 men and their equipment, 33 stretcher cases or 4.5 tons of freight.

The Douglas C-74 Globemaster was developed during the war and eventually delivered in 1946. In 1950 appeared an improved version, the C-124 Globemaster II. A big, four-engined aircraft, it could transport 25 tons of cargo over 1,250 miles (2,000 km) at 310 mph (500 kph). With a reduced load, its range was increased to 6,250 miles (10,000 km).

After the war, the military were looking for an aircraft with the carrying capacity of the C-47 but which could take off and land on short airstrips. With this in mind, de Havilland Canada designed, in 1958, the high-wing DHC-4 Caribou. Powered by two engines, it flew at 220 mph (350 kph), carrying four tons of cargo or thirty soldiers and their equipment. Its normal range was 250 miles (400 km), but with a reduced load its radius of action was increased to over 1,250 miles (2,000 km). In 1964, de Havilland brought out the DHC-5 Buffalo. A high-wing, twin turbo-prop, it flew faster (270 mph/435 kph), went further (2,190 miles/3,500 km) and carried a heavier load (6.3 tons over 500 miles/800 km) than the Caribou. The Buffalo could be used for transporting 40 men or a number of vehicles and guns.

French research in the field of STOL (short take-off and landing) led, in 1961, to the development of the Breguet 941, a four-engined aircraft with jet-flap wings. Flying at 250 mph (400 kph), it could carry 7.2 tons of cargo over distances of 1,120 miles (1,800 km).

1
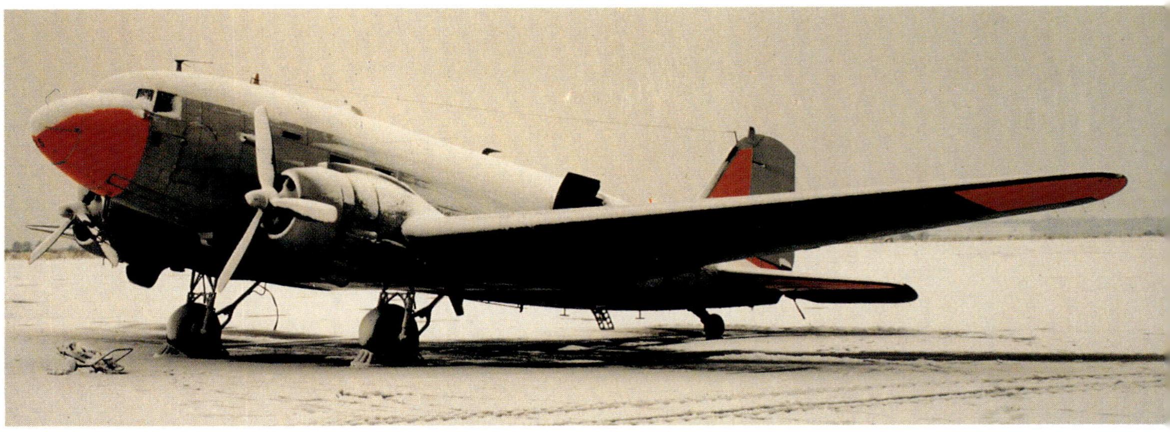

2
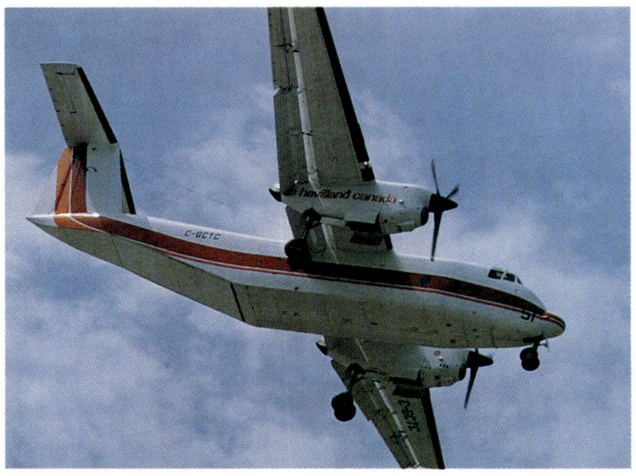

5
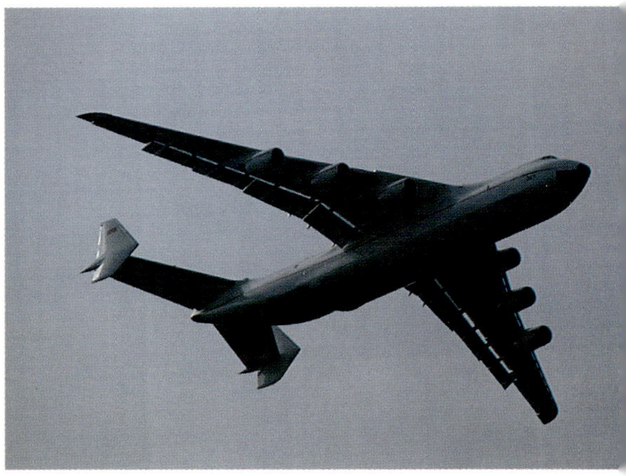

3
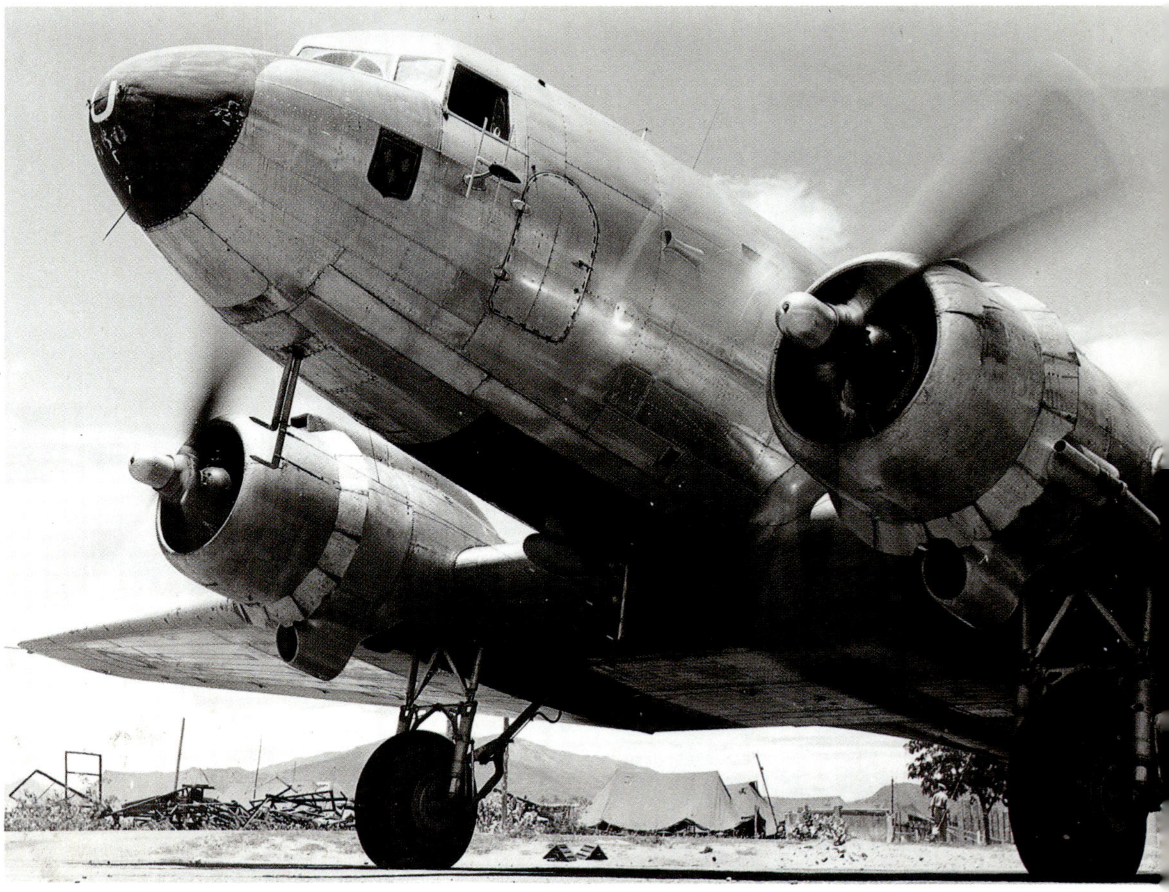

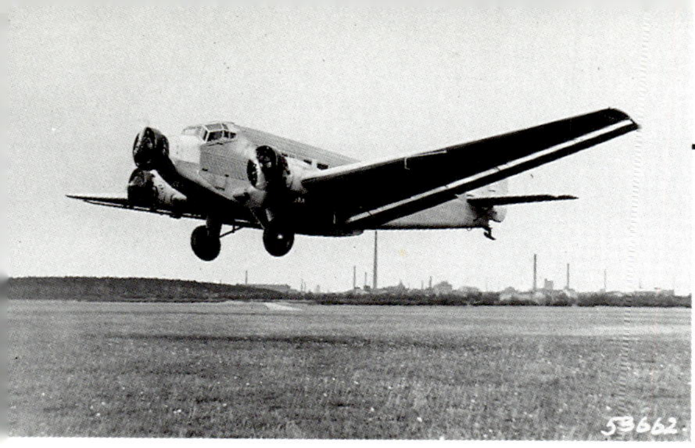

6

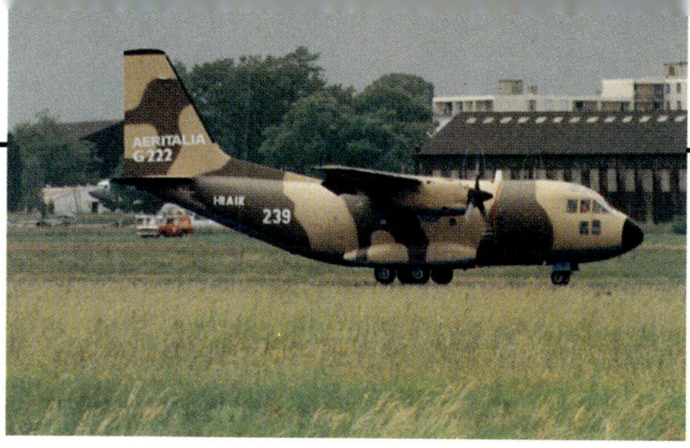

9

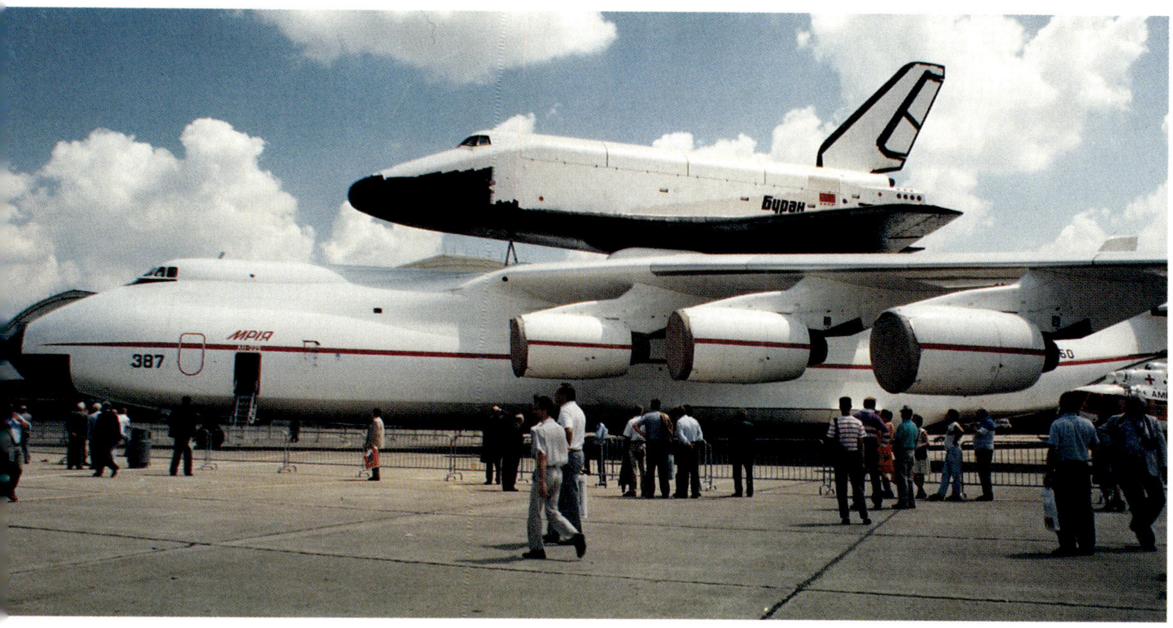

10

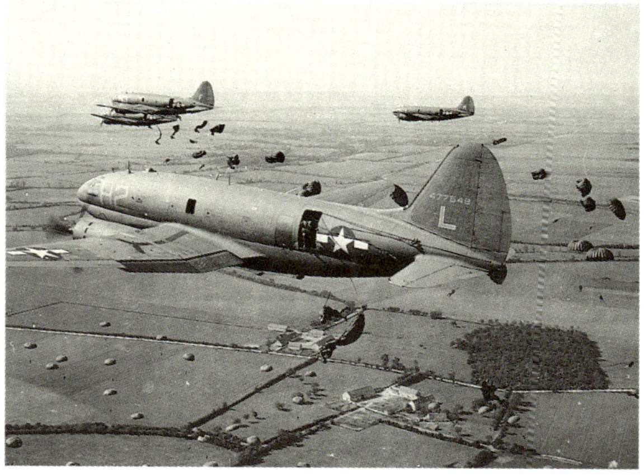
14

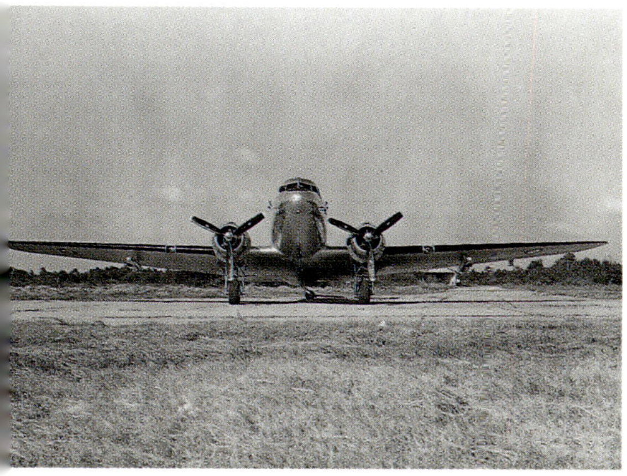
7

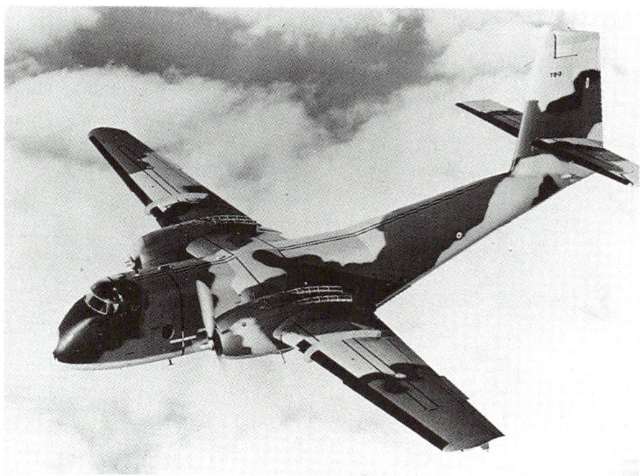
11

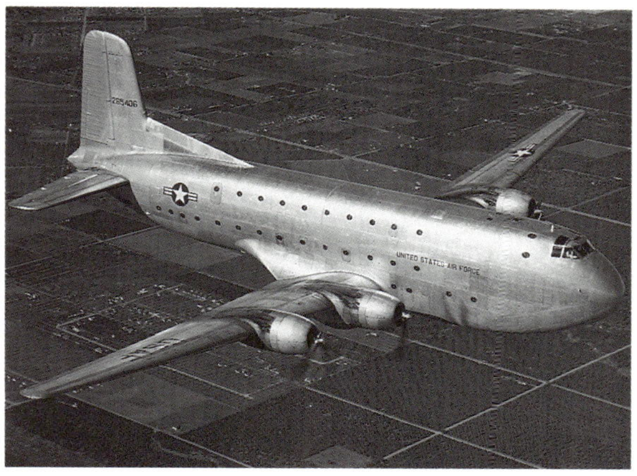
15

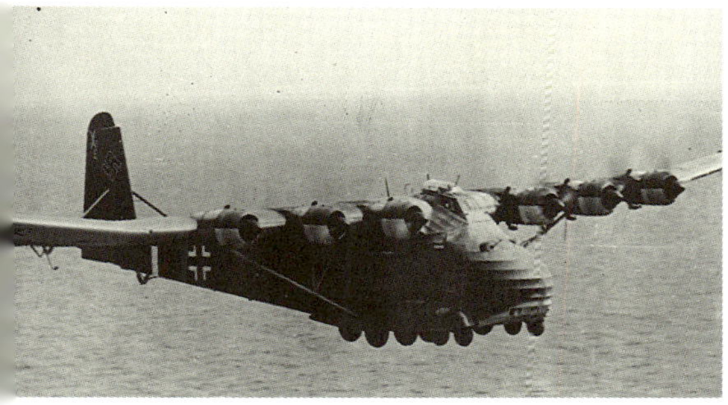
8

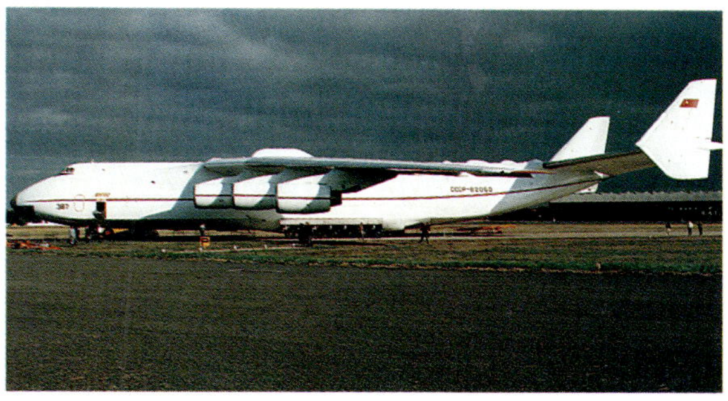
12

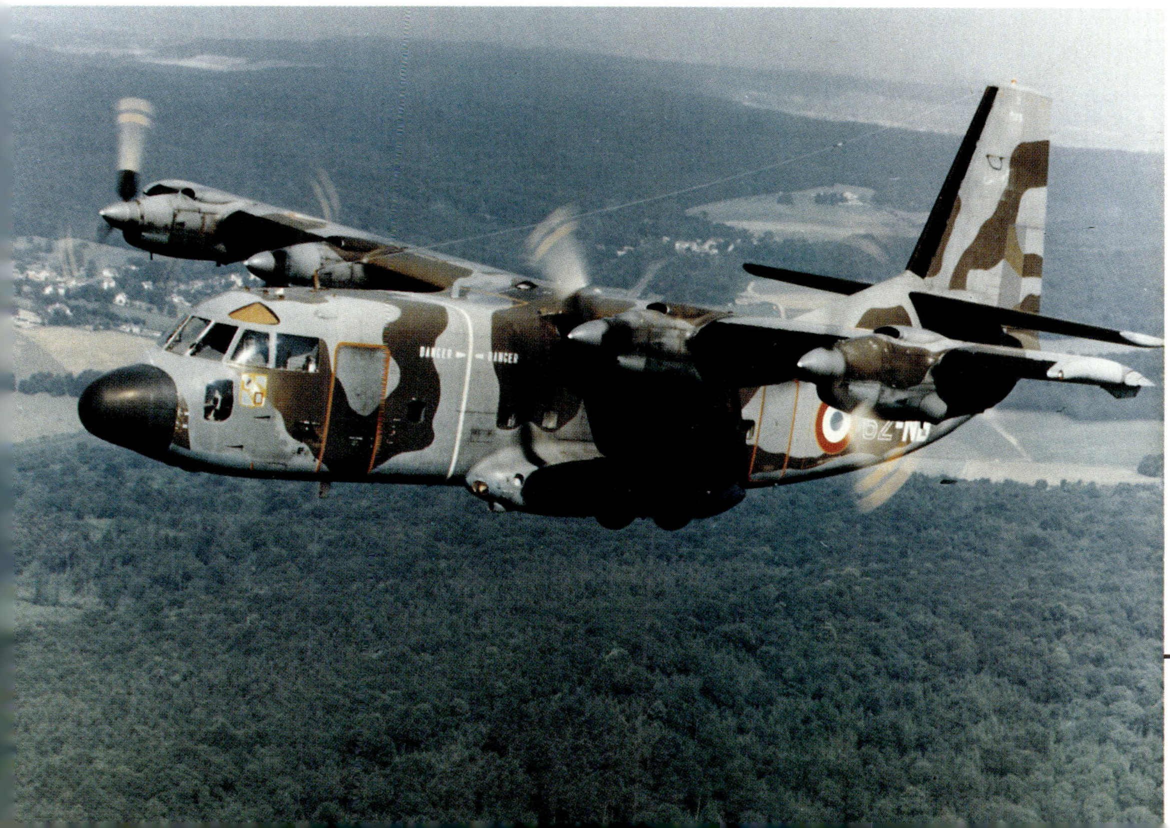
13

In Italy, in 1970 Aeritalia brought out the G.222 military transport, a twin-engined turboprop with a cruising speed of 340 mph (540 kph). It carries 44 passengers, 32 paratroops or five tons of freight and has a range of almost 1,880 miles (3,000 km).

As well as STOL characteristics, the military are always looking for maximum carrying capacity. The champions in this field are now the Ukrainians, with the Antonov An-225, which appeared in 1988. A six-engined aircraft with a record take-off weight of 600 tons, the An-225 can carry 200 tons of cargo at 530 mph (850 kph) over distances of 2,800 miles (4,500 km).

Photo Nos. 1, 3 and 7: Douglas C-47/C-53 (USA)
Photo No. 2: de Havilland DHC-5 Buffalo (Canada)
Photo Nos. 4, 5, 10 and 12: Antonov An-225 (Ukraine)
Photo No. 6: Junkers Ju 52/3m (Germany)
Photo No. 8: Messerschmitt Me 323 Gigant (Germany)
Photo No. 9: Fiat (Aeritalia) G.222 (Italy)
Photo No. 11: de Havilland DHC-4 Caribou (Canada)
Photo No. 13: Breguet Br 941 (France)
Photo No. 14: Curtiss C-46 (USA)
Photo No. 15: Douglas C-124 Globemaster II (USA)

MILITARY TRANSPORT AIRCRAFT

In the post-war years, national armies began to commission new aircraft tailored to their specific transportation needs. In France, studies were carried out by SNCAC for a heavy military transport, the NC 211 Cormoran, a four-engined monster which crashed on its maiden flight. In the event, the Armée de l'Air opted for the Nord 2501 Noratlas to replace its ageing DC-3s. The Noratlas was a twin-engined transport with twin tail booms. It could carry eight tons of equipment or 45 passengers over distances of 1,560 miles (2,500 km) at a speed of 220 mph (350 kph).

In 1959, France and Germany agreed to cooperate on the Transall C-160. Built jointly by Nord-Aviation and three German partners, the high-wing twin-engined transport came into service in 1968. It cruises at close on 375 mph (600 kph), carrying 93 men, 62 stretcher cases, 88 paratroopers or 16 tons of cargo. A new generation of Transalls, introduced in 1981, can be refuelled in flight, giving them a range of 5,000 miles (8,000 km).

In 1961, the RAF re-equipped with a high-wing four-engined transport with twin booms, the Hawker Siddeley A.W.650 Argosy. Fully laden (14 tons) and cruising at 280 mph (450 kph), the Argosy's range was less than 500 miles (800 km), but with a reduced load its range was increased to over 1,560 miles (2,500 km). The Argosy was joined in 1966 by a larger high-wing four-engined transport, the Short Belfast. This aircraft cruised at 310 mph (500 kph), carrying 150 passengers or 36 tons of freight. Its range was 5,300 miles (8,500 km).

In the United States, the Fairchild C-119 Boxcar made its appearance in 1949. A twin-engined aircraft with twin tail booms, it could fly at 250 mph (400 kph), transporting 35-ton loads over distances of between 1,000 and 1,875 miles (1,600 and 3,000 km).

In 1956 Lockheed began supplying the USAF with a new plane which was to be adopted by many of the world's air forces. The C-130 Hercules is a four-engined turboprop with a cruising speed of 390 mph (620 kph). Its range varies from 2,500 to 5,000 miles (4,000 to 8,000 km) depending on the payload. Its maximum capacity is 92 men or 16 tons of cargo.

To the same period belongs the Fairchild C-123 Provider, a twin-engined aircraft with two auxiliary turbojets. It cruised at 190 mph (300 kph) and, with seven tons of cargo, had a range of 1,060 miles (1,700 km).

1
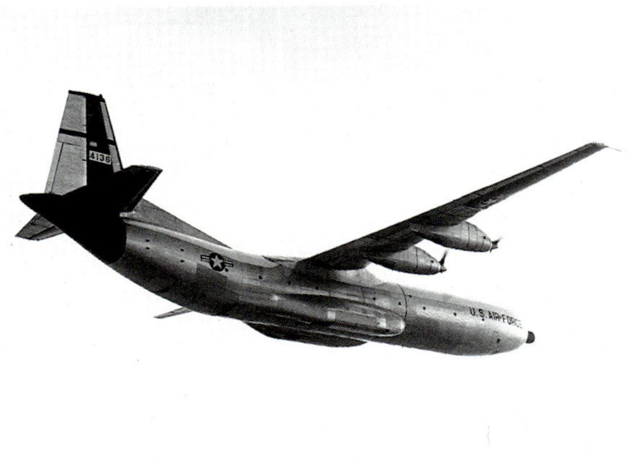

2
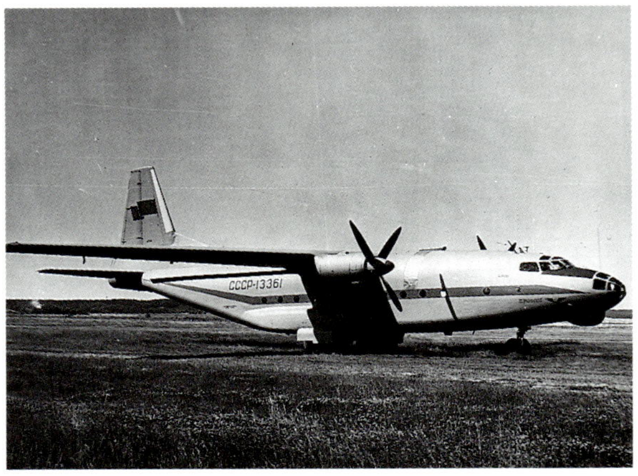

3
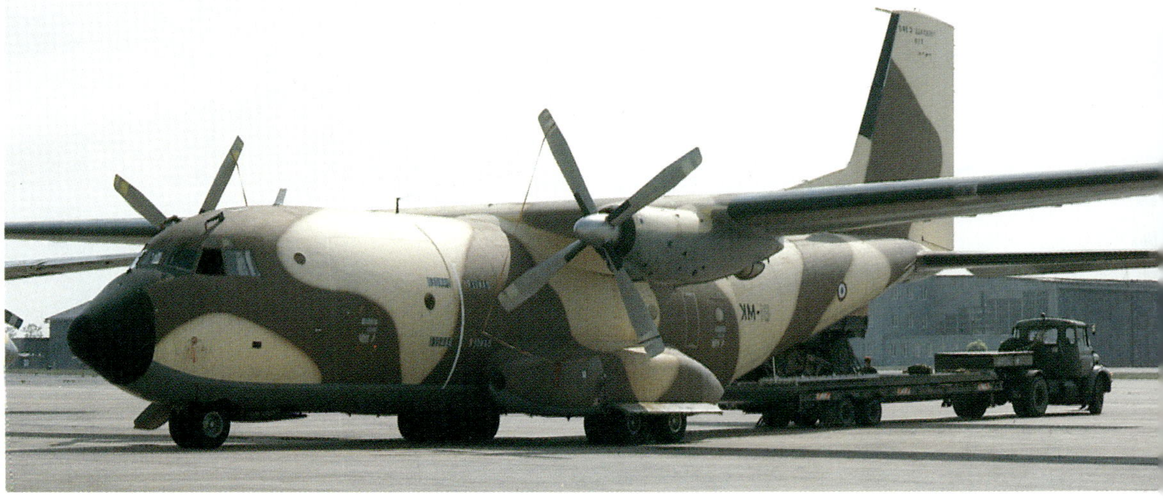

4
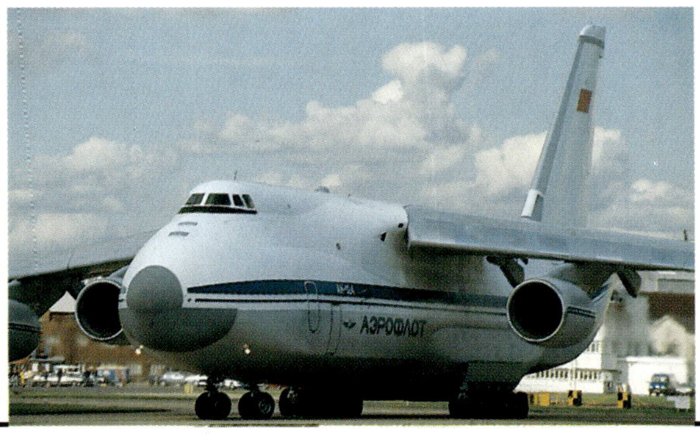

5
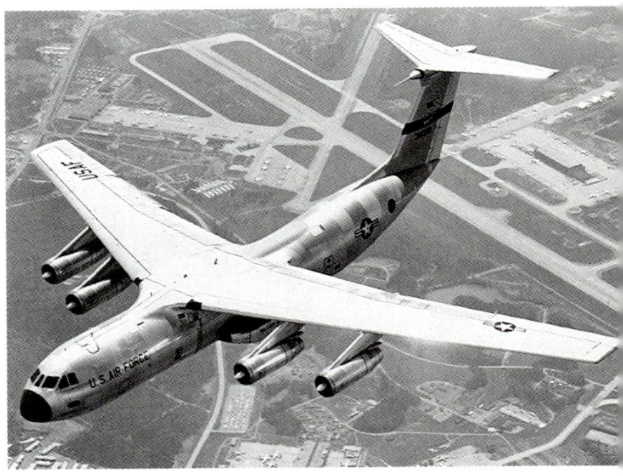

6
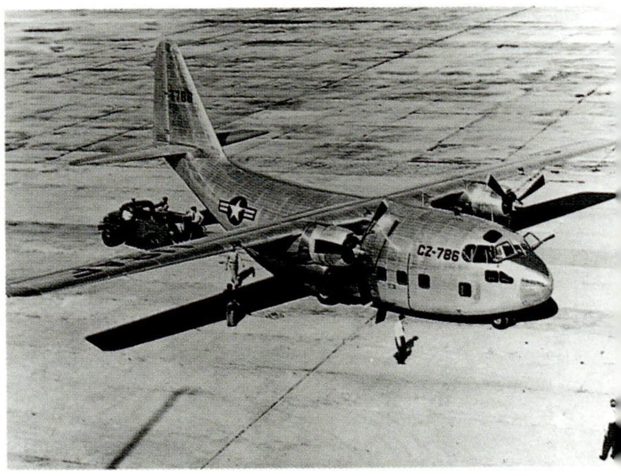

7
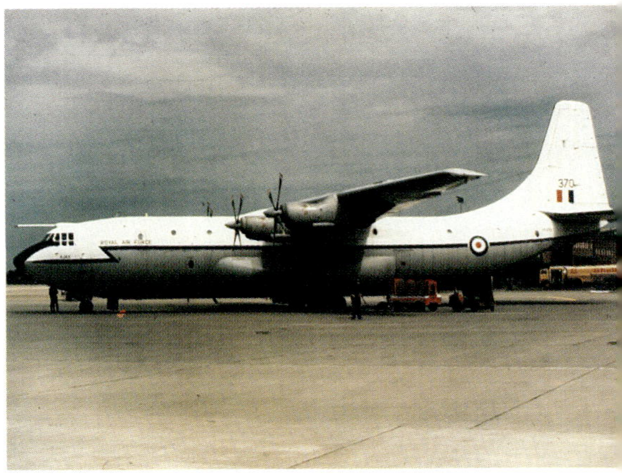

8
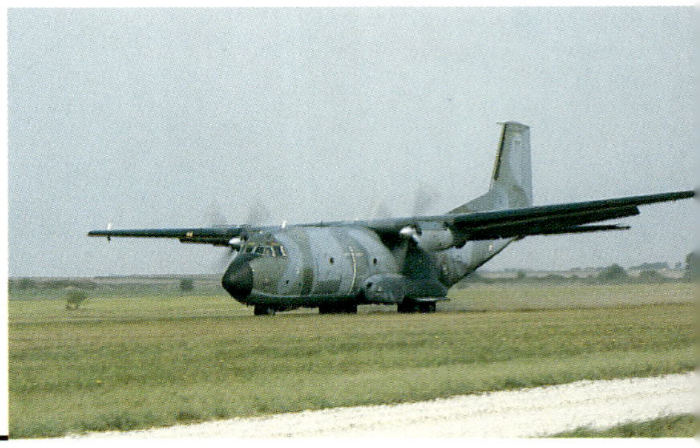

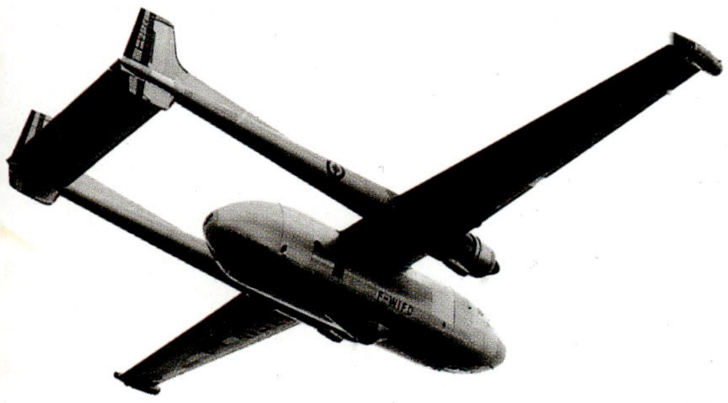
9

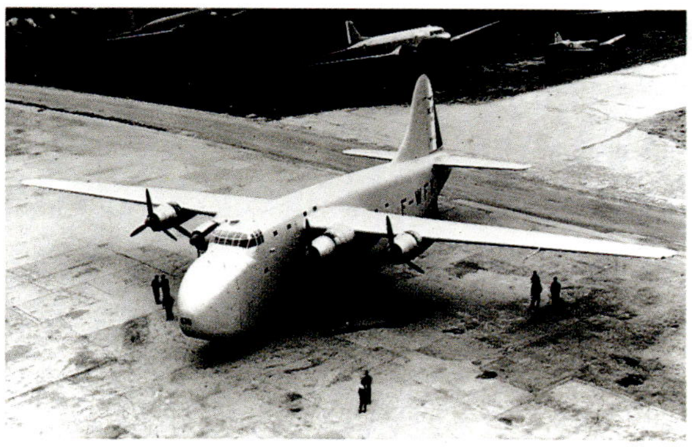
12

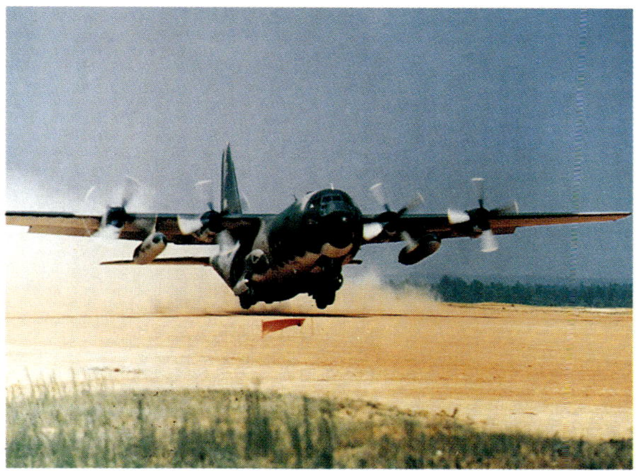
15

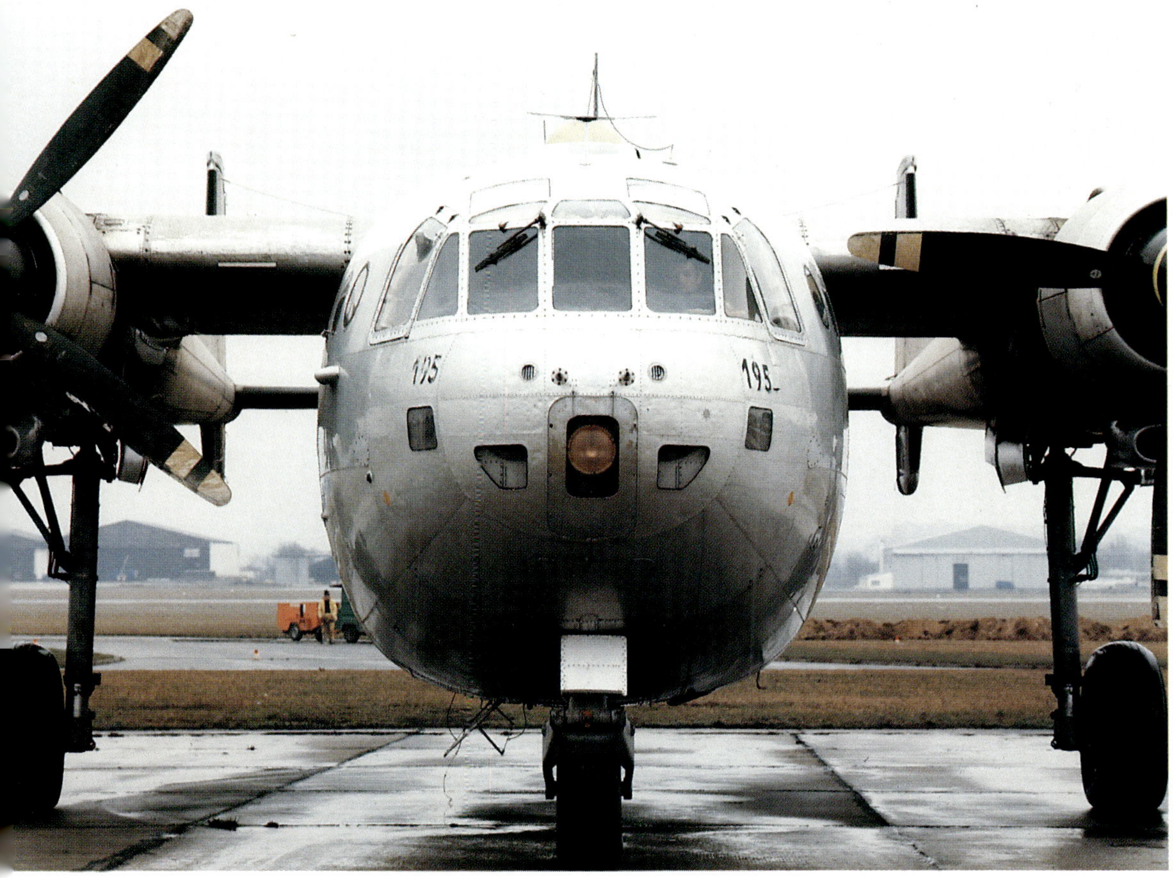
13

For transporting very heavy loads, and in particular strategic missiles, in 1957 Douglas introduced the C-133 Cargomaster, a giant, four-engined transport which could carry a payload of 20 tons. It flew at 360 mph (580 kph) and had a range of almost 4,400 miles (7,000 km). In 1964, the US Air Force began to replace it with the Lockheed C-141 StarLifter. A four-engined jet transport, the StarLifter flies at over 560 mph (900 kph), with a range of 4,000 miles (6,500 km). Its 40-ton capacity means that it can carry 154 infantrymen, 125 paratroopers or 80 stretcher cases.

Photo No. 1: Douglas C-133 Cargomaster (USA)
Photo No. 2: Antonov An-8 (USSR)
Photo Nos. 3 and 8: Transall C-160 (France/Germany)
Photo Nos. 4 and 16: Antonov An-124 (Ukraine)
Photo Nos. 5 and 11: Lockheed C-141 StarLifter (USA)
Photo No. 6: Chase XC-123 (USA)
Photo No. 7: Short Belfast (Great Britain)
Photo Nos. 9 and 13: Nord 2501 Noratlas (France)
Photo Nos. 10 and 15: Lockheed C-130 Hercules (USA)
Photo No. 12: SNCAC NC 211 Cormoran (France)
Photo No. 14: Hawker Siddeley A.W.650 Argosy (Great Britain)

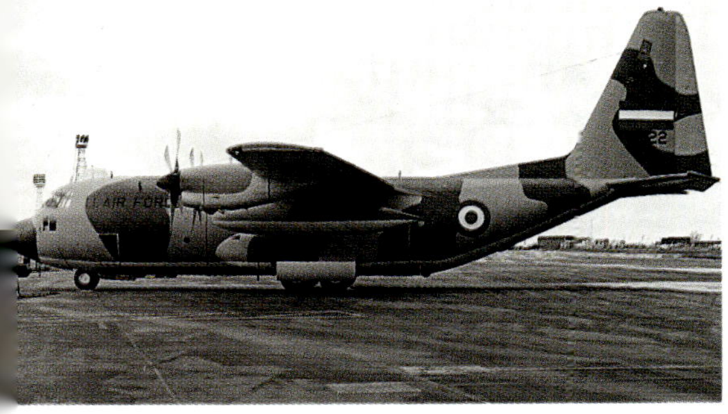
10

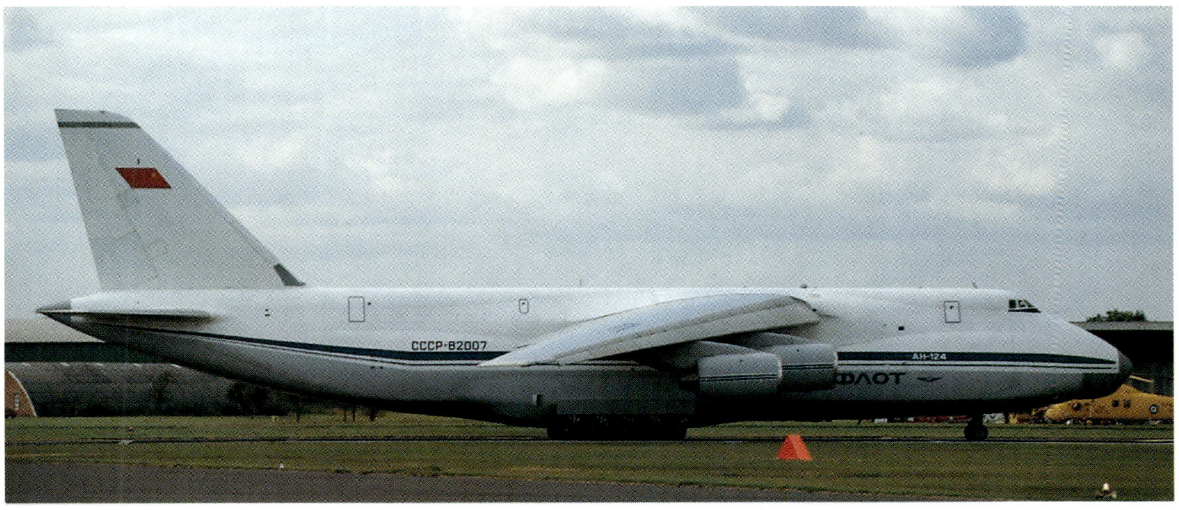
16

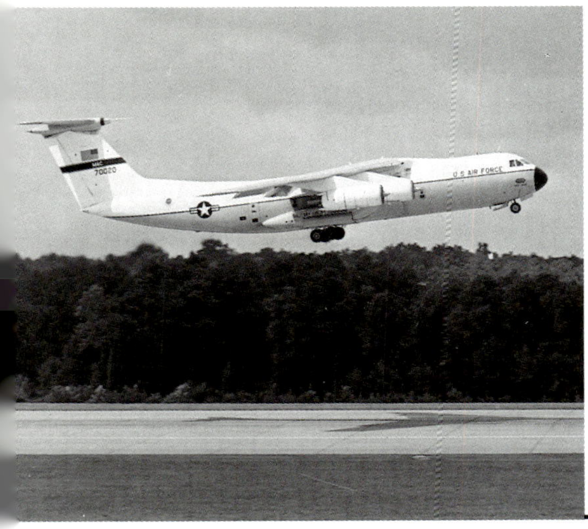
11

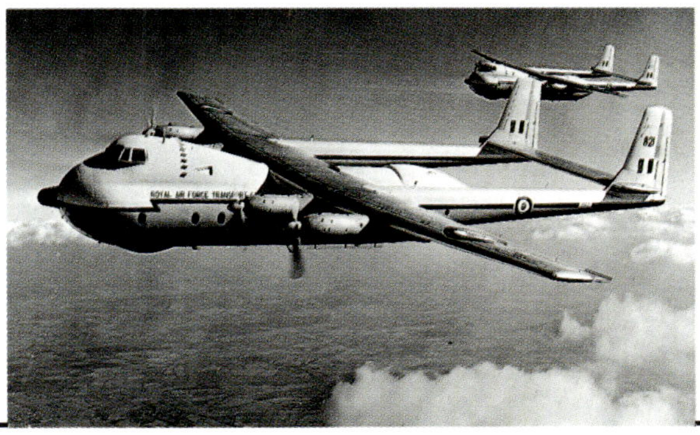
14

5
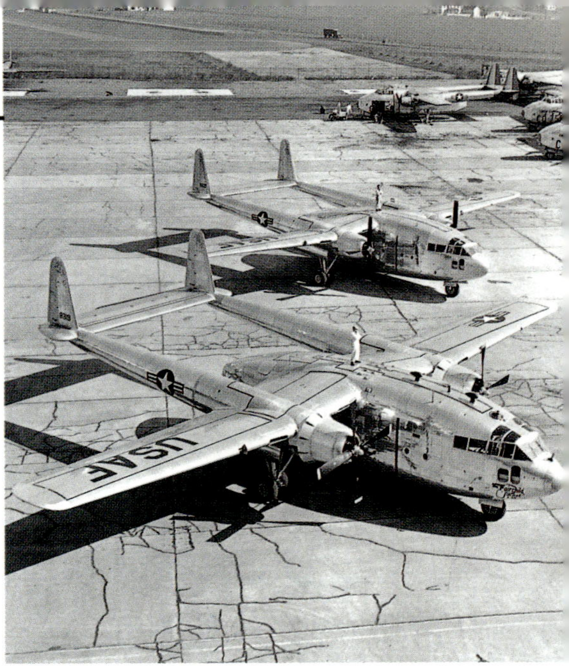

MILITARY TRANSPORT AIRCRAFT

The Soviets built a whole range of planes to meet the logistical and operational requirements of the Red Army. In 1958, hard on the heels of the Antonov An-8 and An-10 models, came the Antonov An-12, a four-engined turboprop, which flew at 440 mph (700 kph) over distances of 2,250 miles (3,600 km) carrying 14 tons of cargo or 100 passengers.

Considerably more capacious is the 1965 Antonov An-22 Antaeus, a four-engined turboprop with a cruising speed of 425 mph (680 kph). Its range is 3,125 miles (5,000 km) with 80 tons of cargo aboard, or 6,900 miles (11,000 km) when carrying a 45-ton load.

Quite different again is the An-72, a twin-jet STOL aircraft, which first appeared in 1977. It carries a load of five tons at around 440 mph (700 kph). Another STOL transport of similar vintage is the An-74. Powered by twin jet engines, it flies at between 375 and 440 mph (600 and 700 kph), carrying a payload of 10 tons over distances ranging from 1,250 to 1,875 miles (2,000 to 3,000 km).

Of similar conception to the American C-141 is the Ilyushin Il-76, a long-range four-engined jet transport, which appeared in 1971. Flying at a maximum of 560 mph (900 kph), it can carry 50 tons of cargo over 2,280 miles (3,650 km). With a reduced load of 20 tons its range extends to 4,560 miles (7,300 km).

To meet the very heaviest transportation needs of the American armed services, Lockheed designed the C-5A Galaxy, which became available in 1969. Carrying a load of 100 tons, this four-engined giant flies at 518 mph (833 kph) and has a range of 3,750 miles (6,000 km). The latest addition is the McDonnell Douglas C-17, which first flew in 1991. A heavy, four-engined tactical transport, the C-17 can carry up to 78 tons at 500 mph (800 kph). With a 71-ton payload, its range is 3,125 miles (5,000 km).

The Japanese developed a STOL military transport, the high-wing Kawasaki C-1A. Powered by twin jet engines, it flew at 500 mph (800 kph), with a payload of eight tons and a range of 800 miles (1,300 km). It could carry 60 infantrymen, 45 paratroopers or 36 stretcher cases.

The Spanish constructor CASA has specialized in lighter aircraft. The 1971 C 212 Aviocar, for instance, can transport 16 passengers or one ton of freight over distances of 1,060 miles (1,700 km), flying at 220 mph (350 kph). More recently, in collaboration with Nurtanio of Indonesia, the

1
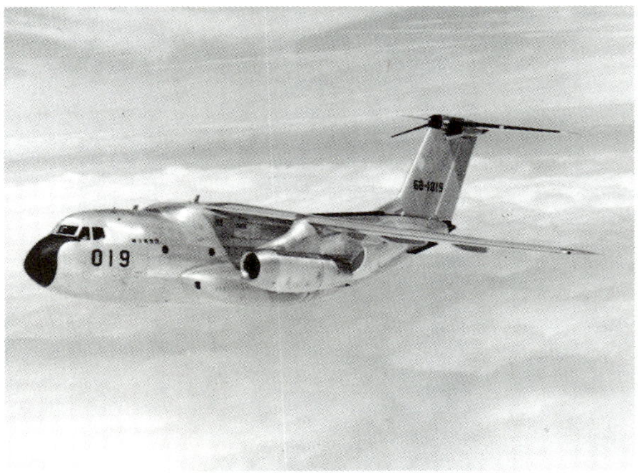

6
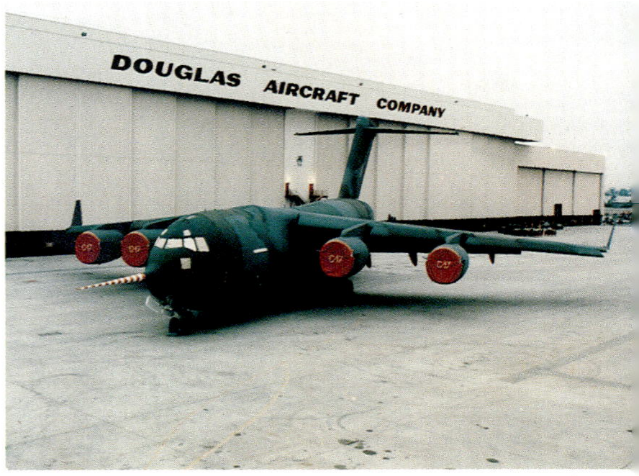

2
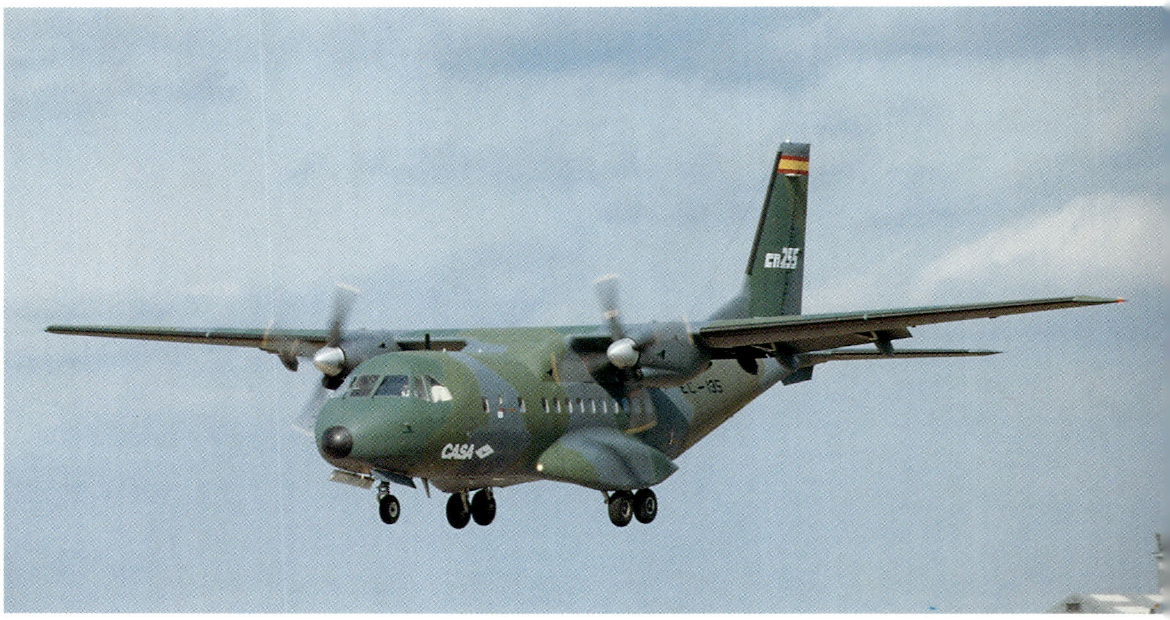

3
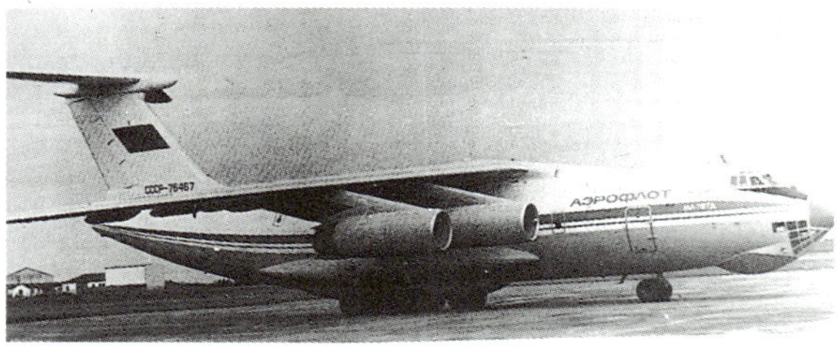

7
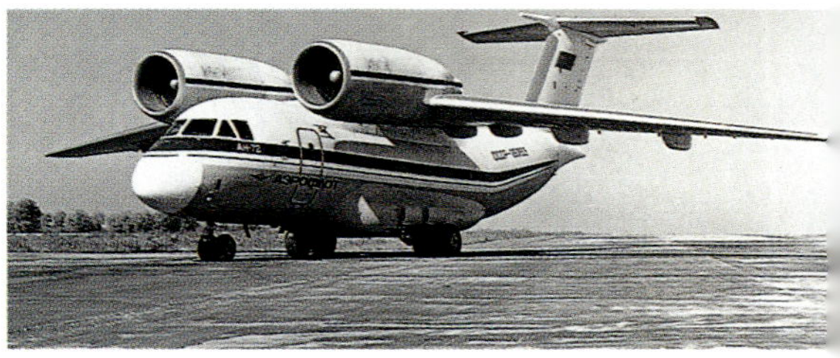

4
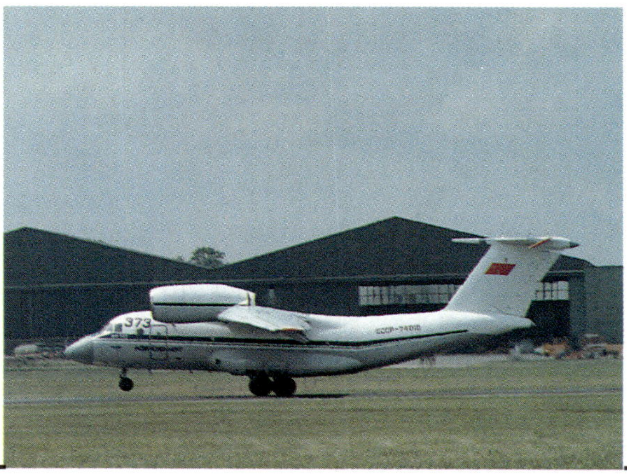

8
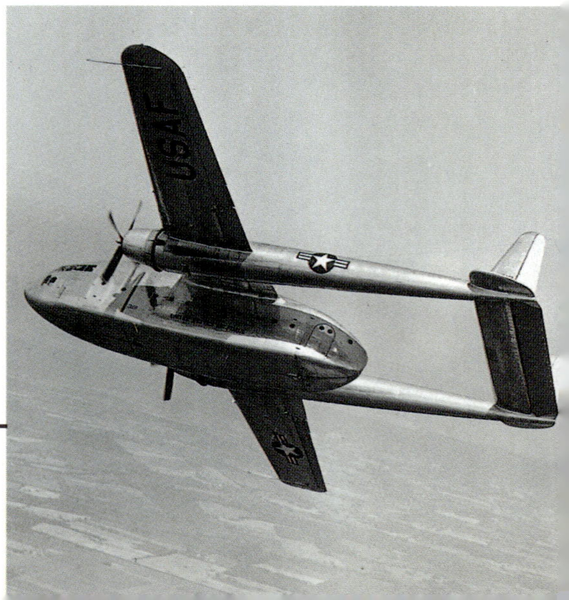

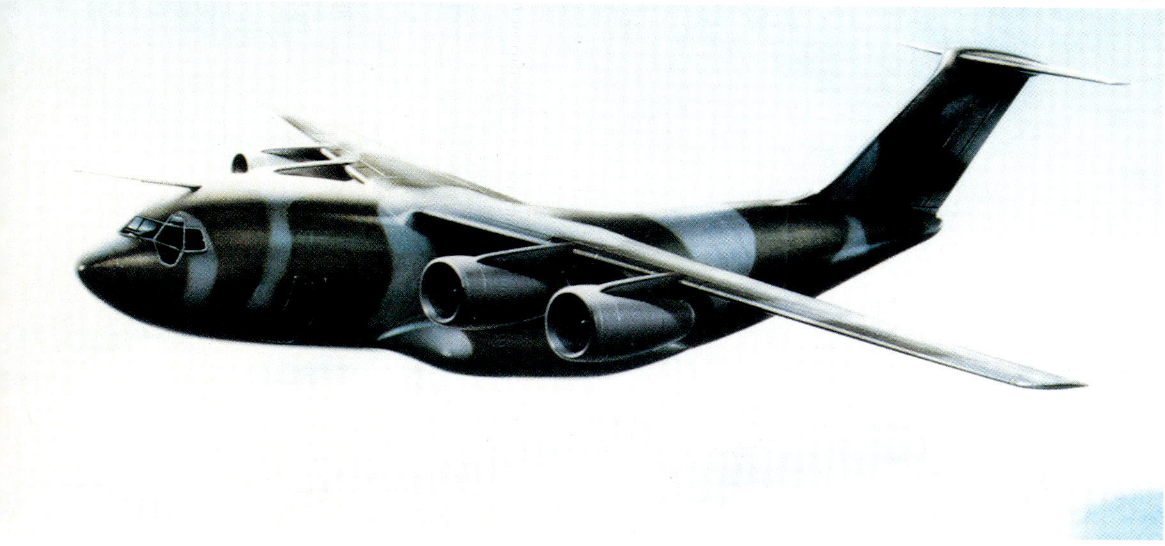
13

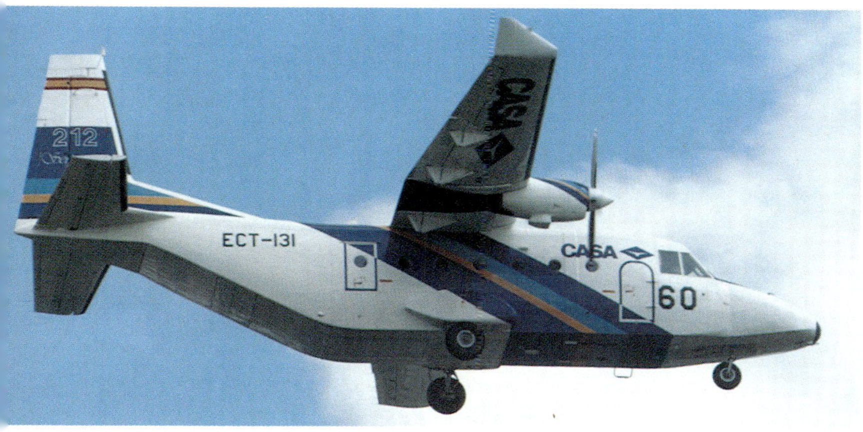

12

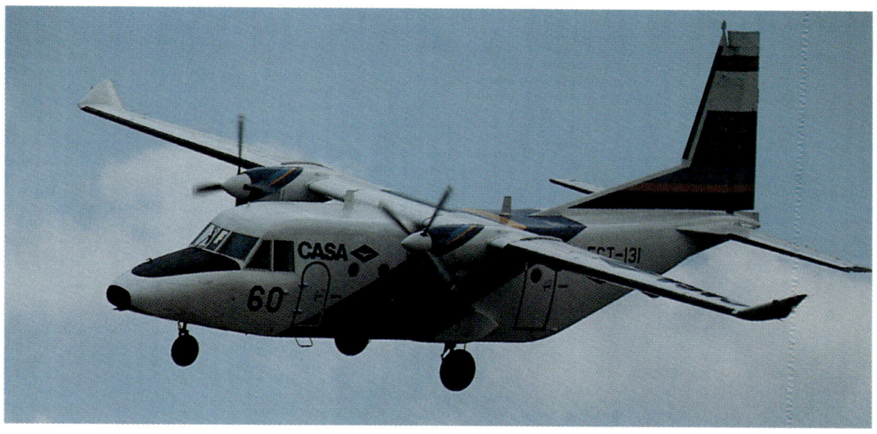

16

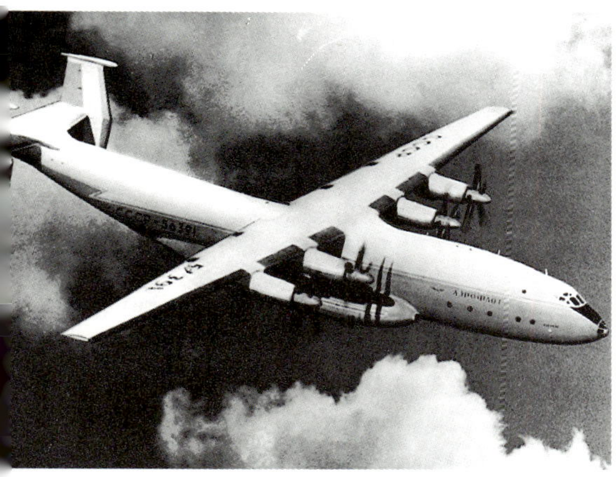
9

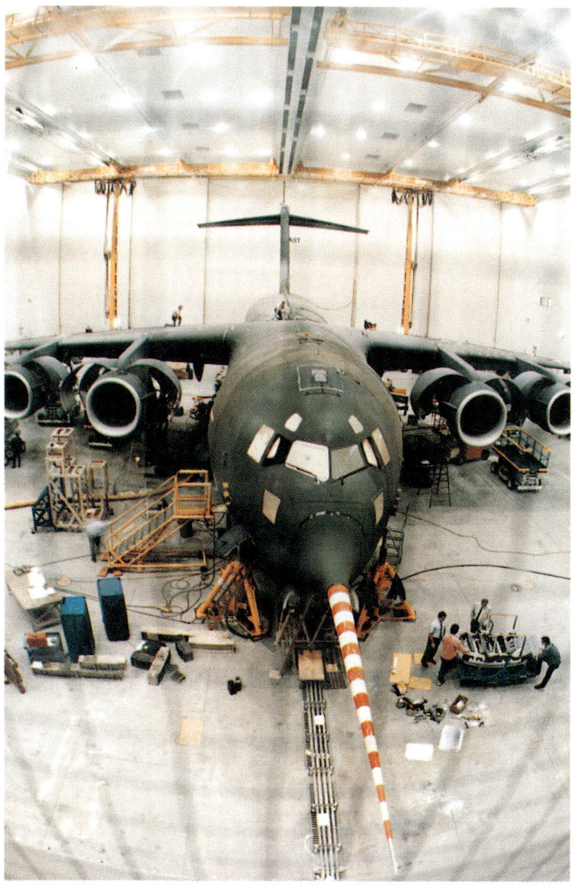
14

company has produced the CN 235 (1983). A high-wing transport powered by twin turboprop engines, it flies at 280 mph (450 kph), carrying 44 passengers for up to 940 miles (1,500 km).

Photo No. 1: Kawasaki C-1A (Japan)
Photo No. 2: Airtech (CASA Nurtanio) CN 235 (Spain/Indonesia)
Photo No. 3: Ilyushin Il-76 (Russia)
Photo No. 4: Antonov An-74 (Ukraine)
Photo Nos. 5 and 8: Fairchild C-119 Flying Boxcar (USA)
Photo Nos. 6 and 14: McDonnell Douglas C-17 (USA)
Photo No. 7: Antonov An-72 (Ukraine)
Photo No. 9: Antonov An-22 (Ukraine)
Photo Nos. 10, 11 and 15: Lockheed C-5 Galaxy (USA)
Photo Nos. 12 and 16: CASA 212 (Spain)
Photo No. 13: Euroflag FLA (Five-nation project)

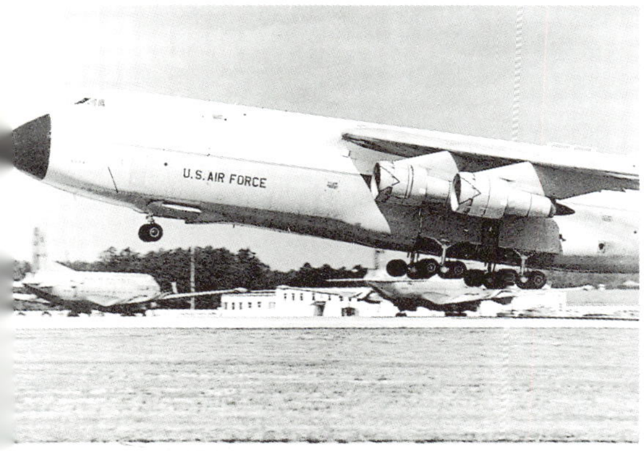

10

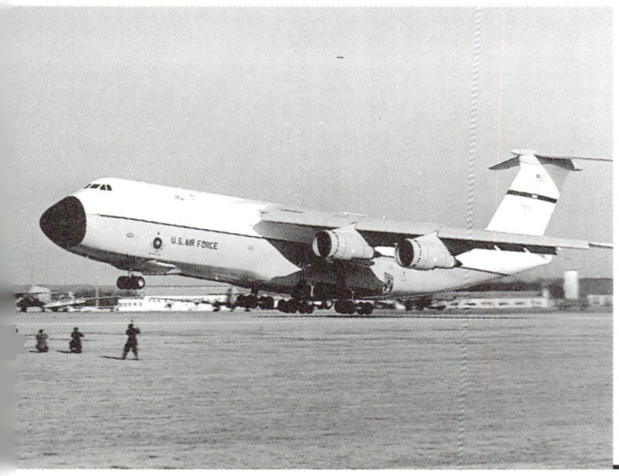
11

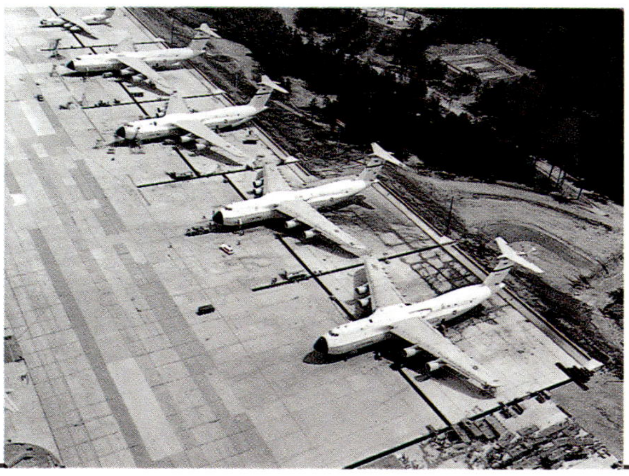
15

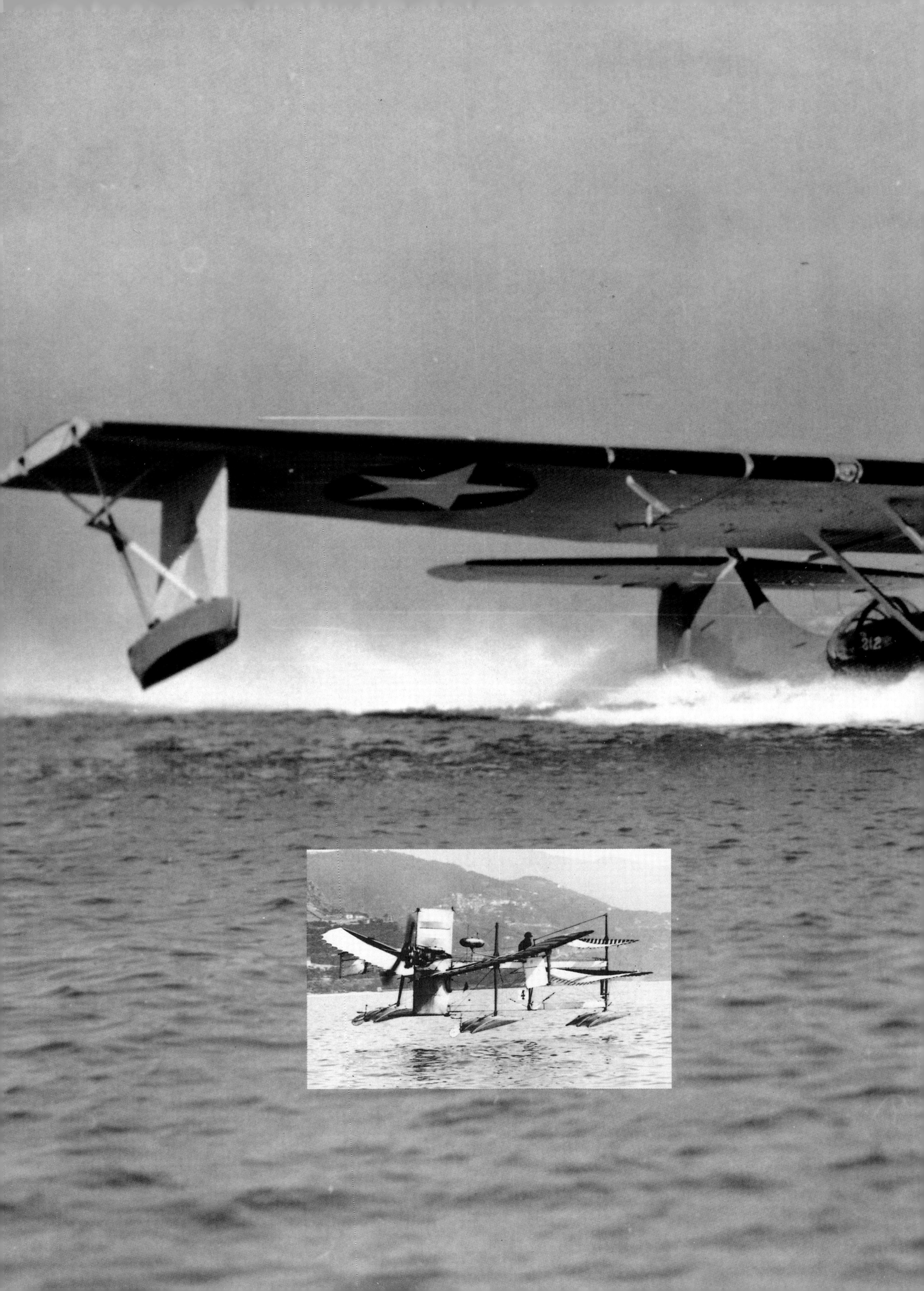

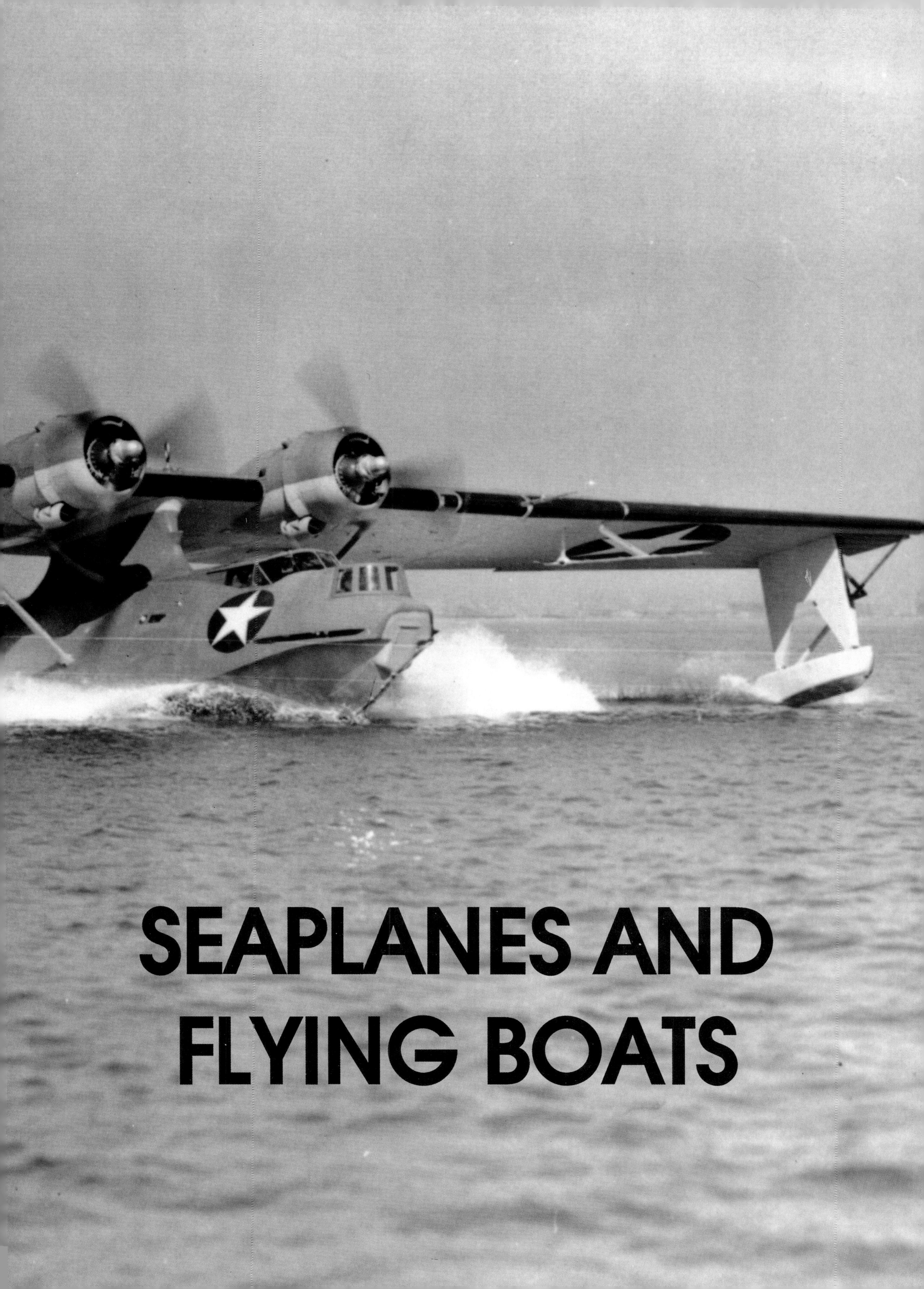

SEAPLANES AND FLYING BOATS

4

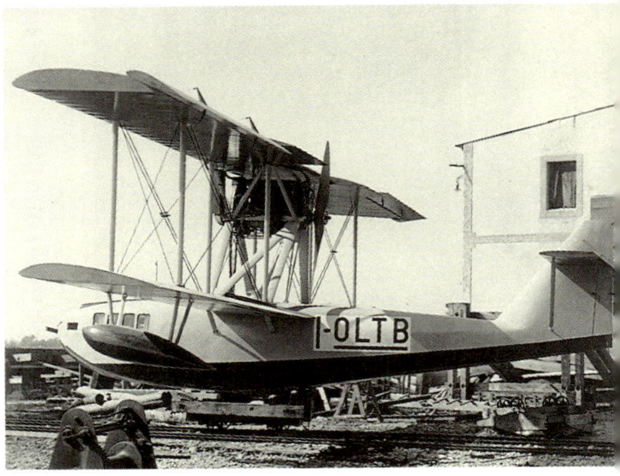

THE EARLY YEARS

The first ever seaplane was built by a Frenchman, Henri Fabre, who in 1910 managed to take off from a lake and fly for 2,600 ft (800 m) at a height of six feet. His wood-and-canvas machine weighed less than 230 lb and flew at under 60 mph (90 kph). During World War I, in 1915, Franco-British Aviation developed a single-engined biplane flying boat for maritime reconnaissance. With its two-man crew, it flew at 68 mph (110 kph) and had a range of 190 miles (300 km). The Italian Macchi M.5 flying boat of 1918 was designed as a fighter. A single-seater biplane powered by one engine, it flew at over 125 mph (200 kph) and had an endurance of three hours 40 minutes. The Germans also produced a seaplane fighter, the two-seater Hansa-Brandenburg W 12 of 1917. It was a single-engined biplane fitted with floats and armed with two or three machine guns. The W 12 had a top speed of 100 mph (160 kph) and could remain airborne for three hours 30 minutes. For reconnaissance duties, the Germans produced the Friedrichshafen F 33 (1916), which saw service over the North Sea and the Channel. A two-seater biplane, it flew at 85 mph (135 kph) and had an endurance of five hours.

After the war, the Italians built a monster flying boat, the Caproni Ca 60 Transaereo, designed to carry 100 passengers across the Atlantic at 80 mph (130 kph). It had nine wings, in sets of three, and was powered by eight engines. However, at the start of its only flight, on Lake Maggiore, it nosed down and crashed into the water.

The Cant 10 Ter of 1926, a single-engined biplane flying boat, could carry four passengers at 93 mph (150 kph) on stages of 375 miles (600 km). From 1926 it was used on the Trieste-Venice-Turin run.

By this time, the Italians had achieved a considerable degree of success in the design of seaplanes, having won the Schneider Trophy (for speed) in 1920 and 1921. But in 1922 victory went to the British, whose entry was the Supermarine Sea Lion. This single-hull biplane could reach speeds of 162 mph (260 kph) and remain in the air for three hours.

Fitted with floats and wheels, the American Douglas DWC World Cruiser was a single-engined two-seater biplane with a cruising speed of 100 mph (160 kph) and a range of 2,200 miles (3,500 km). In 1924, it circled the globe in 175 days and was subsequently ordered by the US Army.

1

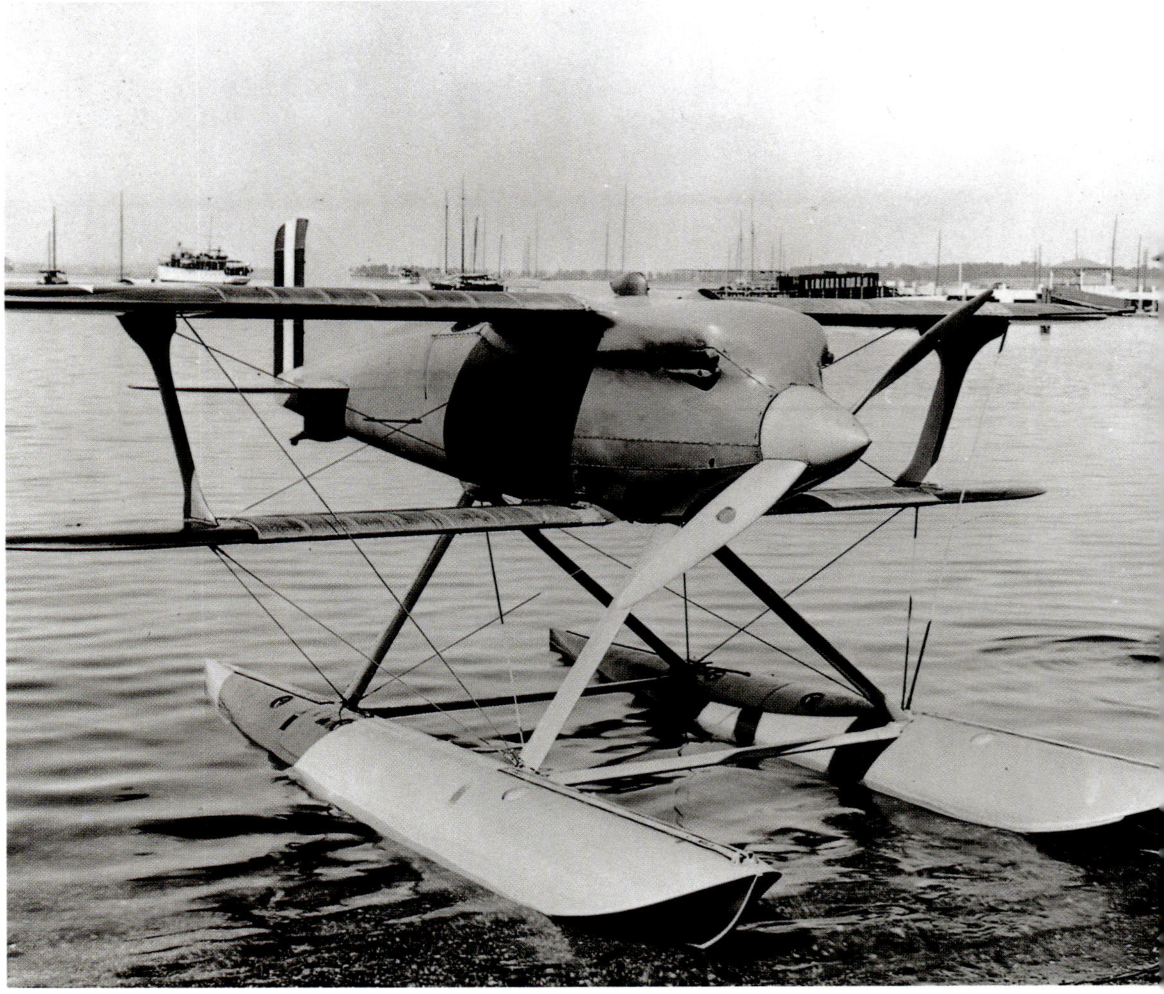

2

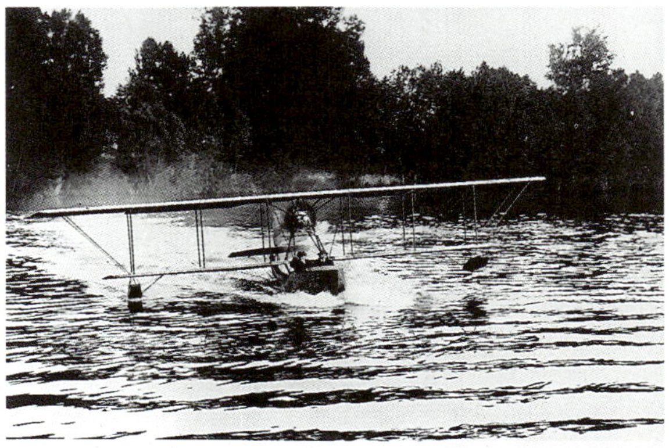

5

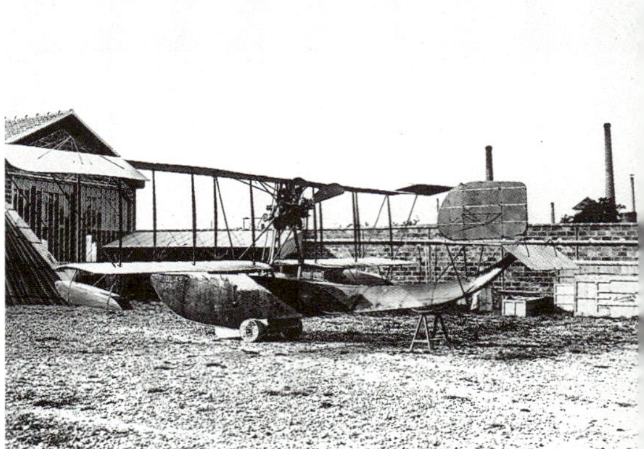

3

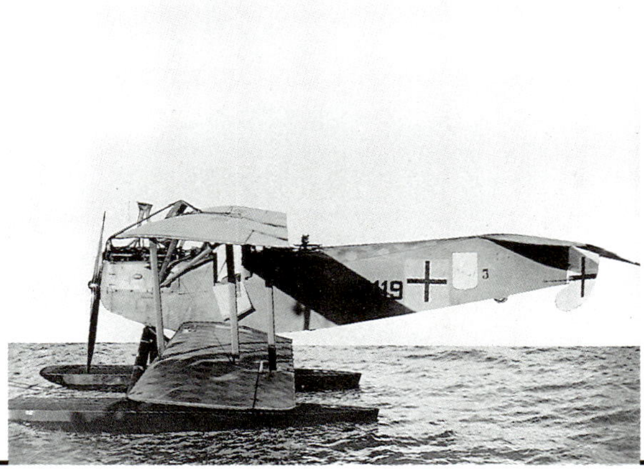

6

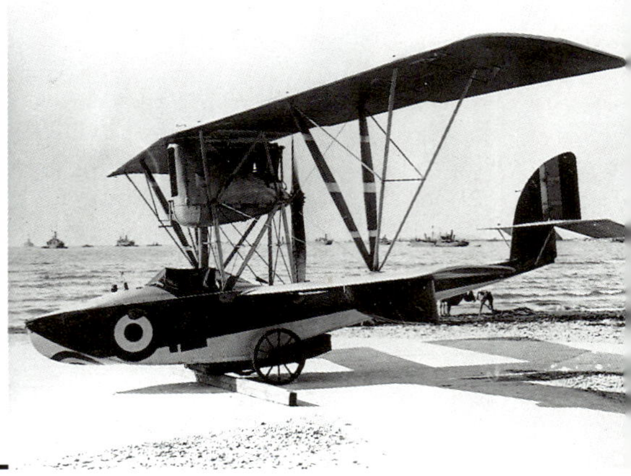

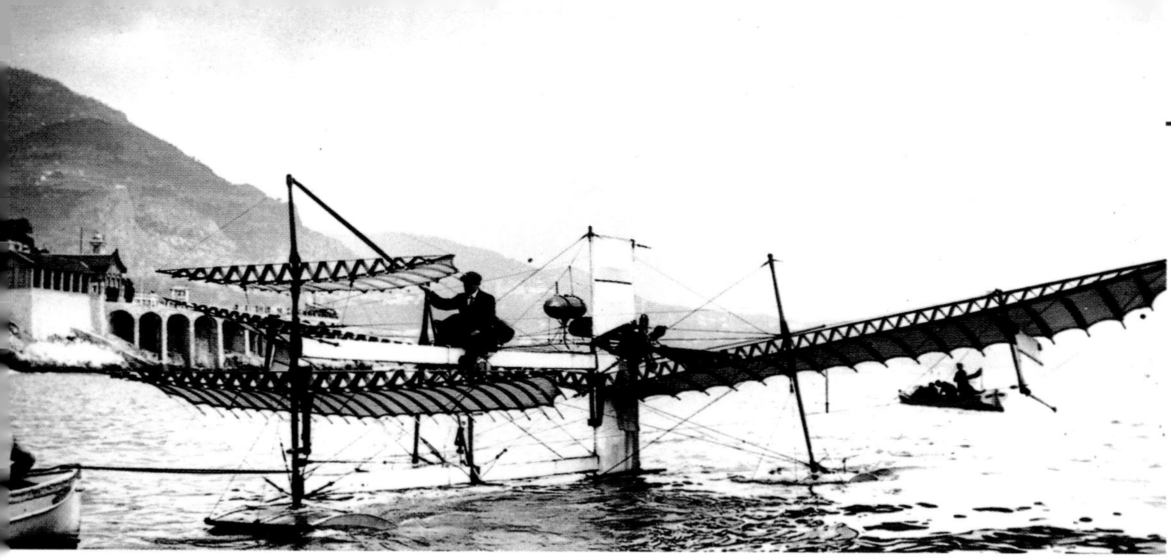
10

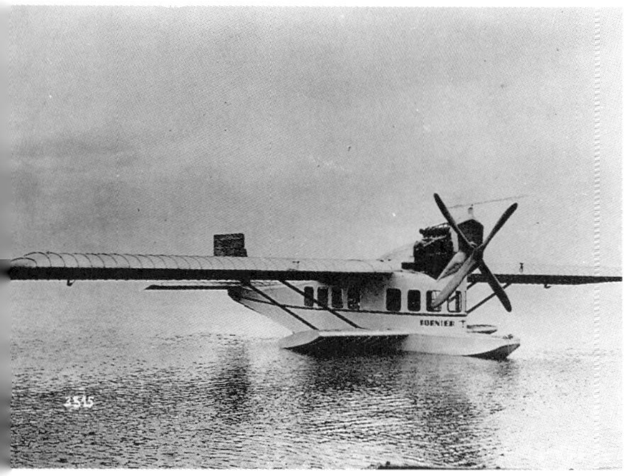
7

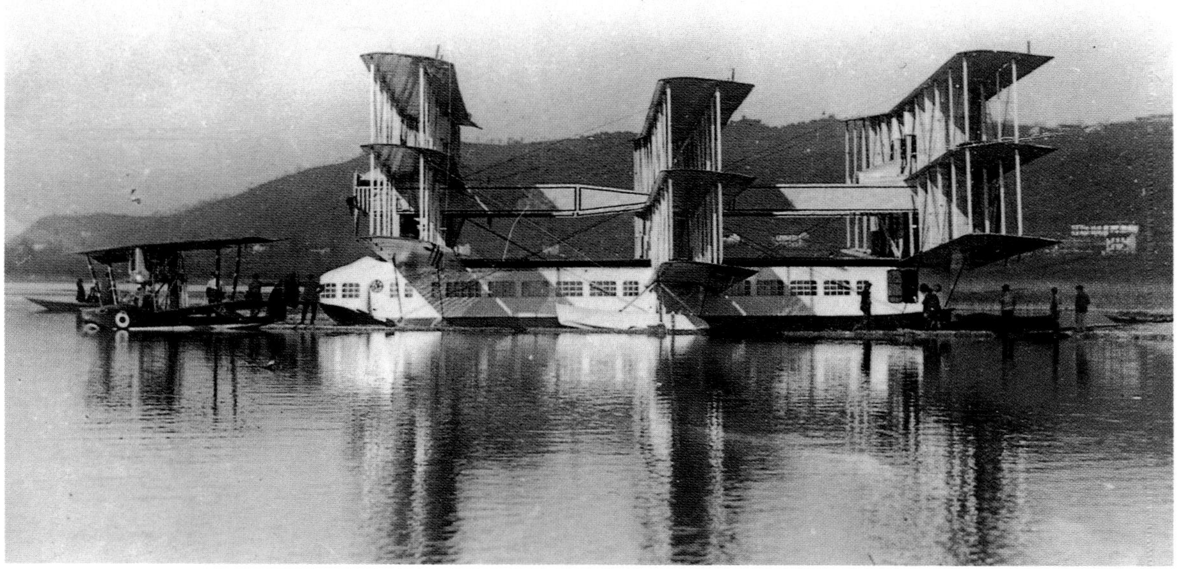
14

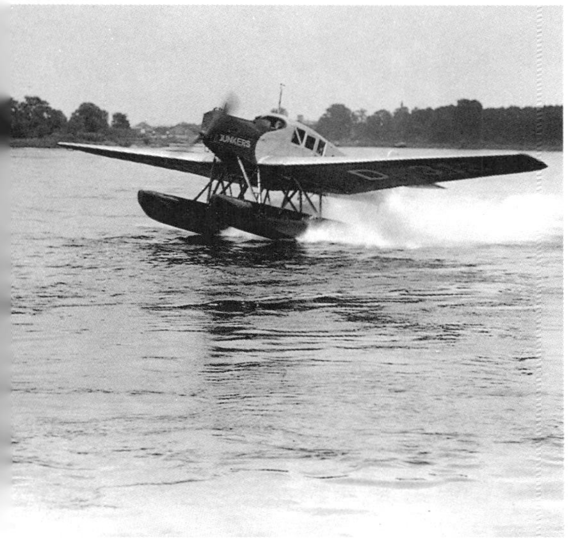
8

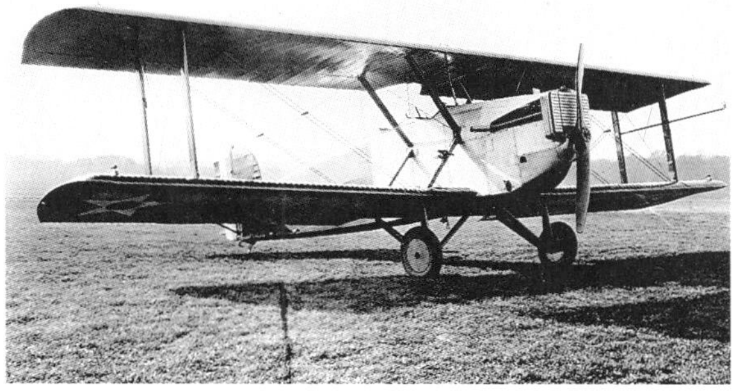
11

For the 1925 Schneider Trophy, Curtiss came up with a seaplane racer, the Army/Curtiss R3C-2. A single-engined biplane, it flew at 266 mph (426 kph) and had a range of 250 miles (400 km). It won the Trophy with Jimmy Doolittle at the controls. In Germany, a four-passenger civilian transport, the Junkers F 13 was fitted with floats and used as a seaplane, but the most original marine aircraft, the Dornier Delphin, made its debut in 1920. It was an all-metal, central-hull flying boat with a high wing, powered by a single engine. The 1924 version, the Delphin II, cruised at 78 mph (125 kph) and carried seven passengers.

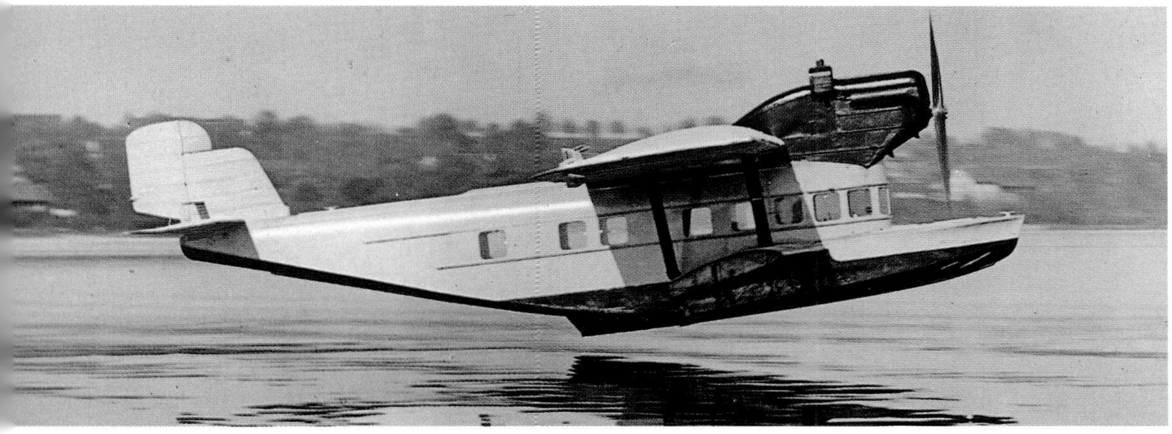
12

Photo No. 1: Army/Curtiss R3C-2 (USA)
Photo Nos. 2 and 5: FBA C (France)
Photo No. 3: Hansa-Brandenburg W12 (Germany)
Photo No. 4: Cant 10 Ter (Italy)
Photo No. 6: Macchi M.5 (Italy)
Photo Nos. 7 and 12: Dornier Delphin II (Germany)
Photo No. 8: Junkers F 13 (Germany)
Photo No. 9: Friedrichshafen F33 L (Germany)
Photo No. 10: Hydravion Fabre (France)
Photo No. 11: Douglas DWC World Cruiser (land version) (USA)
Photo No. 13: Supermarine Sea Lion (Great Britain)
Photo No. 14: Caproni Ca 60 Transaereo (Italy)

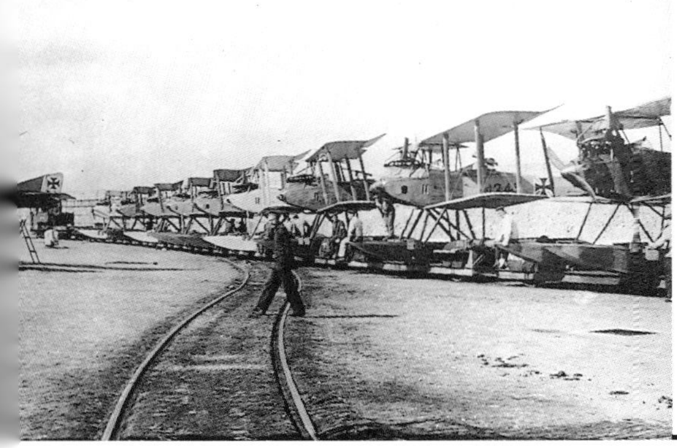
9

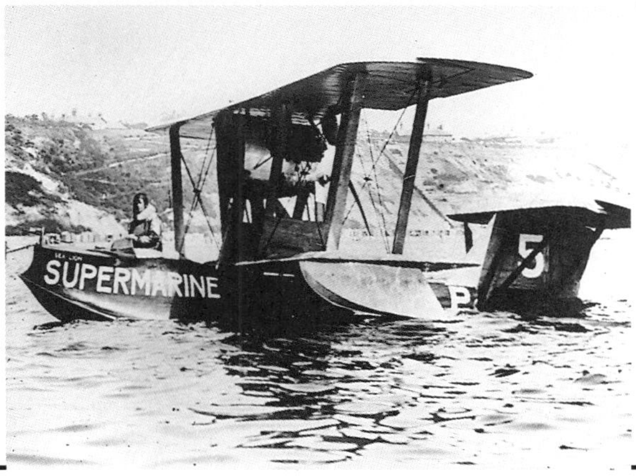

13

THE INTER-WAR YEARS

The Schneider Trophy was an invitation to aircraft constructors to build ever more powerful machines. In 1926, the Italians carried it off with the Macchi M.39, a monoplane with a top speed in excess of 259 mph (415 kph), but the 1927 race was won by the British Supermarine S.5, which recorded 310 mph (499 kph). The two following races, in 1929 and 1931, were won by later versions of the same aircraft, the S.6 and the S.6B, with the result that the trophy was permanently retained by Britain. The S.6 had a top speed of 358 mph (576 kph), the S.6B 408 mph (656 kph). These were the immediate ancestors of the World War II Spitfire.

During this period, flying boats were also set on conquering the transoceanic routes. In 1923, the German Dornier company produced the Wal, a twin-engined aircraft which could fly distances of 1,375 miles (2,200 km) at 112 mph (280 kph) carrying eight to ten passengers. It was followed, in 1926, by the 20-passenger R2 Super Wal and, in 1928, the R4 Super Wal, which cruised at 125 mph (200 kph).

In 1929 came the Dornier Do X, the biggest plane in the world at the time. The take-off weight of this jumbo flying boat was 52 tons. Its 12 engines gave it a range of 1,060 miles (1,700 km) at 120 mph (190 kph). It could accommodate 72 passengers. In 1930 and 1933, the Italians had achieved two record-breaking trans-atlantic flights in the twin-hulled Savoia-Marchetti SM.55. These successes led, in 1932, to the development of a three-engined flying boat, the SM.66, which carried 14 to 18 passengers at speeds of 140 mph (220 kph) and had a range of 1,190 miles (1,900 km).

On the Marseilles-Algiers route, the French began, in 1929, to operate the CAMS 53-1, a biplane flying boat powered by two engines housed in tandem under the upper wing. It carried four passengers at 106 mph (170 kph) and had a range of 700 miles (1,125 km).

To conquer the South Atlantic, Latécoère built the high-wing Laté 300, a four-engined flying boat with a large central hull, which entered service in 1931. It could carry one ton of mail at 100 mph (160 kph), with a range of 3,000 miles (4,800 km). The original Croix du Sud was piloted by Jean Mermoz, lost at sea when the plane disappeared in 1936.

The Blériot 5190 Santos-Dumont was also designed for the South Atlantic service. A high-wing, four-engined flying boat, it had a range of 2,000 miles (3,200 km) at 118 mph (190 kph).

5

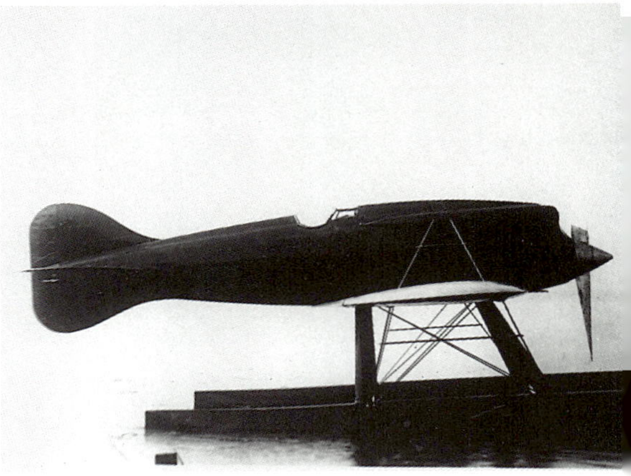

1

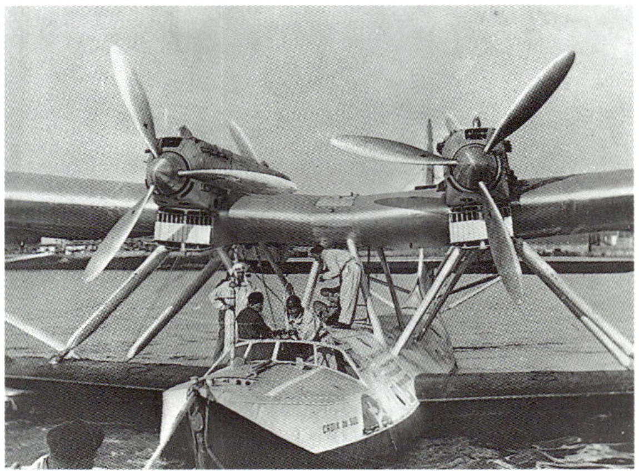

6

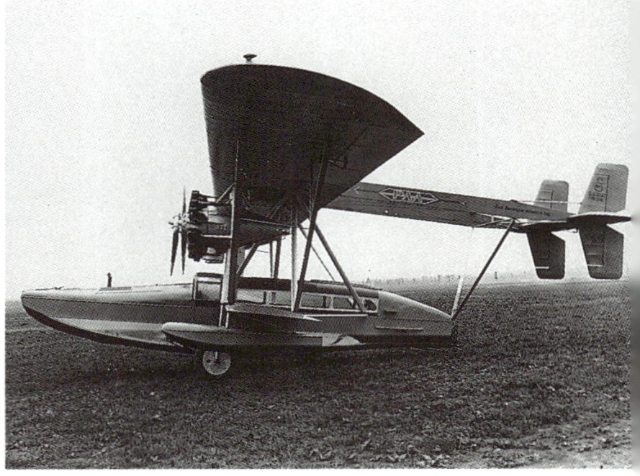

2

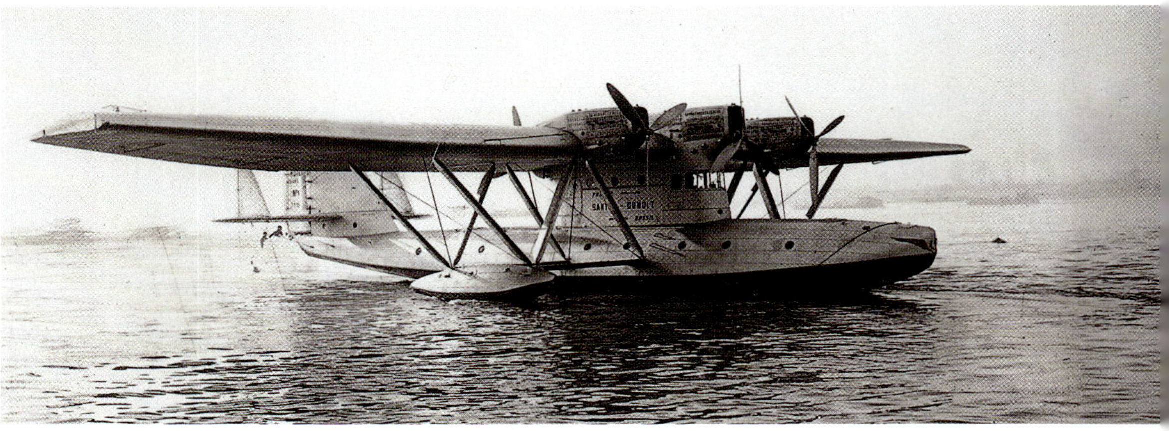

3

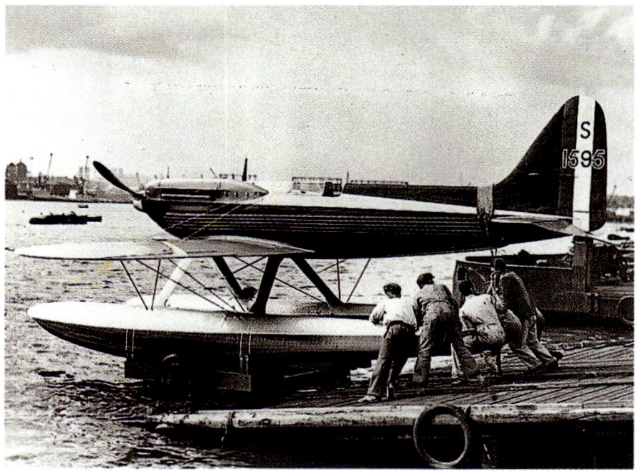

7

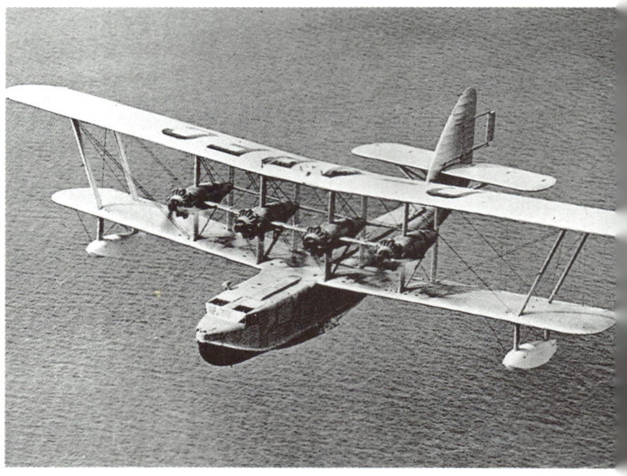

4

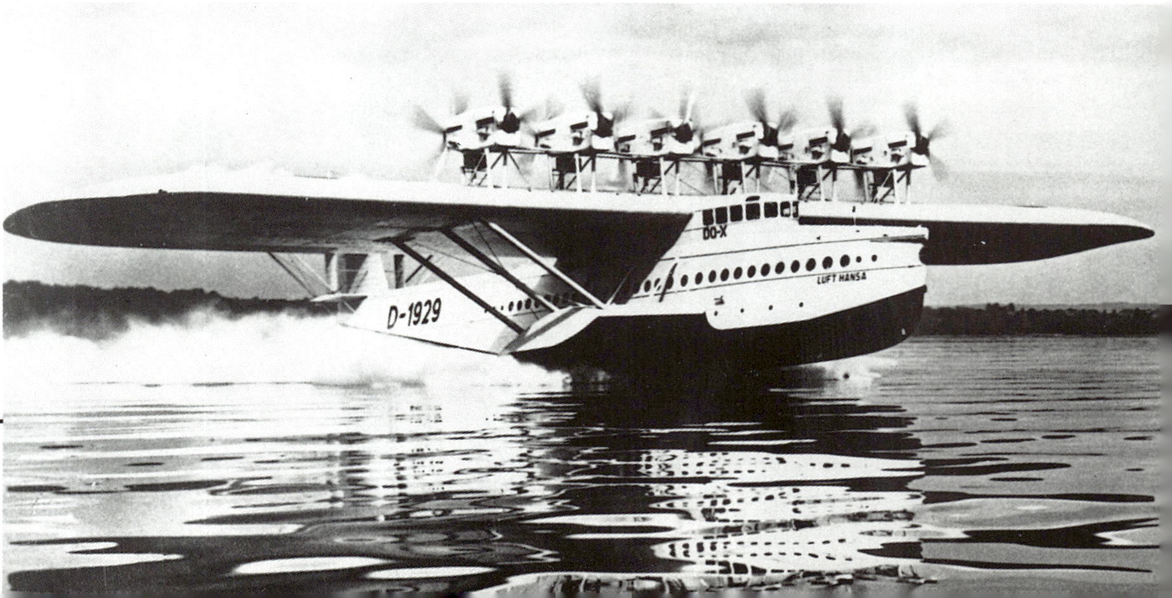

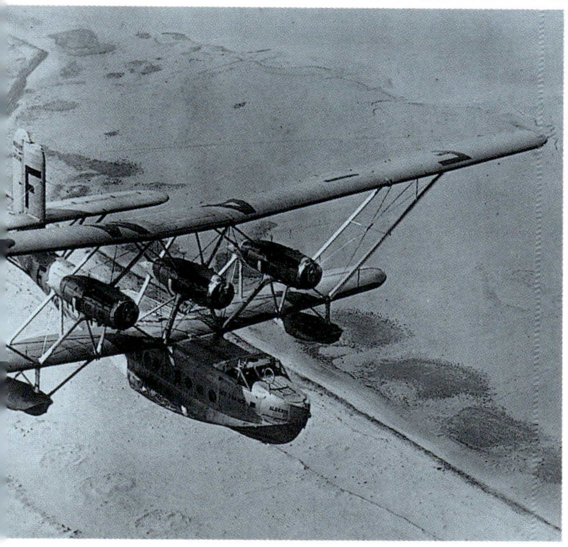

8

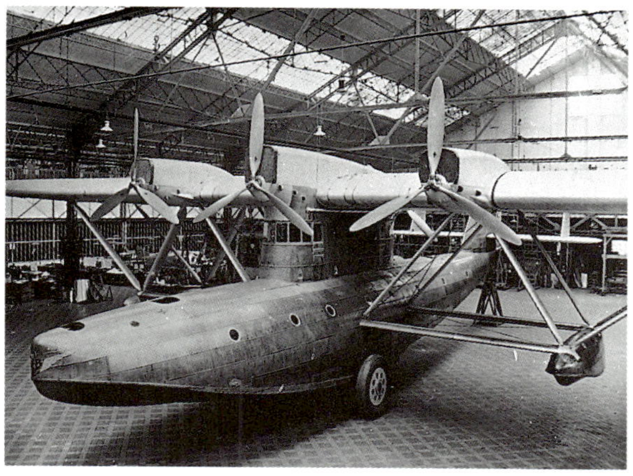

11

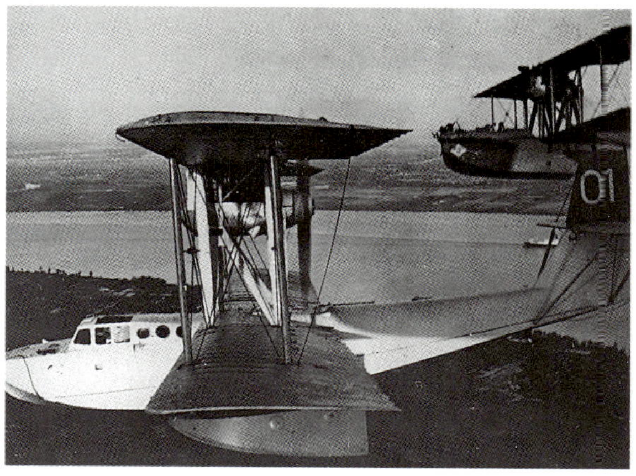

14

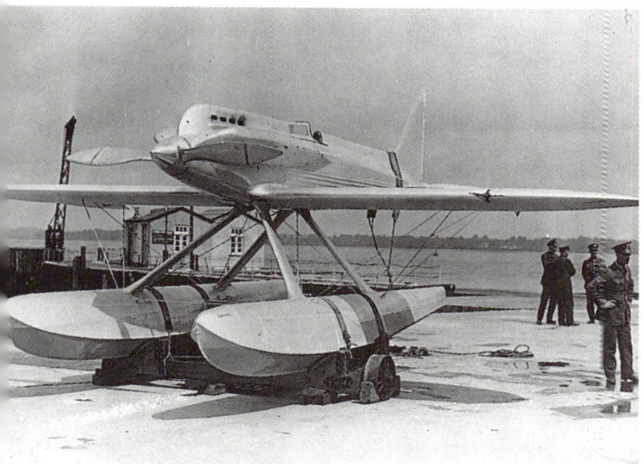

9

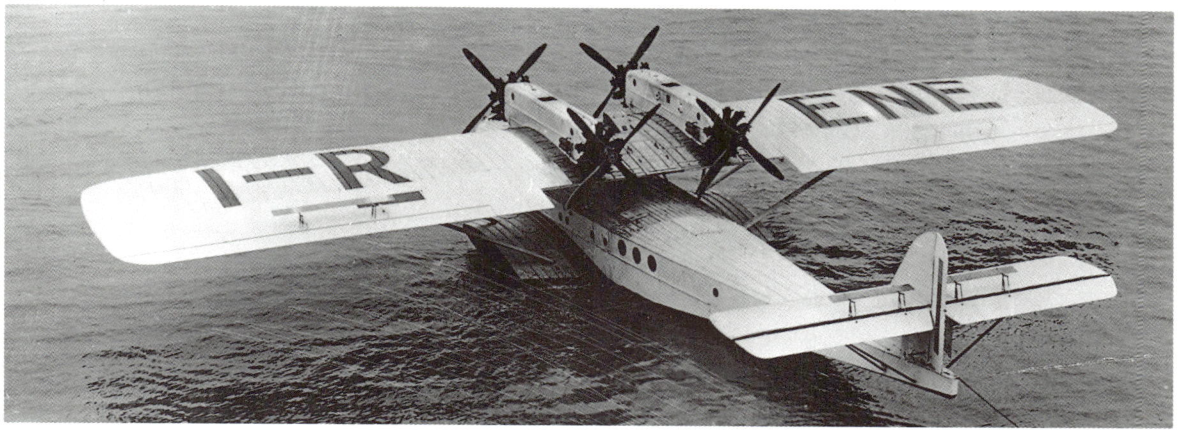

15

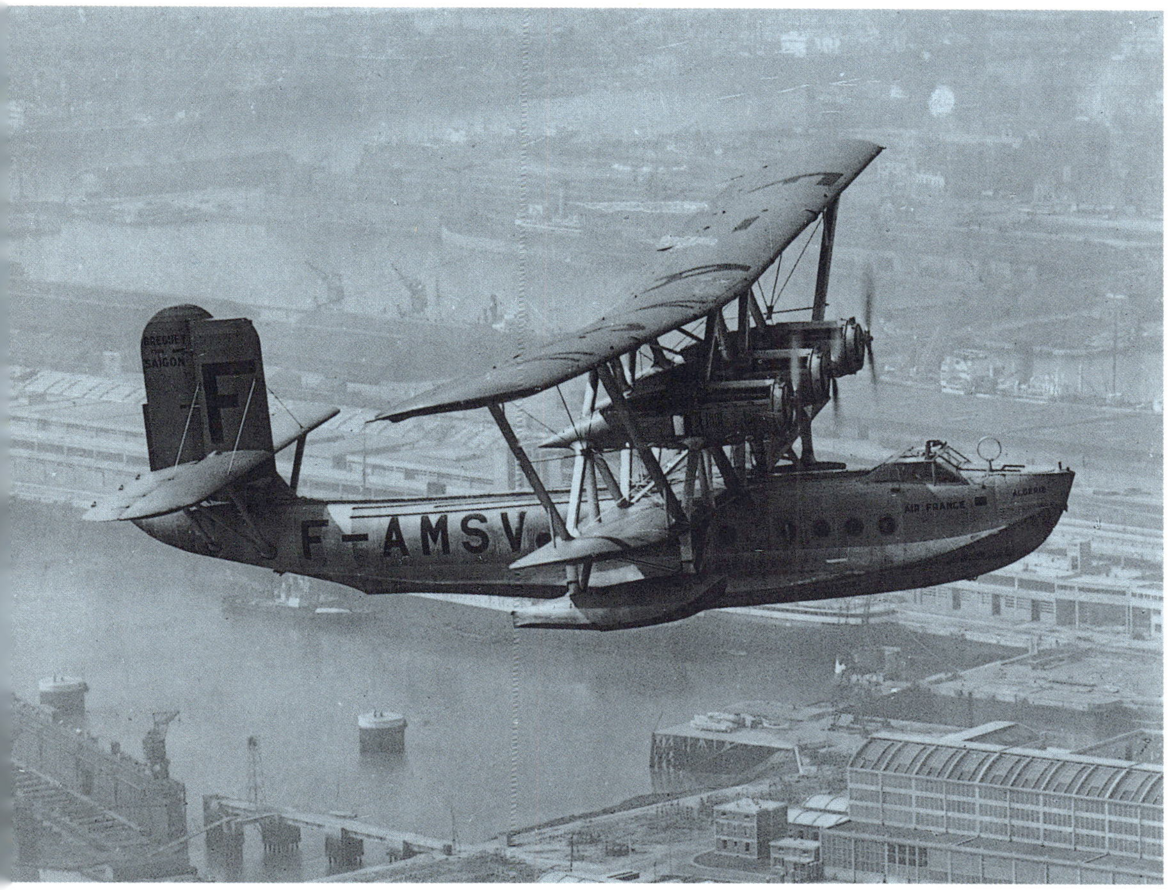

12 Meanwhile, the British were flying the Mediterranean routes with the Short S.8 Calcutta, introduced in 1928. This three-engined, central-hull flying boat carried 15 passengers on stages of 625 miles at 96 mph (155 kph). An enlarged four-engine version, which made its debut in 1931; the S.17 Kent carried just one extra passenger but was a good deal more comfortable. Hot meals were prepared and served in flight.

The French Breguet 530 Saigon was derived from the Short S.8. A metal-hulled biplane powered by three engines, the Saigon had a range of 690 miles (1,100 km), carrying 20 passengers at 125 mph (200 kph).

In the United States, Igor Sikorsky, who had emigrated from Russia, designed an amphibious biplane flying boat, the S-38. It carried eight passengers at 103 mph (165 kph) on flights of up to 600 miles (965 km).

Photo No. 1: Latécoère 300 Croix du Sud (France)
Photo Nos. 2 and 11: Blériot 5190 Santos-Dumont (France)
Photo No. 3: Supermarine S.6B (Great Britain)
Photo No. 4: Dornier Do X (Germany)
Photo No. 5: Macchi M.39 (Italy)
Photo No. 6: Sikorsky S-38 (USA)
Photo No. 7: Short S.17 Kent (Great Britain)
Photo Nos. 8 and 12: Breguet 530 Saigon (France)
Photo No. 9: Supermarine S.5 (Great Britain)
Photo No. 10: Short S.8 Calcutta (Great Britain)
Photo No. 13: Supermarine S.6 (Great Britain)
Photo No. 14: CAMS 53-1 (France)
Photo No. 15: Dornier R4 Super Wal (Germany)

10

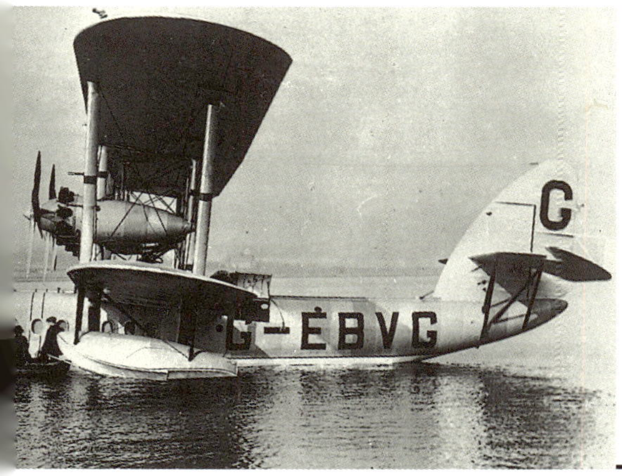

13

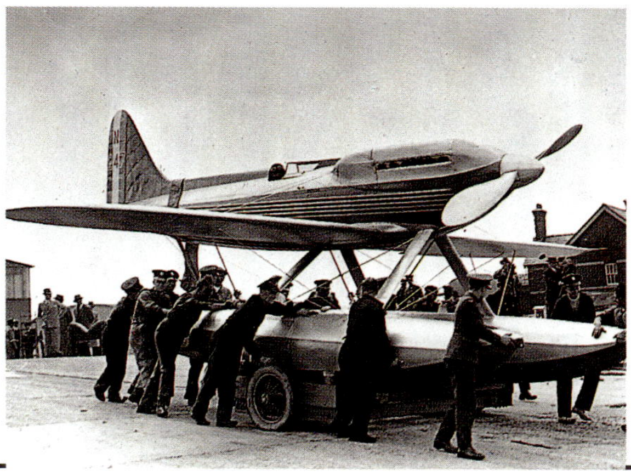

4
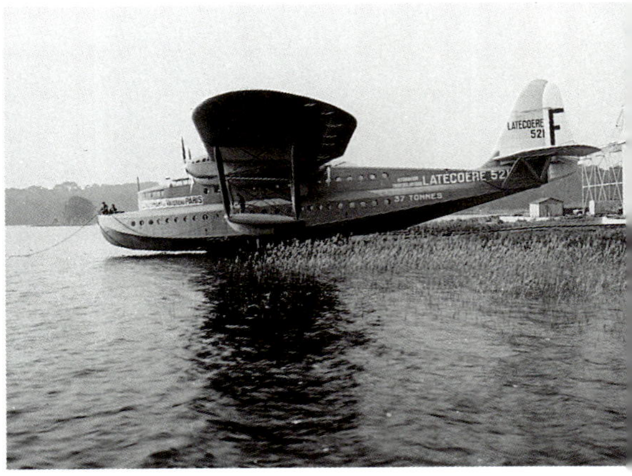

SEAPLANES AND FLYING BOATS

Flying-boat development became a worldwide phenomenon. In 1932, American airlines began to operate the Sikorsky S-43 on Caribbean and Latin American routes. A twin-engined amphibian with a cruising speed of 187 mph (300 kph), the S-43 carried 15 passengers on stages of up to 810 miles (1,300 km). In 1935, PanAm introduced the Sikorsky S-42 on its Pacific routes. A high-wing flying boat powered by four engines, it had a range of 1,190 miles (1,900 km) and carried its 32 passengers at 170 mph (275 kph).

In 1935, the French navy placed an order for the Breguet 521, known as the Bizerte, which flew at 153 mph (245 kph) and had a range of 1,250 miles (2,000 km). It was armed with five machine guns and 660 lb (300 kg) of bombs.

Meanwhile, competition continued on the South Atlantic routes, where in 1935 Latécoère introduced the gigantic Laté 521 *Lieutenant de Vaisseau Paris*, a high-wing single-hull flying boat. Powered by six engines, it had range of 2,500 miles (4,000 km) at 130 mph (210 kph) and could carry up to 70 passengers. In 1937, Lioré et Olivier brought out a four-engined 26-seater flying boat, the LeO H 246. It flew at 160 mph (255 kph) and had a range of 1,875 miles (3,000 km). In 1942, despite the war, SNCASE produced the six-engined SE 200 for the Atlantic run.

Meanwhile, in 1937 the British had thought up an original means of crossing the Atlantic. A big four-engined flying boat, the Short S.21 Maia (cruising speed 146 mph/235 kph, range 856 miles/1,370 km), would take off carrying a smaller four-engined seaplane, the Short S.20 Mercury (cruising speed 187 mph/300 kph, range when launched in mid-air 3,900 miles/6,300 km) on its back. When the right altitude had been reached, the S.21 would turn back, while the S.20 – carrying mail only – continued on its way. In 1938 the Mercury reached Canada from Ireland in 20 hours 20 minutes. Another Short flying boat, the S.23, was introduced in 1936 to fly Imperial Airways' African and Far-Eastern routes. It carried 24 passengers at 187 mph (300 kph) on stages of 750 miles (1,200 km).

In 1937 the Germans also inaugurated postal services across the Atlantic with the Blohm und Voss Ha 139B, a four-engined twin-float seaplane, with a range of 3,300 miles (5,300 km) at 187 mph (300 kph).

On the American side, the Martin company built a big, four-engined flying boat for PanAm, the M-130 China

1
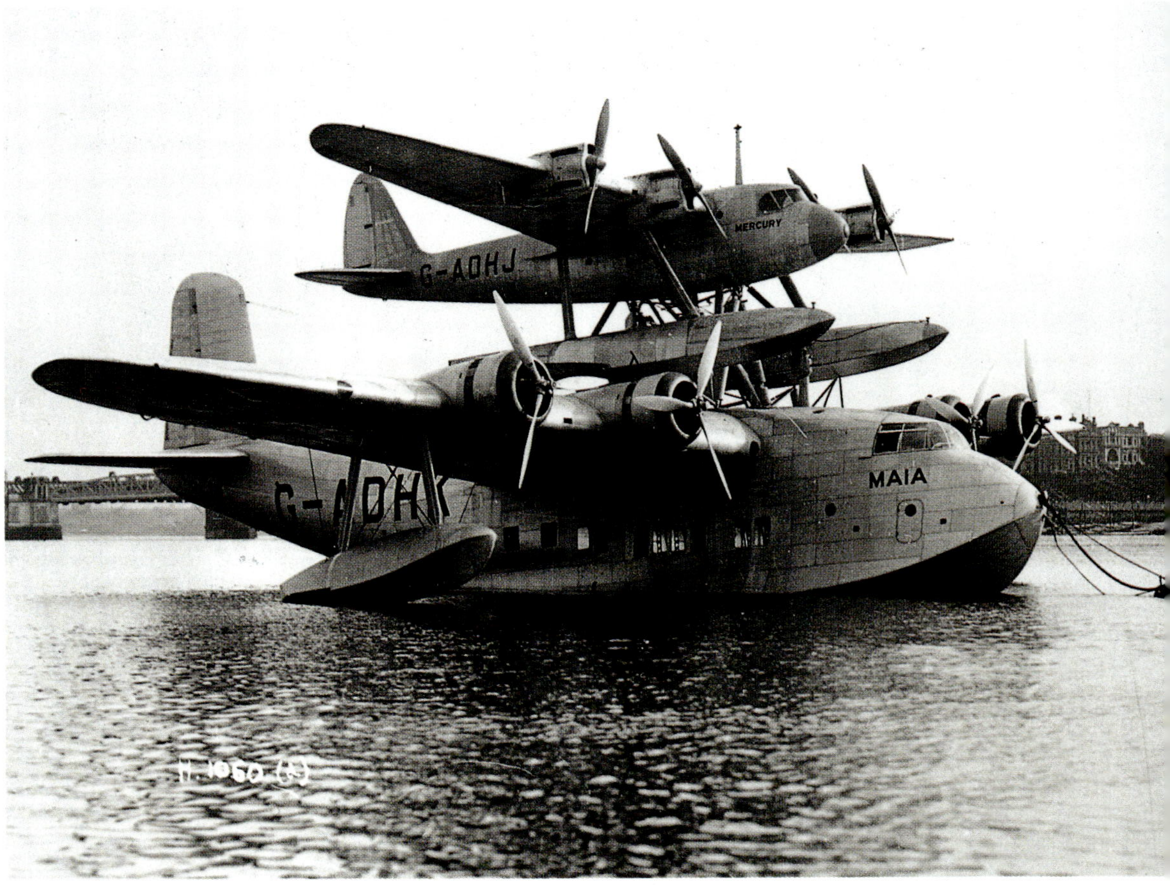

2
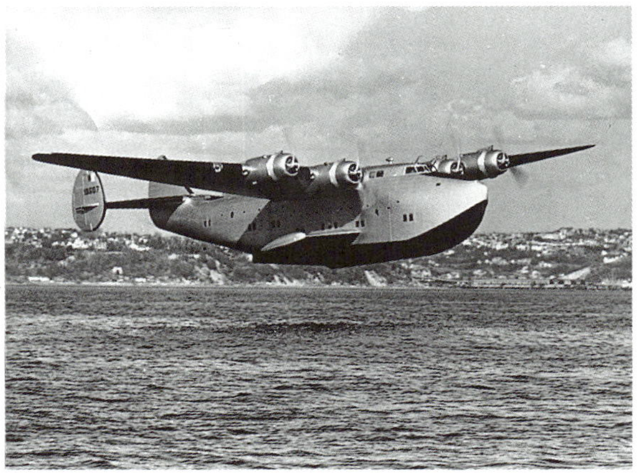

5
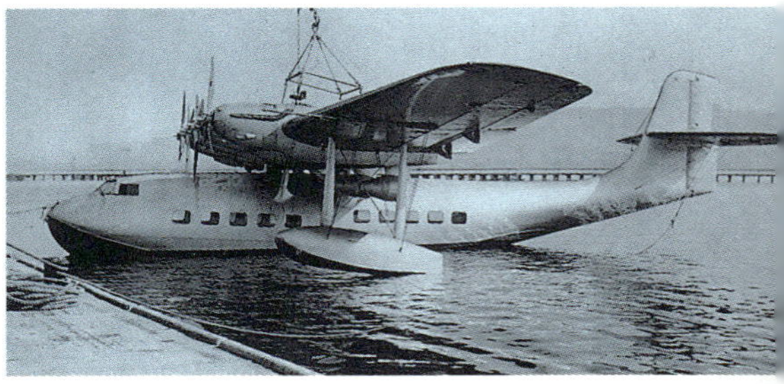

6
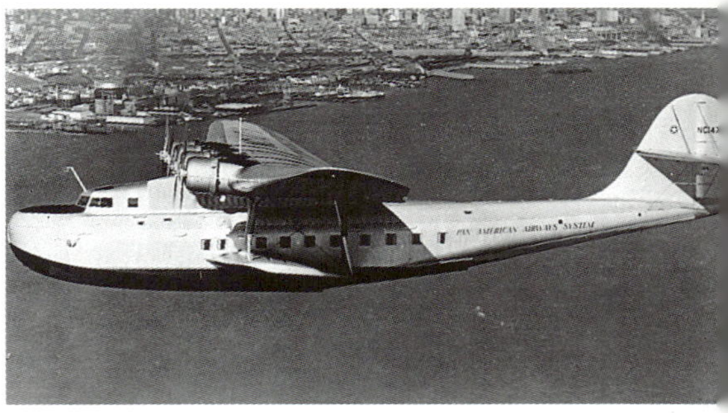

3
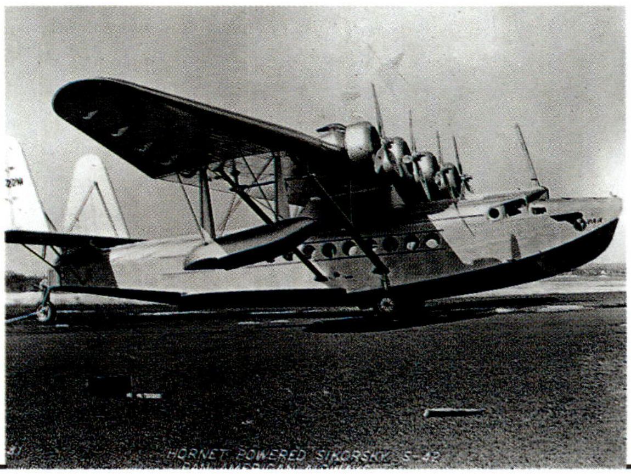

7
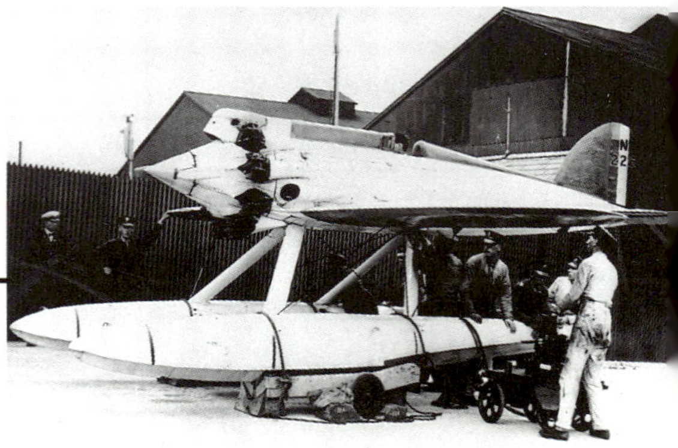

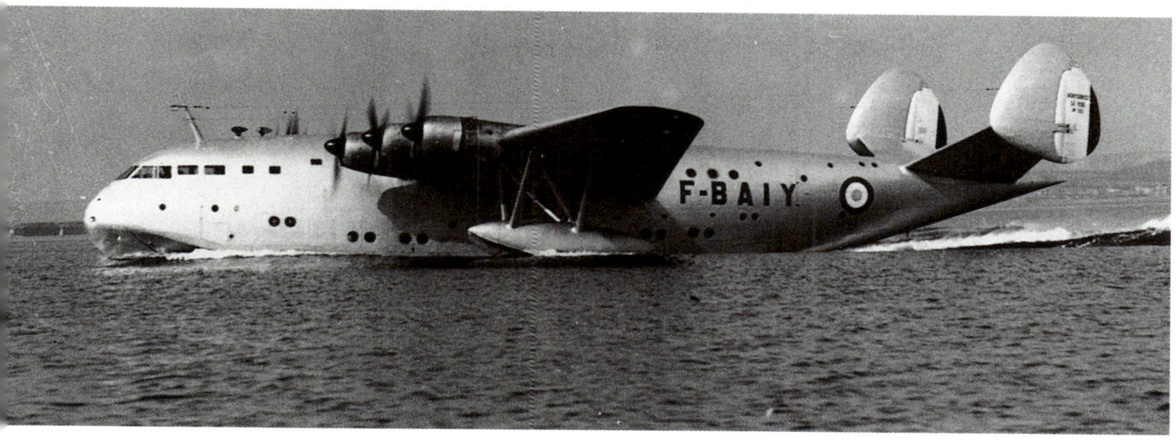

12 Clipper, which could carry 48 passengers at 165 mph (265 kph) on flights of up to 3,125 miles (5,000 km). In 1938, PanAm linked New York to Marseilles with another four-engined flying boat, the Boeing 314. Carrying 74 passengers, it could fly 3,500 miles (5,600 km) at a cruising speed of 187 mph (300 kph).

Then came the war. One of the first aircraft to see action was the 1936 Supermarine Walrus, an amphibious reconnaissance aircraft designed to be catapulted from a ship. A single-engined biplane, it flew at 135 mph (215 kph) and had a range of almost 625 miles (1,000 km)

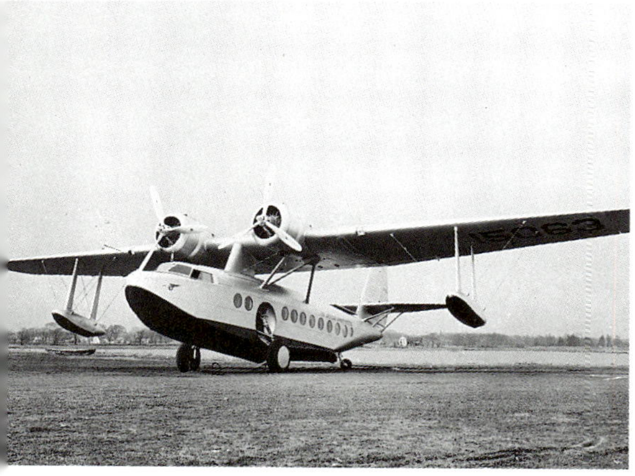

8

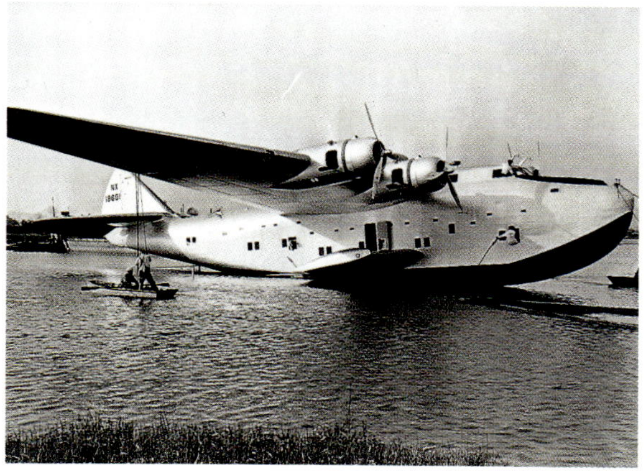

13 **Photo Nos. 1 and 9:** Short S.20/21 Composite, Maia and Mercury (Great Britain)
Photo Nos. 2 and 13: Boeing 314 (USA)
Photo No. 3: Sikorsky S-42 (USA)
Photo No. 4: Latécoère 521 "Lieutenant de Vaisseau Paris" (France)
Photo No. 5: Lioré et Olivier LeO H 246 (France)
Photo No. 6: Martin 130 (USA)
Photo No. 7: Gloster VI racer (Great Britain)
Photo Nos. 8 and 10: Sikorsky S-43 (USA)
Photo No. 11: Supermarine Walrus (Great Britain)
Photo No. 12: SNCASE SE 200 (France)
Photo No. 14: Blohm und Voss Ha 139B (Germany)
Photo No. 15: Breguet Br 521 Bizerte (France)

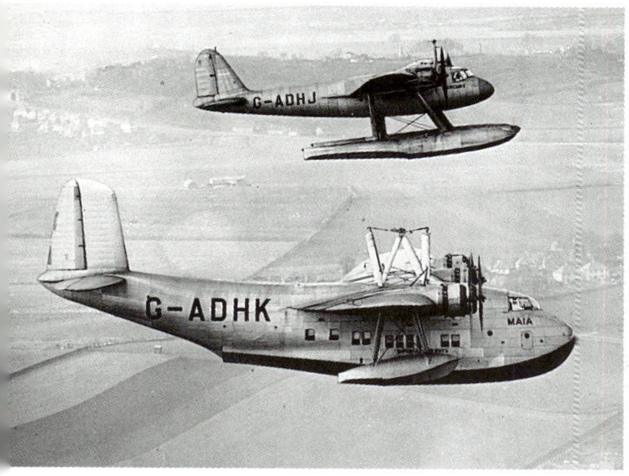

9

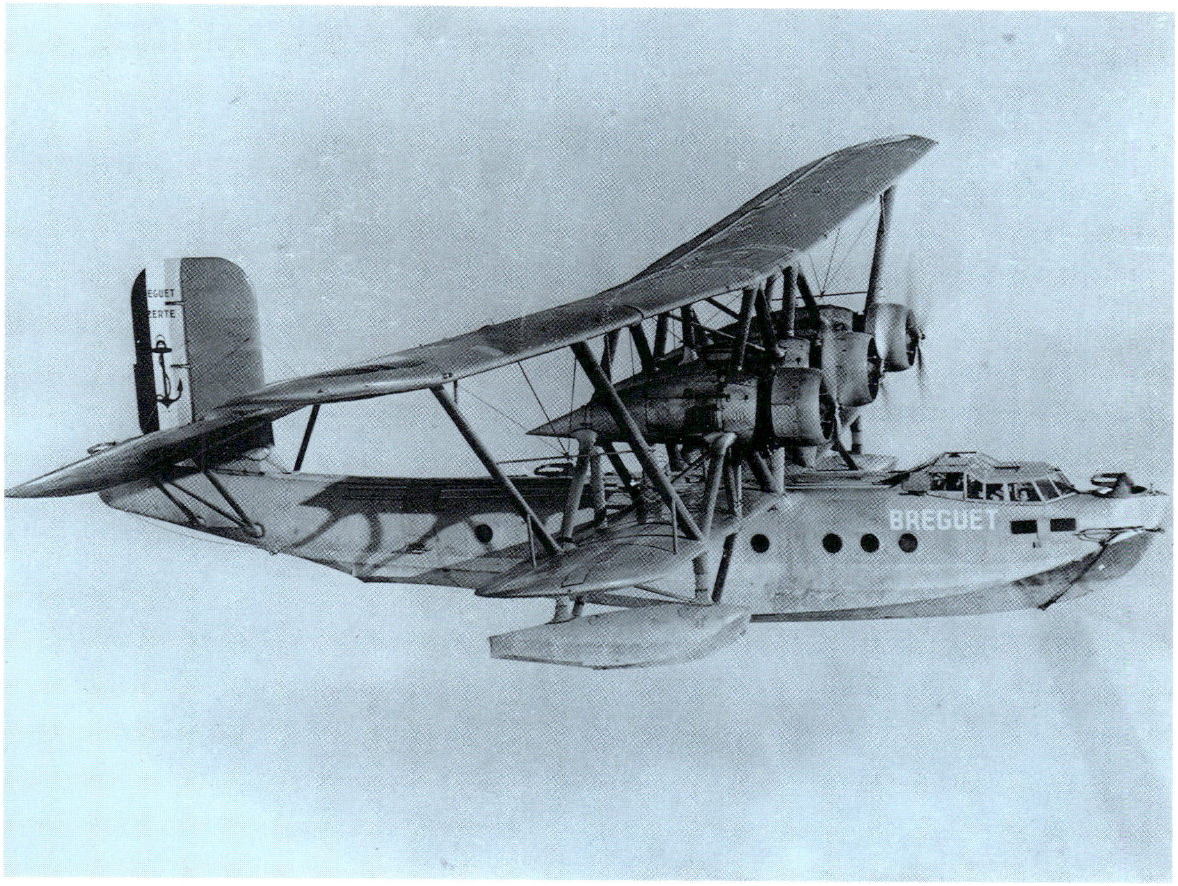

15

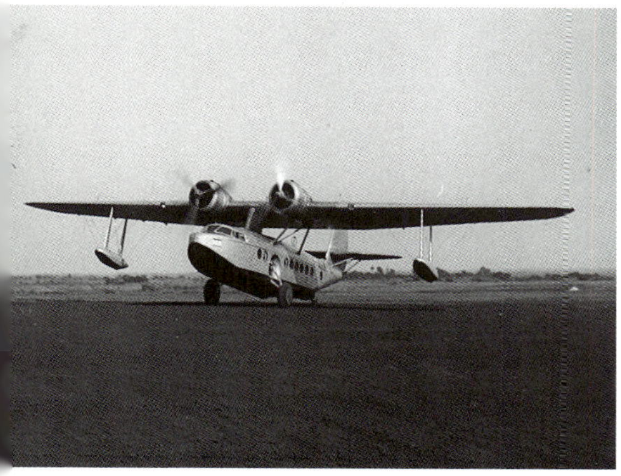

10

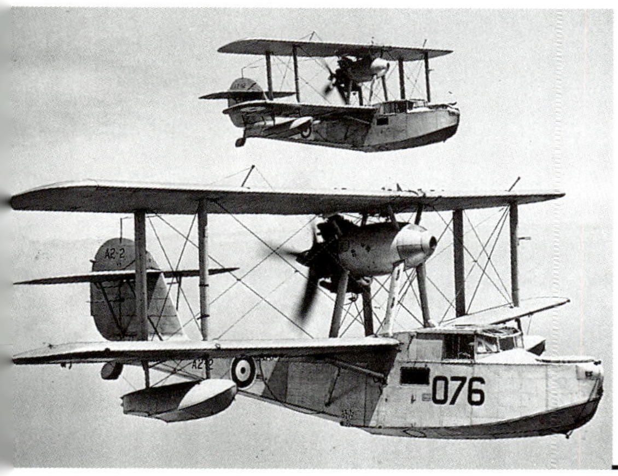

11

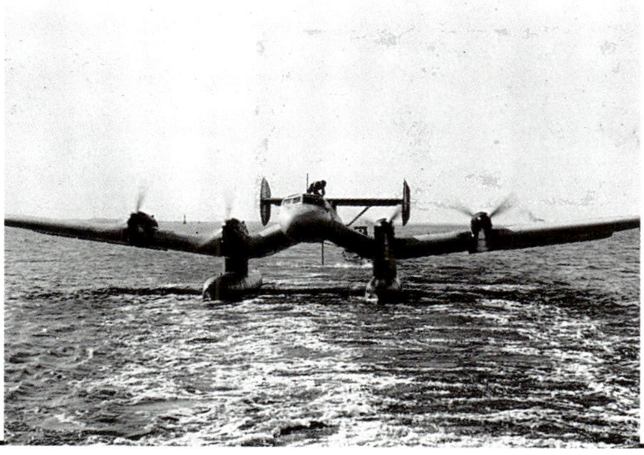

14

THE SECOND WORLD WAR

4

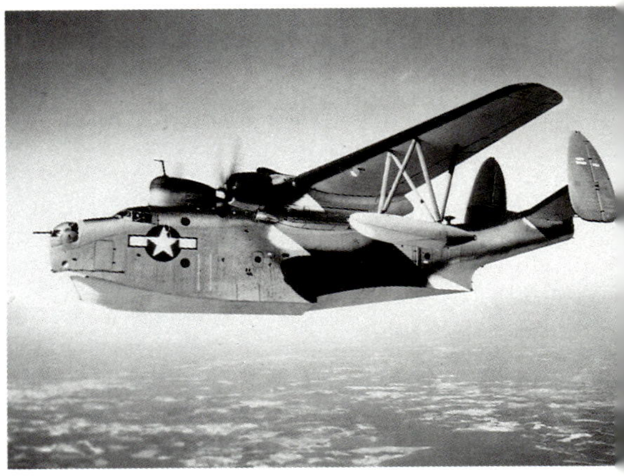

1

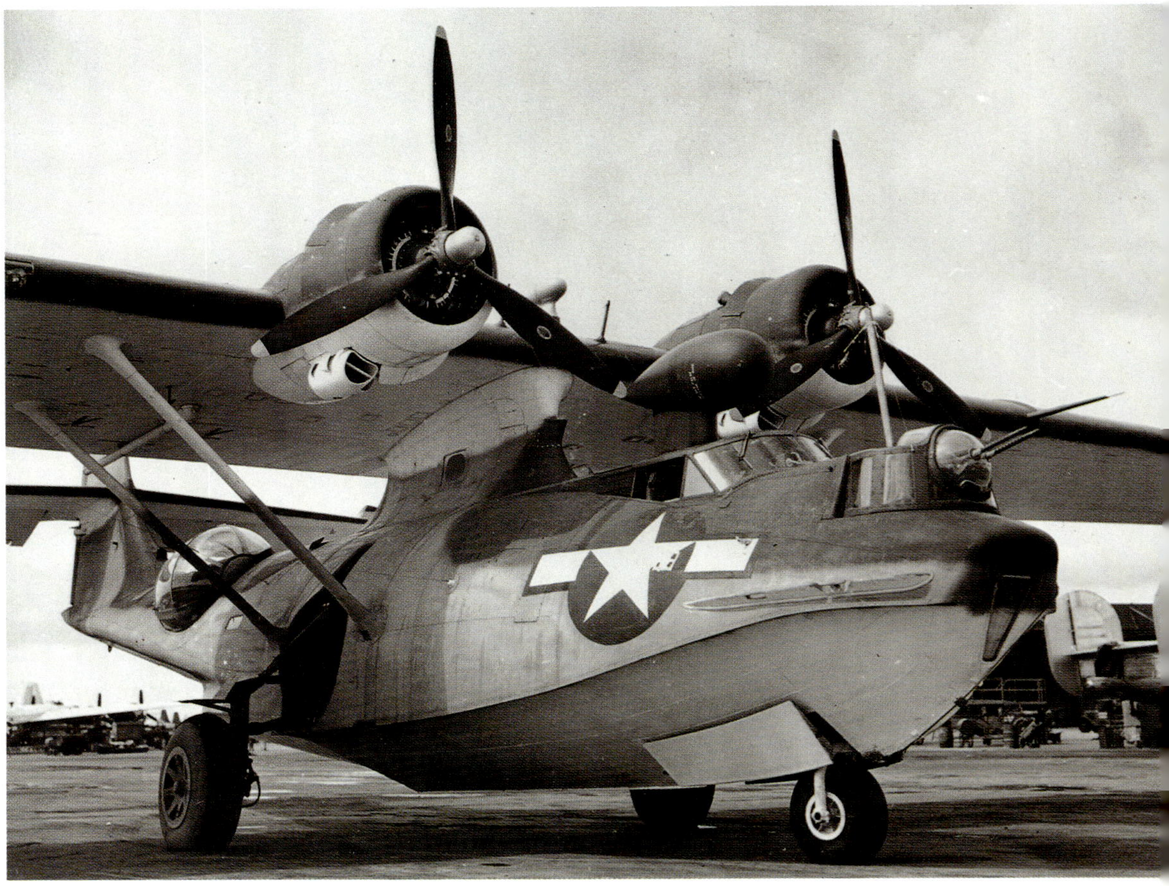

Flying boats played an important role in World War II. On the German side, the Dornier Do 18, unveiled in 1938, was used for reconnaissance. A twin-engined flying boat with a four-man crew, it could cruise at 162 mph (260 kph) over distances of 2,200 miles (3,500 km). The two-man Arado Ar 196 A-1, also employed on reconnaissance duties, was a single-engined seaplane. Armed with cannon, machine guns and 220 lb (100 kg) of bombs, it patrolled at 187 mph (300 kph).

The Heinkel He 115, another seaplane, was powered by twin engines. Intended primarily for torpedo bombing, it also carried two machine guns and 1.5 tons of conventional bombs. It flew at 230 mph (370 kph) and had a range of 2,200 miles (3,500 km).

From 1941, allied convoys had to run the gauntlet of the Blohm und Voss BV 138. A three-engined flying boat with twin tail booms, it was armed with two cannon, machine guns and 660 lb (300 kg) of bombs, and cruised at 178 mph (285 kph) for distances of 2,680 miles (4,300 km).

The biggest flying boat engaged in the conflict was the Blohm und Voss BV 222 Viking, which entered service in 1942. A six-engined flying boat, it flew at 187 mph (300 kph) and had a range of 4,375 miles (7,000 km).

2

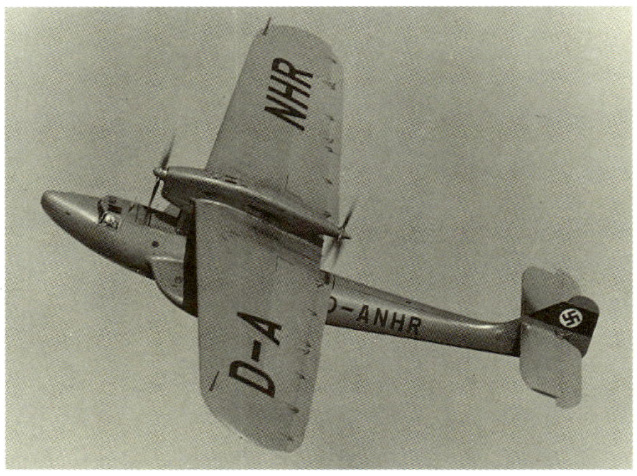

5

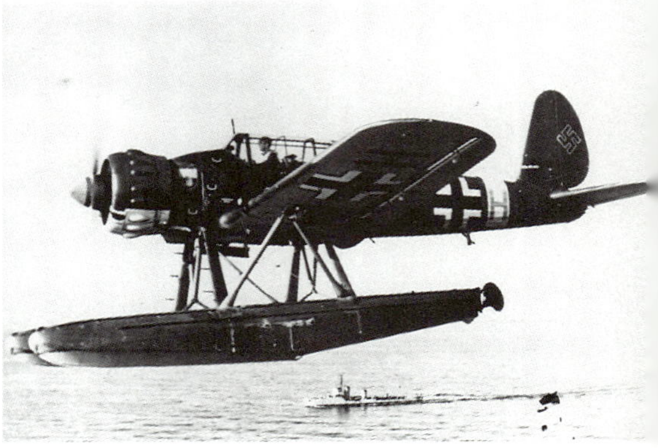

Also on the Axis side, the Italians used the Cant Z.501 flying boat for maritime patrol duties and the Cant Z.506 B Airone (Heron) for attacks on shipping. The Airone was a three-engined seaplane. With a bomb load of 1.2 tons, it flew at 230 mph (370 kph) and had a range of 875 miles (1,400 km). The Japanese made extensive use of marine aircraft in the Pacific. The Kawanishi H6K (1937) and H8K (1942) were both four-engined flying boats used on long-range reconnaissance missions.

For the Allied powers, the British Short Sunderland flying boat had come into service in 1938. A four-engined reconnaissance aircraft with a crew of 13, it carried an armament of seven or more machine guns (earning it the nickname of "Flying Porcupine") and 1,980 lb (900 kg) of bombs. Its speed was 211 mph (338 kph).

3

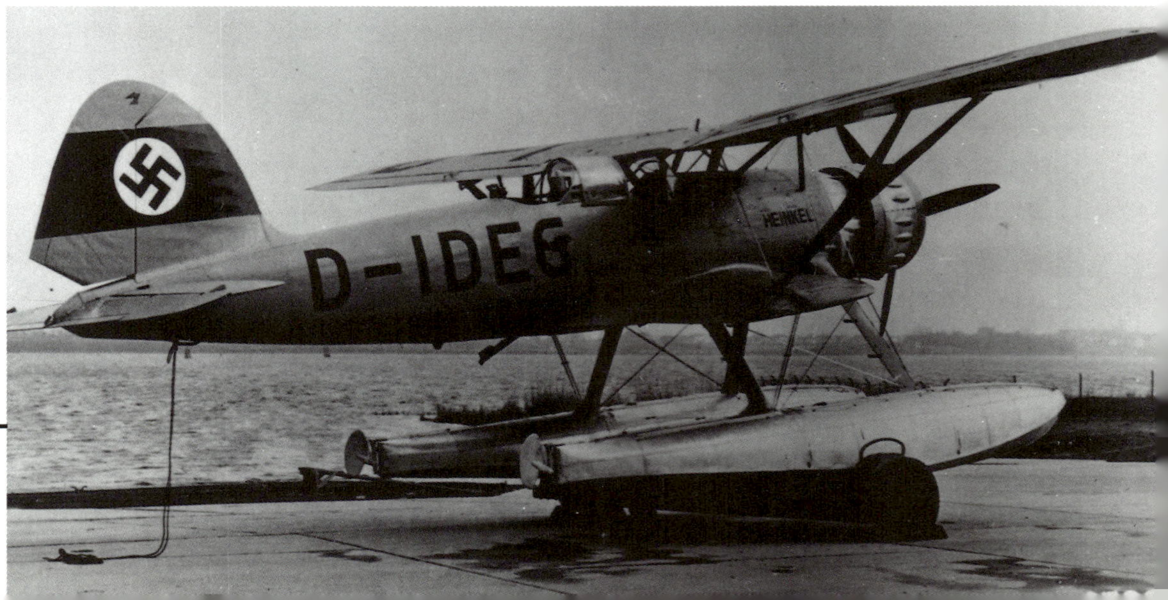

In 1941, the Americans began to deploy the highly adaptable Consolidated PBY Catalina, one of the most celebrated aircraft of the war. A twin-engined flying boat which could also be fitted with a tricycle undercarriage, the "Cat" cruised at up to 175 mph (280 kph) and had the excellent range of 4,000 miles (6,400 km). Its armament

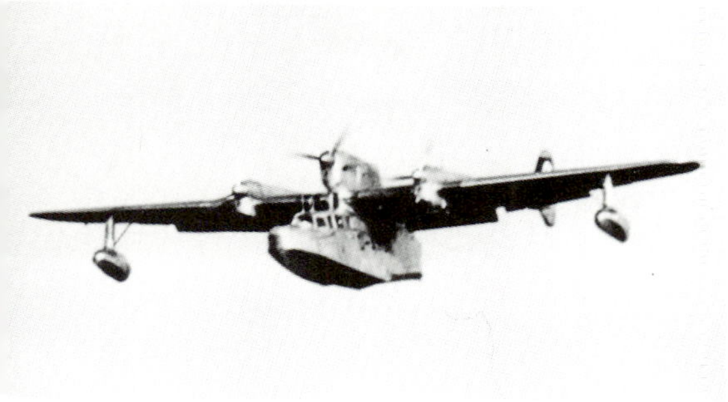
6

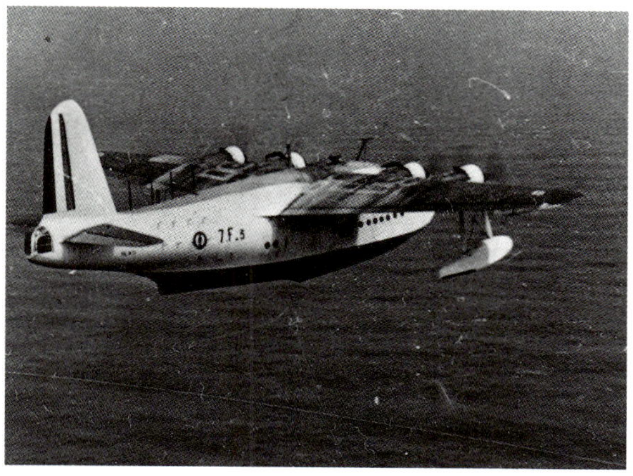
9

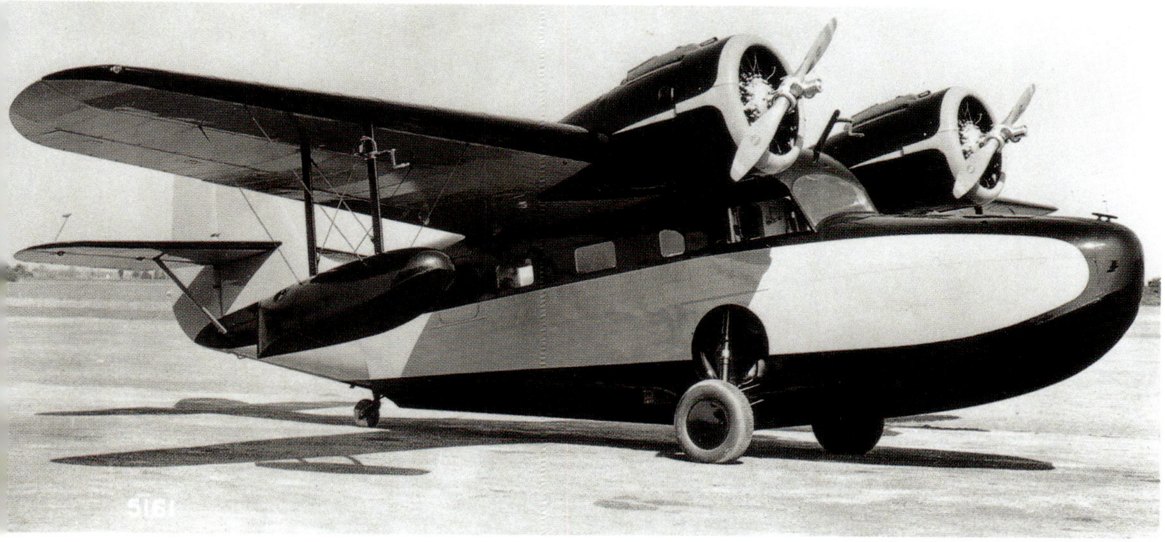
10

consisted of five machine guns and 1.8 tons of bombs. Still bigger was the Consolidated PB2Y Coronado, a four-engined flying boat with a maximum speed of 215 mph (345 kph).

The Martin PBM Mariner (1942) was a twin-engined flying boat. The nine-man crew operated seven machine guns and also carried 1,980 lb (900 kg) of bombs. Cruising at 200 mph (320 kph), it had a range of 2,125 miles (3,400 km).

The Americans also deployed a small, twin-engined amphibious aircraft of civilian origin, the Grumman G-21 Goose (1937). An eight-seater, it cruised at 156 mph (250 kph).

Photo Nos. 1 and 13: Consolidated PBY Catalina (USA)
Photo No. 2: Dornier Do 18 (Germany)
Photo No. 3: Heinkel He 114 (Germany)
Photo No. 4: Martin PBM Mariner (USA)
Photo No. 5: Arado Ar 196 (Germany)
Photo Nos 6 and 11: Blohm und Voss BV 138 (Germany)
Photo No. 7: Blohm und Voss BV 222 Viking (Germany)
Photo No. 8: Cant Z.506 Airone (Italy)
Photo No. 9: Short Sunderland (Great Britain)
Photo No. 10: Grumman G-21 Goose (USA)
Photo No. 12: Kawanishi H8K (Japan)

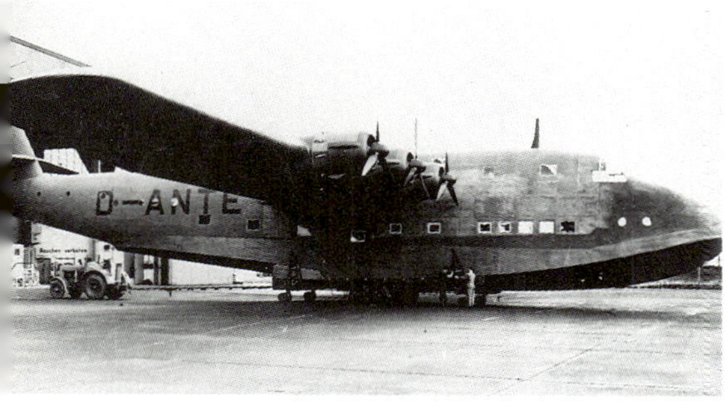
7

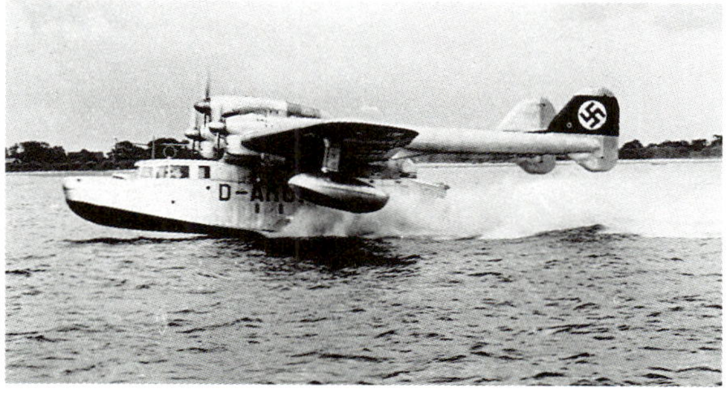
11

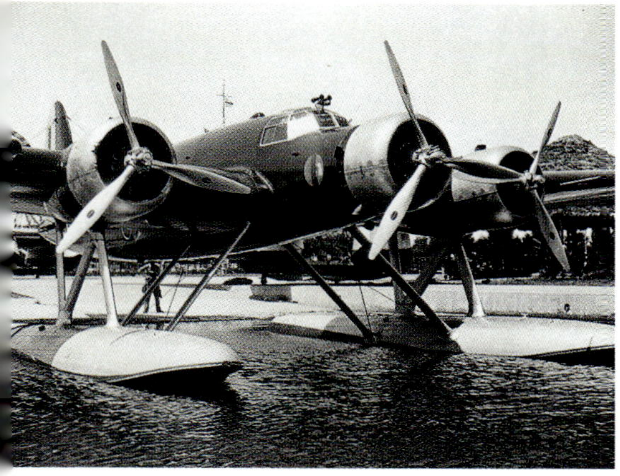
8

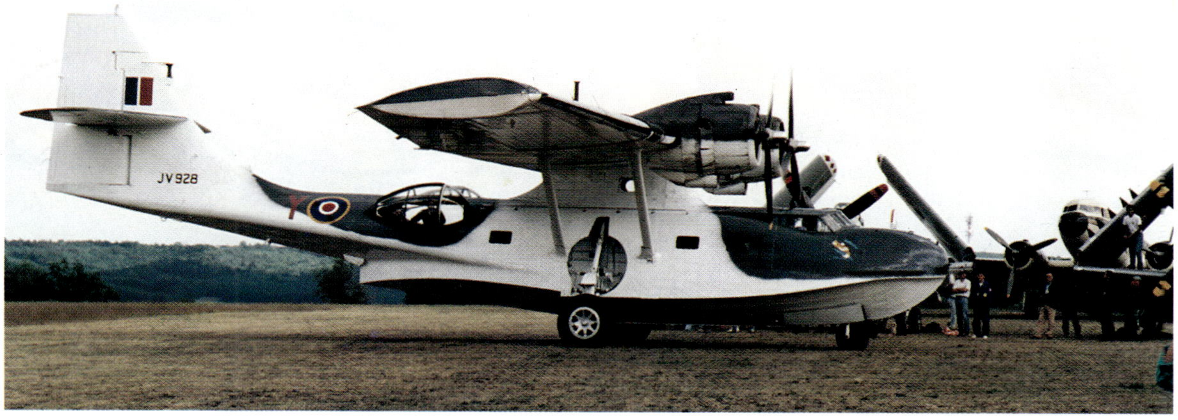
13

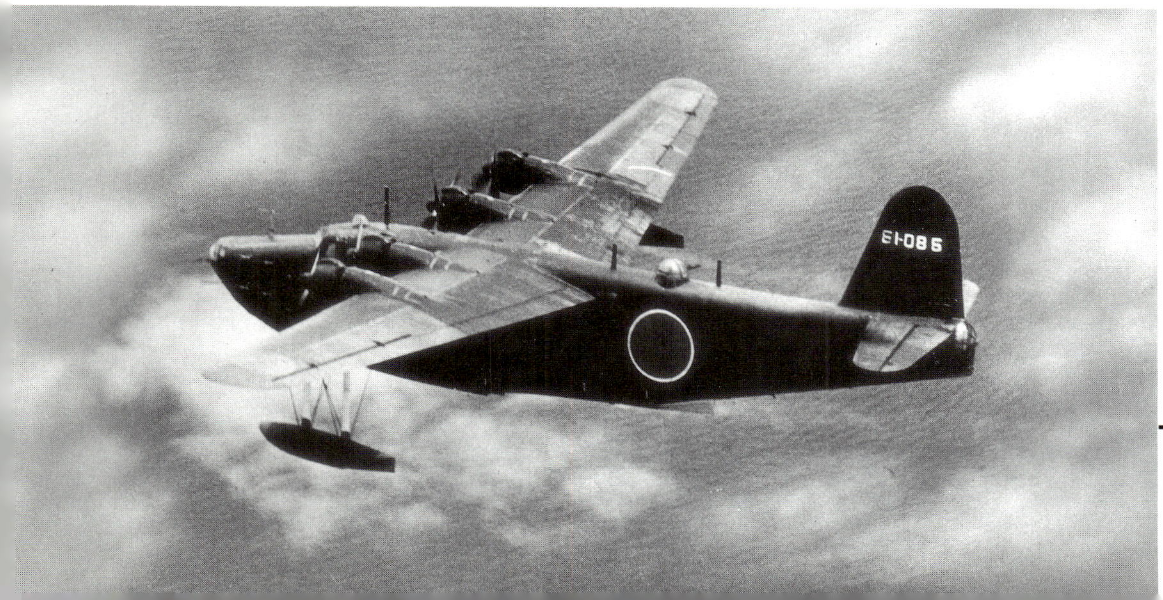
12

4

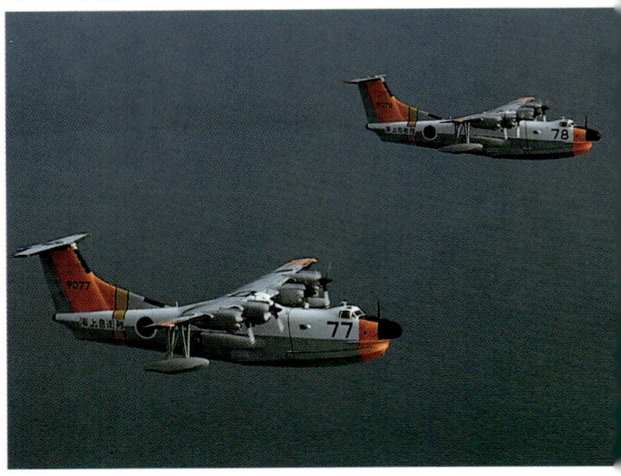

THE POST-WAR PERIOD

During the War, Howard Hughes began work on a giant flying boat conceived for ferrying troops to the Pacific. Of wooden construction, the Hughes HK-1 – dubbed by the media the Spruce Goose – was an eight-engined monster developing 24,000 hp. Though unwanted by the military and completed at Hughes' own expense, it eventually made its one and only flight on 2 November 1947, clearing the water by 50 or 60 feet for almost a mile. It remains to this day the biggest-ever aeroplane.

Another giant flying boat was the British Saunders-Roe S.R.45 Princess, powered by ten engines developing 37,800 hp. Designed to carry 200 passengers over distances of 5,300 miles (8,500 km), it reached 362 mph (580 kph) during test flights.

In 1959, the American Martin P6M SeaMaster became the first-ever jet-powered flying boat. It was also the first to be designed with swept-back wings. Its four engines powered it at speeds of 600 mph (965 kph) over its range of 3,000 miles (4,800 km).

The acknowledged Soviet authority on seaplanes is Beriev. The bureau named after him has designed a whole generation of aircraft, such as the amphibious Be-12 Seagull, which entered service in 1960. Used for maritime patrol duties and capable of carrying eight tons of bombs, this high-wing, twin-engined turboprop can fly at 375 mph (600 kph) and has a range of 2,500 miles (4,000 km). The Be-42 Albatross, which first flew in 1980, is a twin-engined jet. Cruising at 500 mph (800 kph), it has an endurance of nine hours and can carry 37 passengers over distances of 3,125 miles (5,000 km).

Japan, which also has vast territorial waters to patrol, has produced a high-wing, four-engined amphibious aircraft, the Shin Meiwa PS-1 (1972), for anti-submarine and air-sea rescue duties. Armed with bombs, torpedoes or rockets, this aircraft has a range of over 1,250 miles (2,000 km) and a speed of 312 mph (500 kph).

Since 1967 the Canadians have been producing twin-engined amphibious aircraft specifically designed for fighting forest fires. The Canadair CL-215 flies at 180 mph (290 kph), carrying 2,673 litres of water in each of two tanks. In 1989 the company launched the CL-415, a twin-engined turboprop, which carries 6,100 litres in four tanks and can fly at 237 mph (380 kph). These aircraft can also be used for search and rescue missions at sea. In Germany, Dornier have developed a small, high-wing amphibious aircraft, the SeaStar (1984). Powered by twin turboprop engines in tandem configuration, it flies at 246 mph (395 kph), carrying 12 passengers up to 246 miles (395 km).

1

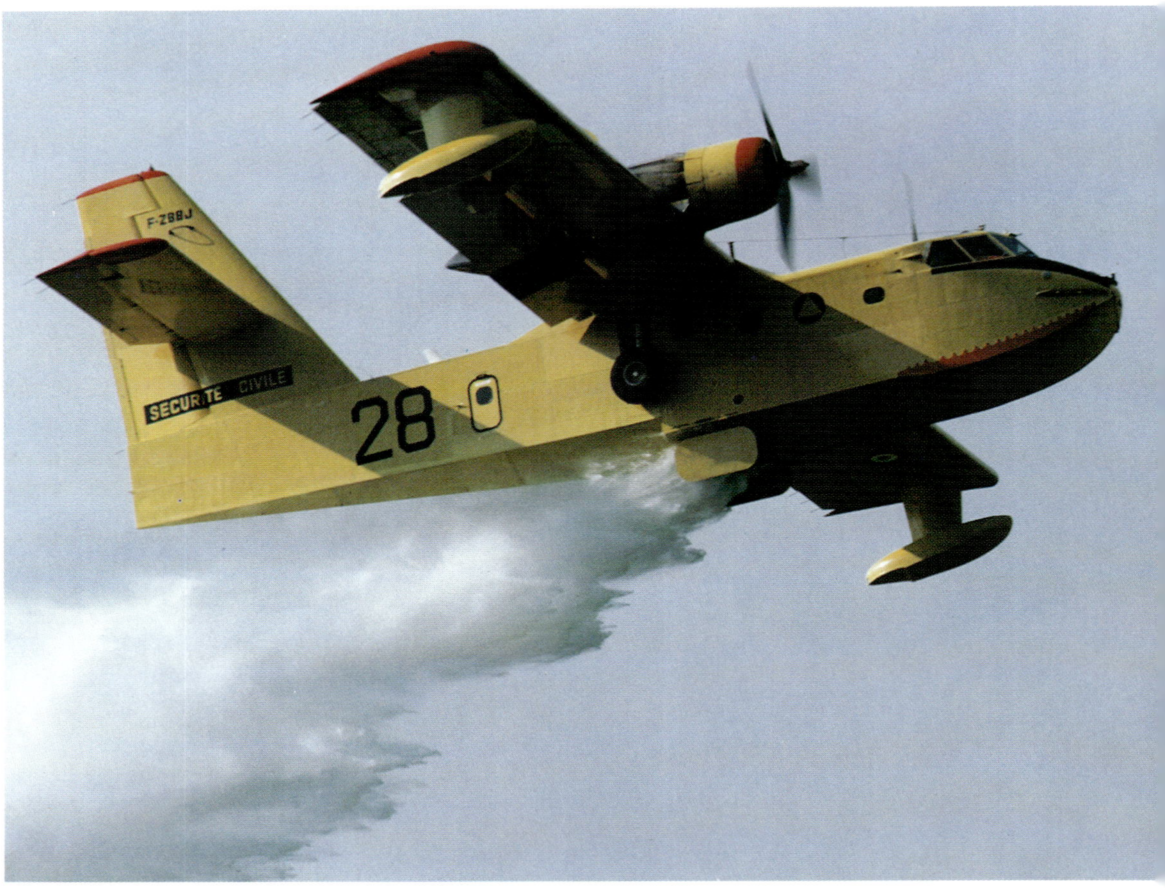

2

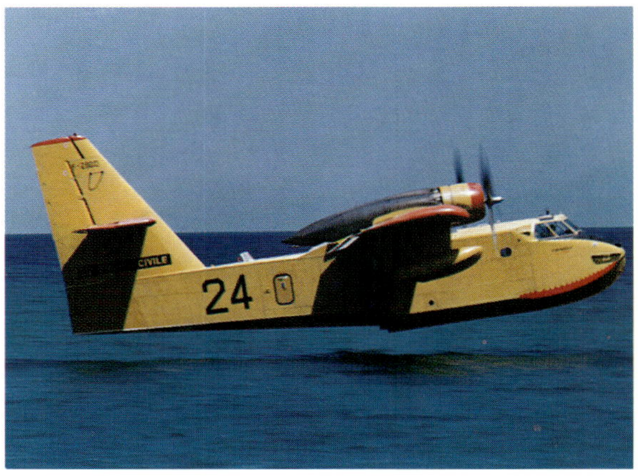

5

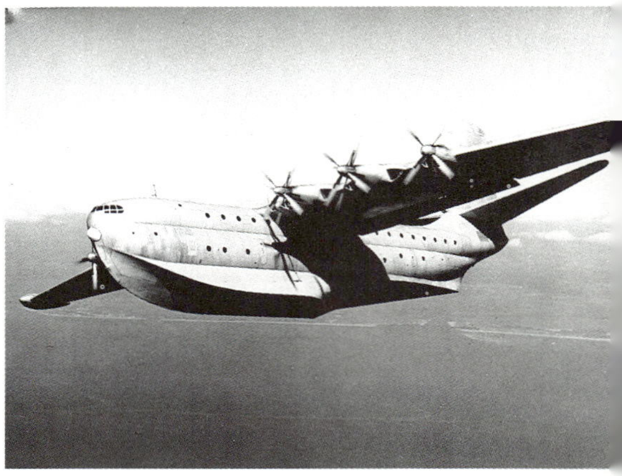

3

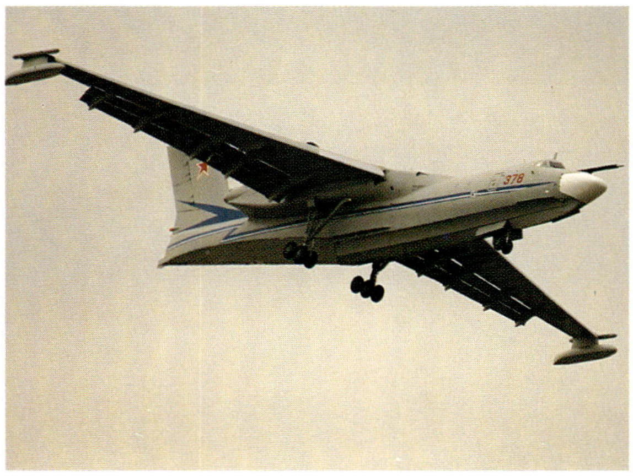

6

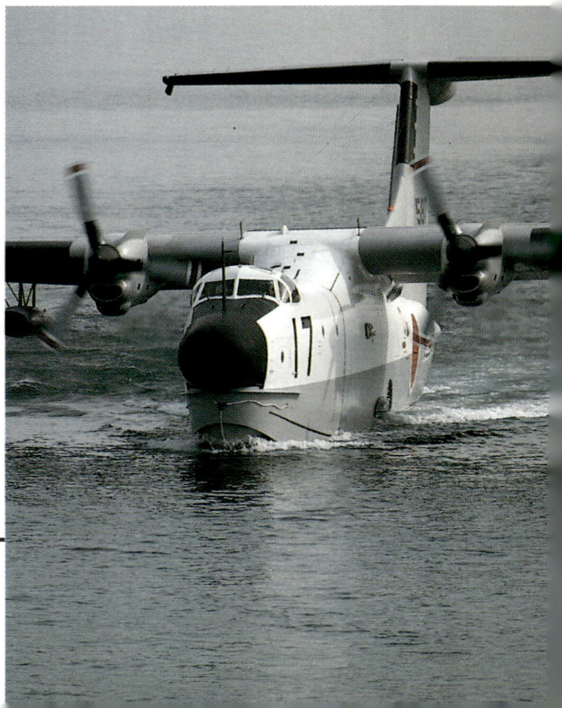

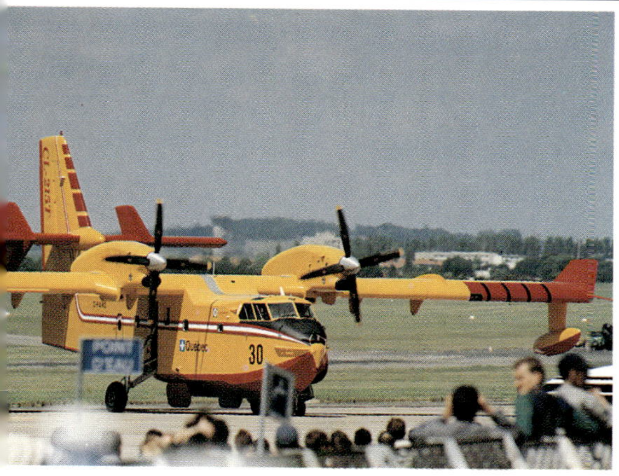

7

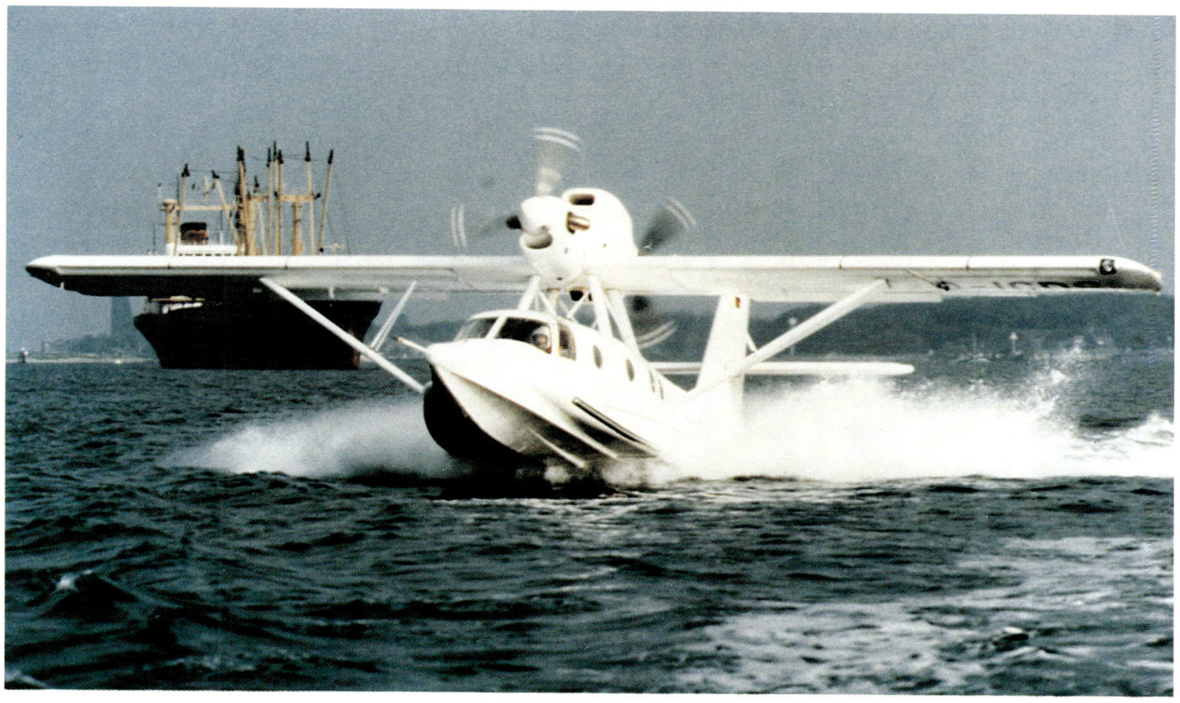

14

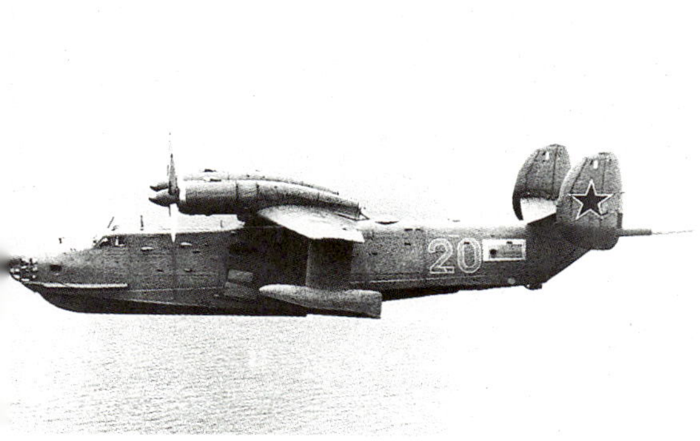

8

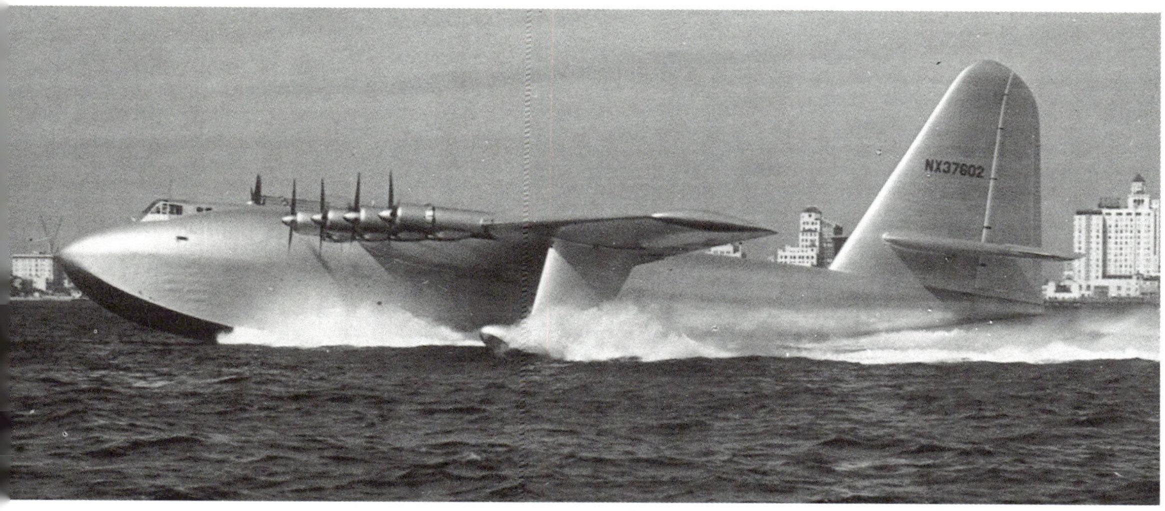

11

Photo Nos. 1 and 2: Canadair CL-215 (Canada)
Photo No. 3: Beriev Be-42 Albatross (Russia)
Photo Nos. 4 and 6: Shin Meiwa PS-1 (Japan)
Photo No. 5: Saunders-Roe SR.45 Princess (Great Britain)
Photo Nos. 7, 10 and 13: Canadair CL-215 T (Cl-415 prototype) (Canada)
Photo No. 8: Beriev Be-12 (Russia)
Photo No. 9: Martin P6M SeaMaster (USA)
Photo No. 11: Hughes HK-1 (USA)
Photo Nos. 12 and 14: Dornier SeaStar (Germany)

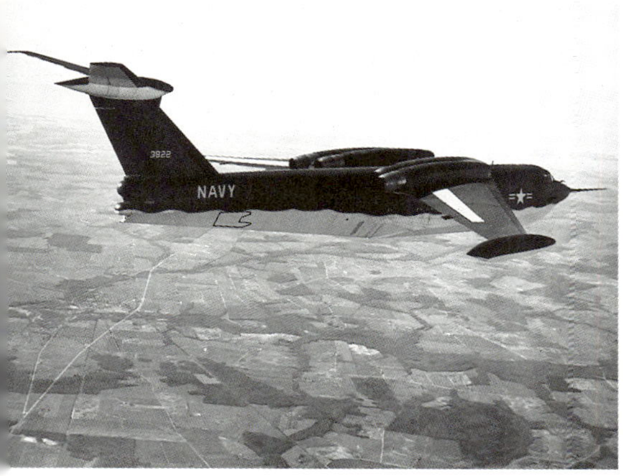

9

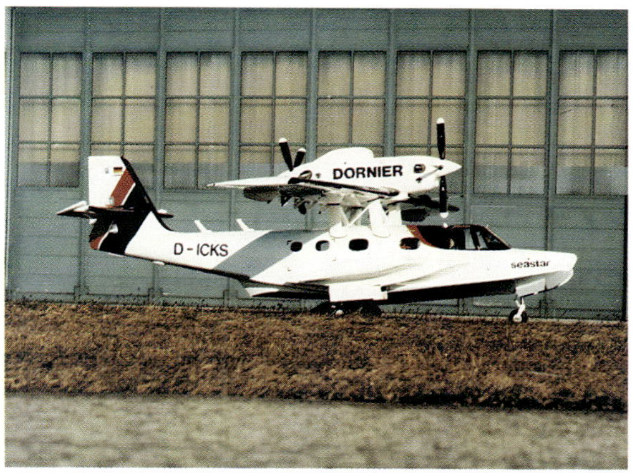

12

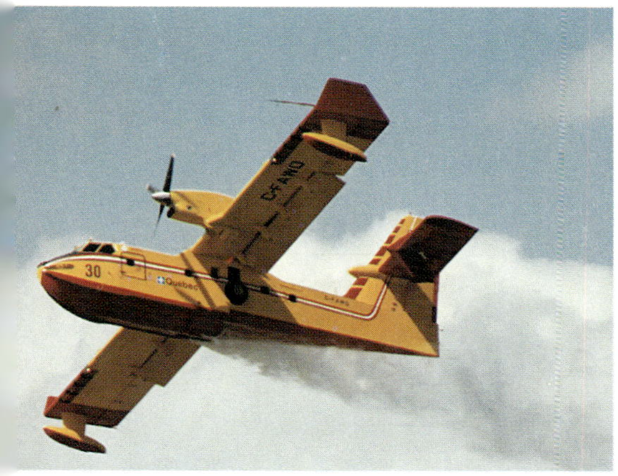

10

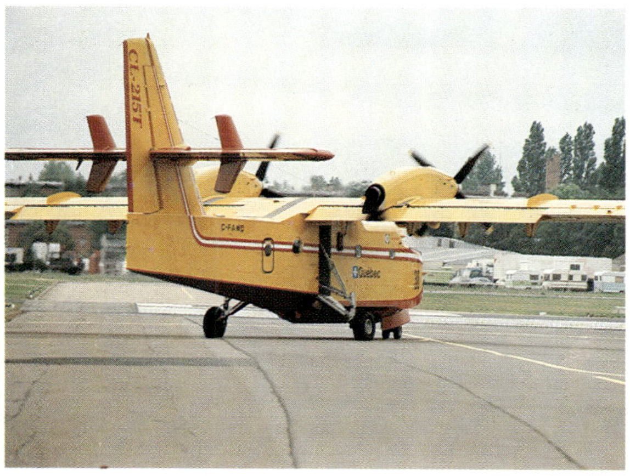

13

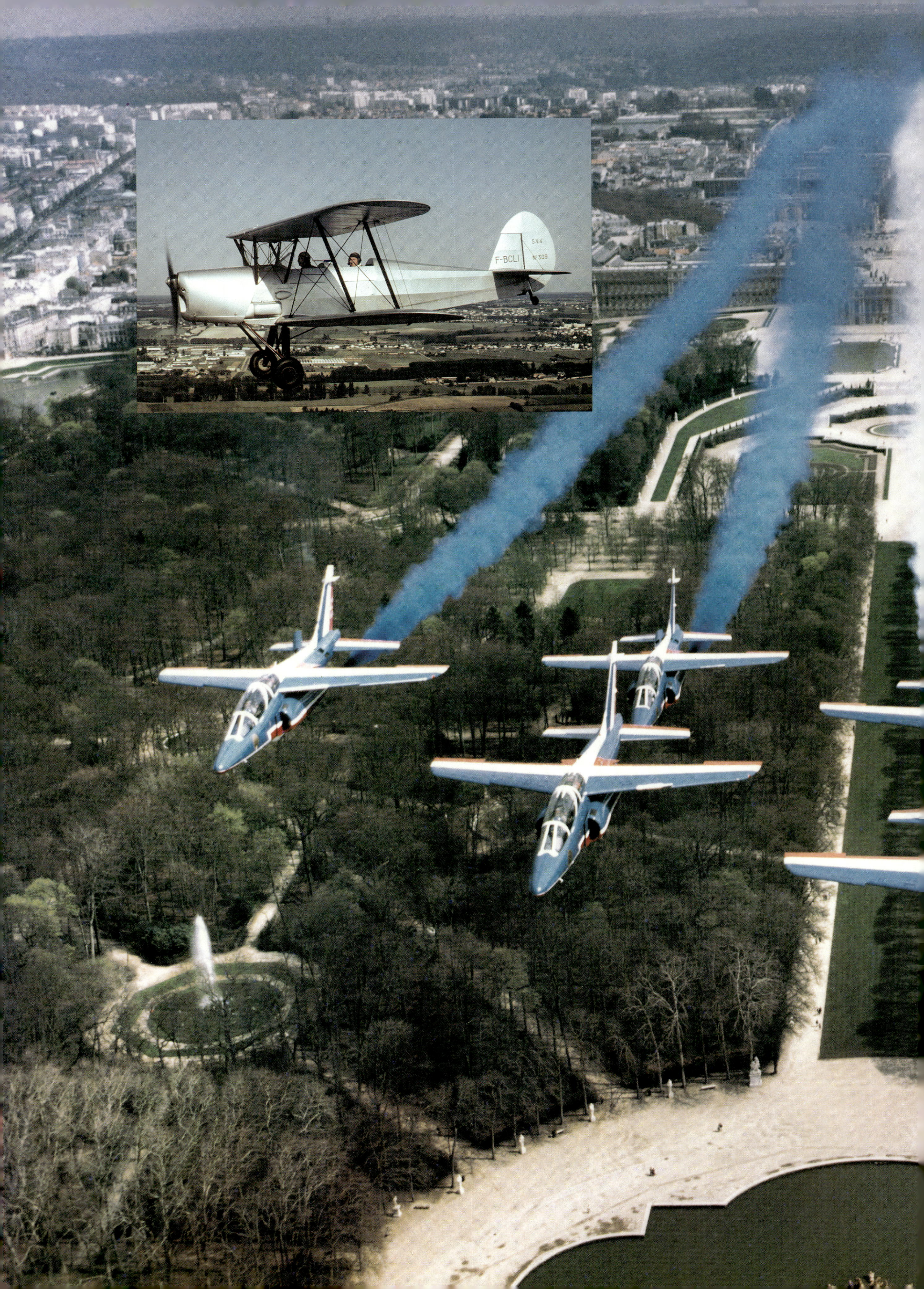
SV4
F-BCLI
N° 309

LEARNING TO FLY

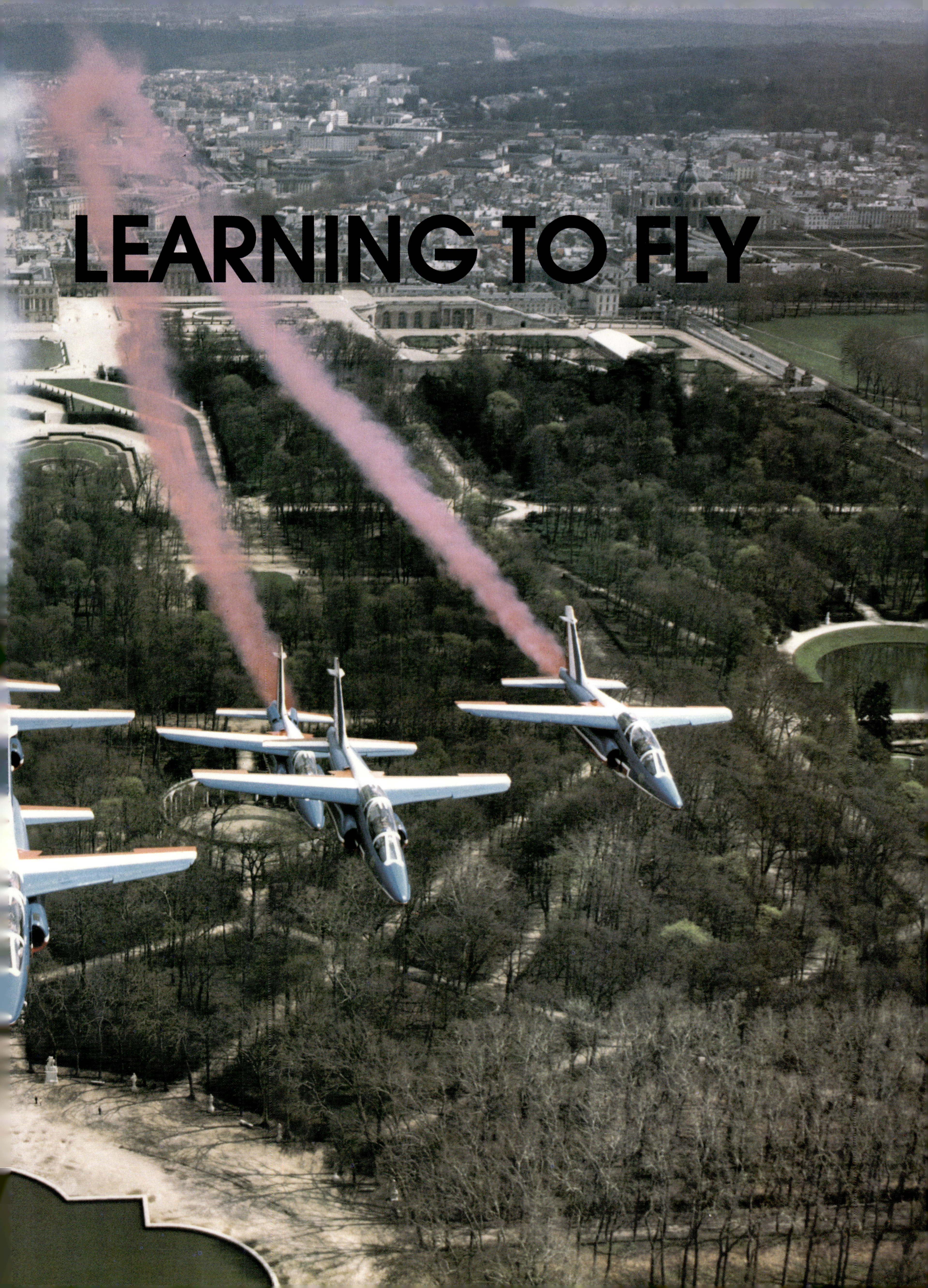

TRAINING AIRCRAFT

4
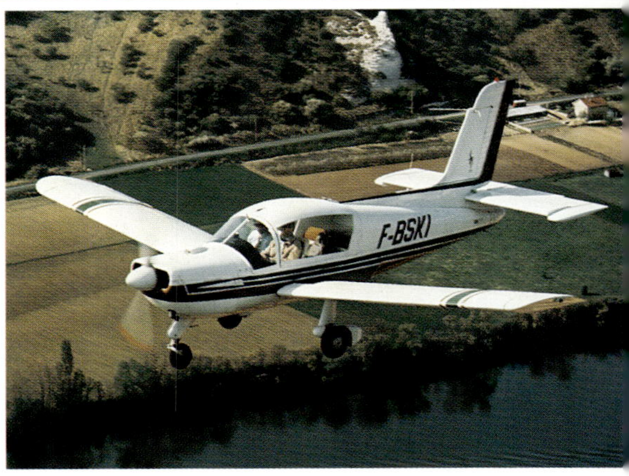

In the 1920s American pilots all learned to fly on board the legendary Jenny, thousands of which were built by Curtiss after 1915. An excellent biplane trainer, the single-engined JN-4 flew at 75 mph (120 kph) and could climb to over 9,800 ft (3,000 m). In 1940, one American trainer was the Ryan PT-20 monoplane, which flew at over 125 mph (200 kph) and had a ceiling in excess of 15,400 ft (4,700 m). The US Army and Navy used the North American T-6 Texan, which was also used by Britain. More than 20,000 units were built. A low-wing, single-engined aircraft with retractable undercarriage, the Texan flew at 212 mph (340 kph) at altitudes of over 24,000 ft (7,300 m).

1
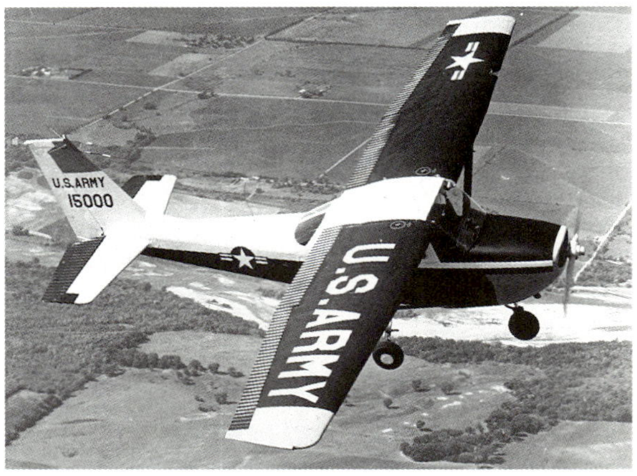

5
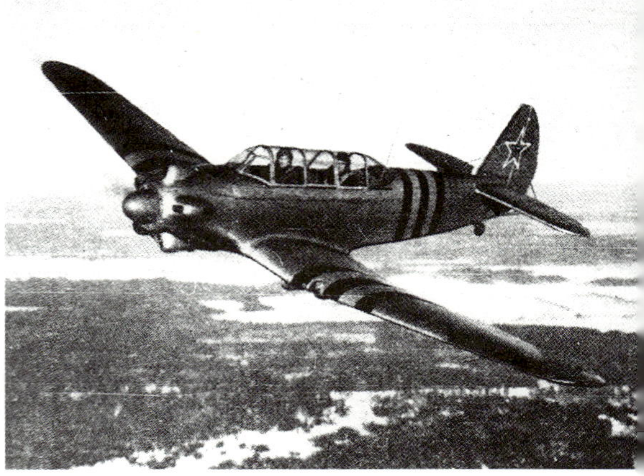

Equally famous was a British biplane trainer, the de Havilland D.H. 82 Tiger Moth. Used to train many of the Empire's pilots after 1931, it was highly manoeuvrable, flying at 110 mph (175 kph) with a ceiling of over 16,400 ft (5,000 m).

After 1947 the Soviets used the Yakovlev Yak-18, a single-engined trainer with a top speed of over 156 mph (250 kph) and a ceiling of 13,000 ft (4,000 m).

2
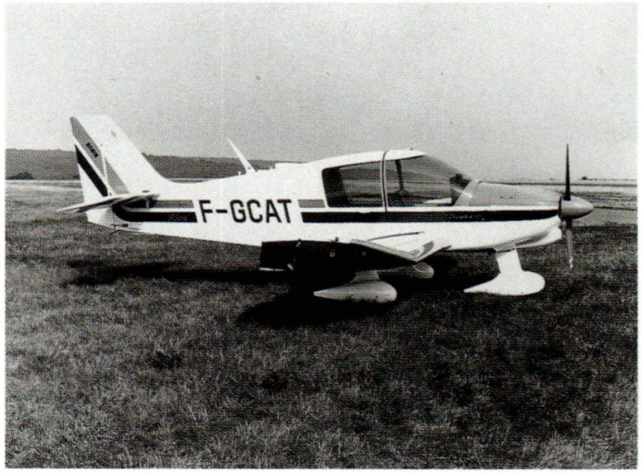

6
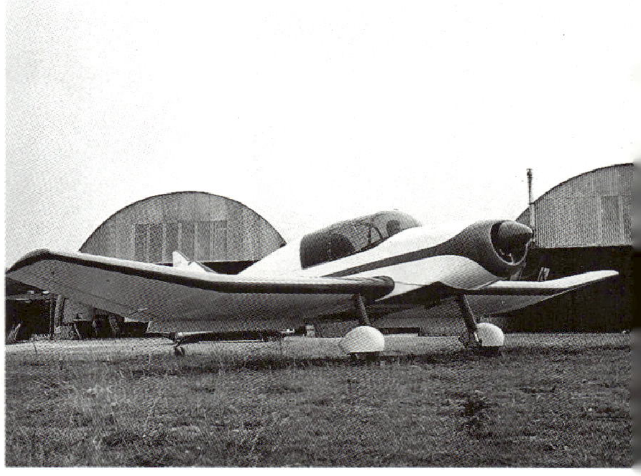

One of the most popular observation and liaison aircraft of World War II was the Piper L-4 Grasshopper, whose top speed was barely 87 mph (140 kph). Since 1955, the Americans have used the Cessna 172 and its military version, the T-41 Mescalero, for basic pilot training. The Cessna is a high-wing, single-engined aircraft with a fixed undercarriage, which reaches speeds of 156 mph (250 kph) and has a ceiling of 16,400 ft (5,000 m).

Pilots of US carrier-borne aircraft train on the Rockwell T-2 Buckeye, which appeared in 1958. Initially a single-engined jet, though subsequently fitted with twin engines, it flies at speeds of 530 mph (850 kph) and can climb to around 39,000 ft (12,000 m). It is being replaced by the Anglo-American T-45 Hawk.

Designed for training jet fighter pilots, the Northrop T-38 Talon made its appearance in 1960. A twin-engined jet, it flies at speeds in excess of 812 mph (1,300 kph) and can reach altitudes of over 52,000 ft (16,000 m).

In 1955 British pilots began training on the BAC Jet Provost a light, single-engined jet which could fly at 468 mph (750 kph) and had a ceiling of 42,600 ft (13,000 m). This aircraft was also used for tactical support, armed with two machine guns and 3,000 lb (1,350 kg) of bombs. This version was called the Strikemaster.

3
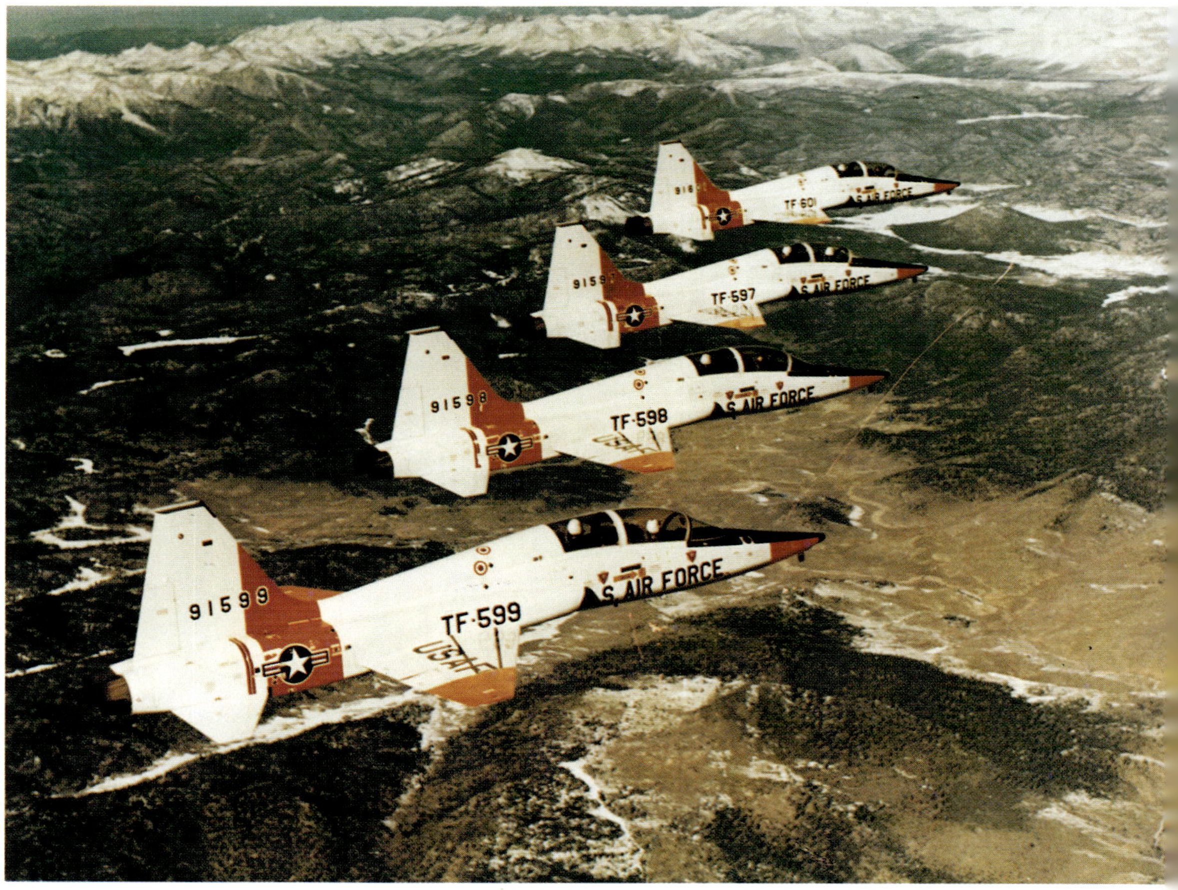

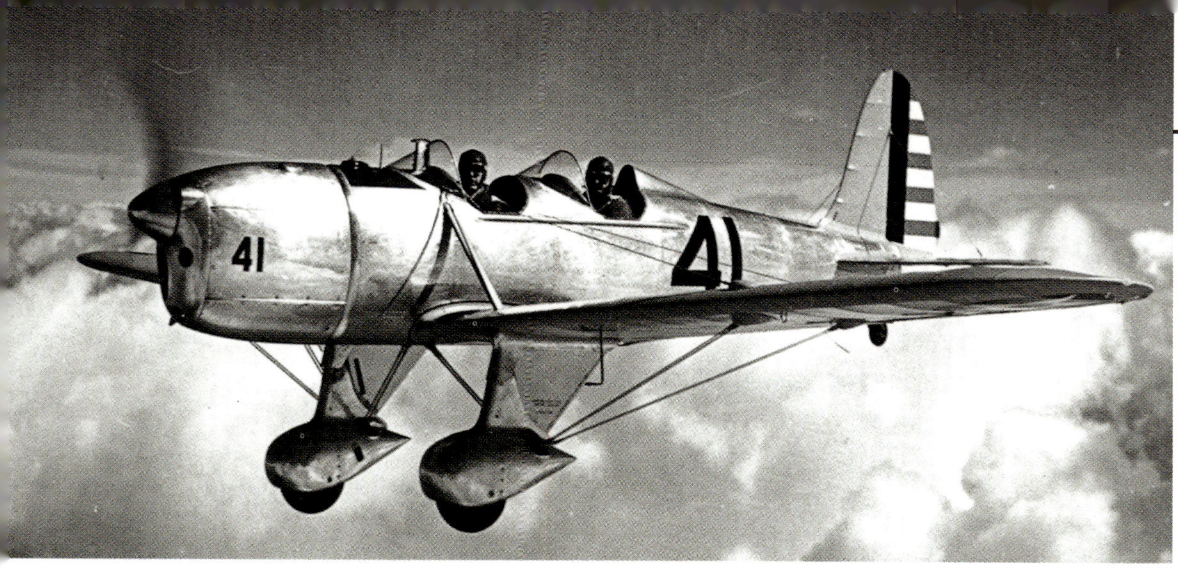

11

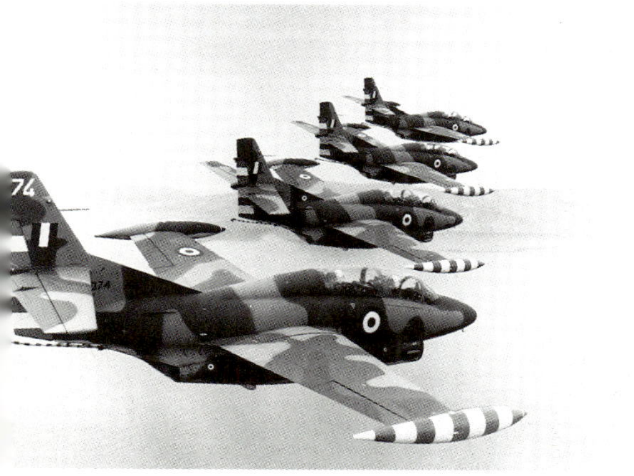

7

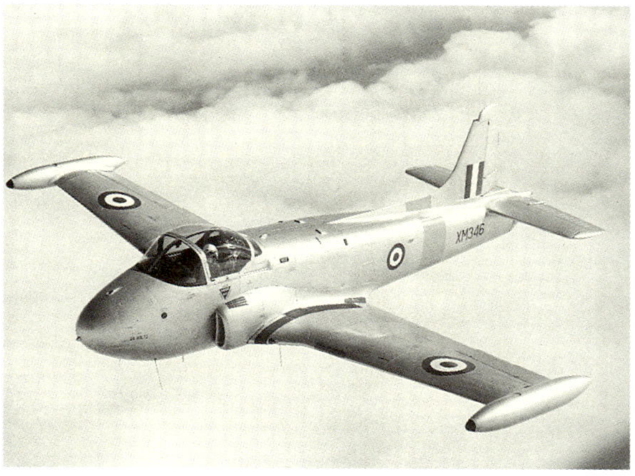

12

French trainers have included the Jodel D.140 Mousquetaire (1958), a low-wing single-engined aircraft with a fixed undercarriage, which flew at 156 mph (250 kph) with four passengers on board. It had a range of 875 miles (1,400 km).

The Socata Rallye Commodore (1961) was another low-wing single-engined aircraft with a fixed undercarriage. It had a maximum speed of 138 mph (221 kph) and carried four passengers on journeys of up to 625 miles (1,000 km). The 1972 Robin DR 400 Dauphin, also a single-engined aircraft with a fixed undercarriage, could carry three passengers at 178 mph (300 kph) over distances of up to 940 miles (1,500 km).

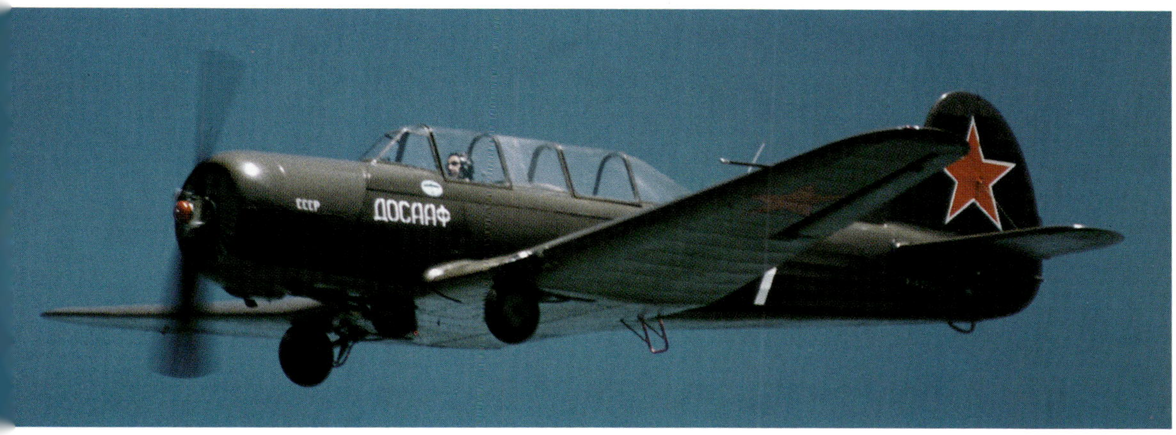

13

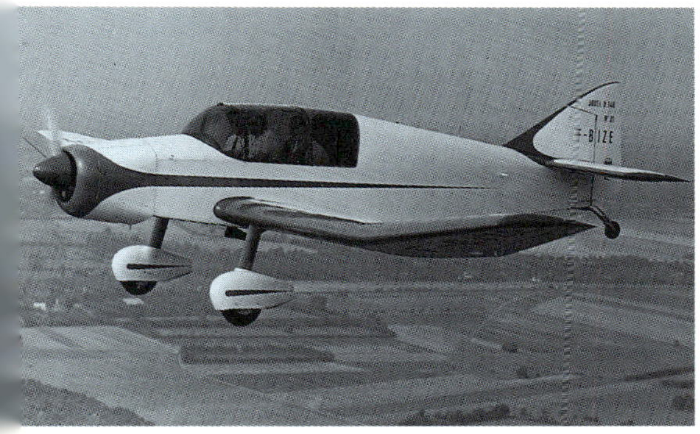

8

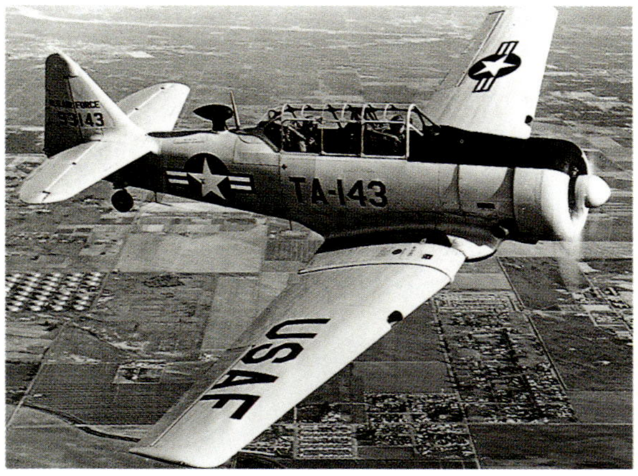

14

Photo No. 1: Cessna T-41B Mescalero (USA)
Photo No. 2: Robin DR 400 Dauphin (France)
Photo No. 3: Northrop T-38 Talon (USA)
Photo No. 4: Socata Rallye Commodore (France)
Photo Nos. 5 and 13: Yakovlev Yak-18 (USSR)
Photo Nos. 6 and 8: Jodel D.140 (France)
Photo No. 7: Rockwell T-2 Buckeye (USA)
Photo No. 9: Curtiss JN-4 Jenny (USA)
Photo Nos. 10 and 14: North American T-6 Texan (USA)
Photo No. 11: Ryan PT-20 (USA)
Photo No. 12: BAC Jet Provost (Great Britain)
Photo No. 15: Piper L-21A Super Cub (USA)
Photo No. 16: de Havilland D.H. 82 Tiger Moth (Great Britain)

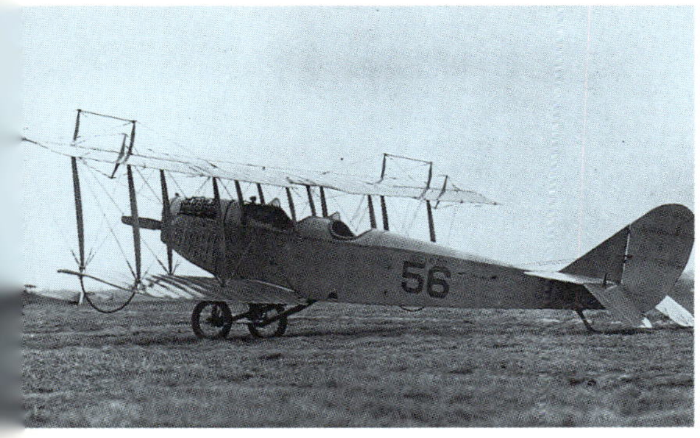

9

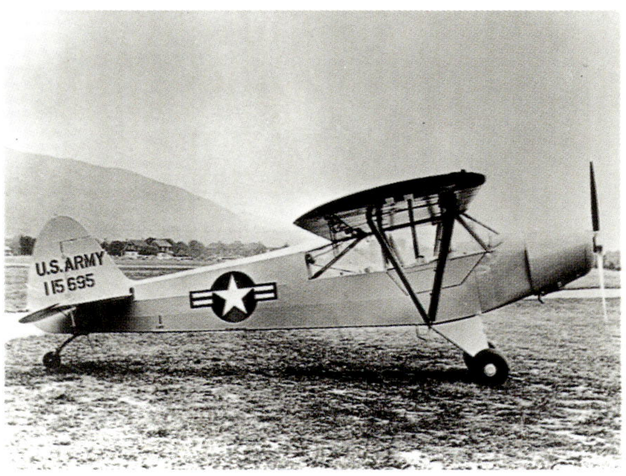

15

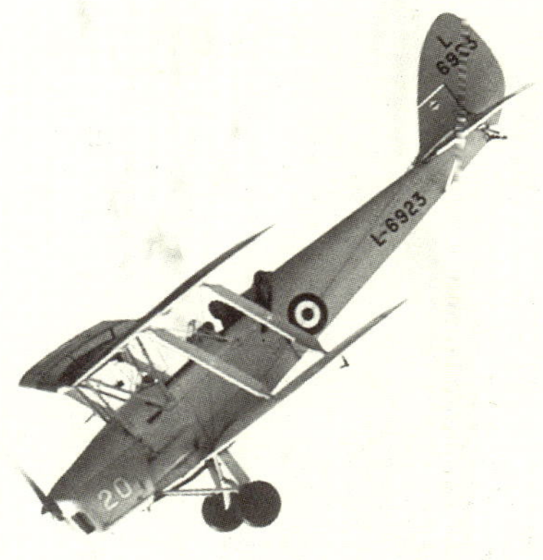

16

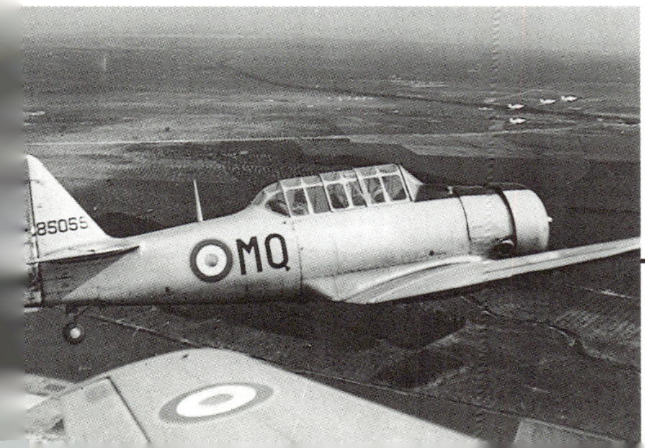

10

5
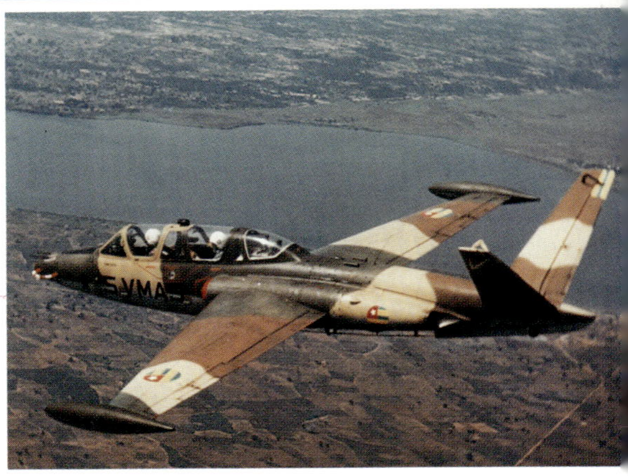

TRAINING AND PRIVATE AIRCRAFT

After the war, in 1945 the French company Nord Aviation built a pre-war Belgian trainer, the Stampe SV.4. A single-engined biplane with a fixed undercarriage, it was capable of 87 mph (140 kph). The de Havilland Canada DHC-1 Chipmunk was a low-wing trainer with a fixed undercarriage. Powered by a single engine, it flew at speeds in excess of 125 mph (200 kph).

The first ever jet trainer made its appearance in 1948. It was the single-engined Lockheed T-33, which had a maximum speed of 590 mph (950 kph) and a ceiling of over 46,000 ft (14,000 m). In 1950, the Soviets brought out the MiG-15UTI two-seater. It could fly at 690 mph (1,100 kph) and climb to 49,200 ft (15,000 m).

The French Max Holste M.H.1521 Broussard made its debut in 1953. It was a high-wing, single-engined liaison aircraft with a fixed undercarriage and could carry five passengers 750 miles (1,200 km) at a cruising speed of 156 mph (250 kph). The Nord 3202 was a single-engined trainer, which appeared in 1959. Designed with a low wing and fixed undercarriage, it flew at over 125 mph (200 kph) and had a range of 560 miles (900 km).

Specifically designed for training was the Potez (subsequently Aérospatiale) Fouga Magister of 1952. This small twin-jet had a cruising speed of 406 mph (650 kph) and a ceiling of 36,000 ft (11,000 m). A modernized Super Magister version was brought out in 1962.

The civilian version of the Morane-Saulnier MS.755 Fleuret/760 Paris was used for training and liaison purposes. A twin-engined jet with seating for four passengers, it made its first flight in 1958. Cruising at 340 mph (550 kph), it had a range of 940 miles (1,500 km).

In 1955, the Italians introduced the Piaggio P.149D training and liaison aircraft. A low wing, single-engined four-seater, it flew at 187 mph (300 kph) and had a range of 690 miles (1,100 km). It was followed in 1973 by a small, high-wing single-engined aircraft with fixed undercarriage, the Aermacchi AM.3C.

Since 1980, the French Armée de l'Air has used the classic single-engined Aérospatiale Epsilon for basic pilot training. It flies at around 230 mph (370 kph) and has a ceiling of 23,000 ft (7,000 m). Pilots then move on to the light, twin-engined Alpha Jet built by Dassault/Dornier. This aircraft reaches speeds in excess of 560 mph (900 kph) and altitudes of 46,000 ft (14,000 m). Armed with a cannon and two machine guns, it was used by the German Luftwaffe as a ground attack aircraft.

1
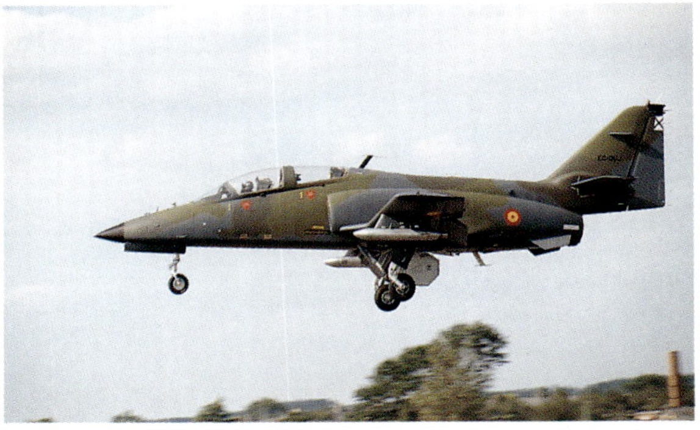

6
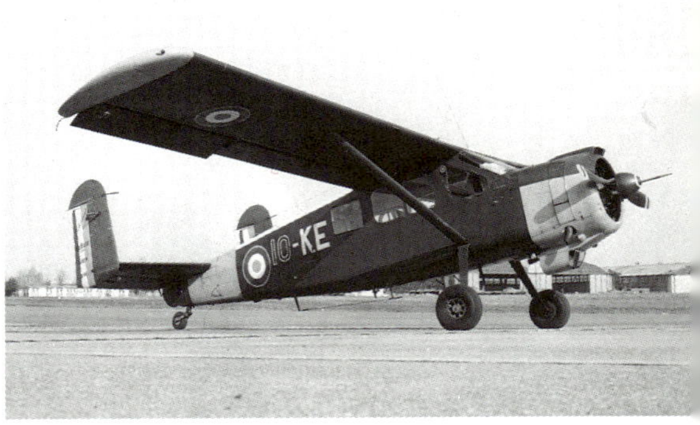

2
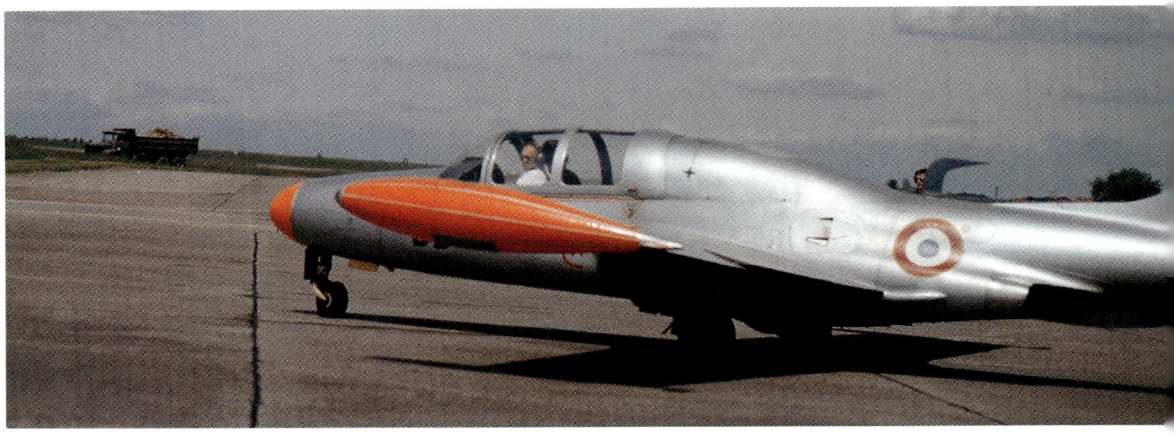

3
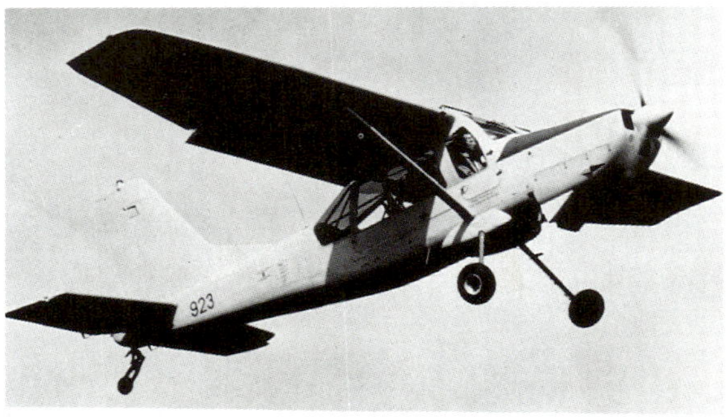

7
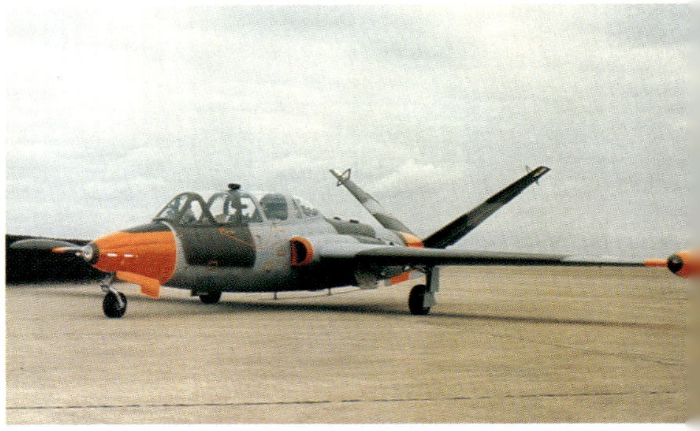

4
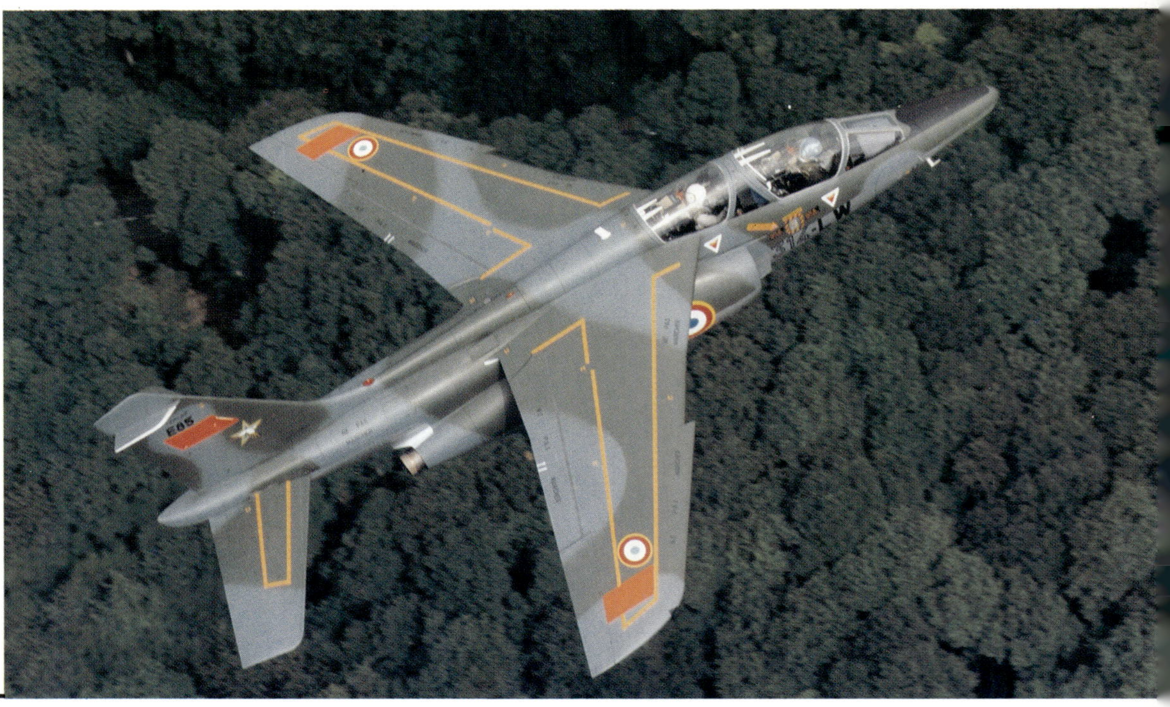

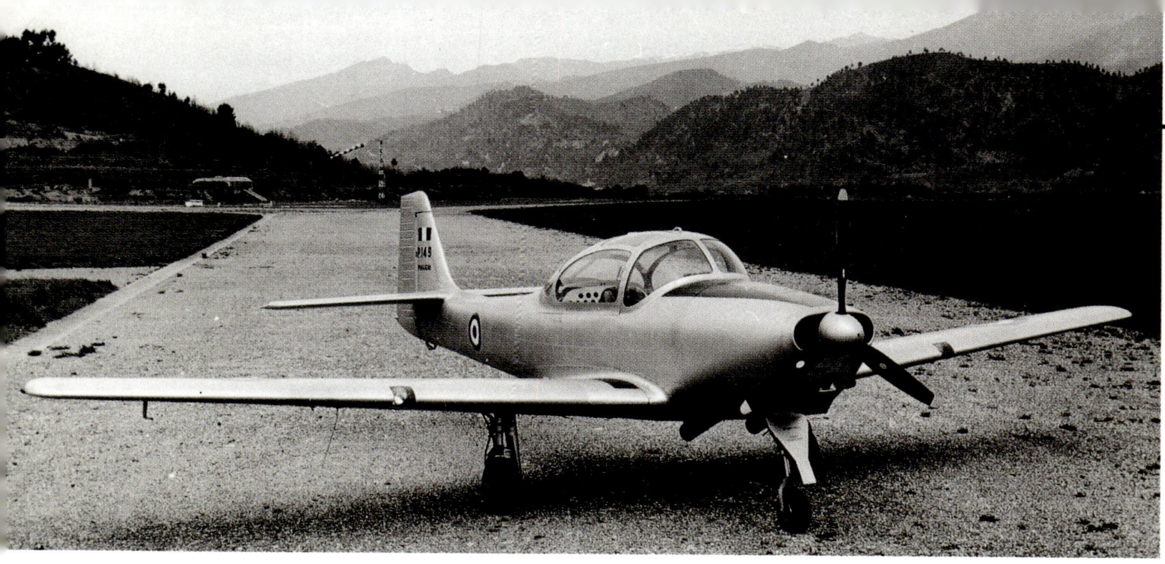

11

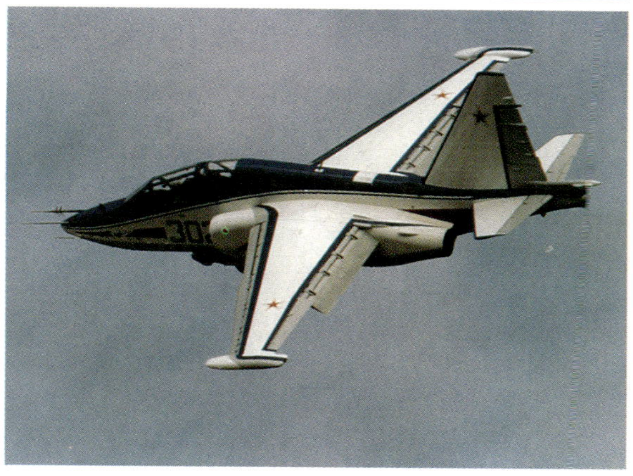

16

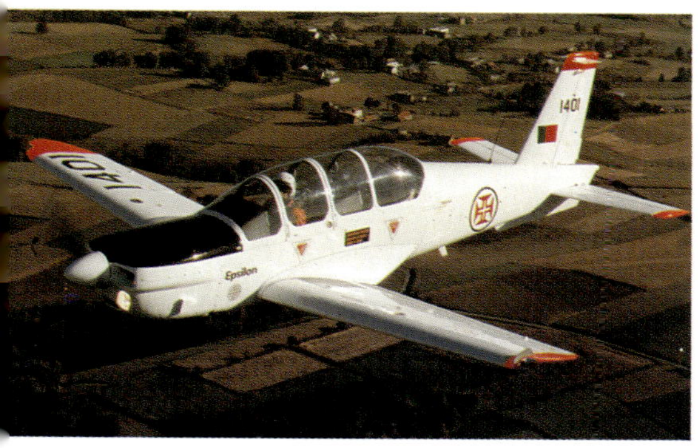

8

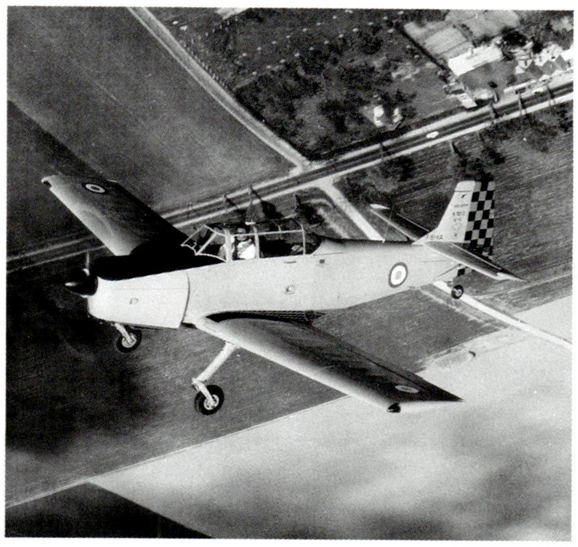

12

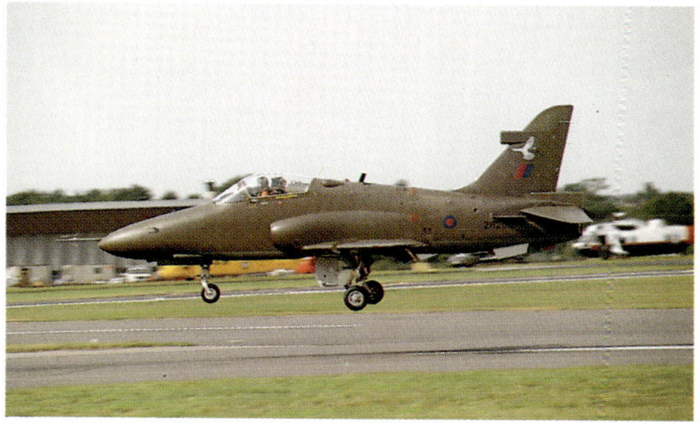

17

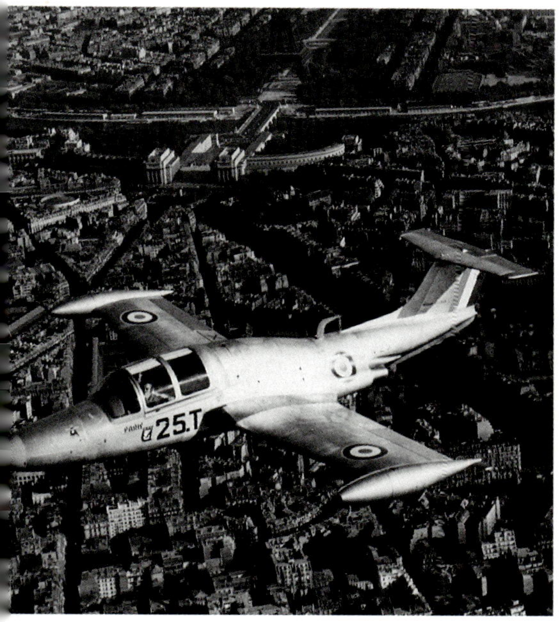

9

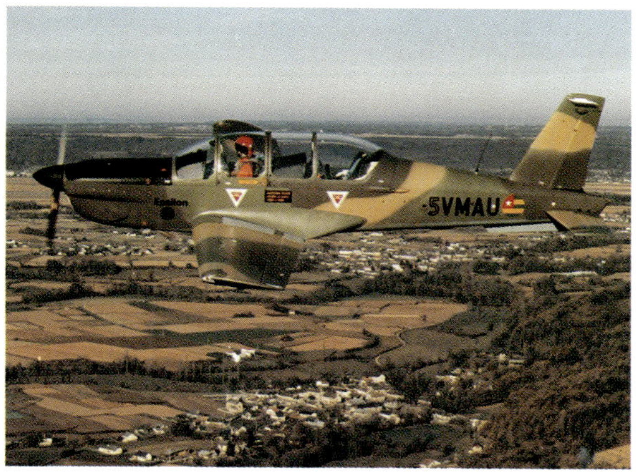

13

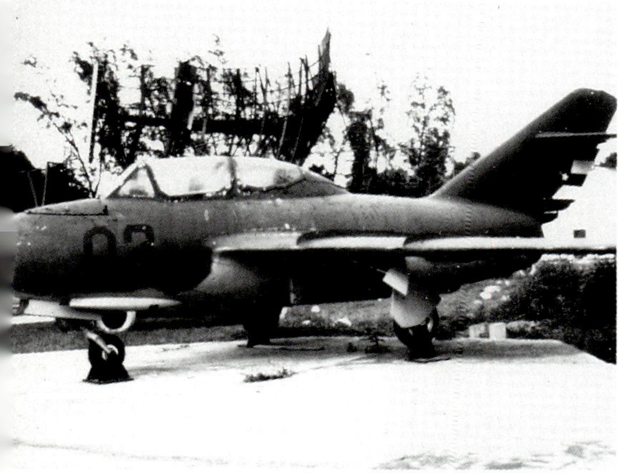

10

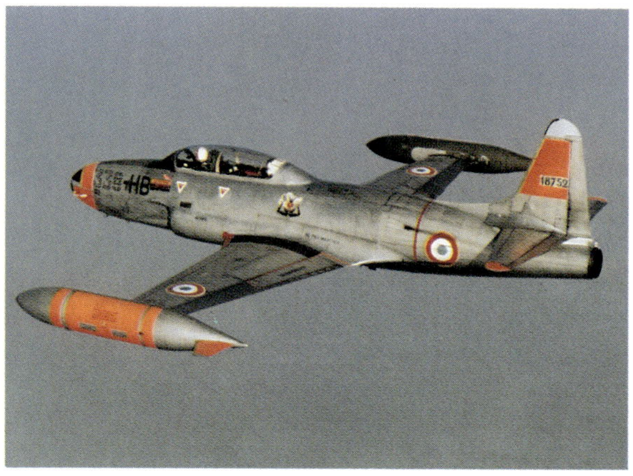

14

Since 1974 British pilots have trained in the British Aerospace Hawk. A single-engined jet used for support duties, it flies at over 625 mph (1,000 kph) and can climb to 49,000 ft (15,000 m). In 1977, Spain unveiled a small, single-engined training and support aircraft, the CASA C-101 Aviojet, which flies at 500 mph (800 kph) and has a ceiling of 42,600 ft (13,000 m). Its range is 1,875 miles (3,000 km).

Finally, in 1960 the Yugoslavs began building a single-engined jet for training and support duties, the Soko G2 Galeb. This was followed in 1978 by the G4 Super Galeb, which flies at over 560 mph (900 kph) and has a range of 1,625 miles (2,600 km).

Photo No. 1: CASA C-101 Aviojet (Spain)
Photo Nos. 2 and 9: Morane-Saulnier MS.760 Paris (France)
Photo No. 3: Aermacchi AM.3C (Italy)
Photo No. 4: Dassault-Dornier Alpha Jet (France)
Photo Nos. 5 and 7: Aérospatiale (Fouga) Magister (France)
Photo No. 6: Max Holste MH 1521 Broussard (France)
Photo Nos. 8 and 13: Aérospatiale Epsilon (France)
Photo No. 10: MiG-15UTI (USSR)
Photo No. 11: Piaggio P.149 (Italy)
Photo No. 12: Nord 3202 (France)
Photo No. 14: Lockheed T-33 (USA)
Photo No. 15: BAe Hawk (Great Britain)
Photo No. 16: Sukhoi Su-28 (Russia)
Photo No. 17: BAe Hawk 200 (single-seater attack version of the Hawk trainer) (Great Britain)
Photo No. 18: de Havilland Canada DHC-1 Chipmunk (Canada)

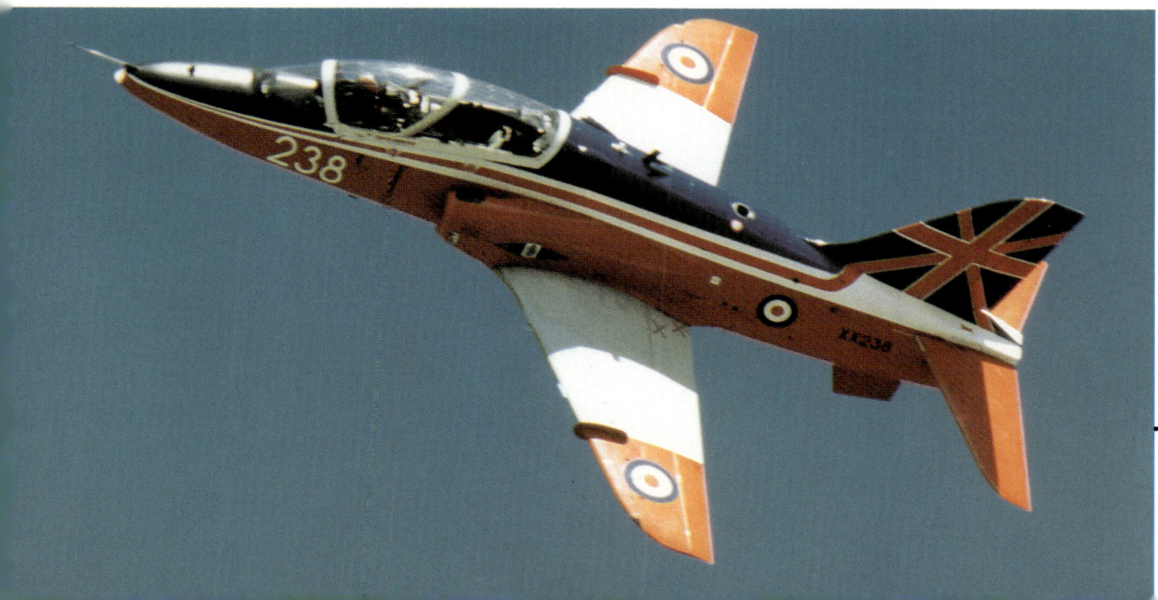

15

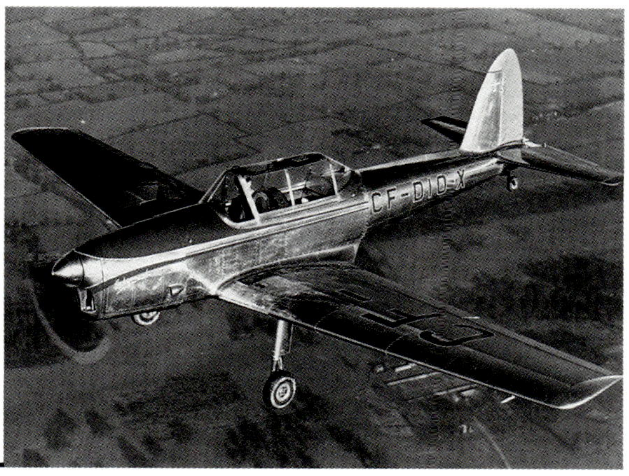

18

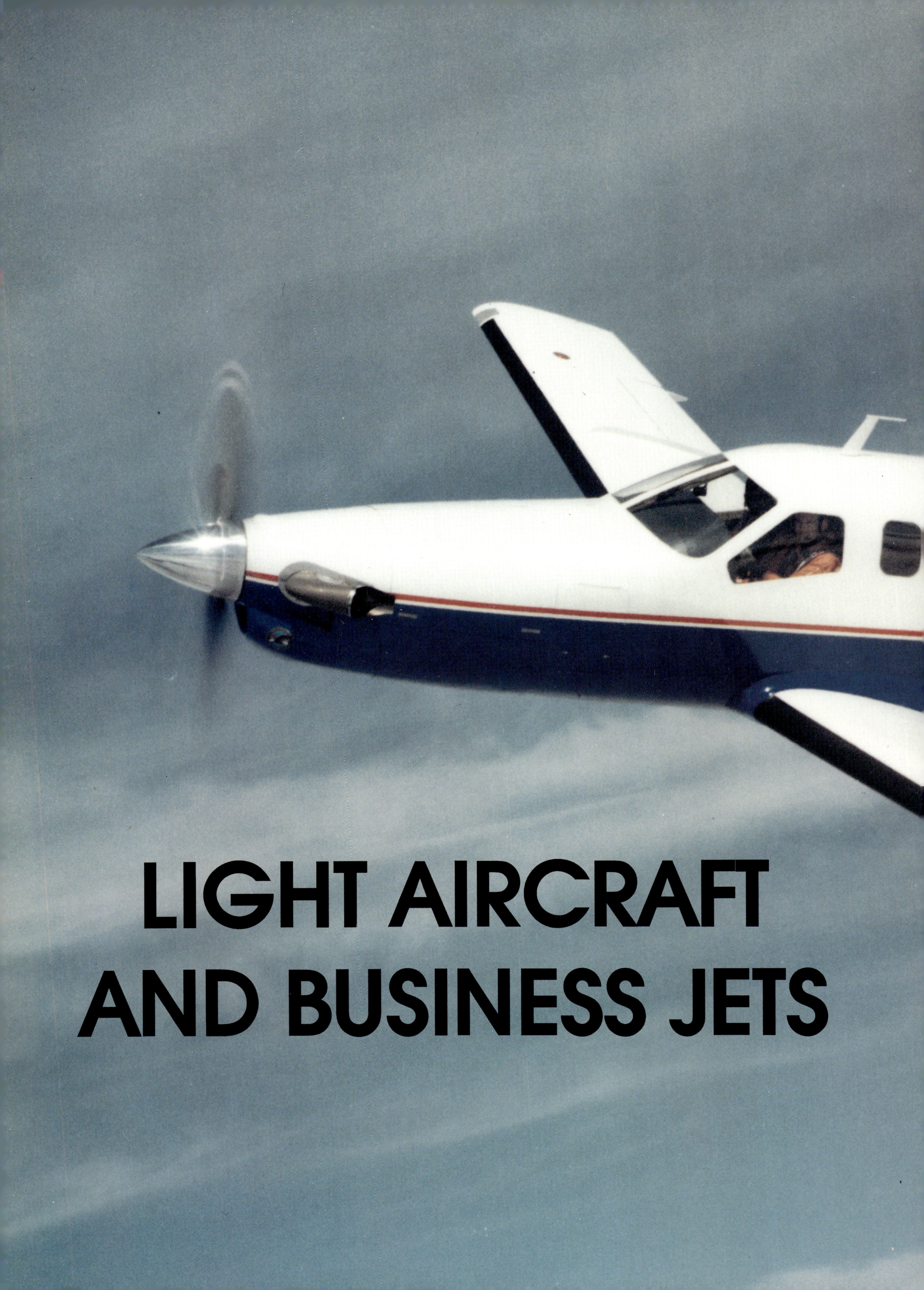

LIGHT AIRCRAFT AND BUSINESS JETS

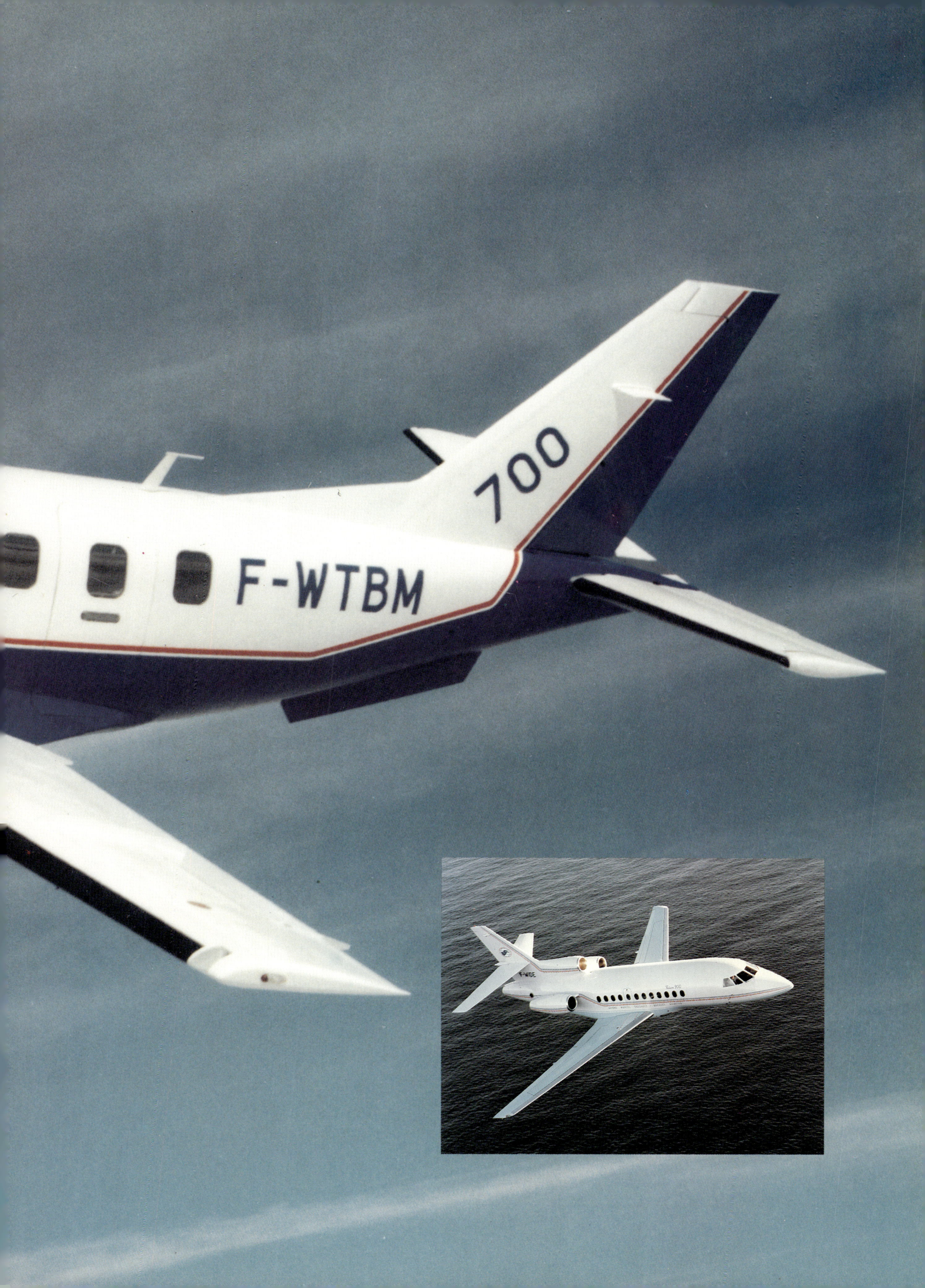
700
F-WTBM

LIGHT AIRCRAFT

Several constructors are active in the light aircraft market. In 1949, the American company Beech brought out the Twin Bonanza, a twin-engined liaison aircraft with retractable undercarriage, which was also adopted by the US Air Force. It was followed in 1958 by the Beech Queen Air, which could carry eight passengers at 250 mph (400 kph) on stages of around 1,250 miles (2,000 km). In 1960, Beech introduced the first of its Baron models. Low-wing, twin-engined aircraft with retractable undercarriage, they were designed to carry four to six passengers at speeds of around 187 mph (300 kph) over distances of up to 560 miles (900 km).

Cessna once produced a whole series of high-wing, single-engined aircraft. The two-seater 150, for instance, which appeared in 1958, had a maximum speed of 115 mph (185 kph) and a range of 560 miles (900 km). Bigger and more powerful was the seven-seater 207 which made its debut in 1970. It flew at 168 mph (270 kph) and had a range of 590 miles (940 km). Cessna have also built twin-engined aircraft.

Another great name in the US light aircraft sector was Piper. In 1959 the company brought out a low-wing, twin-engined aircraft with a retractable undercarriage, the PA-23 Apache, soon followed by the Aztec. In 1964 came the PA-31 Navajo, which carries six to eight passengers at 250 mph (400 kph) on stages of around 1,250 miles (2,000 km).

The PA-31T, dating from 1969, is a twin-engined turboprop with a pressurised cabin, derived from the Navajo. It could fly at over 310 mph (500 kph) and had a range of 1,560 miles (2,500 km) with six to eight passengers on board.

In the single-engined category, Piper brought out the PA-32 Cherokee Six in 1965. This was a fixed-undercarriage aircraft with a cruising speed of 156 mph (250 kph), a range of 560 miles (900 km) and capacity for six passengers. The 1970 PA-24 Comanche was a four-seater. It cruised at 218 mph (350 kph) and had a range of 980 miles (1,570 km).

In France, Socata, the general-aviation division of Aérospatiale, also builds a range of light aircraft. The ST-60 Rallye 7-300 was a seven-seater business aircraft with a low wing and retractable under-carriage. It had a maximum speed of 187 mph (300 kph) and a range of 940 miles (1,500 km).

5
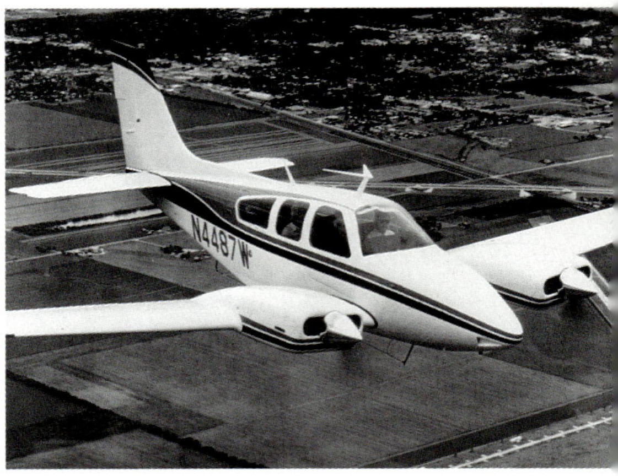

1
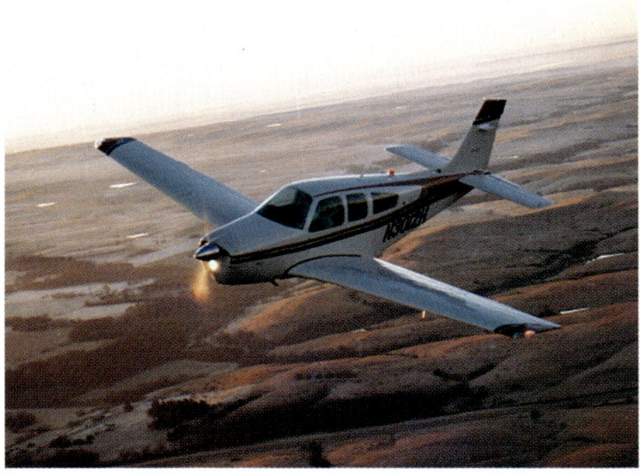

6
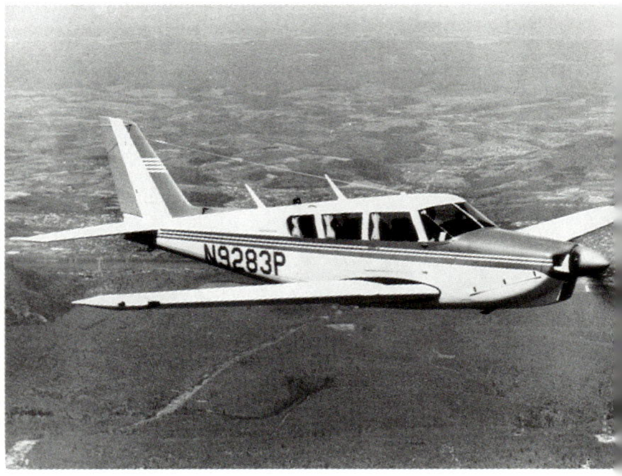

2
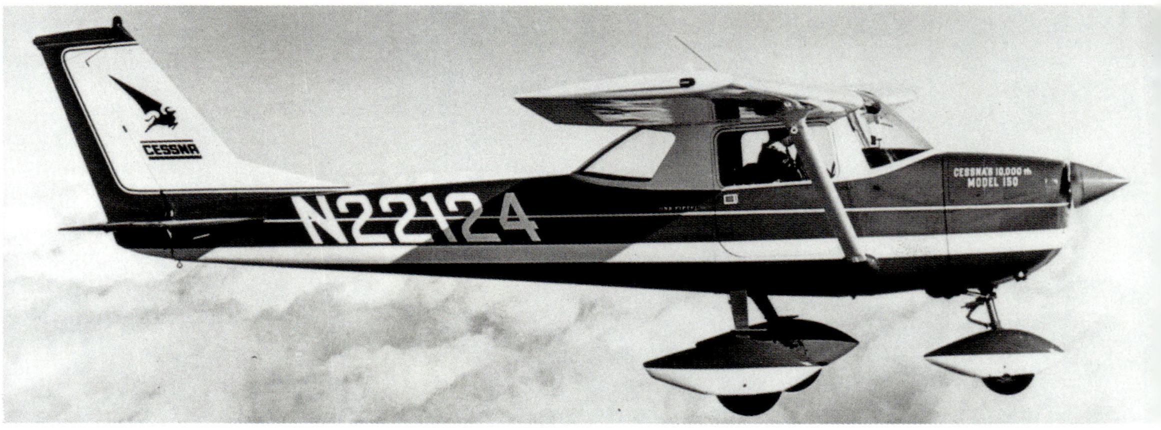

3
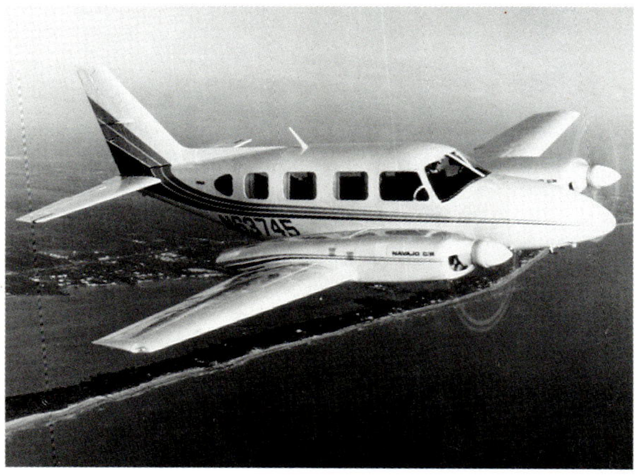

7
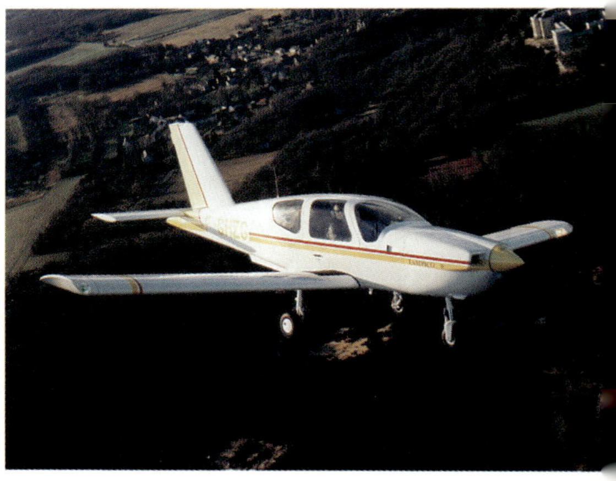

4
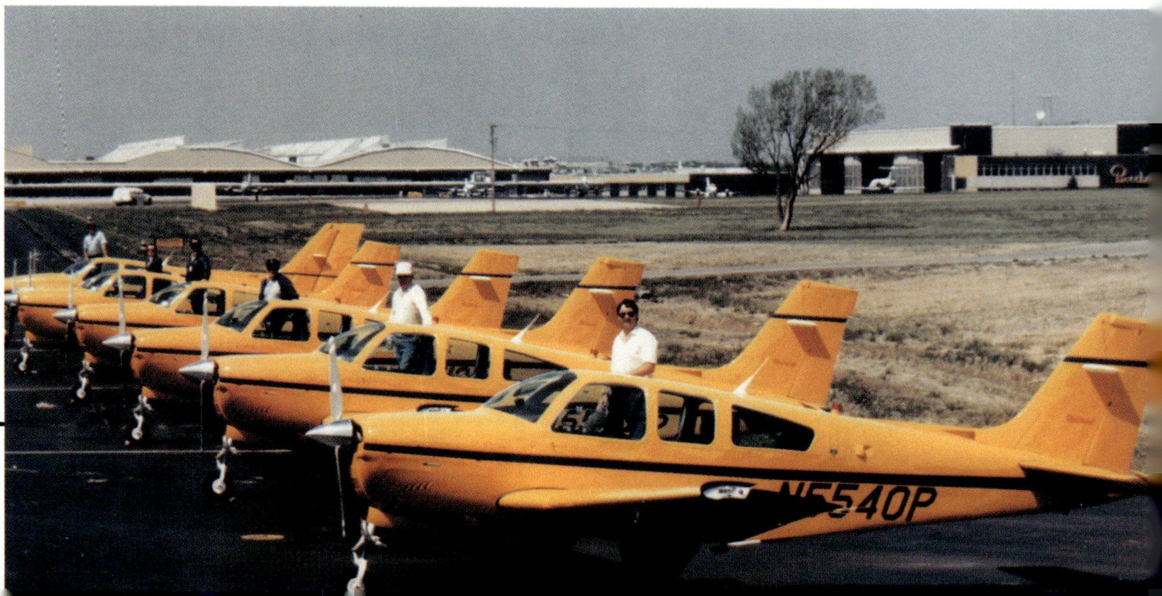

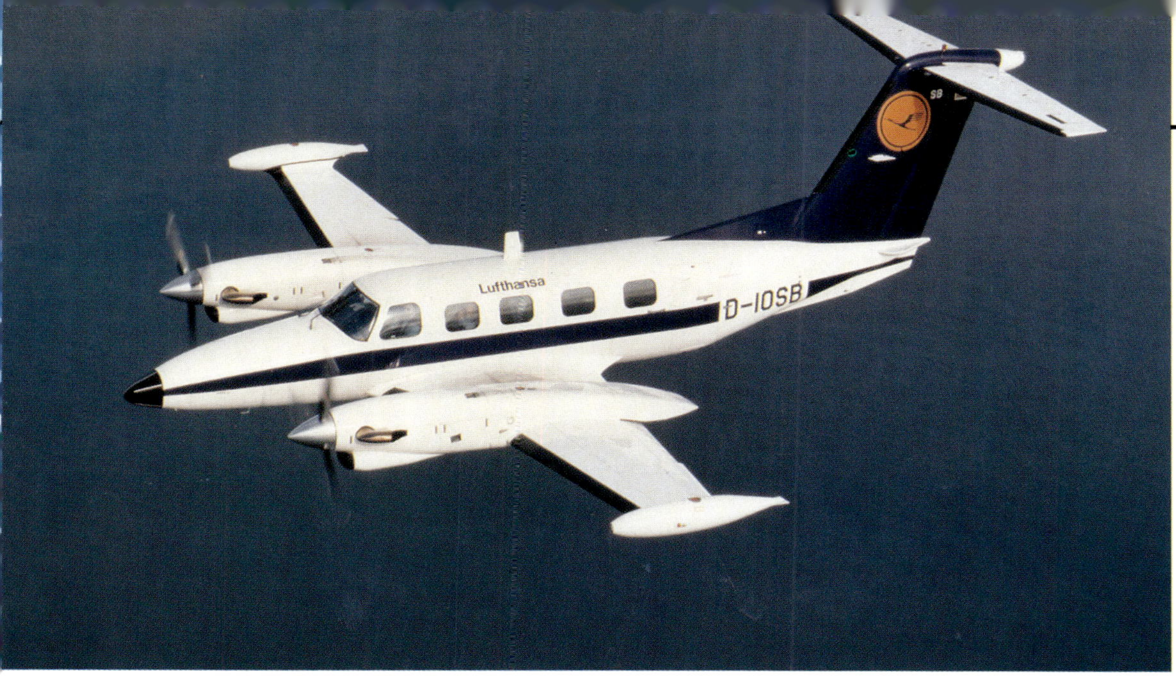

12

Photo Nos. 1 and 4: Beechcraft Bonanza (USA)
Photo No. 2: Cessna 150 (USA)
Photo No. 3: Piper PA-31 Navajo (USA)
Photo Nos. 5 and 15: Beechcraft Baron (USA)
Photo No. 6: Piper PA-24 Comanche (USA)
Photo No. 7: Socata TB.9 Tampico
Photo No. 8: Piper PA-32 Cherokee (USA)
Photo No. 9: Beechcraft Queen Air (USA)
Photo No. 10: Socata Rallye (France)
Photo No. 11: Cessna 207 (USA)
Photo No. 12: Piper Cheyenne (USA)
Photo No. 13: Piper PA-23 Apache (USA)
Photo No. 14: Socata Trinidad (France)

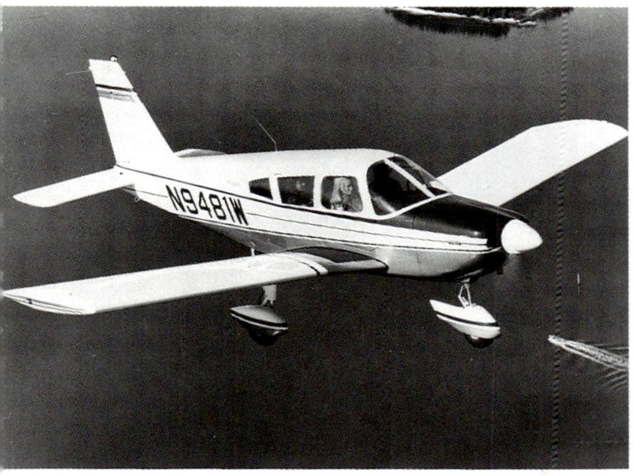

8

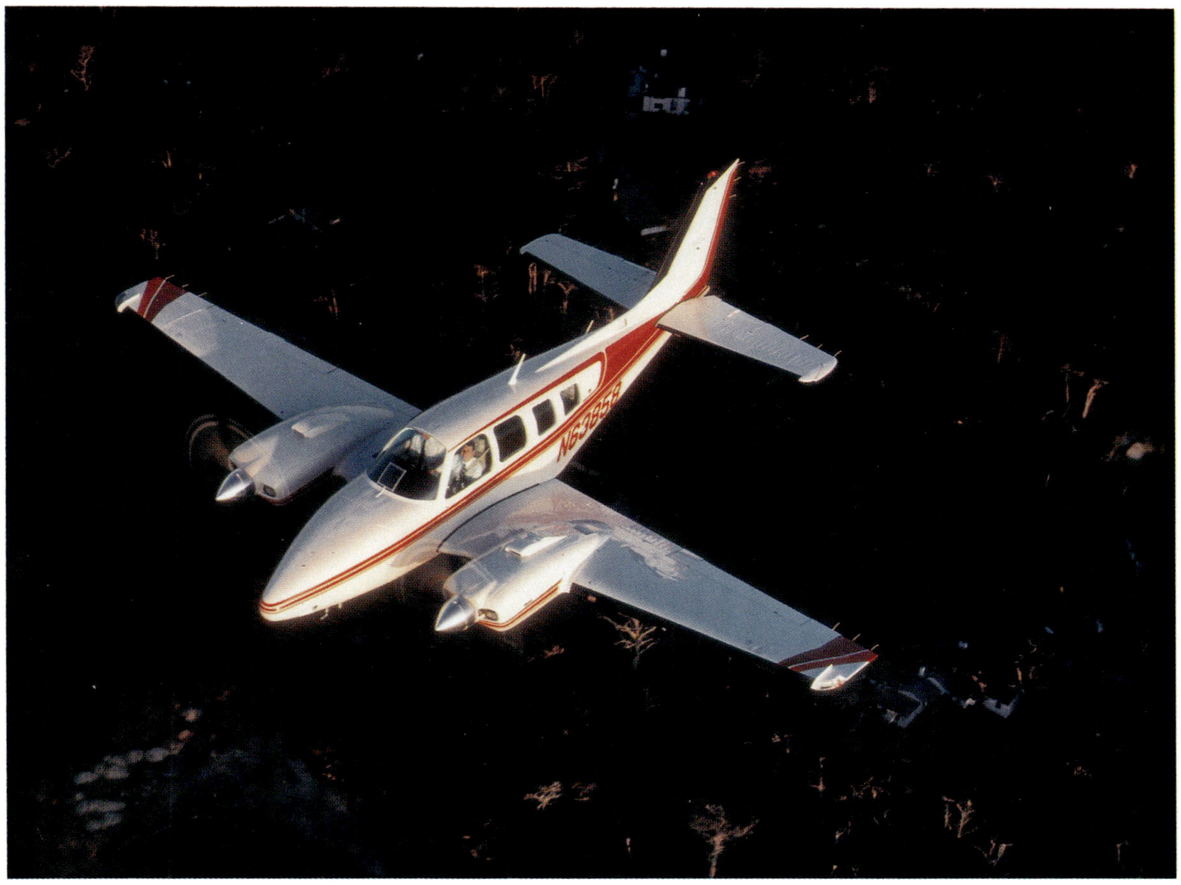

15

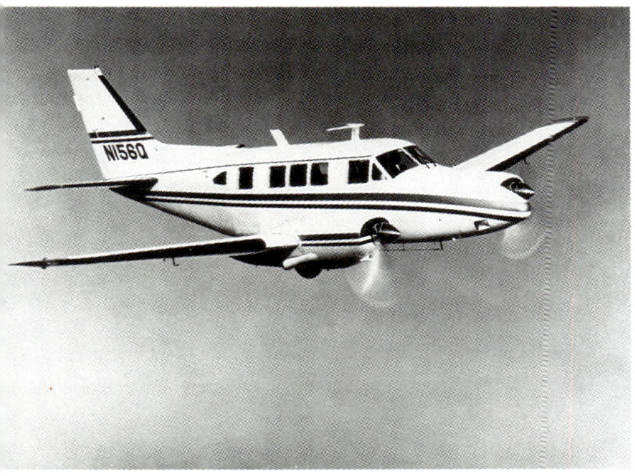

9

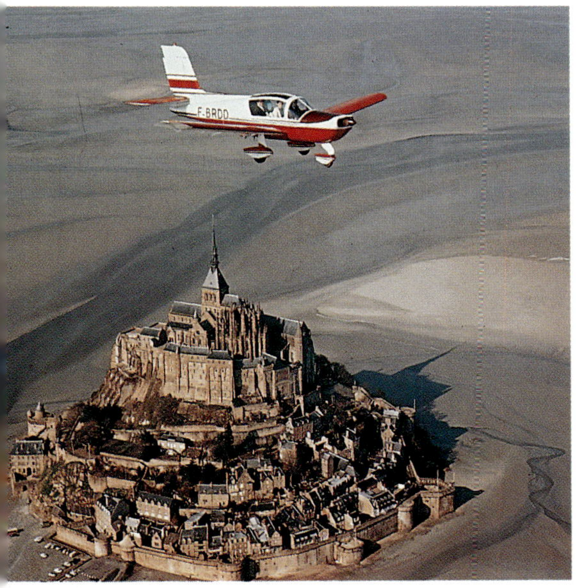

10

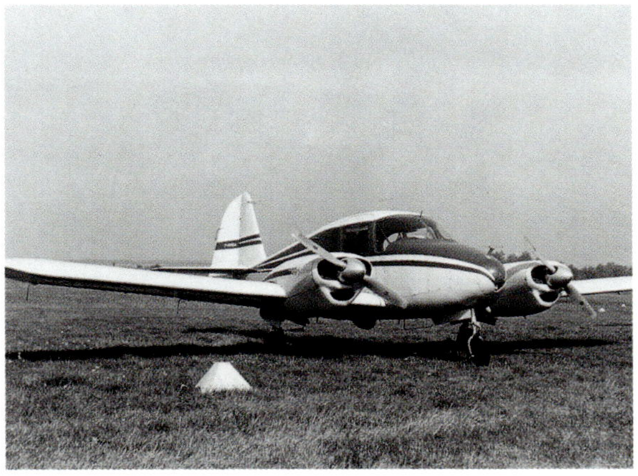

13 The TB-9 Tampico is a basic four-seater single-engined aircraft. Flying at around 125 mph (200 kph), it has a range of over 560 miles (900 km). The TB-10 Tobago is a four-seater business aircraft. It is faster (143 mph/230 kph) and has a range of over 625 miles (1,000 km). Fitted with new engines, the TB-200 version gives better performance in reaching its cruising altitude.

The four-seater retractable undercarriage TB-20 and TB-21 Trinidad models are designed for higher performance. The TB-20 flies at 187 mph (300 kph) and has a range of 1,125 miles (1,800 km). The TB-21 is fitted with a turbo-charger, giving it a cruising speed of 212 mph (340 kph).

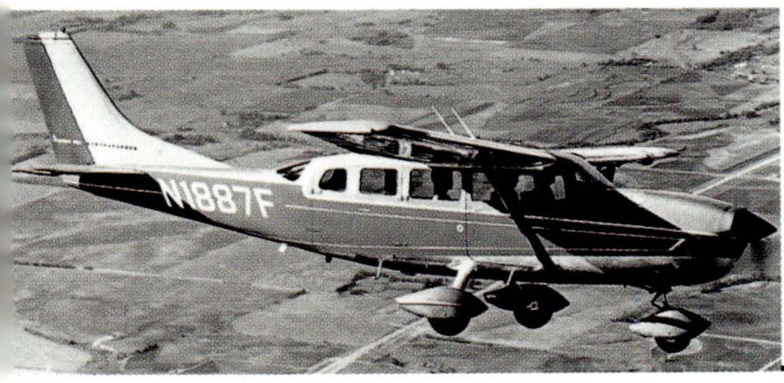

11

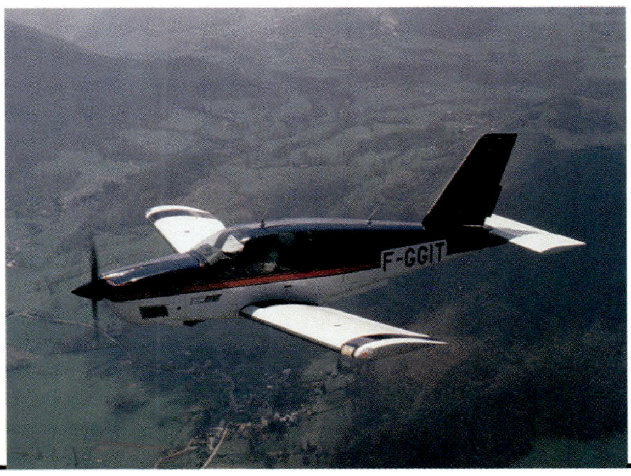

14

Since 1988, Socata have produced the TBM-700, a business aircraft with single turbocharged engine and pressurised cabin. Carrying seven passengers, it cruises at 346 mph (555 kph) on journeys of over 1,250 miles (2,000 km).

5
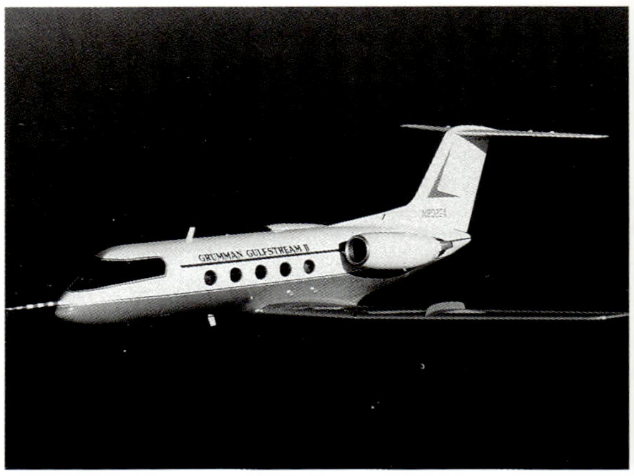

BUSINESS JETS

Business jets form an important category in the United States. One of the first to appear, in 1960, was the ten-seater Lockheed JetStar. Powered by four engines, it cruised at over 530 mph (850 kph) and had a range in excess of 3,125 miles (5,000 km). Its immediate rival was the Rockwell Sabreliner, a twin-engined jet with accommodation for between seven and nine passengers, which flew at 560 mph (900 kph) on flights of over 1,875 miles (3,000 km).

In 1969, another American constructor, Cessna, brought out the six-passenger Citation. Powered by twin jet engines, it cruised at 406 mph (650 kph) and had a range of 1,560 miles (2,500 km). The bigger and more powerful Citation II appeared in 1967. With 10 passengers aboard, it has a range of 1,875 miles (3,000 km). The 1979 Citation III carries up to nine passengers and can cruise at 540 mph (870 kph). The latest are the Citation V, VI, VII and X.

Another range of twin-engined executive jets is produced by the Learjet company. Its 24 model, introduced in 1963, was a fast six-seater with a cruising speed in excess of 530 mph (850 kph) and a range of over 1,690 miles (2,700 km). Fitted with more powerful engines, the 35/36 models can carry four passengers on flights of over 2,800 miles (4,500 km). The 54/55/56 models made their debut in 1980.

In 1965, Gulfstream Aerospace (formerly Grumman) launched the Gulfstream II, a long-haul jet with accommodation for between 10 and 19 passengers. It flies stages of up to 4,375 miles (7,000 km) at speeds of between 500 and 560 mph (800 and 900 kph). Today's Gulfstream V flies 5,757 miles (9,266 km).

In 1986 Beechcraft unveiled a twin turboprop of canard design, the Starship 2000. Carrying from eight to 10 passengers, it flies at 375 mph (600 kph) and has a range of over 1,560 miles (2,500 km).

In 1979, Canadair began producing the Challenger 601, a twin-engined executive jet with a top speed of over 530 mph (850 kph) and capacity for 19 passengers. With four passengers it has a range of 4,000 miles (6,400 km).

Since 1967, British Aerospace has been producing the HS.125, a twin-engined jet with seating for six to eight passengers. It flies at 525 mph (845 kph) on stages of 2,200 miles (3,500 km). The HS.125 has been updated several times, the latest version being the BAe 1000, a 15-seater jet with a range of around 4,060 miles (6,500 km).

French constructors are also active in this field. The SN-600 Corvette was designed by Aérospatiale in 1970. A small, twin-engined jet with seating for between eight and 12 passengers, it flies at over 440 mph (700 kph) and has a range of 1,690 miles (2,700 km). Dassault entered the field in 1961 with the Mystère/Falcon-20, another twin-engined jet with a maximum speed in excess of 530 mph (850 kph) and a range of over 2,200 miles (3,500 km). It

1
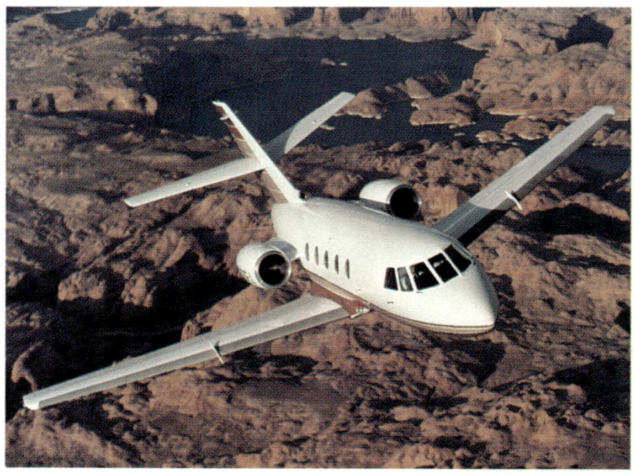

6
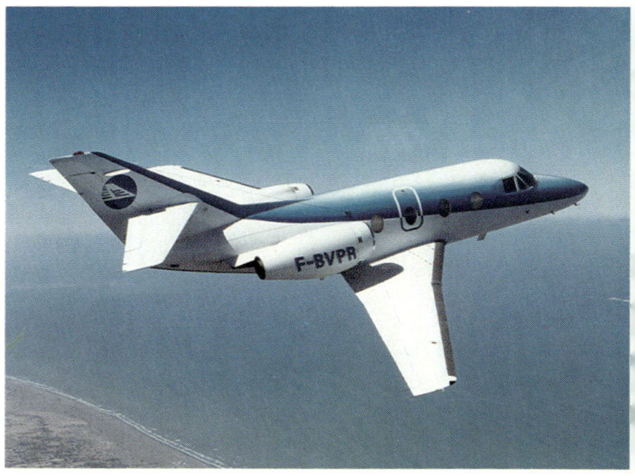

2
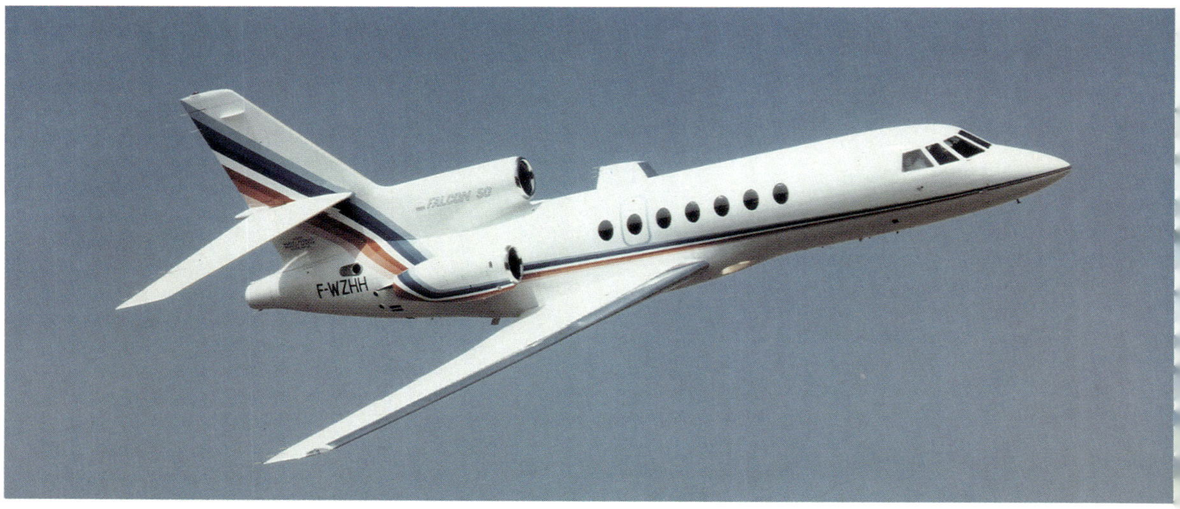

3
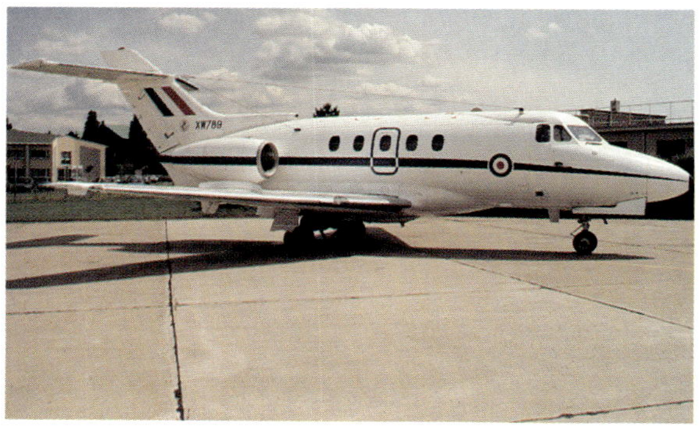

7
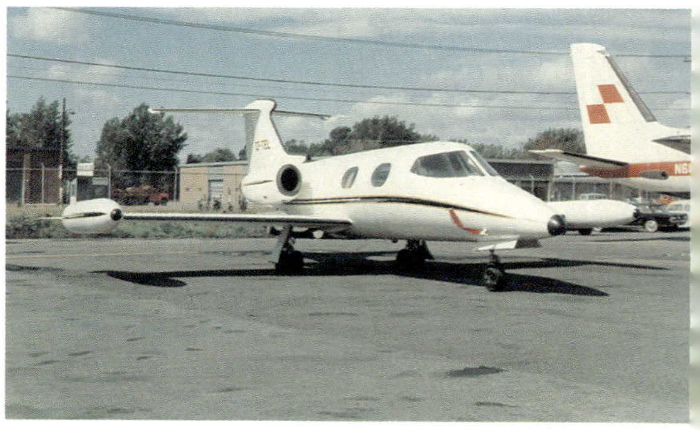

4
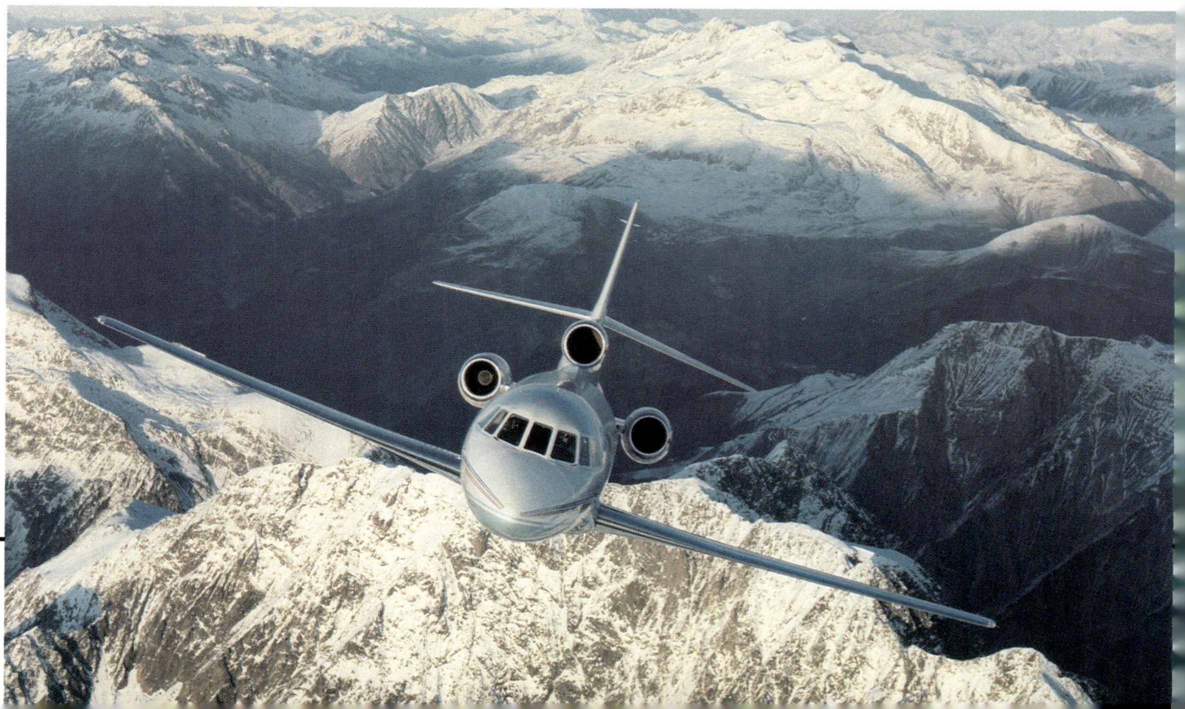

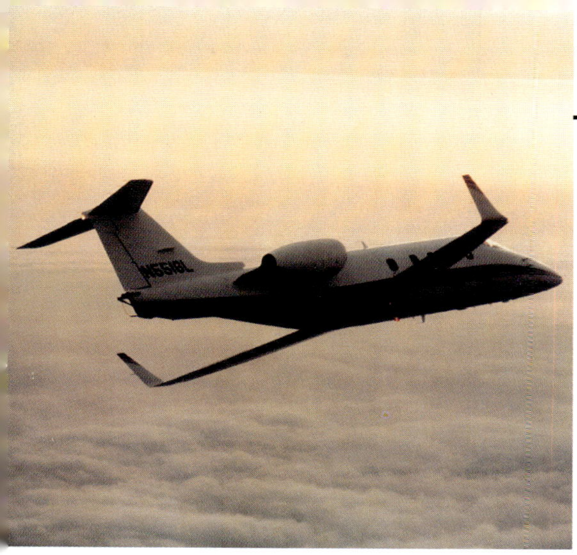

8

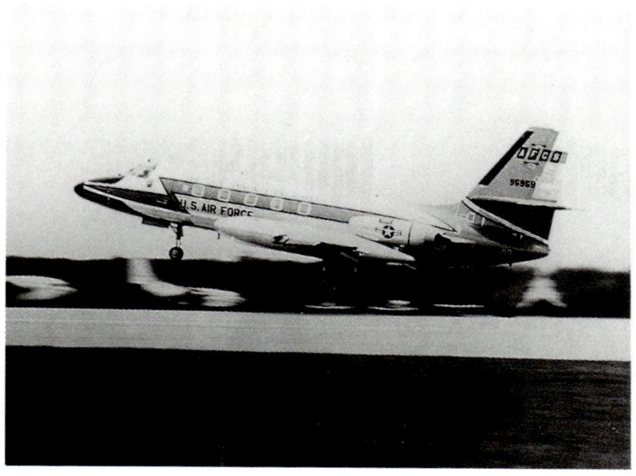

13

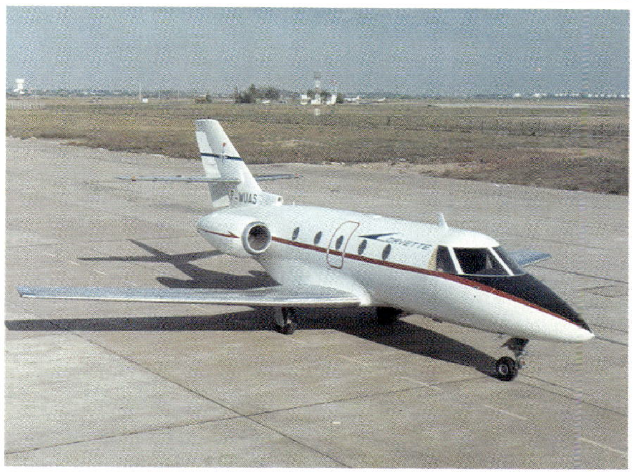

16

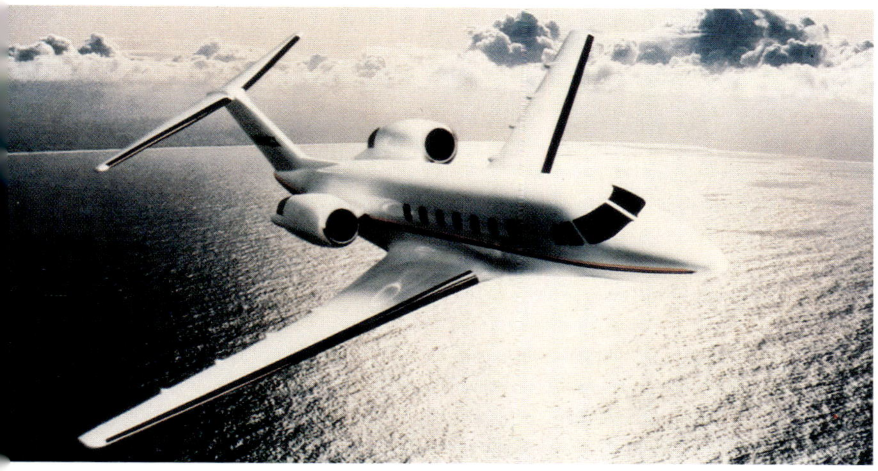

12

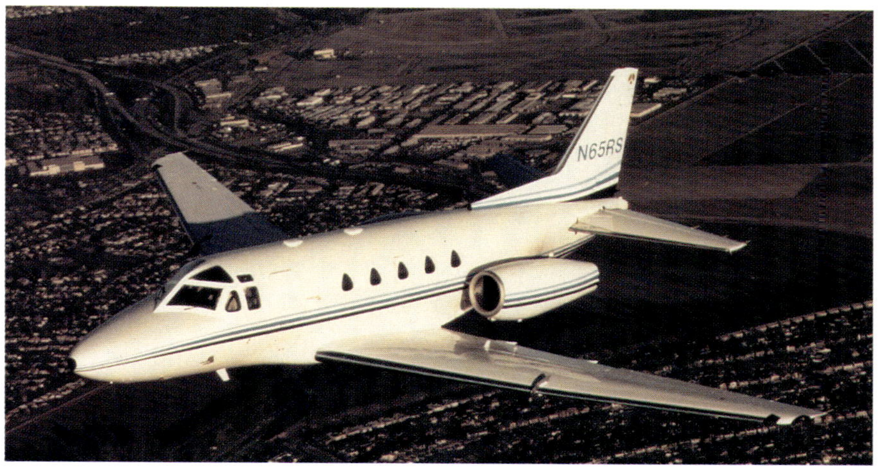

17

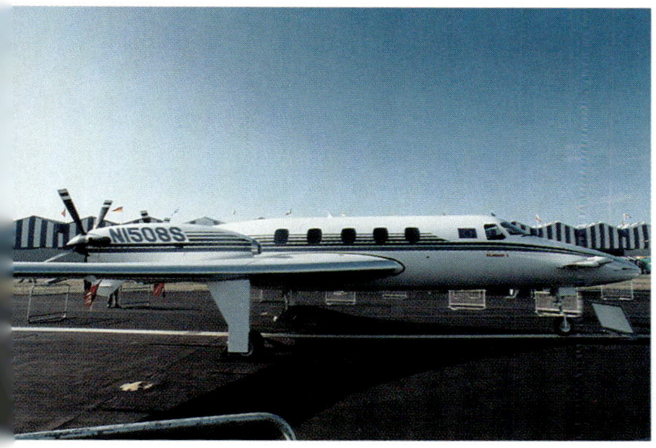

9

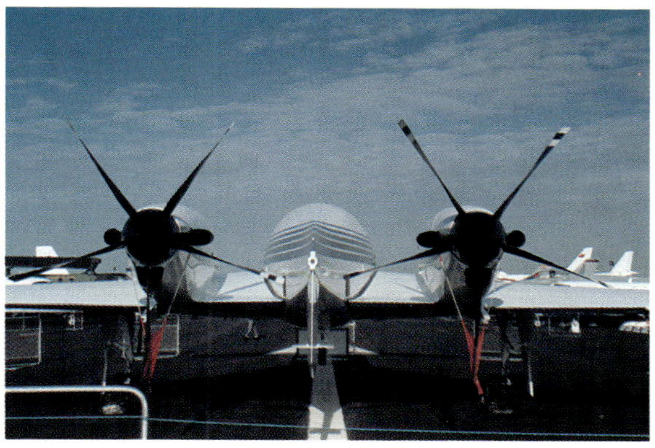

14

carries 10 passengers. The smaller Mystère/Falcon-10, which has seating for four passengers, has a similar range and a cruising speed of over 560 mph (900 kph). In 1976, Dassault brought out the Mystère/Falcon-50, a three-engined jet with a cruising speed of over 530 mph (850 kph). The latest in the range is the 1984 Falcon 900, another three-engined jet, with accommodation for 19 passengers. It cruises at 590 mph (950 kph) and, with eight passengers aboard, has a range of 4,560 miles (7,300 km).

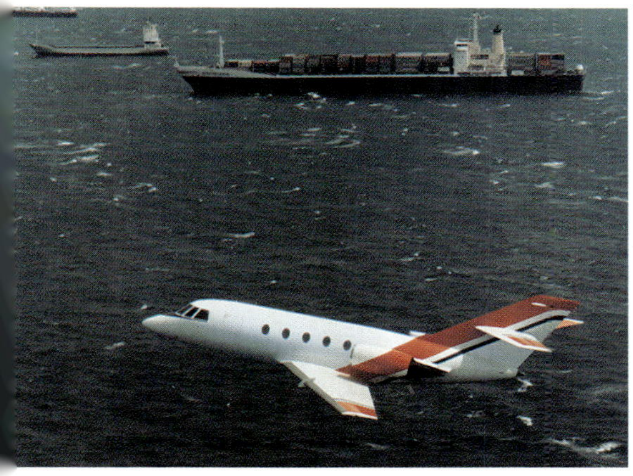

10

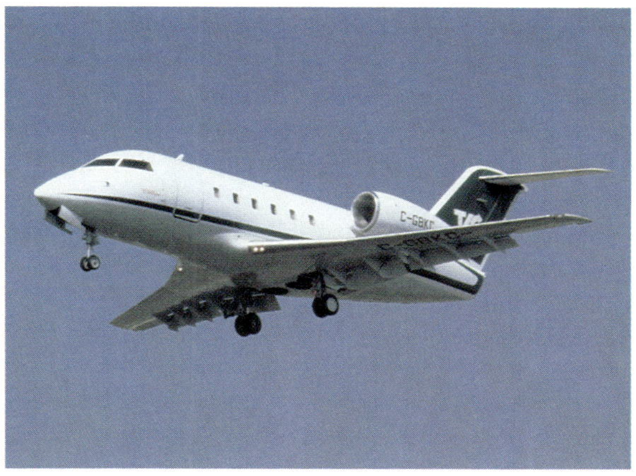

15

Photo Nos. 1, 10 and 18: Dassault Mystère-Falcon 20 (France)
Photo No. 2: Dassault Mystère-Falcon 50 (France)
Photo No. 3: Hawker Siddeley HS.125 (Great Britain)
Photo No. 4: Dassault Mystère-Falcon 900 (France)
Photo No. 5: Gulfstream II (USA)
Photo No. 6: Dassault Mystère-Falcon 10 (France)
Photo No. 7: Learjet 24 (USA)
Photo No. 8: Learjet 50 (USA)
Photo Nos. 9 and 14: Beechcraft Starship 2000 (USA)
Photo No. 11: Learjet 35 (USA)
Photo No. 12: Cessna Citation X (USA)
Photo No. 13: Lockheed JetStar (USA)
Photo No. 15: Canadair Challenger (Canada)
Photo No. 16: Aérospatiale Corvette (France)
Photo No. 17: Rockwell Sabreliner (USA)

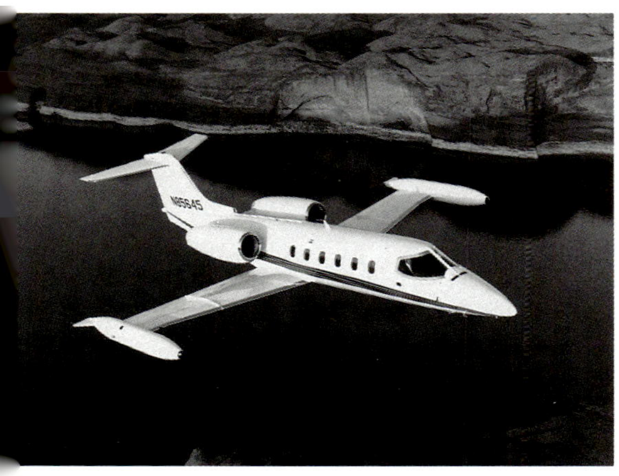

11

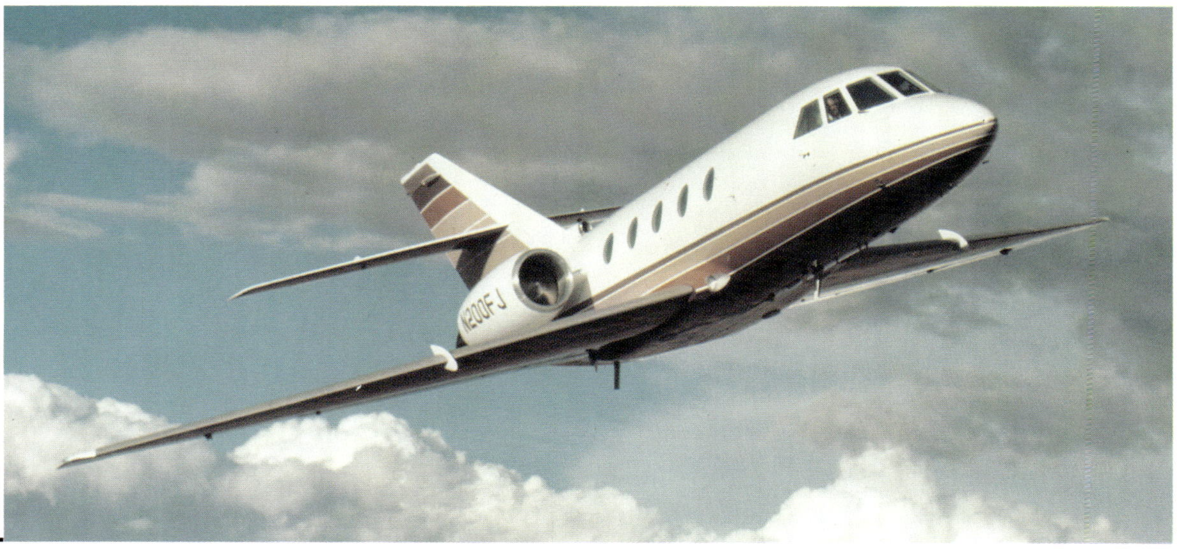

18

VERTICAL FLIGHT

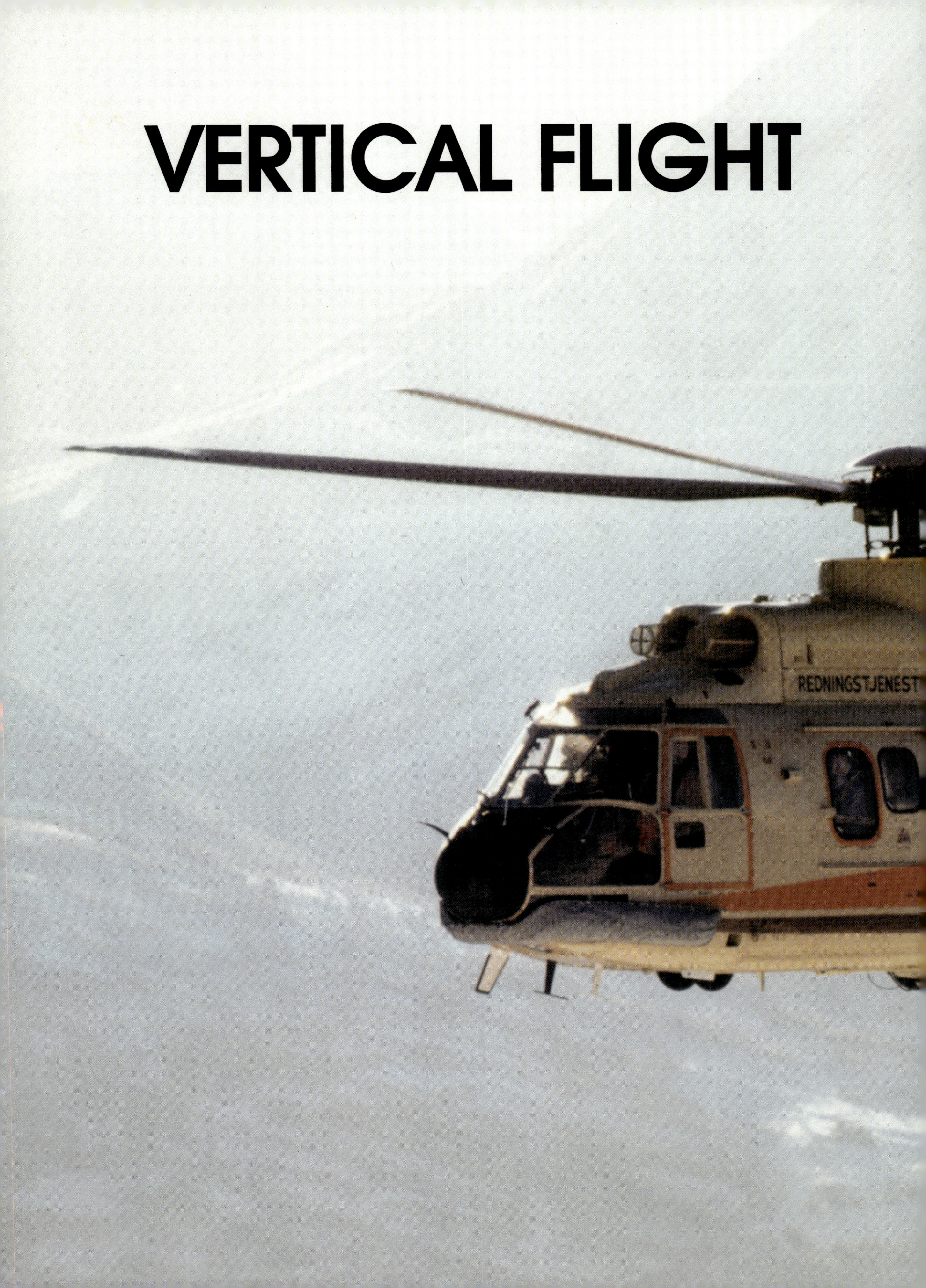

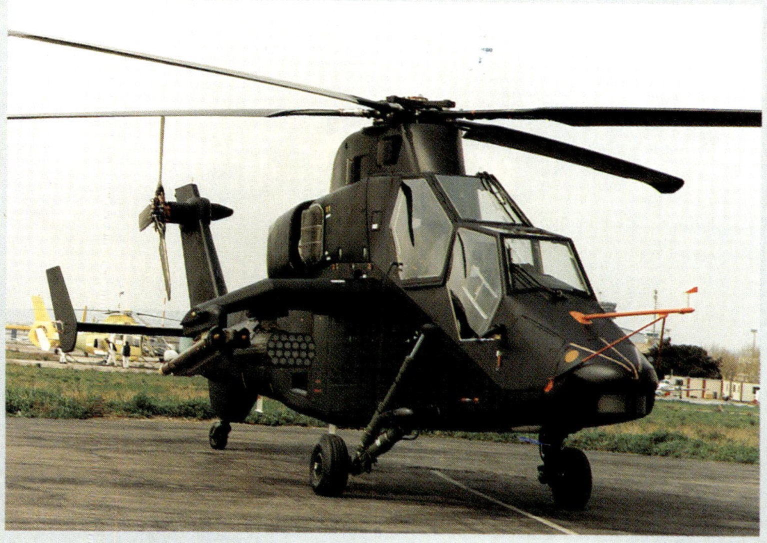

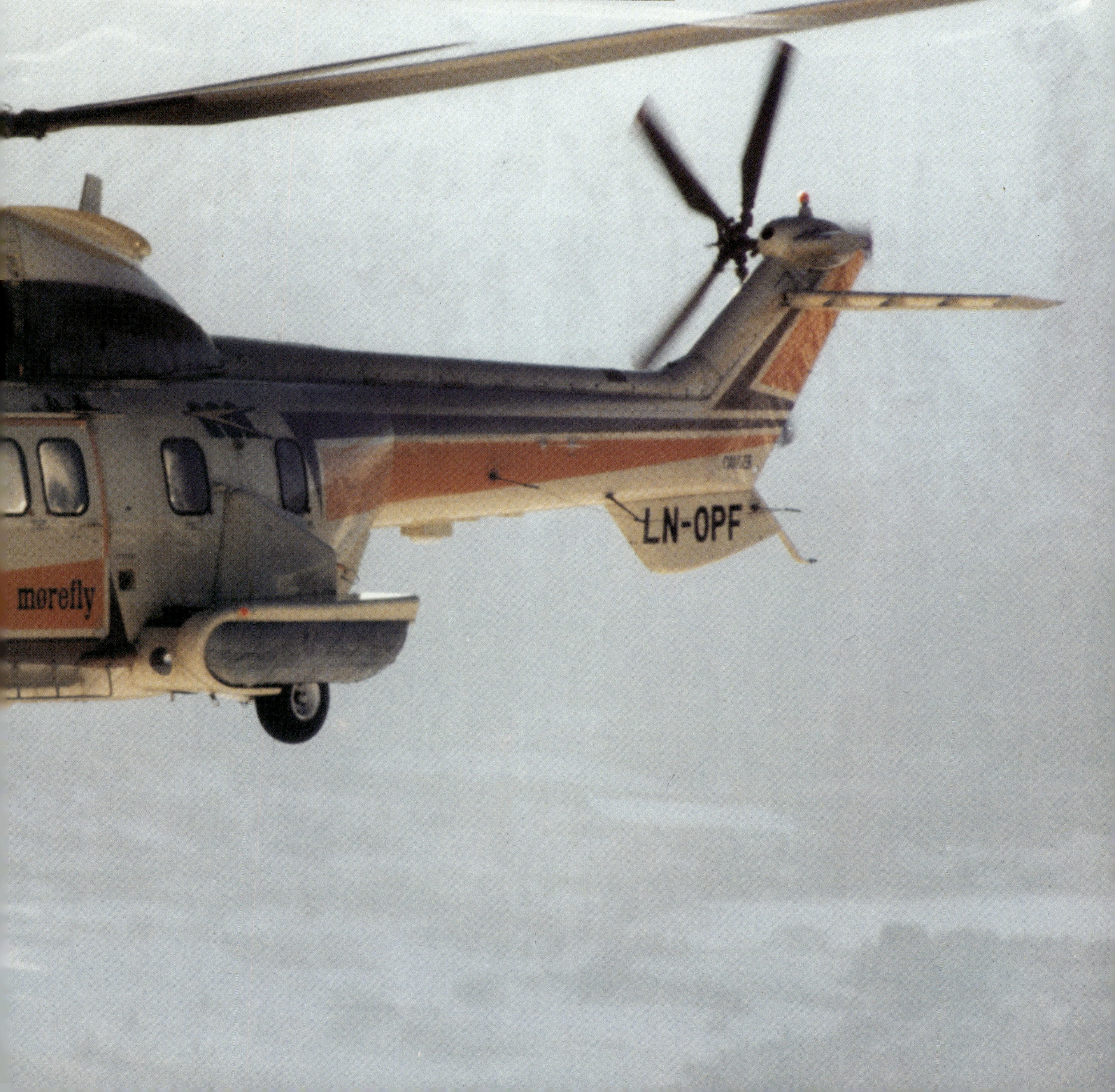
LN-OPF
mørefly

HELICOPTERS AND AUTOGYROS

4

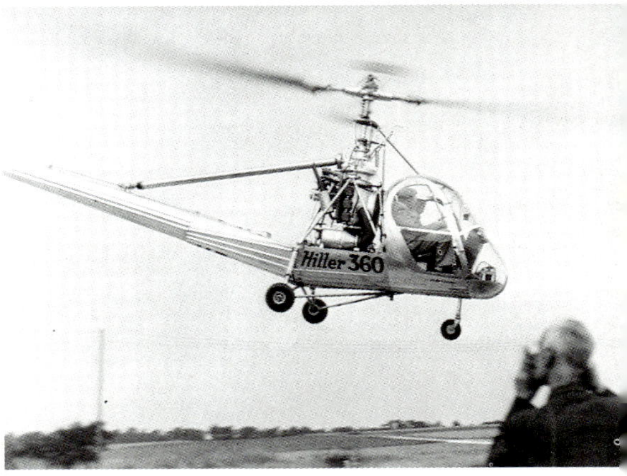

The first inventor to have envisioned vertical flight was that universal genius Leonardo da Vinci, at the end of the 15th century. But he lacked an engine for the machine he had in mind.

At the beginning of this century several fragile contraptions were built, some of which even managed to get clear of the ground, such as the French mechanic Paul Cornu's *Hélicoptère* (1907). In the same year, Louis Breguet's *Gyroplane* rose three feet into the air. But not until 1922 did vertical flight become a serious proposition, when the Frenchman Etienne Oemichen introduced his version of the helicopter. Meanwhile, in 1921 Louis Breguet had returned to his earlier experiments, and his Gyroplane G 11E of 1935 set new distance and altitude records. From 1924, the Spaniard Juan de la Cierva concentrated on developing an autogyro, an aircraft in which the wing is replaced by freely rotating horizontal vanes and which therefore has to taxi to take off.

In the United States, the Russian emigré Igor Sikorsky first flew his Vought-Sikorsky VS-300 helicopter in 1939. From this was derived the 1944 VS-316/R-4 used by the American army. The year 1946 saw the advent of the Bell 47, which flew at 87 mph (140 kph), and the very similar Hiller 360. In 1951, the French constructor SNCASO began developing the SO.1220 Djinn, a small helicopter adopted by the French army.

Meanwhile, back in the United States Sikorsky was building increasingly heavy military helicopters, the S-55/H-19 and S-58/H-34, which cruised at 100 mph (160 kph) with 20 passengers on board. These were followed, in 1959, by the S-61, a six-ton machine with a carrying capacity of 32 passengers and a cruising speed of over 162 mph (260 kph). In 1952, another American constructor, Piasecki, began supplying the army with a helicopter powered by two rotors working in tandem, the HRP-2/H-21 Workhorse, better known as the Flying Banana. It was capable of over 125 mph (200 kph).

Thereafter helicopters became more specialized. In 1961, for instance, Boeing-Vertol introduced the CH-47 Chinook. A transport helicopter with two turboshafts driving tandem rotors, the Chinook could carry 44 soldiers at speeds of 162 mph (260 kph) and had a range of 1,250 miles (2,000 km). In 1965 Bell brought out a combat helicopter, the 209 HueyCobra. A twin-engined Sea Cobra version with coupled turboshaft engines was used by the US Marine Corps, and flew at 173 mph (278 kph).

1

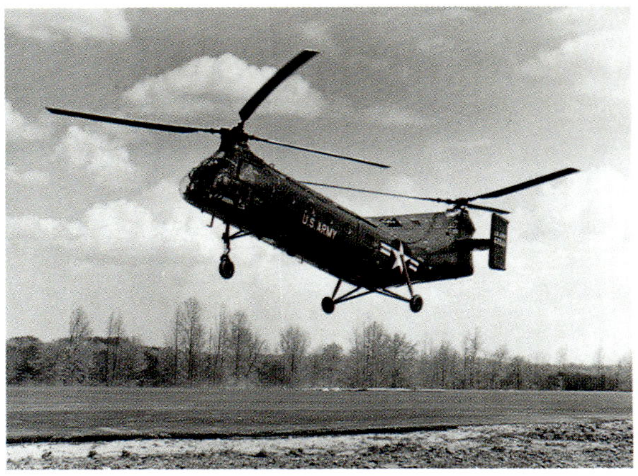

5

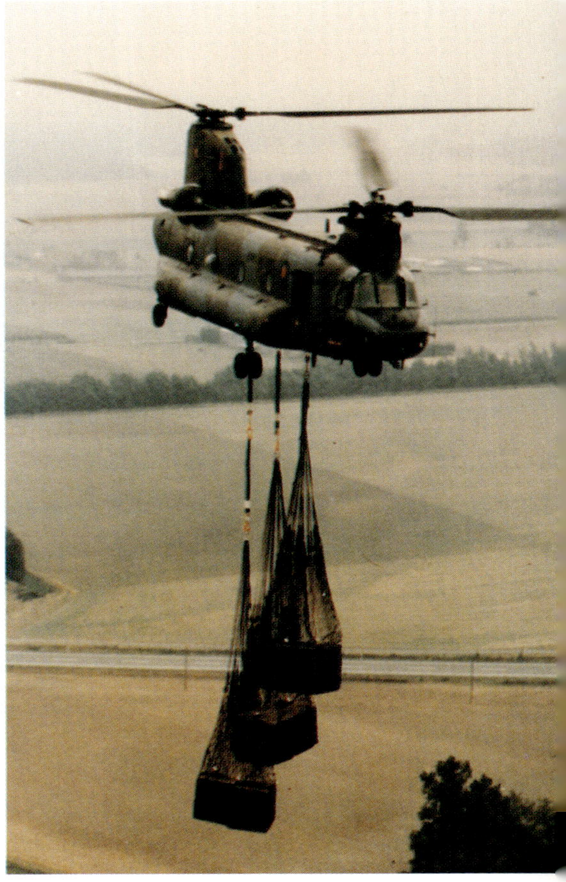

2

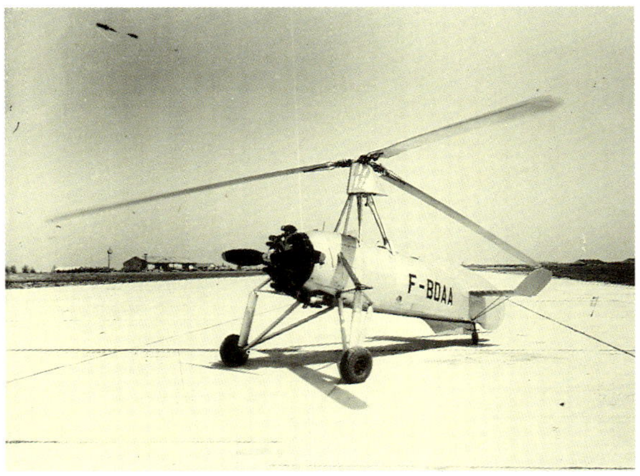

3

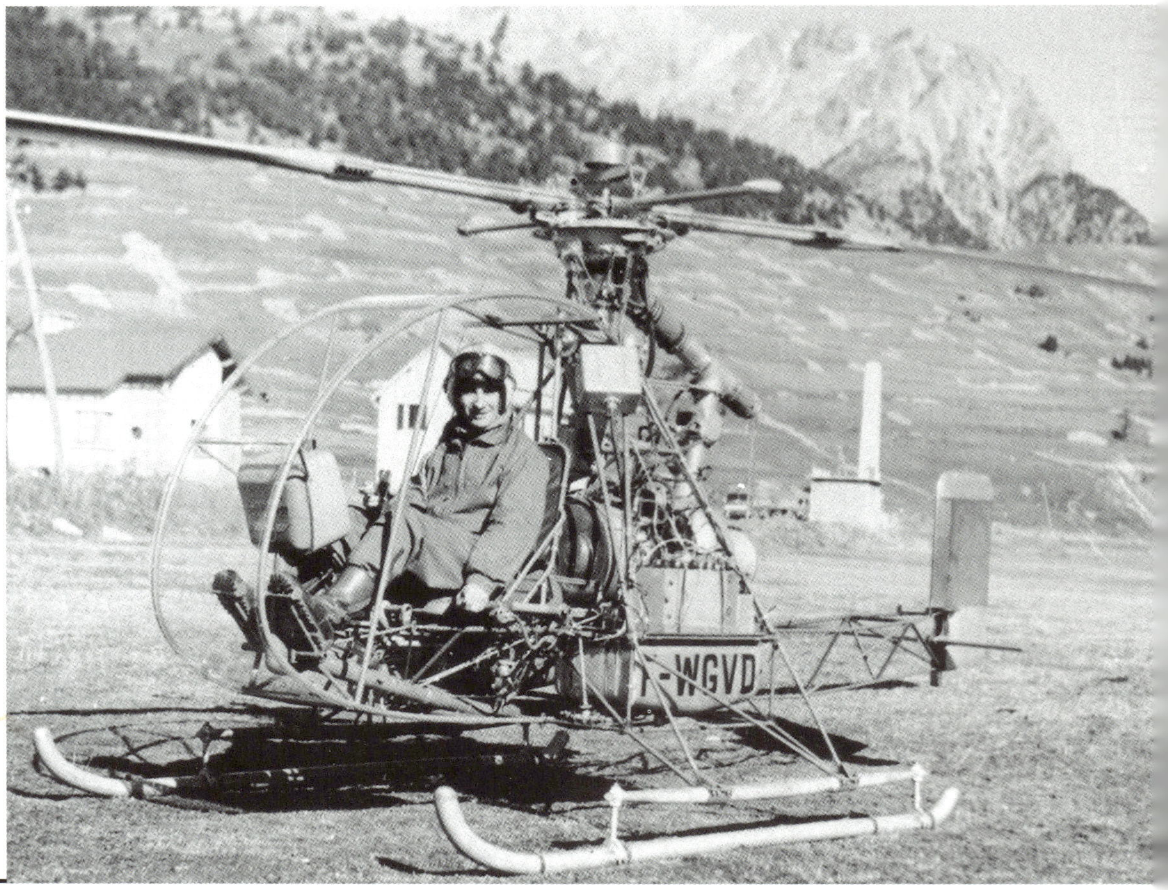

11

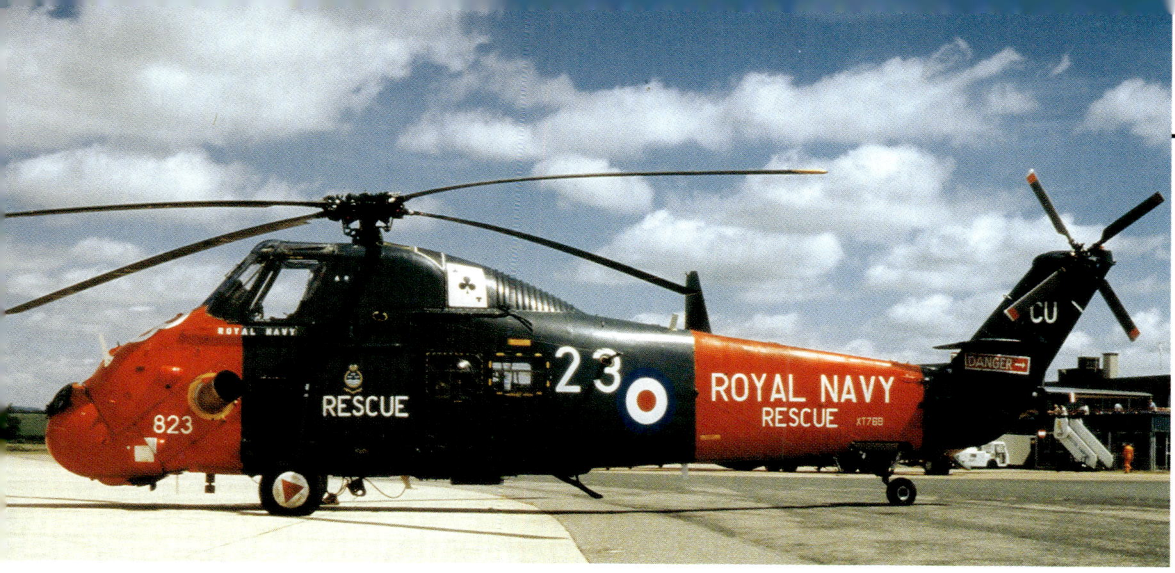

Photo No. 1: Piasecki "Flying Banana" (USA)
Photo No. 2: Cierva C.30 autogyro (Spain)
Photo No. 3: SNCASO Djinn (France)
Photo No. 4: Hiller 360 (USA)
Photo No. 5: Boeing Vertol CH-47 Chinook (USA)
Photo No. 6: Bell 47 (USA)
Photo No. 7: Breguet Type III Gyroplane (France)
Photo No. 8: Sikorsky S-55 (USA)
Photo No. 9: Oemichen (with gas bag) (France)
Photo No. 10: Bell AH-1 Cobra (USA)
Photo No. 11: Westland Wessex (Great Britain)
Photo No. 12: Sikorsky R-4 (USA)
Photo No. 13: Cornu's Hélicoptère (France)
Photo No. 14: Sikorsky S-61 (USA)

6

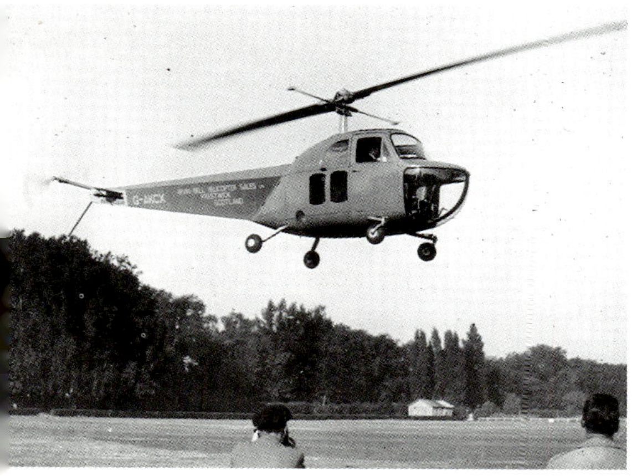

12

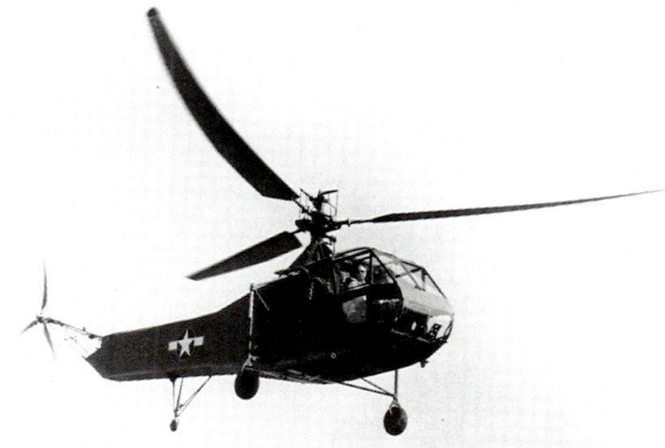

10

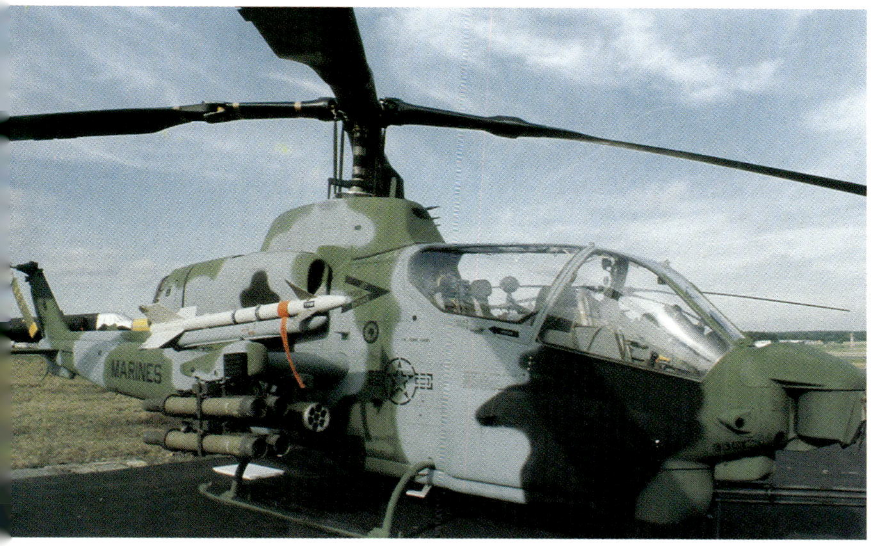

13

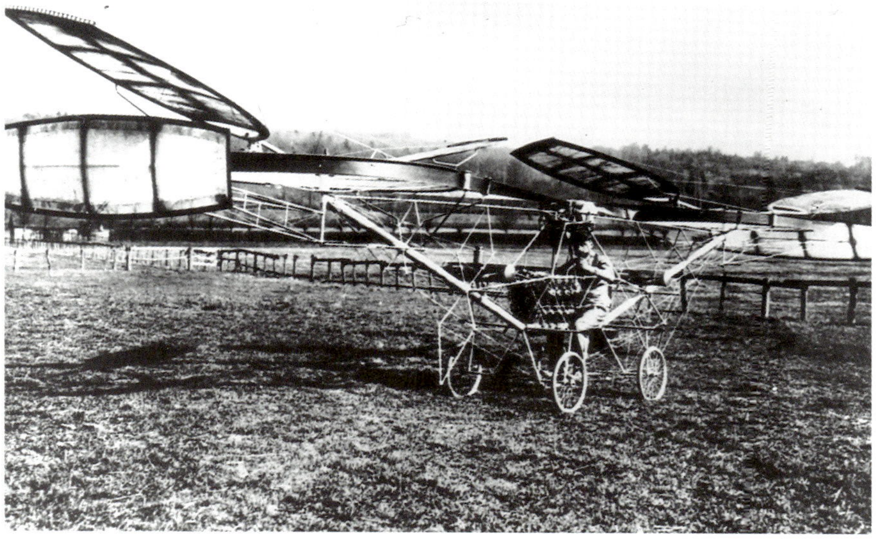

7

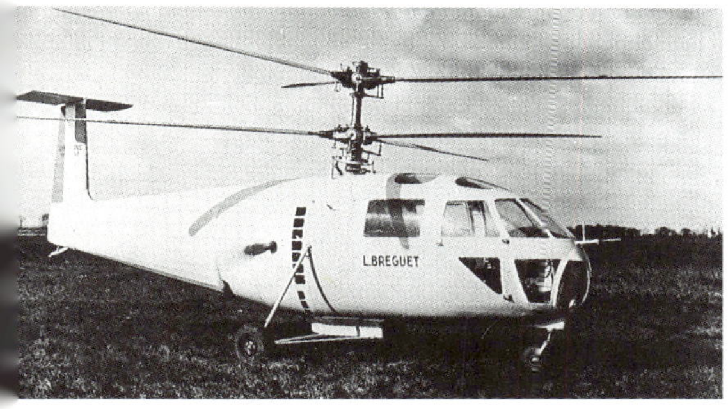

8

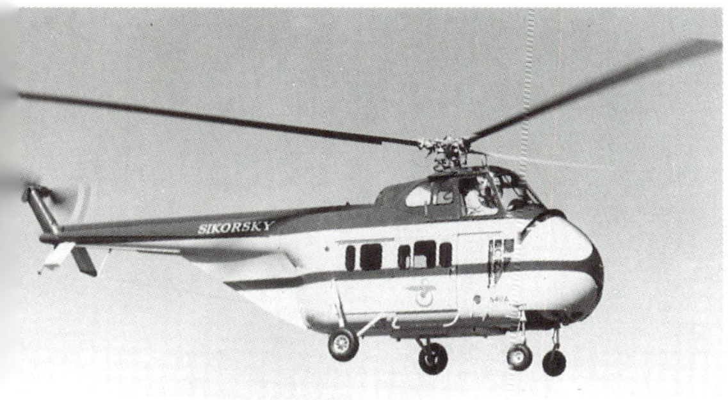

9

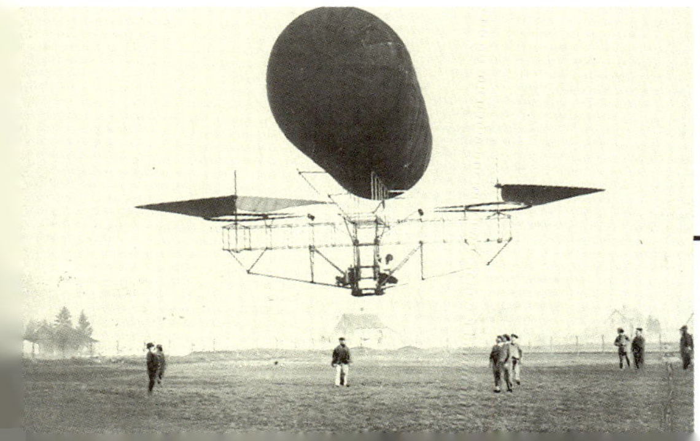

14

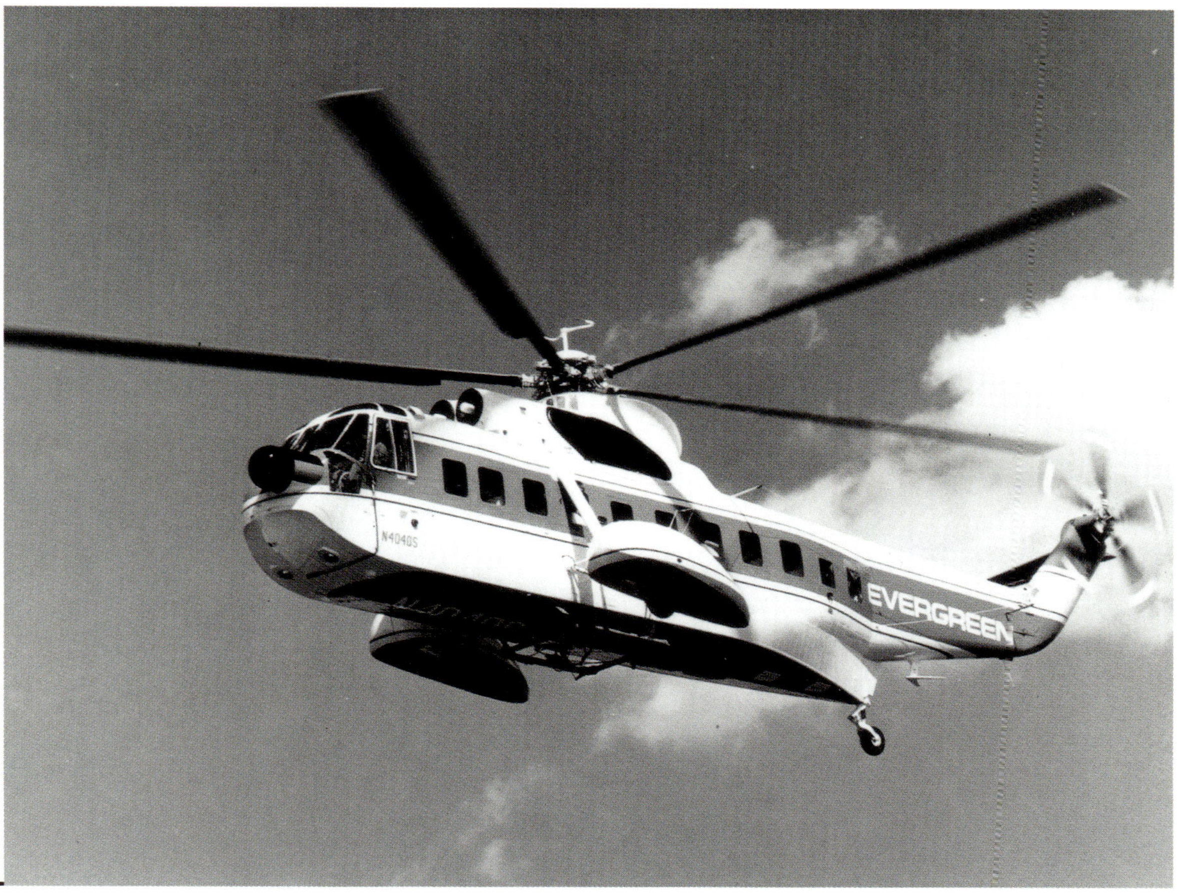

4

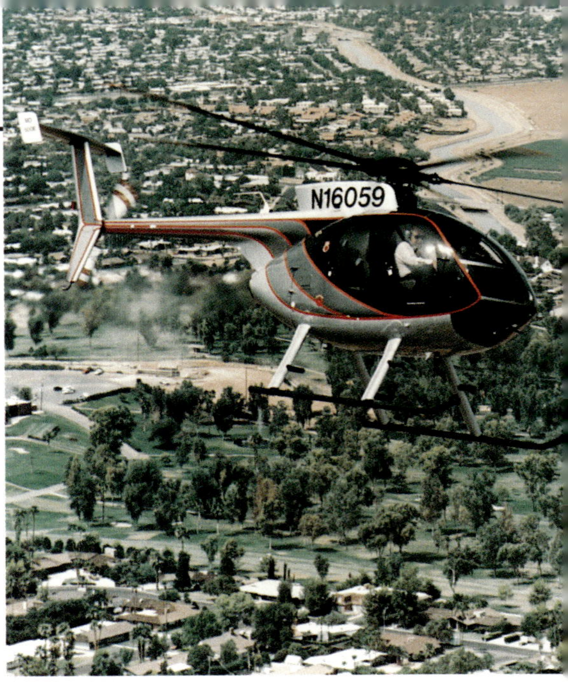

HELICOPTERS

The year 1956 saw the maiden flight of the Bell Huey, which in various versions was to become the most popular helicopter in the world. It had a maximum speed of 125 mph (200 kph) and a range of 250 miles (400 km). Early versions were designed to carry 10 passengers, later ones up to 15. The UH-1 Iroquois was intensively deployed in Vietnam. A lighter U.S. helicopter is the single-turboshaft Hughes 500. A six-seater, it can be armed with a machine gun or grenade launcher. The Defender version carries four anti-tank missiles.

In 1955, Aérospatiale of France introduced the SA 318 Alouette II, a single-turboshaft five-seater with a cruising speed of over 125 mph (200 kph). It was followed by the seven-seater SA 319 Alouette III and, in 1969, the heavier SA 330 Puma. This is a twin-turboshaft medium transport helicopter with a maximum speed of 175 mph (280 kph) and a range of 375 miles (600 km). It can carry 20 infantrymen or three tons of equipment. The Puma can be armed with missiles for anti-tank duties. In 1967, in conjunction with Westland, Aérospatiale also began producing the five-seater SA 341 Gazelle. Powered by a single turboshaft, it reaches speeds of 175 mph (280 kph).

Another joint Aérospatiale/Westland venture was the Lynx, which went into production in 1971. Cruising at over 187 mph (300 kph), this helicopter can carry ten armed soldiers, 13 passengers or various types of weaponry. Since 1967 the German firm of MBB has been manufacturing the Bo 105, a light, twin-turboshaft six-seater. It flies at 150 mph (240 kph) and can deliver six anti-tank missiles. Later came the German/Japanese BK 117, for 7 to 10 passengers and a range of 156 miles (250 km). Aérospatiale and MBB helicopters are now marketed by the new Franco-German group Eurocopter. In Italy, in 1965 Agusta designed the single-seater A.106 for anti-submarine warfare. It flies at 112 mph (180 kph), carrying two torpedoes.

In 1953, the Soviet constructor Mil began producing the Mi-4, different versions of which carried 1.8 tons of cargo or 11 passengers at 100 mph (160 kph). Its range varied from 156 to 250 miles (250 to 400 km). The 1960 Mi-8 was a twin-turbine-engined helicopter with room for 28 passengers and a range of 312 miles (500 km). It flew at 162 mph (260 kph) and could be armed with cannon, rockets or missiles. Over 10,000 were built. The 1957 Mi-6 was a much larger beast. Laden with 70 passengers or 12 tons of freight, it cruised at 156 mph over a range of 625 miles (1,000 km).

In 1954, another Soviet constructor, Kamov, began building a small liaison helicopter for the Red Army, the Ka-15.

1

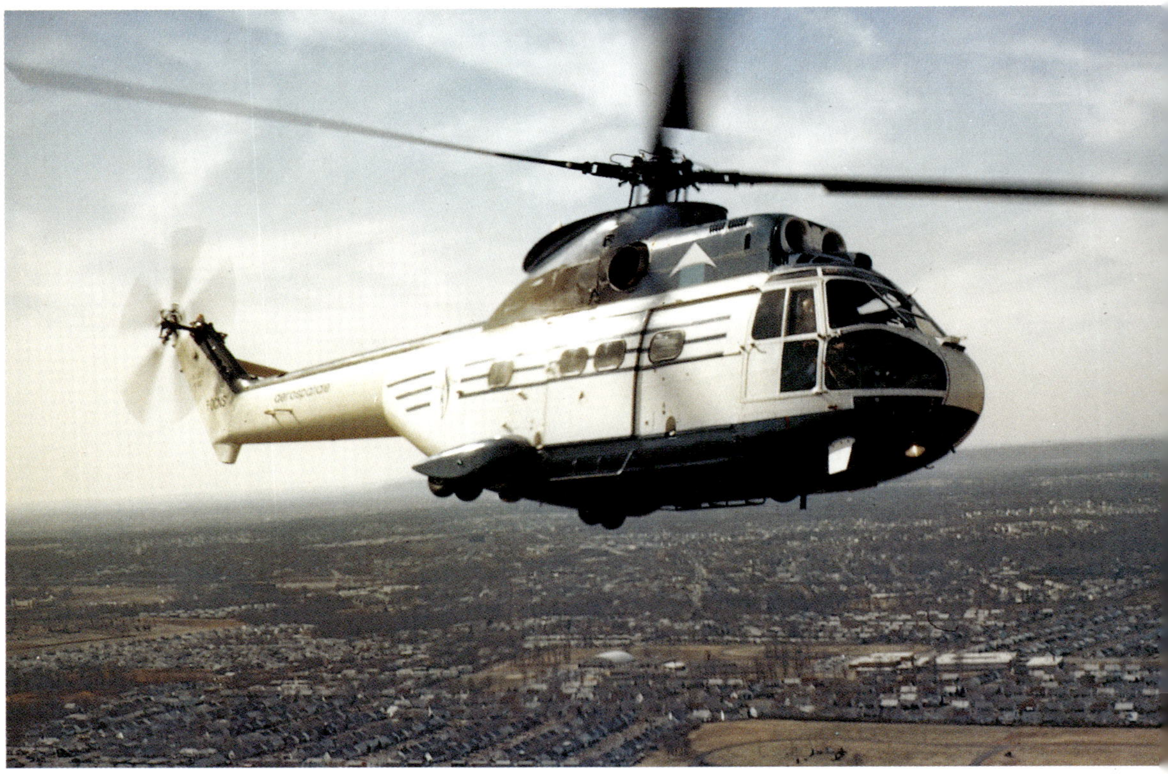

2

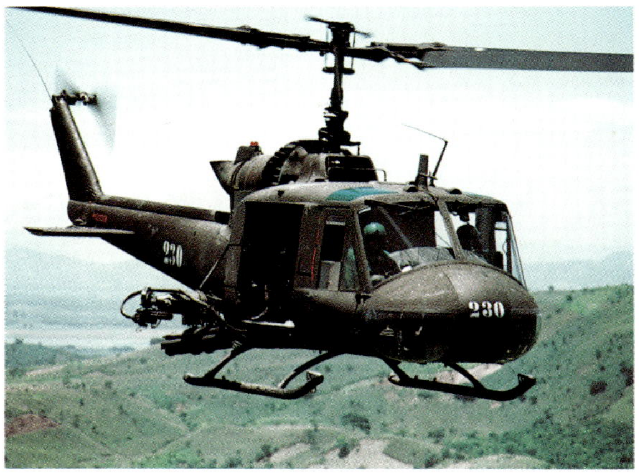

5

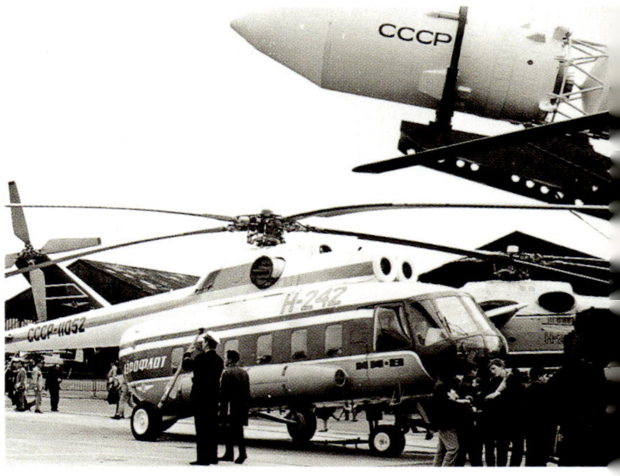

3

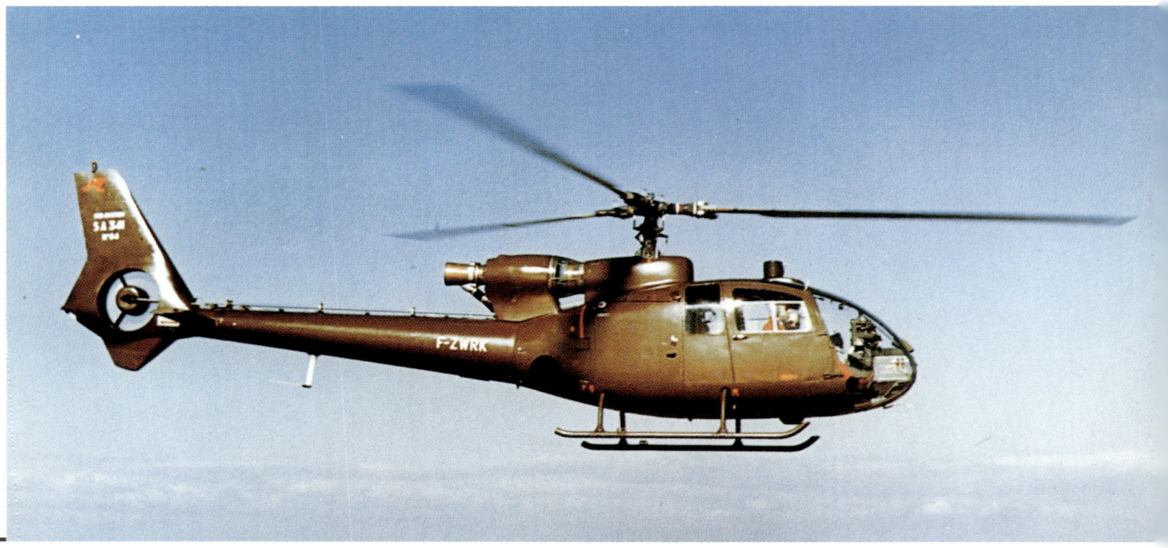

6

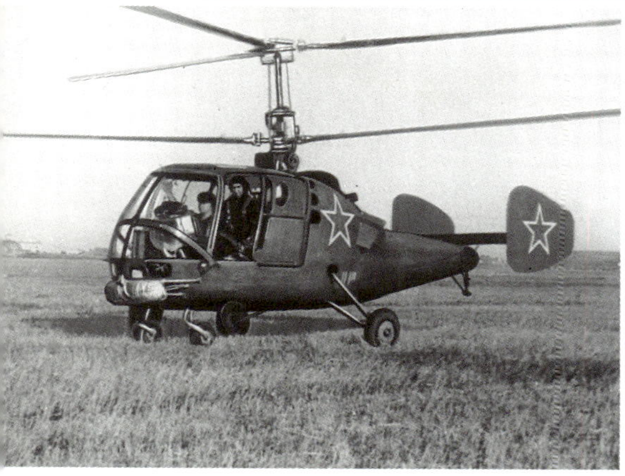

7

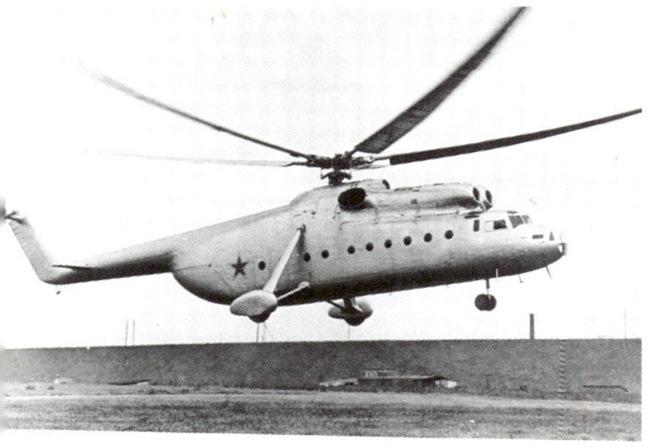

14

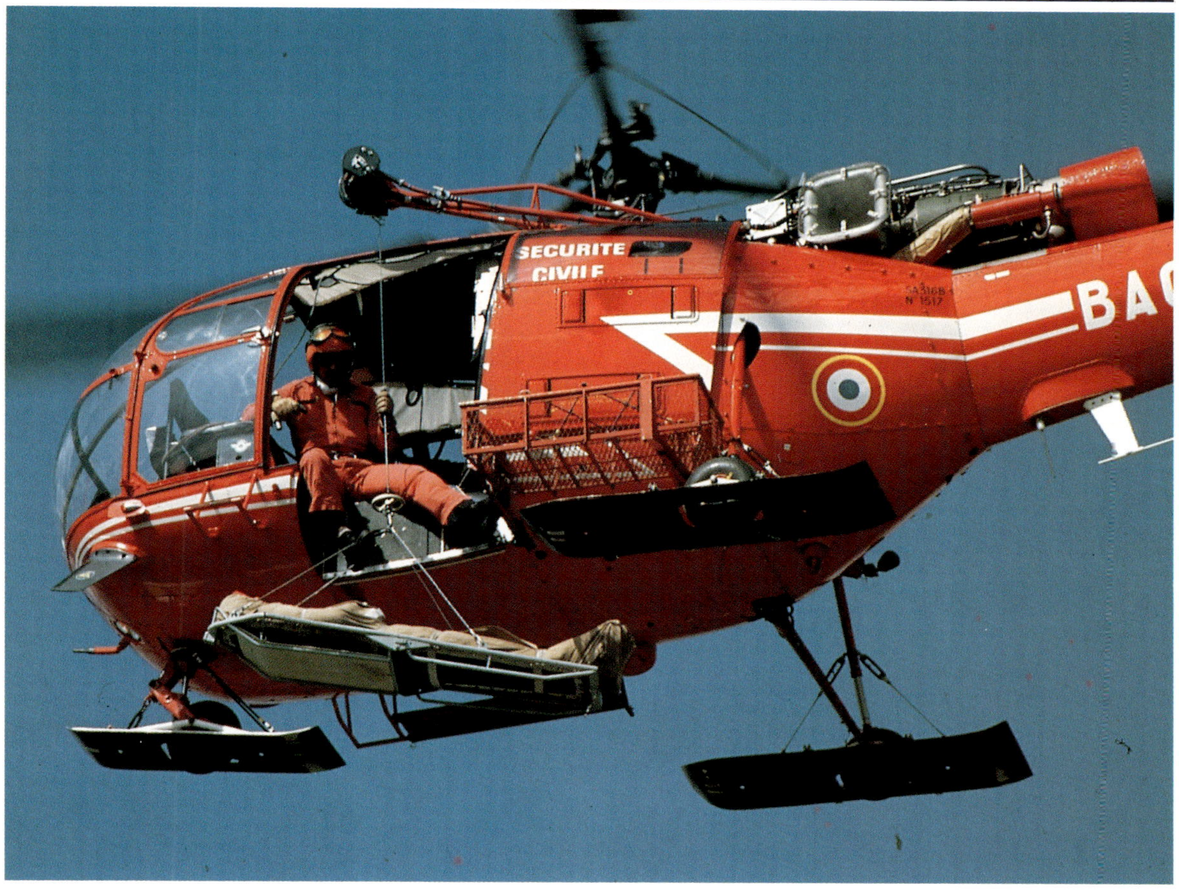

8

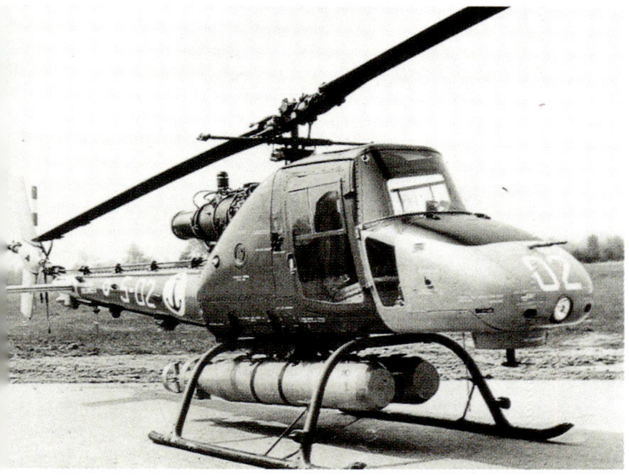

12

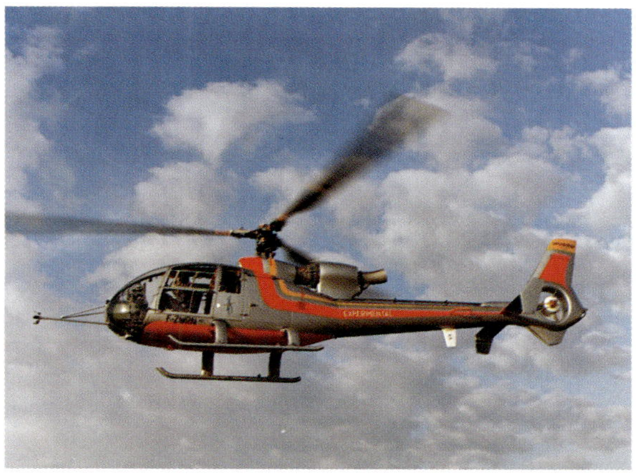

Photo No. 1: Aérospatiale SA 330 Puma (France)
Photo No. 2: Bell UH-1 Iroquois (USA)
Photo Nos. 3 and 12: Aérospatiale SA 341 Gazelle (France)
Photo No. 4: Hughes 500 (USA)
Photo No. 5: Mil Mi-8 (Russia)
Photo No. 6: Kamov Ka-15 (Russia)
Photo No. 7: Mil Mi-6 (Russia)
Photo No. 8: Agusta A.106 (Italy)
Photo No. 9: Westland Lynx (Great Britain)
Photo No. 10: Mil Mi-4 (Russia)
Photo No. 11: Eurocopter Bo 105 (Germany)
Photo No. 13: Eurocopter/Kawasaki BK 117 (Germany/Japan)
Photo No. 14: Aérospatiale SA 319 Alouette III (France)

9

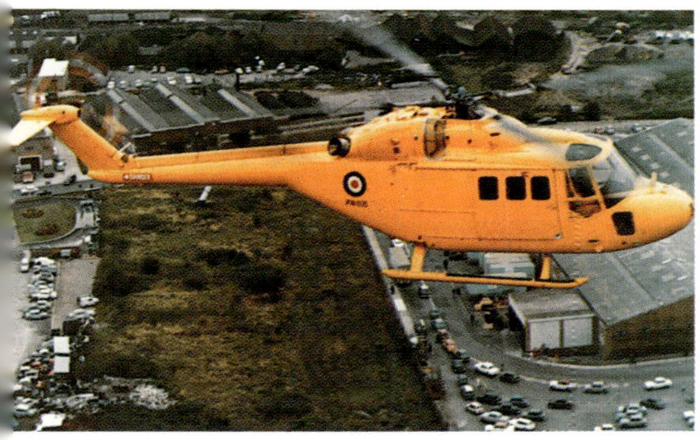

13

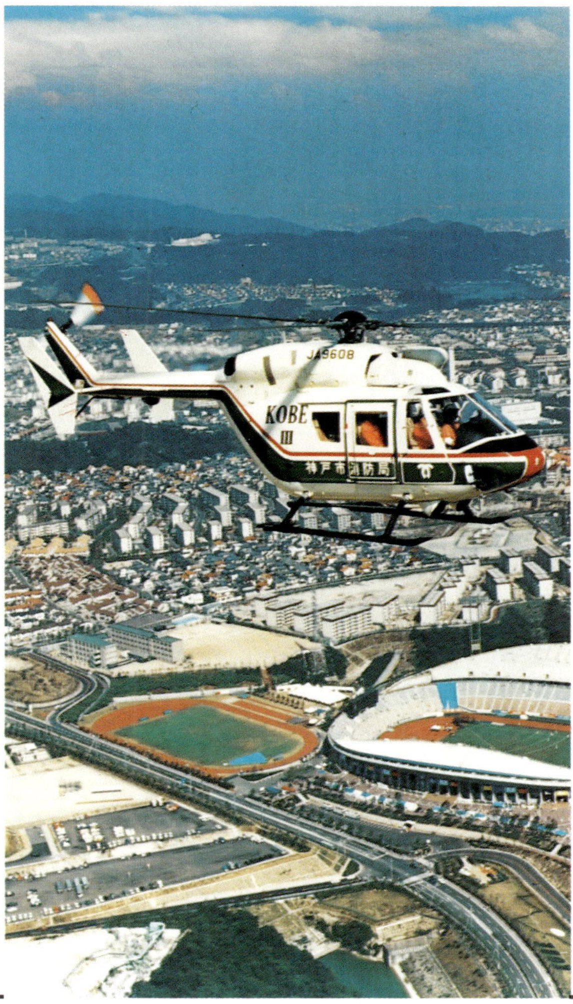

10

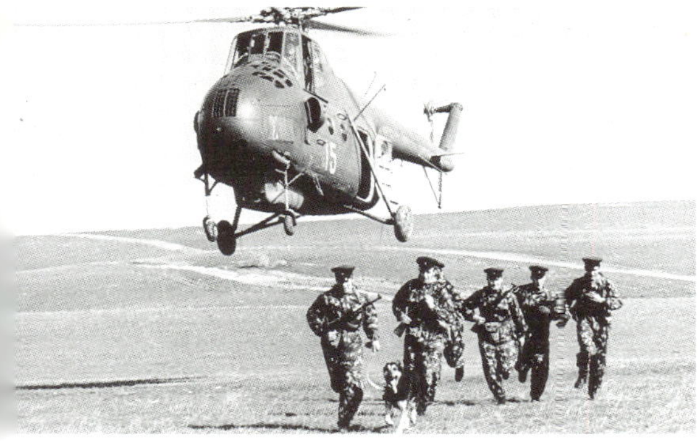

11

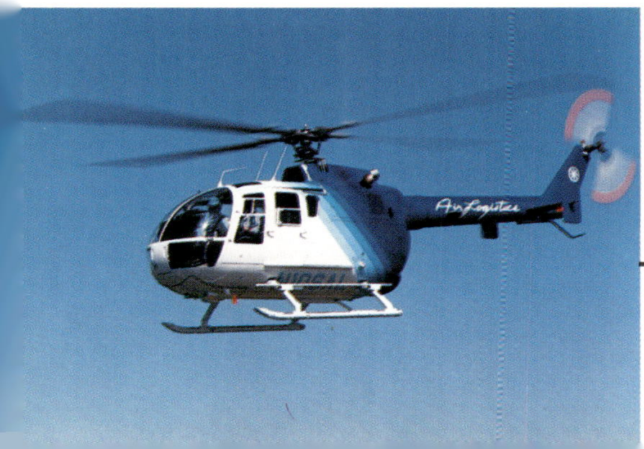

HELICOPTERS

Aérospatiale's biggest helicopter, the SA 321 Super Frelon, came into service in 1962, designed for anti-submarine warfare and reconnaissance duties. Powered by three turboshafts, it flies at over 168 mph (270 kph) and has an endurance of four hours. Armament consists of four torpedoes or Exocet missiles. Alternatively, it can transport 37 passengers in addition to its two pilots.

More recently, Aérospatiale has brought out the AS 350 Ecureuil/Astar (1965), a light, single-engined six-seater with a top speed of 140 mph (225 kph), and a twin-engined version of the same helicopter, the AS 350 Ecureuil/Twinstar. The AS 550 and 555 Fennec are military derivatives of the Ecureuil, able to carry 20-mm cannon, rockets or anti-tank missiles. The 1969 SA 315 Lama, consisting of an Alouette II airframe fitted with the more powerful Alouette III engine, is intended for high-altitude missions. In 1972 it reached a ceiling of 40,809 ft (12,442 m).

The AS 365 Dauphin, introduced in 1972, is a twin-turboshaft helicopter with seating for between 10 and 14 passengers and a cruising speed of 175 mph (280 kph). It is used by the US Coast Guard for search and rescue missions, and can be armed with anti-ship missiles. The AS 332 Super Puma (1978) is another twin-turboshaft helicopter. It cruises at 163 mph (262 kph) for up to 530 miles (850 km) with 25 passengers on board. A military version, the Cougar, can carry up to 29 troops or be fitted with cannon or rocket launchers.

In 1961, Bell began marketing civilian versions of the Huey, the single-engined 205 and 214 models. They had capacity for 15 and 19 passengers respectively, flying at 143 mph (230 kph) over distances of 463 miles (745 km). The Bell 206 JetRanger, a light, single-engined helicopter with seating for between five and seven, was a civilian version of the Kiowa, while the Bell 212 is a twin-engined version of the 205. It carries 14 passengers at 125 mph (200 kph) on stages of up to 275 miles (440 km). These helicopters are now all made in Canada.

Sikorsky in 1965 unveiled the S-65/CH-53. Powered by two or three turboshafts, this big helicopter can carry 55 infantrymen, two jeeps or a 105mm field gun. In 1976 came the S-76, a twin-engined civilian helicopter with carrying capacity for 12 passengers and a top speed of 166 mph (269 kph). In 1982 McDonnell Douglas (formerly Hughes) brought out the MD-530, an updated and more powerful version of the 500. The Italian company Agusta began production in 1971 of the A.109, a versatile twin-

1
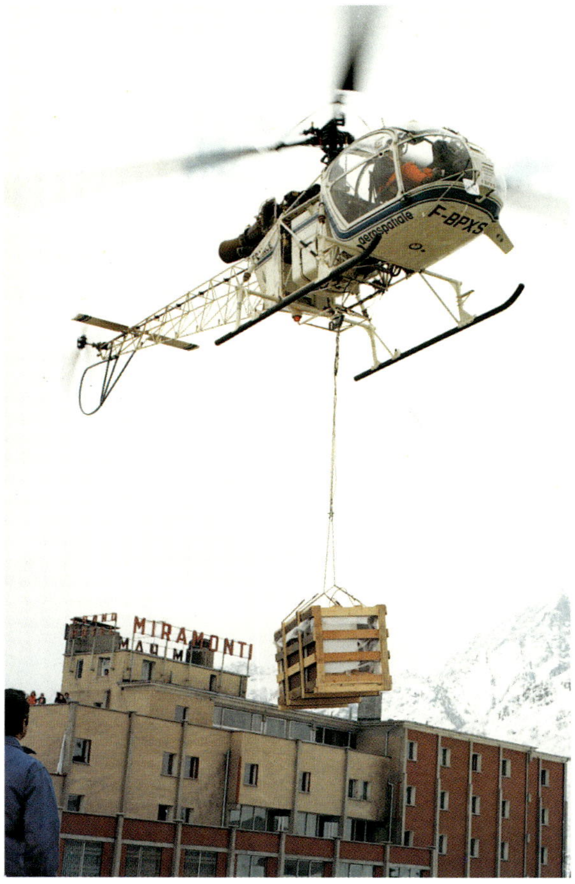

2
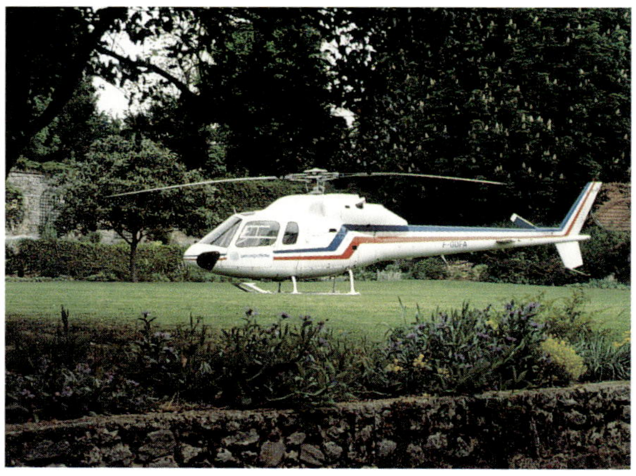

3
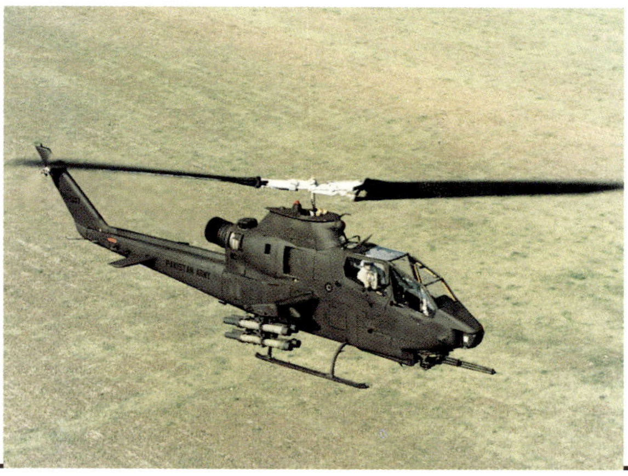

4
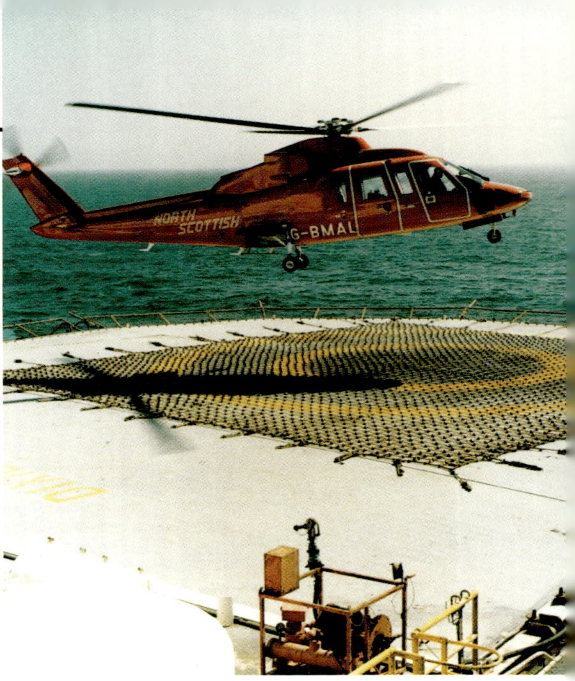

5
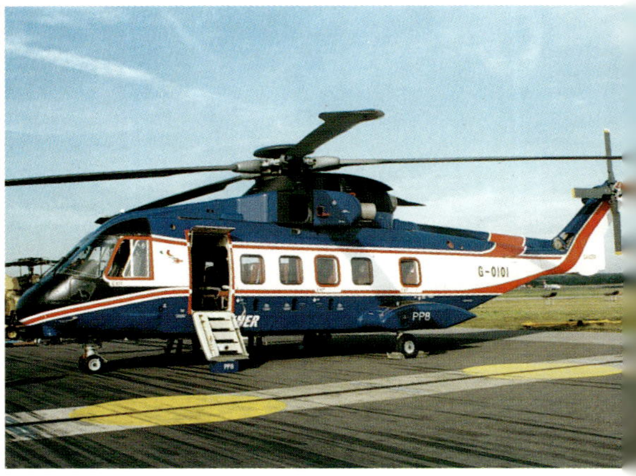

6
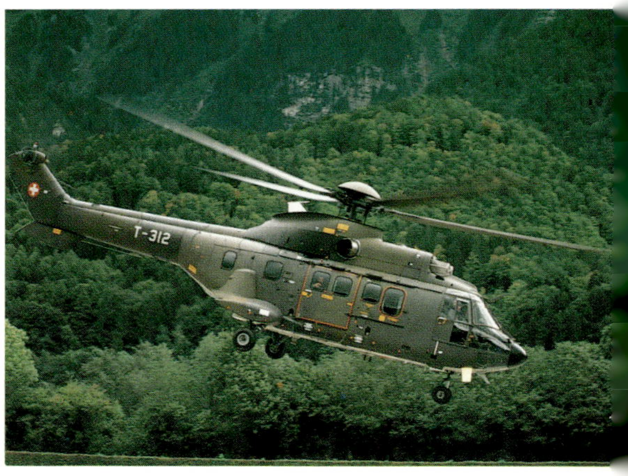

7
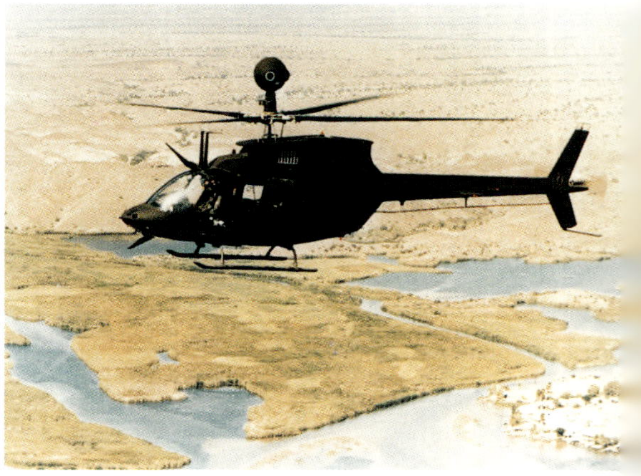

8
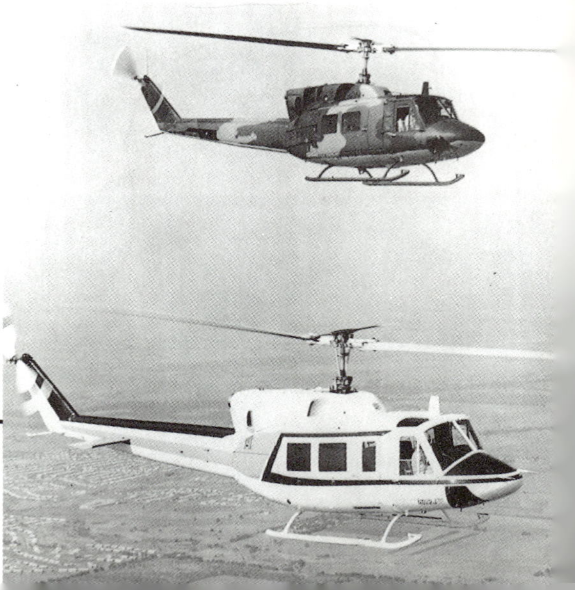

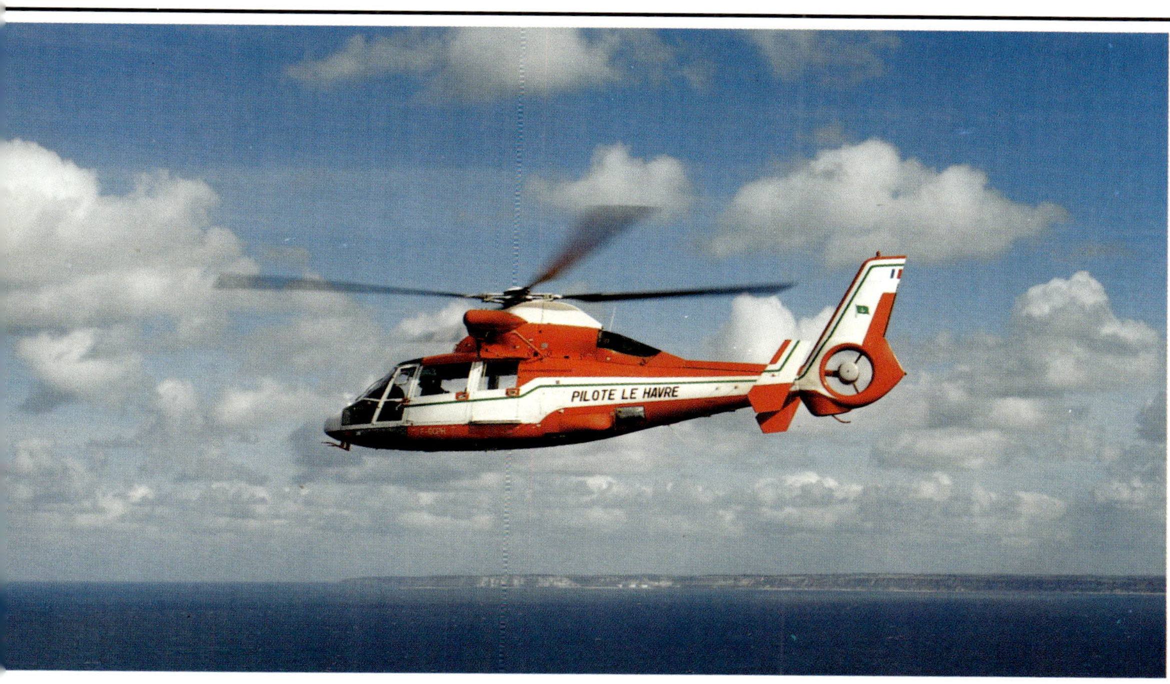

11

engined helicopter. The civilian version carries eight passengers, while the Hirundo military model can transport seven infantrymen or be fitted to fire anti-tank missiles. With Westland, Agusta is also involved in the EH.101 programme. Together, they designed a three-engined transport and maritime reconnaissance helicopter, which first flew in 1987. Cruising at 187 mph (300 kph), it can carry 30 men or six tons of equipment for distances of up to 1,500 miles (2,400 km).

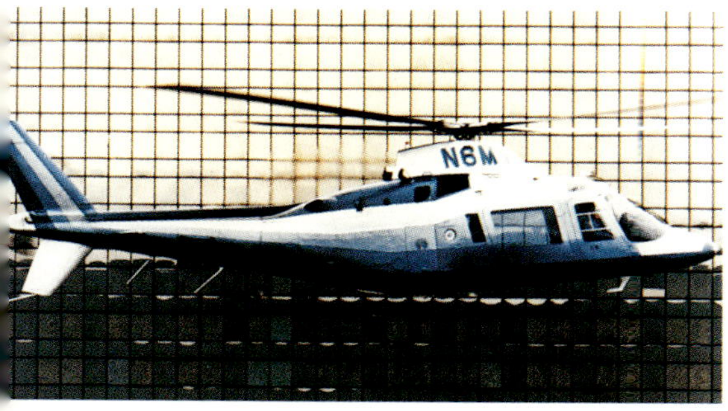

9

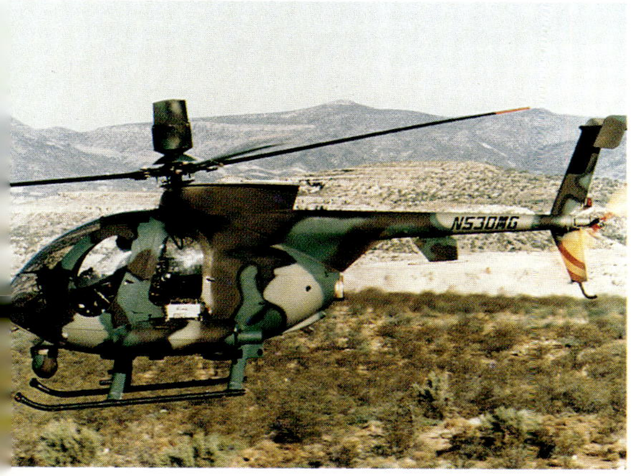

10

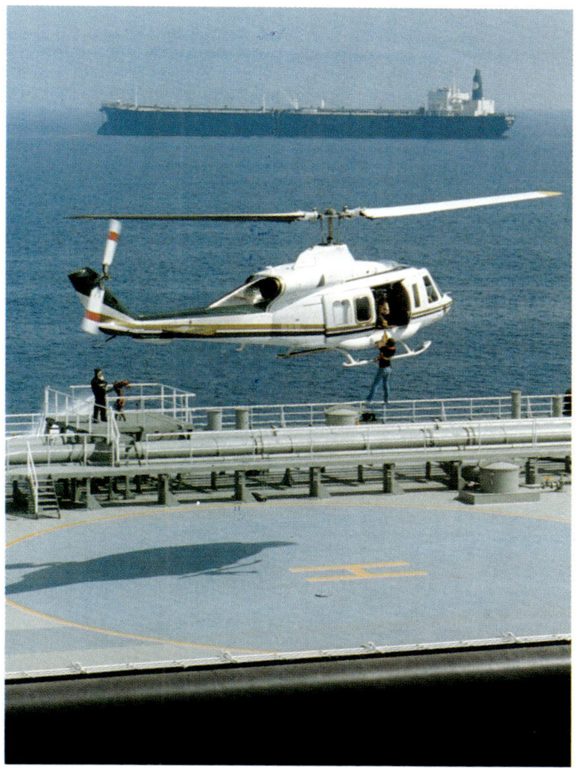

12 The Russian Mil Mi-26 is by far the most capable helicopter. This 23,000-horsepower machine can carry 22 tons of cargo at 183 mph (295 kph).

Photo No. 1: Aérospatiale SA 315 Lama (France)
Photo No. 2: Aérospatiale Ecureuil (France)
Photo No. 3: Bell HueyCobra (USA)
Photo No. 4: Sikorsky S-76 (USA)
Photo No. 5: EHI EH.101 (airline version) (GB/Italy)
Photo No. 6: Aérospatiale AS 332 Super Puma (France)
Photo No. 7: OH-58D Kiowa (USA)
Photo No. 8: Bell 212 (USA)
Photo No. 9: Agusta A.109 (Italy)
Photo No. 10: McDonnell Douglas MD-530 (USA)
Photo No. 11: Aérospatiale AS 365 Dauphin (France)
Photo No. 12: Bell 214 (USA)
Photo No. 13: Aérospatiale SA 321 Super Frelon (France)
Photo No. 14: Sikorsky CH-53E (USA)
Photo No. 15: Mi-26 (Russia)

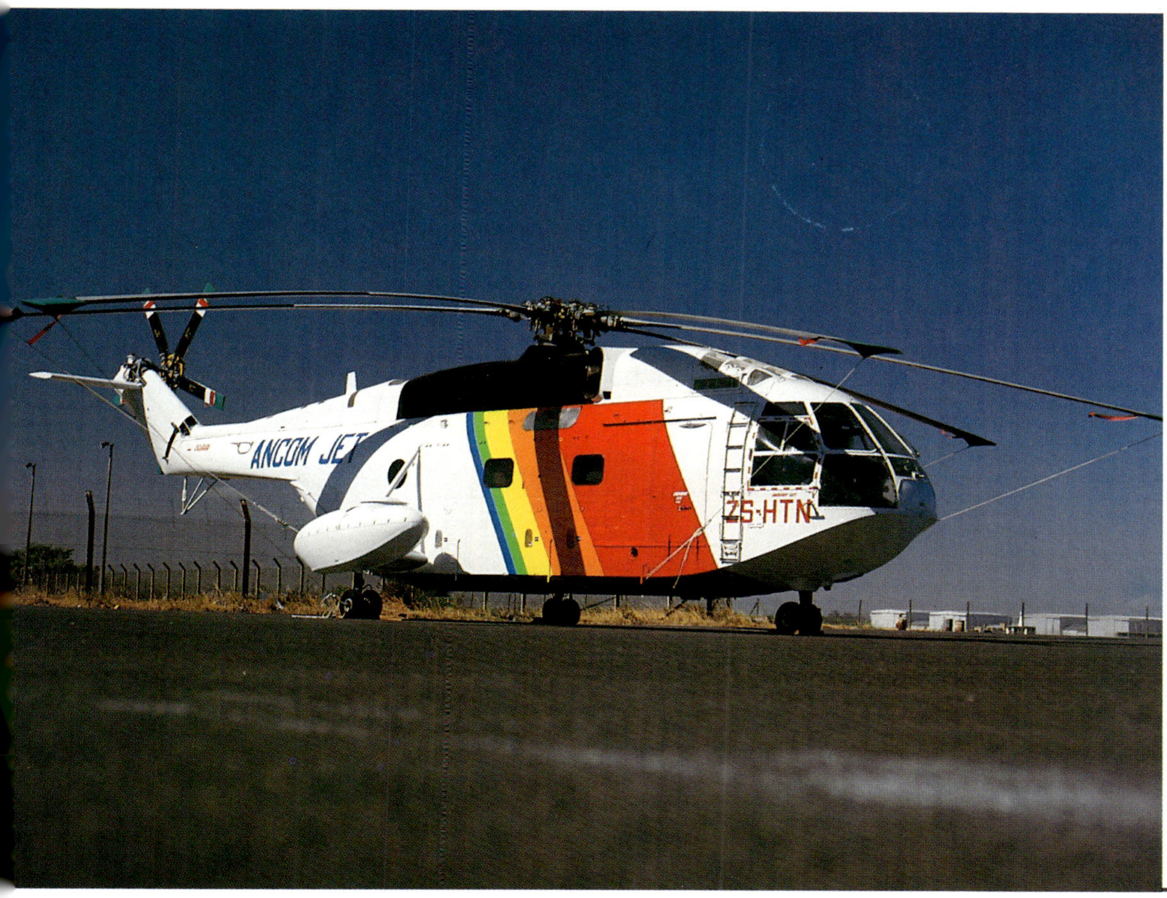

13

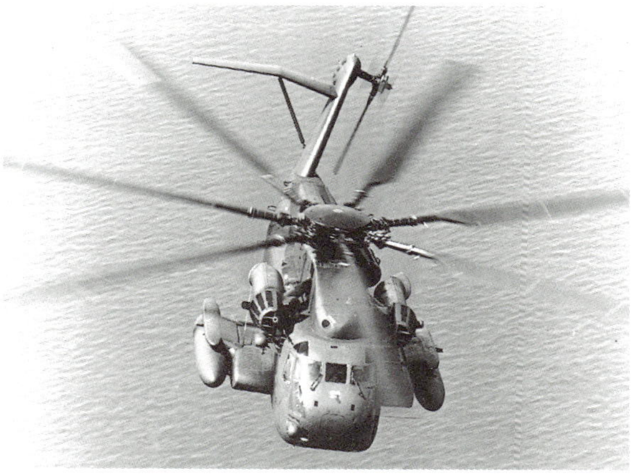

14

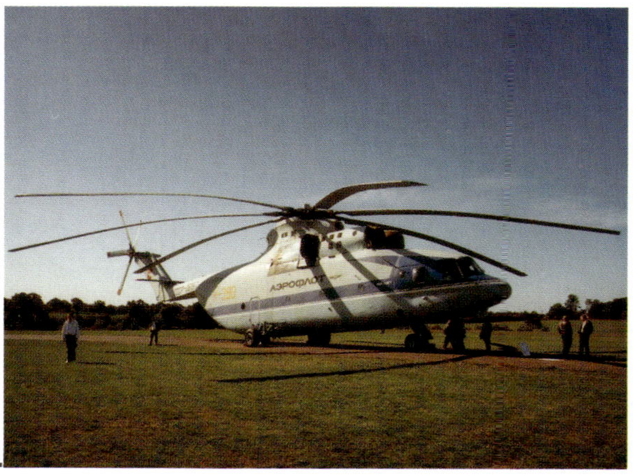

15

5
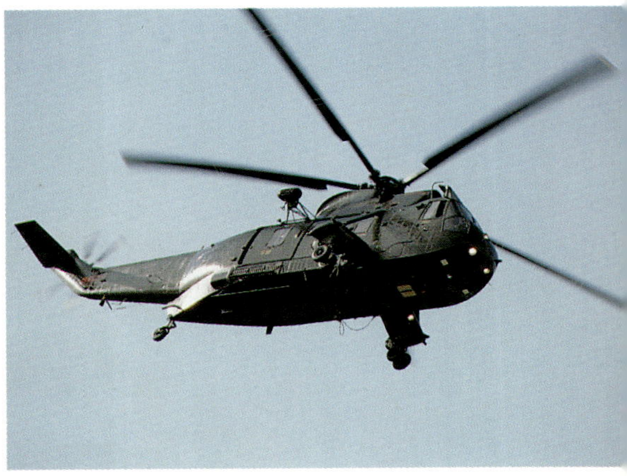

HELICOPTERS

In 1969 the Soviet design bureau named for M.I. Mil introduced the Mi-14, an amphibious twin-turboshaft helicopter designed for maritime patrol duties with a cruising speed in excess of 125 mph (200 kph) and endurance of six hours. It can deliver torpedoes, bombs and depth charges. It was followed, in 1972, by the Mi-24, a twin-engined attack helicopter heavily armed with nose-mounted guns and guided missiles of various types. It can also carry eight commandos and fly at over 206 mph (330 kph), with a radius of action of 100 miles (160 km). Another combat helicopter, the Mi-28, made its debut in 1982. A two-seater armed with a 30-mm cannon, rockets and 16 anti-tank missiles, it has a range of 293 miles (470 km) and a cruising speed of 168 mph (270 kph).

In Poland, PZL-Swidnik began in 1979 to produce the W-3 Sokol, which carries 12 passengers or two tons of cargo. It can also be armed with two 23-mm cannon, rockets and anti-tank missiles. It cruises at 156 mph (250 kph) and has a range of 437 miles (700 km).

Another helicopter designed for anti-tank warfare is the twin-turbine A.129 Mangusta, brought out by the Italian Agusta company in 1983. A two-seater with a speed of up to 196 mph (315 kph), it carries eight anti-tank missiles, machine guns, cannon and rockets.

In Britain, Westland began in 1961 to manufacture the Sea King, a derivative of the Sikorsky S-61, for maritime reconnaissance and anti-submarine warfare. Powered by twin turboshafts, it flies at over 125 mph (200 kph) to deliver highly specialized weaponry. The Commando version can transport 28 men over distances of 375 miles (600 km). A Westland Lynx holds the world helicopter speed record at 249 mph (401 kph).

Aérospatiale has also designed combat helicopters in recent years. The 1985 AS 565 Panther is a tactical version of the Dauphin, capable of transporting eight to ten troops or carrying out support-and-protection duties or anti-tank strikes using Hot missiles. Within the Eurocopter consortium, France and Germany are together building a two-seater, twin-engined combat helicopter known as the Tiger. Support-and-protection and anti-tank versions should become available in 1997. The Eurocopter group is also marketing the new Bo 108. Powered by twin turboshafts, this helicopter carries four to six passengers, flies at 156 mph (250 kph) and has a range of 500 miles (800 km). Another project in which Eurocopter is involved – with Agusta and Fokker – is the NH 90 programme. The aim is to bring out a tactical transport helicopter (TTH), and a marine reconnaissance version (NFH) by the end of the century. In the United States, in 1978 Bell began

1
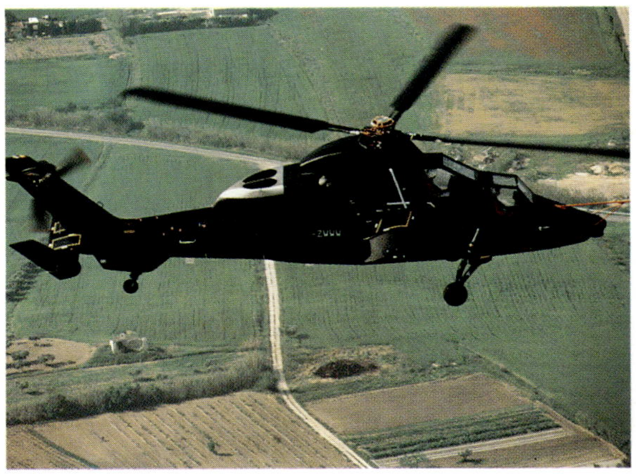

6
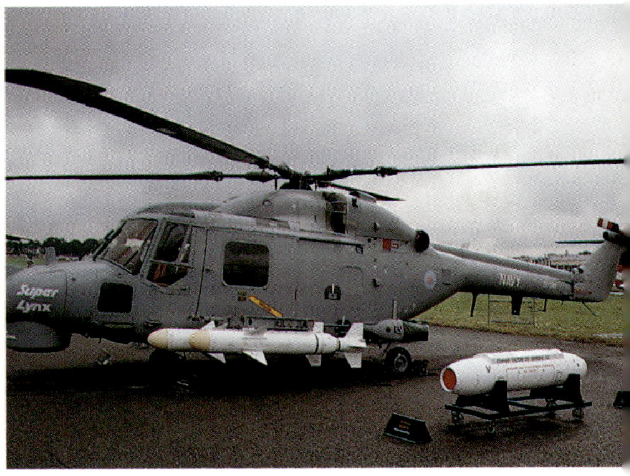

2
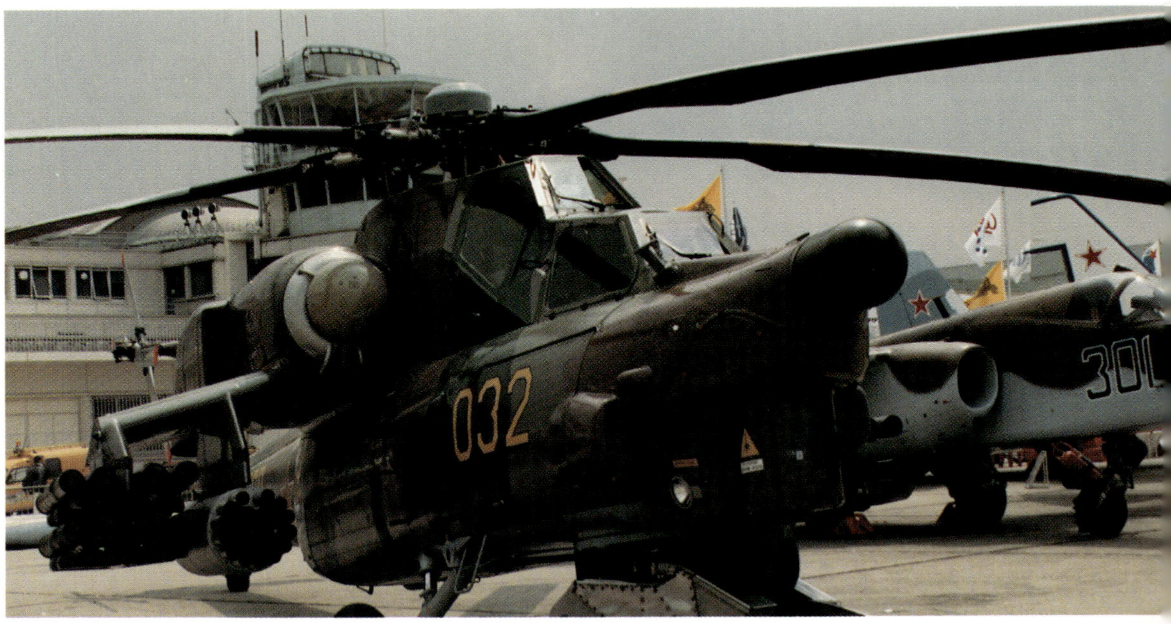

3
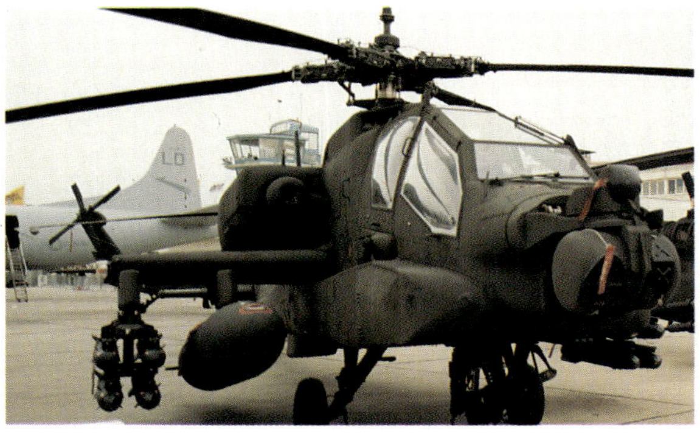

7
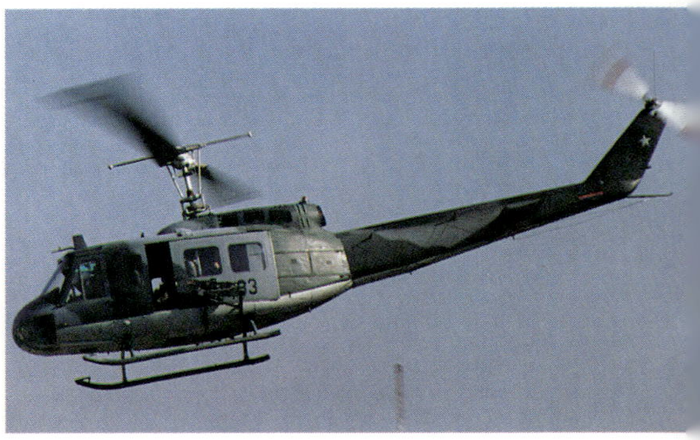

4
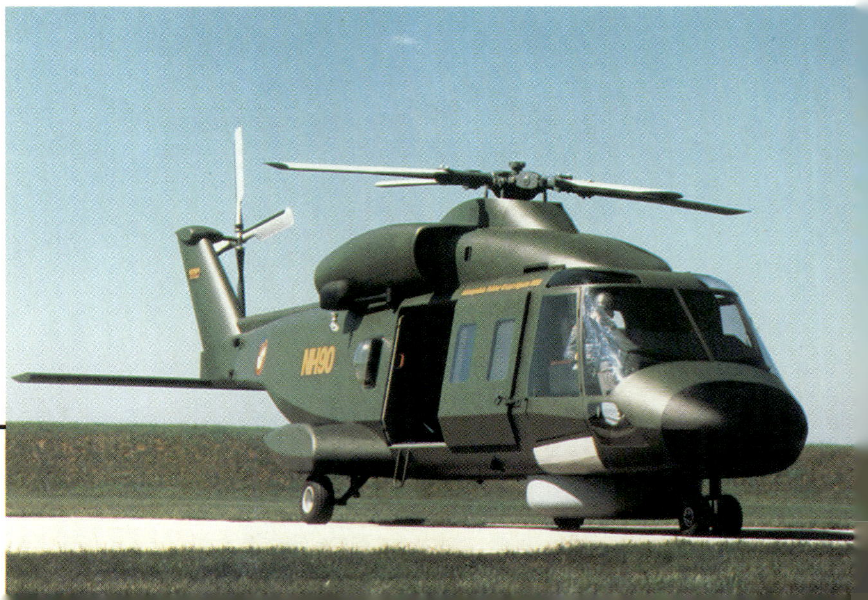

8

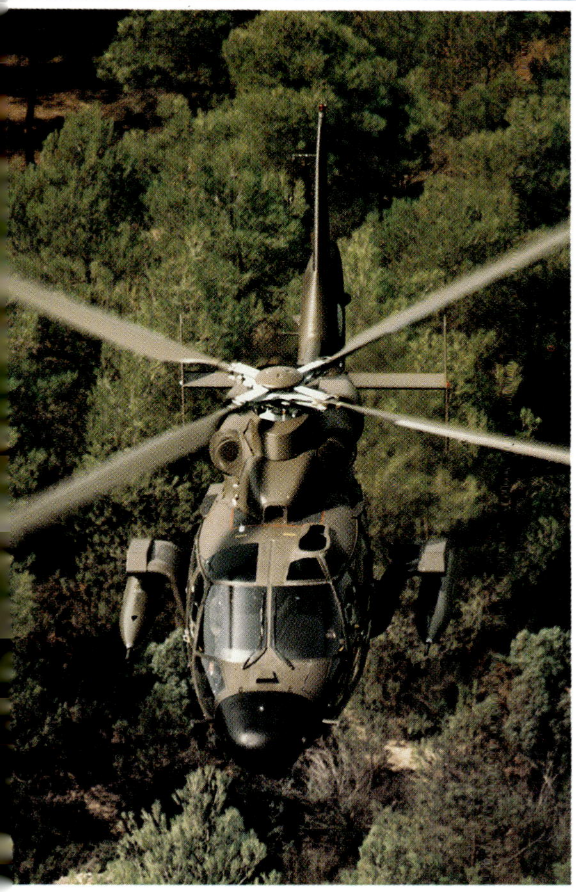

11

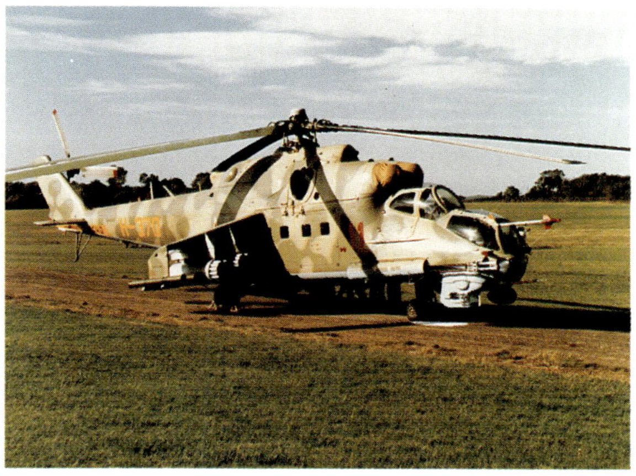

12

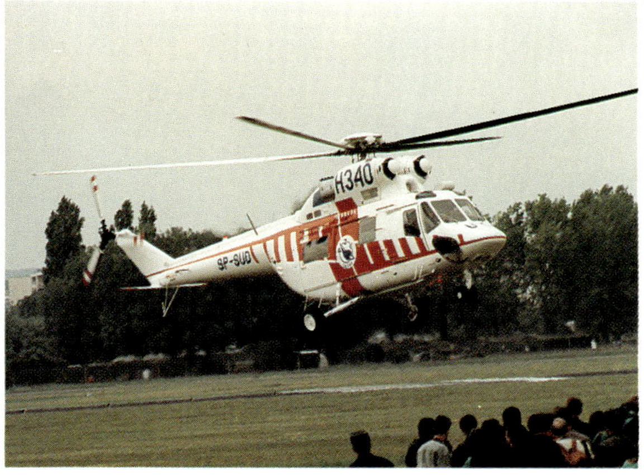

manufacturing a fast, twin-engined helicopter, the 222. This has been replaced by the 230, made by Bell Canada.

The McDonnell Douglas AH-64 Apache (1975) is an attack helicopter armed with a 30-mm cannon and 16 anti-tank missiles. It flies at up to 182 mph (293 kph). Finally, the Sikorsky UH-60 Black Hawk and SH-60 Sea Hawk helicopters have been in service since 1978. They can be used to transport 11 infantrymen on stages up to 187 miles (300 km) or to deliver weapons of various kinds.

13

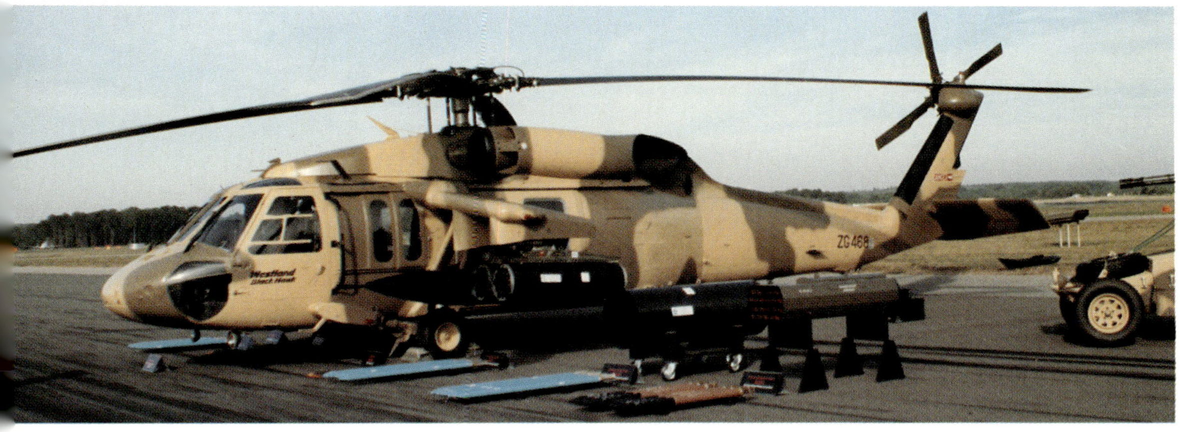

Photo No. 1: Eurocopter Tiger (France/Germany)
Photo No. 2: Mil Mi-28 (Russia)
Photo No. 3: McDonnell Douglas AH-64 Apache (USA)
Photo No. 4: Agusta/Eurocopter/Fokker NH 90
Photo No. 5: Westland Commando (Great Britain)
Photo No. 6: Westland Super Lynx (Great Britain)
Photo No. 7: Bell UH-1 Huey (USA)
Photo No. 8: Aérospatiale AS 565 Panther (France)
Photo No. 9: Mil Mi-14 (Russia)
Photo No. 10: Eurocopter Bo 108 (Germany)
Photo No. 11: Mil Mi-24 (Russia)
Photo No. 12: PZL W-3 Sokol (Poland)
Photo No. 13: Sikorsky UH-60 Black Hawk (USA)
Photo No. 14: Agusta A.129 Mangusta (Italy)

9

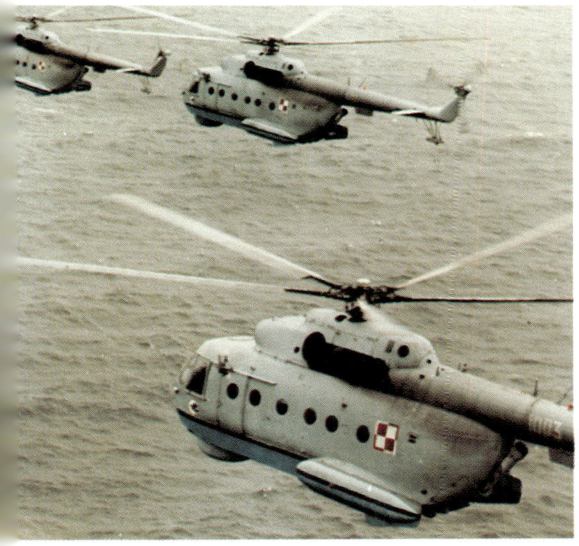

10

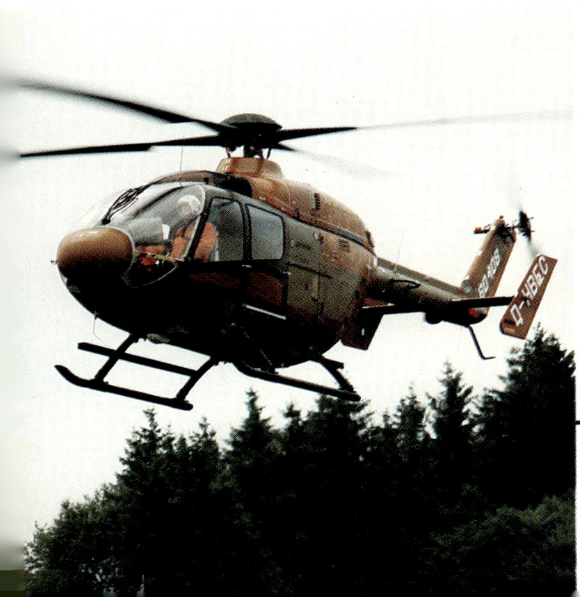

14

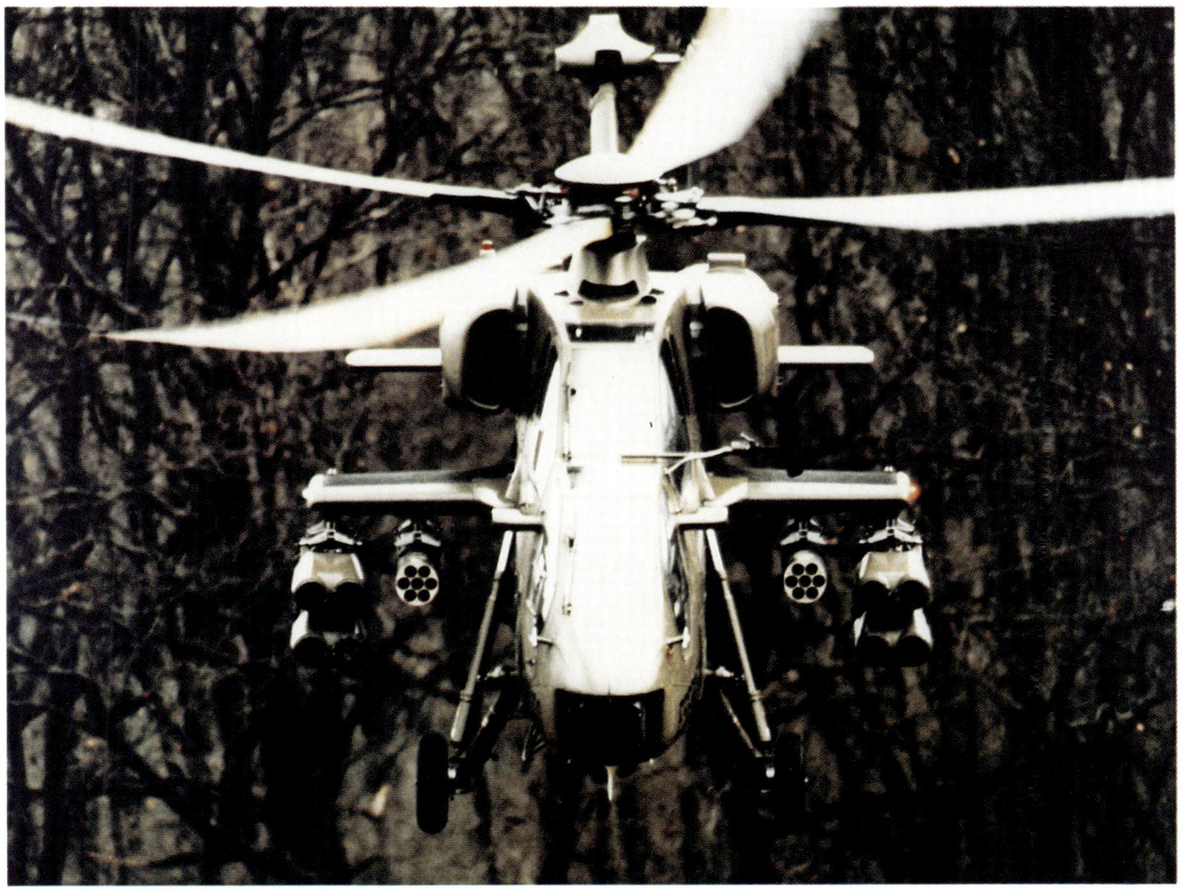

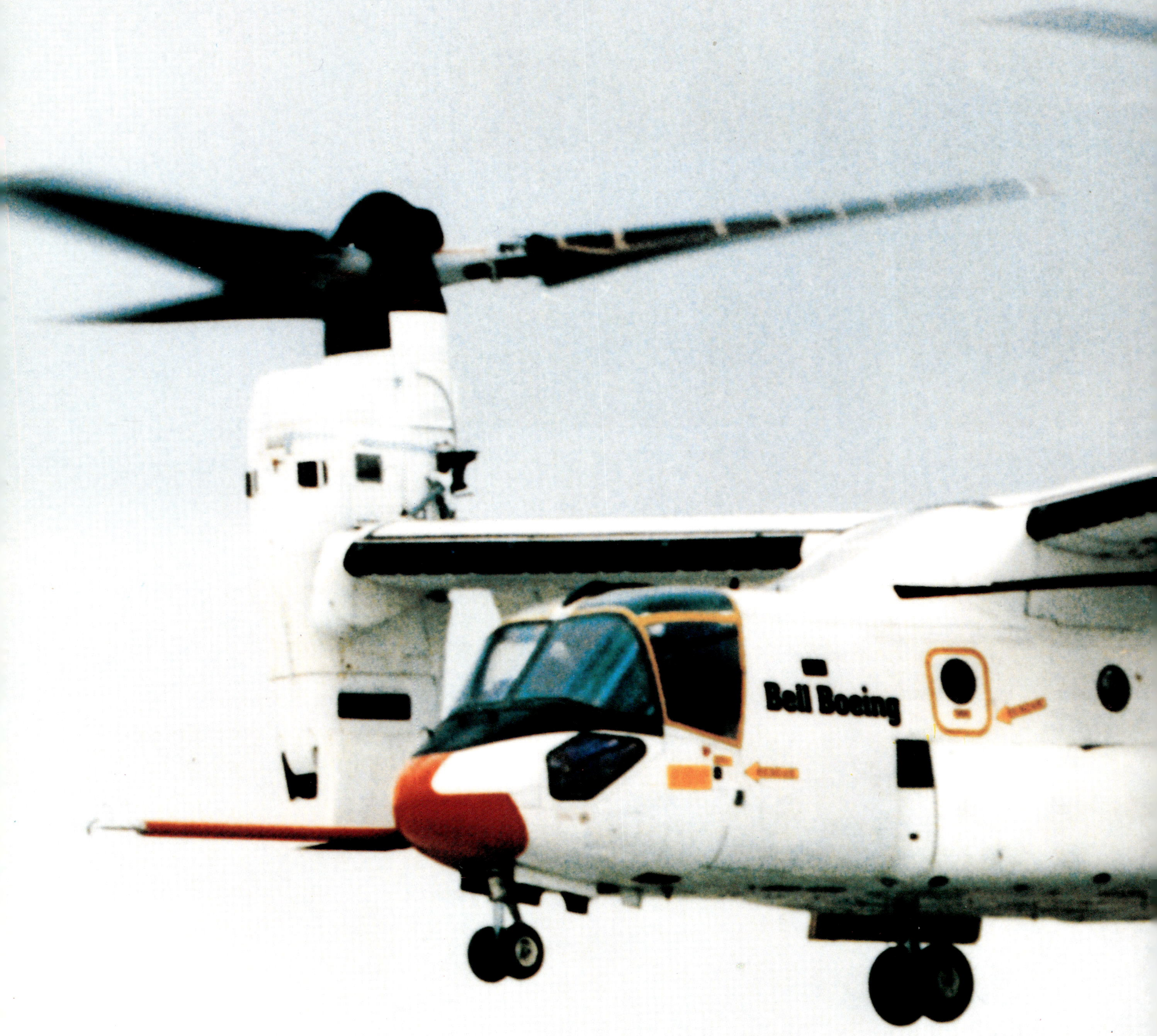

SOME EXCEPTIONAL FLYING MACHINES

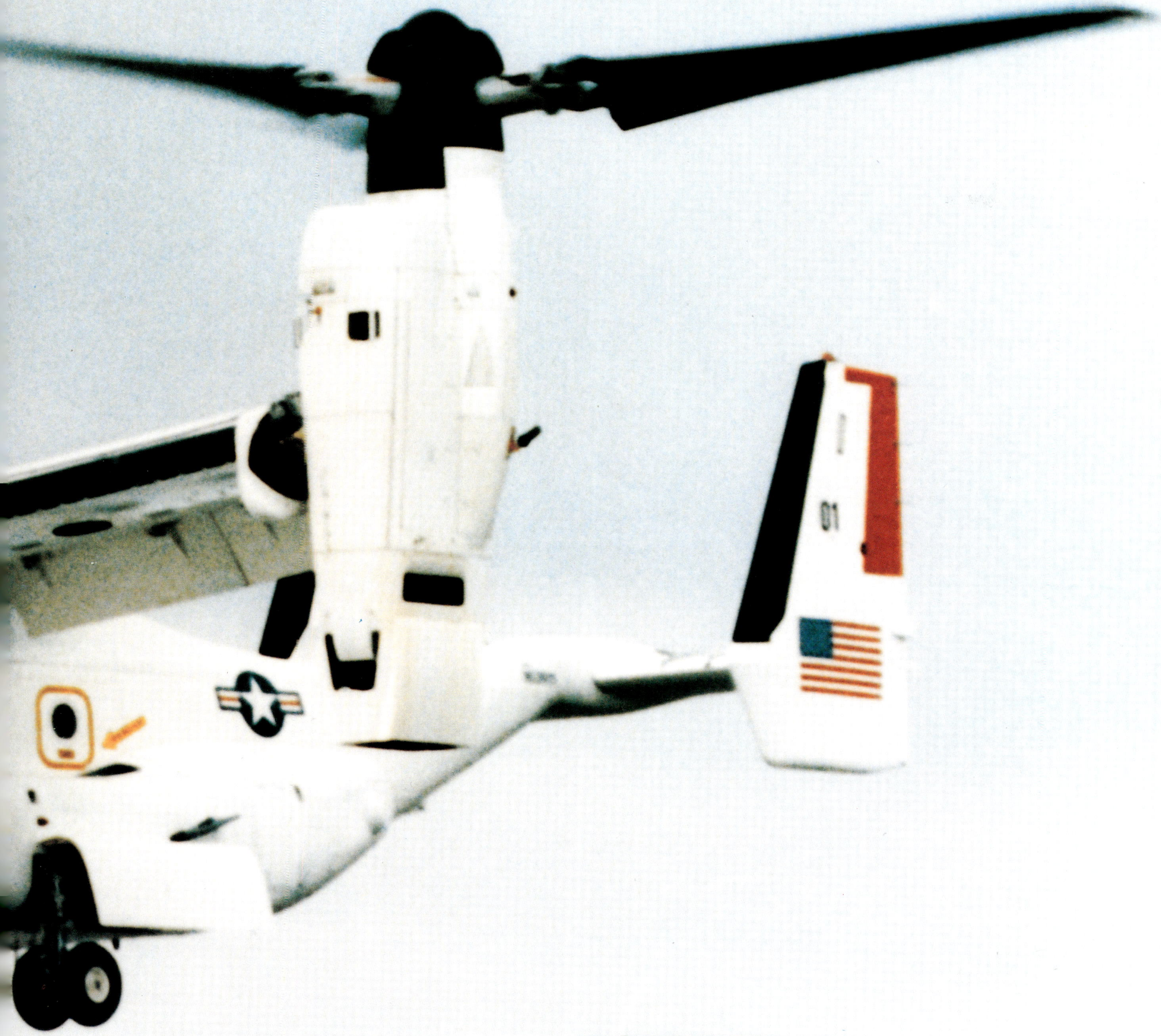
01

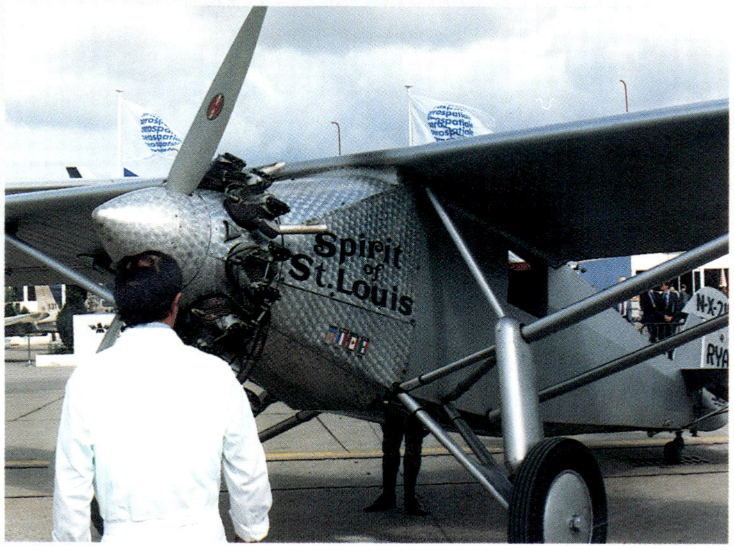
Spirit
of
St. Louis

5

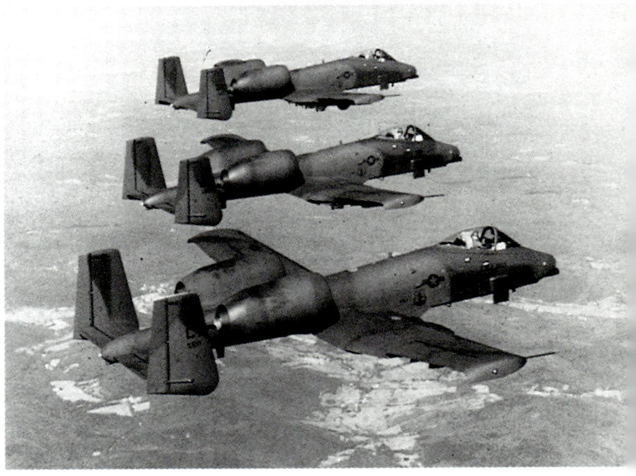

AERONAUTICAL INNOVATIONS

The Pou-du-Ciel (Sky Louse, or Flying Flea) was a miniature light aircraft brought out in 1933. A single-seater, its top speed was no more than 62.5 mph (100 kph).

The oddest-looking of German warplanes was undoubtedly the Blohm und Voss BV 141 of 1938. It consisted of a fuselage bearing only the single engine, the tail fin and a half-tailplane on the port side, while a separate crew nacelle was mounted on the starboard wing. Used as an observation aircraft, it flew at 250 mph (400 kph) and had a ceiling of 29,500 ft (9,000 m).

The Yokosuka MXY-7 Ohka (Cherry Blossom) suicide plane was introduced by the Japanese in 1945. Launched from a bomber with 2,640 lb (1,200 kg) of high explosive in the nose, it was propelled in its final death dive by three rocket motors, hitting its target at 580 mph (930 kph). Its range was 25 miles (40 km). Another last-throw weapon was the German Bachem Ba 349, a rocket-propelled aircraft introduced in 1945 to intercept Allied bombers. It reached speeds of 625 mph (1,000 kph).

In the 1950s the US aircraft industry began to design vertical take-off aircraft. The propeller-driven Convair XFY-1 Pogo, Lockheed XFV-1 and Ryan X-13 Vertijet all approached the problem in the same way, taking off straight up from a vertical position. A similar French experiment, the jet-propelled SNECMA C-450 Coléoptère (Beetle) crashed on its first take-off. This solution soon gave way to aircraft with rotatable engine exhaust ports able to direct thrust downwards. The twin-engined Aérospatiale N-500 (1967) was of this type, flying at speeds of 220 mph (350 kph). Similar in design was the 1957 Short SC.1, a prototype which paved the way for the Hawker Siddeley (now British Aerospace) Harrier and Sea Harrier. A single-engined single-seater jet, the Harrier has been in service with the RAF since 1969. Armed with 30-mm cannon, bombs or missiles, it flies sorties of up to 722 miles (1,162 km) at speeds approaching 750 mph (1,200 kph). The Soviet equivalent is the Yakovlev Yak-38, which reaches 862 mph (1,380 kph).

In 1962 Dassault built the Mirage III-V Balzac, with one jet engine for forward propulsion and eight to provide lift, but it was not developed beyond the prototype stage.

The Bell-Boeing V-22 Osprey, which has two swivel engines, first flew in 1989. It was designed for the US Navy, Marines and Air Force, to fly many missions carrying a 10-ton payload 2,073 miles (3,336 km) at 361 mph (582 kph).

A series of amazing aircraft, the Leduc 0.10 through to 0.22 was used in the years 1947 to 1958 to study the possibilities of the ramjet.

1

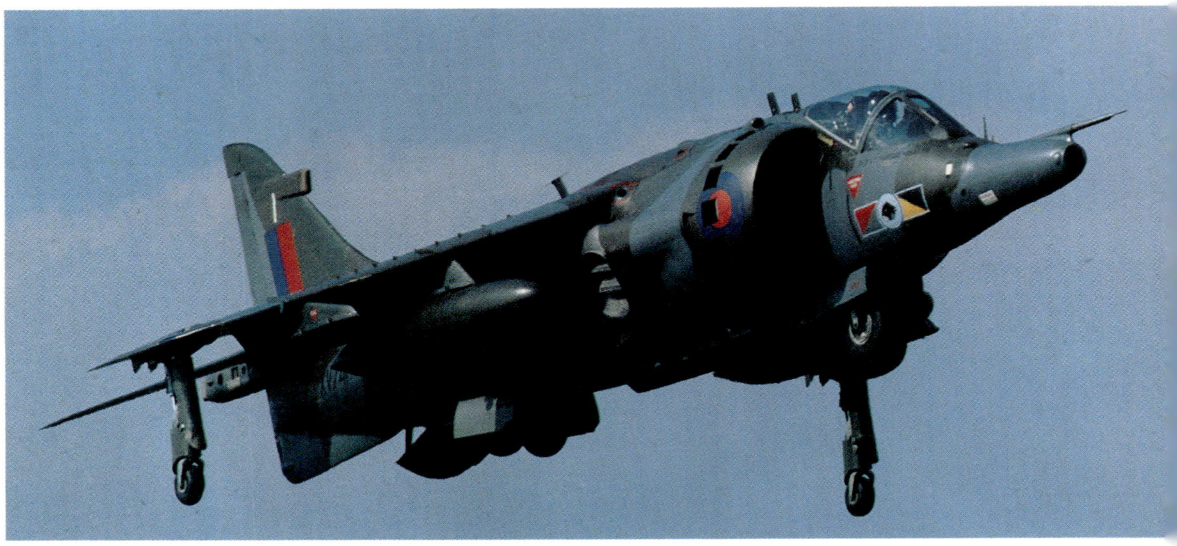

2

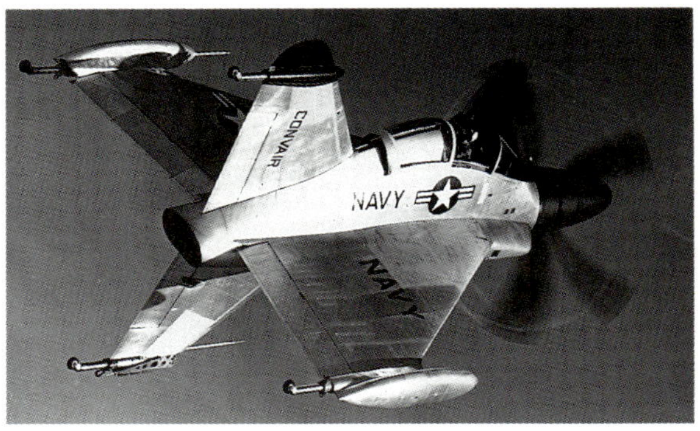

6

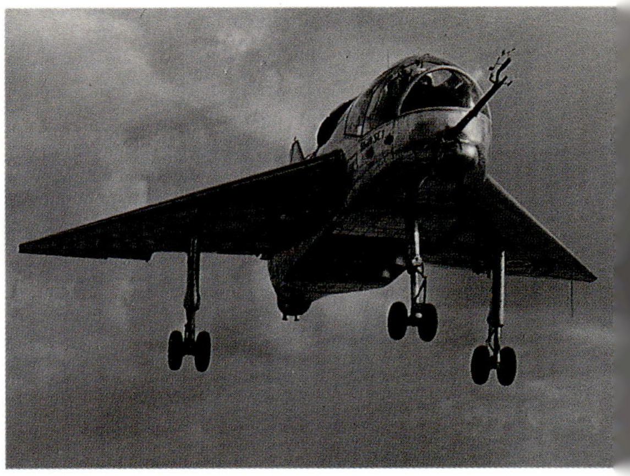

3

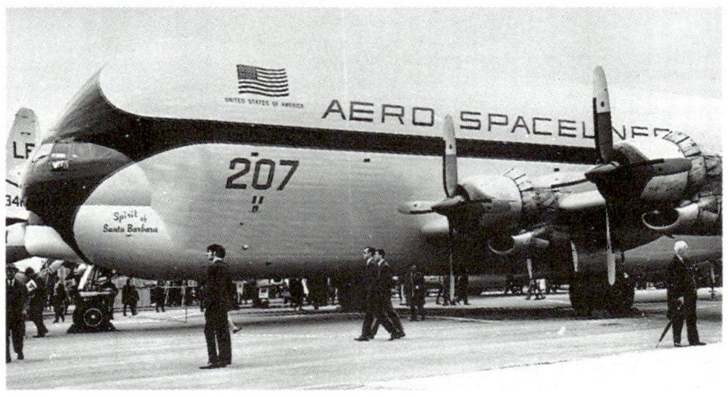

7

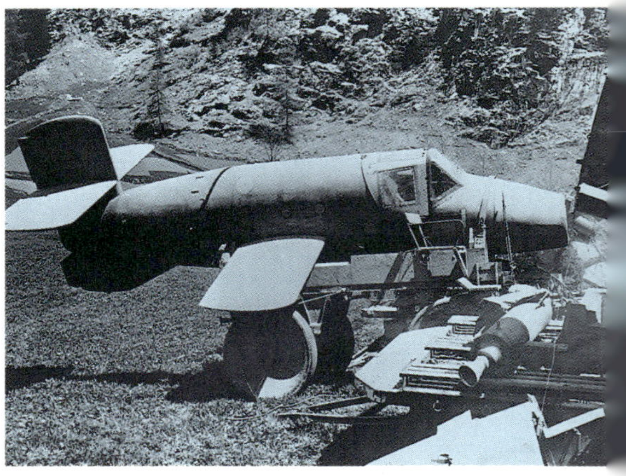

4

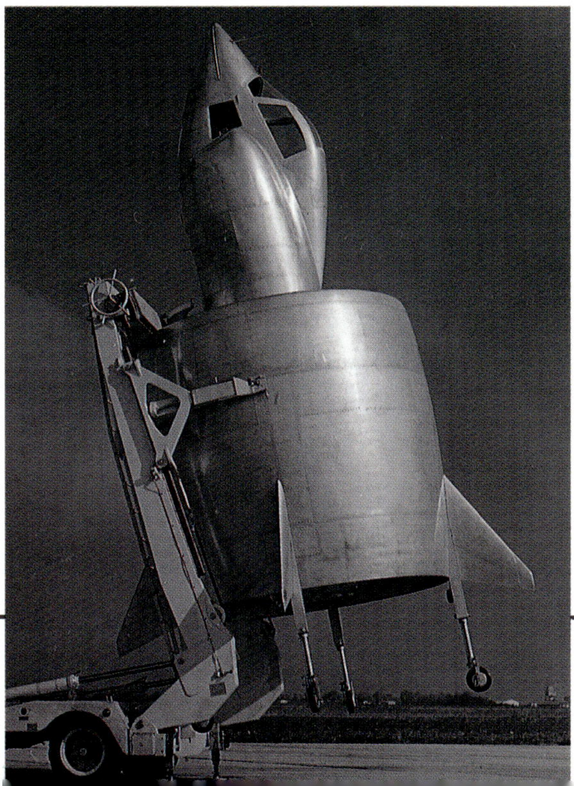

8

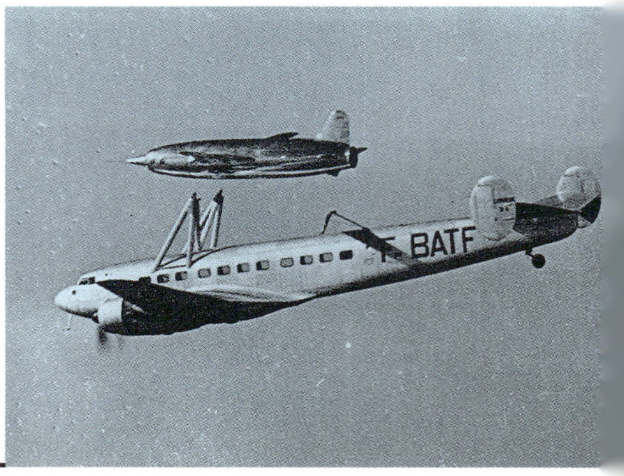

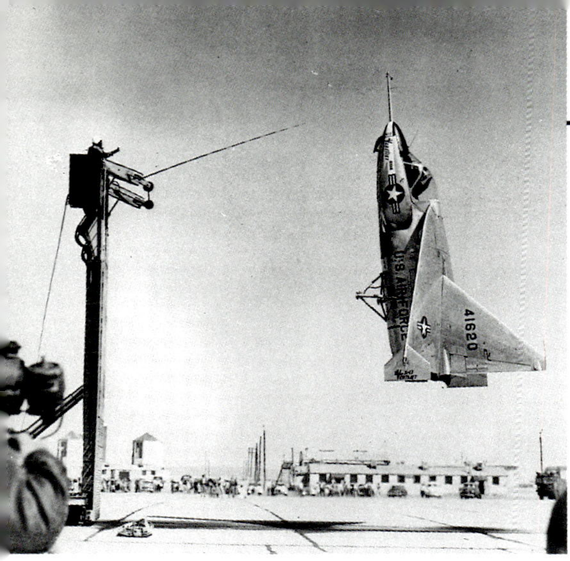

9

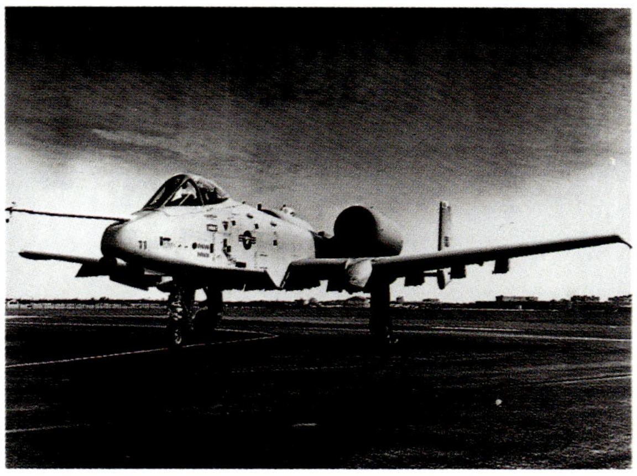

13

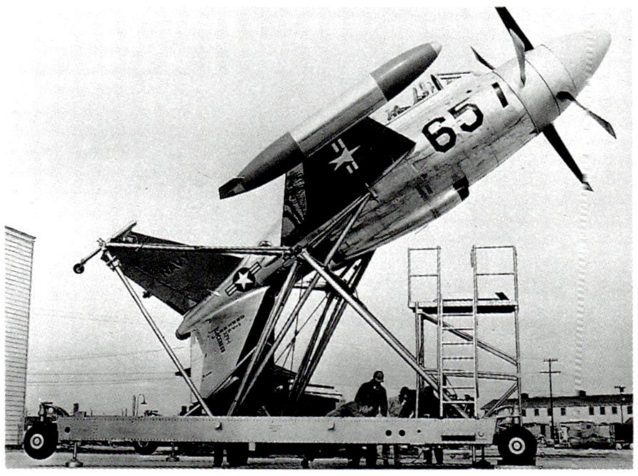

17

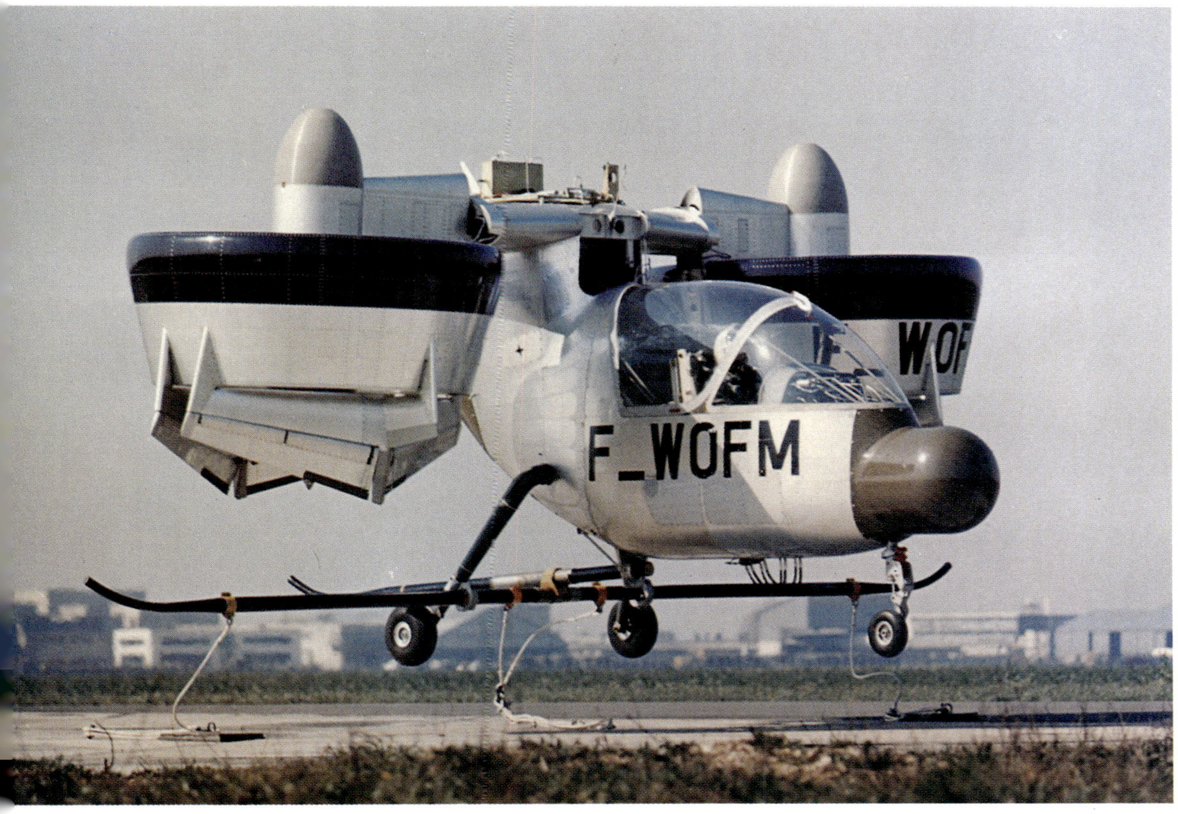

14 The Fairchild Republic A-10 Thunderbolt II is a monoplane with twin engines on the rear fuselage. Designed for anti-tank warfare, it flies at 420 mph (676 kph), carrying a multiple 30-mm cannon, bombs, missiles and rockets.

Derived from the Boeing 377, the Guppy is a four-engined heavy transport aircraft capable of carrying 24 tons of cargo. It has a range of 510 miles (815 km) and flies at around 280 mph (450 kph).

Photo Nos. 1, 16 and 18: BAe Harrier (Great Britain)
Photo No. 2: Convair XFY-1 Pogo (USA)
Photo No. 3: Aero Spacelines Mini Guppy (USA)
Photo No. 4: SNECMA 450 Coléoptère (France)
Photo Nos. 5 and 13: Fairchild Republic A-10 Thunderbolt II (USA)
Photo No. 6: Short SC.1 (Great Britain)
Photo No. 7: Bachem Ba 349 Natter (Germany)
Photo No. 8: Leduc 0.10 (France)
Photo No. 9: Ryan X-13 Vertijet (USA)
Photo No. 10: Yakovlev Yak-38 (Russia)
Photo No. 11: Yokosuka MXY-7 Ohka 22 (Japan)
Photo No. 12: Dassault Balzac (France)
Photo No. 14: Nord Aviation N-500 (France)
Photo No. 15: Blohm und Voss BV 141 (Germany)
Photo No. 17: Lockheed XFV-1 (USA)
Photo No. 19: Pou-du-Ciel (Sky Louse, or Flying Flea) (France)

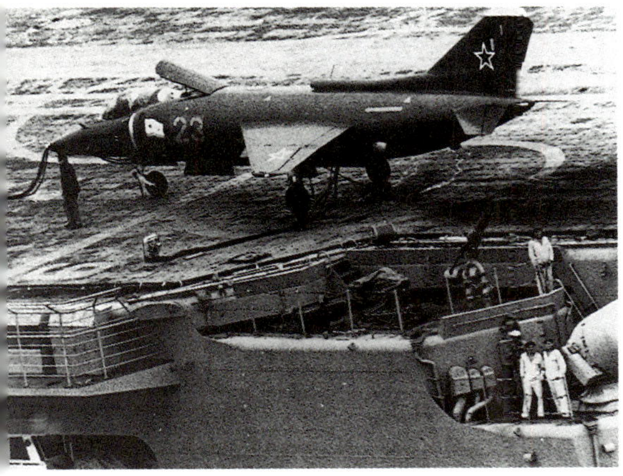

10

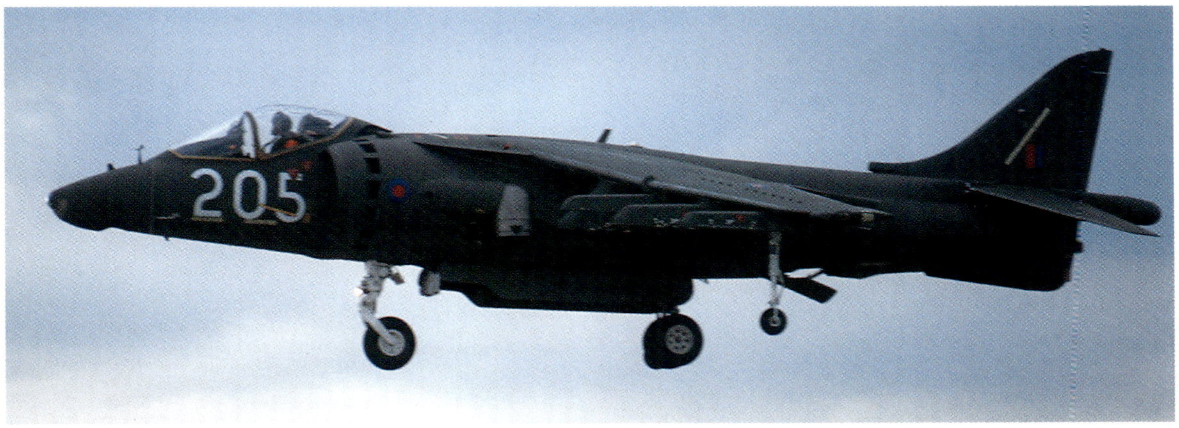

18

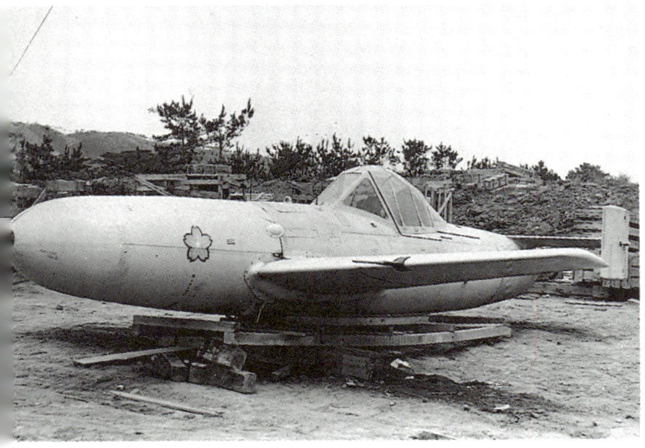

11

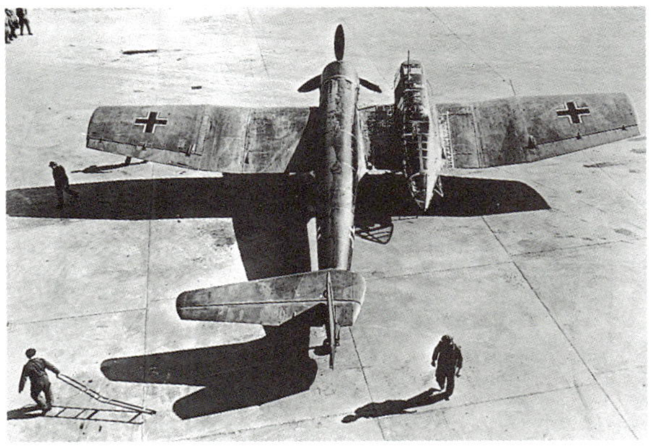

15

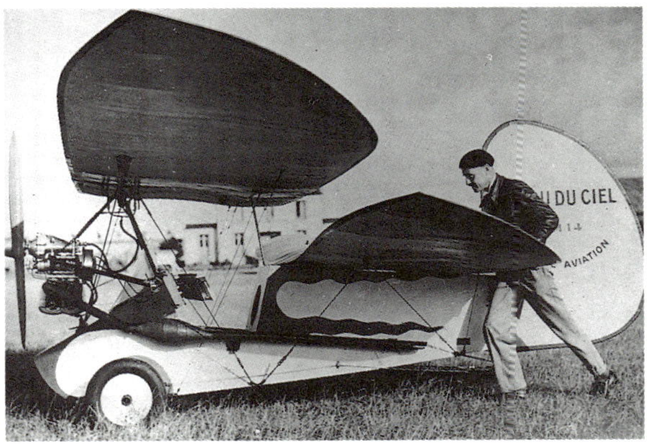

19

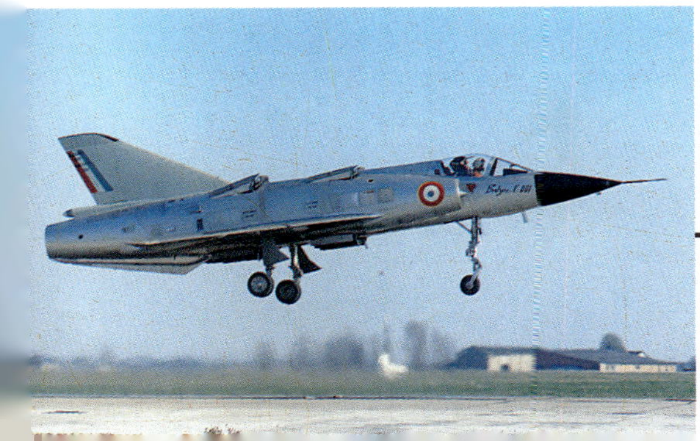

12

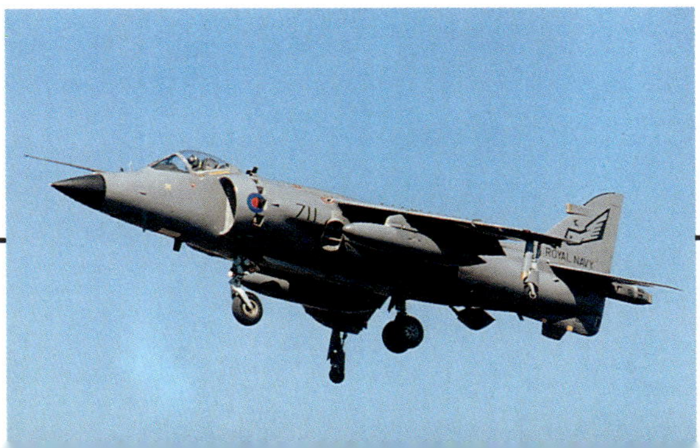

16

TRAIL BLAZERS AND RECORD BREAKERS

After Blériot's 1909 Channel crossing, the second great challenge in aviation history was the Atlantic. In 1919, a converted Vickers Vimy biplane bomber, piloted by Alcock and Brown, made the journey between Newfoundland and Ireland, 1,890 miles (3,024 km) in 16 hours 27 minutes. It remained to link Paris and New York. On 8 May 1927, the French aviators Nungesser and Coli disappeared over the Atlantic after setting off from Le Bourget in a Levasseur PL.8, the *Oiseau Blanc* (White Bird). Not long after, on 20 May 1927, the American Charles Lindbergh made the crossing in the opposite direction, taking 33 hours 30 minutes. His mount, the Ryan *Spirit of Saint Louis,* was a single-engined high-wing aircraft with a cruising speed of 112 mph (180 kph) and a range of 4,125 miles (6,600 km). On 3 September 1930, the Frenchmen Costes and Bellonte made the first crossing from Paris to New York, their Breguet XIX Super TR taking 37 hours 18 minutes. This single-engined biplane had a top speed of 153 mph (245 kph) and a range of 5,940 miles (9,500 km).

Meanwhile, the Italians had begun a series of record-breaking flights. Back in 1927, a twin-hull flying boat, the twin-engined Savoia-Marchetti S.55, flew from north Italy to New York via Africa, Rio de Janeiro and the Caribbean.

In 1928, René Couzinet designed the C-70 *Arc-en-ciel* (Rainbow), a three-engined monoplane with a fixed undercarriage. On 16 January 1933, with Jean Mermoz at the controls, it crossed the South Atlantic from Saint-Louis-du-Sénégal to Natal, Brazil. Cruising at 175 mph with six people on board, the aircraft took 14 hours 27 minutes.

The world speed record was another great challenge. In 1910, a Blériot flew at over 62.5 mph (100 kph), and in 1913 a Deperdussin broke the 125-mph (200-kph) barrier. In 1930, the Americans began to compete for the Thompson Trophy, a trial of sheer speed. The winner in 1932 was the Gee Bee R-1, a single-seater monoplane, whose 800-hp engine gave it a top speed of over 296 mph (475 kph).

In 1947, the Bell X-1 experimental aircraft was launched from a B-29 bomber with Chuck Yeager at the controls. Propelled by a rocket engine, it at last broke the sound barrier and, in 1953, a later version reached a speed of 1,650 mph (2,655 kph).

4
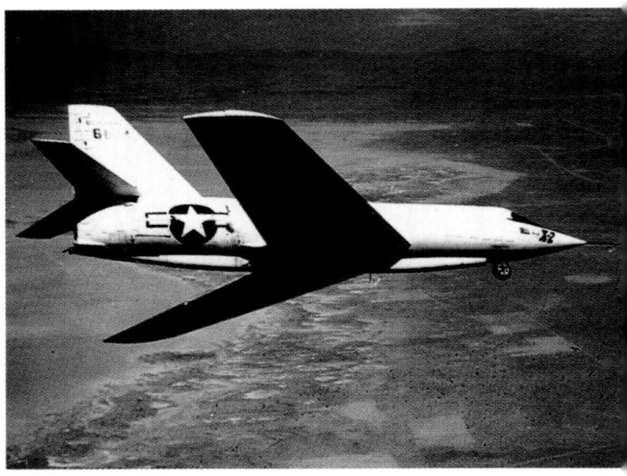

1
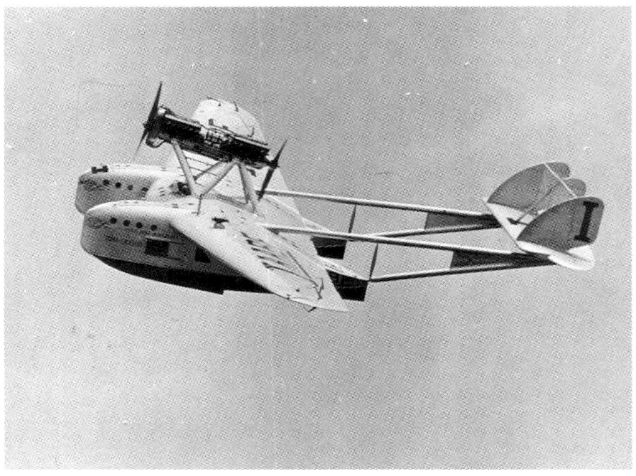

5
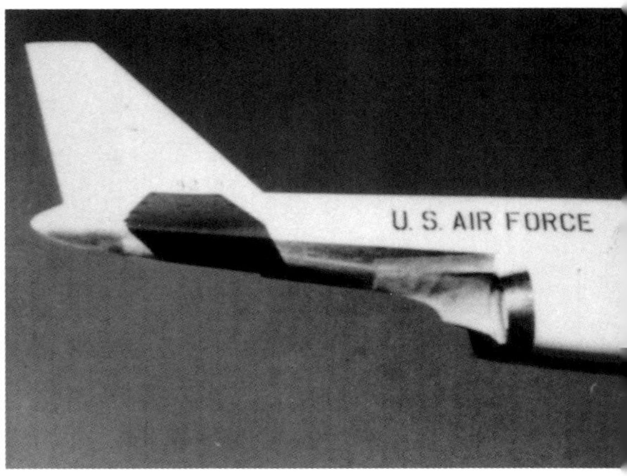

2
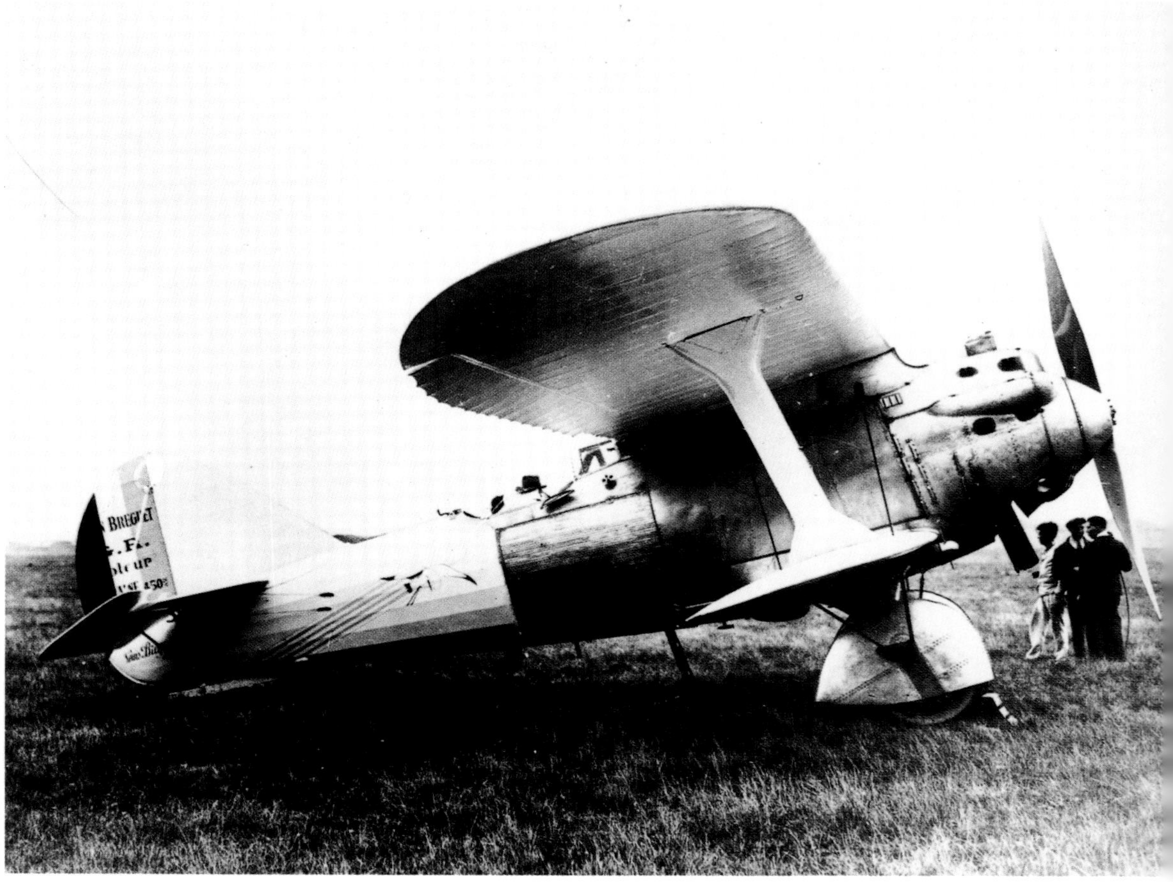

3
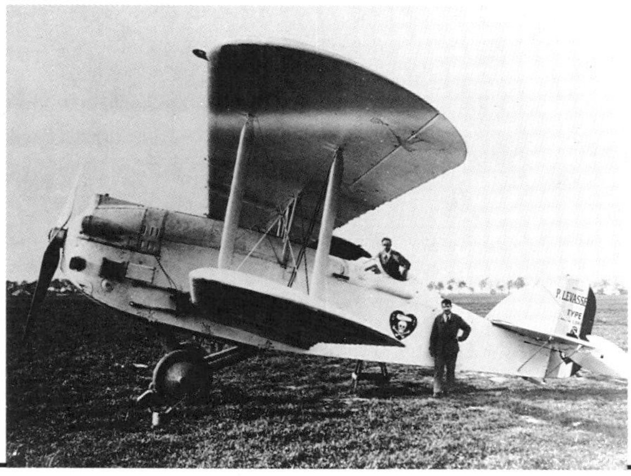

6
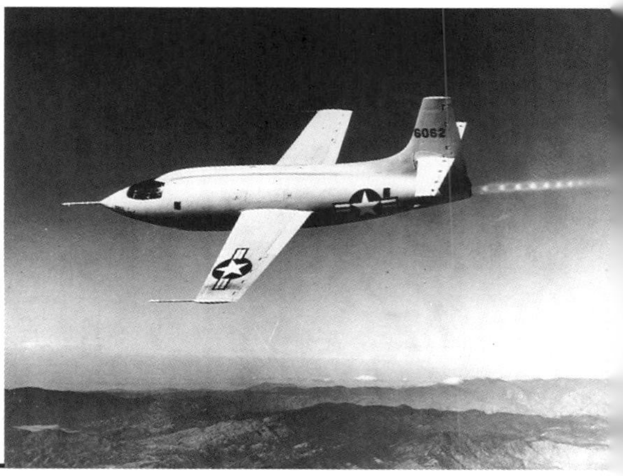

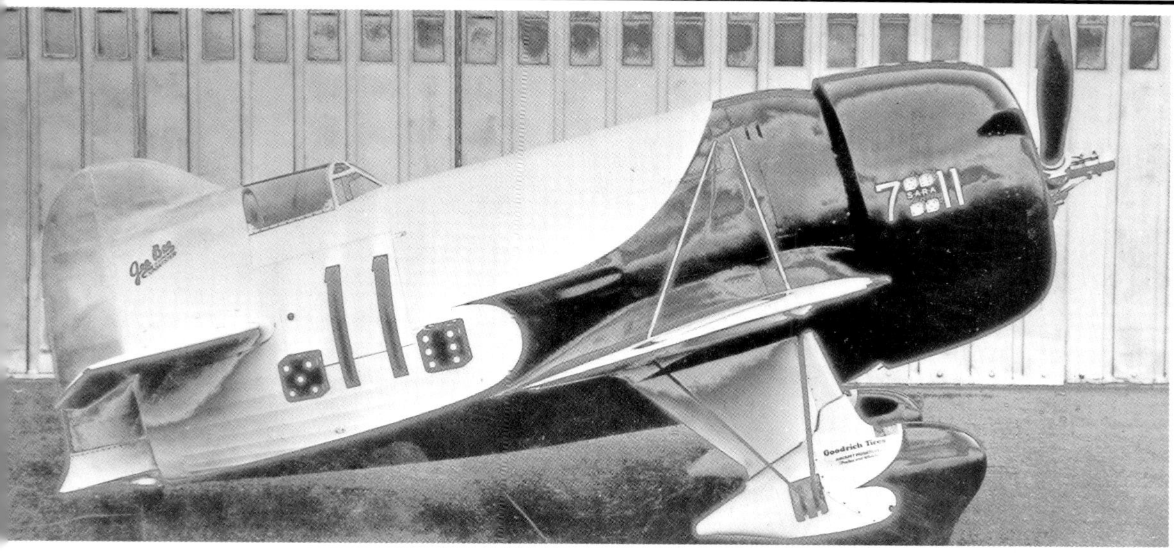

8

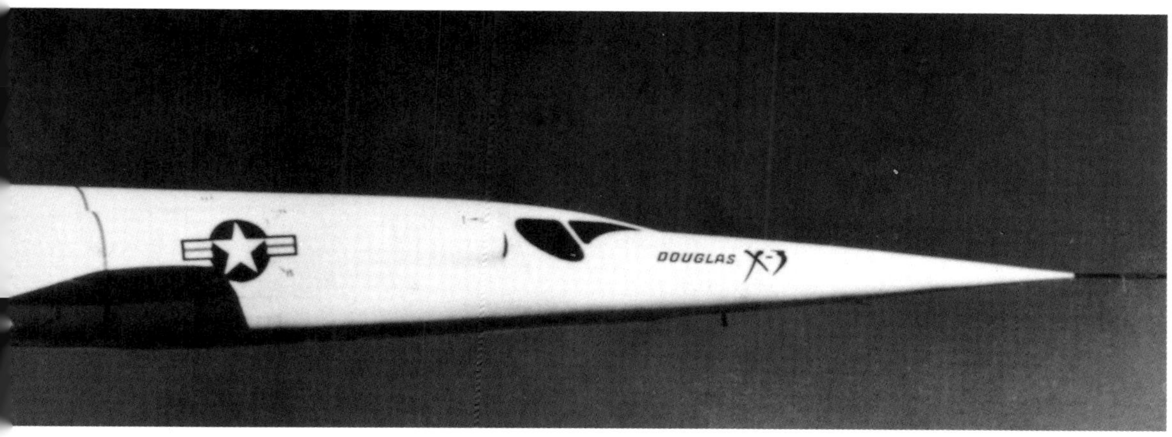

Launched in similar fashion in 1956, the Bell X-2 flew at Mach 3.2. In contrast, the Douglas X-3, first flown in August 1954, never exceeded the speed of sound. Finally, in 1967, the North American X-15, launched from a B-52 bomber and propelled by rockets, set a record of 4,534 mph (7,297 kph). In 1962 an X-15 had reached 314,750 feet (95,936 m).

Research of this kind has opened up all kinds of possibilities. The transport aircraft of the future are now on the drawing board. They include the Alliance, a supersonic airliner intended to supersede Concorde. Carrying over 200 passengers, it will cover distances of up to 7,500 miles (12,000 km) at speeds in excess of 1,250 mph (2,000 kph). Another aircraft in the planning stage at Aérospatiale is the hypersonic AGV (high-speed plane), which by the year 2020 could be transporting 150 passengers at speeds of over 1,875 mph (3,000 kph).

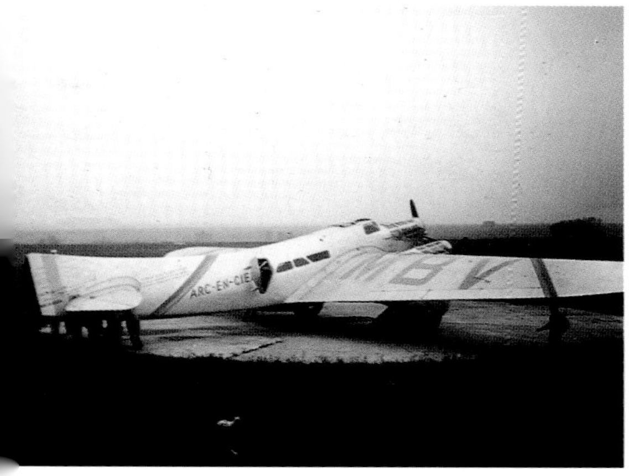

7

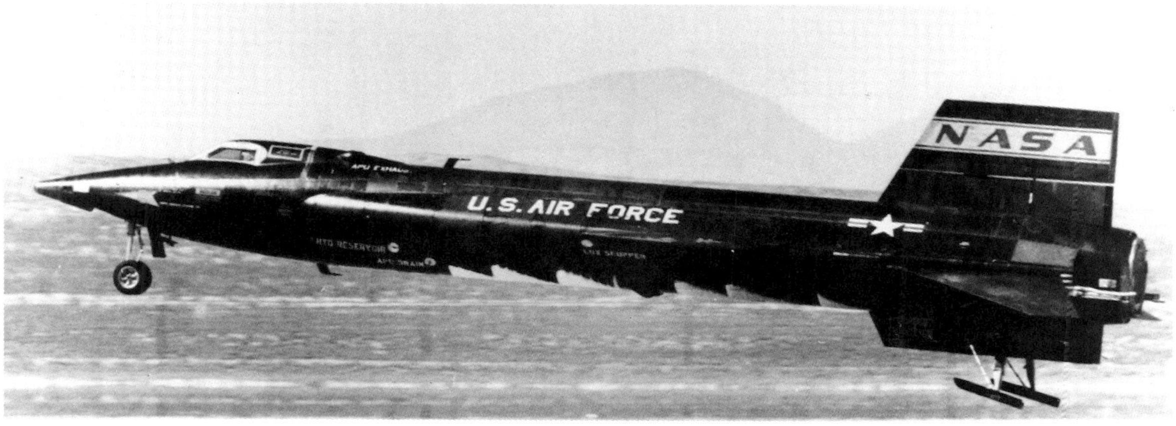

10

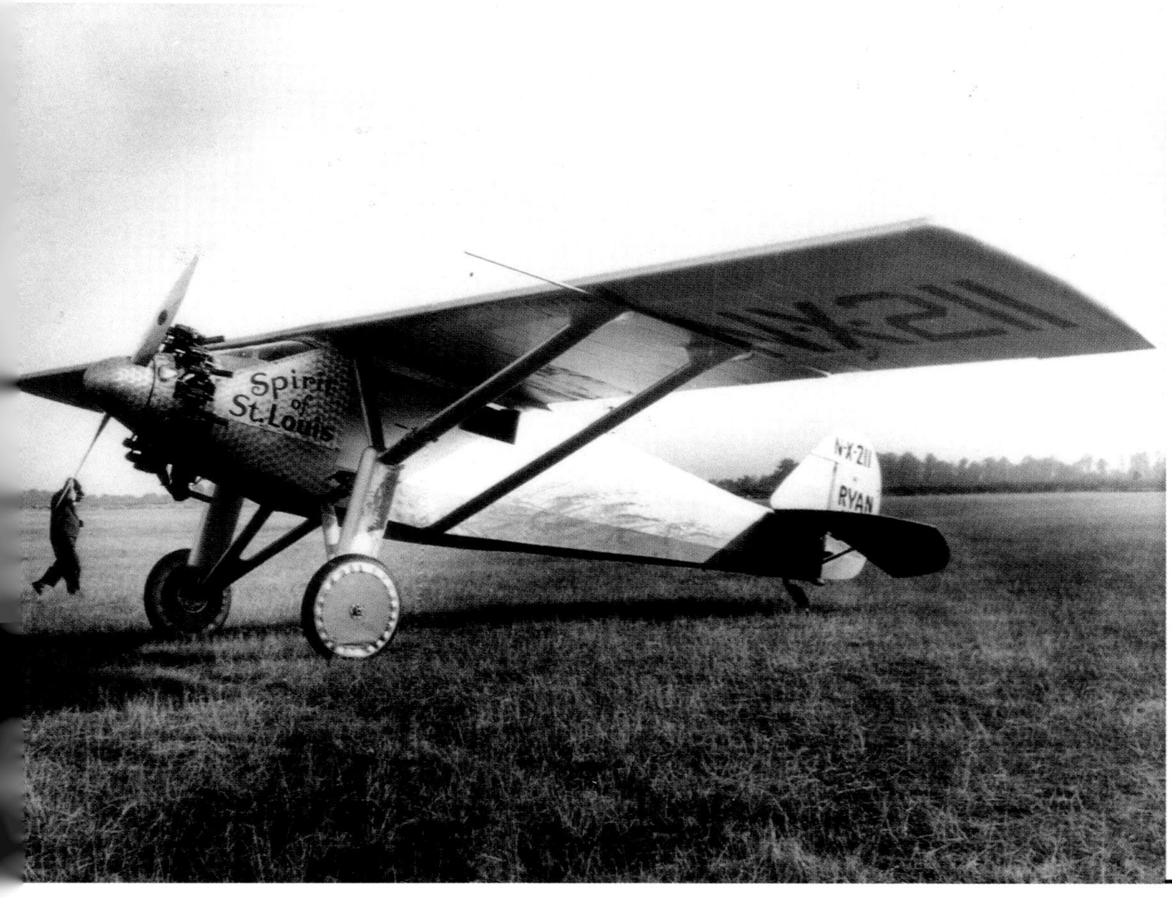

9

Photo No. 1: Savoia-Marchetti S.55 (Italy)
Photo No. 2: Breguet Br XIX Super TR (Costes and Bellonte) (France)
Photo No. 3: Lavasseur P. 8 *Oiseau Blanc* (White Bird) (Nungesser and Coli) (France)
Photo No. 4: Bell X-2 (USA)
Photo No. 5: Douglas X-3 Stiletto (USA)
Photo No. 6: Bell X-1 (USA)
Photo No. 7: Couzinet 70 *Arc en ciel* (France)
Photo No. 8: Gee Bee R-1 (USA)
Photo No. 9: Ryan *Spirit of Saint Louis* (USA)
Photo No. 10: North American X-15 (USA)

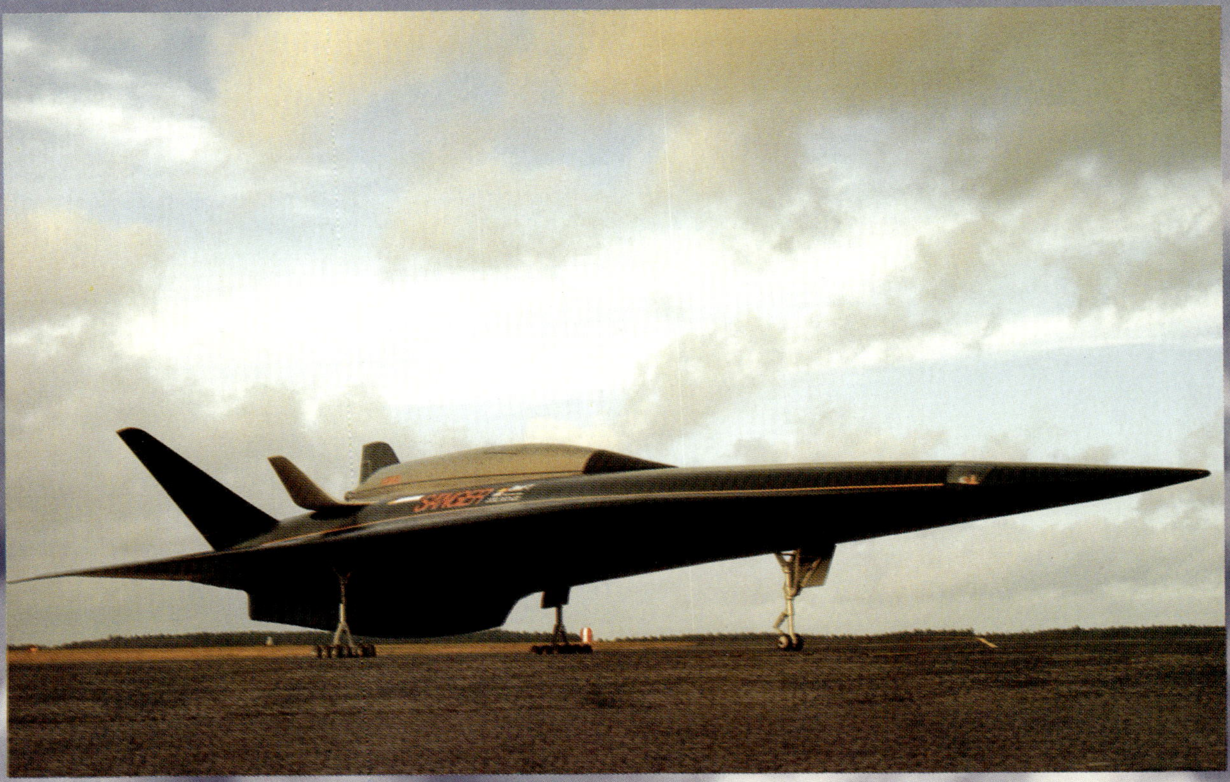

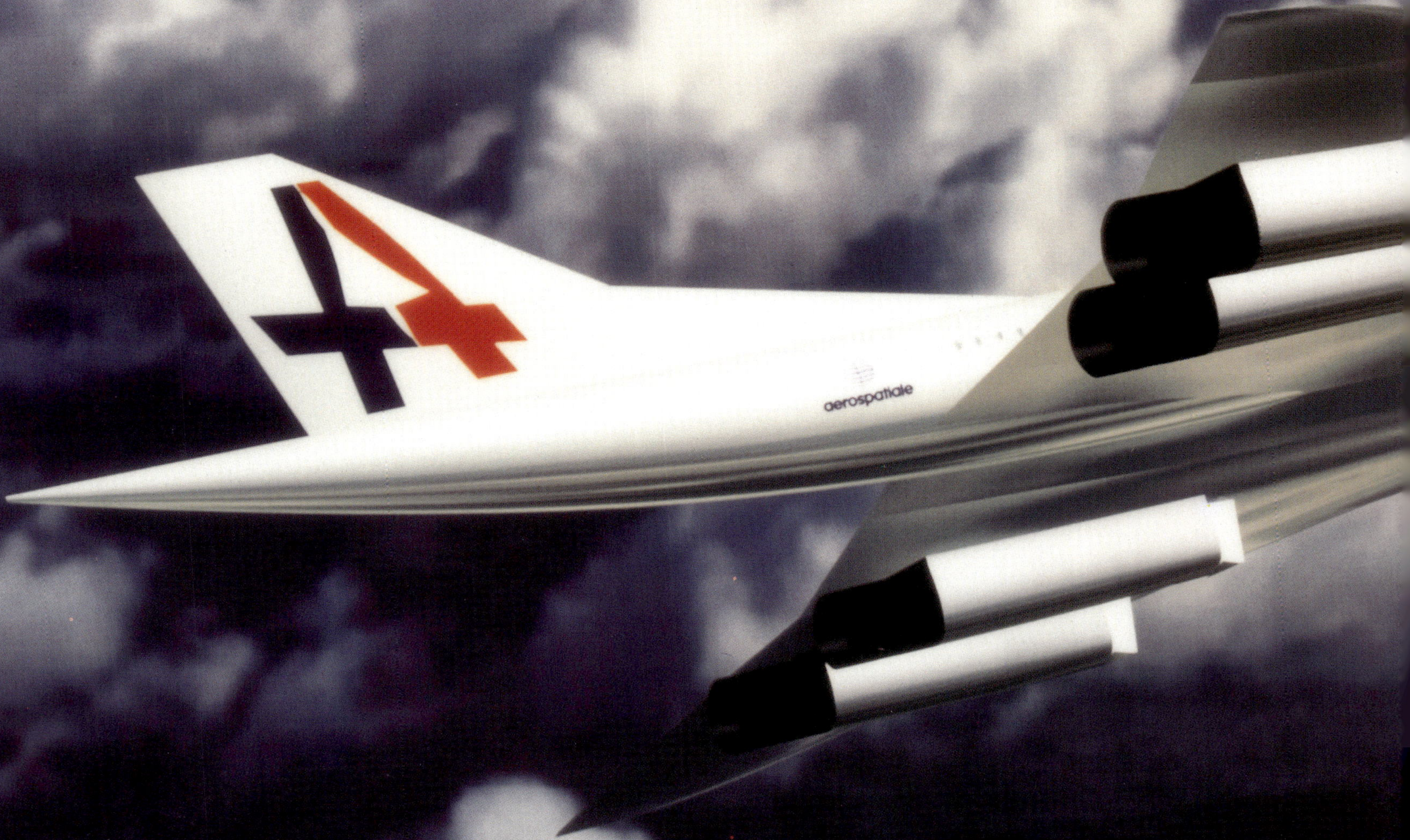

THE SHAPE OF THINGS TO COME

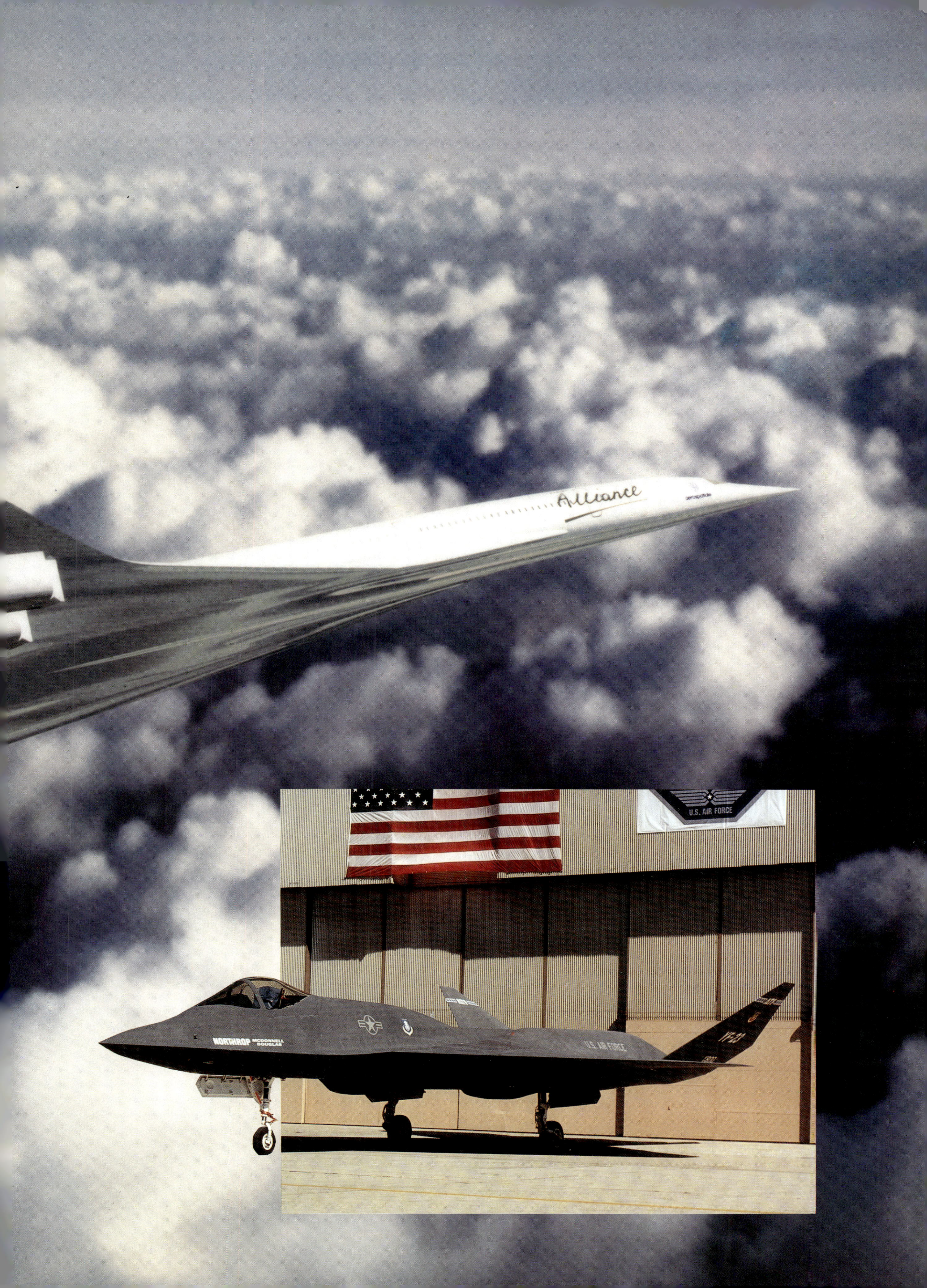
Alliance
U.S. AIR FORCE
NORTHROP McDONNELL DOUGLAS
U.S. AIR FORCE
YF-23

AIRCRAFT OF THE FUTURE

5
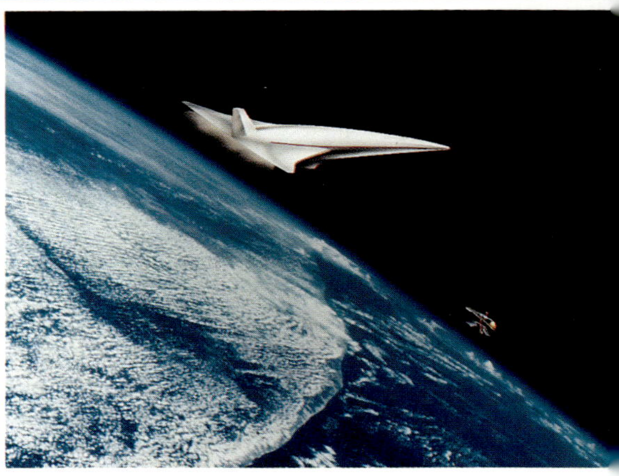

Nothing can stop further progress in air transport. The 21st century will inevitably see the appearance of new types of aircraft as technological advances in different fields give fresh impetus to the aeronautics industry.

The continuing quest for speed will result in a successor to the supersonic Franco-British Concorde. Already, Aérospatiale, British Aerospace and Boeing have plans for an aircraft that will fly at much the same speed as Concorde (slightly over 1,250 mph/2,000 kph), but further (7,500 miles/12,000 km) and with greatly increased carrying capacity (200-300 passengers). They are calling it the Alliance. But, because of the high costs of development, it is likely that the supersonic airliner of the future will be the fruit of even wider international cooperation, involving the Germans, Americans, British, French, Italians, Japanese, Russians, and others. At the same time, giant airliners carrying between 500 and 600 people should be in production by the end of the century, both in Europe and the United States. The Airbus consortium of Aérospatiale, British Aerospace, Deutsche Aerospace and CASA may have unveiled the A350 or the A2000, while Boeing and McDonnell Douglas may be building successors to the 747 and the proposed MD-12.

For transporting major aircraft components, Airbus-Industrie has commissioned Latécoère to build a super jet-powered Guppy, to take over from the propeller-driven Guppies currently in service.

Looking further ahead to 2025-2030, the lessons learned from the European space plane Hermes will give rise to hypersonic transport aircraft. They may fly within the atmosphere, like Aérospatiale's planned ram-jet AGV (high-speed plane), or venture out into space, like Deutsche Aerospace's Sänger, British Aerospace's Hotol or Aérospatiale's STS-2000. In the regional transport field, DASA, Aérospatiale and Alenia are currently designing the Regioliner, a twin-engined jet with capacity for between 92 and 122 passengers, to meet a growing need. The Europeans are also working on the Eurofar, a convertible aircraft – half aeroplane, half helicopter – of similar conception to the American V-22 Osprey. Future combat aircraft will be faster, more agile and increasingly difficult to detect. Air forces will also be equipped with new transport planes such as the European FLA twin-engined jet, currently under study. It should eventually supersede the Transall and the C-130 Hercules.

1
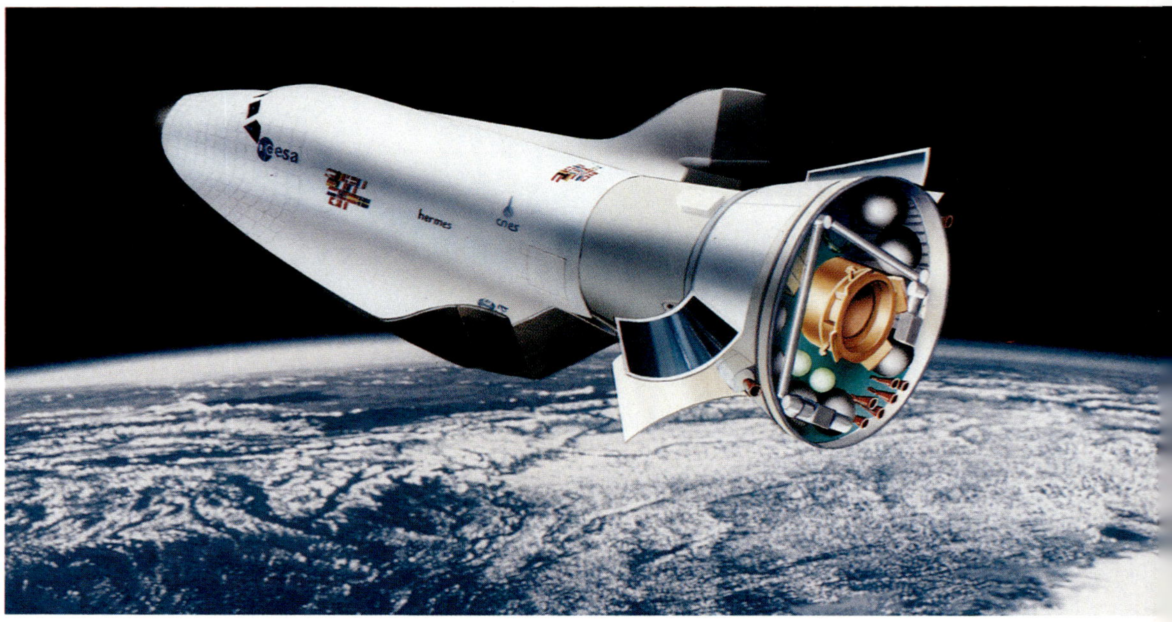

2
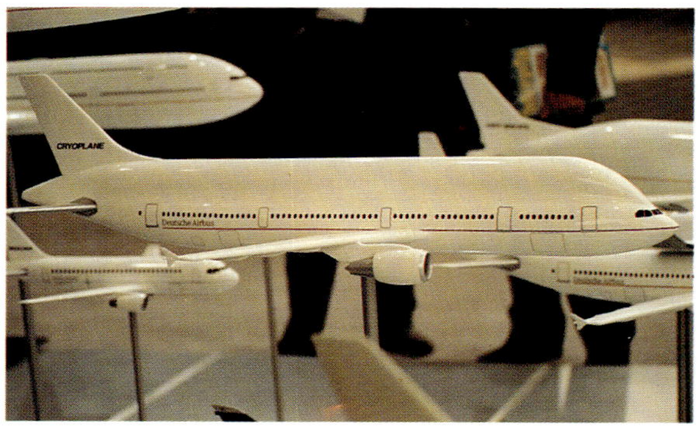

6
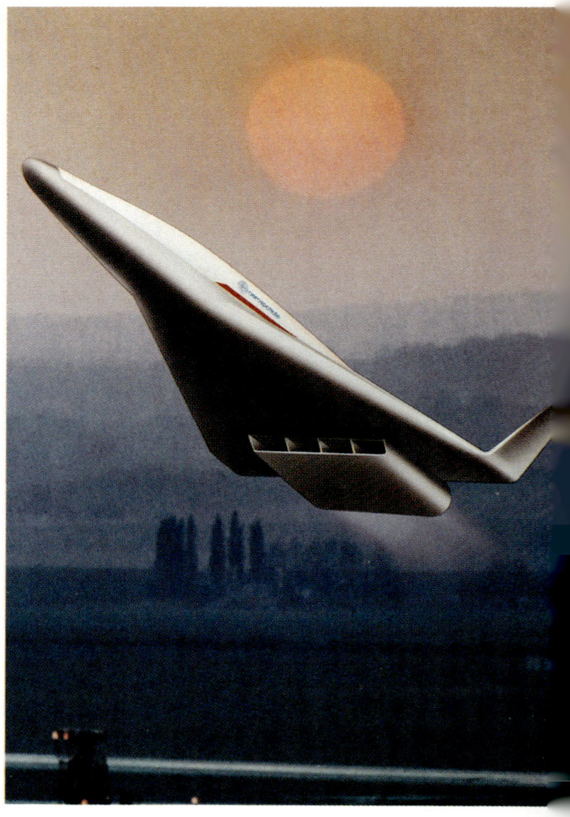

3
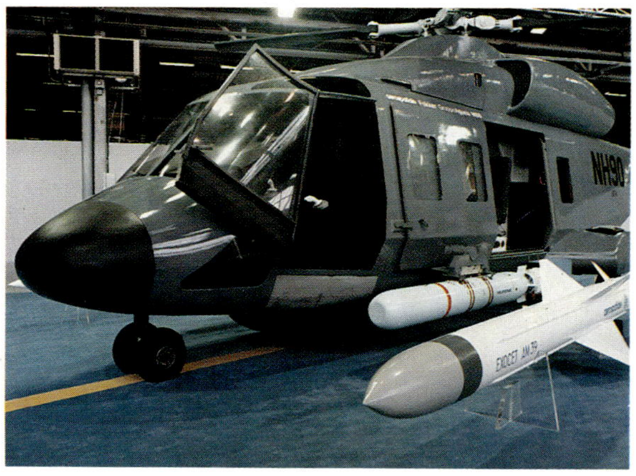

4
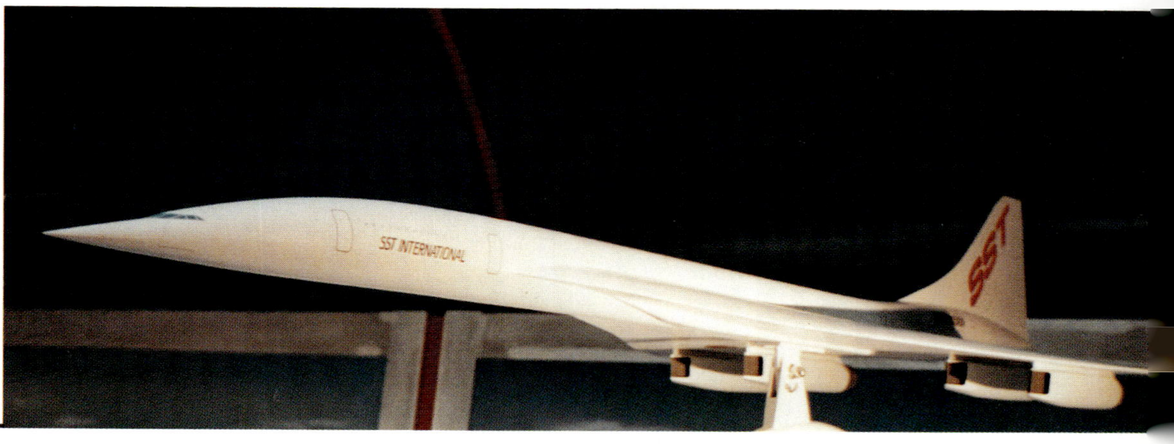

9

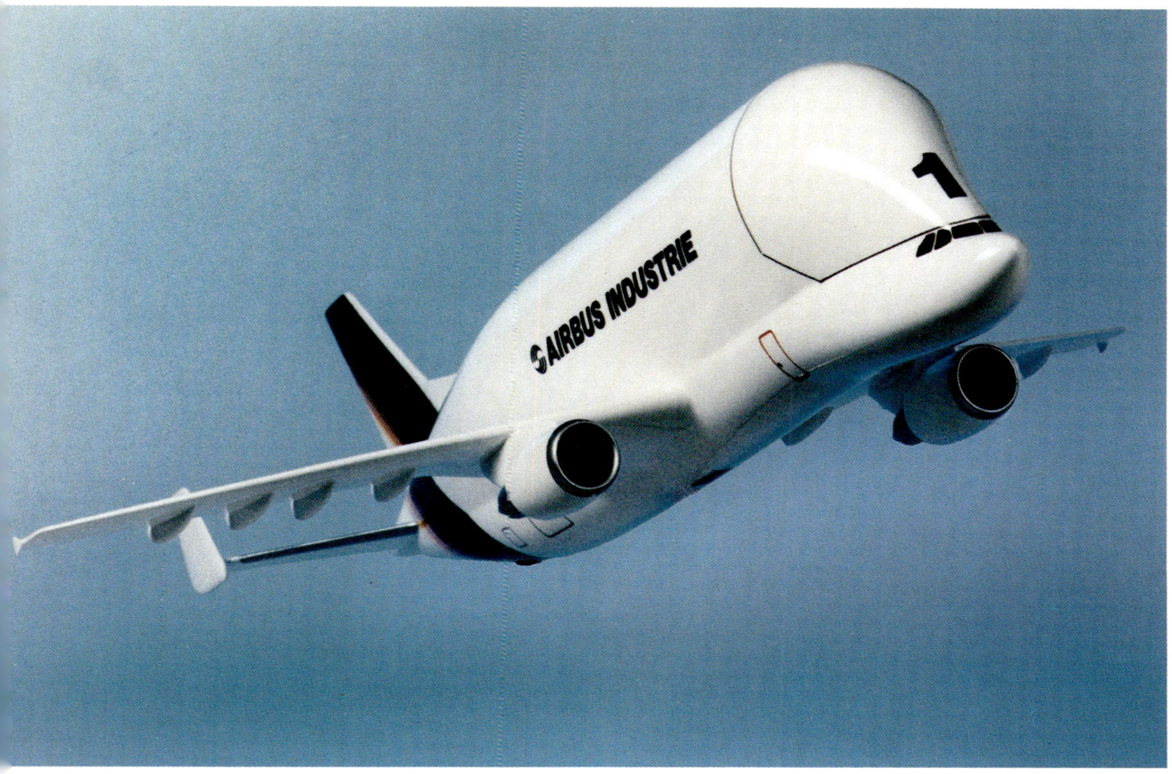

7

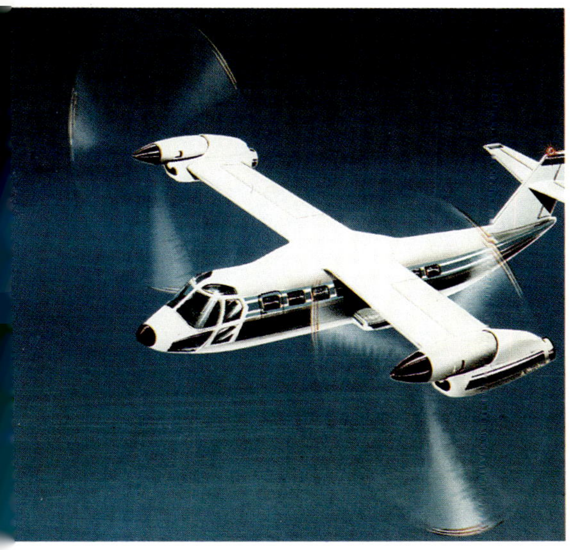

12

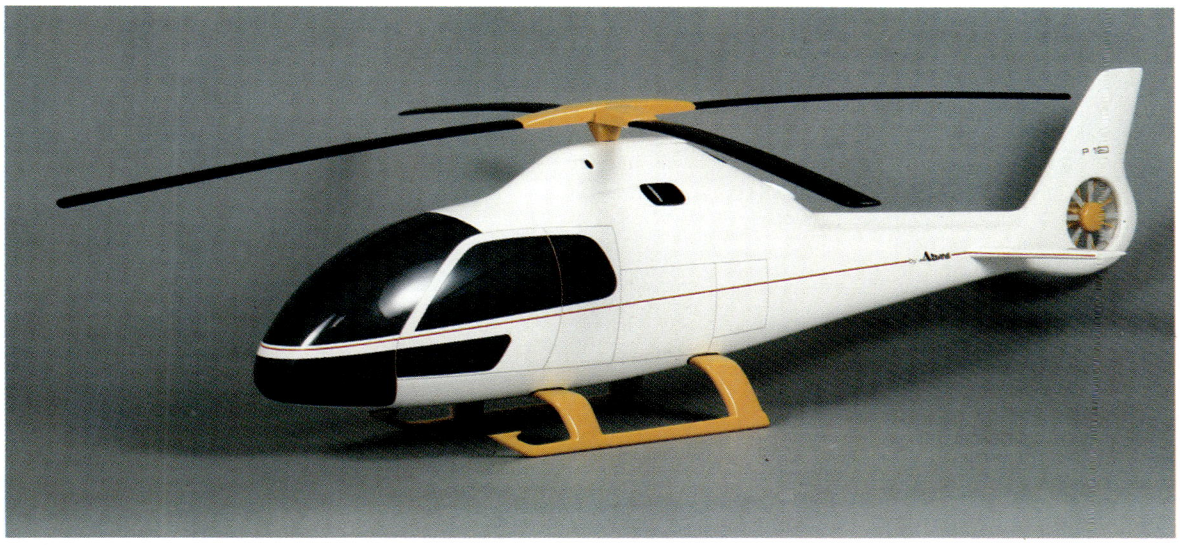

10

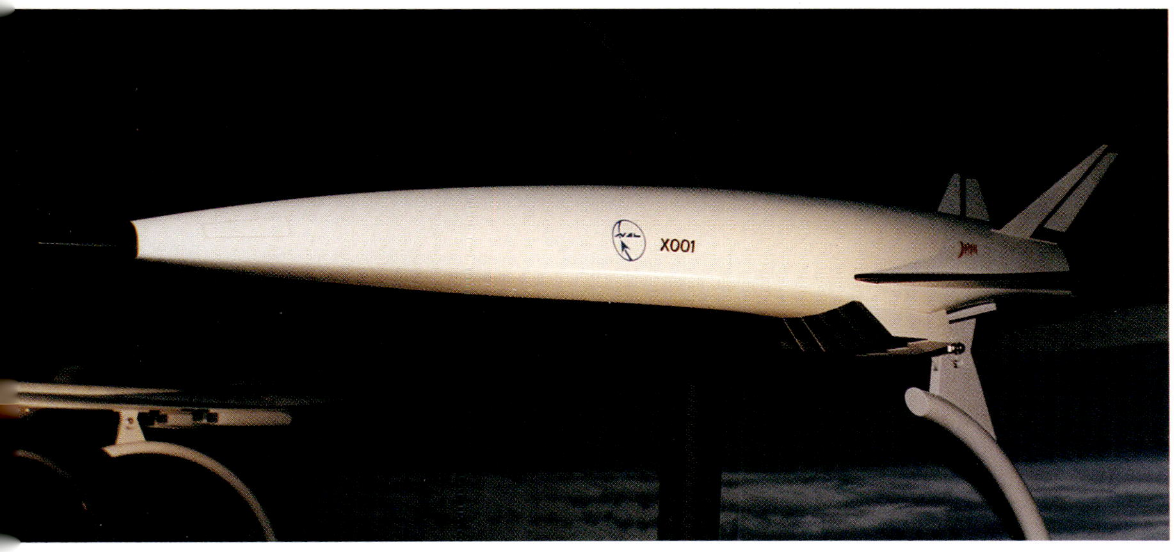

Photo No. 1: Hermes aerospacecraft (France, Germany, Italy)
Photo No. 2: Aérospatiale Cryoplane (France)
Photo No. 3: NH 90 (France, Germany, Italy, Netherlands)
Photo No. 4: SST International (Japan)
Photo no. 5: Aérospatiale Oriflamme (France)
Photo No. 6: Aérospatiale STS 2000 (France)
Photo No. 7: Eurofar convertible aircraft (France, Germany, Great Britain, Italy, Spain)
Photo No. 8: Aérospatiale Alemia DASA Regioliner (France, Germany, Italy)
Photo No. 9: Satic Super Flipper (France, Germany)
Photo No. 10: X001 (Japan)
Photo No. 11: DASA A2000 (Germany)
Photo No. 12: P.120L (China, France, Germany, Singapore)

8

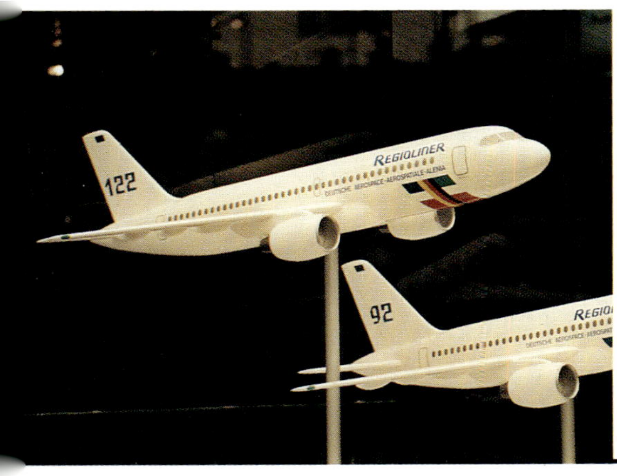

11

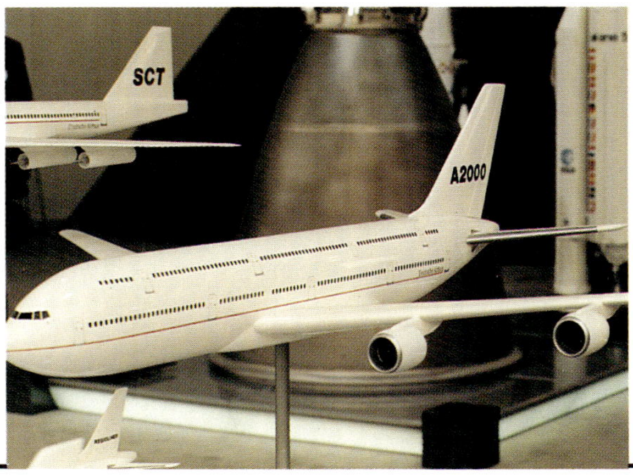

PHOTOGRAPHIC CREDITS

Aviaplans, F. Robineau, Dassault, Aérospatiale, O. Bigel, K. Tokunaga, DACT, E. Moreau, J. Petit, SHAA, Musée de l'Air, Patrick Bunce and Greenborough Associates.

The publishers would like to thank the archivists of the French Air Force history department and those of the Musée de l'Air for their valuable assistance.

Produced by Copyright-Studio for CLB Publishing Ltd.
Design: Nicole Leymaire
Production: Catherine Bataille
Translated from the French by Simon Knight, in assocation with
First Edition Translations Ltd, Cambridge, UK.
Edited by David Gibbon

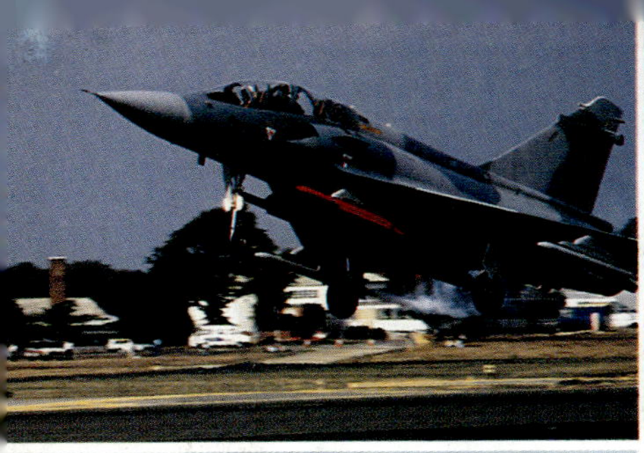
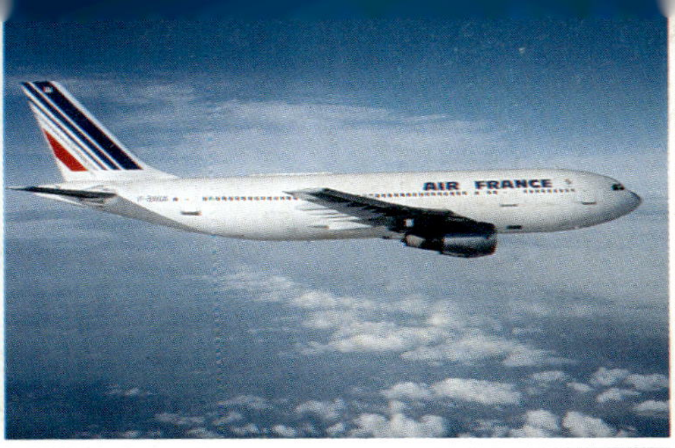
AIR FRANCE
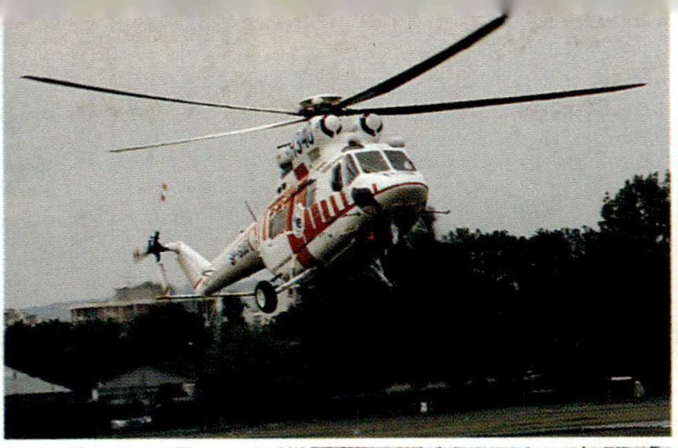
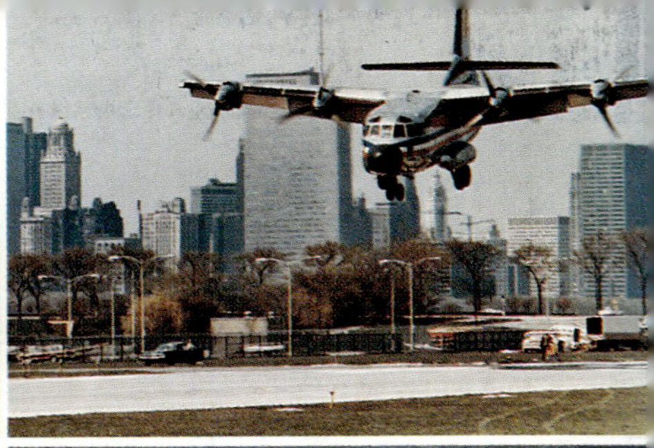
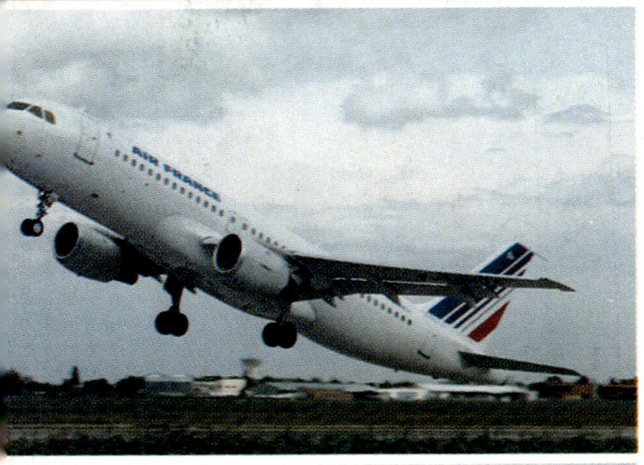
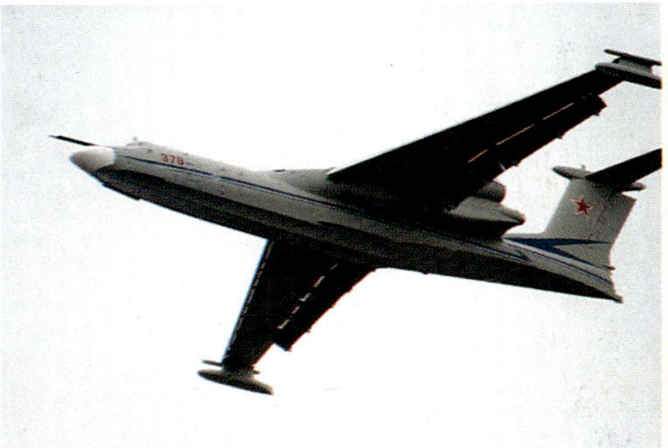
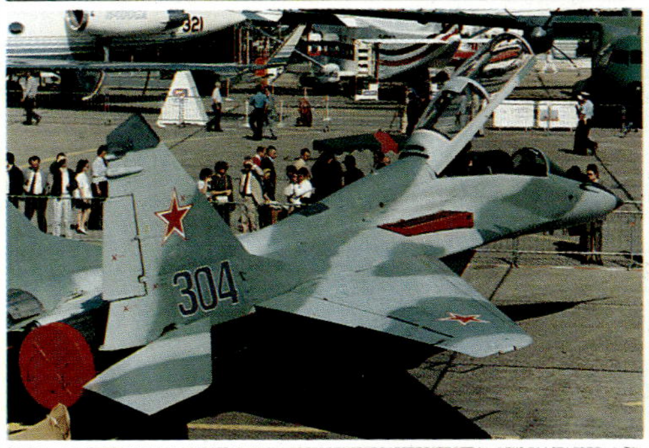
304
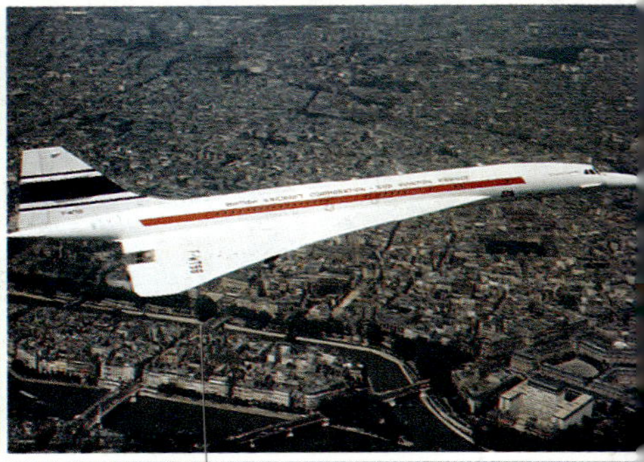
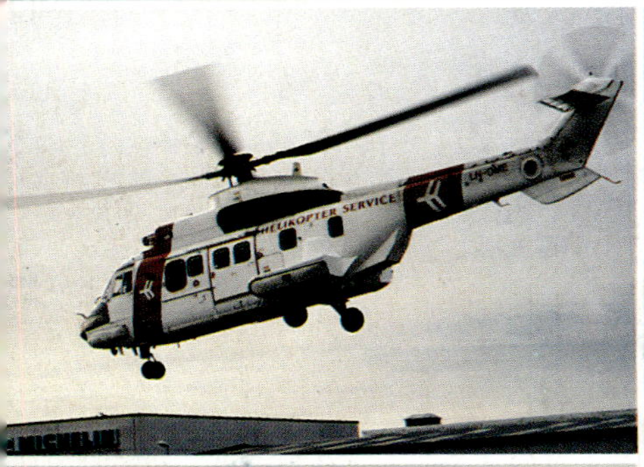
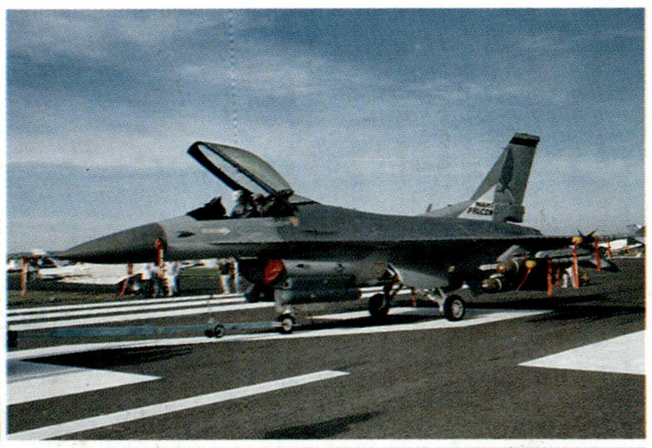
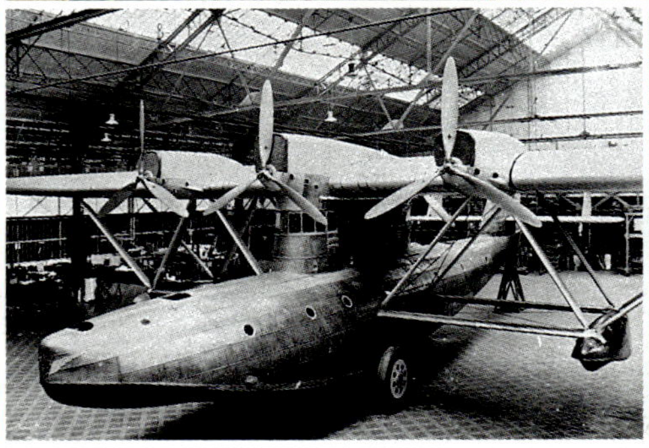
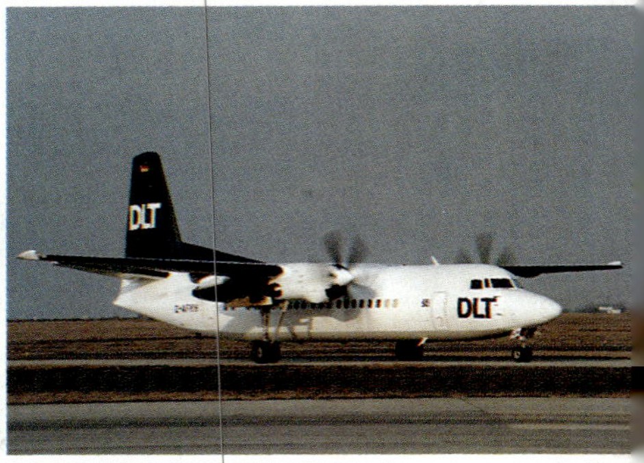
DLT
DLT
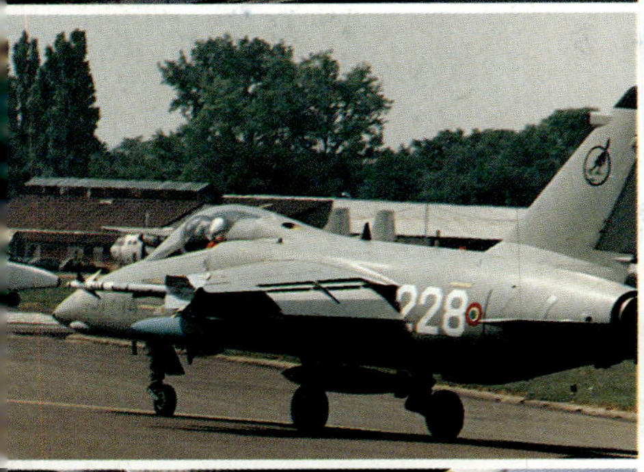
228
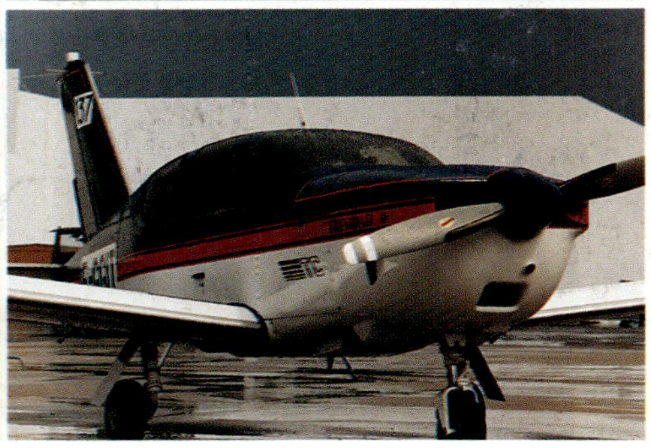
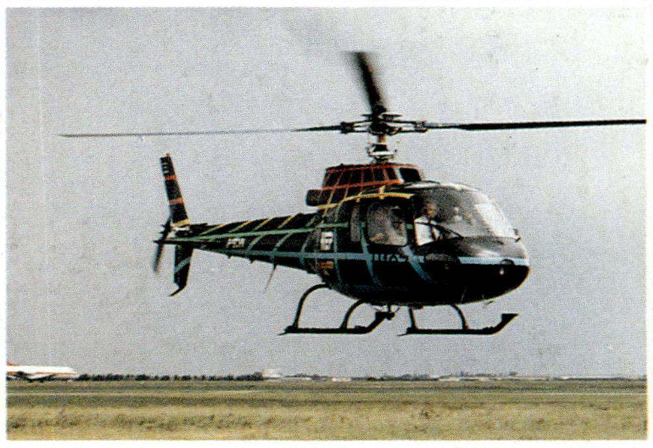
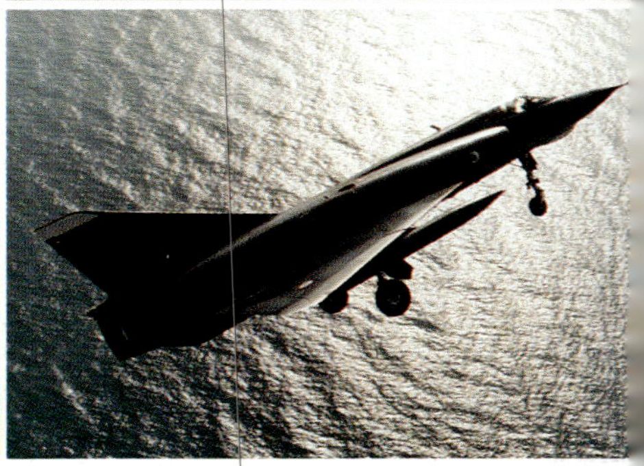
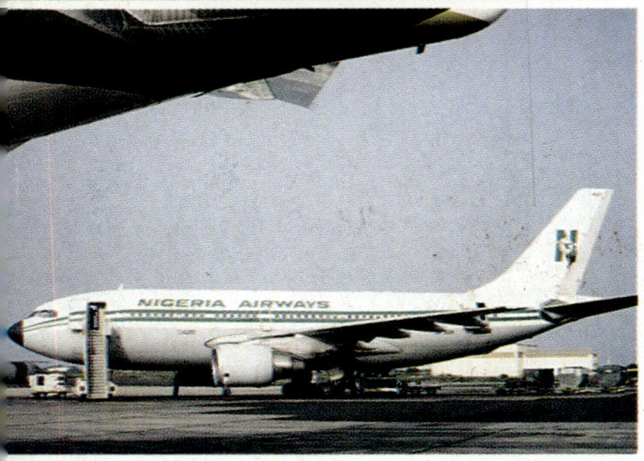
NIGERIA AIRWAYS
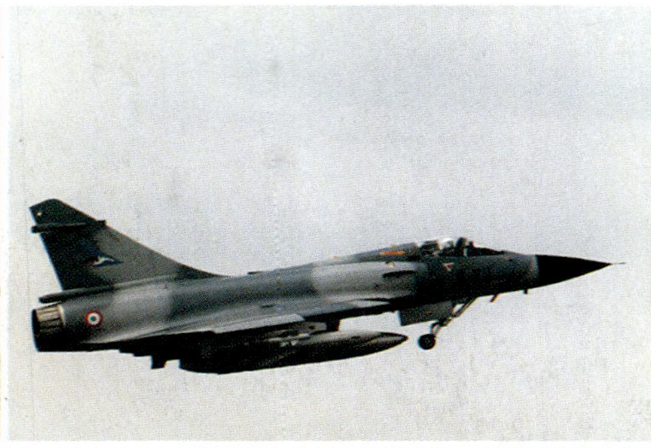
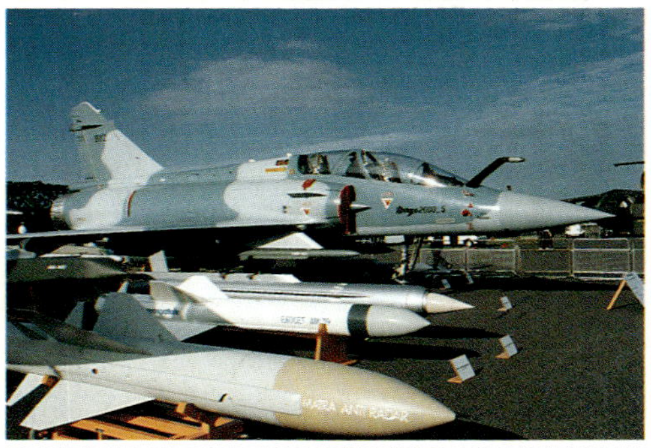
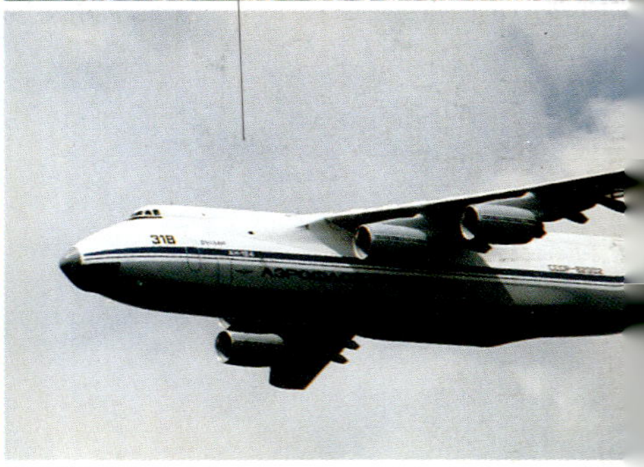
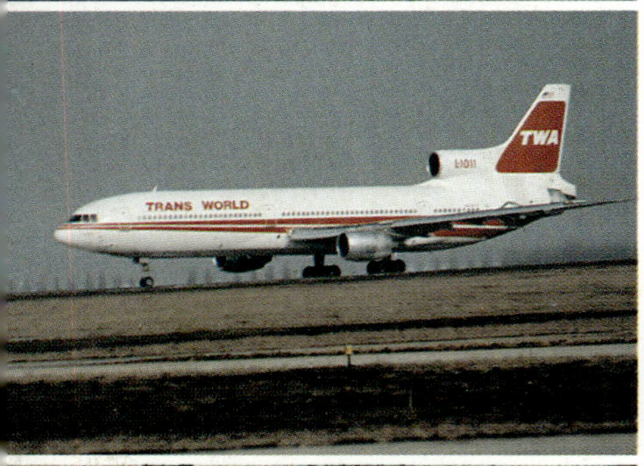
TWA
TRANS WORLD
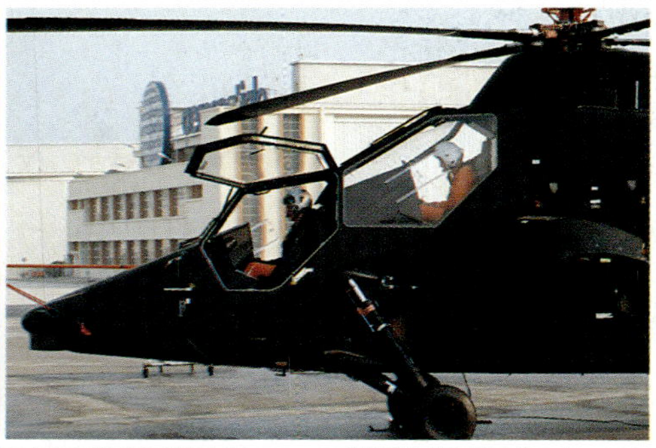
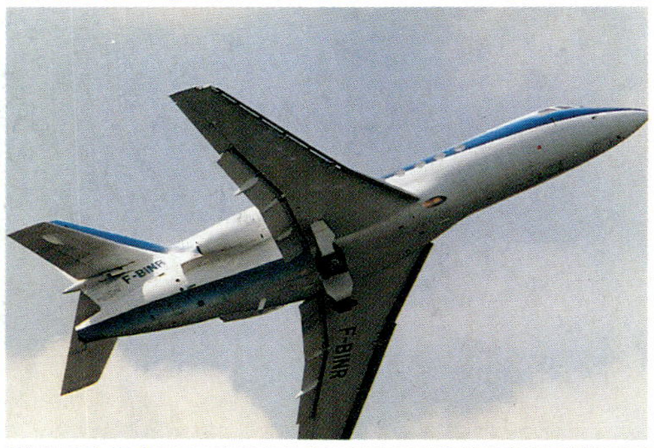
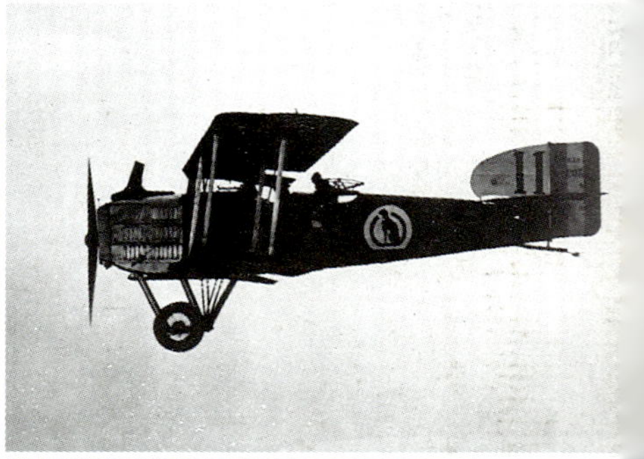
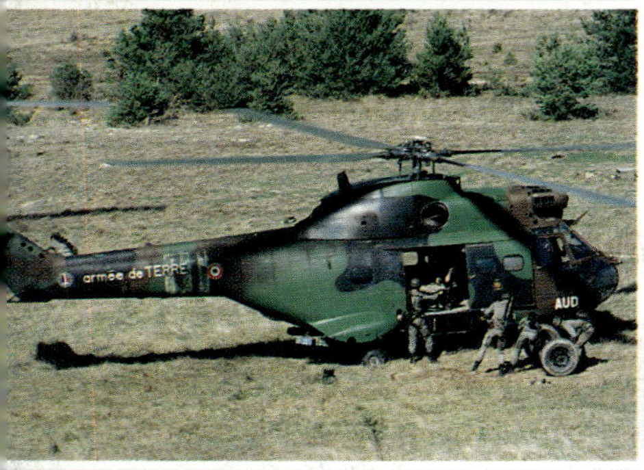
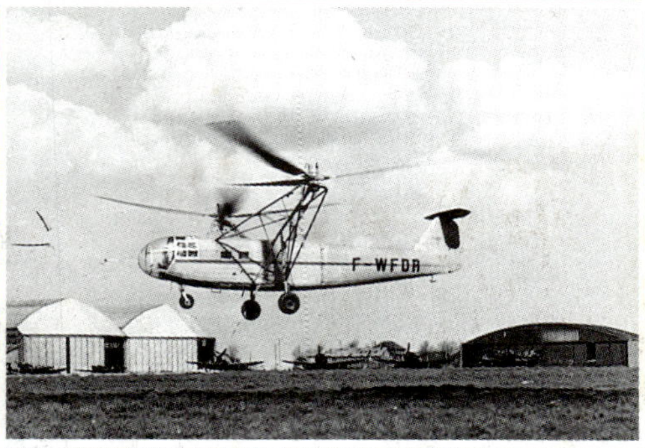
F-WFDA
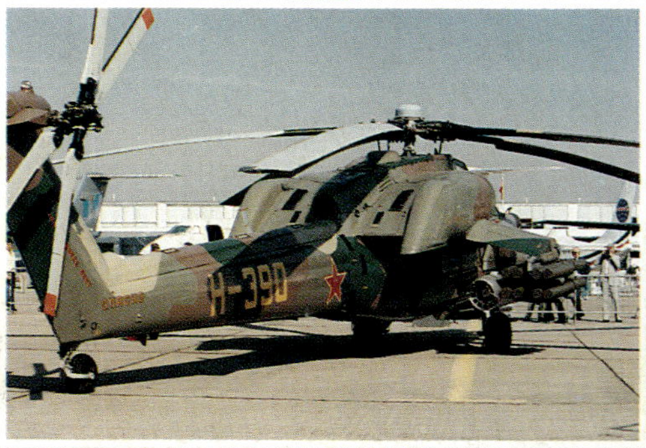
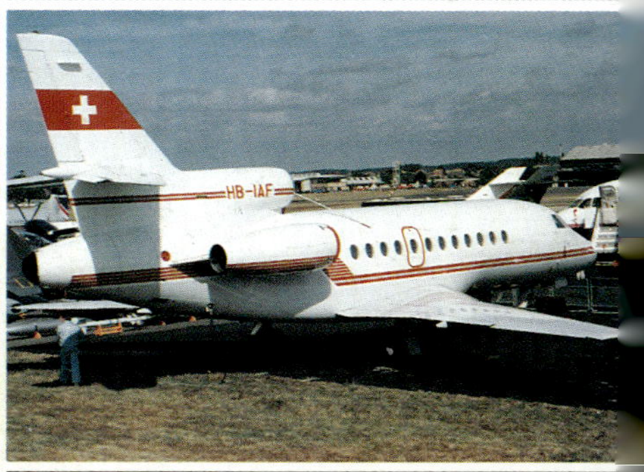
HB-IAF
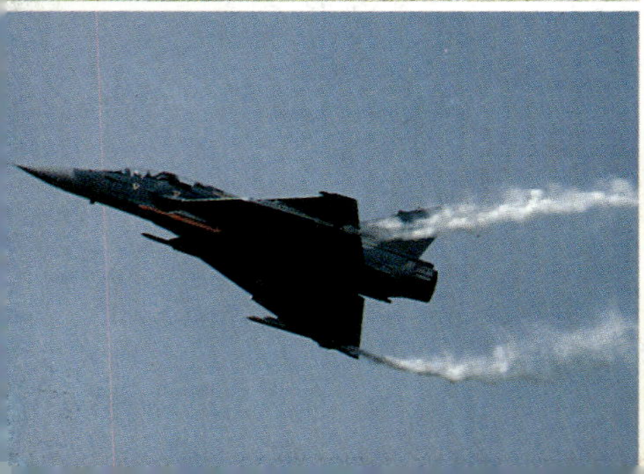
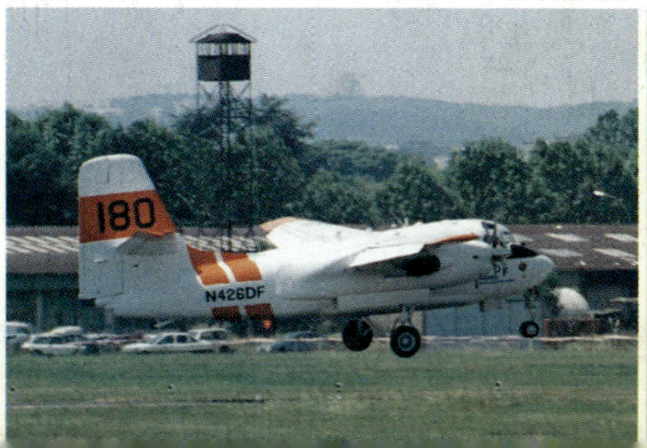
180
N426DF
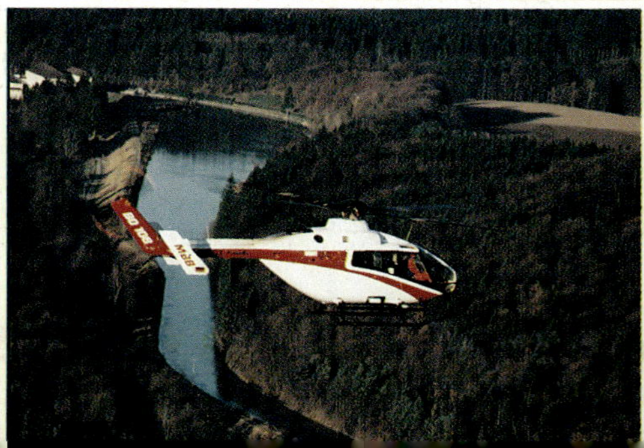
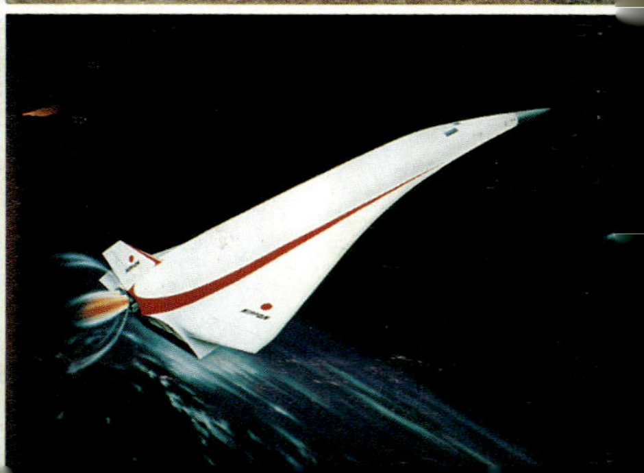